A Textbook of
Modern Spanish

A Textbook of

Modern Spanish

As now written and spoken in Castile and the Spanish American Republics

---

By

Marathon Montrose Ramsey

former Professor of Romance Languages in Columbian University (The George Washington University)

Revised by

Robert K. Spaulding

Professor of Spanish in The University of California at Berkeley

Holt, Rinehart and Winston

New York

LIBRARY OF CONGRESS CATALOG CARD NUMBER: 56–5658
PRINTED IN THE UNITED STATES OF AMERICA

89 090 1918

ISBN: 0-03-016150-9

Reviser's Preface

Marathon Montrose Ramsey (born September 28, 1866 at Newton, Massachusetts) was the only child of Elise Amélie Teulon Ramsey and Samuel Ramsey, who was for many years chief clerk in the Surgeon General's office of the War Department, although he had been trained for the ministry and the legal profession. Throughout his life he engaged in scholarly pursuits and in 1892 he published with G. P. Putnam's Sons *The English Language and English Grammar,* a volume of 571 pages. It is not surprising, then, that he himself educated his son at home. From mid-October, 1887, to the end of June, 1888, young Ramsey was in Europe. He spent the winter in Seville and Madrid, the spring in Italy where, in addition to languages, he studied drawing under the direction of an Italian artist. His tour included a short stay in Paris before he sailed for New York from Antwerp. This was his only trip outside the United States. His European visit, though comparatively short, was very profitable for, because of his father's connections, he had the entrée of cultivated circles. On June 3, 1889, he married Agnes Craig of Washington, D. C. Not many months after his marriage, Ramsey was given a position in the Military Information Bureau of the War Department, a position he held for almost six years. In the *Columbian Call,* a journal published by the students of the Columbian University, issue for January 30, 1897, we read: "during Professor Ramsey's incumbency eleven publications were issued by the Military Information Division...in the preparation of which Professor Ramsey played a very important part. His most permanent work, however, was the organization of the technical military library, now numbering 4,000 volumes, the classified catalogue of which, printed in September, 1896, being his latest official work under the War Department". He served as chief translator for the International American Conference (more popularly called the Pan American Conference) held in Washington during the fall, winter and spring of 1889-1890, under the leadership of William E. Curtis, former American ambassador to Spain.

After a few years as Instructor in Romance Languages in the Columbian University, Ramsey was promoted to the rank of professor in that institution (1894). After 1898 and until 1900 he was director of the summer school and he also served as secretary of the faculty and president of the Graduate Club. From 1900 to 1901 he was fellow by courtesy of The Johns Hopkins University, where he was preparing for the Ph. D. degree. In 1901 he became Assistant Professor of Romance Languages in Leland Stanford Junior University. Two years later illness brought on by overwork forced him to resign this position and terminate his teaching career.

In addition to his work with the War Department and his teaching duties Professor Ramsey, in the short period of eight years, prepared the following works, published, with the exception noted, by Henry Holt and Company: *A Textbook of Modern Spanish,* 1894; *The Island of Cuba* (with Lt. Andrew Rowan), 1896; *An Elementary Spanish Reader,* 1897; *Progressive Exercises in Spanish Prose Composition,* 1900; *Lo esencial del lenguaje castellano* (Silver Burdett and Company), 1900; *A Spanish Grammar with Exercises,* 1902. He also contributed articles on Spanish and Spanish-American literature to *Johnson's Universal Cyclopaedia,* pp. 645-648 and 643-645, respectively, and on Latin-American literature to the *Encyclopaedia of the World's Best Literature,* edited by Charles Dudley Warner, pp. 8903-8928. *A Hand Dictionary of the Modern Spanish and English Languages,* never completed, was announced as "in preparation" and he prepared the manuscript of a *Manual of Spanish Phonetics and Orthography.* He also tried his hand at the composition of poems and short stories. Not all his energies were expended on his publications, however: numerous statements and countless anecdotes reveal that he was a great teacher. He was the recipient of the order of Isabel la Católica and, it seems, of the degree of L. H. D. from the University of Nicaragua.

So far as can be ascertained after a lapse of fifty-odd years, *A Textbook of Modern Spanish* was written during the author's spare time between the years 1889 or 1890 and 1893. His diary indicates that the manuscript was forwarded to the publishers in May, 1893, and the contract for publication is dated August 15 of the same year. During the years the *Textbook* was in preparation its author served as full-time employee of the War Department by day and attended night classes in the Corcoran Scientific School of the Columbian University which, having in June, 1893, issued him a diploma as graduate of the French and German Departments, granted him a B. S. degree the same year the *Textbook* appeared (1894). His chief subjects, according to the program of the graduating exercises, were chemistry, physics and astronomy. At the ceremony Ramsey read a paper entitled "Language and Science". The following year he received an M. A. degree from the Columbian University.

With his thorough training both in languages and in sciences, it is not surprising that Professor Ramsey should produce a work as accurate and scholarly as is the *Textbook*. What is surprising, indeed, is that, with his other activities, he found time to write the Spanish grammar which at the time of publication was generally acclaimed by reviewers and teachers "because of the very great advance it shows over all existing Spanish grammars in English". Down through the years Spanish teachers continue to refer to Ramsey as "the ultimate and best accessible authority".

The title page of the original volume declares it to be a textbook of modern Spanish as now written and spoken in Castile and the Spanish-American republics. This inclusive statement of purpose implies that literary Spanish and colloquial Spanish go together in the constitution of the tongue and that they may not be identical. It further recognizes that the language of Spanish America can not be ignored in any treatment of Spanish and assumes that there are differences. In addition to pushing farther in the direction of the traits of American Spanish (which to a considerable extent are characteristic of folk speech) I hope above all that in the course of the revision — and in emphasis of the author's declared intention — I have called attention of readers to the restrictions of use of many phenomena of Spanish, now limiting them to conversational usage, now to elegant style.

Part I, which dealt with the principles of pronunciation and orthography, has been retained in the revision. *Part II,* which consisted of twenty preliminary lessons with exercises and was designed to teach the beginning student the fundamentals of grammar and prepare him for more advanced study in the third division of the original edition, has been suppressed. But those portions which contained material of value to the advanced student or teacher have been blended with the more detailed explanation of the corresponding points in what Professor Ramsey called *Part III: More Extended Treatment.* That division, revised and expanded by the addition of pertinent illustrations and discussion brought over from earlier chapters, is now labeled *Part II: Forms and Uses.* This merger has been made in the belief that in a book intended primarily for reference and classroom work with students already well grounded in the basic principles of grammar, all points — minor and major — of one topic should be treated together. In combining the two sections duplication has been held fairly close to the minimum. All exercises and vocabularies have been omitted.

Though Professor Ramsey often used as illustrations passages from literary or scientific works of his own day (e.g., § **4.7**), in general he does not cite their source. Observant students, however, recognize some: the second example of § **4.7** comes from Pérez Galdós, **Marianela,** XVII; the fourth of § **9.58** from Palacio Valdés, **La hermana San Sulpicio,** XVI; the last of § **25.27** from chapter XII of the same novel; the last of § **18.8** probably from chapter V; etc. Since many have expressed regret that the source of the illustrations is not more generally indicated, I have, in keeping with contemporary practice, almost invariably listed both author and text, with the subdivision thereof, of the examples that I have added. Thus students may judge for themselves the suitability of a new illustration and readily see how much illustrative material has been added.

In the half century and more that has passed since the publication of the *Textbook,* an entirely new concept of the function of the grammarian has been established: he is today the recorder of usage, not the judge and promulgator of its correctness. It has not been my intention to convert the *Textbook* into a mere record of usage, since it is hoped that the proper scholars will see to the publication of a statistical survey of which the preliminary findings may be viewed in the *Spanish Syntax List* of Hayward Keniston, Henry Holt and Company, New York, 1937. In an effort to bring Professor Ramsey's work more nearly abreast of current thinking, I have, however, softened the force of numerous statements. Elasticity of correct grammatical expression is, in living use, rather greater than it was formerly the fashion to concede. In fact the insertion of "often", "usually", "frequently", "may" and the like appears in retrospect to have been one of the chief modifications of the statement of principles.

Since the publication of the *Textbook* knowledge of the subject has greatly increased. Consequently I have expanded the treatment at several points and in a few cases rewritten the discussion. Some of the lesser modifications represent only the author's treatment of the same points in his *Spanish Grammar* (1902), where he introduced such changes in the discussions as were dictated by experience accumulated in the eight years following the publication of his *Textbook.* The number of changes found necessary for the revision is after all relatively insignificant, however, and attests the truth of the words of a reviewer of 1895 who praised "the fullness, clearness, and precision of statement everywhere shown" *(The Nation,* January 24, 1895, p. 75). I hope that users of the book in its revised form will continue to find in it those features which have for so long made it a *vade mecum* of students of the subject and that it will continue to be true, as that early reviewer said, that "no serious student of Spanish can afford to be without Prof. Ramsey's work".

To Mrs. Birdie K. Hewitt, M. A., I here express my thanks for the collection of illustrations which enabled me to draw conclusions as to usage at more than a few points.

I am truly grateful to Mrs. Agnes Craig Ramsey for her cooperative spirit and assistance. She has informed me of facts and made available to me material that would otherwise have remained totally beyond my reach and ken.

R. K. S.
The University of California at Berkeley

Introduction

The peninsula bounded by the Pyrenees, the Mediterranean and the waters of the Atlantic is a geographical unity, but a unity in no other respect. From the remotest ages it has been the battle-ground of races, religions and languages the most diverse. Basques, Celtiberians, Phœnicians, Romans, Suevi, Goths, Franks, Arabs and Mauritanians have successively contributed to the population, the language and the monuments of the peninsula. The mountainous nature of the country and its long separation into kingdoms and provinces have prevented a feeling of national unity and fostered local rivalries and jealousies. The inhabitants of the several districts regard themselves as Castilians, Andalusians, Catalonians or Galicians rather than as Spaniards. They refuse to their sovereign the title of King of Spain, and place a confederate stamp upon his official designation *"Rey de las Españas"*, King of *the Spains.*

The comprehensive words "Spain" and "Spanish" are misleading except when used as geographical or political designations; for the diversity of the climate and natural features of the country is equalled by that of the characteristics and language of the inhabitants. Strictly speaking there is no *Spanish* language. To say nothing of Portuguese, the diversities of dialect are so great that Catalán, Andaluz and Gallego are mutually unintelligible; and all degrees of variety lie between these extremes. The central position of Castile, and the political ascendency acquired by it as early as the XIth century have caused the dialect there spoken to be acknowledged as the typical language of Spain. It has been cultivated with the greatest care and embodies the most extensive and valuable part of the literature of all Spain. It is to Castilian that foreigners refer when they speak of "Spanish". It is generally in Spain, and in Spanish America universally, spoken of as *la lengua castellana.* In this work the English terms "Spanish" and "Spanish language" will be employed as synonymous with *el castellano* and *la lengua castellana.*

Since Spain enjoyed fully 600 years of peace and prosperity as a

Roman province, it became more thoroughly Latinized than any other part of the Empire outside of Italy. It moreover was accorded a gentler colonial policy than any other province. Everything possible was done to conciliate the good will, to further the interests and to secure the loyalty of the Spaniards. Cities were founded and placed upon the footing of the highly favored municipalities of ancient Latium; and Spain became the richest and most important Roman province. Not only were the material interests of its people thus carefully fostered, but every attention was given to learning and literature.* Latin of the very purest type was spoken in Spain; her orators were admired even in the Forum at Rome, and among her authors were classics like the two Senecas, Lucan, Martial and Quintilian. Spain had thus the advantage of having for the basis of her language a pure classic Latin, which probably no other dependency outside of the immediate vicinity of Rome ever possessed in like degree. To this circumstance it is partly to be attributed that Spanish is in its most prominent feature, the inflections, much nearer Latin than its more direct descendant, Italian; and that were it not for the simplification of orthography introduced by the Spanish Academy, Spanish would have the honor (which now belongs to its near neighbor, Portuguese) of being the most like Latin of the principal Romance languages.

Two other languages have had a large influence in the formation of Spanish — Gothic, which is also found largely in all the other languages of Latin stock, and Arabic, which Spanish and Portuguese alone possess. The Arabs (or Moors, as they are usually called) held possession of a large part of the Iberian peninsula for nearly 800 years, and their intellectual superiority could not fail to produce a powerful and lasting impression on the language and character of the conquered nation.

The tendency of all language is to become simplified by use. The "numbers infinite of many-lettered" forms assumed in successive ages by the Sanskrit verb became 1,400 or less in classic Greek; its younger sister, Latin, had a maximum of 395, while the modern Spanish verb has at the utmost 62 distinguishable forms.† Spanish, moreover, has lost all case distinctions except in three pronouns, while the comparison of adjectives and adverbs now applies to but eight words.

The simplified condition of the language as now written does not

* M. Schele de Vere, "Grammar of the Spanish Language", 1854, p. 198.

† See Chapter XVIII, § 18.2.

justify the devoting of a large part of a textbook to the mere forms and definitions of words, reserving their usage for a second part called "syntax" *(putting together),* as was necessary in Greek and Latin, and has generally been followed blindly by modern grammarians. In this work the forms of words and their uses are exhibited together.

It may be necessary to state that Spanish, as written and spoken in the new world, is no further different from the mother tongue of Castile than the English of the educated classes of the United States differs from that spoken at the court of St. James. Some slight variations of pronunciation, still slighter changes of spelling, and an occasional word of native Indian origin, are about the only distinguishing features in both cases.

The present course of events, tending to bring the United States into more intimate relations with the Latin republics of the South, calls for instruction in the Spanish language, more practical and in greater detail than is afforded by any work now in use. An effort has been made to combine in the following pages as far as possible the special advantages of a progressive series of lessons and exercises, and of a systematic treatise on grammar. The beginner will find the first elements of the language exhibited so simply as to offer no difficulty or discouragement at the outset; and great pains have been taken to explain each point when first presented. The work is thus progressive in its method, and no statement presupposes the knowledge contained in a subsequent one. The only knowledge presupposed is an acquaintance with the most general distinctions and terms of grammar common to all languages.

It is obvious, however, that in such a method only the simplest principles and sentences can be exhibited in the beginning. The irregularities, anomalies and apparent absurdities which cause the beginner so much perplexity, are deferred until added knowledge and experience prepare him to grapple with them. As an example, the nominatives of the personal pronouns are shown in the second lesson; the objective forms are deferred to the first chapter of Part III; while the complexities of their enclitic use and duplicate objective forms are withheld until Chapter XXVII. The forms and uses of the various moods and tenses are learned and practised, one at a time, before any complete paradigm is presented; and the most useful irregular verbs are inserted by degrees before they are considered as a class.

To one who bestows only a hasty glance, this postponement of difficulties may give the impression that the work has no method or arrangement, when in fact its arrangement has been the subject of a special care and study, the constant endeavor having been to introduce nothing at a point where it cannot be appreciated.

Although the work is divided into three parts, it must not be imagined that any one of them forms a complete treatise independent of the others. Part I contains the principles of orthography and pronunciation which must be thoroughly assimilated before the study of the grammar and lexicology of the language is commenced. Part II contains twenty Lessons of moderate length, with exercises, which lead gradually up to the more extended treatment contained in Part III. Part III is divided into twenty Chapters of length varying with the requirements of the subjects under consideration, with exercises at intervals. It is not intended that each or any of these chapters is to be assigned as a *lesson.* Let the student undertake so much as his circumstances enable him to learn thoroughly. The author believes that Exercises, to test the student's progress at every step, and give opportunity to practise what he has learned, are among the most important agencies in education, and ought never to be evaded. He has, however, in preparing them, endeavored to avoid tedious and puerile iteration. Exercises in translating from Spanish into English have been omitted, from a conviction that this purpose can be better attained by a Progressive Reader, beginning with sentences of the most elementary character. Such a reader is now in preparation.

The work will also be found available as a systematic grammar and book of reference. By means of the Index, the student can find any particular point (as, for example, the neuter article or the pluperfect subjunctive) without having to read anything else.

The author desires to express his gratitude and indebtedness to Dr. José Ignacio Rodríguez, of the Bureau of the American Republics, to Mr. Edmundo J. Plaza, Secretary of the Mexican Legation at Washington, to Prof. M. Schele de Vere, of the University of Virginia, and to Mr. Bernardino Goicoechea, of New York, for valuable suggestions made during the preparation of this work.

COLUMBIAN UNIVERSITY,
WASHINGTON, *March,* 1894.

Useful Works of Reference

Consultation of the following titles, which deal primarily with modern Spanish, can be of great profit to teachers and students of Spanish:

Academia Española, *Gramática de la lengua española,* Madrid, Espasa-Calpe, S.A., 1931.

Alonso, Amado and Henríquez Ureña, Pedro, *Gramática castellana, Primer curso,* tercera edición, Editorial Losada, S.A., Buenos Aires, 1943; *Segundo curso,* tercera edición, Editorial Losada, S.A., Buenos Aires, 1943.

Bello, Andrés-Cuervo, Rufino José, *Gramática de la lengua castellana destinada al uso de los americanos,* décimonovena edición, Paris, R. Roger y F. Chernoviz, 1918. (There are many later printings.)

Bouzet, Jean, *Grammaire Espagnole,* Paris, Eugène Belin, n.d.

Cuervo, Rufino José, *Apuntaciones críticas sobre el lenguaje bogotano,* séptima edición, Bogotá, Editorial "El Gráfico," 1939.

Fernández, Salvador, *Gramática española, Los sonidos, el nombre y el pronombre,* Manuales de la Revista de Occidente, Madrid, 1951.

Gili Gaya, Samuel, *Curso superior de sintaxis española,* segunda edición, Barcelona, 1948.

Harmer, L. C. and Norton, F. J., *A Manual of Modern Spanish,* London University Tutorial Press Ltd., 1935.

Kany, Charles E., *American-Spanish Syntax,* Chicago, University of Chicago Press, n.d.

Keniston, Hayward, *Spanish Syntax List,* Henry Holt and Company, 1937.

Lenz, Rodolfo, *La oración y sus partes,* tercera edición, Madrid, 1935.

Navarro Tomás, Tomás, *Manual de pronunciación española,* cuarta edición, Madrid, 1932 (the standard work on Spanish pronunciation; there exists a simplified form of it in English: Navarro Tomás, Tomás and Espinosa, Aurelio M., *A Primer of Spanish Pronunciation,* Chicago-New York-Boston, Benj. H. Sanborn and Company, 1927).

Salvá, Vicente, *Gramática de la lengua castellana,* décimacuarta edición, Garnier Hermanos, Paris, n.d.

Spaulding, Robert K., *Syntax of the Spanish Verb,* New York, Henry Holt and Company, n.d.

The titles listed below, which are historical in approach, will mention incidentally features of modern Spanish grammar:

Entwistle, William J., *The Spanish Language,* London, Faber and Faber Ltd., 1936.

García de Diego, Vicente, *Gramática histórica española,* Editorial Gredos, Madrid, 1951.

Hanssen, Federico, *Gramática histórica de la lengua castellana,* Halle a.S., Max Miemeyer, 1913 or Buenos Aires, "El Ateneo," 1945.

Lapesa, Rafael, *Historia de la lengua española,* tercera edición corregida y aumentada, Madrid, 1955.

Menéndez Pidal, Ramón, *Manual de gramática histórica española,* séptima edición, Madrid, Espasa-Calpe, S.A., 1944.

Oliver Asín, Jaime, *Historia de la lengua española,* sexta edición, [Madrid], 1941.

Spaulding, Robert K., *How Spanish Grew,* Berkeley and Los Angeles, University of California Press, second printing, 1948.

Trend, J. B., *The Language and History of Spain,* Hutchinson's University Library, London, n.d.

Contents

PART I: ORTHOGRAPHY AND PRONUNCIATION

PART II: FORMS AND USES

APPENDICES

A Textbook of Modern Spanish

PART I

ORTHOGRAPHY AND PRONUNCIATION

Orthography and Pronunciation

THE ALPHABET

1. The alphabet recognized by the Spanish Academy[1] contains 25 simple and 4 compound letters, which are alike regarded as representing distinct sounds. To these may be added **w**[2] (names: **v doble, doble u**), employed principally in foreign words, to which **k** is also confined.

The forms of the letters are the same as in English:

CHARACTERS	NAMES	PRONUNCIATION	CHARACTERS	NAMES	PRONUNCIATION
a	a	*ah*[3]	**ñ**	eñe	*ain'yey*
b	be	*bay*	**o**	o	*oh*
c	ce	*thay*	**p**	pe	*pay*
ch	che	*chay*	**q**	cu	*coo*
d	de	*day*	**r**	ere	*ai'rey*
e	e	*ay*	**rr**	erre	*air'rey*
f	efe	*ai'fey*	**s**	ese	*ai'sey*
g	ge	*hay*[4]	**t**	te	*tay*
h	hache	*ah'chey*	**u**	u	*oo*
i	i	*ee*	**v**	ve *or* uve	*vay*
j	jota	*ho'tah*[4]	**x**	equis	*ai'kees*
k	ka	*kah*	**y**	i griega (*i.e., Greek i*) *or* ye	*ee greeay'ga* or *yay*
l	ele	*ai'ley*			
ll	elle	*ail'yey*			
m	eme	*ai'mey*	**z**	zeta	*thay'tah*
n	ene	*ai'ney*			

[1] The Royal Spanish Academy, founded in 1713 by the Duke of Escalona, is composed of 36 (formerly 30) members. Its object is to improve and preserve the Spanish language. The Grammar and Dictionary published by it are the official standards of the language.

[2] **W** appears in a few Spanish proper names like **Wamba** and **Witiza,** which are also written **Vamba** and **Vitiza** respectively.

[3] The English equivalents are only approximate at best. **E** does not end with the "off-glide" of English *ey* in *they, ay* in *bay, hay,* etc.

[4] Guttural *h,* pronounced nearly like German **ch** in **Buch.** Its sound will be represented in this work by *'h.*

2. The sound of each letter (simple or compound) is relatively unchanging, except **c** and **g**, which, as in English, have two or more sounds.

VOWELS

3. Great importance is attached to the vowels in Spanish; their sounds are full and clear, while those of the consonants are often obscure or even suppressed. The vowels have the following values:

A sounds approximately like *a* in *ah.*[1]
E sounds approximately like *a* in *hay.*[2]
I sounds approximately like *ee* in *bee.*
O sounds approximately like *o* in *hope.*[3]
U sounds approximately like *oo* in *room.*
Y, when a vowel, is equivalent to **i.**

These vowels, although somewhat fainter when not stressed, always retain the same character of sound.

REMARK. **Y** has the value of a vowel only when standing alone, as in **y** *and* or at the end of a word, as in **ley** *law.* It never occurs between consonants, its place being then taken by **i: sistema** *system,* **oxígeno** *oxygen.* (See also § **23,** 3, REMARK.)

In Chile **y** was formerly discarded as a vowel, **i** being used instead. This usage was quite general in Peru, Ecuador, Colombia and Venezuela. Survivals of this orthography, which in the past had official approval, are still met with.

4. The gradually descending scale of the audibility or strength of the vowels is the following: **a, o, e, i, u.** Thus, **a, o, e** are traditionally called strong vowels and **i, u,** weak vowels.

DIPHTHONGS AND TRIPHTHONGS

5. A diphthong is a combination, in either order, of a vowel and a semivowel. The vowels are **a, e, i, o, u** (cf. § 4); the semivowels are **i** when pronounced approximately like the **i** of *collier, union* or the y of *they, boy* and **u** when pronounced approximately like the **u** of *penguin, queen* and *out.*

A triphthong is a combination of the vowel **a** or **e** preceded by

---

[1] The sound of Spanish **a** is midway between *a* in *father* and *that.*
[2] See § **1**, note 3.
[3] But without the diphthongal glide with which *o* is often pronounced in English.

the semivowel **i** or **u** and followed by the semivowel **i** (or **y**, orthographically).

From the point of view of spelling diphthongs and triphthongs are considered to constitute single syllables. Vowels in any other combination constitute separate syllables, from the point of view of spelling. In rapid speech, however, and often in poetry combinations that make separate syllables in writing are treated as forming single syllables.

6. The following is a list of all the orthographic diphthongs and triphthongs in the language. The diphthongs in the one column are the reverse of those in the other:

DIPHTHONGS

ai, ay	aire, hay	**ia**	seria, diablo
au	pausa, caudal	**ua**	cuanto, agua
oi, oy	sois, hoy	**io**	estudio, atención
ou	bou	**uo**	evacuo, evacuó
ei, ey	pleito, ley	**ie**	piedra, anuncie
eu	feudo, deuda	**ue**	pues, fuego
iu	viuda, triunfo	**ui, uy**	ruido, muy

TRIPHTHONGS

iai	apreciáis	**uai, uay**	averiguáis, Paraguay
iei	apreciéis	**uei, uey**	averigüéis, buey

REMARK. Pure Castilian words do not end in **au, ou, eu** or **iu. Bou,** the only example in the language, is a Catalan borrowing. Proper names like **Arbeu, Arrau,** etc., are non-Castilian in origin.

7. It has been shown (§ 3) that y as a vowel is equal to **i.** Whenever a diphthong or triphthong ending in **i** comes at the end of a word, in spelling the **i** is changed to y, as exhibited above (§ **6**).

This, however was formerly not the general usage in Chile, Peru, Ecuador, Colombia and Venezuela. See § **3**, REMARK.

8. The diphthongs **ue, ie** do not begin words; **ue** is preceded by **h** (silent),[1] while the **i** of **ie** is changed to **y.** These changes do not

[1] This usage is a relic of an old rule, observed long ago when **u** represented both the sound of *v* (consonant) and *u* (vowel), in order to show that in such case **u** had the vowel sound. It is now adhered to merely from custom. Before **ie** h was formerly used in a similar way, since **i** represented both the sound of **y** (consonant) and **i** (vowel). The older spelling survives in **hielo, hiedra** (variant form **yedra**) and in **hierba** (also spelled **yerba**). The **h** of **hiedra** and **hierba** may in part represent the Latin words from which they come (*hedera, herba*).

affect the pronunciation, and are merely a requirement of Spanish orthography:

hueso bone	**huevo** egg	**huérfano** orphan
yerro error	**yendo** going	**yegua** mare

REMARK. There are words beginning with **hie,** but they do not come under this principle; with them the **h** is, or represents, an original part of the word:

hiena	GREEK *ὕαινα*	hyena
hierro	LATIN *ferrum*	iron
hiel	LATIN *fel*	gall

9. Adjacent vowels which are not diphthongs in writing are nevertheless very much run together in rapid speech. This also occurs in the case of concurrent vowels or diphthongs in different words, and where two vowels are separated by silent **h,** and causes the foreigner much perplexity at first on hearing the spoken language. For example:

la sola‿idea	mi‿acción	suba‿usted	¿sabe‿usted?
sólo‿eso	mi‿hija	a‿hora	la‿hora
socio‿ausente			

REMARK. The assimilation is more complete when the concurrent vowels are identical; as in:

sería‿agradable	de‿eso	mi‿ida	esta‿acción

10. As a diphthong or triphthong is considered a single syllable, it is sometimes necessary to place the written accent over that syllable. In that case the accent mark must be placed over the vowel; when placed over **i** or **u** the diphthong then become two syllables. Thus **uo** in **continuo** *continuous* and **continuó** *he continued* is a diphthong, but not in **continúo** *I continue;* so **ia** in **seria** *serious* is a diphthong, but not in **sería** *would be.* (For the written accent or accent mark see §§ **21** ff.)

11. If the vowels are **i** and **u** the accent mark, if necessary, must be placed over the last vowel; if placed over the first one, the diphthong is dissolved. Thus **ui** in **fuí** is a diphthong, as is **iu** in **Feliú** (a Catalan proper name). (For the use of the accent mark see § **30**.)

In many forms of verbs in **uir** the **u** and **i** are frequently pronounced as separate syllables. In the past it was not unusual to write **huído** instead of **huido,** etc.

In spite of the spelling, **flúido** is normally pronounced as a word of two syllables: "flwido".

REMARK. The learner is cautioned against allowing the **u** of the diphthong **ui** to be heard as a vowel; it should have the consonant value of the English *w*:

luir	pronounced practically *lweer*	not	*loo-ir*
muy	" " *mwee*	"	*moo-ee*
huir	" " *weer*	"	*oo-eer*
constituir	" " *constitweer*	"	*constitoo-eer*

12. Where several words are formed from the same stem, it will be found that the vowels **e** and **o** are often changed to **ie** and **ue** respectively when they receive the stress in pronunciation; and, conversely, when the diphthong is relieved of the stress, the original vowel resumes its place. This alternation pervades the language, being especially noticeable in the forms taken by Latin words in Spanish, and in the formation of derivatives; but it does not apply in every case. Examples:

LATIN	WITH STRESS	WITHOUT STRESS
festa	fiesta *feast*	festivo *festive*
certum	cierto *certain*	certidumbre *certainty*
refero	refiero *I refer*	referencia *reference*
arden(t)s	ardiente *burning*	ardentía *phosphorescence*
cornu	cuerno *horn*	cornudo *horned*
forum	fuero *forum*	forense *forensic*
hortus	huerto *kitchen garden*	hortaliza *garden truck*
fon(t)s	fuente *fountain, spring*	fontanoso *containing springs*

13. When an initial **e** or **o** is thus expanded, the resulting diphthongs **ie** and **ue** are respectively changed to **ye** and **hue** (in accordance with the orthographic requirement given in § **8**):

LATIN	SPANISH	GREEK	SPANISH
equa	yegua *mare*	ὀρφανός	huérfano *orphan*
error	yerro *error*		
ovum	huevo *egg*		

14. CONSONANTS

F, k, m and **n** have nearly the same value in Spanish as in English.

B has nearly the same but not quite so forcible a sound as in

English when it follows a pause in speaking or the nasal sounds written **m** or **n** (**¡Basta!, ambos, un barco**); in other cases the lips do not touch each other; the breath is allowed to escape between them (**haba, habla, árbol, el barco, objeto**).

C has two sounds. Before **e** and **i** it is pronounced approximately like *th* in *thin.* In all other cases it has the sound of *k.*

REMARK. The pronunciation of **c** and **z** like *th* is comparatively modern, dating from the eighteenth century or later. It is peculiarly Castilian, as distinguished from the common speech of Andalusia, Catalonia, Valencia, the Basque Provinces and Galicia; it has not found its way into Portuguese, and in Spanish America it is generally regarded as affected and pedantic if used by the people born there. In the last-named part of the globe the usual pronunciation of **c** before **e** and **i,** and of **z** in all cases, is that of *c* in *city, precede.*

C is frequently omitted before **c** and **t** in pronunciation. This elision has been the cause of many shortened forms which are now correct, such as: **contrato** *contract;* **objeto** *object;* **afición** *affection.*

Ch is now everywhere pronounced nearly like *ch* in *church.* In words of Greek ancestry it formerly represented also the *k* sound of the *ch* of *echo,* but this sound is now written in the manner prescribed for the sound of *k* in the table at the end of this section.

REMARK. In proper names of non-Castilian origin final **ch** is at times pronounced like *k:* **Escrich, Roch.**

D ordinarily has a tinge of the sound of *th* in *then* because the tip of the tongue only gently touches the edge of the upper incisors without entirely shutting off the passage for the breath. Between vowels and at the end of words this sound is more apparent, becoming almost exactly like *th* in *then.* When it follows a pause in speaking, the sound of **n** or **l,** it has however practically the sound of English *d* (**Don Domingo, molde**).

REMARK. Both **d** and **t** before **r** have the forcible sound, obtained by pressing the tongue against the teeth, much heard in the Irish brogue.

D is often elided in familiar speech when occurring between vowels or at the end of words; as: **pegao** for **pegado, sentío** for **sentido, tomá** for **tomad, Madrí** for **Madrid, usté** (even **uté**) for **usted,** etc. Two identical vowels coalesce when thus brought together; as: **pue** for **puede, to** for **todo, na** for **nada.** Of these, the contraction **ado** = **ao** is the most frequent.

G has more than one sound. Before **e** and **i** it has the sound of strongly aspirated *h*, nearly like the German *ch* in *Buch*. In all other cases it either sounds approximately (see the first part of statement for **B**) like *g* in *go* when it follows a pause in speaking or **n** (**Galicia es un reino; tengo, un gato**), or, as in all other circumstances, contact of soft palate and tongue is not complete and the breath escapes through the narrow passage left between the back of the tongue and the soft palate (see the latter part of the statement for **B**): **¿Dónde se halla Galicia?, hago, casa grande, rasgo.**

In order to obtain either of the latter sounds of **g** before **e** and **i, u** is interpolated between **g** and the vowel. In this case the **u** is silent; if it must be pronounced, a dieresis (¨) is placed over it; as in: **agüero, vergüenza.**

Among the uneducated people **g** and **b** are interchangeable before **u**, or are even silent altogether. Thus **aguja** is transformed into *abuja* or *ahuja;* and conversely **abuelo** become *agüelo* or *ahuelo,* and **bueno,** *güeno* or *hueno.* Similarly **hueco, huero, huerta,** become *güeco, güero, güerta.*

H is entirely silent (except in dialectal pronunciations wherein **h** is still pronounced at the beginning of a word when it derives from Latin *f* (**humo** from *fumum,* **haba** from *fabam,* etc.).

J has the same sound which **g** has before **e** and **i;** as in: **enjambre, hijo, juego, jefe, jirafa.**

REMARK. In Chile, Peru and Ecuador, and indeed throughout most of the Pacific coast of South America, it was formerly the rule to use **j** in all cases where the guttural sound occurs, hence to use it instead of **g** before **e** and **i**; as in

jeneral *for* general vijía *for* vigía pájina *for* página

L is made by putting the tip of the tongue against the sockets of the upper incisors, the remainder of the tongue lying almost flat. Thus Spanish **l** does not have the "hollow" sound of *l* in such English words as *false, tool,* where the back of the tongue rises toward the palate.

Ll has approximately the sound of the letters *lli* in the English *million,* which is written in Spanish **millón.**

In Andalusia (and even in Madrid) and most parts of Spanish America, **ll** is pronounced like *y* in the English *beyond;* hence **caballo** = *cabayo,* **pollo** = *poyo.* But this pronunciation is not considered the most elegant.

N. In Andalusia, Galicia, Catalonia, even in other parts of Spain and in many parts of Spanish America, notably Cuba, final **n** is given a nasal sound almost identical with the French *an, on,* etc. But this the student is not advised to adopt.

REMARK. Final **ny** in proper names of Catalan origin is pronounced as *n* (especially by those conscious of its ancestry) or as *ni:* **Capmany, Castany, Fortuny.**

Ñ has approximately the sound of the letters *ni* in the English *pinion,* written in Spanish **piñón.**

NOTE. The mark over **ñ** is called **la** (or **el**) **tilde** in Spanish.

P is pronounced without the puff of breath that often accompanies this sound in English. The **p** of initial **ps (psicología)** is silent.

Q only occurs before **ue** and **ui,** and sounds like *k,* the following **u** being always silent.

R is articulated by touching the top of the tongue to the sockets of the upper incisors. It is forcibly rolled at the beginning of words and after **l, n** and **s.**

Rr invariably has the forcibly rolled sound.

REMARK I. Special care must be taken to distinguish between **r** and **rr,** as very ludicrous mistakes are liable to arise from confusing them; thus **pera** is a *pear,* **perra** a *female dog.*

REMARK II. In compound words made up of one ending in a vowel plus one beginning with **r,** the latter is doubled in writing, thus preserving the sound it would have at the beginning of a word: **Monterrey** (monte + rey), **pararrayos** (para + rayos), **prorrata** (pro + rata), etc.

S has normally the hissing sound of *s* in *say, case.* When it is followed in rapid speech by the sounds of **b, d, g, l, m, n,** it is often pronounced approximately like the *s* of *cause* **(esbozo, los barcos, desde, tres días, trasgo, las gorras, isla, dos lagos, mismo, pocas manos, asno, muchos niños).** When it is followed by **r,** it tends to disappear and the number of trills of **r** increases as a consequence (thus **los reyes** becomes practically **lorreyes).**

REMARK. No word or syllable in Spanish begins with **s** followed by a consonant, and many Spaniards experience great difficulty in uttering such a combination without prefixing a vowel.

S at the end of syllables is frequently dropped or pronounced like aspirated *h* in Andalusia and Spanish America. Thus: *Eh'pañol* for **español,** *deh'puéh* for **después,** *¡a lo'hueno' corru'co' de almendrah'!* for **¡a los buenos corruscos de almendras!** *get your nice macaroons!* a familiar street vender's cry. This is restricted to the uneducated classes or to familiar language.

T is pronounced with the tip of the tongue against the upper teeth rather than the gums (as in English) and, like **p**, is not accompanied by the breathing sound.

V is pronounced like **B** (see the statement above), the two letters being interchangeable so far as concerns pronunciation: **¡Vaya!, convidar, un vaso, mover, el vaso.**

W is pronounced according to its value in the language from which the word containing it is taken. Hence **Wágner** = *Vágner,* and **Wáshington** = *Uáshington.*

X has approximately the sound of *x* in *wax, axle,* though more like *gs* than *ks.*

REMARK. In many words **x** had formerly the sound of the Spanish **j**, but according to modern orthography the **x** in those words is replaced by **j**. Thus what were formerly written *xefe, baxo, relox,* are now spelled **jefe, bajo, reloj.**[1] The spellings **México, mexicano,** preferred by some to **Méjico, mejicano,** are a survival of the older system.

The prefix **ex,** when followed by a consonant other than **h,** is very generally pronounced *es,* as *escelente* for **excelente.**

Y is a consonant only at the beginning of a word or syllable; it then has the same value as in English, but is pronounced with greater tension of the organs of speech.

In many localities consonantal **y** has nearly the sound of *z* in *azure* (the French *j*), and even that of English *j* in *joke.*

Z sounds like *th* in *thin.* With the exception of its own name and a few other words, it never occurs before **e** or **i,** but only before **a, o** and **u,** the consonants **b, c, g, m** and **n,** and at the end of a word.

In Andalusia and Spanish America **z** is given the sound of *c* in *city, precede,* as has been explained under **C.**

---

[1] **Reloj** (from the Latin *horologium*) is the general term for *timekeeper,* and means both *watch* and *clock.* The final **j** is now silent, the chief instance of a silent consonant other than **h** in literary Spanish. The word is therefore sometimes written **reló;** its plural is regular—**relojes.**

15.

TABLE SHOWING THE MANNER OF REPRESENTING CERTAIN CONSONANTAL SOUNDS BEFORE THE SEVERAL VOWELS

	a	e	i	o	u
Sound of *k*	ca	que	qui	co	cu
Sound of *th*	za	ce	ci	zo	zu
Sound of *g*	ga	gue	gui	go	gu
Sound of *h*	ja	ge(je)	gi(ji)	jo	ju
Sound of *kw*	cua	cue	cui	cuo	
Sound of *gw*	gua	güe	güi	guo	

DOUBLE LETTERS

16. The Spanish Academy long ago suppressed double consonants in writing where one alone is pronounced.[1]

17. **C** and **n** are the only consonants now doubled, and that only when both are pronounced; as: **acción, ennoblecer, perenne.**

18. **Cc** can occur only before **e** and **i,** and is pronounced *k'th;* as: **accessible, occidente.**

19. **Ll** and **rr** are not considered double letters but distinct signs for particular sounds.

20. Latin and English *mm* stand as **nm** in Spanish:
inmersión immersion **inmenso** immense **inmortal** immortal

THE ACCENT MARK

21. In Spanish as in English, in words of two or more syllables, some one is pronounced more forcibly than the others. This forcible utterance will be called *stress;* the mark for showing it in writing or print (´) will be called the *written accent* or *accent mark.*

---

[1] Thus **s** is no longer written double: even in the case of verb forms ending in **s** followed by the pronoun **se** it is customary (but not universal) to write only one (**démoselo** for **démosselo** *let us give it to him*). But **nn** is regularly retained in **dénnoslo** *give it to us,* etc.

As it would be too laborious in writing to place an accent mark over every word, and as words of similar terminations are generally stressed alike, they have been grouped into classes, which, from their uniformity, do not need the written accent. Only words that are in some way exceptional require the accent mark.

22. The various ways of making this classification have caused the changes which have taken place during the last two centuries in the system of written accentuation. The one last adopted proceeds upon the following general principles:

a. The greater part of words ending in a vowel are stressed on the penultimate.

b. The greater part of words ending in **n** or **s**[1] are stressed on the penultimate. (Because most words ending in **s** are plurals, and the adding of **s** or **es** in the plural does not change the original stress; and most words ending in **n** are parts of verbs, and nearly all parts of verbs are stressed on the penultimate.)

c. The greater part of words ending in other consonants than **n** or **s** are stressed on the last syllable.

d. Words stressed on any syllable before the antepenultimate are usually compounds: **bébaselo, escribiéndonosla.**

NOTE. As of September, 1952, the Spanish Academy decreed certain reforms in spelling and accentuation, including the omission of the accent mark in **fuí, fué, dió, vió;** in infinitives like **embaír, sonreír** and **desoír;** and in the first word of compounds like **décimoséptimo.** Only time will determine whether the reforms are generally adopted. They have not been followed in this work.

23. From these general principles are deduced the following rules governing the written accent:

1. All words ending in a vowel or in **n** or **s**[1] which are stressed on the penultimate, bear no accent mark:

teme	margen	martes
toma	imagen	crisis
suspiro	volumen	vecinos

[1] Verb forms usually follow the spelling of the infinitive or the majority of forms, though not infrequently each is subjected to the applicable rule: **reuno, –es, –e** or **reúno, –es, –e** (from **reunir**); **maullo, –as, –a** or **maúllo, –as, –a** (from **maullar**), etc. But **reunimos, reunís; maullamos, maulláis,** etc.

2. All words ending in a vowel, or in **n** or **s**, which are stressed on the last syllable, must bear the accent mark on that syllable:

café	motín	atrás
amó	vaivén	revés
Perú	renglón	pedís
contendrá	alquitrán	además

3. All words ending in a consonant other than **n** or **s**, and which are stressed on the last syllable, do not bear the accent mark:

alud	reloj	peral
esperar	altivez	verdegay
Abel	Edom	Habacuc

REMARK. Final **y**, although sounded as a vowel, is considered a consonant for the purposes of written accentuation.

4. All words ending in a consonant other than **n** or **s**, and which are stressed on the penultimate, must bear the accent mark:

áspid	ángel	mármol
ítem	cráter	nácar
clímax	lápiz	alférez

5. All words stressed on a syllable previous to the penultimate, must bear the accent mark:

ciénaga	músico	héroe
artículos	pirámide	régimen
línea	atmósfera	paseábamos[1]

24. It is to be remembered (1) that in writing a diphthong or a triphthong is considered one syllable (cf. §§ 4 ff.); (2) that in writing other combinations of vowels form separate syllables; (3) that an accent mark on **i** or **u** followed or preceded by any other vowel means that the vowels do not form a diphthong or part of a triphthong but separate syllables.

25. These peculiarities give rise to the following special rules for words containing diphthongs or triphthongs:

1. The presence of a diphthong or triphthong in a syllable which would naturally be stressed, does not affect the written accentuation of the word:

heroico	envainan	enviuda
piocha	empeine	arruina
cuenca	Ceuta	pierden

[1] Regardless of the rules given in § 23 the accent mark is omitted from capital letters by the majority of printers nowadays.

2. If a syllable requiring the written accent contains a diphthong or triphthong, the accent mark must be placed over the vowel; or, in the case of a diphthong composed of **i** and **u** over the last:

buscapié	piélago	después
parabién	huéspedes	estudiáis
benjuí	Cáucaso	semidiós

3. Whenever the **i** or **u** of two or more successive vowels is stressed, the accent mark must be placed over said vowel to show that there is no diphthong or triphthong, as the case may be:

ataúd	país	raíz	poesía
días	mío	acentúo	creído
continúan	poesías	decíais	temíais
roído	dúo	leía	alelíes
aúlla	saúco	egoísmo	período
increíble	paraíso		

26. The tenses of the verb which bear the accent mark, retain it when one or more pronouns are added to them (§ 3.57):

fuése	vióse	rogóles
pidiómelo	conmovíla	andaráse

27. When one or more pronouns are added to any part of a verb so as to shift the stressed syllable to the antepenultimate, or still farther from the end, the stressed syllable must be then marked:

dándomelos	comérselo	habiéndoseme
conseguírnoslos	consiguiéndonoslas	castíguesemele

28. When two Spanish words are combined, each retains its original accent. This also applies to an adverb formed from an adjective by adding **mente:**

décimoséptimo, *from* décimo *and* séptimo
cortésmente, *from* cortés *and* mente
lícitamente, *from* lícita *and* mente

29. The preposition **a** and the conjunctions **e, o, u** formerly bore the accent mark from custom, and not for any orthoepic reason.

30. No words of one syllable bear the written accent, with the exception of the two classes of words following:

a. Monosyllabic preterite forms of verbs. (The accent mark is used here in imitation of the great majority of verbs where it is called for: **comí, averigüé, comió,** etc. For a similar reason the accent mark is usually printed on **riáis, fiáis,** etc.).

fuí fué vió rió[1]

b. Where there are two monosyllables of identical form, the more emphatic one is often distinguished by the written accent. When so used, the accent is termed *diacritic*:

dé give (*subjunctive of* **dar**)	**de** of, from
él he, him	**el** the
mí me	**mi** my
más more	**mas** but
sé I know, be (*command*)	**se** oneself
sí yes, oneself	**si** if
tú you	**tu** your

31. This practice, formerly more general, is often extended to **té** *tea* (**te** *you*), **són** *sound* (**son** *are*), **pára** *stops* (**para** *for*), etc. The accent mark regularly distinguishes the adverb (**sólo**) from the adjective (**solo**).

32. The diacritic accent mark is used to distinguish demonstrative pronouns used substantively:

éste this one	**este** this
ése that one	**ese** that
aquél that one yonder	**aquel** that (yonder)[2]

33. To distinguish the interrogative or exclamatory from the relative use of pronouns and adverbs:

cómo how?	**como** as
cuál which?	**cual** which
cuán how!	**cuan** as
cuándo when?	**cuando** when
cuánto how much?	**cuanto** as much
cúyo whose?	**cuyo** whose
dónde where?	**donde** where
qué what?	**que** that, which
quién who? whom?	**quien** who, whom

[1] Usage with regard to an accent mark in forms like **huis, huido** (< **huir**), **riáis,** (< **reír**), cannot be said to be uniform.

[2] When followed by **que**, and with the meaning of *he that, the one that,* the accent mark is usually omitted: **este que, ese que, aquel que** (see § **5.35**).

34. And finally when any of the pronouns or adverbs in the preceding section are repeated as correlatives:

cuándo por una parte, **cuándo** por otra	*now* in one place, *now* in another
Quién lloraba, **quién** rezaba.	*One* wept, *another* prayed.
Cuáles leían, **cuáles** fumaban.	*Some* were reading, *others* smoking.

35. There are many pairs of words composed of the same letters, but stressed differently both in speaking and writing. In these the written accent is not diacritic (cf. § 30, b), but indicates the pronunciation. For example:

tenia, tenía	cortes, cortés	anden, andén
pie, píe	veras, verás	picaron, picarón

36. The adverb **aun,** when it follows the verb to which it belongs is usually pronounced in two syllables, and the dissolution of the diphthong is shown by the accent mark: **aún.** When it precedes the verb it is usually a diphthong and has no accent mark (see the more complete statement of § **30.27**):

¿Aun no ha llegado?	No ha llegado aún.

37. In English one syllable of a word is often stressed at the expense of the vowels in the other syllables; thus *reciprocal* is pronounced so that it is impossible to tell what are the precise sounds of the last two vowels. But in Spanish the original quality of a vowel is not appreciably changed or lost because it does not receive the principal stress.

38. Special care should be exercised by the English-speaking foreigner in distinguishing the vowel terminations of Spanish words, especially **o** and **a,** pronouncing them clearly, yet without special emphasis when not stressed. The change of a final vowel often constitutes the only difference between two inflectional forms of a verb, or two nouns of widely different meaning; while the distinction of gender depends entirely upon the vowels **o** and **a.** The following pairs of nouns may serve as an example and an exercise:

abuelo grandfather	**abuela** grandmother
barro mud	**barra** bar, ingot

cardo thistle
cargo charge, employment
copo snowflake
cuarto room, apartment
dicho saying
duelo duel
grano grain
hilo thread
huelgo breath, wind
músico musician
naranjo orange tree
puerto port, harbor
seno bosom
tino skill, tact
velo veil

carda wool card
carga load
copa wineglass
cuarta quarter
dicha luck
duela barrel stave
grana cochineal
hila lint
huelga strike *(of laborers)*
música music
naranja orange *(fruit)*
puerta door, gate
sena senna
tina vat, bathtub
vela candle

39. The following words will exercise the learner in pronunciation, as well as serve as examples of the present system of accentuation. To aid the student in distinguishing the syllable to be stressed, the stressed vowel is in boldface type when not indicated by the written accent:

Querétaro, vástago, búscame, monosílabo, crepúsculo; Panamá, consagré, partí, partió, frenesí, baladí, quinqué, biricú; máscara, sábado; Bolívar, áspid, cónsul, memorándum, Madrid, arroz, zarzal, mujer; aman, amarán, partirán, sartén, almidón, atún, ningún, alguien, virgen, orden, origen, resumen, colon, Colón, batan, batán, amen, amén; bien, también, cien, recién; letras, vidas, además, compás, portugués, Dios, semidiós, pues, después, obús, énfasis, montes, montés, delfines, delfinés, tomas, Tomás, fines, finés; averiguáis, averiguaréis.

Pirineos, Mediterráneo, bajaes, bacalao, empleo, corroen, canoa, deseos, aérea, erróneo, hectárea, baúl, desvarío, tenían, lidian, lee, lea, ley, leí, insinúan, decíais, delirio, sitio, acaricia, atestigua, fatuos, amortiguan, averigüé, veréis, acaricié, gradue, gradúe, caen, Caén, hay, ahí, Túy, muy, Luis, cáustico.

40. DIVISION OF SYLLABLES

This is only required in dividing a word at the end of a line, and usage differs essentially from the English.

1. The fundamental principle is to make syllables end in a vowel as far as possible; therefore a single consonant occurring between vowels is joined to the vowel or vowels which follow:

ca-ra-co-les   flu-xión   re-ba-ño   fle-xi-bi-li-dad

2. The characters **ch, ll, rr** and **ñ**, being considered as simple consonants, follow the above rule:

mu-cha-cho ba-ta-lla bu-lló ba-rre-ño ci-ga-rro

REMARK. Double **c** and **n** are divided as in English:

ac-ce-so ac-ción en-no-ble-cer in-ne-ga-ble

3. Prepositional prefixes form separate syllables, as in

ab-ne-gar ex-pre-sar des-a-gra-da-ble con-ce-bir

Except when the prefix comes before **s** followed by a consonant, in which case the **s** is joined to the prefix:

abs-te-ner cons-tan-te ins-pi-rar pers-pi-ca-cia
ab-sol-ver con-sul-tar in-sis-tir per-se-guir

4. Vowels forming a diphthong or triphthong must not be separated:

jui-cio a-güe-ro guar-dia des-pre-ciéis

Concurrent vowels which cannot form diphthongs or triphthongs, and diphthongs or triphthongs dissolved by the accent mark, form separate syllables:

le-er re-al a-ta-úd tra-ído da-rí-ais

5. The liquid consonants **l** and **r**, when preceded by any consonant other than **s**, must not be separated from that consonant, except in uniting parts of compound words. Thus:

ha-blar po-dría cé-le-bre si-glo
sub-lu-nar sub-ra-yar ab-ro-gar es-la-bón

6. Two separate consonants standing between vowels are divided; as:

ac-ta cuer-da yer-ba chas-co pron-to

7. When a syllable consists of a single vowel, it should not stand alone at the end or beginning of a line, as would be the case in **o-cupar, a-rreglar, ganzú-a.**

CAPITALS AND PUNCTUATION

41. The use of capitals is much the same as in English, the chief exception being that no adjective, whatever be its derivation, begins with a capital letter, except in titles or at the beginning of a sentence:

el continente **sudamericano**	the *South American* continent
la bandera **chilena**	the *Chilean* flag
las hermosuras **sevillanas**	the *Seville* belles
las tablas **alfonsíes**	the *Alphonsine* tables (astronomical)

a. In titles of periodicals both nouns and adjectives are usually capitalized, particularly if they stand side by side:

La España Moderna	*Modern Spain*
El Correo	*The Mail*
Revista de filología hispánica *or* **Revista de Filología Hispánica**	*Review of Hispanic Philology*

b. In other titles ordinarily only the first word is capitalized (except for proper names and at times in short titles):

Peñas arriba	*Up the Crags*
La vida es sueño	*Life Is a Dream*
Sangre y arena	*Blood and Sand*
Historia de la literatura española	*History of Spanish Literature*

c. In geographic names made up of a common noun and an adjective the latter is regularly capitalized, the former often is:

la República Argentina	the Argentine Republic
el mar Rojo *or* el Mar Rojo	the Red Sea
el Río Bravo *(perhaps through influence of English)*	the Rio Grande
el Nuevo Mundo	the New World
la Sierra Nevada	the Sierra Nevada

BUT

el río Ebro	the Ebro river
el lago Titicaca	Lake Titicaca
el estrecho de Magallanes	the Straits of Magellan
el monte Vesubio	Mount Vesuvius

d. In geographical names made up of the definite article and a noun, the latter is regularly capitalized, the former often is, whether the noun be common or proper:

El Paso	El Paso
La Línea	La Línea *(near Gibraltar)*
Lugo y La Coruña	Lugo and Corunna
En esta ría está El Ferrol.	On this estuary is El Ferrol.

e. Other combinations are represented by **El Paso del Norte, Las Navas de Tolosa, El Cabo** *(Cape)* **de San** *(occasionally* **san)** **Vicente,** etc.

42. The pronoun **yo** *I* is written with a small initial except at the beginning of a sentence or quotation:

Dijo el duque, "**Yo,** y **yo** sólo, soy el dueño aquí."	Said the duke, "*I,* and *I* alone am master here."

43. The punctuation is the same in both languages, except that in the case of an interrogation or exclamation, an inverted point (¿ ¡) is placed at the beginning of the sentence or clause in addition to the usual sign at the end, as will be seen throughout this book. (Moreover, since some sentences are to a degree both interrogations and exclamations, a combination of signs (¿. . . ¡, ¡. . . ?) will be encountered on occasion.) In this way the reader is apprised in advance as to the nature of a sentence, and can modulate his voice accordingly. The use of the dash instead of the quotation marks of English and in general to indicate a change of speaker is customary. Example: **Lo que me parece — dijo Galiani — es que está usted triste.** *"What I think," said Galiani, "is that you are sad."* If the quotation ends the paragraph, the second dash is omitted.

The use of the colon for the forward projection of the idea is more frequent than in present-day English: **Yo soy un malvado: lo confieso.** (Valera, **Pepita Jiménez, Paralipómenos**) *I am a villain. I confess it.*

a. The names of the chief punctuation marks of Spanish are the following:

punto, punto final period (.)
dos puntos colon (:)
punto y coma semicolon (;)
puntos suspensivos suspension points (. . .)
coma comma (,)
principio de interrogación (¿)
fin de interrogación (?)
principio de exclamación *(or* **admiración)** (¡)
fin de exclamación *(or* **admiración)** (!)
comillas quotation marks (« », " ")
guión hyphen (-)
raya dash (—)
crema *(or* **diéresis)** diaeresis (¨)
paréntesis parentheses ( )
paréntesis rectangular *(or* **cuadrado)** bracket ([*or*])
corchete brace ({ *or* })
estrellita *(or* **asterisco)** asterisk (*)
calderón *(or* **párrafo)** paragraph (¶ *or* §)
cruz *(or* **obelisco)** dagger (†)

b. In writing figures the period is used to separate groups of three digits and the comma serves as a decimal point: **1.234** = 1,234 and **5,6** = 5.6.

A Textbook of Modern Spanish

PART II

FORMS AND USES

I

Peculiarities Of Nouns

PLURAL

1.1. The plurals of all Spanish nouns, pronouns, adjectives and participles end in s. We shall here consider the nouns under the following subdivisions:

1. Nouns ending in an unstressed vowel or diphthong merely add **s**:

el caballo the horse	**los caballos** the horses
la casa the house	**las casas** the houses
el indio the Indian	**los indios** the Indians
la tribu the tribe	**las tribus** the tribes

2. Nouns of more than one syllable which end in stressed **e, o, u** and the monosyllables **pie** *foot* and **te** *tea* likewise add **s**:

el canapé the couch	**los canapés** the couches
el landó the landau	**los landós** the landaus
el tisú the tissue	**los tisús** the tissues
el pie the foot	**los pies** the feet
el te the tea	**los tes** the teas

3. Nouns which end in a consonant insert **e** as a connecting vowel before adding **s**:

el balcón the balcony	**los balcones** the balconies
la flor the flower	**las flores** the flowers

REMARK. Final **c** is changed to **qu** to preserve the hard sound before **e**; and final **z** is changed to **c** (§ **15**):

el frac the dress coat	**los fraques** the dress coats
la cruz the cross	**las cruces** the crosses

4. Nouns which end in stressed **a, i** or a stressed diphthong of which the last letter is y add **es**:

el bajá the pasha	**los bajaes** the pashas
el rubí the ruby	**los rubíes** the rubies
el rey the king	**los reyes** the kings

REMARK. The following words, of foreign origin, are exceptions: **papá, papás; mamá, mamás; sofá, sofás.** There are a few others of rare occurrence.

5. The names of the letters of the alphabet (which are all feminine) add **es:**

las aes, bees or **bes, ees** or **es, íes, oes, úes** *the a's, b's, e's, i's, o's, u's*

6. Polysyllabic nouns which end in unstressed **is** or **es,** pure Latin terms and family names which end in **z** and are not stressed on the last syllable usually do not change in the plural. The article suffices to distinguish the plural from the singular:

la crisis the crisis	**las crisis** the crises
el paréntesis the parenthesis	**los paréntesis** the parentheses
el lunes (the) Monday	**los lunes** (the) Mondays
el déficit the deficit	**los déficit** the deficits
el ultimátum the ultimatum	**los ultimátum** the ultimata
Martínez (*a family name*)	**los Martínez** the Martinez

REMARK. Family names ending in an unstressed vowel may or may not change in the plural: **Los Medina(s)** *the Medinas.* All others usually follow the rules of § **1.1** but may remain unchanged.

1.2. The addition of **s** or **es** in forming the plural does not change the spoken stress of the words. But the addition of **es** does affect the written accent mark of words which end in **n, s** or a stressed vowel; for when **es** is added, a written accent may have to be omitted or added (see § **23**):

el cañón the cannon	**los cañones** the cannons
el joven the young man	**los jóvenes** the young men
la virgen the virgin, maid	**las vírgenes** the virgins, maids
el semidiós the demigod	**los semidioses** the demigods
el bajá the pasha	**los bajaes** the pashas

REMARK. There are few exceptions: **el carácter** *the character* (plural: **los caracteres**); **el régimen** *the government, rule* (plural: **los regímenes**); **el espécimen** *the specimen* (plural: **los especímenes**).

GENDER

1.3. In Spanish there are three genders: masculine, feminine and neuter. The latter applies only to pronouns, adjectives and participles. (See § 2.47.) Every noun, whether denoting an animate or inanimate object, or an abstraction is either masculine or feminine. There are no available rules for determining the gender of Spanish nouns. The gender of many nouns must be learned separately for each noun, in the same manner as the spelling of many words in English. It is true there is usually a reason for the gender assigned to a word, but it must often be sought in the language from which the word is derived, and it may be obscure or untraceable.

But few of the languages of the world maintain a grammatical distinction of masculine and feminine genders—at the outset probably an accident of form. Still fewer divide the masculine into two, thus making a masculine, a feminine and a neuter. These three genders were recognized in Latin; but the languages derived from it have allowed the neuter generally to sink back into the masculine, and so masculine nouns are greatly in the majority. Spanish and Portuguese are the only Romance tongues which retain any really noticeable trace of the neuter.

English is the only language that bases grammatical gender on the nature of things—males are masculine, females feminine, and everything else neuter. But in other languages various considerations play important rôles. The broad natural distinction is pretty well maintained as regards human beings and large and well-known animals; but beyond these a gender is assigned to each object with little regard to its nature.

Nevertheless there are some general considerations which are of great aid to the learner:

I. As REGARDS SIGNIFICATION:

1.4. Names and designations of men, and the males of many animals, are masculine, irrespective of termination:

el monarca the monarch
el cardenal the cardinal
el cura the priest
el centinela the sentinel
el caballo the horse
el león the lion

Similarly, designations of females are feminine:

la reina the queen
la ninfa the nymph
la hurí the houri
la lavandera the laundress
la vaca the cow
la gallina the hen

These rules outweigh all others.

1.5. The proper names of countries, districts or divisions of territory are masculine, except when they terminate in unaccented **a:**

El Perú ha sido desgraciado.	Peru has been unfortunate.
Chile es largo y estrecho.	Chile is long and narrow.
Aragón está limitado al norte por los Pirineos.	Aragon is bounded on the north by the Pyrenees.
El Canadá es un dominio británico.	Canada is a British dominion.
España está colocada en el extremo sudoeste de Europa.	Spain is placed in the extreme southwest of Europe.
Australia no ha sido enteramente explorada.	Australia has not been entirely explored.

1.6. The proper names of oceans, rivers, mountains and mountain chains are masculine, irrespective of termination, except in those cases where the name is a mere epithet, properly feminine, and not originally a proper name:

el Atlántico the Atlantic
el Tajo the Tagus
el Amazonas the Amazon
el Sena the Seine
el Magdalena the Magdalena River
los Andes the Andes
el Etna Mt. Etna
el Himalaya the Himalaya Mountains

BUT

la Sierra Nevada the Sierra Nevada
la Silla (*mountain range in Chile*)

There have been reputable authors who give the feminine gender to names of rivers ending in **a**: **la Sena, la Mosela.** Usage, however, is to the contrary. It is to be noted that the fuller forms **el Río de la Plata, el Río de la Magdalena, el Río de las Amazonas,** when shortened are **el Plata, el Magdalena, el Amazonas.** This second form has sometimes caused the first to be forgotten; thus no one says today **el Río de los Manzanares,** as it no doubt was at first, but **el Manzanares.**[1]

1.7. With respect to the proper names of cities, towns and villages, no absolute rules for determining gender can be given. The greater number follow the gender of their termination; i.e., they are masculine except when they end in **a.** But even those in a are usually considered masculine when they stand for the inhabitants of the city; while the same name is sometimes treated as masculine and at other times as feminine (cf. §31.29) :

Jerez es famoso por sus vinos.	Jerez is famous for its wines.
Toledo está casi circundada por el Tajo.	Toledo is almost surrounded by the Tagus.

[1] Small stream on which Madrid is situated.

Nueva York; Nueva Orleans.	New York; New Orleans.
Lugo y Orense están colocadas sobre el Miño.	Lugo and Orense are placed on the Miño River.
Madrid está situado en una extensa planicie.	Madrid is situated on an extensive plain.
Sevilla es hermosa.	Seville is beautiful.
Todo Sevilla está interesado.	All Seville is interested.
Nueva York, el Nueva York propiamente dicho, es una isla. (Camba, **La ciudad automática, Rascacielos,** I)	New York, New York proper, is an island.

1.8. Infinitives, phrases and indeclinable parts of speech used for the nonce as nouns (like the English expressions *the ups and downs, the why and wherefore, the ifs and ands*) belong to the class of neuters which return to the masculine:

el comer y beber	eating and drinking
el sí; **el** pero	the affirmative; the but (*objection*)
el pro y **el** contra	the pro and con

1.9. The names of the letters of any alphabet are feminine, as connected with **la letra** *the letter.* Thus: **la a, una B grande, las cees; la guímel** (third letter of the Hebrew alphabet), **la delta, la omega.** Nevertheless some authors treat the letters of the Greek and Hebrew alphabets as masculine, and **delta,** when applied to the triangular island at the mouth of a river, is masculine, according to the Academy:

el delta del Nilo	the Nile delta

See § **1.23** for vowels used as nouns.

II. As regards termination:

1.10. Nouns ending in **o** are masculine, except **la mano** *the hand,* **la nao** *the ship (poet.),* **la radio** *the radio,* **la seo** *the church (provinc.);* **modelo** in the sense of artist's model, **reo** *culprit* and **testigo** *witness* take either **el** or **la** as the case may require. **La contralto** *the contralto,* **la soprano** *the soprano* are used in reference to women singers. **La foto** is an abbreviation of **la fotografía.**

Those ending in **a** are principally feminine. Except: **el día** *the day,*

el planeta *the planet,* **el mapa**[1] *the map* and a number of words largely of Greek origin which end in **ma,**[2] such as:

el programa the program	**el dilema** the dilemma
el fantasma the phantom	**el lema** the lemma

Nouns ending in **dad, tad, tud, ión, umbre, ie,** are feminine.[3] In addition, the genders of a large number of nouns will be found in the list of terminations given in § 32.15.

NOTE. These are all the rules of any value which can be given. The learner will sometimes be helped by the etymology of the word in question; but the simplest and easiest way is to learn the appropriate article in connection with each noun, and associate them together. The only resource in all cases of doubt is the dictionary.

1.11. Nouns designating rank or relationship are used in the masculine plural to denote individuals of both sexes:

los reyes	the king and queen
los presidentes	the president and lady
los esposos	the husband and wife
mis padres	my parents, my father and mother
mis parientes	my relations (*of both sexes*)
los señores	the gentleman (*or* gentlemen) and lady (*or* ladies)
los señores Vargas	Mr. and Mrs. Vargas
los niños	the children (*boys and girls*)
los hijos de V.	your children (*sons and daughters*)

1.12. A large number of nouns ending in **o** change it to **a** to form the feminine. This is especially exemplified in nouns of relationship, as will be seen in the following list:

el abuelo the grandfather	**la abuela** the grandmother
el nieto the grandson	**la nieta** the granddaughter
el hijo the son	**la hija** the daughter

---

1 The rare **la mapa** means "that which is outstanding of its kind."

2 This **ma** was in Greek *ματ mat* (nominative *μα ma*), the *t* being the sign of the neuter gender and corresponding to Latin i*d*, illu*d*, istu*d* or English i*t*, tha*t*, wha*t*. Other "Greek nouns" in frequent use are: **clima** *climate,* **diagrama** *diagram,* **dogma** *dogma,* **drama** *drama,* **enigma** *enigma,* **idioma** *language,* **poema** *poem,* **problema** *problem,* **síntoma** *symptom,* **sistema** *system,* **telegrama** *telegram.*

3 In most words **-ión** is indicative of feminine gender. However, there are exceptions: **el sarampión** *the measles,* etc.

el **hermano** the brother	la **hermana** the sister
el **tío** the uncle	la **tía** the aunt
el **sobrino** the nephew	la **sobrina** the niece
el **primo** the cousin *(male)*	la **prima** the cousin *(female)*
el **suegro** the father-in-law	la **suegra** the mother-in-law
el **cuñado** the brother-in-law	la **cuñada** the sister-in-law
el **viudo** the widower	la **viuda** the widow
el **soltero** the bachelor	la **soltera** the unmarried lady
el **muchacho** the boy	la **muchacha** the girl
el **niño** the boy child, the boy	la **niña** the girl child, the girl
el **huérfano** the orphan *(male)*	la **huérfana** the orphan *(female)*
el **amigo** the friend *(male)*	la **amiga** the friend *(female)*
el **conocido** the acquaintance *(male)*	la **conocida** the acquaintance *(female)*
el **cocinero** the cook *(male)*	la **cocinera** the cook *(female)*
el **criado** the servant *(male)*	la **criada** the servant girl, the maid
el **vecino** the neighbor *(male)*	la **vecina** the neighbor *(female)*
el **parroquiano** the customer *(male)*	la **parroquiana** the customer *(female)*

1.13. In nouns denoting persons or animals, the distinction of gender is usually a natural one. The feminine form is obtained in various ways, corresponding for the most part to the formation of the feminine of adjectives.

a. Nouns in a remain unchanged, and take the article **el** or **la** as the case may require:

el **artista** the artist	la **artista** the artist
el **centinela** the sentinel	la **centinela**[1] the sentinel
el **compatriota** the compatriot	la **compatriota** the compatriot
el **espía** the spy	la **espía** the spy
el **indígena** the native	la **indígena** the native

b. A few nouns of other endings than a have a common form for both genders:

el **cómplice** the accomplice	la **cómplice** the accomplice
el **hereje** the heretic	la **hereje** the heretic
el **joven** the youth, young man	la **joven** the young girl
el **mártir** the martyr	la **mártir** the martyr
el **reo** the culprit, criminal	la **reo** the culprit, criminal
el **testigo** the witness	la **testigo** the witness
el **tigre** the tiger	la **tigre** the tigress

[1] But **la centinela** is sometimes used in speaking of a man.

c. The majority of nouns in **o** change it to **a** to form the feminine:

el **brujo** the wizard	la **bruja** the witch
el **gato** the tomcat	la **gata** the she-cat
el **mozo** the young fellow, lad	la **moza** the young girl, lass
el **tendero** the shopkeeper	la **tendera** the shopkeeper
el **pasajero** the passenger	la **pasajera** the passenger

d. The majority of nouns in **e** change that ending to **a:**

el **elefante** the elephant	la **elefanta** the elephant
el **farsante** the humbug	la **farsanta** the humbug
el **gigante** the giant	la **giganta** the giantess
el **monje** the monk	la **monja** the nun
el **pariente** the relative	la **parienta** the relative
el **sastre** the tailor	la **sastra** the tailoress

REMARK. By strict analogy, the terminations **–ante, –ente, –iente, –yente** formed from the Latin present participle should be invariable, and are often so written by purists to whom forms like **estudianta, presidenta, asistenta, acompañanta,** are not entirely acceptable. However, **la infanta** *the princess royal* is never *la infante.* Cf. § **20.1.**

e. Most of those in **d, l, n, r,** s and **z** add **a:**

el **huésped** the guest, boarder	la **huéspeda** the guest, boarder
el **colegial** the collegian	la **colegiala** the collegian
el **león** the lion	la **leona** the lioness
el **autor** the author	la **autora** the authoress
el **doctor** the doctor	la **doctora** the doctress
el **marqués** the marquis	la **marquesa** the marchioness
el **rapaz** the little boy	la **rapaza** the little girl

f. The following add **-esa** to the stem of the masculine after removing a terminal vowel:

el **abad** the abbot	la **abadesa** the abbess
el **alcaide** the warden	la **alcaidesa** the warden's wife
el **alcalde** the mayor	la **alcaldesa** the mayor's wife
el **barón** the baron	la **baronesa** the baroness
el **conde** the earl	la **condesa** the countess
el **duque** the duke	la **duquesa** the duchess

g. The following add **-isa** to the masculine stem:

el **diácono** the deacon	la **diaconisa** the deaconess
el **poeta** the poet	la **poetisa** the poetess
el **profeta** the prophet	la **profetisa** the prophetess
el **sacerdote** the priest	la **sacerdotisa** the priestess

h. The following are too irregular for classification:

don (Appendix I, f.)	**doña**
el **actor** the actor	la **actriz** the actress
el **emperador** the emperor	la **emperatriz** the empress
el **gallo** the cock	la **gallina** the hen
el **héroe** the hero	la **heroína** the heroine
el **jabalí** the wild boar	la **jabalina** the wild sow
el **príncipe** the prince	la **princesa** the princess
el **rey** the king	la **reina** the queen

i. The following have a distinct form for the feminine:

el **caballero** the gentleman	la **dama** the lady
el **caballo** the horse	la **yegua** (Lat. *equa*) the mare
el **hombre** the man	la **mujer** the woman
el **macho** male (of animals)	la **hembra** the female (animals)
el **marido** the husband	la **esposa** the wife
el **padre** the father	la **madre** the mother
el **toro**, el **buey** the bull, the ox	la **vaca** the cow
el **varón** male (of persons)	la **hembra** the female (persons)
el **yerno** the son-in-law	la **nuera** the daughter-in-law

1.14. There are certain nouns which, without change of termination or of gender, may apply equally to males or females. Such nouns are called *epicene*[1]:

Su Majestad el rey. Su Majestad la Reina.	His Majesty the King. Her Majesty the Queen.
Su hermano es una persona discreta.	His brother is a discreet person.
Su hija de V. es un ángel.	Your daughter is an angel.

1.15. The names of many animals are of this nature. Thus we say **la zorra** *the fox;* **la ardilla** *the squirrel;* **la zebra** *the zebra;* **la jaca** *the pony;* **la llama** *the llama;* and **el gorila** *the gorilla;* **el ratón** *the mouse;* **el coyote** *the coyote;* **el gavilán** *the hawk,* whether applied to males or females. When it is necessary to distinguish sex, we add **macho** *male* or **hembra** *female,* as the case may be:

---

[1] In such cases, adjectives and participles regularly revert to the natural gender of the person represented:

Contento su Majestad, no hay quien sea contra nosotros.	If his Majesty is satisfied, there is no one who can oppose us.
Su Ilustrísima está muy ilusionado. (Benavente, **Pepa Doncel,** I, 2.)	His worship is full of illusions.

la comadreja **macho**	the *male* weasel
el adive **hembra**	the *she*-jackal
el milano **hembra**	the *female* hawk

REMARK I. We may also say **el macho de la comadreja, la hembra del adive,** etc., which construction, although less usual, is more correct, since it avoids the incongruity of a masculine article before a feminine noun and vice versa. The objection is not valid, however, when **macho** or **hembra** stands in the predicate:

Esta cotorra es macho.	This parrot is a male.
Esos canarios deben ser hembras.	Those canaries must be females.

REMARK II. In some of the above words and also in the case of **boa** *boa,* **puma** *puma* usage varies: **la** *or* **el boa, la** *or* **el puma.**

1.16. Some feminine nouns in **a** denoting things may be applied to persons, in which case they take either **el** or **la** according to sex:

la atalaya the watchtower	**el atalaya** the lookout, watchman
la ayuda the aid	**el ayuda** the assistant, aide
la bestia the beast	**el bestia** the beastly man
la calavera the skull	**el calavera** the madcap
la canalla the rabble	**el canalla** the despicable man
la escolta the escort, convoy	**el escolta** the individual escort *(man)*
la espada the sword	**el espada** the matador
la gallina the hen	**el gallina** the cowardly man
la guardarropa the wardrobe	**el guardarropa** the master of the king's wardrobe
la guardia the guard *(corps)*	**el guardia** the guard, guardsman
la guía the guide *(inanimate thing)*	**el** or **la guía** the guide
la máscara the mask	**el** or **la máscara** the masker
la policía the police	**el policía** the policeman
la recluta the recruiting	**el recluta** the recruit
la trompeta the trumpet	**el trompeta** the trumpeter
la veleta the weather vane	**el veleta** the changeable man
la vigía the lookout	**el vigía** the lookout or watchman
la vista the sight, view	**el vista** the customs inspector
una ordenanza an ordinance	**un ordenanza** an orderly

1.17. Where a noun that has both a masculine and a feminine form is placed in the predicate after another noun, or is in apposition to it, it should agree with the first noun in gender:

El alba es **la precursora** del día.	The dawn is the harbinger of day.
Mi primo será **nuestro guía.**	My cousin will be our guide.

La naturaleza ha sido **nuestra guía.**	Nature has been our guide.
El sueño, hermano menor de la muerte.	Sleep, the half-sister of death.

1.18. A few nouns are occasionally used in either gender by some standard authors; the following is a list of these, the preferable gender being placed first:

el, la azúcar*	the sugar
el, la calor*	the heat
el, la color*	the color
el, la cutis*	the skin
la, el dote	the dowry, marriage portion
las dotes intelectuales	intellectual endowments
el, la fin*	the end
el, la linde	the boundary, limit
el, la mar *(fem. in elevated style, and in many nautical phrases)*	the sea
la, el margen	the margin, edge, brink
el, la origen*	the origin, source
el, la pro*	the benefit, advantage
el, la puente*	the bridge
la, el tilde	the tilde, any small thing

NOTE. Those designated by an asterisk are now rarely feminine.

REMARK. In the spoken language, especially in America, **el sartén** *the frying pan,* is used instead of the preferred **la sartén.**

1.19. Arte is feminine in the phrase **las bellas artes** *the fine arts,* but is nowadays likely to be masculine otherwise, though the feminine is invariably possible and most often encountered in the plural. It is commonly masculine in:

el arte diabólico	the black art
el arte dramático	the drama

1.20. Orden varies in gender according as its meaning varies. It is masculine when it means *arrangement, style,* and feminine when signifying a precept, command or organization:

los órdenes arquitectónicos	the orders of architecture
el orden corintio, dórico	the Corinthian, Doric order
Fulano es amante del orden.	So-and-so is a lover of order.
Ha tomado las sagradas órdenes.	He has taken holy orders.

El rey ha expedido una orden. — The king has issued an order.
la Orden de Alcántara, de Isabel la Católica — the Order of Alcantara, of Isabella, the Catholic

1.21. Certain nouns mostly denoting things have different meanings according as they vary in gender:

el canal the canal, channel, trench	**la canal** the gutter, conduit, *sometimes* channel, *etc.*
el cometa the comet	**la cometa** the [toy] kite
el consonante the rhyme word	**la consonante** the consonant
el crisma the holy oil	**la crisma** the head[1] *(vulgar)*
el cólera the cholera	**la cólera** the anger
el corte the cut, edge	**la corte** the court, metropolis
el capital capital *(money)*	**la capital** the capital *(city)*
el frente front, head	**la frente** the forehead
el moral mulberry tree	**la moral** morals, the moral
el parte dispatch, message *(telegram, etc.)*	**la parte** the part, portion
el pendiente earring	**la pendiente** slope
el pez fish[2] *(in the water)*	**la pez** pitch
el tema the theme, subject	**la tema** the fixed idea
el vocal the voting member	**la vocal** the vowel

1.22. Many nouns have two terminations, **o** and **a,** with corresponding change of gender, some of which are, by uneducated people or dialectally, often employed interchangeably without affecting the meaning:

aguatocho, aguatocha fire engine
barreno, barrena auger
bolso, bolsa purse
caldero, caldera cauldron
capacho, capacha hamper
carrasco, carrasca live oak
cayado, cayada shepherd's crook
cencerro, cencerra mulebell
chocolatero, chocolatera chocolate pot
cribo, criba sieve
conventículo, conventícula conventicle
embrollo, embrolla fraud, snare
escardillo, escardilla weeding hook
estampido, estampida crack, report
lejío, lejía lye
mirlo, mirla blackbird
pardillo, pardilla linnet
saco, saca sack
tajuelo, tajuela low stool

---

[1] Because it is the part christened. The people say: **te rompo la crisma** (*or* **el bautismo**). *I'll break your head.*

[2] *Fish,* in the market and kitchen, is **pescado.**

Remark. In general, however, the individuals of such pairs differ in meaning, as can be seen from the following columns:

fruto fruit *(on tree or in a figurative sense)*	**fruta** fruit *(after it is gathered)*
leño piece of timber, log	**leña** firewood, kindling
madero board	**madera** wood
ramo bough, branch *(when broken off or in a figurative sense)*	**rama** bough, branch *(on the tree)*
grito single shout, cry	**grita** shouting, outcry
cesto basket *(large)*	**cesta** basket *(small)*
jarro pitcher, jug *(narrow-mouthed with handle)*	**jarra** jar *(wide-mouthed with handles)*
gorro cap *(without visor)*	**gorra** cap *(with visor)*
guitarro guitar *(small)*	**guitarra** guitar *(large)*

1.23. As stated in § **1.9**, the names of the letters of any alphabet are feminine, agreeing with **letra** understood. The vowels used as words (prepositions and conjunctions) retain this gender:

La e es la segunda de las vocales.	*E* is the second of the vowels.
Se necesita **una a** delante del acusativo.	*An a* is needed before the accusative.
La o se convierte en **u** delante del sonido de **o.**	*O* is changed to *u* before the sound of *o*.

1.24. All other indeclinable words are regarded as masculine, irrespective of termination and of the fact that nearly all descriptive terms which could apply to the word are feminine (such as **palabra, dicción, voz, preposición, interjección, conjunción, partícula,** etc.):

El ya da aquí la idea de sorpresa.	*The ya* here expreses surprise.
El además tiene en este caso la fuerza de adverbio.	*Además* has in this case the value of an adverb.
Esos peros y **cuandos** me dan rabia.	*Those buts* and *ifs* of yours set me wild.

Remark. Still, if such feminine descriptive word occur near the indeclinable word in question, it may be treated as feminine:

Para esto empleamos en unas locuciones la preposición **a** y en otras **la para.**	For this we employ in some constructions the preposition *a* and in others *para*.
La oh es una de las interjecciones que denotan dolor.	*Oh* is one of the interjections that denote pain.

NUMBER

1.25. The only deviations from the principles given in §§ **1.1** and **1.2** with regard to the plurals of nouns concern those of foreign origin and compound nouns:

Lord, as a title of nobility, becomes **lores:**

la cámara de **los lores**	the House of *Lords*

club *club* becomes **clubes** or **clubs.**
mitin *meeting* becomes **mítines** or **mitins.**

Foreign family names are invariable in the plural, unless they have a termination common to Spanish and are pronounced as Spanish words:

los **Browning,** los dos **Húmboldt**	the *Brownings,* the two *Humboldts*
los **Racines,** las **Brontes**	the *Racines,* the *Brontë sisters*

Hidalgo *gentleman of the nobility* formerly changed to **hijosdalgo,** but in present-day Spanish the plural is **hidalgos.**

Ricohombre *state councillor* has **ricoshombres** for the plural.

Gentilhombre *court gentleman* very properly becomes **gentileshombres,** since **gentil** is an adjective.

Remark. In the formation of the plural of compound nouns made up of an adjective and a noun or of two nouns it might appear that both parts are usually pluralized but exceptions are numerous and are best learned by experience. The plural of nouns compounded of verb and noun is the same as the singular. Cf. § **32.7.**

El sordomudo *the deafmute,* becomes **los sordomudos** *the deafmutes.*
El altavoz *the loudspeaker* becomes **los altavoces** in the plural.
El padrenuestro *the Lord's Prayer* has **los padrenuestros** as its plural.
El arco iris *the rainbow* makes **los arcos iris** in the plural.
El avemaría *the Hail Mary, bead of the rosary* is **los avemarías** in the plural.
El barreminas *the minesweeper* becomes **los barreminas** in the plural.
El colocaminas *the minelayer* has **los colocaminas** for its plural.
El saltamontes *the grasshopper* is **los saltamontes** in the plural.

1.26. In speaking of a thing which is found singly in a number of individuals, it is most often placed in the singular in Spanish—contrary to the English usage, especially when dealing with a part of the body or an article of clothing:

Ambos máscaras se quitaron **la careta.**	Both maskers took off *their dominos.*
Se tiñeron **la cara** y las manos.	They dyed *their faces* and hands.
Todos los animales tienen **cabeza.**	All animals have *heads.*
Todos los animales tienen pies.	All animals have feet.

REMARK. To say **todos los animales tienen cabezas** would convey the idea that each one has several heads. However, when there is no chance for equivocation, the plural is used:

Salieron con las cabezas rotas.	They got away with their heads broken.
Quitaron las sillas a los caballos.	They took the saddles off the horses.

1.27. Some nouns have a secondary acceptation when used in the plural. Therefore the plurals of these nouns have two values: first, as true plurals of the primitive meaning; secondly, as expressing a new idea. Such nouns are:

alfiler pin	**alfileres** pin money
baqueta ramrod	**baquetas** drumsticks
conveniencia suitability, propriety	**conveniencias** perquisites
corcho cork	**corchos** clogs
corte court	**cortes** Spanish parliament
día day	**días** saint's day (§ **12.66**)
letra letter, handwriting	**letras** literary attainments
mano hand	**manos** manual labor
salud health	**saludes** compliments, greetings

1.28. It is hardly correct to say that certain nouns are used exclusively in the singular, or in the plural; nevertheless there are many nouns which are rarely, if ever, found in any but one number:

1. The following are seldom used in the singular:

aborígenes aborigines	**despabileras** snuffers
afueras outskirts	**enaguas** petticoat, skirt
alrededores environs	**esponsales** betrothal
anales annals	**exequias** obsequies
andas stretcher, litter	**expensas** expense
andurriales byways	**gafas** spectacles
añicos flinders, bits	**grizas** fragments
antepasados ancestors	**modales** manners, deportment
arras earnest money	**pantalones** trousers
caídos arrears of taxes	**tenazas** tongs
calofríos shivering, shudders	**tijeras** scissors
calzas breeches	**tinieblas** darkness
comestibles food, eatables	**víveres** provisions
dádivas gifts	

2. Those nouns which are relatively rarely used in the plural either denote objects of which but one example exists, or are abstract nouns

expressing qualities, sciences, trades, etc. The following may serve as examples:

la envidia envy	**la previsión** foresight
la fisiología physiology	**la prontitud** promptness
el infierno hell	**la vejez** old age

However, the plural of abstract nouns is frequent in the meaning of instances of the quality named: **crueldades** *acts of cruelty,* **envidias** *exhibitions of envy,* etc.

DISTINCTIONS BETWEEN SUBJECT AND OBJECT

1.29. In English the distinction between a noun as subject and as object is shown by its location; in Latin the distinction was made by means of case endings, irrespective of location. In Spanish, however, case endings are lacking as in English, while location has about as little effect upon the meaning as in Latin. The Spaniards, therefore, cannot easily distinguish between subject and object, and do not always succeed as clearly as might be desired.

a. The chief device in Spanish for distinguishing a noun as direct object (accusative) is by placing the preposition **a** before it. But as this preposition is the regular sign of the indirect object (dative), its application to a direct object vacillates between an endeavor on the one hand to prevent the noun from being mistaken for subject, if the preposition were omitted, and on the other, to prevent its being mistaken for the indirect object, if the preposition were employed. The effects of these restricting influences will be presented in detail.

b. The preposition **a** as the sign of the direct object has no force as a preposition and conveys no meaning, but is now often a mere grammatical device. In its other uses—namely, to designate the recipient of an action (indirect object) and to denote time, place or direction—it has a true prepositional value and is to be translated by *on, at* or *to.* For the purposes of this chapter the former use will be termed "the distinctive **a**" and the latter "the prepositional **a**." The use of **a** with direct objects originated in its use with indirect objects. The line of distinction between the two kinds of objects is at times very tenuous.

1.30. The distinctive a applies primarily to nouns representing determinate, known persons or to things personified:

Oía detrás de él **a** sus perseguidores.	He heard his pursuers behind him.
El general B., después de haber derrotado **a** los rebeldes en muchos	General B., after having routed the rebels in many encounters, entered

encuentros, entró en la capital el 8 de mayo.	the capital on the 8th of May.
El asesino corrió tras el vehículo y cuando tuvo a tiro seguro a su víctima, disparó el revólver.	The assassin ran after the carriage and, when he got his victim in sure range, fired his revolver.
Se ha arrestado ya por sospechas de connivencia **a** trece individuos.	They have already arrested thirteen persons upon suspicions of being accomplices.
Quería ver por última vez **a** su esposa y **a** sus hijos.	He wished to see his wife and children for the last time.
Procuró hacer olvidar **a** la niña su orfandad y su abandono. (Palacio Valdés, **La hija de Natalia,** III, 1)	He tried to make the child forget her orphaned state and her loneliness.
Es un soldado que honra **a** su nación.	He is a soldier who honors his nation.
Las aves saludan **a** la Aurora.	The birds salute the dawn.
Llamó en vano **a** la muerte.	He invoked death in vain.

Remark. Personification (and consequent use of **a**) is very common with **obedecer** *obey:* **obedecer (a) la regla** *to obey the rule,* **resistir** *resist:* **resistir (a) los ruegos de un amigo** *to resist the entreaties of a friend,* and occurs not infrequently with **contestar** *answer:* **contestar (a) la carta** *to answer the letter,* and with verbs of like meaning. Whether through personification or otherwise, **renunciar** *renounce* is very regularly followed by **a: renunciar (a) la dicha** *to renounce happiness,* as is also **sobrevivir** *survive:* **sobrevivir al desastre** *to survive the disaster.*

1.31. The distinctive **a** is therefore required before proper names of persons under such circumstances:

Enviaré **a** Diego en su lugar.	I will send James in his place.
Pablo y Juan aparecieron entonces a la derecha del camino, llevando **a** Benito como un cuerpo inerte.	Paul and John then appeared to the right of the road, carrying Benedict like an inanimate body.
Admiro mucho **a** Wáshington.	I admire Washington very much.

1.32. It is further required before demonstrative, interrogative, relative or adjective pronouns denoting persons:

¿A dónde llevan **a** ése? (Baroja, **La dama errante,** XXVI)	Where are they taking that fellow?
No hallaron allí **a** ninguno de los obreros.	They did not find any of the workmen there.

¿Has conocido **a** nadie que tanto sepa? (Pérez de Ayala, **Prometeo,** IV)	Have you ever known anyone who knows so much?
¿Esperas **a** alguien? (Benavente, **Lo cursi,** I, 1)	Are you waiting for someone?
Vimos **a** unos sumamente afanados, desidiosos **a** otros.	We saw some extremely diligent, others indolent.
¿**A** quién recomienda el juez?	Whom does the judge recommend?
No es más que un avaro **a** quien nadie estima. (Palacio Valdés, **Los cármenes de Granada,** II, 8)	He is only a miser whom no one respects.
Saludé **a** cada una de las señoras.	I saluted each of the ladies.
¿**A** cuál de las dos has querido más: **a** Felisa o **a** Socorro? (Palacio Valdés, **Seducción**)	Which of the two did you love more: Felisa or Socorro?

REMARK. In colloquial style there is a tendency to omit **a** with interrogative words standing at the beginning of their clause:

Vamos, Luisón, ¿cuál de las tres escogerías? (Palacio Valdés, **Sinfonía pastoral, Scherzo,** II)	Come, Louie, which of the three would you choose?
¿Cuántos hombres de ésos conoces tú? (Pereda, **La puchera,** XXXI)	How many men of that sort do you know?

1.33. **A** is also required before personal pronouns in the redundant construction or in contrast:

Me dejó **a** mí triste por alegrar **a** ella.	He left me sad so as to cheer her.
Me olvida **a** mí cuando le ve **a** él.	She forgets me when she sees him.

1.34. Before words explaining an objective personal pronoun:

Nos acogieron muy bien **a** mi hermana y **a** mí.	They received my sister and me very kindly.
Los miraban de reojo **a** la joven y **a** él.	They looked sidewise at the girl and him.

1.35. When the direct object of a verb is a geographical proper name, it takes the distinctive **a** (at least in conservative literary usage)—unless it be one which is regularly preceded by the definite article, in which case the preposition is not used. Present-day usage inclines toward omission of **a** in all cases.

He visitado **a** Medellín.	I have visited Medellín.
Deseamos ver **a** París.	We wish to see Paris.

Subió el Amazonas desde su embocadura hasta sus fuentes. — He ascended the Amazon from its mouth to its source.

Cambiáronse los más afectuosos discursos con motivo de la amistad que une a Chile y la República Argentina. — The most friendly speeches were spoken on both sides about the friendship which unites Chile and the Argentine Republic.

1.36. The distinctive **a** is not invariably used before nouns denoting persons when preceded by a numeral or before numerals denoting persons:

Derrotó trescientos enemigos con cuarenta escaramuzadores. — He routed three hundred of the enemy with forty skirmishers.

¿No quedó flotando alguno? —preguntó José. —Sí, vimos tres o cuatro. (Palacio Valdés, **José,** VIII.) — "Didn't someone remain afloat?" asked Joseph. "Yes, we saw three or four."

1.37. Before the indefinite article, use and omission of **a** seem about equally frequent, though perhaps the latter may be expected more confidently (cf. § **1.41**) :

Barraba vió un hombre que se movía a pie, en el campo, cargado con un bulto voluminoso. (Payró, **Cuentos de Pago chico,** VIII.) — Barraba saw a man moving, afoot, out in the country, carrying a bulky object.

Por la ventana vió **a** un hombre que corría a campo traviesa. (Baroja, **La feria de los discretos,** VIII.) — Through the window he saw a man running across country.

Al volver, en el camino vimos una mujer con un niño en brazos. (Baroja, **El mundo es ansí,** III, 3.) — On returning we saw on the road a woman with a child in her arms.

Vió venir hacia él un hombre que no tardó en reconocer. (Palacio Valdés, **Los majos de Cádiz,** XV.) — He saw coming toward him a man whom he was not long in recognizing.

Pronto se desvaneció esta duda al ver doblar la esquina **a** un hombre. (**Idem,** XV.) — Soon this hesitation vanished on seeing a man turn the corner.

A duras penas encontramos un guardia, que nos indicó la latitud a que nos encontrábamos. (Camba, **El baño de los ingleses, in Londres.**) — With difficulty we found a policeman who told us our latitude.

1.38. The use of the distinctive **a** with names of animals is highly variable. However, if the speaker regards the animal as capable of reasoning, as is at times shown by the context, he will be likely to use the distinctive **a**:

La cocinera mata la gallina.	The cook kills the fowl.
Guisa el pollo.	She cooks the chicken.
Ahuyenta los gatos que le molestan con sus maullidos.	He frightens away the cats that bother him with their mewings.
Arma una trampa para coger **a** la zorra.	He sets a trap to catch the fox.
La bala hirió al tigre en la cadera.	The ball struck the tiger in the flank.
El niño estaba acariciando **al** gato, el cual contestaba con susurros de contento.	The boy was fondling the cat, which answered with purrs of contentment.

Remark. The not infrequent use of **a** in situations like the following is probably due to adaptation to a formula requiring the use of **a** (§ **1.30**) or to a desire to single out the object (§ **1.40**):

Hacía trotar y galopar **a** la bestia, espoleándola con los talones. (Valera, **Juanita la larga, IV.**)	She would make the animal trot and gallop, spurring it with her heels.
Toda la noche estuvo oyendo mugir **a** una vaca que le habían quitado el ternero. (Miró, **Nuestro Padre San Daniel, Oleza y el enviado, VI.**)	All night she continued to hear the mooing of a cow whose calf they had taken away from it.

1.39. When the distinctive **a** would come before a word beginning with **a** and after a word ending with a vowel, it is sometimes omitted in writing:

Vió aquella ninfa.	He saw that nymph.
Logró ver **a** aquella ninfa.	He succeeded in seeing that nymph.

Remark. But if the object is a proper name, the **a** (whether it is prepositional or distinctive) is never omitted:

Encontré a Alfredo.	I met Alfred.
Ha ido a Argel.	He has gone to Algiers.

1.40. When both subject and direct object denote things, the object sometimes takes the distinctive **a** when ambiguity would otherwise result on account of the freedom allowed in Spanish in the order of words. In practice this usage occurs principally with **preceder** *precede,* **seguir** *follow,* **exceder** *exceed,* **igualar** *equal,* **superar** *surpa* and verbs of equivalent meaning. **Exceder** is also followed by **de** in phrases like **exceder de veinte** *exceed twenty.*

El bullicio siguió **al** silencio. **Al** silencio siguió el bullicio.	Tumult succeeded the silence.
El silencio siguió **al** bullicio. **Al** bullicio siguió el silencio.	Silence succeeded the tumult.
Alcanzó **al** vapor el yate.	The yacht overtook the steamer.
Alcanzó el vapor **al** yate.	The steamer overtook the yacht.

But if one of the terms is a person, as is usually the case, there is no danger of ambiguity, because when the person is the object it is necessarily distinguished by **a:**

Por fin venció el joven su pasión al juego.	The young man finally overcame his passion for gambling.
Por fin venció **al** joven su pasión al juego.	The passion for gambling at length overcame the young man.

REMARK. It may not be amiss to repeat that, in such cases, if the meaning of the words be such as not to admit of double meaning, there is no need of the distinctive **a:**

El río en este lugar había minado la ribera.	At this place the river had undermined the bank.
Animaba su rostro una sonrisa de inefable bondad.	A smile of ineffable kindness illuminated her face.

1.41. The employment of the distinctive **a** before a direct object denoting a person, depends largely upon the individuality attached to the object by the speaker:

Aguardo un criado.	I am waiting for a servant *(unknown.)*
Aguardo **a** un criado.	I am waiting for a servant *(known).*
Fueron a buscar un médico experimentado que conociera bien las enfermedades del país.	They went to look for an experienced physician who would be acquainted with the diseases of the country.
Fueron a buscar **a** un médico extranjero, que gozaba de una gran reputación.	They went for a foreign physician who enjoyed a great reputation.
Allí hallará amigos que le acojan bien.	He will find friends there who will receive him well.
Halló **a** amigos que le acogieron bien.	He found friends who received him well.
Vamos a llamar el médico. (Palacio Valdés, Santa Rogelia, VI.)	Let us call the doctor.

REMARK. Just as verbs normally having a person as an object may retain **a** before an object which is a thing (§ **1.30**), so those verbs which frequently have a thing as object may not have **a** when the object is a common noun representing a person (§ **1.45**). The absence of **a** in such situations is probably due primarily to the nature of the verbal idea and not to the mere presence after a verb of another phrase, especially an indirect object, with **a**, which circumstance is sometimes adduced as the sole reason.

Mandaron el chico al seminario de Lancia. (Palacio Valdés, **La fe, I.**)	They sent the boy to the seminary at Lancia.
Que conduzcan inmediatamente esta joven a la cárcel. (Palacio Valdés, **Marta y María, XIII.**)	Have them conduct this young woman to jail immediately.
Uno de los consejos que dió a su hijo fué el de enviar al Africa todos los cautivos. (Menéndez Pidal, **Orígenes del español,** § 89, 1)	One of the pieces of advice that he gave to his son was to send all the captives to Africa.

So **a** will often be lacking with a verb used in less than its literal sense:

¿Tú ves Joaquín? (Benavente, **Al natural,** I, 8)	Consider the case of Joaquín.

As the illustrations below suggest, it is not invariably true that the direct object dispenses with **a** when the verb has also an indirect object or other phrase beginning with that preposition, even if ambiguity may theoretically result:

Lleva usted **a** sus chicos a la escuela, al teatro, y al cine, y es un gusto ver cómo se instruyen y se divierten. (Camba, **La rana viajera, España,** V.)	You take your children to school, to the theater, to the movies, and it is a pleasure to see how they learn and have a good time.
La Brenda presentó **a** las francesas a las demás señoras del hotel. (Baroja, **César o nada,** I, 9.)	La Brenda introduced the French women to the other ladies in the hotel.
Señoras, presento a ustedes **al** señor Jiménez. (Palacio Valdés, **La hija de Natalia,** I, 4.)	Ladies, I present Mr. Jiménez to you.

1.42. For this reason the distinctive **a** is not customarily used before plural nouns and collective nouns which denote a general class and not particular individuals:

El presidente aguardará la vuelta del ministro de guerra antes de nombrar los oficiales para el ejército.	The President will await the return of the Secretary of War before nominating the officers of the army.

La escuela de la guerra es la que forma los grandes generales.	The school of practical warfare is what forms great generals.
Toca al pueblo elegir sus diputados al congreso.	It devolves upon the people to elect their representatives to Congress.
Yo he conocido paisanos de Villoria muy despiertos. (Palacio Valdés, **Sinfonía pastoral, Presto finale, II.**)	I have known peasants from Villoria who were very wide-awake.
Como los labriegos no sabían utilizar estos aparatos, tuvieron que traer mecánicos y electricistas. (Baroja, **El mundo es ansí,** I, 1.)	As the farmers didn't know how to use these pieces of apparatus, they had to bring mechanics and electricians.
Pues yo he tratado españoles de casi todas partes. (Camba, **La rana viajera, Alemania,** VII.)	Well, I have associated with Spaniards from almost everywhere.
Ya enviaré yo gente de confianza que te acompañe. (Pérez de Ayala, **Luz de domingo,** II.)	Of course, I shall send confidential people to go with you.
Me chocó ver tanta gente en la calle. (Baroja, **El mundo es ansí,** III, 4.)	It struck me to see so many people in the street.
La anciana amaba los niños.	The old lady loved children.

BUT

La anciana amaba a sus hijos.	The old lady loved her children.

1.43. Verbs of **naming, calling, considering,** etc. may take two direct objects, the true object and the predicate or thing asserted. The true object takes the distinctive **a:**

Llamaba música **a** los rebuznos que emitía.	He called the brays which he uttered, music.
Consideramos pura pérdida de tiempo **a** la lectura de semejantes obras.	We consider the reading of such works pure waste of time.

1.44. When a noun is compared by means of **como** with the direct object of a verb, it may receive or discard the distinctive **a** according to taste:

Le festejaron como **a** un príncipe.	They regaled him like a prince.
La acogieron como **a** una hermana.	They received her like a sister.
Le miran como padre, y él los trata como hijos.	They look upon him as a father, and he treats them as if they were his children.

1.45. Certain verbs usually applying only to things may have a double meaning when applied to persons, according as the object is preceded by the distinctive **a** or not:

Los romanos robaron las sabinas.	The Romans carried off the Sabine women.
Las gitanas roban los niños.	The gipsy women steal children.
Las gitanas roban **a** los niños.	The gipsy women rob the children.
Esta mujer ha perdido su hijo.	This woman has lost her son.
Esta mujer perderá **a** su hijo.	This woman will spoil her son.
Por su negligencia perdió **a** su **hijo.**	By his negligence he caused his son's ruin.
Mi hija quiere un cochero.	My daughter wants a coachman.
Mi hija quiere **a** un cochero.	My daughter loves a coachman.

REMARK. It is not true that **a** is never used with **perder** if it means *lose:*

Una infeliz mujer que había perdido **a** su marido sollozaba en un rincón. (Palacio Valdés, **José,** XVI.)	An unfortunate woman who had lost her husband was sobbing in a corner.
¿Y usted perdió **a** alguno de su familia en el naufragio? (Benavente, **Los malhechores del bien,** I, 14.)	And you lost someone of your family in the shipwreck?

1.46. **Tener** takes the distinctive **a** when it means *to hold,* but not when meaning *to have, possess:*

Dos asistentes tuvieron **al** enfermo mientras que el cirujano hizo la operación.	Two assistants held the patient while the surgeon performed the operation.
Tengo un cocinero experimentado.	I have an experienced cook.
Tenemos un hermano en el extranjero.	We have a brother who lives abroad.

REMARK. Idiomatically, the object of **tener** may take the distinctive **a** if **tener** is merely equivalent to the verb *to be:*

Tengo **a** mi chiquillo muy enfermo.	My little boy is very ill.
Tenemos **a** nuestro hermano en el extranjero.	Our brother is now abroad.
No tengo **a** nadie que me importe en el mundo . . . ¿Parientes? . . . ¡Dios nos libre! (Benavente, **La honradez de la cerradura,** I, 1, 3.)	I haven't anyone in the world that matters to me. . . Relatives?. . . God save us!

II

The Articles. The Neuter Gender

2.1. The articles in Spanish, as in all the languages of the European continent which have any, vary in form to indicate gender and number. The singular is as follows:

	MASCULINE	FEMININE
DEFINITE ARTICLE:	**el** the	**la** the
INDEFINITE ARTICLE:	**un** a *or* an	**una** a *or* an

In the plural, the definite article has the following forms, agreeing with the nouns which they accompany:

MASCULINE	FEMININE
los the	**las** the
los hombres the men	**las niñas** the girls

2.2. Masculine nouns require a masculine, feminine nouns a feminine article:

el hombre the man
un hombre a man
la niña the girl
una niña a girl

EXCEPTION. Feminine nouns beginning with stressed **a** or **ha** take **el** in the singular, instead of **la**, when the article immediately precedes. **El** is here of different origin from the masculine article of the same form and its use does not by any means change the gender of the noun (cf. § 2.5 note).

el agua the water
el hacha the axe
el arpa the harp
el aya the governess
el aula the classroom

BUT

la ambición the ambition
la hamaca the hammock
la alhaja the jewel
la audacia the audacity

REMARK. This change is not made properly before adjectives of like form: **la alta casa** *the high house*. Cf. also **la Ana, la Angela,** etc., in women's names.

2.3. At present, even in literary style, **un** is often used for **una** under the same circumstances. The Spanish Academy now considers such usage permissible though not preferable:[1]

un hacha *an* axe	**un** arpa *a* harp

2.4. When the masculine singular form of the definite article, **el,** comes immediately after the prepositions **a** or **de,** the **e** is elided, and **a el, de el,** become respectively **al, del.** These are now the only contractions of the kind in the written language:

al coche; **del** jardín	*to the* carriage; *from the* garden

2.5. The definite article is merely a demonstrative adjective abbreviated.[2] Since it is a shortened form and frequently used, it is in value weaker than the demonstrative **este,** etc. While the demonstrative character of the latter is direct, that of the article is logical or mental. Their nature is the same, as will be seen by comparison of the following examples:

Esta demostración que voy a exponer...	*This* demonstration which I am about to present...
La demostración que voy a exponer...	*The* demonstration which I am about to present...
Aquellas colinas que protegen la rada contra los vientos del este...	*Those* hills which protect the roadstead against the easterly winds...
Las colinas que protegen la rada contra los vientos del este...	*The* hills which protect the roadstead against the easterly winds...

Latin and Russian have no definite article, but the demonstratives *ille* in the former and *tot* in the latter are often used with the value of an article. The article in the principal Romance languages is some modification of Latin *ille.*

2.6. The definite article is applied, in both Spanish and English, as follows:

---

[1] Cf. § **7.10,** Remark.

[2] An early form of the definite article in Spanish was **elle** (which in the course of time became **el**), **ela, elo, elos, elas.** The initial **e** was subsequently discarded from the last four. But **ela** before words beginning with **a** lost the final **a** instead of the initial **e,** a usage which still holds good before nouns which begin with stressed **a.**

a. To some particular person, thing or idea which has been spoken of or which is known to, or understood by, the person addressed:

el contrato susodicho	*the* aforementioned contract
La ciudad está triste ahora.	*The* city is dull now.
¿A qué hora estará abierto **el** mercado?	At what time will *the* market be open?
Allí está un sereno en la esquina.	There is a night watchman on the corner.
Allí está **el** sereno en la esquina.	There is *the* night watchman on the corner.

b. To any of the elements or features of nature, of which only one can be supposed to be under consideration:

el cielo, **la** tierra, **el** horizonte	*the* sky, *the* earth, *the* horizon
el sol, **el** alba, **la** vía láctea	*the* sun, *the* dawn, *the* milky way
el arco iris, **el** fuego fatuo	*the* rainbow, *the* will-o'-the-wisp
pasar **el** meridiano, estar en **el** cenit	to pass *the* meridian, to be in *the* zenith

c. To single animals, plants and gems, as representatives of their respective species:

La zorra es celebrada por su astucia.	*The* fox is celebrated for his cunning.
La cigüeña es un ave de paso.	*The* stork is a bird of passage.
El nenúfar es una de **las** más graciosas plantas acuáticas.	*The* water lily is one of *the* most graceful aquatic plants.
El topacio es una piedra trasparente de un hermoso color amarillo.	*The* topaz is a transparent stone of a beautiful yellow color.

d. To an individual taken as a representative of any of the divisions of the human race or of society:

el chino, **el** negro, **el** indio	*the* Chinaman, *the* Negro, *the* Indian
el sereno, **el** fabriquero, **el** lechuguino	*the* night watchman, *the* manufacturer, *the* dude
los intereses **del** obrero	*the* interests of *the* workingman

e. To any of the members or faculties of man, taken in a general sense:

el hígado, **el** corazón	*the* liver, *the* heart
la memoria, **el** alma	*the* memory, *the* soul
El estómago es un órgano de que mucho se abusa.	*The* stomach is a much-abused organ.

f. To nouns restricted in the extent of their application by any defining words:

la flor **del** cacto	*the* flower of *the* cactus
El huevo **del** colibrí es más pequeño que un garbanzo.	*The* egg of *the* hummingbird is smaller than a chick-pea.
el interés con que se mira esta cuestión	*the* interest with which this question is regarded
los locales donde se encuentra dicha formación mineral	*the* localities where this mineral formation is found

g. To epithets or nicknames immediately following a proper name of a person:

Pedro **el** Cruel	Peter *the* Cruel
Isabel **la** Católica	Isabella *the* Catholic
Alejandro **el** Grande	Alexander *the* Great

h. To names of oceans, seas and rivers:

el Pacífico, **el** Adriático, **el** Mediterráneo	*the* Pacific, *the* Adriatic, *the* Mediterranean
el Río de la Plata, **el** Río Bravo del Norte	*the* Plata River, *the* Rio Grande

2.7. The leading difference between the Spanish and the English use of the definite article is that it is employed in Spanish before any noun used in a general sense as the representative of the entire class or species to which it belongs:

El hombre es mortal.	Man is mortal.
El pan es nutritivo.	Bread is nutritious.
Las flores son el adorno de la tierra.	Flowers are the ornament of the earth.
Los caballos son animales útiles.	Horses are useful animals.
La ciencia moderna ha sometido **al** tiempo y **al** espacio.	Modern science has conquered time and space.
Los estragos **del** tiempo.	The ravages of time.
El dedo **del** destino nos señala una carrera larga, próspera y brillante.	The finger of destiny points out to us a long, prosperous and brilliant career.
Los aztecas conocían **el** oro, **la** plata, **el** cobre y **el** estaño, pero no sabían labrar **el** hierro.	The Aztecs were acquainted with gold, silver, copper and tin, but they did not know how to work iron.
El porfirio es más duro que **el** grafito.	Porphyry is harder than graphite.

2.8. The same is true when the nouns represent, not visible objects, but abstractions:

El tiempo es precioso.	Time is precious.
El sueño es necesario al hombre.	Sleep is necessary to man.
La prudencia es una parte importante **del** valor.	Prudence is an important part of valor.
He escrito una obra sobre **la** mineralogía.	I have written a work on mineralogy.
Las riquezas y **el** lujo fomentan **la** molicie y **la** pereza.	Riches and luxury nourish effeminacy and idleness.
La historia demuestra que **la** violencia hace los tiranos, **la** dulce autoridad hace los reyes.	History demonstrates that violence makes tyrants, mild authority makes kings.

2.9. As a verbal noun, formed of the infinitive of a verb, expresses an act in an abstract manner, it is often preceded by the masculine article **el** (cf. § **19.27**):

El hablar demasiado es su falta principal.	Talking too much is his principal fault.
El comer y **el** beber son necesarios a **la** vida.	Eating and drinking are necessary to life.
El leer alto es buena práctica.	Reading aloud is good practice.
Su enfermedad proviene **del** excesivo fumar.	His illness proceeds from excessive smoking.

2.10. The article is generally repeated before each noun. When the nouns are of different genders or numbers and stand as separate entities of primary importance in the sentence, each should have the article. When, however, the nouns are closely connected in meaning, the article may be more elegantly omitted before all but the first noun:

Tengo una casa y un jardín.	I have a house and garden.
El padre y la madre tienen un coche y un caballo.	The father and mother have a horse and carriage.
La energía y celo que exhibe son admirables.	The energy and zeal which he exhibits are admirable.
El descuido y negligencia del coronel han sido fatales al regimiento.	The carelessness and negligence of the colonel have been fatal to the regiment.
la erudición y estudio que caracterizan sus producciones literarias	the learning and research which characterize his literary productions

2.11. When several nouns refer to the mental properties of a person, the article may be omitted before all but the first; but if the nouns denote the actual possessions of the person, each requires the appropriate article:

el celo *(m.)*, inteligencia *(f.)* y honradez *(f.)* del empleado	the zeal, intelligence and probity of the clerk
el sombrero, las botas y la petaca del empleado	the hat, boots and cigar case of the clerk

2.12. The article should not be repeated after **o**, *or*, before a noun which is merely a synonym or explanation of the preceding noun:

el vestíbulo o entrada de la casa	The vestibule or entry of the house
Nueva Gerona es la capital o ciudad principal de la Isla de Pinos.	New Gerona is the capital or the principal town of the Isle of Pines.

2.13. When the noun is used partitively, that is, when only a portion of a substance or class is under consideration, the article is omitted in both languages:

En la sierra costanera hay extensas canteras de mármol y alabastro.	In the coast chain there are extensive quarries of marble and alabaster.
Los densos bosques rinden cinchona, zarzaparrilla, copaiba, caucho, resina, cedro, caoba y palos de tinte.	The dense forests produce cinchona, sarsaparilla, copaiba, rubber, resin, cedar, mahogany and dyewoods.
Valparaíso es notable por su riqueza dando cebada, frijoles, trébol, frutas, trigo y cáñamo.	Valparaiso is notable for its fertility, producing barley, beans, clover, fruits, wheat and hemp.

REMARK. The use of the definite article with names of languages responds to this principle, even though there is a tendency nowadays to omit it without regard to possible distinctions of meaning. Omission is the rule after **en**, to a slightly less degree after **de** and very regularly after forms of **hablar**, in view of the frequency of phrases like **este señor habla español** *this gentleman speaks (some) Spanish* [as contrasted with **este señor habla bien el español** *this gentleman speaks Spanish (as a whole) well*]:

Estaba yo bastante adelantado en latín. Así como aquél era mi primer año en geometría era el tercero de latín, porque mi padre tenía la manía culta de que si no sabía latín no sabría bien nunca castellano. La diferencia consistía	I was quite advanced in Latin. While that was my first year in geometry it was the third in Latin, because my father had the learned notion that if I didn't know (some) Latin I would never know Castilian well. The difference consisted in the

en que ahora estudiaba el latín para aprobar.... El profesor... quería que "cuando fuera a examinarme supiera más latín que el profesor." (Sender, **Crónica del alba**)	fact that I was now studying Latin (as a whole) to pass.... The teacher...wanted me, "when I went to be examined, to know more Latin than the teacher."
Esta palabra viene del griego.	This word comes from Greek.
Hablaba el francés a la perfección. (Palacio Valdés, **Años de juventud del doctor Angélico**, XII)	He spoke French to perfection.

2.14. The so-called partitive **de** is hardly frequent in Spanish and when it is used the noun is likely to be limited by a demonstrative, possessive or indefinite adjective:

No nacen **de** estos hombres todos los días. (Pérez Galdós, **El amigo Manso**, III)	*(Any of)* these men are not born every day.
Déme **de** esos papeles de votar. (Benavente, **El primo Román**, II, 6)	Give me *some of* those ballots.
Nos van a traer **de** un vino muy rico. (Benavente, **Señora ama**, II, 4)	They are going to bring us *some* fine wine.
Diéronle **de** un brebaje. (Pérez Galdós, **Torquemada en la cruz**, I, 1)	They gave him a potion.

2.15. The definite article is required in Spanish before adjectives employed as nouns and representing an entire class:

El bueno no siempre se escapa de la calumnia.	*The good man* does not always escape calumny.
Los ricos deben ser caritativos con **los pobres.**	*The rich* should be charitable to *the poor.*
Los sabios son modestos, y **los valientes,** misericordiosos.	*The wise* are modest, and *the brave,* merciful.

2.16. The definite article is usually used before the four cardinal points, and the names of the days of the week and month (except in dating letters):

el sur *or* **el** mediodía	South
el oeste, **el** poniente *or* occidente	West
Llegué aquí **el** sábado.	I got here Saturday.
todos **los** domingos	every Sunday
Saldrá **el** 24 de junio.	He will start the 24th of June.

En el almuerzo del domingo, doña Trina agasajó a sus huéspedes con un principio extraordinario. (Pérez de Ayala, **La caída de los Limones,** XI, in **Prometeo**)
At the Sunday luncheon Doña Trina regaled her boarders with a special entrée.

Acordóse entonces de que el día siguiente era domingo. (Pérez Galdós, **Torquemada en la hoguera,** IV)
He remembered then that the following day was Sunday.

2.17. The definite article is required in Spanish before many nouns, when they are governed by a preposition, which discard it in English:

a **la** ciudad, a **la** iglesia	to town, to church
a **la** escuela, a **la** clase	to school, to class
al mercado, **al** Congreso	to market, to Congress
en **la** ciudad, en **la** iglesia	in town, in church
en **el** colegio, en **la** escuela	at college, at school.
a **la** noche, **al** cuidado de	at (*or* by) night, in care of

2.18. The article may be separated from its noun by adjectives, adjective phrases, or qualifying phrases having the value of adjectives:

Subiendo por **el** pendiente y mal trazado **sendero.**
Ascending by *the* steep and irregular *path.*

La sin par **corrección** de dibujo.
The unequaled *correctness* of drawing.

Los en verdad atrevidos **pensamientos de D. Cosmos.**
The truly daring *thoughts of Don Cosmos.*

Se adelantó a recibir las llaves de **la** poco ha orgullosa y ahora rendida **ciudad** morisca.
He advanced to receive the keys of *the* lately haughty but now surrendered *city* of the Moors.

2.19. The definite article is occasionally used before an entire clause preceded by the conjunction **que** (cf. § **23.65**):

Y contribuía no menos al mismo resultado **el que** el tío Lucas sabía, quería y podía dirigir la molienda. (Alarcón, **El sombrero de tres picos,** VI)
And there contributed no less to the same result *that* Uncle Lucas knew how, wanted to and was physically able to direct the milling.

2.20. The contractions **al** and **del** are not used when the article is part of a title considered as quoted:

¿Ha visto V. la extraordinaria de **El Globo** (*or* del **Globo**)?	Have you seen the extra edition of "The Globe" (*or* the "Globe")?
Rodrigo Díaz de Vivar es generalmente conocido bajo el sobrenombre de **el Cid** (*or* del **Cid**).	Rodrigo Diaz de Vivar is generally known by the surname of *the Cid* (*or* the *Cid*).
Pocas comedias de Calderón aventajan a **"El** postrer duelo de España."	Few of Calderon's comedies surpass "The Last Sorrow of Spain."

2.21. In general, the proper names of nations or countries, cities, towns and villages are used without the definite article but to this general rule there are exceptions. Some names, such as **Venezuela, Méjico, Chile,** etc., never take the article; while, on the contrary there are certain names of countries, and even of cities and towns, which are often preceded by the definite article, at least in conservative literary usage. Of these the following are the most frequently met with:

el Brasil Brazil
el Cairo Cairo
el Callao Callao
el Canadá Canada
la Coruña Corunna
el Ecuador Ecuador
el Ferrol Ferrol
la Florida Florida
la Guaira Guayra
la Habana Havana
el Havre Havre
el Japón Japan
la Mancha *(a Spanish province)*
el Paraguay Paraguay
el Perú Peru
la Rioja *(a Spanish province)*
el Uruguay Uruguay

REMARK. Instead of **los Estados Unidos** *the United States* with a verb in the plural form, it is relatively frequent, in journalistic usage, to omit the article, the verb then being singular:

Estados Unidos pidió a las otras repúblicas americanas que redujeran las tarifas aduaneras.	The United States asked the other American republics to reduce the customs duties.

2.22. The name of a country preferably takes the article when stress is laid upon its extent, power or dignity. Thus the article would be superfluous in the following sentence, since it speaks of an ordinary occurrence:

El embajador de **la** Francia presentó sus credenciales al presidente.	The ambassador of France presented his credentials to the president.

But it would be very properly used, and add emphasis, in the following connection:

El embajador se quejó de no haber sido tratado con las distinciones debidas a un representante de **la** Francia.	The ambassador complained of not having been treated with the distinction due to a representative of France.

2.23. The definite article is required if the name of the country is qualified by an adjective or adjectival phrase:

la España **meridional**	*Southern* Spain
el Asia **rusa**	*Russian* Asia
la Guayana **holandesa**	*Dutch* Guiana
la India **del siglo XX**	*twentieth-century* India

If the name of the country is not a proper name, but a descriptive title, the definite article is also required:

los Países Bajos	the Netherlands
los Estados Unidos	the United States
la República Argentina	the Argentine Republic

2.24. Names of rivers and mountains require the definite article:

el Vesubio; el Hélicon; el Chimborazo	Vesuvius; Mt. Helicon; Chimborazo
los Alpes; los Andes; los Pirineos	the Alps; the Andes; the Pyrenees
el Tajo; el San Lorenzo; el Misurí	the Tagus; the St. Lawrence; the Missouri

2.25. Proper names of persons and animals, not preceded by an adjective, do not take the definite article; when qualified by an adjective the article is employed:

Juan, Pedro y José salieron **a la** pesca.	John, Peter and Joseph went out fishing.
Don Quijote ensilló a Rocinante.	Don Quixote saddled Rozinante.
la pequeña Lolita	little Lolita
el viejo Tomás	old Thomas

REMARK. The adjective **Santo** is an exception in the names of saints, in which it is considered part of the name:

el día de San Juan	St. John's Day *(midsummer)*

2.26. When a proper name is preceded by an adjective, the preposition **de** is sometimes interpolated (cf. §§ **29.20, 30.52**):

la **tonta de Juana**	that *silly Jane*
El **pobre de Benito** no sabía qué parte tomar.	*Poor Benedict* did not know what course to adopt.

2.27. Given and family names of women sometimes take the definite article in very familiar conversation, often to refer to a person previously mentioned. In reports of legal proceedings, the article is sometimes used before a proper name of either a man or woman and then has the value of English *the said.* Furthermore, the definite article is not infrequently placed before the names of women in public life, such as actresses or writers. In most cases the use of the definite article implies a certain jocularity and lack of respect:

He visto a la Mariquita en la ópera.	I saw Mariquita at the opera.
Cuando vea V. a la Pérez, dígale que quiero verla.	When you see that Pérez girl, tell her I want to see her.
Y declaró el Menéndez que había visto al Pepe Blanco en la noche del viernes, etc.	And this Menéndez testified that he had seen the said Pepe Blanco on Friday night, etc.
La Pardo Bazán está todavía demasiado próxima a nosotros para que sus escritos de actualidad no parezcan viejas. (Nelken, **Las escritoras españolas,** IX, 2)	Pardo Bazán is still too near to us for her writings on contemporary events not to seem stale.

2.28. The proper names of the following classic Italian poets take the definite article in imitation of Italian usage:

el Petrarca, el Ariosto, el Tasso, el Dante[1]	Petrarch, Ariosto, Tasso, Dante

REMARK. The names of modern Italians do not take the article.

2.29. The definite article is used before a common noun in an apostrophe:

Don Tiburcio, el cura párroco, les gritó desde el camino: — ¡Eh, **los** segadores! ¿Cómo marcha esa siega? (Palacio Valdés, **Sinfonía pastoral, Adagio cantábile,** V)	Don Tiburcio, the parish priest, shouted to them from the road, "Oh, reapers! How is the reaping going?"

[1] In Italian *il Petrarca, l'Ariosto, il Tasso* and *l'Alighieri* (preferably not ***il*** *Dante,* since *Dante* is not a family name).

Al poco rato se abrió una de las ventanas iluminadas de la casa y se presentó en ella una figura de hombre, que gritó: —¡Eh, **los** náufragos! ¡Adelante! (Baroja, **Las inquietudes de Shanti Andía,** VII, 6)	Shortly one of the lighted windows opened and a man's figure presented itself in it, shouting, "Oh, shipwrecked sailors! Come in!"

2.30. Proper names may take the definite article when they are used as common nouns to express the character of the individual; or to denote his statue, his book, his writings, etc.:

Bolívar es **el** Wáshington de Colombia.	Bolivar is the Washington of Colombia.
El señor Quintana es **el** Solón de la República Argentina.	Mr. Quintana is the Solon of the Argentine Republic.
la Venus de Médici, **el** Apolo del Belvidere	the Venus of Medici, the Apollo Belvidere
Tráigame V. **el** Salvá.	Bring me Salvá.
Quiero pedir prestado **el** Plinio de su señor padre.	I want to borrow your father's Pliny.
¿Ha leído V. **el** Quijote o **el** Gil Blas?	Have you read Don Quixote or Gil Blas?

REMARK. The definite article is not used before the titles of **Don, Doña, fray** *brother* (of a religious order), **frey** *brother* (of a military order), **sor** *sister* (of nuns) and **San** or **Santo, Santa,** *Saint;* and the foreign titles of **monsieur, monseñor, míster, madama, miss, sir, lord** or **milord, ladi** or **miladi.** Before all other titles the definite article is required when the individual is spoken of; but not when he is addressed (cf. Appendix I):

la señora y las señoritas de Medina	Mrs. Medina and the Misses Medina
el coronel Vaquero	Colonel Vaquero
la hermana San Sulpicio	Sister St. Sulpicio
el senador Valera	Senator Valera

2.31. The indefinite article is preferably not used in Spanish before nouns in the predicate when they are employed as adjectives to express some quality or character of the subject:

Soy **español** y **soldado.**	I am *a* Spaniard and *a* soldier.
¿Es **sastre** su hermano de V.?	Is your brother *a* tailor?
No señor, es **comerciante.**	No, sir, he is *a* merchant.
Su marido es **título.**	Her husband is *a* nobleman.
Don Joaquín es **francmasón.**	Joachim is *a* mason (freemason).

REMARK. The article is employed, however, before the predicate noun when the latter is specified by an adjective or qualifying phrase:

Es **un** gran embustero.	He is a *great* liar.
Soy **un** sastre desgraciado.	I am an *unfortunate* tailor.
Soy **un** español de familia noble.	I am a Spaniard *of noble family.*

But if an adjective and noun occur together so frequently as to become a kind of stereotyped expression, the article is omitted:

Es **buen católico.**	He is *a* good Catholic.
Es **gran orador.**	He is *a* great orator.
Es **ama de llaves** en casa del Sr. B.	She is housekeeper at Mr. B.'s.

Moreover, the predicate noun takes an article when it is emphatic and its quality is considered as a leading characteristic. Thus to say of a person **es cobarde,** merely charges him with cowardice; but to say, **es un cobarde,** conveys the idea that cowardice is a dominant fault:

Son unos mentecatos si piensan así.	They are downright fools if they think so.
Su hermano es un holgazán.	His brother is a regular do-nothing.

2.32. The article is omitted before a few nouns preceded by a verb of motion or rest, the noun usually having a special sense:

Voy a casa, a misa, a palacio.	I am going home, to mass, to the palace.
Estar en casa; salir de casa.	To be at home; to leave home.
Al volver de caza.	On returning from hunting.

2.33. It is omitted before many nouns used in an indeterminate sense, with a verb, and expressing a concrete idea:

No tengo tiempo para mirarlo.	I haven't *the* time to look at it.
Tenía gran inclinación de pegarle un tiro.	I had *a* great mind to fire at him.
Tengo intención de ir allí.	I intend to go there.
Dar filo a un útil.	To put *an* edge on a tool.
Quiere ver mundo.	He wants to see *the* world.
Es tiempo de que Juan piense en tomar mujer.	It is time for John to think of taking *a* wife.
Pedro ha abierto escuela.	Peter has opened *a* school.
José ha puesto tienda.	Joseph has set up *a* store.
¿Sabe V. si la hija lleva dote?	Do you know if the daughter has *a* dowry?

REMARK. The use of the indefinite article with abstract nouns, usually as objects of verb or preposition, though very frequent, is by some authorities condemned as a Gallicism:

Hemos empleado una precaución extraordinaria.	We have used extra caution.
Ha demostrado un afán laudable.	He has displayed praiseworthy energy.
He prestado a su descripción una atención minuciosa.	I paid minute attention to his description.
Hablamos de los dolores ajenos con una gran frialdad.	We talk of other people's sufferings with great calmness.

2.34. A noun after **ser** in an impersonal sentence is not usually preceded by an article:

Es lástima; es error.	It is *a* pity; it is *a* mistake.
Es verdad; es mentira.	It is true [*lit.* truth]; it is *a* lie.
Es costumbre del país.	It is *the* custom of the country.

2.35. A noun after the preposition **sin** is not generally preceded by the indefinite article. **Sin** followed thus by a noun is often equivalent to the English adjective formed by adding *-less* to the noun:

Da el dinero al hombre sin decir palabra.	He gives the man the money without saying *a* word.
No quiero ir a la ciudad sin sombrero.	I do not want to go to the city without *a* hat.
un rey sin reino	a king without *a* kingdom
un príncipe sin dinero	a money*less* prince
un muchacho sin amigos	a friend*less* boy
Esta carta está sin faltas.	This letter is fault*less.*

2.36. The article is often omitted in enumerations:

Viejos y niños escuchaban con atención sus palabras.	Old and young listened attentively to his words.
Padre e hijo fueron a cual más temerosos de Dios.	Father and son were equally pious.

2.37. The definite article is frequently omitted in proverbs, of which a terse style is a leading characteristic:

Dádivas quebrantan peñas.	Gifts move mountains.
A menudo pagan justos por pecadores.	The innocent often pay for the guilty.
Pobreza no es vileza.	Poverty is no crime.
Huéspeda hermosa, mal para la bolsa.	A handsome landlady is bad for the purse.

2.38. **Casa,** unaccompanied by any article, and preceded by a preposition, takes the place of the English elliptical manner of refering to a person's residence or place of business by placing his name in the possessive; when no possessor is indicated, **casa** is equivalent to the English *home,* also unspecified as to ownership:

Vengo de casa de mi cuñado.	I am coming from my brother-in-law's.
Compro pan en casa de A.	I buy bread at A.'s.
Voy a casa ahora.	I am going home now.
Manda los muchachos a casa.	He sends the boys home.
¿Está en casa su hermano de V.?	Is your brother at home?
Mi mujer está en casa de su madre.	My wife is at her mother's.

2.39. It is usual to omit both definite and indefinite article before a noun in apposition (i.e., when it is explanatory of a preceding noun):

En la primavera de 1877, D. F. P. Moreno, explorador argentino de considerable reputación, visitó los lagos que forman las cabeceras del río Santa Cruz.	In the spring of 1877, Don F. P. Moreno, *an* Argentine explorer of considerable note, visited the lakes which form the head-waters of the River Santa Cruz.
Valparaíso, puerto principal de Chile, es uno de los más grandes emporios del comercio de Sud América.	Valparaiso, *the* principal port of Chile, is one of the greatest commercial emporiums of South America.
Del curuguati, planta parásita, se hacen sogas y cables.	From the curuguaty, *a* parasitic plant, are made ropes and cables.
Quito, capital del Ecuador, posee un clima delicioso.	Quito, *the* capital of Ecuador, has a delightful climate.
El presidente del Gobierno Provisional, señor Alcalá Zamora, y el ministro de Gobernación, don Miguel Maura, jefes de los católicos republicanos, dimitieron en plena sesión. (Madariaga, **España,** II, 1, 3)	The president of the Provisional Government, Mr. Alcalá Zamora, and the Minister of the Interior, Mr. Miguel Maura, *the* leaders of the Republican catholics, resigned in the middle of the session.

Remark. The definite article, however, is used before the noun in apposition when it merely serves to identify a person who is well known to speaker but not to hearers:

Mi hermano **el** ingeniero.	My brother *the* engineer.
Stanley **el** explorador africano.	Stanley *the* African explorer.

El señor Édison, **el** célebre inventor norteamericano.	Mr. Edison, *the* celebrated American inventor.

2.40. When the noun in apposition is modified by a superlative adjective, the definite article is required, unless the adjective be one of those which have a separate form for the superlative or which embody a superlative meaning:[1]

Antioquia, provincia la más rica de Colombia.	Antioquia, the richest province of Colombia.
Santa María, la colonia más antigua del continente sudamericano, fué fundada en el Golfo de Darién, en el año 1510.	Santa Maria, the oldest colony of the South American continent, was founded in the Gulf of Darien in 1510.
El Brasil, último país de Sud América en declarar la independencia,...	Brazil, the last country of South America to declare independence,...
El Cayambe, único volcán situado inmediatamente debajo del ecuador, es una de las cimas principales de la Cordillera Oriental.	Cayambe, the only volcano situated directly under the equator, is one of the principal peaks of the Eastern Chain.

2.41. Neither definite nor indefinite article is employed at the head of printed titles of books and articles:

Nuevo método práctico para aprender el alemán	*A* New Practical Method for Learning German
Tratado elemental de mecánica	*An* Elementary Treatise on Mechanics
Historia de la conquista de Méjico	*The* History of the Conquest of Mexico

2.42. The article is omitted before a noun in many phrases of an adverbial or prepositional character:

con motivo de su mala salud	on account of his ill health
a esquina de la Calle Ancha	on *the* corner of Broad Street
en nombre de Dios	in *the* name of God
a orillas del Guadiana	on *the* banks of the Guadiana
en gran manera	in *a* high degree
a tiro de piedra de la casa	at *a* stone's throw from the house
Salí con objeto de buscarle.	I went out with *the* intention of looking for him.

---

1 See also § 8.40.

THE NEUTER GENDER

2.43. It has been seen that nouns have but two genders, masculine and feminine. The neuter gender applies to the definite article, the personal pronoun of the third person, adjectives, past participles, the adjective pronouns, and occasionally to adverbs. It is, moreover, limited to the singular number.

2.44. The only separate neuter forms are those of the three demonstrative pronouns, **esto, eso, aquello;** the definite article, **lo;** and the personal pronoun of the third person singular, **ello,** *acc.* **lo:**

Esto me agrada más.	*This* pleases me more.
Eso no me parece practicable.	*That* does not seem feasible to me.
Aquello ya no sucede en el día de hoy.	*That* no longer happens nowadays.
Lo hermoso debe combinarse con **lo** útil.	*The* beautiful must be combined with *the* useful.
No hicieron caso de **ello.**	They took no notice of *it.*
En cuanto a mí, no **lo** creo.	As for me, I do not believe *it.*

2.45. Some other adjective pronouns, although lacking a separate form for the neuter, employ the masculine with a neuter value:

todo everything	**mucho** much
tanto so much	**poco** little
demasiado too much	**harto** quite enough

When so used, these words are referred to by neuter pronouns:

Aunque tengo poco, estoy contento con **eso.**	Although I have little, I am content with *that.*
Debe haber algo de misterioso en su conducta, mas yo no acierto a descubrir**lo.**	There must be something mysterious in his conduct, but I do not succeed in discovering *it.*
Aprendió mucho en el colegio, pero en saliendo de él **lo** olvidó.	He learned a great deal at college, but he forgot *it* on leaving.

2.46. The neuters of the remaining adjective pronouns, and of adjectives and past participles, are formed by prefixing the neuter article **lo:**

lo mío, lo suyo	what is mine, his
lo ameno, lo distinguido	what is agreeable, distinguished

The effect of placing **lo** before such words is to form a substantive phrase expressing the quality in question considered abstractly:

Como no parecía dudable **lo referido** por el indio.	As *what was told* by the Indian did not seem questionable.
La lana de la llama nunca está grasienta ni sucia como la del carnero, y la parte tomada de los lomos rivaliza con ella en **lo sedoso y suave.**	The wool of the llama is never greasy or dirty like that of the sheep, and the part taken from the flanks rivals the latter in *softness and silkiness.*
Todo esto me parece pecaminoso olvido de **lo eterno** por **lo temporal.**	All this seems to me a sinful forgetfulness of *what is eternal* for *what is temporal.*

REMARK. **Lo** may be similarly (though rarely) applied to a noun to show that its quality is taken abstractly:

Si el poeta se ciñe a la verdad, ¿de qué le sirve **lo poeta?**	If the poet limits himself to the truth, of what use is *his being a poet?*
En Isabel la católica no era menos grande **lo mujer** que **lo reina.**	In Isabella the Catholic *her character as a woman* was no less great than *her character as a queen.*
Estos institutos militares religiosos, en que se confundían **lo monje y lo caballero,...**	These military-religious institutes, in which *monasticism* and *knighthood* were combined,...

2.47. The so-called neuter form of the article, **lo,** is used only before adjectives, participles or adjective pronouns to express their value taken abstractly as nouns. An adverb may intervene:

Lo útil.	What is useful, utility.
Lo agradable.	What is agreeable, agreeableness.
Lo mío.	Whatever is mine, my property.
Lo americano.	Whatever is American.
Lo hecho; lo dicho.	What is done; what has been said.
En lo pasado.	In the past.
Han hecho lo posible.	They have done what was possible.
Según lo determinado.	According to what has been determined.
Lo claro de la frase.	The clearness of the phrase.
Lo curioso del asunto.	The curious part of the matter.
Hemos proveído lo necesario.	We have provided what is necessary.
Preferimos lo útil a lo puramente ornamental.	We prefer the useful to the purely ornamental.

2.48. The substantive nature of the adjective or participle preceded by **lo** is especially manifest when followed by **de** and a noun.

Such constructions generally require the employment of a noun in rendering them into English:

V. sabe **lo firme** de mi resolución.	You know *the firmness* of my resolve.
La marea estaba en **lo más bajo** del reflujo.	The tide was at *the lowest* ebb.
Traté de demostrarle **lo necio** y **lo inútil** del proyecto.	I tried to prove to him *the folly* and *uselessness* of the project.
Continuaba leyendo el estudiante sin considerar **lo avanzado** de la hora.	The student kept on reading without considering *the lateness* of the hour.

2.49. A curious modification of the neuter applied to adjectives is met with when they are followed by the relative **que** and **ser, estar,** or any of their substitutes. In that case the adjective does not agree with the neuter **lo,** but with the noun subject of the relative clause; or more strictly, **lo** does not agree with the adjective. The construction can be better exemplified than defined. It cannot be translated literally:

Lo melancólica que está **la ciudad.**	The sadness that pervades the city.
Lo convenientes que fueron en otros tiempos, y **lo** útiles que pueden ser todavía.	Their suitableness in other days, and their possible utility still.
Lo quiméricos que nos parecían **todos sus proyectos.**	The visionary character which seemed to us inherent in all his plans.
Lo divertida que se pasó **la noche.**	The entertaining manner in which they passed the night.
Lo enfermas que se sienten.	The severity of their illness.
Lo indiferentes que se mostraban.	The degree of indifference which they exhibited.
Lo desprovista que se halla de municiones **la fortaleza.**	The limited supply of munitions in the fortress.

REMARK. The same construction is likewise applicable to adverbs:

Lo bien que habla.	The able manner in which he speaks.
Lo aprisa que corrían.	The rapidity with which they ran.
Lo diestramente que desvió el golpe.	The dextrous manner in which he parried the stroke.

2.50. The construction **lo** + adjective often has practically the exclamatory value of **qué** or **cuán** *how*:

Ahora que fué preciso separarme de doña **Isabelita**, comprendí de repente **lo** muy querida que se había hecho para mí en menos de dos semanas.

Now that it was necessary to part from Isabelita, I suddenly realized how very dear she had become to me in less than two weeks.

No puede V. figurarse **lo** hermosa que se ha puesto **mi hija** desde que V. **la** vió.

You cannot imagine how beautiful my daughter has grown since you saw her.

REMARK. By transposing the order, it will be seen that the construction is similar to the absolute use of **lo** explained in § **5.47**:

¡Lo que es hermosa aquella actriz!

How beautiful that actress is!

No me conoció por lo que yo venía disfrazado.

He did not recognize me because I was so [thoroughly] disguised.

2.51. The neuter forms of the pronouns (**esto, eso, aquello,** and **ello,** *acc.* **lo**) do not refer to single words, but reproduce entire previous clauses or propositions:

Si se hubiera sabido en Chárleston que el hijo de Juan Gárdner se había puesto al servicio del ejército nordista, seguramente hubiera tenido **esto** fatales consecuencias para el dueño de la plantación de Bella Vista.

If it had been known in Charleston that the son of John Gardner had entered the Northern army, *this* [*knowledge*] would certainly have had fatal consequences for the master of Bellview plantation.

Eso parece estar en contradicción consigo mismo.

That appears to be in contradiction with itself.

Todo **ello** indicaba, como es fácil comprender, que las autoridades no estaban dispuestas a hacer nada.

It all indicated, as is easily understood, that the authorities were not disposed to do anything.

Se habla de una gran derrota sufrida por las armas de los aliados; pero no se da crédito a **ello**.

There is talk of a great defeat suffered by the armies of the allies; but no credit is given to *it*.

Me dijeron que la tropa acababa de fusilar a los dos contrabandistas, y que el pueblo había querido impedir**lo**.

They told me that the soldiers had just shot the two smugglers, and that the populace had wanted to prevent *it*.

2.52. By extension, **ello** may represent an idea that has not been expressed, but is only in the mind of the speaker:

Ello es que debemos mirarnos como muy afortunados.

The fact is, we ought to consider ourselves very lucky.

Ello es que siempre su conducta ha sido para mí un misterio. — *The fact* is, his conduct has always been a mystery to me.

Ello era que la sangre corría de ambos campeones. — *The fact* was that blood was flowing from both combatants.

REMARK. **Ello** occasionally stands isolated at the beginning of a sentence, with the value of *in fact* (cf. § 3.25):

Ello, es preciso indagar qué vida lleva. — Fact is, it is necessary to find out what kind of life he leads.

2.53. It is customary, after a second verb, to repeat a predicate noun, adjective, participle or adverb by means of the neuter **lo** (cf. § 3.61):

La noche fué tan tranquila como **lo** había sido el día. — The night was as calm as the day had been.

Esta constelación no está situada tan cerca del polo antárctico como la estrella polar **lo** está del polo norte. — This constellation is not situated so near to the Antarctic pole as the pole star is to the north pole.

Se comprende que una costa tan expuesta a los golpes del huracán, y batida de frente, **lo** fuera con una fuerza de que ninguna descripción puede dar idea. — It is plain that a coast so exposed to the fury of the hurricane, and beaten upon directly, would be so with a violence that no description can give an idea of.

Mi hermano se precia de ser poeta; mas ni **lo** es ni **lo** será nunca. — My brother flatters himself that he is a poet; but he neither is nor ever will be one.

REMARK. When the noun is not predicate, the demonstrative may agree with it:

Si gozo de buena **salud, la** debo al ejercicio y a la temperancia. — If I enjoy good *health,* I owe *it* to exercise and temperance.

Si estoy bueno, **lo** debo al ejercicio y a la temperancia. — If I am well, I owe it to exercise and temperance.

2.54. Although the infinitive, when used as a verbal noun, is preceded by the masculine article, it is nevertheless logically a neuter, and is therefore reproduced by a neuter pronoun:

Estábamos determinados a **partir,** pero hubo dificultades en **ello,** y tuvimos que diferir**lo.** — We were prepared to start, but there were obstacles to our doing so, and we had to postpone it.

El **estar** tan ignorante y embrutecida una parte del pueblo es muy de- — The fact of a part of the people being so ignorant and degraded is plorable, y no podemos atribuir**lo** a otra cosa que a la distribución desigual del dinero. — deplorable, and we cannot attribute it to aught else than the unequal distribution of money.

REMARK. If we were to substitute true nouns for the above infinitives, the pronouns would be masculine or feminine accordingly, as required:

Estábamos determinados a la **partida,** pero tuvimos que diferir**la.** — We were prepared for the departure, but had to postpone it.

La **ignorancia** y el **embrutecimiento** de una parte del pueblo son muy deplorables, y no podemos atri**buirlos** a otra cosa, etc. — The ignorance and degradation of a part of the people are very deplorable, and we cannot attribute them to aught else, etc.

2.55. The neuter **ello** is the only one of the personal pronouns that lacks a terminal form in the accusative; hence although we may say in the masculine:

Yo le conozco a él. — I know him.

We cannot say in the neuter:

Yo lo entiendo a *ello.* — I understand it.

But in the dative it has two forms:

Como no pareciese suficiente lo declarado por los testigos, se creyó necesario agregarle *(or* agregar a ello) el reconocimiento de los peritos. — As the testimony of the witnesses did not seem sufficient, it was thought necessary to add to it the opinion of the experts.

A lo dado no se le debe mirar ni el pelo, ni el tamaño. *(Refrán)* — We must not look a gift-horse in the mouth. *(Proverb)*

2.56. In the southern countries of South America particularly **lo de** frequently has the meaning of **casa de** in Castilian usage:

Para ir a **lo de Galván** tenía que tomar la misma dirección que para **lo de don Fabio.** (Güiraldes, **Don Segundo Sombra,** III) — To go to *Galván's (house, place, ranch)* I had to take the same direction as to go to *Don Fabio's.*

Voy a ir hasta *El Cardón;* hasta **lo de Eduardito.** (Lynch, **Los caranchos de la Florida,** X) — I am going as far as *El Cardón;* as far as *Edward's.*

2.57. The feminine form of the personal, possessive, demonstrative and some other pronouns and of the articles is idiomatically used in innumerable phrases without reference to any stated or even understood antecedent:

Hay soplones que van con el cuento al señor cura... ¡y ya sabéis cómo **las** gasta don Tiburcio! (Palacio Valdés, **Sinfonía pastoral, Adagio cantábile,** IX)

There are talebearers that go to the priest with the story... and you well know how Don Tiburcio acts.

Esos cocineros saben mucho; lo sirven muy caliente, con una salsa picante, y luego es **ella.** (Benavente, **Lo cursi,** I, 2)

Those cooks are pretty smart: they serve it very hot, with a highly-seasoned sauce, and then there is the deuce to pay.

¡**La** han hecho ustedes buena! ¿Y cómo me presento yo en gorra y zapatillas al presidente? (Palacio Valdés, **La hermana San Sulpicio,** I)

Now you have done it! How can I present myself to the president in a cap and bedroom slippers?

Pero dejando esto a un lado, yo no **las** tengo todas conmigo. (Valera, **Juanita la larga,** XIII)

But leaving this aside, I am not easy in mind.

Era público y notorio que se **la** tenía jurada. (Payró, **Justicia salomónica,** in **Nuevos cuentos de Pago Chico)**

It was public and notorious that he had it in for you *(or* that he had sworn revenge).

Esos chicos quejillones siempre se salen con **la suya.** (Unamuno, **Recuerdos de niñez y de mocedad, I,** 5)

Those complaining children always have their own way *(or* get what they want).

¡Vaya, vaya! ¿Conque **ésas** tenemos? Le deseo a usted buena suerte. (Benavente, **Por las nubes,** I, 5)

Well, well! So that's what's up? I wish you good luck.

¡Calla!... ¡Asunción!... —La niña modernista. **Esa** es otra. (Benavente, **Lo cursi,** II, 5)

Hush! Here comes Asunción! —The up-to-date girl. Worse yet and more of it.

¡**La** de cosas que debo hacer mañana! (Benavente, **Rosas de otoño,** II, 4)

The number of things I must do tomorrow!

Presumían, por el aire que llevábamos, que habíamos hecho **alguna** muy gorda. (Pereda, **Peñas arriba,** XX)

They presumed by our attitude that we had done something extra special.

Yo le juro que no vuelve a hacernos **otra.** (Pérez Galdós, **Fortunata y Jacinta,** II, 6, 10)

I swear to you that she won't play another of her tricks on us.

Infierno y cielo están aquí. Aquí pagamos tarde o temprano todas **las** que hemos hecho. (Pérez Galdós, **Torquemada en la hoguera,** III)	Heaven and Hell are here. Here sooner or later we pay for all the tricks that we have played.

REMARK. The construction discussed in § 2.57 is often called the "neuter feminine."

III
Personal Pronouns

3.1. Spanish, in common with most languages, originally had only two personal pronouns of the second person: **tú** *you* (archaic *thou*) for the singular and **vos** *you* (archaic *ye*) for the plural. But it is equally true that in those languages these two pronouns have either become obsolete or their use is greatly restricted, while other expressions have taken their places in polite speech. At present the following are in use in Spanish:

Pronouns of the Second person	Sing.	**tú**	you (thou)
		vos	you
		usted	you
	Plur.	**vosotros** *(masc.)*	you (ye)
		vosotras *(fem.)*	you (ye)
		ustedes	you

3.2. **Tú** *you* is used only: in sacred or poetical style or in addressing near relations, very intimate friends, small children and animals. Its use implies an intimacy, familiarity or even patronizing attitude which is not wisely assumed without due consideration of the circumstances. In effect, its use is comparable to that of the given name in English.

3.3. **Vos** *you* (now used only as a singular, although still joined to the second person plural of verbs) is in Castilian usage employed:

in representation of antique style; occasionally in translations from English and French, to represent the second person plural address of those languages; and interchangeably with **tú** in addressing the Deity. On the other hand, the use of **vos** to address one person is, in spoken usage or its written counterpart, very wide-spread among even semi-literate people in much of Spanish America (especially in Argentina and Uruguay) with the exception of the greater part of Mexico, Peru, Cuba, Puerto Rico, Santo Domingo and Panama. (For the verb forms used with **vos** in Spanish America see **§ 13.8, REMARK II.**)

3.4. Vosotros, -as (formed by adding **otros, -as** to **vos**) is the plural of **tú** and **vos**, and in Castilian is used in addressing two or more persons to whom **tú** or **vos** would apply. It is, moreover, sometimes used by public speakers and in the pulpit.

In the south of Spain, and in the New World generally, **vosotros, -as,** the corresponding object **os,** possessive **vuestro** and the second person plural verb forms of Castilian, have been replaced, especially in non-literary use, by **ustedes,** the corresponding objects, possessives and the third person plural verb form.

3.5. Usted (*plur.* **ustedes**) represents the conventional English *you* under all circumstances. It is the universal respectful address of society, and the only one the foreigner is ever likely to employ or hear addressed to him, unless he marries a native or forms intimate friendships. It is a contraction of **vuestra merced** *your grace (plur.* **vuestras mercedes**) and therefore requires the verb in the third person, as would be the case in English if we were to use the same way of addressing people.

Compare for example the usage in speaking to a judge or nobleman: *your Honor has said . . . ; does your Lordship believe . . . ?*

It is often abbreviated to **V.** or **Vd.** or **Ud.** for the singular, and **VV., Vs.** or **Vds.** or **Uds.** for the plural. In the original edition of the grammar the author used the form he found in the printed page from which he took the example. The reviser has likewise quoted what he found. These signs are always to be read **usted** and **ustedes,** just as *Mr.* in English is read *mister* and *M.* in French, *monsieur.*

3.6. The remaining personal pronouns are:

yo	I
él *(masc.)*	he, it
ella *(fem.)*	she, it
nos	we
nosotros *(masc.)* **nosotras** *(fem.)*	we
ellos *(masc.)* **ellas** *(fem.)*	they

3.7. **Nos** is no longer used in the nominative case except by sovereigns, tribunals, officers of Church and State, etc., when speaking or writing in their official capacity, and, though very rarely, by authors and editors, in the same manner as the English royal and editorial *we*.

3.8. **Nosotros, -as** (formed by adding **otros, -as** to **nos**) is to be used for *we* in its proper sense, the masculine form referring to males, the feminine to females; the masculine **nosotros** is used in speaking as the mouthpiece of a mixed company.

Nevertheless, a lady may say **nosotras** of a mixed company; which, although not theoretically correct, probably arises from the habit of saying **nosotras** in girlhood, speaking of herself and playmates—*we girls*. But the tendency nowadays is for women to use **nosotros** to the total exclusion of the feminine form.

3.9. **Ellos** applies to men and to mixed companies; **ellas,** to females only.

3.10. As the terminations of Spanish verbs vary for each person, the subject pronouns are usually dispensed with, except when required to give emphasis or prevent vagueness.

¿Tiene el hombre un revólver?	Has the man a revolver?
Sí, tiene.	Yes, *he* has.
¿Quién tiene un burro?	Who has a donkey?
Yo tengo un burro.	*I* have a donkey.
¿Qué quiere **ella?**	What does *she* want?
Quiere la rosa.	*She* wants the rose.

DECLENSION

3.11. A noun in Spanish never varies in form as in Latin, except to make the plural. Adjectives, articles and participles never have more than four forms; namely, the masculine and feminine respectively of the singular and plural. There is therefore little trace left of the case endings of Latin so far as these parts of speech are concerned.

3.12. The personal pronouns are the only words in Spanish which retain distinctions of case. In their full inflection they have four cases:

The **nominative,** or subject.
The **dative,**[1] or indirect object.
The **accusative,**[1] or direct object.
The **prepositional,** i.e. when governed by any preposition.

However, there is not always a separate form for each case; but the student must strive to keep them distinct in his mind even though they be identical on paper.

3.13.

TABLE OF PERSONAL PRONOUNS AND THEIR INFLECTION

			NOMINATIVE	DATIVE	ACCUSATIVE	PREPOSITIONAL
SING.	1st p.		**yo**	**me**	**me**	**mí**
	2d p.		**tú**	**te**	**te**	**ti**
	3d p.	masc.	**él**	**le**	**le, lo**	**él**
		fem.	**ella**	**le, la**	**la**	**ella**
		neut.	**ello**	**le**[2]	**lo**	**ello**
PLUR.	1st p.	masc.	**nosotros**	**nos**	**nos**	**nosotros**
		fem.	**nosotras**	**nos**	**nos**	**nosotras**
	2d p.	masc.	**vosotros**	**os**	**os**	**vosotros**
		fem.	**vosotras**	**os**	**os**	**vosotras**
	3d p.	masc.	**ellos**	**les**	**los, les**	**ellos**
		fem.	**ellas**	**les, las**	**las**	**ellas**
Reflexive substitute for 3d person, common to both numbers.			[*none*]	**se**	**se**	**sí**

Usted, like nouns, is invariable, except for number.

[1] The terms *accusative* and *dative* will also, for the sake of brevity, be employed as synonyms of *direct* and *indirect object* in speaking of nouns. But when so employed they will not denote any special forms, as in the case of the personal pronouns, but merely the nature of their grammatical dependence upon a verb.

[2] The use of the neuter **le** appears in phrases like **¿Qué le vamos a hacer? (¿Qué le hemos de hacer?)** *What are we going to do about it? (What can we do about it?)*. **No hay que darle vueltas.** *There's no use talking about it,* and in exclamations like **Andale (Andele, etc.)** *Come, Come on,* so frequent in Mexico.

USE OF THE CASES

The student is already familiar with the nominatives of the personal pronouns, and with the circumstance of their usual omission except when required for emphasis, contrast or perspicuity. We have, therefore, to deal only with the objective forms.

3.14. The dative and accusative pronouns ordinarily *precede* all forms of the verb except the infinitive, present participle, and imperative positive (which will be explained hereafter).

REMARK. It is to be observed that the dative and accusative forms of these pronouns are identical except in the case of the third person; it is therefore in this person only that the distinction between the usages of the dative and accusative can be shown.

Dative

3.15. The leading use of the dative is to denote the person *to* whom anything is given, told, shown, or in any way conveyed or imparted:

Ella **me** habla.	She speaks *to me.*
Yo **te** escribiré.	I will write *to you.*
Les digo; **les** doy.	I say *to them;* I give [to] *them.*
He visto a mi hermana y **le** he hablado del asunto.	I have seen my sister and have spoken *to her* of the matter.
Nos parece probable.	It seems *to us* probable.
¿Qué **le** ha sucedido?	What has happened *to him?*

3.16. A verb which takes a dative pronoun (indirect object) may also govern a direct object at the same time:

Ella me enseña sus **dibujos.**	She shows me her *drawings.*
Te escribiré una **carta.**	I will write you a *letter.*
Les digo la **verdad.**	I tell them the *truth.*
Le he dado algunas **rosas.**	I have given her some *roses.*
Le prestaré el **dinero** que necesita.	I will lend him the *money* he needs.

3.17. As the Spanish dative combines in a measure the functions of both the Latin dative and ablative (literally, *give-to-ive* and *take-from-ive*), it is further employed in cases where something is taken away from anyone (cf. § 3.45):

Me han comprado mis géneros.	They have bought my goods *from me.*
El aullido de los perros **nos** quita el sueño.	The howling of the dogs deprives *us* of sleep.
Le he ganado la apuesta.	I have won the bet *from him.*

3.18. The dative is further used to represent the person for whose benefit or advantage anything is done:

Les ha procurado colocaciones.	He has procured *them* situations.
Te compraré un reloj.	I will buy *you* a watch.
Dice que **me** buscará un criado.	He says he will look for a servant *for me.*

3.19. After **ser** used impersonally, a dative personal pronoun may be employed to denote the person *to* whom the impersonal expression is applicable:

Le será fácil probar la coartada.	It will be easy *for him* to prove an alibi.
Caballeros, **me** es imposible escribir mientras Vds. hablan.	Gentlemen, it is impossible *for me* to write while you talk.

3.20. The dative case is confined to the personal pronouns; no other words have any distinction of case. Therefore when the indirect object is any other pronoun, or a noun, the relation is expressed by a preposition—generally **a**:

He hablado **a mi hermana.**	I have spoken *to my sister.*
Le he hablado.	I have spoken *to her.*
Escribiré **a los Sres. padres de V.**	I will write *to your parents.*
Les escribiré.	I will write *to them.*
El ruido quita el sueño **a mi padre.**	The noise deprives *my father* of sleep.
Han robado la capa **a mi amigo.**	They stole the cloak *from my friend.*
He procurado **a** (*or* **para**) **mi hijo** un empleo en el Ministerio de Guerra.	I have procured *my son* a position in the War Department.

Accusative

3.21. The accusative form is used when the pronoun is the direct object of any action:

Yo **la** llamo.	I call *her.*
No **nos** ven.	They do not see *us.*
Los he vendido.	I have sold *them.*
Ella **le** ha acogido cordialmente.	She received *him* cordially.
Ya no **los** tememos.	We no longer fear *them.*

Prepositional

3.22. When the pronoun is governed by a preposition, the prepositional form is required. This, it is to be noted, is the same as the nominative, in all but the first and second persons singular (and, we may add, the reflexive pronoun of the third person, which has no nominative):

Es evidente que hablan **de mí.**	It is evident they are speaking *of me.*
Mira **hacia ti.**	He looks *toward you.*
Quiere venir con **nosotros.**	He wants to come *with us.*
Iremos **sin él.**	We will go *without him.*
Llegaremos **después de ellas.**	We will arrive *after them.*
¿Han traído una carta dirigida **a mí?**	Have they brought a letter addressed *to me?*

GENDER

3.23. The personal pronouns of the third person always assume the gender of the nouns which they represent, although it is not apparent in the dative where no distinction of gender is made. Consequently, as in Spanish all existing things are either masculine or feminine, *it,* applied to either of them, must be represented by the appropriate case of **él** or **ella** (which is only occasionally expressed as subject):

Quiero vender mi casa. Es bonita y cómoda; recientemente **la** he mandado pintar, y **le** he agregado una ala.	I want to sell my *house. It* is pretty and comfortable; I have recently had *it* painted, and have added an ell to *it.*
¿Dónde está la taza? —**La** he roto.	Where is the *cup?* —I broke *it.*
¿Tiene V. mis plumas? —**Las** tengo.	Have you my *pens?* —I have *them.*
En el fondo . . . se destaca una sierra azul bastante lejana, y en **ella** algunas casas blancas. (Baroja, **El mundo es ansí,** II, 4)	In the background . . . a blue *range of mountains,* quite distant, stands out, and on *it* some white houses
¿Ha leído V. los **libros?** —**Los** he leído.	Have you read the *books?* —I have read *them.*
¿Ve V. a los **soldados?** —**Los** veo, y veo a un oficial con **ellos.**	Do you see the *soldiers?* —I see *them,* and see an officer with *them.*

3.24. It will be observed that **él** has two forms for the accusative singular: **le** and **lo.** According to the prevailing usage of the language,

le relates to a male person or a masculine thing personified, **lo** to any other masculine noun:[1]

Busco a mi criado pero no **le** hallo.	I look for my *servant,* but do not find *him.*
Busco mi **sombrero** pero no **lo** hallo.	I look for my *hat,* but do not find *it.*
¿Quiere V. mi abanico? —No **lo** quiero.	Do you want my *fan?* —I do not want *it.*
¿Dónde está el **muchacho? le** necesito.	Where is the *boy?* I want *him.*
Pega al **perro** y **lo** mata.	He beats the *dog* and kills *him.*

3.25. **Ello** has a value of *it* only as representing a subject referred to, or the substance of something said, and never a visible, tangible thing. It therefore refers to situations or statements, but not to nouns. It is seldom expressed as subject.[2] The accusative of **ello (lo)** must not be confused with the accusative of the masculine pronoun **él,** of similar form:

¿Qué es **ello?**	What is *it?*
No **lo** haré.	I shall not do *it (thing proposed).*
Sí, **lo** creo.	Yes, I believe *it (what you say).*
Convengo en **ello.**	I agree to *it (condition made).*
No creo en **ello.**	I don't believe in *it.*
No tenemos evidencia alguna de **ello.**	We have no evidence whatever of *it.*

Remark. **Ello** formerly had a greater variety of uses, some of which survive, at least in rustic usage, especially in Spanish America. One of these uses is as a vague and evasive reference to the matter at hand: **¡Bárbaros, más que bárbaros! —También es cierto; pero ello, don Román, pongámonos en los casos.** (Pereda, **Don Gonzalo González de la Gonzalera,** I) *Savages, worse than savages! —That is true too; but as for that* (or *perhaps*), *let us consider the circumstances.* See also § 2.52.

---

[1] The usage of the accusative masculine forms **le** and **lo** is very irregular. Many reputable modern writers use **lo** of persons as well as of things, and others employ **le** in reference to inanimate objects. The dominant practice is that given above. The use of **les** for **los** is sometimes met with, and dative feminine forms **la** and **las** are in use. The subject will be exhaustively discussed hereafter. See next chapter.

[2] In fact it is seldom that any word is used in Spanish corresponding to English *it* as subject:

Es tarde.	*It* is late.	**No es probable.**	*It* is not likely.
Es evidente.	*It* is evident.	**Está bien.**	*It* is all right.
Es singular.	*It* is strange.	**¿Quién es?**	Who is *it?*

REFLEXIVE PRONOUNS

3.26. The objective cases of the personal pronouns of the first and second persons are used reflexively when the subject of the sentence is of the same person as the pronoun:

Me he cortado.	I have cut *myself.*
Me hallo sin dinero.	I find *myself* without money.
Me he mandado hacer una capa.	I have had a cloak made *for myself.*
¿De quién habla V.? —Hablo **de mí.**	Of whom are you speaking? —I am speaking *of myself.*
Si lo haces, **te** pondrás en ridículo.	If you do it you will make *yourself* ridiculous.
¿**Os** llamáis sabios?	Do you call *yourselves* wise?
Nos hemos armado; si nos acometen, **nos** defenderemos.	We have armed *ourselves;* if they attack us we will defend *ourselves.*

3.27. If in similar reflexive expressions the subject is of the third person, the reflexive pronoun **se** is used as object, whatever be the gender or number of the subject:

Se cree hombre de gran importancia.	He thinks *himself* a man of great importance.
Ella **se** compra un vestido nuevo.	She buys *herself* a new dress.
Se procuran sillas.	They procure *themselves* chairs.
El muchacho **se** hace un silbato.	The boy makes *himself* a whistle.
¿**Se** afeita V. antes de almorzar?	Do you shave *yourself* before breakfast?
Ellas **se** dedican al estudio de la música.	They devote *themselves* to the study of music.
Vds. **se** incomodan inútilmente.	You disturb *yourselves* needlessly.

3.28. The objective cases of the personal pronouns of the third person, including **usted,** always designate a different individual or thing from the subject:

Ella **la** llama.	She calls *her.*
Ella **se** llama Paca.	She calls *herself* Fanny.
V. **le** engaña.	You deceive *him.*
V. **se** engaña.	You deceive *yourself.*
Vds. **los** incomodan.	You disturb *them.*
Vds. **se** incomodan.	You disturb *yourselves.*
El capitán habla siempre de **ella.**	The captain is always talking of *her.*
El capitán habla siempre de **sí.**	The captain is always talking about *himself.*

El hombre pone el libro delante de **sí** sobre la mesa. — The man lays the book on the table before *him.*

El mozo entra y pone una botella de vino delante de **él.** — The waiter comes in and places a bottle of wine before *him.*

El guardia los ve venir hacia **sí.** — The guard sees them coming towards *him.*

REMARK. However, the reflexive **sí** may be applied to an object different from the subject of the sentence, provided **sí** be closely preceded by the noun to which it refers, and the meaning be not obscured:

Para diferenciar a los vegetales entre **sí,** el botánico atiende en primer lugar al desarrollo de la semilla. — In order to distinguish plants from *one another,* the botanist considers in the first place the development of the seed.

3.29. When **mí, ti, sí** are governed by **con,** *with,* it is joined to them, and **go** is added to the combination, producing the peculiar forms **conmigo, contigo, consigo:**

¿Quiere V. venir **conmigo?** — Do you want to come *with me?*

Quiero hablar **contigo.** — I want to speak *with you.*

Mi hermana está enfadada **consigo.** — My sister is angry *with herself.*

Mi hermana está enfadada con ella. — My sister is angry with her *(some other lady).*

Llevan víveres **consigo.** — They carry provisions *with them.*

The explanation of this is that the Latin *cum, with,* was affixed to personal pronouns: *mecum, tecum, secum, nobiscum, vobiscum.* The first three of these have been preserved in modern Italian with the forms of *meco, teco, seco.* In old Spanish they appear as *nosco, vosco;* subsequently these became obsolete, and the origin of the others being forgotten, the preposition **con** was again added.

3.30. The distinction between **sí** and **él, ella,** etc. (cf. § 3.28, end) is not strictly observed, as the latter tend to usurp the rôle of the reflexive pronoun in speech and in the less careful writers:

María intentaba crearse una vida para **ella** sola. (Baroja, **La dama errante,** I) — Mary was attempting to create a life for *herself* alone.

Su antiguo sistema era el bueno: que cada uno pescase para **él.** (Blasco Ibáñez, **Cañas y barro,** VII) — His old system was the good one: let each one fish for *himself.*

Vieron venir hacia **ellos** un señor de blancas patillas. (Blasco Ibáñez, **Los muertos mandan,** III) — They saw a gentleman with white side whiskers coming toward *them.*

Griegos y semitas tenían el instinto fuerte de vivir, inventaban dioses para **ellos**, un paraíso exclusivamente suyo. (Baroja, **El árbol de la ciencia**, IV, 3)

Greeks and Semites had a strong instinct for life, they invented gods for *themselves,* a paradise exclusively their own.

Hablaba para **ella** misma, para distraerse con sus propias palabras. (Gálvez, **Nacha Regules**, I)

She was talking to *herself,* to distract herself with her own words.

Ve venir a **él** una mora y un guía renegado. (Madariaga, **España**, I, 19)

He sees a Moorish woman and a renegade guide coming to *him.*

TERMINAL DATIVE AND ACCUSATIVE

3.31. The dative and accusative forms, being short and of weak sound, are not sufficiently sonorous to bear any degree of emphasis; and moreover the dative, not having a distinction of gender, is often not precise enough to prevent ambiguity. It is clear that something further is often necessary.

This lack is supplied by the use of the prepositional case (which is fuller in form and maintains throughout a distinction of gender) preceded by the preposition **a.** This will be called the *terminal* dative or accusative, since it may follow any form of the verb without being appended to it. The **a** in this case is merely a grammatical device, and has no prepositional value. The terminal forms, although stronger in sound, are exactly equivalent in meaning to the simple forms:

SINGULAR				PLURAL			
		SIMPLE	TERMINAL			SIMPLE	TERMINAL
1 p.	Dat.	**me**	**a mí**	1 p.	Dat.	**nos**	**a nosotros, –as**
	Acc.	**me**			Acc.	**nos**	
2 p.	Dat.	**te**	**a ti**	2 p.	Dat.	**os**	**a vosotros, –as**
	Acc.	**te**			Acc.	**os**	
3 p. M.	Dat.	**le**	**a él**	3 p. M.	Dat.	**les**	**a ellos**
	Acc.	**le, lo**			Acc.	**les, los**	
3 p. F.	Dat.	**le**	**a ella**	3 p. F.	Dat.	**les**	**a ellas**
	Acc.	**la**			Acc.	**las**	

The terminal form is used in two ways: *1st,* as a substitute for the simple form; *2nd,* in addition to and in conjunction with it.

3.32. It is seldom used as a mere substitute, except in the following instances, where it is the only construction admissible:

a. In answering a question, where the answer is to be the direct or indirect object of a verb expressed in the question, but left to be understood in the answer:

¿A quién ha visto V.?	Whom did you see?
A él, a ella, a Vd., a ellos, etc.	*Him, her, you, them,* etc.
¿A quién ha entregado V. la carta?	To whom did you deliver the letter?
A él, a ella, a ellas, etc.	*To him, to her, to them,* etc.

b. Where two or more objective pronouns are brought into direct contrast:

No (le) busca **a Vd.** sino **a mí.**	He does not seek *you* but *me.*
El tigre no (nos) ve **a nosotros** ni nosotros **a él.**	The tiger does not see *us,* nor we *him.*

c. Where the direct object of a verb is a pronoun of the first or second person, the indirect object, if a pronoun, usually assumes the terminal form:

Me han recomendado **a V.**	They have recommended me *to you.*
Me han enviado **a ti.**	They have sent me *to you.*
¿Por qué te han enviado **a mí?**	Why have they sent you *to me?*
Vuestro general os ha entregado **a nosotros.**	Your general has delivered you *to us.*

d. When the direct object is a pronoun used reflexively, and the indirect object is any other personal pronoun, the latter often assumes the terminal form:

Me he ofrecido **a él** como guía.	I offered myself *to him* as guide.
Se recomienda **a ellos.**	He recommends himself *to them.*
Se dirige **a mí** *or* Se me dirige.	He addresses himself *to me.*
Se ha presentado **a nosotros** *(or* Se nos ha presentado) en un estado deplorable de embriaguez.	He presented himself *to us* in a deplorable state of intoxication.

3.33. A personal pronoun representing the terminus of a motion expressed by an intransitive verb is put in the prepositional case and preceded by **a.** This construction is not the terminal dative, the **a** having a true prepositional value:

Viene a mí y me da una esquela. Dice que me ha mandado un paquete, pero **no ha llegado a mí.**	He *comes to me* and gives me a note. He says he sent me a package, but it *has not reached me.*
Anita, la chiquilla te llama. —**Voy a ella** ahora.	Annie, the baby is calling you. —I *am going to her* now.

REMARK. In no other class of cases will it be advisable to use the terminal form alone; in the few other instances where it might be employed, the double construction explained below would be equally applicable and generally preferable.

REDUNDANT CONSTRUCTION

3.34. The use of the terminal form for the purpose of emphasis or clearness is as an addition to the simple form. This we will call the *redundant* construction. The combinations are:

	DATIVE	ACCUSATIVE
SINGULAR	**me...a mí**	**me...a mí**
	te...a ti	**te...a ti**
	le... { **a él** / **a ella** / **a V.** }	**le...a él** *(animate)*
		lo...a él *(inanimate)*
		la...a ella
		le...a V. *(masc.)*
		la...a V. *(fem.)*
PLURAL	**nos...** { **a nosotros** / **a nosotras** }	**nos...** { **a nosotros** / **a nosotras** }
	os... { **a vosotros** / **a vosotras** }	**os...** { **a vosotros** / **a vosotras** }
	les... { **a ellos**[1] / **a ellas** / **a Vds.** }	**los...a ellos**
		las...a ellas
		los...a Vds.
		las...a Vds.

[1] The use of **le...a ellos,** etc., or plural noun (cf. § 3.36) is of long standing and appears in some standard writers but is not considered correct: **Eso le ha ocurrido a los más insignes autores.** (Wast, **Vocación de escritor,** IV, 7) *This has happened to the most noted authors.* **La opinión popular le importa muy poco a los gobiernos.** (Benavente, **La escuela de las princesas,** I, 10) *Popular opinion matters very little to governments.*

3.35. Either pronoun may come first, but greater emphasis is conveyed when the terminal form precedes. Where the simple form is first, the verb is placed between the two pronouns; otherwise the verb follows both:

Le enseño **a ella** el castellano.	I am teaching her Spanish.
Les escribiré **a ellas** una relación circunstanciada del suceso.	I will write them a detailed account of the occurrence.
¿**A él** qué **le** importa?	What does it matter to *him?*
A ellos no **les** diré nada.	I shall not tell *them* anything.
A mí me parece que el hombre es loco.	It seems to *me* that the man is mad.
Me parece **a mí** que no llegará hoy.	It seems to me he will not arrive today.
¿No **le** recibirá V. **a él**?	Won't you receive him?
No **nos** convidarán **a nosotros.**	They won't invite *us.*
Te mandaré **a ti** la próxima vez.	I will send *you* the next time.
Le han concedido **a él** una pensión, y las niegan a personas que verdaderamente las merecen.	They have granted *him* a pension, and refuse them to persons who really deserve them.

3.36. This usage is so general that it is often carried to excess. It is commoner with indirect objects than with direct. It is furthermore extended to nouns and other pronouns, in which event the noun is preceded by **a** and accompanies the simple objective pronoun:

No **les** parece conveniente **a las señoras.**	It does not seem proper to the ladies.
No **le** dan nada **al mozo.**	They give nothing to the waiter.
Llamadle al juez. (Baroja, **El árbol de la ciencia,** V, 9)	Call the judge.
¿Cómo **le** van a defender **a ése?** (Benavente, **El primo Román,** I, 8)	How are they going to defend that fellow?

EMPLOYMENT OF **USTED** AND ITS SUBSTITUTES

3.37. **Usted,** being grammatically a noun, is invariable except as regards number. Still, it is practically employed as a personal pronoun, and will be discussed here as such.

3.38. Both for clearness and courtesy **usted** should appear at least once in every sentence relating to the second person, except familiarly in very short ones where there is no danger of ambiguity:

¿Qué dice? ¿Qué quiere?	What do you say? What do you want?
¿Cómo está su señor padre?	How is your father?
¿Quiere fumar?	Have a smoke?
Me hace un gran favor.	You do me a great favor.
Yo le prestaré lo necesario si quiere.	I will lend you the necessary [amount] if you wish.

3.39. As subject, **usted** is usually expressed once near the beginning of the sentence, and afterwards left to be understood, except when required for clearness:

Vd. tiene talento, pero no quiere estudiar.	You have talent, but you won't study.
¿Cuándo enviará V. a su hermano los libros que le ha prometido?	When will you send your brother the books you have promised him?

3.40. **Usted** appears as object only when governed by a preposition. In the dative and accusative its place is taken by the datives and accusatives of **él** or **ella,** according to the sex of the person addressed:

No partiremos sin Vds.	We will not start without you.
Tengo gran confianza en V.	I have great confidence in you.
No he recibido de V. ninguna carta.	I have not received any letters from you.
Ninguno de Vds. ha hallado la solución del enigma.	None of you has found the solution of the enigma.
Ya que ha venido V., **le** diré algo que **le** será interesante.	Now that you have come, I will tell *you* something that will be interesting *to you.*
¿No creen Vds. que **les** pagaré?	Do you not believe I will pay *you?*
Vd. me ha engañado, pero yo **la** perdono.	You deceived me, but I forgive *you (fem.).*
Señoras: celebro hallar**las** reunidas. (Benavente, **Pepa Doncel,** III, 11)	Ladies: I am happy to find *you* together.

3.41. But if **usted** has not previously appeared in the sentence, or if the person referred to is not sufficiently apparent, **a Vd., a Vds.,** is added to the personal pronoun, in the same manner as the redundant construction previously explained:

Le esperaré **a V.** mañana.	I shall expect *you* tomorrow.
Ya **la** comprendo **a V.,** señorita.	Now I understand *you,* Miss.
Les digo **a Vds.** la pura verdad.	I am telling *you* the plain truth.

¿Qué **le** ha dicho **a V.** su hermano?	What has your brother told *you?*
Su señor hermano cree que yo no **le** pagaré **a V.**	Your brother believes that I will not pay *you.*
Sólo venía a **verles a ustedes.** (Benavente, **La honradez de la cerradura,** I, 3)	I was only coming to see *you.*

3.42. Still, **a Vd.** will be found as the sole object of the verb, and the objective pronoun sometimes appears unattended by **a Vd.,** when **Vd.** has not previously appeared in the sentence. So that the following three modes of expression are admissible, the first being relatively familiar (occasionally even to the verge of disrespect) and the third the most usual:

Le devolveré el libro.	I will return *you* the book.
Devolveré **a V.** el libro.	I will return the book *to you.*
Le devolveré **a V.** el libro.	" " " " " " "

REMARK. The objective forms **a V., a Vds.,** are required under the same circumstances as those enumerated in §§ 3.32–3.33:

He venido a V.	I have come to you.
Me dirijo a Vds.	I address myself to you.

3.43. As **usted** requires the third person, the reflexive **sí** is applicable to it in the same manner as to any word used in the third person, and with the same restrictions:

¿**Se** ha quemado **V.**?	Have *you* burned *yourself?*
V. se pondrá en ridículo.	*You* will make *yourself* ridiculous.
Vds. se cansarán innecesariamente.	*You* will tire *yourselves* unnecessarily.
¿No ve **V.** la taza delante de **sí**?	Don't *you* see the cup before *you?*
¿No ve V. que la taza está delante de V.[1]?	Don't you see that the cup is before you?
¿No ve V. la taza delante de él?	Don't you see the cup before him?

3.44. Although **usted** does not exhibit the gender of the person it represents, all variable words which qualify or relate to it agree in gender as well as number with the person represented:

V. es rico y dichoso. V. es rica y dichosa. Vds. son ricas y dichosas.	You are rich and happy.

[1] **V.** is here required because there is a change of subject.

La considero a V. como muy afortunada. Las considero a Vds. como muy afortunadas.	I consider you very lucky.

NOTE. There can be no definite rule prescribed as to how often **usted** should appear in a long sentence or address. The student must simply strive to attain clearness on the one hand, and on the other to avoid undue repetition.

DATIVE OF ADVANTAGE OR DISADVANTAGE

3.45. Verbal expressions of advantage or disadvantage require the dative of the person and the accusative of the thing, in the same manner as verbs of giving and imparting. The construction applies to nouns as well as to pronouns. When any preposition is required in English to express this relation, it is generally *for* or *from* (cf. §§ **3.17, 3.18**):

Les consigue una audiencia.	He secures *them* an audience.
Me quita el sueño.	He deprives *me* of sleep.
Nos han robado el dinero.	They have stolen the money *from us.*
Me toma mis libros.	He takes my books *from me.*
¿Está en casa tu hermano? —Me parece que sí. ¿**Le** quieres algo? (Martínez Sierra, **Mamá,** III)	Is your brother at home? —I think so. Do you want something *of him?*
Le compran sus géneros.	They buy his wares *from him.*
Me llevan mis flores.	They carry off my flowers [*from me*].
Dije a mi padre mi deseo de aprender a montar. No quise ocultar**le** que Pepita me había excitado a ello. (Valera, **Pepita Jiménez,** 4 de mayo)	I told my father of my desire to learn to ride. I did not try to conceal *from him* that Pepita had urged me.
Ocultad vuestra felicidad **a todo el mundo.** (Benavente, **Al fin, mujer,** I, 1, 1)	Conceal your happiness *from everybody.*
El paisaje no **le** merecía la menor atención. (Baroja, **El mundo es así,** I)	The landscape wasn't worthy of the slightest attention *from him.*

3.46. In many cases Spanish employs the dative of a person and the accusative of a thing. On the other hand in English the person is oftener accusative and the thing is preceded by a preposition,—generally *for:*

Le pide a V. una propina.	He asks you for a gratuity.
Le agradezco a V. su buena voluntad.	I thank you for your good will.
Me alaba mi aplicación.	He praises me for my assiduity.
¿Ha pagado V. al sastre la levita?	Did you pay the tailor for the coat?
Se la he pagado hoy.	I paid him for it today.
Nadie le conocía renta o propiedad de donde se sustentase. (Palacio Valdés, **José,** III)	No one knew him to have income or property by which to support himself.
¿Qué le encuentras a ese muchacho? (Baroja, **El aprendiz de conspirador,** II, 5)	What do you see in that boy?

3.47. The ethical dative or dative of interest is a secondary use of the dative case, where it appears in connection with other objective pronouns; it frequently seems superfluous and cannot be rendered into English, but indicates an interest—more or less faint—taken in the matter by the person represented by the pronoun. Its use extends to nouns also:

Avisaré a su padre y él **me** le dará una buena paliza.	I shall tell his father, and he will give him a good caning *for me.*
Póngan**mele** (pongan-me-le) **Vds.** sábanas limpias.	You put clean sheets under him *for me. (Said by doctor to nurses.)*
Échatemelo (echa-te-me-lo).	Toss it to me.
Los muchachos se **me** llevan **mis** flores.	The boys carry off my flowers *(from me for themselves).*

PRONOUN FOLLOWED BY A NOUN IN APPOSITION

3.48. When the pronoun is subject and followed by a noun in apposition which limits or defines it, the definite article is interpolated between the pronoun and said noun:

Yo el rey lo mando.	*I, the king,* command it.
Nosotros los mejicanos somos muy pundonorosos.	*We Mexicans* are very touchy.
Vds. los artistas tienen grandes privilegios.	*You artists* have great privileges.

3.49. Frequently the pronoun is suppressed, the verb retaining the person and number which it would have if the pronoun were given:

Los nordistas pensamos de un modo diferente.	*We* northerners think differently.
Sois los sudamericanos muy progresivos.	*You* South Americans are very progressive.
Tendremos el gusto los liberales de presenciar el cambio.	*We* liberals will have the pleasure of witnessing the change.
Ninguna le hemos visto. (Pérez de Ayala, **Prometeo,** IV)	None *of us* has seen him.
Nadie nacemos zabijondos [=sabihondos]. (Alvarez Quintero, **El genio alegre,** I)	Nobody (among *us*) is born knowing it all.
El día que cada uno fuéramos un tirano para nosotros mismos, todos los hombres serían igualmente libres. (Benavente, **La escuela de las princesas,** II, 9)	The day that each one of *us* should be a tyrant to himself, all men would be equally free.
La señora se ha muerto como podemos morirnos cualquiera. (Benavente, **La honradez de la cerradura,** I, **Cuadro segundo**)	The lady has died just as each one of *us* may die.
Uno tendrá su historia (¡quién no la tenemos, si fuéramos a ver!) (**Idem,** II, **Cuadro quinto, escena segunda**)	A fellow may have his history (who of *us* doesn't have one, if we looked into it!)
Hoy a casi nadie le ocurre algo digno de ser contado. La generalidad de los hombres nadamos en el océano de la vulgaridad. (Baroja, **Las inquietudes de Shanti Andía,** I, 1)	Today anything worthy of being related happens to almost no one. The majority of *us* men swim in the ocean of the commonplace.

3.50. When an objective personal pronoun is accompanied by a noun in apposition, the following is the mode of expression used:

Claro, a **nosotras las mujeres** nos engañan con mucha facilidad.	Clearly they deceive *us women* very easily.
Las locuras humanas llevan mucho dinero a las arcas de **Vds. los abogados.**	The follies of mankind put much money into the coffers of *you lawyers.*

INTENSIFICATION BY MISMO

3.51. The nominative forms of all the pronouns may be intensified by the addition of the appropriate form of **mismo** *self* which is varied like all adjectives in **o:**

Yo **mismo,** yo **misma.**	I *myself.*
Tú **mismo,** tú **misma.**	You *yourself.*
Él **mismo,** ella **misma.**	He *himself,* she *herself.*
Nosotros **mismos,** nosotras **mismas.**	We *ourselves.*
Usted **mismo,** usted **misma.**	You *yourself.*
Ustedes **mismos,** ustedes **mismas.**	You *yourselves.*

3.52. Mismo may be applied to nouns in the same manner:

El emperador **mismo.**	The emperor *himself.*
Su madre **misma** lo ha dicho.	His mother *herself* said it.
Procura castigar a los culpables **mismos.**	He seeks to punish the offenders *themselves.*

3.53. The appropriate form of **mismo** may be used, when great emphasis is needed, to intensify the prepositional case or the compound forms of the dative and accusative; but it is not applicable to the simple dative and accusative forms:

Con su terquedad, caballero, no perjudicará V. a nadie sino a **sí mismo.**	With your obstinacy, Sir, you will injure nobody but *yourself.*
Veo que en vez de engañar a V., me he engañado a **mí mismo.**	I see that instead of deceiving you I have deceived *myself.*
El que enseña bien a otro se enseña también a **sí mismo.**	He who teaches another well teaches *himself* also.
Nos hemos perdido a **nosotros mismos.**	We have ruined our *own selves.*

TWO PRONOUNS AS OBJECTS

3.54. When a verb has two objects, both may be pronouns. In such case they appear together, with no word intervening and so take the same place with regard to the verb as a single pronoun. The dative precedes the accusative, with the exception that the reflexive **se** always stands first, whatever may be its function:

No **te lo** daré; no **te la** daré.	I will not give *it to you.*
Creo que **me lo** prestará.	I think he will lend *it to me.*
Nos los promete; **nos las** promete.	He promises *them to us.*
Se lo aplica.	He applies *it to himself.*

Se me figura que...	It seems to me that...
Se nos muestra como un estilista superior. (Sánchez Cantón, prologue to edition of **El Conde Lucanor)**	He exhibits *himself to us* as a superior stylist.

REMARK I. Among the untaught, however, **me se** and **te se** are frequently used instead of **se me** and **se te** respectively. Moreover, in the event of combination of **me, nos, te, os** with **le, les,** or of **te** with **me, nos,** the arrangement will invariably be **me le(s), nos le(s), te le(s), os le(s), te me, te nos,** regardless of which is direct and which is indirect object (cf. § **3.32** *c.).*

REMARK II. There is a tendency, more pronounced in colloquial than in literary language and perhaps more frequent in Spanish America than in Spain, to use a direct or indirect object form instead of a preposition plus a personal pronoun when the verb already has a reflexive pronoun as direct object (cf. § **29.17** *d*): **Solía ir a reunírseles.** (Gallegos, **Canaima,** XII, **Angulos cruzados)** = **Solía ir a reunirse con ellos** *or* **a ellos.** *He was accustomed to go and join them.* **Apoderándoselo, sin hacer caso de las protestas de los mestizos, se dirigió a su choza.** (Idem, XVIII, **El racional)** = **Apoderándose de él,** etc. *Taking possession of it, without heeding the protests of the half-breeds, he went to his shanty.*

3.55. If both objects be pronouns of the third person, the dative, of either number, assumes the form **se,** which is of different origin from the reflexive **se:**

le le, les le	*become*	**se le**	le les, les les	*become*	**se les**
le la, les la	"	**se la**	le los, les los	"	**se los**
le lo, les lo	"	**se lo**	le las, les las	"	**se las**

Abro la carta y **se la** leo.	I open the letter and read *it to him (to her, etc.).*
Su cuñado de V. quiere comprar mi casa, pero yo no **se la** vendo.	You brother-in-law wishes to buy my house, but I will not sell *it to him.*
El coronel ha olvidado sus quevedos; mi criado **se los** llevará.	The colonel has forgotten his glasses; my servant will take *them to him.*
Ya he escrito la carta, pero aun no **se la** he enviado.	I have already written the letter, but have not yet sent *it to them.*

3.56. The redundant construction is applicable to the dative when there are two pronouns as objects, in the same manner as when there is but one. Its use extends to a noun (cf. §§ **3.35-3.36**):

No **me** lo ha dicho **a mí.**	He has not told it *to me.*
Ya **se** lo he dicho **a ellas.**	I have already told it *to them.*

Espero hoy a mi hijo; **se le** presentaré **a V.** mañana.	I expect my son today; I will introduce him *to you* tomorrow.
Se lo explicaré **a Vds.**	I will explain it *to you.*
Haré los marcos hoy, y **se** los mandaré **a V.** mañana.	I will make the frames today and send them *to you* tomorrow.
¿Cuándo **nos** lo prestará V. **a nosotros?**	When will you lend it *to us?*
No **se** las daré **a ellas** antes de mañana.	I will not give them *to them* until tomorrow.
Ofréceselas **a esta señora.** (Benavente, **Campo de armiño,** I, 9)	Offer them *to this lady.*
Se lo dejará todo **a los museos.** *(Idem,* III, 1)	He will leave everything *to the museums.*
Sacó el frasco de sales, **se** lo hicieron oler **a la enferma.** (Palacio Valdés, **Los cármenes de Granada,** I, 2)	He got out the vial of smelling salts, they made *the sick woman* smell it.
¿Con qué cara te **le** presentarás mañana **a Santos?** (Gallegos, **Doña Bárbara,** II, 10)	In what light will you present yourself *to Santos* tomorrow?

3.57. When one or more objective pronouns of simple form are governed by an infinitive, they are either affixed to it so as to make one word or they immediately precede the verb which governs the infinitive; the former being the more usual construction:

Quiere **hablarme.** **Me quiere** hablar.	He wants to *speak to me.*
Viene a **buscarlos.** **Los viene** a buscar.	She is coming to *look for them.*
Voy a **decírselo.** **Se lo voy** a decir.	I am going to *tell it to him.*
Ella ha prometido **enseñármelo.** Ella **me lo ha prometido** enseñar.	She has promised to *teach it to me.*
Necesito **consultarle** a V. **Le necesito** consultar a V.	I need to *consult you.*
Quiero **llevarla** al teatro. **La quiero** llevar al teatro.	I want to *take her* to the theater.

3.58. Frequently a pronoun may depend either upon the infinitive or the preceding verb, according to the meaning intended; in which case each pronoun accompanies the verb to which it belongs:

Será inútil escribirle.	It will be useless to write to him.
Le será inútil escribir.	It will be useless for him to write.

Nos será difícil procurarlos.	It will be difficult for us to procure them.
Será difícil procurárnoslos.	It will be difficult to procure them for us.
Nos será difícil procurárselos.	It will be difficult for us to procure them for him.
No les parece prudente intentarlo.	It does not seem prudent to them to attempt it.

3.59. Between the prepositional form and the preposition preceding it, nothing whatever should intervene. Consequently when two or more prepositionals are the objects of the same verb, the preposition must be repeated before each. Otherwise the nominative form will be used:

Nos busca **a** V. y **a** mí.	He is looking for you and me.
Quiere vengar la ofensa hecha **a** su hermano y **a** sí mismo.	He wishes to avenge the injury done to his brother and himself.

REMARK. The preposition **entre,** however, cannot be thus repeated since its meaning is reciprocal. In modern usage the subject forms of the personal pronouns follow it[1]:

Entre tú y **yo** *(occasionally* Entre **ti** y mí).	Between you and *me.*
Entre él y **yo.**	Between him and *me.*
Este informe queda entre V. y **yo.**	This information is between **you** and *me.*
La amistad que existe entre mi hermano y **tú.**	The friendship that exists between my brother and *you.*

THE ACCUSATIVE OF SUBSTITUTION

3.60. The forms **le** or **lo, la, los, las,** serve to recall a previous noun without repeating it. When this is done in English it is by some such indefinite word as *one, any, some, such:*

Alega que no tiene **influencia,** pero yo creo que **la** tiene.	He alleges that he has no influence, but I believe that he has.
Compraré **billetes si los** hay todavía. —Ya no **los** hay.	I shall buy tickets if there still are any. —There are no more.
En Boston hay **casinos** de damas como **los** hay de hombres aquí.	In Boston there are women's clubs as there are of men here.

[1] The subject forms are also used with **excepto** *except;* **incluso** *including;* **menos** *except;* **salvo** *except;* **excepto (menos, salvo) yo** *except me;* **incluso tú** *including you.*

¿Tiene V. **vino** de Manzanilla? —Sí señor, **lo** tengo, y de primera clase.	Have you any Manzanilla wine? —Yes, sir, I have, and first class.
¿Quién quiere **agua?** —**La** quiero yo.	Who wants water? —I do.
¿Tiene V. **ganas** de comer? —**Las** tengo y urgentes.	Have you an appetite? —I have, and a pressing one.
Grandes **derechos** parece usted tener. —Sin duda cree usted tener**los** mayores. (Martínez Sierra, **Madrigal,** II)	You seem to have great rights.— Doubtless you think you have greater ones.
Amigos somos [tu familia y yo] desde que ni tú ni yo levantábamos una vara del suelo... Que tú **lo** eres nuestro tampoco hay que dudarlo. (Palacio Valdés, **La aldea perdida,** I)	[Your family and I] have been friends since you and I were mere children... And there is no need of doubting, either, that you are ours [our friend].

3.61. The neuter form **lo** serves similarly to recall an adjective, a noun taken in an indeterminate sense with an adjective value, or an entire phrase or statement (cf. § 2.53), and is then often equivalent to the English *so:*

Ella está mala, pero no **lo** parece.	She is sick, but she does not look so.
El alcalde, pues supe después que **lo** era, *etc.*	The alcalde, for I afterwards learned that he was one, *etc.*
Su paso era ligero, porque **lo** era su corazón.	His step was light because his heart was.
O es cura o va a ser**lo.**	Either he is a priest or he is going to be one.
Eres linda, pero **lo** serías mucho más si no te abandonaras tanto. (Gallegos, **Doña Bárbara,** I, 11)	You are pretty, but you would be much more so if you didn't neglect yourself so much.
Considero necesario, como **lo** considera también la comisión, conservar intacta la cláusula.	I consider it necessary, as does the committee also, to preserve the clause unchanged.

3.62. This neuter **lo** accompanies the verb **ser** in answers, to represent the predicate of the question:

¿Son Vds. los soldados que prendieron al espía? —**Lo** somos.	Are you the soldiers who took the spy? —We are.
¿Es V. la madre de este niño? —**Lo** soy.	Are you the mother of this child? —I am.
¿Es V. madre? —**Lo** soy.	Are you a mother? —I am.

¿Me engaño, señorita, en creerla mi sobrina? —No, señor, **lo** soy en efecto.	Am I mistaken, Miss, in believing you to be my niece? —No, sir; I am indeed she.
¿Es ella la dueña de la casa? —No **lo** es.	Is she the mistress of the house?—She is not.

REMARK. This manner of answering is, however, rather formal; in ordinary style the answers would be **sí señor, no señora,** etc. Moreover, some authorities believe that if the noun refers to a specific person, the personal pronoun should agree with such noun in gender and number. Then the answers to the first two questions above would be **Los somos** and **La soy** respectively.

IV

Personal Pronouns (contin.)

4.1. The objective forms of the personal pronouns are applicable only in connection with a verb or a verbal derivative. When they precede the verb, they stand separately; when they follow, they are appended to the verb. This latter use is called *enclitic.* Some forms of the verb require the enclitic use; with others it is inadmissible; while in a large class of cases it is optional. Yet when optional, the use of enclitics is rhetorical and distinctive of a literary, as opposed to a colloquial, style. In one or another dialects of northern Spain, however, enclitic use is still normal to the spoken language. Moreover these enclitics are not applicable, under all circumstances, even to the same verbal form. Hence their employment is rather rare.

We will treat the various verbal forms in detail.

Indicative:

4.2. With the indicative mood, the enclitic use of the pronouns is optional (with the distinction indicated above), although most frequently found in connection with the imperfect and preterite tenses.

The choice depends upon the location of the verb, the general principle requiring it to stand at the beginning of the sentence or clause:

Dígolo porque creo en la justicia de su pretensión.	I say it because I believe in the justice of his claim.
Preparábaseles una recepción regia.	They were preparing a regal reception for them.
Mandóles que se detuviesen.	He ordered them to stop.
Recibiósele con extraordinarias demostraciones de júbilo.	He was received with unusual expressions of joy.

4.3. When the verb, at the beginning of an independent clause, is preceded by one of the conjunctions **y, o, mas** or **pero,** the enclitic use is quite permissible:

Apoyóse la joven en el respaldo del sillón, **y púsose** a mirar con una curiosidad infantil los papeles que arreglaba el anciano.	The young girl leaned upon the back of the easy chair, and began to look with childish curiosity at the papers which the old man was arranging.
Desterraban a los demás, **o encerrábanlos** en los calabozos.	They banished the rest, or incarcerated them in dungeons.
Al principio estas palabras le hicieron temer una nueva emboscada; **pero desvanecióse** esta idea cuando oyó la voz de, *etc.*	At first these words made him fear a fresh ambuscade, but this idea was dispelled when he head the voice of, *etc.*

4.4. As stated in § 4.2, an enclitic pronoun may follow a verb at the beginning of any clause of a sentence, when the preceding clause expresses a subordinate idea and is complete in itself:

A pesar de todo este progreso legislativo y literario, **hallábase** España en los últimos tiempos del reinado de Enrique IV en uno de aquellos períodos de abatimiento que inspiran melancólicos presagios sobre la suerte futura de una nación.	In spite of all this legislative and literary progress, Spain found herself towards the end of the reign of Henry IV in one of those periods of depression which inspire melancholy forebodings with regard to the future fate of a nation.

4.5. If the sentence begins with an absolute clause, an indicative verb immediately following may therefore receive an enclitic pronoun:

Envuelto en su capa negra, y calado su sombrero hasta los ojos, **veía-**	Muffled up in his black cloak, and with his hat thrust down over his

sele horas enteras recargado contra el palo mayor. — eyes, he was seen for whole hours leaning against the mainmast.

Admirándose de tan extraño género de locura, **fuéronselo** a mirar desde lejos. — Wondering at such a strange kind of madness, they went to look at it from a distance.

4.6. In narrative style, where a number of complete clauses occur in succession, without connecting conjunctions, an enclitic may of course follow a verb at the beginning of any one of them:

Sintió pasos, **detúvose,** y escuchó atentamente. — He heard footsteps, stopped, and listened attentively.

Dórale un brillante sol sus mieses, **riéganle** claros manantiales sus huertas, y a su rededor se levantan los montes que como inmensos biombos la separan del resto del mundo. — A bright sun gilds its harvests, clear streams water its orchards, and around it rise the mountains which like immense screens separate it from the rest of the world.

4.7. Such at least has been the preferred use of the literary language. In theory the pronoun should be enclitic only after a pause but it is questionable whether writers of the following felt a pause before the verb form. Similar instances are very frequently encountered:

Veinte años antes **habíase** casado con una joven de Cáceres. — Twenty years before, he had married a young woman of Cáceres.

Largo rato después **hallábase** en el mismo sitio cuando acertó a pasar Teodoro Golfín. (Pérez Galdós, **Marianela,** XVII) — A long while afterwards, she was still in the same place, when Theodore Golfín happened to come along.

Odiaba a sus ministros, y entre dientes **llamábales** mil veces presidiarios. (Castelar) — He hated his ministers and muttered that they were convicts a thousand times over.

La negra silueta del pueblo **dibujábase** a lo lejos, y una torrecilla **alzábase** sobre él, destacando su espadaña con precisión del fondo oscuro de la noche. (Palacio Valdés) — The dark outline of the village was visible in the distance and a steeple loomed up above it with its spire sharply outlined against the dark background of the night.

La reunión **dividióse** instantáneamente en dos bandos. (Blasco Ibáñez, **Guapeza valenciana,** II, in **Cuentos valencianos**) — The gathering divided into two factions instantaneously.

Su fundación **parecíale** mezquina. (Pérez de Ayala, **El anticristo,** in **Bajo el signo de Artemisa**) — Her establishment seemed small to her.

Habla Larra, porfía, suplica; ella **muéstrase** inexorable. (Azorín, **Larra,** in **Lecturas españolas**) — Larra speaks, insists, begs; she acts (remains) inflexible.

Subjunctive:

4.8. The enclitic use of the objective pronouns is inapplicable to the subjunctive mood (with the exception of the present tense when used imperatively) :

Es importante que se quede al alcance de la voz. — It is important that he remain within call.

Las damas le suplicaron que las dejase partir aquella misma noche. — The ladies begged him to let them set out that very night.

Imperative and its substitutes:

4.9. The simple imperative always requires the enclitic use:

Dámelo presto. — Give it to me quick.

Háblanos con franqueza, ¿cuál de los dos quieres más? — Tell us candidly, which of the two do you like best?

Idos en seguida. — Depart at once.

4.10. The subjunctive mood used imperatively requires the enclitic pronouns when it is employed affirmatively and is the first word in the clause (cf. § 23.53) :

Déjela Vd. — Let her alone.

Díganme Vds. lo que les parece. — Tell me what you think.

Busquémoslo por este lado. — Let us look for it on this side.

Díganselo, si quieren. — Let them tell him so, if they want to.

REMARK. But when the subjunctive is not the first word and when it is used negatively, as in forbidding, the objective pronouns precede:

Que **me lo traigan** vivo o muerto. — Let them bring him to me dead or alive.

¡Propicia **se te muestre** la fortuna! — May fortune be kind to you!

Usted **lo** pase bien. — Goodbye.

Malos demonios **te lleven.** (Pérez de Ayala, **Prometeo,** I) — May the devil take you.

Dios **te dé** paciencia para soportar a nuestra querida familia. (Benavente, **Campo de armiño,** II, 4) — God give you patience to endure our dear family.

4.11. The simple infinitive and present participle require the enclitic use:

No había medio de **orientarse.**	There was no way of getting their bearings.
No querían **dejarse** ver.	They did not wish to let themselves be seen.
Curioso sería explicar aquí cómo acerté a complacer a todos, sin **proponérmelo,** sin **saberlo,** y por casualidad.	It would be curious to explain here how I managed to please them all, unintentionally, unwittingly, and by chance.
Creyéndole muerto el moro pasó adelante.	The Moor, thinking him dead, passed on.
Esto es para ti, primita, decía, **poniéndoselo** en la boca.	This is for you, cousin, he said, putting it in her mouth.

4.12. Any verb in the indicative (especially the modal auxiliaries **deber, ir a, poder** and **querer**), when governing an infinitive or a present participle may be preceded by an objective pronoun or pronouns which logically belong to the dependent verb. In such cases the pronoun may be appended to the dependent verb or to the governing verb. Thus there are three possible constructions, the third being restricted to literary usage (cf. § 4.14):

Le salieron a encontrar. Salieron a **encontrarle.** **Saliéronle** a encontrar.	They went out to meet him.
Se lo debo entregar inmediatamente. Debo **entregárselo** inmediatamente. **Déboselo** entregar inmediatamente.	I must deliver it to him at once.
Se estaba armando para la pelea. Estaba **armándose** para la pelea. **Estábase** armando para la pelea.	He was arming himself for the combat.

REMARK. When the location of the governing verb precludes its taking an enclitic, there remain of course but two locations for the pronoun:

¿Qué **me va** V. a dar? ¿Qué va V. a **darme?**	What are you going to give me?
No **lo alcanzo** a comprender. No alcanzo a **comprenderlo.**	I am unable to understand it.

4.13. The governing verb of this construction may be an infinitive or a present participle:

Espero **volverle** a ver pronto. Espero volver a **verle** pronto.	I hope to see him again soon.

Mañana tendré el gusto de **venirla** a buscar a V. Mañana tendré el gusto de venir a **buscarla** a V.	Tomorrow I shall have the pleasure of coming by for you.
Quisiera **poderlos** encontrar. Quisiera poder **encontrarlos.**	I should like to be able to find them.
Estándome divirtiendo de este modo... Estando **divirtiéndome** de este modo...	While I was engaged in amusing myself in this way...

4.14. In the case of the compound tenses formed by **haber** and a past participle, the objective pronoun accompanies the auxiliary,—preceding it or being appended to it, according as the circumstances permit:

Me he equivocado sin duda. **Heme** equivocado sin duda. *(But not* he equivocádo*me)*	I am doubtless mistaken.
Largo tiempo **le habíamos** aguardado. **Habíamosle** aguardado largo tiempo. *(But not* habíamos aguardádo*le)*	We had waited for him a long time.
Los habían de haber aprendido. **Habíanlos** de haber aprendido. Habían de **haberlos** aprendido. *(But not* haber aprendído*los)*	They were to have learned them.

4.15. The only allowable deviation from the above is when, to avoid repetition, the auxiliary is understood after having been previously expressed:

Era un propietario rico de Cáceres, donde había nacido y **criádose.**	He was a rich landowner of Cáceres, where he was born and brought up.
Habiéndose levantado el príncipe, y **armádose** para el torneo, llamó a su escudero, joven listo y despejado, *etc.*	The prince, having arisen and armed himself for the tournament, called his squire, a bright and clever young man, *etc.*
Habían encontrado a los rebeldes en cuatro escaramuzas, y **vencídolos** en cada punto.	They had met the rebels in four skirmishes and defeated them at every point.

Así que hubo llamado a los guardias y **entregádoles** su prisionero, compuso lo mejor que pudo su ropa desgarrada y se dirigió rápidamente al castillo.

When he had called the guards and turned his prisoner over to them, he arranged as best he could his torn clothing and hastened to the castle.

REMARK. This deviation does not apply to a past participle used adjectively with **ser** or **estar:**

Los competidores afortunados fueron admitidos, y presentados a ellos (*not* presentádos*les*) los premios.

The successful competitors were admitted and the prizes presented to them.

Están ya elegidas las organizaciones cívicas y militares que han de tomar parte de la ceremonia, y asignados a ellos (*not* asignádos*les*) los puestos que deben ocupar en la procesión.

The civic and military organizations which are to take part in the ceremony are already decided upon, and their places in the procession assigned to them.

But when the past participle is used adjectively with **tener** (as a substitute for **haber**), the enclitic use is admissible:

La comisión tiene ya preparado su informe y **presentádolo** al congreso.

The committee has already prepared its report and presented it to the congress.

Los abogados tienen cotejada la evidencia y **puéstala** por escrito.

The lawyers have collated the evidence and committed it to writing.

REDUNDANT USE OF THE OBJECTIVE PERSONAL PRONOUNS

4.16. We have seen (§ 3.34) that both the simple and the compound objective form of a personal pronoun may be used at the same time representing a single object. This is required either for the clearness of the sentence, to give vivacity to a contrast, or to call the attention more markedly to a particular object:

Sigue tu gusto e inclinación, y déja**me a mí** seguir el mío.

Follow your own pleasure and inclination and let me follow mine.

Este acontecimiento no **nos** parecía **a nosotros** tan lamentable como a él.

This occurence did not seem to us so lamentable as it did to him.

Mudanzas que no harían mella en hombres de una sensibilidad menos delicada, **le** abatirían **a él** por completo.

Reverses which would not affect men of less delicate sensibilities, would overcome him completely.

El se quedaba inmóvil como una estatua, mientras **a mí me** temblaban las piernas de miedo.	He remained motionless as a statue, while my knees trembled with fear.

4.17. When a noun object, terminal form of personal pronoun (§ 3.31) or other pronoun object is placed before the verb, it is repeated by the proper object form of the corresponding personal pronoun, which shows that the noun, etc., is the object. The rule is sometimes extended to relative and interrogative pronouns, even though position before the verb is normal to them:

La **atmósfera** la componía una densa niebla que se extendía y alzaba en la altura, interceptando la vista del cielo.	The air was composed of a dense fog which spread and rose upwards, intercepting the view of the sky.
En 1849 volvió a Bundelkund, donde se casó con una noble india, cuyo **corazón lo** había herido como el suyo la desgracia de su patria.	In 1849 he returned to Bundelkund, where he married an Indian noblewoman whose heart had been wounded like his own by the misfortune of their native land.
A los **desertores los** han indultado de la pena de muerte.	They have reprieved the deserters from the penalty of death.
Al **príncipe le** han matado.	They have killed the prince.
A los **modernos les** sucede lo contrario.	The contrary happens to moderns.
A **mí me** gusta el jugo de tomate.	I like tomato juice.
Las tribus de estas comarcas habían permanecido en estado salvaje, refractarias a toda idea de civilización e impacientes por sacudir el yugo europeo. **Esto lo** sabía perfectamente Nana Sahib, y allí había buscado asilo para librarse de las pesquisas de la policía inglesa y esperar la hora de suscitar el movimiento insurreccional.	The tribes of these regions had remained in a savage state, refractory to all idea of civilization and impatient to shake off the European yoke. This, Nana Sahib knew perfectly, and he had sought a refuge there to escape the pursuit of the English police and to await the hour for instigating the insurrectionary movement.
Por mí, si estuviera en su lugar —decía otra a **quien le** pesaba mucho menos —no me disgustaría poco ni mucho. (Palacio Valdés, **José,** XIV)	"So far as I am concerned, if I were in her place," said another whom it grieved much less, "it wouldn't disturb me at all."
¿Y a **quién le** debes este triunfo? (Benavente, **La gobernadora,** III, 7)	And to whom do you owe this triumph?

4.18. But an accusative pronoun may precede, though it rarely does, when it is the real object of the verb, and the noun is introduced afterwards by way of explanation:

Los demolieron hasta sus cimientos aquellos edificios, obras maestras de la arquitectura.	They demolished them to their foundations, those buildings, masterpieces of architecture.
Los plantaron allá en el corazón del continente, la fe y los lirios de Francia, exigiendo para ellos el homenaje de las antiguas razas indígenas.	They planted them there in the heart of the American continent, the faith and the lilies of France, and demanded for them the homage of the ancient native races.

4.19. The use of the redundant pronoun is not considered good style after a relative which is direct object of a following verb, unless the pronoun is separated from the relative by words which would tend to break the connection:

En este castillo se guarda la espada del héroe nacional Wallace, arma que en esta edad afeminada hay pocos brazos que **la** pudieran manejar.	In this castle is kept the sword of the national hero Wallace, a weapon which in this effeminate age there are few arms able to wield.
¿Quién eres tú que lo preguntas, y en un idioma que, por estas partes, hay muy pocos que **lo** entienden?	Who are you who ask it, and in a language which few in these parts understand?
Una palabra nueva, terminada en ismo, que no **la** conociera nadie, era para él un regalo de los dioses. (Baroja, **La dama errante**, VI)	A new word, ending in ism, which nobody knew, was for him a gift of the gods.

4.20. By means of this repetition, ambiguity may often be avoided and the object of the verb in relative clauses distinguished:

Llegaron a un patio cuadrado, cercado de celdas pequeñas, que cada una de ellas **la** ocupaba uno de los presidiarios.	They came to a quadrangular court, surrounded by small cells, each of which was occupied by one of the convicts.
Y María, como a quien más **le** importaba, advirtió a su marido en secreto que no se fuese.	And Mary, like one to whom it mattered most, warned her husband secretly not to go.
La derrota del enemigo fué decidida y terminada por un ataque sobre la retaguardia de su ala derecha,	The rout of the enemy was decided and completed by an attack on the rear of his right flank, which ma-

maniobra que mucho **la** favorecía la desigualdad del terreno. — neuvre was much aided by the unevenness of the ground.

Fué entonces necesario desbandar a la mayor parte del ejército a causa del continuo frío, que **lo** hizo aquel invierno excesivo. — It was then necessary to disband the greater part of the army on account of the continued cold, which was excessive that winter.

Se ha querido notar una analogía inadmisible entre el delito político y el de deserción, que Weiss **la** rechaza con tanta verdad como elocuencia. — Attempt has been made to establish an untenable analogy between treason and desertion, which [analogy] Weiss rejects with as much truth as eloquence.

4.21. In many other cases this is necessary to show whether a noun is subject or object, when the location does not make it self-evident:

Manuscritos antiguos y medio borrados, que durante siglos enteros habían yacido desapercibidos en algún monasterio o en una de las grandes bibliotecas públicas, **los** buscaba y leía con avidez extraordinaria. — Old half-obliterated manuscripts which had lain for centuries unnoticed in some monastery or in some of the great public libraries, he sought out and read with extraordinary avidity.

Los iberos se esparcieron probablemente en un tiempo por toda la península, y esto **lo** prueba el nombre de muchas ciudades, montañas y ríos. — The Iberians probably at one time spread over the entire peninsula, and this is proved by the names of many cities, mountains and rivers.

Al tiempo que querían dar los remos al agua, porque velas **no las** tenían, llegó a la orilla del mar un bergantín. — At the moment when they were about to dip their oars in the water, for sails they had none, a two-masted vessel came up to the shore.

Remark. The first impression conveyed by **porque velas no tenían** would be that **velas** is the subject of **tenían,** which mistake is at once prevented by the objective **las.**

ALTERNATIVE OBJECTIVE FORMS OF THE PERSONAL PRONOUNS

4.22. The vacillation in the use of the objective forms of the personal pronouns of the third person is a grave defect in Spanish. While in some instances there are only single forms about which there is no dispute, in others there are double or alternative forms, with regard to whose use there is the utmost diversity of opinion.

The admissible forms of the objective personal pronouns of the third person are as follows:

		MASC.	FEM.	NEUT.
SINGULAR	Dative	le	le *or* la	le
	Accusative	le *and* lo	la	lo
PLURAL	Dative	les	les *or* las	[none]
	Accusative	los *or* les	las	[none]

a. In regard to these alternative forms, some authorities insist on the exclusive use of the one, in each pair, and others maintain the equally exclusive right of the other. The usage of the majority of careful writers of today is that set forth in detail below.

b. The greatest disagreement is about the two forms, **le** and **lo**, of the accusative masculine.[1] Some writers disapprove of **le**, others will not tolerate **lo**. The use of **lo** is preferred to that of **le** in most of Spanish America and in parts of Spain (especially the south and indeed everywhere outside of Castile), at least among those who are not influenced by the language of literature and the teaching of the schools.

4.23. A safe medium, which is generally followed by careful writers, is to apply **le** to persons and **lo** to things, when of the masculine gender:

Compré un solar y luego **lo** vendí por dos veces la suma que me había costado.	I bought a building lot and then sold it for twice the sum it had cost me.
Al cumplir mi hijo veinte años **le** mandé a viajar por Europa.	When my son reached the age of twenty, I sent him to travel in Europe.

4.24. In addition to persons, **le** is applicable to the more important animals when considered as intelligent beings:

Soltó al perro y **le** condujo a la pista del fugitivo.	He loosed the dog and led him to the fugitive's trail.
Sin embargo el perro continuaba	Nevertheless the dog continued bark-

[1] This disagreement is so extensive as to have given rise to the terms **leístas,** to denote the advocates of **le,** and **loístas,** applied to those who favor **lo.**

ladrando, sin que pudieran hacerle callar ni las caricias ni las amenazas. — ing, and neither caresses nor threats could make him keep quiet.

4.25. Otherwise animals are represented by **lo,** and even the larger animals when they are not considered as taking any voluntary part in the action:

El conejo, sin pensar en dar gracias a su libertador, se echó á correr con tanta prisa que pronto **lo** perdió de vista el sacerdote. — The rabbit, without a thought of gratitude to his deliverer, ran off with such speed that the priest soon lost sight of him.

El dragón se apeó de su caballo y **lo** ató entre los matorrales. — The dragoon dismounted from his horse and tied him in the thicket.

4.26. So a human being, when acted upon as an inanimate object, is often represented by **lo:**

Levantaron al borracho y **lo** llevaron a casa. — They raised the drunken man and carried him home.

Dirigió un sablazo a su adversario que **lo** partió por medio. — He aimed a stroke at his opponent which cut him in two.

Los lacayos arrojaron al ladrón por encima del almenaje y **lo** hicieron añicos. — The lackeys threw the thief over the battlements and dashed him to pieces.

Remark. Thus, in speaking of a deceased young man we could say **lo perdieron sus padres** *his parents lost him;* while of a young man who has gone to the bad we might say **el descuido e indulgencia de sus padres le perdieron** *the remissness and indulgence of his parents ruined him.*

4.27. On the other hand, an inanimate thing of the masculine gender, when personified, may properly be represented by **le.** Some writers use it to refer to any masculine singular antecedent:

El objeto del arte es la creación de la belleza, y **le** humilla quien **le** somete a otro fin. — The purpose of Art is the creation of beauty, and he humiliates it who subjects it to any other use.

Nos dió Pepita un espectáculo sencillo y poético que yo había visto cuando niño, aunque no **le** recordaba. (Valéra, **Pepita Jiménez, 4 de mayo)** — Pepita gave us a simple and poetic spectacle that I had seen when I was a child, though I didn't recall it.

4.28. The usual form of the masculine plural of the personal pronoun is **los,** but the form **les** occurs as an accusative in so many writers of repute that it must be accepted. When employed, it is mostly restricted to persons, or things personified:

Era la noche fría de tal modo, que **les** obligó a buscar reparos para el hielo. (Cervantes)	The night was so cold that it obliged them to seek shelter against the frost.
Les forzaba a partir la poca seguridad de la playa. (*Idem*)	The insufficient safety of the beach forced them to depart.
Necesitan una guía que **les** conduzca por el inmenso campo de nuestra literatura. (Gil y Zárate)	They need a guide to lead them through the vast field of our literature.
Volvió a abrazar**les** Torquemada, diciéndoles con melosa voz, —Hijos míos, sed buenos. (Pérez Galdós, **Torquemada en la hoguera,** VIII)	Torquemada again embraced them, saying with a honeyed voice, "My children, be good."
La estupefacción **les** tenía mudos. (Palacio Valdés, **Sinfonía pastoral, Presto finale,** VI)	Stupefaction kept them silent.

4.29. The form **les** is expected when it is the object of the reflexive substitute for passive (§ **21.40**) :

Eran tan pocos que apenas se **les** hubiera creído capaces de atacar un castillo medianamente forticado.	They were so few in number that one could hardly have thought them able to assault a castle only tolerably fortified.

4.30. The dative of the feminine personal pronoun of the third person is properly **le** in the singular and **les** in the plural. But the forms **la** and **las** are in use as applied to persons:

En vano intentaba persuadirla de semejante desatino, porque Berta se irritaba y **la** imponía silencio.	In vain did she attempt to persuade her against such an imprudence, for Bertha became angry and imposed silence upon her.
No hacía mucho tiempo que estaba allí cuando vió a sus dos hermanas que con dificultad trataban de abrirse un camino por el tropel de hombres y carruajes, y **las** hizo una señal para que le aguardasen.	He had not been there long when he saw his two sisters trying with difficulty to force their way through the throng of men and vehicles, and made a sign to them to wait for him.
Me acerco poco a Pepita; apenas **la** hablo. (Valera, **Pepita Jiménez, 20 de abril**)	I go near Pepita very seldom; I scarcely talk to her.

Las pregunto si están contentas de Madrid y qué tal marchan sus negocios. (Pardo Bazán, **La sirena negra,** I)	I ask them if they are happy in Madrid and how their affairs are going.
Como no llamaba tampoco para que **la** llevasen el chocolate, fué a ver si **la** pasaba algo. (Benavente, **La honradez de la cerradura,** I, 2, 2)	As she didn't call either for them to take her chocolate to her, she went to see if something was wrong with her.

REMARK. D. Andrés Bello suggests that, since **le** and **les** are common to the masculine dative, the employment of **la** and **las** as feminine forms would be convenient for the sake of distinction. But this necessity is already provided for by the redundant construction (§ **3.34**):

Encontré a D. Pedro con su esposa y **la** di (le di a ella) un ramillete.	I met Don Pedro and his wife and gave her a bouquet.
Cuando por fin conseguí verla, estaba presente su primo, de modo que no quise decir**la** (decirle a ella) nada de lo que tenía pensado.	When at last I succeeded in seeing her, her cousin was present, so that I would not tell her anything of what I had intended.

4.31. (1) There is a tendency, not yet thoroughly studied, to use **le** with certain verbs where **la** would be expected, especially if the subject is a thing. Usage seemingly considers the person to participate only indirectly in the action. Often it will be observable that the verb is not then employed in its most literal sense. See § **4.32** for a partial list of these special verbs. (2) Moreover, **le** is by some authors preferred to **la** before a verb which begins with **(h)a.** (3) There are also writers who generally consider an infinitive or a **que** clause the direct object of a verb and the person concerned the indirect object. Cf. § **19.32.** Possibly these uses are at times influenced by others involving the same verbs in which the object is indisputably indirect. Examples of the constructions mentioned in the three divisions of this paragraph will be given under three headings:

GROUP ONE

Rogelia paseaba su mirada por el grupo... **Le** sorprendió no ver a Perico. (Palacio Valdés, **Santa Rogelia,** I, 3)	Rogelia gazed about the group... It surprised *her* not to see Perico.
En la calle de Atocha **le** cogió la	On Atocha Street the rain caught up

lluvia y se vió necesitada a refugiarse en un portal. (Idem, III, 7)

with *her* and she was obliged to take shelter in a doorway.

—¿Qué le pasa a esta señorita? —¿Qué le ha de pasar? El tiro... —¿Eh? ¿**Le** ha dado? (Benavente, **Al natural,** II, 4)

"What is the matter with this young lady?" "What do you expect? The shot..." "What? It struck *her*?"

La abuela no vendrá porque ya **le** fatiga el andar mucho. (Linares Rivas, **La raza,** II, 11)

Grandmother will not come because walking a great deal now fatigues *her*.

¿Vas a pegar**le** después de lo que la pobre está sufriendo? (Dicenta, **Juan José,** II, 8)

Are you going to beat *her* after what the poor woman is suffering?

Su naturaleza nerviosa y ardiente era incapaz de dominar las más leves impresiones, mucho menos las que como ésta **le** tocaban en lo vivo del corazón. (Palacio Valdés, **Maximina,** XIII)

Her nervous, ardent nature was incapable of dominating the slightest impressions, much less those which, like this one, touched *her* to the heart.

Cuando hablé del anillo de Saturno, Maruja dijo: —Tonterías. **Le** molestaba que la atención de todos la acaparara yo. (Sender, **Crónica del alba)**

When I spoke of the ring of Saturn, Maruja said: "Rubbish." It annoyed her that I should monopolize everyone's attention.

Group two

Juana la larga..., gracias a su constante actividad, buen orden y economía, en todo lo cual su hija **le** ayudaba con inteligencia y celo, había mejorado de posición. (Valera, **Juanita la larga,** V)

Juana la larga..., thanks to her constant activity, capability and economy, in all of which her daughter aided *her* with intelligence and zeal, had improved her position.

Por lo pronto determinó no salir a paseo sola, pretextando que temía **le** acometiese un desmayo como el que le había amagado. (Palacio Valdés, **Maximina,** XIX, end)

For the time being she determined not to go out to walk alone, giving as a reason that she feared that a fainting fit like that one which had threatened *her* might attack *her*.

Mamá tiene miedo. **Le** asusta disgustarse con esas señoras. (Benavente, **Pepa Doncel,** II, 1, 1)

Mother is afraid. It frightens *her* to fall out with those ladies.

GROUP THREE

¿No comprenden que esa pobre mujer estará aterrada viendo esto? ¿Por qué **le** hacen sufrir? (Pérez de Ayala, **Luz de domingo,** IV)	Don't you understand that that poor woman will be terrified to see this? Why do you make *her* suffer?
Todavía estaba doña Javiera en muy buena edad. . .aunque la vida sedentaria **le** había hecho engrosar. (Peréz Galdós, **El amigo Manso,** III)	Doña Javiera was still at a very good age. . .although the sedentary life had made *her* grow stout.
Quedóse meditando en que su destino no **le** permitía salir de aquel círculo de personas que en los últimos tiempos la había rodeado. (Pérez Galdós, **Fortunata y Jacinta,** IV, 3, 7)	She continued to meditate on the fact that her fate did not permit *her* to leave that group of persons that had surrounded her of late.
Juanita no fué nunca a la miga, pero su madre **le** enseñó a coser y a bordar primorosamente. (Valera, **Juanita la larga,** IV)	Juanita never went to school but her mother taught *her* to sew and to embroider beautifully.
Doña Inés, entusiasmada, se allanó hasta el extremo de mandar**le** que cuando estuviesen las dos solitas la tutease. (Valera, **Juanita la larga,** XXIII, end)	Doña Inés, grown enthusiastic, acquiesced to the extreme of ordering her to address *her* in the familiar form when the two were all alone.
¡Con qué gozo pasó Julita a ocuparse en el adorno y tocado de su cuñada! Ella eligió el traje que había de ponerse, y **le** ayudó a vestírselo, ella la peinó a la moda. (Palacio Valdés, **Maximina,** II)	With what satisfaction Julita went in to concern herself with the dressing and coiffure of her sister-in-law! She chose the dress she was to wear, and helped *her* to put it on, she arranged her hair stylishly.
Ambas corrieron buen rato hasta que la fatiga **les** obligó a aflojar el paso. (*Idem,* XIX, end)	Both ran for quite a spell until fatigue obliged *them* to slow down.
Se complace en decir a todo el mundo todo lo malo que ella dice que dicen de uno. Tendré que prohibir**le** que ponga los pies en mi casa. (Benavente, **Titania,** I, 2, 1)	She takes pleasure in telling every one all the evil that *she* says they say about one. I shall have to forbid *her* to set foot in my house.

4.32. Some of the verbs which may have the construction treated in § 4.31, divisions 1 and 2 (that is, the dative forms of the personal pronouns rather than the accusative) are listed below. Some verbs in the list apply to both division 1 and 2. The use of **le** for **la** is usually found when the verb is used in a meaning to some extent figurative. In such cases the subject is a thing.

acometer	asustar	encantar	molestar
acompañar	ayudar	enseñar	pegar
afligir	coger	estorbar	preocupar
aguardar	complacer	fascinar	sorprender
alcanzar	convencer	fatigar	seducir
amenazar	dar	indignar	tocar
asistir	distraer	interesar	tranquilizar

V

Possessives Interrogatives Demonstratives

POSSESSIVE ADJECTIVES

5.1. The full inflection of the possessive adjectives is given below. **Mi, tu** and **su,** from their terminations, can have but one form for both genders, while **nuestro** and **vuestro** vary like any adjective in **o:**

SING.	**mi**	my
PLUR.	**mis**	
SING.	**tu**	your
PLUR.	**tus**	
SING.	**su**	his, her, your, their, its
PLUR.	**sus**	
SING.	**nuestro, –a**	our
PLUR.	**nuestros, –as**	
SING.	**vuestro, –a**	your
PLUR.	**vuestros, –as**	

5.2. There is but one possessive adjective for both the singular and plural of the third person. This possessive, as has already been shown (§ 3.5), must also do duty for the second person:

SING.	**su**	his, her, its, their, your
PLUR.	**sus**	

5.3. As **su** corresponds to so many different nominatives, it is often equivocal; and whenever there is danger of ambiguity the possessor is often more clearly specified. This is done by replacing **su** by the definite article before the noun, and placing the appropriate personal pronoun, preceded by **de**, after the noun:

SING.	**la casa de él**	his house
	la casa de ella	her house
	la casa de ellos	their *(masc.)* house
	la casa de ellas	their *(fem.)* house
	la casa de usted	your *(sing.)* house
	la casa de ustedes	your *(plur.)* house
PLUR.	**las casas de él**	his houses
	las casas de ella	her houses
	las casas de ellos	their *(masc.)* houses
	las casas de ellas	their *(fem.)* houses
	las casas de usted	your *(sing.)* houses
	las casas de ustedes	your *(plur.)* houses

REMARK. As in Spanish all existing things are either masculine or feminine, *its,* in the above connection, must be **de él** or **de ella.**

5.4. The learner can easily judge when the ambiguity would be such as to require the definite article + **de él, de ella,** etc., which is really very seldom. On the other hand, the definite article + **de V.** or **de VV.** is often employed, at least in Spain, both for clearness and courtesy, unless **V.** or **VV.** has previously appeared in the sentence. In such cases it is generally not repeated.

REMARK. A redundant construction, **su casa de él, su casa de V.,** is also met with. **Su casa de él, de ella,** etc., however, is considered colloquial; while **su casa de V., de VV.,** is very frequent, **usted** being considered as added in such cases by way of compliment.

5.5. In addition to those already given, the possessive adjectives have fuller forms when they follow a noun or stand alone. They are then varied like adjectives ending in **o:**

REFERRING TO ONE POSSESSOR	1st p.	**mío, –a; –os, –as**	mine, my
	2nd p.	**tuyo, –a; –os, –as**	yours, your
	3rd p.	**suyo, –a; –os, –as**	his, hers, her, its; yours, your
REFERRING TO MORE THAN ONE POSSESSOR	1st p.	**nuestro, –a; –os, –as**	ours, our
	2nd p.	**vuestro, –a; –os, –as**	yours, your
	3rd p.	**suyo, –a; –os, –as**	theirs, their; yours, your

5.6. The possessive adjective is placed after the noun for the sake of emphasis, in spirited language, in contrast, and for rhetorical effect; the noun in that case is regularly accompanied by the definite article:

el derecho mío	my right
la influencia suya	his influence
Según el parecer nuestro	according to *our* opinion
el amor nuestro a la patria	our love for the country

5.7. But in some expressions of general character, ocurring so frequently as to have become familiar phrases, the article is omitted:

de parte mía	on my part
a casa nuestra	to our house
a fe mía	on my word
a pesar suyo	in spite of them
a costa suya	at his expense
a instancias suyas	at his entreaty
Mira en torno suyo.	He looks around him.

5.8. The Spanish usage corresponds to the English in such expressions as the following, **mío, tuyo, suyo,** etc., serving regularly as predicate adjectives:

El dinero es mío.	The money is mine.
El caballo castaño es suyo.	The chestnut horse is his.
Tuya es la culpa.	Yours is the blame.
¿De quién es este diccionario? —Mío.	Whose is the dictionary? —Mine.

5.9. In such cases **suyo** may be replaced by the appropriate personal pronoun preceded by **de,** when ambiguity would otherwise result:

El libro con pasta de cuero de becerro es **de él, de ella.**	The book bound in calf is *his, hers.*

La pluma de oro es **de V.** — The gold pen is *yours.*
Las casas de ladrillo son **de ellos.** — The brick houses are *theirs.*
Los abanicos de gasa son **de ellas.** — The gauze fans are *theirs.*
La culpa no es **mía, sino de V.** — The fault is not *mine,* but *yours.*

5.10. The possessives of the first person, i.e. **mío** and **nuestro,** when employed in direct address, regularly follow the noun, provided said noun be not accompanied by an adjective:

¡Hijo mío! –Sí, madre mía. — My son! –Yes, mother.
Amigos míos; oyentes míos. — My friends; my hearers.
Padre nuestro que estás en los cielos. — Our Father who are in heaven.

5.11. But if an adjective accompanies the noun, either form may be used, with this distinction, as above stated, that the fuller form is more emphatic, and therefore more affectionate:

Mi querido hijo.
Querido hijo mío. } My dear son.

5.12. The possessive adjective follows the noun when taken in an indeterminate sense. It then corresponds to the English idiomatic expressions *of mine, of ours, of his,* etc.:

Un antiguo conocido **mío, nuestro.** — An old acquaintance *of mine, of ours.*
Busca a un **criado suyo.** — He is looking for a servant *of his.*
Un amigo **nuestro** español. — A Spanish friend *of ours.*

5.13. When this usage occurs after the verb **ser,** the indefinite article is omitted unless the noun be qualified by an emphatic adjective:

Son parroquianos nuestros. — They are customers of ours.
Es buen amigo mío, suyo. — He is *a* good friend of mine, of his.
Es **un** fiel y estimado amigo mío, suyo. — He is *a* faithful and valued friend of mine, of his.

We may also say:

Es amigo mío y de mi padre. — He is *a* friend of mine and of my father's.
Es vecino nuestro, y del ministro mejicano. — He is *a* neighbor of ours and of the Mexican Minister's.

5.14. The possessive adjective of the first person very often precedes the noun in direct address in most of Spanish America, as it occasionally does in Spain. Position before the noun is, moreover, the rule in addressing one's superior in the armed forces:

¡Pero m'hija! ¡Pero criatura! ¡Pero Negra, no seas ansina! (Lynch, **El inglés de los güesos,** VII)	But my dear! But child! But Negra, don't be like that!
¡Mi chiquilla! ¡Si supieras la alegría que me das! (Benavente, **Pepa Doncel,** III, 2)	My child! If you knew the joy you are giving me!
¿Los juicios no son públicos, si acaso? —Son públicos y muy públicos, sí, mi señora. (Payró, **Justicia salomónica,** in **Nuevos Cuentos de Pago Chico**)	The trials are not public, by chance? They are public and very public, yes, my lady.
El sargento se acercó al grupo, y, encarándose con uno de ellos, dijo: Mi general. (Baroja, **Zalacaín el aventurero,** II, 9)	The sergeant approached the group and, facing one of them, said: "General."

REMARK I. The use of **mi, tu, su,** etc., in combination with the indefinite article or a demonstrative adjective is relatively unusual in literary Spanish (though perhaps it is less rare in Spanish America than in Spain): **un su abuelo, aquel su abuelo** (Coloma, **Pequeñeces,** I, 3) *a grandfather of his, that grandfather of his;* **esta su manía** (Palacio Valdés, **La fe,** VII) *this mania of his;* **un su amigo** (Madariaga, **España,** I, 2, 18) *a friend of his.*

REMARK II. The use of the definite article in combination with **mi, tu, su,** etc., formerly general in Spanish, is, in modern times, a trait of dialects of the north and northwest of Spain (Asturias, Santander, etc.): **la mi alcoba, los sus vestiducos** (Pereda, **Sotileza,** X) *my bedroom, her clothes;* **el su nombre, del su padre** (Pérez de Ayala, **Exodo,** in **Bajo el signo de Artemisa)** *his name, from his father.*

5.15. The full forms of the possessive adjectives are frequently used in cases where, in English, the preposition *of* or *from* and a personal pronoun would be required:

Salieron en busca **suya.**	They went out in search *of him.*
Todavía no he recibido carta **suya.**	I have not yet received a letter *from him.*

5.16. The possessive adjective should be repeated before each noun, unless it refers to the same person or object (cf. § **31.24**):

Mi tío, mi tía y mi prima están en Guayaquil.	My uncle, aunt and cousin are in Guayaquil.
Señor mío y amigo.	Sir and friend.
Mi amigo y colega, el Sr. Gómez.	My friend and colleague Mr. Gomez.

5.17. When the subject of the sentence is of the third person, **su** (alone) and **suyo** regularly refer to the subject, so that the possessions of another third person are likely to be expressed by **de él, de ella, de Vd.,** etc., either alone or in connection with **su:**

V. no ha tomado el sombrero de él sino el suyo.	You have not taken his hat but your own.
El no ha tomado el sombrero de V. sino el suyo.	He has not taken your hat but his own.
Mi hermano ha venido a pedir a V. un libro suyo.	My brother has come to ask you for a book of his.

REMARK. In general (though it is only a generalization), in the spoken usage of Spanish America, however, **su** and **suyo** mean *your(s); his, her(s)* are expressed by **de él, de ella, etc.** In Spain on the other hand *your(s)* is likely to be expressed by **el (la, etc.). . . de usted** or **su(s) de usted.**

5.18. The possessive adjective may be strengthened by the addition of the appropriate form of the adjective **propio** *own* (cf. § **9.73**) :

Vivo en mi propia casa.	I live in my own house.
Ella enseña a sus propios niños.	She teaches her own children.
Engrandecen su propia importancia.	They magnify their own importance.

REMARK. **Propio** is occasionally, though rarely, used interchangeably with **mismo** to intensify a noun or personal pronoun:

El propio lo ha hecho.	He himself has done it.

ADJECTIVES USED AS PRONOUNS

5.19. In Spanish any adjective or past participle may stand alone, either employed as a noun or referring to a noun understood or previously expressed. This usage is not common in English except in the plural, where we say: *the rich and the poor; the righteous, the wicked.* Usually in the singular, and often in the plural, we express the noun or indicate it by the use of *one, ones:*

el viejo, una vieja	the old man, an old woman
un anciano, una anciana[1]	an elderly gentleman, an aged lady
el rico, los ricos	the rich man, the rich
el enfermo, la enferma	the sick person *(male and female)*

[1] **Anciano** is more respectful than **viejo,** and is therefore preferable in polite language when applied to persons. *Old,* relating to the length of existence of anything, is rendered by **antiguo: un antiguo amigo** *a friend of long standing.*

POSSESSIVE PRONOUNS

5.20. This usage applies to the forms of the possessive pronouns **mío, tuyo, suyo, nuestro, vuestro.** When these stand in the place of nouns, they are regularly accompanied by the definite article, both agreeing with the thing possessed:

Entre su familia y **la mía** existe una amistad muy estrecha.	A very close friendship exists between his family and *mine.*
Los amigos de V. y **los nuestros.**	Your friends and *ours.*
Ese sujeto no está contento con gastar su propio tiempo, sino que quiere también gastar **el mío.**	That individual is not satisfied with wasting his own time, but wishes to waste *mine* too.
Mi casa es semejante a **la suya.**	My house is similar to *his.*

REMARK. The possessive pronoun may be similarly reinforced by the addition of the proper form of **propio:**

He cuidado de su honor como del mío propio. (Pérez Galdós, **El abuelo,** V, 1)	I have looked after her reputation as after my own.
Y el príncipe tiene tan poca prisa por casarse contra todas las conveniencias. — Menos la suya propia. (Benavente, **La escuela de las princesas,** I, 2)	And the prince is in so little haste to marry in spite of all the advantages. — Except his own.

5.21. When necessary for the clearness of the sentence, **suyo** may be replaced by the appropriate personal pronoun preceded by **de,** the article still agreeing with the thing possessed:

Nuestros amigos y **los de V.**	Our friends and *yours.*
Mi casa está cerca de **la de ella.**	My house is near *hers.*
Ha cambiado su caballo por **el de ellas.**	He has exchanged his horse for *theirs* (the ladies').

5.22. When **uno** represents a noun previously expressed, it is not apocopated, even though followed by an adjective (cf. § **9.60**) ; but an adjective used as a noun representing a person, requires the apocopated form:

Si V. no tiene paraguas, le prestaré uno viejo mío.	If you have no umbrella, I will lend you an old one of mine.
Esposo mío, este abrigo que tengo está algo raído, además de estar fuera de moda; necesito uno nuevo.	Husband, this cloak of mine is rather shabby, besides being out of fashion; I want a new one.

Que **un rico** no tiene cuidados no es verdad. — It is not true that *a rich man* has no cares.

5.23. When adjectives or past participles are used after the verb *to be,* they may or may not take the definite article; the distinction being that *without* the article the mere value indicated is expressed, while *with* the article it is expressed as belonging to a particular object (or objects) understood:

Estas manzanas son agrias. — These apples are sour.
Estas manzanas son **las agrias.** — These apples are *the sour ones.*
Este abanico está roto. — This fan is broken.
Este abanico es **el roto.** — This fan is *the broken one.*

5.24. The same principle applies to the possessive forms: without the article they merely express ownership; with it, some particular possession:[1]

Aquella finca es mía. — That estate is mine *(belongs to me).*
Aquella finca es la mía. — That estate is mine *(the one belonging to me).*
La pluma de oro es la mía. — The gold pen is *mine.*
Estos niños son los míos. — These are my children.

5.25. Used absolutely in the masculine plural, the possessive pronouns denote the persons (friends, relations, servants, etc.) connected with anyone:

Los míos. — My people, my friends, my party.
¿Cómo están V. y los suyos? — How are you and yours?
¿Va V. a llevar a los suyos consigo? — Are you going to take your folks with you?
El coronel conduce los suyos a la brecha. — The colonel leads his men to the breach.
Me parece que el honorable Delegado considera solamente los intereses de los suyos. — It seems to me that the Hon. Delegate cares only for the interest of his own constituents.

DEMONSTRATIVE ADJECTIVES

5.26. There are four demonstrative adjectives in Spanish: **este,**

[1] It may also be said that absence of the article distinguishes the possessor, that presence of the article distinguishes the possession.

ese, aquel and **el** (which is the same as the definite article).[1] They agree with the noun they relate to, in the same manner as adjectives:

	MASC.	FEM.	
SING.	**este**	**esta**	this
	ese	**esa**	that *(near you)*
	aquel	**aquella**	that *(yonder)*
PLUR.	**estos**	**estas**	these
	esos	**esas**	those *(near you)*
	aquellos	**aquellas**	those *(yonder)*

5.27. **Este** denotes what is near to, or associated with, the speaker; **ese**, what is near to, or associated with, the person spoken to; and **aquel**, what is remote from both. They usually precede the nouns to which they belong but they may follow, in which case the definite article precedes the noun (cf. § **5.30**):

Este libro que yo tengo.	This book which I have.
Esta ciudad en donde yo estoy.	This city where I am.
Ese libro que V. tiene.	That book which you have.
Esa ciudad en donde está V.	That city where you are.
Aquel libro que mi tío tiene.	That book which my uncle has.
Aquella ciudad en donde está mi tío.	That city where my uncle is.
El gringo este es muy ladino. (Payró, **Pago Chico**, XII)	This foreigner is very sly.
Si viviera **el cura aquel** de mi parroquia, le demostraría que yo no puedo perder nada. (Alas, **Protesto**, IV, in **El Señor; y lo demás son cuentos**)	If that parish priest of mine were alive, I would prove to him that I can't lose anything.
En una misma fecha cayeron, pues, dos cosas seculares, **el trono aquel** y **la tienda aquella**. (Pérez Galdós, **Fortunata y Jacinta**, II, 1, 1)	At one and the same date there collapsed then, two secular things, that throne and that store.

5.28. Similarly, **este** refers to a subject mentioned by the speaker; **ese**, to one mentioned by the person addressed; and **aquel**, to the ideas of a third person:

Este ejemplo que he citado.	This example which I have cited.
Esa opinión que tiene V.	That opinion which you hold.
Aquella doctrina de San Pablo.	That doctrine of St. Paul's.

[1] The five forms of the article, **el, la, lo, los, las,** are derived from the Latin demonstrative adjective pronoun *il*le, il*la*, il*lud*; acc. plur., il*los*, il*las*. This explains the employment of the article as a demonstrative in Spanish.

5.29. With reference to time, **este** relates to the present, **ese** to a period relatively near, while **aquel** applies to a remote time:

Esta mañana, este año, este siglo.	This morning, year, century.
Esa época, esos años.	That epoch, those years.
Aquel suceso; aquellos siglos.	That occurrence; those centuries.
En esas horas estará en París.	By that time he will be in Paris.
Aquellos días no los llegaremos a ver.	Those days we shall not live to see.

5.30. **Ese** (like Latin *iste*) occasionally implies contempt, especially when placed after a noun, which in that event takes the definite article:

Ese chicuelo chillón.	That squalling brat.
Esas truchas de criadas a servir.	Those worthless servant girls.
El gaitero ese.	That confounded bagpiper.
La taimada esa.	That slyboots.

DEMONSTRATIVE PRONOUNS

5.31. When the demonstrative adjectives **este, ese** and **aquel** do not modify a noun they bear an accent mark in writing (excepting the neuter forms, cf. § 5.36). They then have the function of pronouns:

Este caballo y **aquél.**	This horse and *that one* yonder.
Esa escopeta de V. y **ésta** mía.	That gun of yours and *this one* of mine.
¿Quiere V. aquellos libros o **ésos?**	Do you want those books [over there] or *those* [near you]?
¿Quién es **ése?**	Who is *that* [fellow]?

5.32. In referring to two persons or things, **éste** is equivalent to **the latter,** and **aquél, the former;** the order of reference therefore is usually the reverse of the English:

César y Cicerón son igualmente célebres en la historia romana; **éste** por su elocuencia, **aquél** por su valor.	Cicero and Caesar are equally celebrated in Roman history; *the former* for his eloquence, *the latter* for his valor.
Una mujer hermosa gusta a los ojos; una mujer buena gusta al corazón.	A handsome woman pleases the eyes; a good woman pleases the heart.
Si **aquélla** es una joya, **ésta** es un tesoro.	If *the former* is a jewel, *the latter* is a treasure.

5.33. When there is danger of mistaking which of two nouns is the subject of a verb in a dependent clause, the one intended is reproduced by a demonstrative—**éste** applying to the nearest, and **ése** to the farthest one:

Si la nación no ama al rey, es porque se deja (éste *or* ésa) llevar de perniciosas influencias.	If the nation does not love the king, it is because (he *or* it) allows (himself *or* itself) to be led astray by evil influences.

5.34. In business style, **en ésta** and **en ésa** are used elliptically, the word **ciudad** *city* or **plaza** *market* being understood:

En ésta los precios de géneros extranjeros suben sin vacilar a causa del aumento de derechos de importación.	Prices of foreign goods are steadily rising *here* on account of increase in import duties.
¿Cómo van los negocios **en ésa?**	How is business *with you?*

5.35. When followed, without an intervening comma, by a preposition or by **que, este, ese, aquel,** being then only "logical" or weakened demonstratives (see below), that is, practically definite articles, are most often printed without an accent mark nowadays:

Con el traje de aldeano me parecía usted mejor que con este de caballero. (Pérez de Ayala, **Prometeo,** IV)	In the villager's costume you looked better to me than in this gentleman's.
Voy un momento a consultar una apuntación. —¿No será esta que te dejas aquí? (Benavente, **Titania,** II, 4)	I am going to consult a note for a moment. — May it not be this one that you are leaving here?
Transcurrieron otros quince días y llegó aquel en que nuestro héroe debía de abandonar el lecho. (Alarcón, **El capitán Veneno,** III, 3)	Another fortnight passed and there arrived that day on which our hero was to leave his bed.
¡Dichoso aquel que apartado de los negocios y libre de todo cuidado cultiva los campos de sus padres. (Palacio Valdés, **La novela de un novelista,** XXXII)	Happy [is] he who, far from business affairs and free of all care, tills the lands of his forefathers!
No hice caso de una protesta de desprendimiento hidalgo, de esas que en situaciones análogas tiene todo español. (Pardo Bazán, **La sirena negra,** VI)	I paid no attention to a protest of noble disinterestedness, [one of] those which every Spaniard makes in comparable situations.

5.36. The neuter forms, **esto, eso** and **aquello,** are only used as pronouns. They do not refer to tangible objects, but to some statement, remark or abstract idea:

¿Ha leído V. esto?	Have you read this?
Eso es.	That's it.
Eso parece impracticable.	That (which you propose) seems impracticable.
Eso es siempre deseable.	That is always desirable.
Aquello del filósofo griego.	That [thought] of the Greek philosopher.
Aquello no es de ninguna consecuencia.	That is of no consequence.

5.37. The neuter of the possessive pronouns denotes property collectively and abstractly:

He ganado lo mío honradamente.	I have gained my possessions honestly.
No desea sino lo suyo.	He wants only what belongs to him.

5.38. Eso forms an integral part of the frequently used phrase **y eso que,** which means *even though* or its equivalent:

Dos años había pasado en Vergara, donde la congregación tenía colegio, y en los dos años no había hecho más que suspirar por su patria. **Y eso que** para la salud le probaba muy bien el país. (Palacio Valdés, **La hermana San Sulpicio,** III)	She had spent two years in Vergara, where the order had a school, and in the two years she had done nothing but sigh for her native soil, *even though* the country proved very good for her health.
Ahí viene, **y eso que** le dije bien claro que esperara. (Martínez Sierra, **Madrigal,** II)	There he comes, *even though* I told him very clearly to wait.
¡Y es que esta luz cruda no le favorece a usted nada!... **Y eso que** no tiene usted ni una cana. (Benavente, **Al natural,** II, 5)	And the truth is that this crude light doesn't favor you at all! *In spite of the fact that* you haven't a single gray hair (still it doesn't help your appearance).

THE LOGICAL PRONOUN **EL**

5.39. From the Latin pronoun *ille, illa, illud,* is derived a set of forms which has three separate uses and appears in the grammars under three distinct names. Preceding a noun, or adjective used as a noun, it is called the *definite article.* As the representative of a person or thing, it appears in fuller forms as the *personal pronoun of the third person.* With these two uses the student is already familiar.

Used most often as the antecedent of a relative, but always referring to some noun or statement preceding, it has the use of a demonstrative; it is, however, only circumstantially a demonstrative, as it does not point out, but refers to, a noun. It may thus be called the *logical pronoun.*

5.40. **El** in its several forms, when used as a pronoun, does not accompany a noun, but serves to avoid the repetition of one; it is equivalent to the English *that, the one,* referring to something already mentioned or understood:

Mi casa y la que V. ve.	My house and the one which you see.
El jardín de mi casa, y el de la que V. ha comprado.	The garden of my house and that of the one which you have bought.
La pluma de acero y la de oro.	The steel pen and the gold one.
Este potro es el de que le he hablado a V.	This colt is the one about which I spoke to you.
¿No es esa escopeta la que le va a regalar a V. su tío?	Is not that gun the one your uncle is going to give you?
El coche de mi padre y el de su amigo.	My father's carriage and that of his friend.
Los cigarros de V. o los de su señor hermano.	Your cigars or those of your brother.

REMARK. The last two examples might be expressed in English by using the possessive, but in Spanish there is only one mode of expression:

Los cigarros de V. o los de su señor hermano.	Your cigars or your brother's.
No tengo mi escopeta sino la de mi vecino.	I have not my gun but my neighbor's.

5.41. The logical pronoun similarly denotes persons, and is used instead of the personal pronouns **él, ella, ellos, ellas,** when a relative pronoun follows:

Los que hablan son guatemaltecos.	Those who are speaking are natives of Guatemala.
El que desea mucho, siempre es pobre.	He who desires much is always poor.

Las que me ha indicado V. son primas mías. — Those [ladies] whom you have pointed out to me are cousins of mine.

Aquel soldado es el que ha matado a mi perro. — That soldier is the one who killed my dog.

La de quien VV. hablan es mi hermana. — She of whom you speak is my sister.

5.42. But when the relative following is governed by a preposition, **aquel** is more usual as an antecedent than **el**, when referring to persons:

Aquel de quien he recibido esta carta. — He from whom I have received this letter.

Aquella a quien adoro. — She whom I adore.

Aquellos con quienes hemos hablado no apoyan la medida. — Those with whom we have spoken do not favor the measure.

5.43. The masculine singular of the logical pronoun, **el**, coalesces with **de** and **a** in the same manner as when it is the definite article. (The personal pronoun, **él**, of stronger stress, does not do so):

Los que viven en el hemisferio austral ven al sol describir su arco diurno por encima del horizonte del norte y no por encima **del** del[1] sur. — Those who live in the southern hemisphere see the sun describe its daily arc above the horizon of the north and not above that of the south.

Al que tiene, se dará; y **al** que no tiene, aun lo que tiene, se le quitará. — To him that hath shall be given; and from him that hath not shall be taken away even that which he hath.

¿A qué teatro iremos? — **Al** del Duque.[2] — What theater shall we go to? — To the Duke's.

5.44. The neuter form **lo** refers only to a previous idea, thought or sentence, and not to any person or thing. Its principal use is to supply the antecedent before a relative pronoun, which in English is contained in the pronoun *what,* which is always expressed in full in Spanish by **lo que:**[3]

---

[1] It is also frequent, presumably for the sake of euphony, to write **de el del.**

[2] A theater in Seville, named in honor of the Duke of Montpensier.

[3] A very common idiomatic use of **lo que** is in the phrase **lo que es** *as for, so far as concerns,* etc.: **Lo que es tú, veo que no pierdes la costumbre.** (Martínez Sierra, **Primavera en otoño,** near end) *As for you I see that you haven't lost the habit.*

Eso es exactamente lo que quiero. — That is exactly what I want.

¿Ha leído V. lo que he copiado? — Have you read what I have copied?

Si lo que dice es verdad,... — If what he says is true,...

Estas circunstancias han ayudado materialmente a hacer a Inglaterra lo que es en la actualidad. — These circumstances have aided materially in making England what she is at present.

5.45. Either part of the expression **lo que** may be governed by a preposition, which in either case precedes the entire expression. In English a preposition governing the relative part of *what* is placed at the end of the phrase:

No puedo formar concepto de lo que dirá. — I can not form a conjecture of what he will say.

V. encontrará las costumbres muy diferentes de lo que espera. — You will find the customs very different from what you expect.

Eso es exactamente **en lo que** yo estaba pensando. — That is exactly *what* I was thinking *about.*

Es imposible prever **a lo que** la tiranía pueda incitarlos. — It is impossible to foresee *what* tyranny may drive them *to.*

NOTE. In the last two examples the preposition governs **que,** although standing before **lo;** the construction resembles that explained at § **5.65.**

5.46. When each member of the expression **lo que** is governed by a separate preposition, both prepositions precede **lo,** the one applying to **que** being placed last. But this is a clumsy construction, and should be avoided whenever possible:

Es difícil conciliar lo que refiere el profesor, **con a lo que** hemos estado acostumbrados. — It is difficult to reconcile what the professor says *with what* we have been accustomed *to.*

No tengo ningún recuerdo **de a lo que** V. se refiere (*better* de eso a que V. se refiere). — I have no recollection *of what* you refer *to.*

5.47. Lo que, in exclamations, direct or indirect, expresses manner or quantity, thus being equivalent to **cómo** or **cuánto:**

¡**Lo que** ciega a los hombres la codicia! — *How* cupidity blinds men!

¡**Lo que** vale la influencia política! — *How much* political influence is worth!

¡**Lo que** es tener buena ropa! — *What a fine thing* it is to have good clothes!

Mostró bien en el gesto **lo que** le contrariaba aquella visita. (Valera, **Pepita Jiménez, Paralipómenos**)	He showed clearly in his expression *how (much)* that visit annoyed him.
Y no sabrá él nunca **lo que** le aprecio. (Benavente, **Al fin, mujer, I, 2, 1**)	And he will never know *how much* I think of him.

5.48. **Lo** is used elliptically with **de** to represent *the question, the affair of;* thus:

Es lo de siempre.	It is the old story (that of always).
lo del arancel	the tariff question
concerniente a lo de Pierra	concerning the Pierra affair

INTERROGATIVE ADJECTIVES, PRONOUNS AND ADVERBS

5.49. Interrogative adjectives and pronouns have usually been considered after the relatives, but the interrogative usage is the original one. The forms of the words are the same, except that they bear an accent mark in interrogative usage:

¿**Quién** ha ganado el premio gordo?	*Who* has won the grand prize?
Queremos saber **quién** ha ganado el premio gordo.	We wish to know *who* has won the grand prize.
No sabemos **quién** ha ganado el premio gordo.	We do not know *who* has won the grand prize.
El diario de hoy nos dirá **quién** lo ha ganado.	Today's paper will tell us *who* has won it.

REMARK. The first example is called a direct interrogation; the others indirect interrogations. In both of these the interrogative use is distinguished in Spanish by the written accent. This not only applies to pronouns but also to certain adverbs which are used interrogatively as well as relatively:

ADJECTIVES AND PRONOUNS				ADVERBS			
INTERROGATIVE		RELATIVE		INTERROGATIVE		RELATIVE	
quién	who?	**quien**	who	**cuándo**	when?	**cuando**	when
cuál	which?	**cual**	which	**cómo**	how?	**como**	as
qué	what?	**que**	that	**dónde**	where?	**donde**	where
cúyo *(rare, archaic)*	whose?	**cuyo**	whose	**por qué**	why?	**porque**	because
cuánto	how much?	**cuanto**	as much				

NOTE. The adjectives and pronouns in the table above, with the exception of the invariable **que,** vary in the same manner as adjectives of like termination and conform to the same laws of agreement. The adverbs are, of course, invariable.

5.50. Quién is used only as a pronoun and is restricted to persons:

¿Quién llama?	Who calls?
¿A quiénes ha ajustado V.?	Whom (what persons) have you hired?

5.51. Qué may precede nouns representing either persons or things. Used alone, it always has a neuter value:

¿**Qué** ser humano, **qué** animal, **qué** planta o piedra no demuestra la providencia de Dios?	*What* human being, *what* animal, *what* plant or stone does not show the providence of God?
¿**Qué** falta en sus obras? Nada.	*What* is lacking in his works? Nothing.
No sabemos **qué** pasó. (Menéndez Pidal, **La España del Cid,** II, 6, 2)	We don't know *what* happened.

After a pause, **qué** at times has practically the value of **por qué:**

¿**Qué** vamos a engañarnos? (Benavente, **La honradez de la cerradura,** II, 3, 3)	*Why* should we deceive each other?

5.52. Popularly **qué cosa** is occasionally used for **qué** in its neuter value:

¿**Qué cosa** ha dicho V.? ¿**Qué cosa?**	*What* did you say? *What?*
¿**Qué cosa** es? ¿**Qué cosa** quiere?	*What* is it? *What* does he want?
¿**Qué cosa** es "anacronismo"?	*What* is "anachronism"?

5.53. Cuál (plural **cuáles**) *which* is applicable to persons or things, or may be used alone as referring to either. It queries *a certain one* (or *ones*) of a number indicated or understood:

¿Cuál de los caballos va V. a comprar, el bayo o el negro?	Which horse are you going to buy, the bay or the black one?
¿Cuál de los caminos conduce a Bemba?	Which road leads to Bemba?
¿Cuál necesita V., éste o aquél?	Which do you want, this or that?
¿Cuáles de sus casas ha vendido Vd.?	Which of your houses have you sold?

5.54. **Cuál** takes the place of **qué** *what* before the verb *to be,* when the noun follows, except when a mere definition of a word is asked for:

¿Cuál es la fecha de su carta?	What is the date of his letter?
¿Cuáles son los deberes de un cónsul?	What are the duties of a consul?
¿Cuál será el resultado?	What will be the result?
¿Qué es el panteísmo?	What is pantheism?
¿Qué es la diferenciación del homogéneo?	What is the differentiation of the homogeneous?
¿Qué *(i.e.* qué cosa) es el peligro que os espanta sino una infundada aprehensión?	What is the danger that appalls you but an unfounded fear?
Vds. hablan de precauciones, pero ¿cuál *(not* qué) es el peligro que les espanta?	You speak of caution, but what **is** the danger that appalls you?

5.55. In spite of a theoretical distinction between **qué** and **cuál** as interrogative adjectives, the latter properly implying selection from a group known to both speaker and person spoken to, the use of **cuál** as such has become quite infrequent in Spain (where **qué** expresses both meanings), though it survives more widely in Spanish America:

Lo que quisiera en aquel momento era tener mucho talento y mucha ciencia para convencerle de la verdad de la revelación. ¿De cuál revelación? —le había preguntado el hidalgo. —¿Cómo de cuál revelación? (Palacio Valdés, **La fe,** V)	What he would like at that moment was to have a great deal of ability and knowledge to convince him of the truth of the revelation. "Of which revelation?" the nobleman had asked him. —What do you mean, of which revelation?
¿Está la señorita? —¿Cuál señorita? Alvarez Quintero, **El genio alegre,** III)	Is the lady in? —Which lady?
Yo iba a darte las gracias esta noche en el baile. — ¿Cuál baile? . . . Si hay baile, no iré yo. (Azuela, **Los de abajo,** XIV)	I was going to thank you tonight at the dance. — What dance? . . . If there is a dance, I am not going.

5.56. **Cuánto** (varied like adjectives in **o**) means *how much* in the singular and *how many* in the plural:

¿Cuánto dinero ha recibido V.?	How much money have you received?
No le diré a V. cuánto.	I will not tell you how much.
¿Cuánta gasolina necesitan Vds.?	How much gasoline do you need?
¿Cuántos días hay en mayo?	How many days are there in May?

5.57. **Cúyo** (varied like adjectives in **o**) corresponds to *whose.* Its interrogative use is now rare (except possibly in some parts of South America), and even then this usage is limited almost entirely to cases where **cúyo** is followed by the verb **ser.** In other connections the meaning is expressed by **de quién,** or a different form is given to the inquiry by using **qué:**

¿De quién es este sombrero? ¿Cúyo es este sombrero?	Whose is this hat?
¿De quién es aquel hermoso edificio? ¿Cúyo es aquel hermoso edificio?	Whose is that handsome building?
¿De quién es hijo ese joven?[1]	Whose son is that lad?
¿Qué cuadro ha ganado el premio?	Whose picture has won the prize?
¿Qué historia de España prefiere V.? *or* ¿Quién es el autor de la historia de España que V. prefiere?[1]	Whose history of Spain do you prefer?

5.58. **Qué** and **cuánto** are also used in exclamations. These are but an extension of the interrogative use, and differ only in punctuation and the fact that they do not ask for information. The two kinds of sentences pass into each other so imperceptibly that it is sometimes difficult to distinguish them.

5.59. **Qué** is employed in exclamations with the meaning of *what!;* before an adverb, or an adjective not accompanying a noun, it is rendered *how!:*[2]

¡Qué feliz es V.!	How happy you are!
¡Qué dicha! ¡Qué lujo!	What luck! What luxury!
¡Qué grandiosa vista!	What a magnificent view!
¡Qué elegante biblioteca tiene su señor padre!	What an elegant library your father has!

[1] Such expressions are **¿cúyo hijo es ese joven? ¿cúya historia de España prefiere V.?** are not now considered admissible, although recommended by their brevity and the example of various classic authors.

[2] Though it rarely makes an appearance in the literary language, **que** is often inserted in the colloquial language between the phrase containing **qué** and a following verb: **¡Qué rico que debía estar el maestro!** (Unamuno, **Recuerdos de niñez y de mocedad,** I, 4) *How rich the teacher must have been!*

¡Qué bien habla!	How well he speaks!
¡Con qué acierto teclea!	With what accuracy she fingers (manipulates the keys)!

5.60. Greater emphasis or vivacity is imparted by placing an adjective after a noun preceded by **qué** and interpolating **más** or **tan:**

¡Qué tinta más mala!	What bad ink!
¡Qué lugar tan silencioso, tan poético!	What a quiet, poetical place!
¡Qué obra tan digna de admiración!	What an admirable work!

5.61. In an exclamatory sentence **qué de** + noun has the meaning of *how many* or its equivalent:

¡**Qué de fatigas** comenzaron para mí! (Palacio Valdés, **La hermana San Sulpicio,** VII)	*How many trials* began for me!
¡Pero cuánto ha visto usted en este mundo, amigo Mendizábal, y **qué de cosas** habrá presenciado tan trágicas, tan interesantes! (Pérez Galdós, **Miau,** XII)	But how much you have seen in this world, friend Mendizábal, and *how many* tragic, interesting *things* you must have witnessed!
¡Qué de pleitos, qué de trapisondas! (Benavente, **Los malhechores del bien,** I, 4)	What a lot of lawsuits, what a lot of snarls!

5.62. Cuánto, when used in exclamations, is shortened to **cuán** before adjectives and before adverbs. Outside of literary style **cuán** is usually replaced by **qué** (cf. § 5.59). Otherwise it is inflected regularly:

¡Cuánto ha cambiado su señorita hermana!	How much your sister has changed!
¡Cuánto sabe! ¡**Cuán docto** es!	How much he knows! *How learned* he is!
¡**Cuán** fácilmente lo hace!	*How easily* he does it!
¡Cuántas vidas inocentes han sido sacrificadas en el altar del fanatismo!	How many innocent lives have been sacrificed on the altar of fanaticism!

5.63. In questions **cuánto** may be resolved into **qué tanto,** and **cuán** into **qué tan:**

¿Qué tanto dista del puerto la ciudad?	How far is the city from the port?
Qué tan arraigado es este sentimiento muy pocas personas en América lo saben.	How deep-rooted this feeling is, few persons in America know.

REMARK. In exclamations this substitution can only be employed by separating **qué** from **tan:**

¡Qué acción tan generosa aquélla!	What a generous action that [was]!
¡Qué alma tan noble!	What a noble soul!

5.64. In like manner **cuál** may be resolved into **qué tal,** which is more usual than the change of **cuánto** just mentioned. Where the meaning permits, there is a distinction between **cuál** and **qué tal;** the former questions the identity, the latter the quality, of the person or thing:

¿Cuál es la casa que V. habita?	What house do you live in?
¿Qué tal es la casa que V. habita?	What kind of a house do you live in?
Si estos son los vencidos, ¿qué tales serán los vencedores?	If these are the vanquished, what kind of men may the victors be?
¿Cuáles son los vencedores?	Who (*i.e.* which) are the victors?

REMARK. Nowadays **qué tal** is most often used to ask for a valuation, with frequent ellipse of the verb: **¿Qué tal?** *How are things going?* **¿Qué tal el viaje?** *How was the trip?* **¿Qué tal ha dormido usted?** *How did you sleep?*

5.65. A preposition that logically precedes a relative clause may be prefixed to its antecedent:

¡De los extravíos que es capaz una imaginación exaltada (*instead of* los extravíos de que)!	Oh the extravagances of which an exalted imagination is capable!
Sé al blanco que tiras (*instead of* sé el blanco a que tiras).	I know what you are aiming at.
Era cosa de ver con la presteza que acometió los comestibles.	It was a sight to see the celerity with which he attacked the eatables.
La joven echó de ver con la insistencia que yo la miraba.	The young girl noticed the intentness with which I looked at her.
No quiero referir en las muchas ocasiones que yo le he prestado ayuda.	I will not mention the many occasions on which I have given him assistance.

VI

Parts Of The Body

6.1. In speaking of the parts of the body of man or beast, the Spanish usage differs considerably from the English, the chief deviation consisting in a less frequent use of the possessive adjectives and a preference for the definite article over the indefinite article. The same modes of expression that apply to parts of the body are also extended to articles of clothing *on the person.*

6.2. When one's own hand, foot, coat, etc., is the direct object of a verb, the appropriate article and not the possessive adjective precedes the part in question:

El ha perdido **el** brazo derecho.	He has lost *his* right arm.
El niño abre **los** ojos.	The child opens *its* eyes.
Ella bajó **la** cabeza.	She bowed *her* head.
Mete **la** mano en **el** bolsillo.	He puts *his* hand in *his* pocket.
Recibió una herida en **el** pecho.	He received a wound in *his* chest.

REMARK. The possessive is really unnecessary here, as there can be no doubt as to whose right arm he has lost, or whose eyes the child opens, etc.

6.3. After **tener** *to have* or an equivalent, the definite and not the indefinite article is used, unless the latter is required as a numeral. This construction with **tener** is often employed in connections where it would not be used in English:

Tenía la nariz larga y la boca ancha.	He had *a* long nose and *a* wide mouth.
Llevaba la barba entera.	He wore *a* full beard.
El tiene las piernas demasiado largas.	His legs are too long.
Ella tiene los dientes blancos y pequeños.	She has small, white teeth.
Tenía los cabellos desordenados.	Her hair was disarranged.
Tengo los ojos cansados.	My eyes are tired.

V. tiene los ojos demasiado pequeños.	Your eyes are too small.
Mi hermano tiene las manos llenas de verrugas.	My brother's hands are covered with warts.
Ella tiene las encías ulceradas.	She has ulcerated gums.
Llevo **un** diente postizo.	I have *one* false tooth.
Tengo **un** pie estropeado.	I have *a* crippled foot.
Ha perdido **un** ojo.	He has lost *an* eye.

6.4. When the part referred to is expressed by the plural or a general term, the article *may* be omitted, except in indicating a passing state:

Tiene ojos azules, facciones delgadas y pelo rubio.	She has blue eyes, delicate features and blond hair.
Ya podrían comprarte unos guantes de lana. Tienes las manos heladitas. (Pérez Galdós, **Miau,** II)	They might well buy you some woolen gloves. Your hands are frozen.

6.5. When the limbs, etc., of another are acted upon, the verb takes the person as the indirect,[1] and the parts of his body or clothing as the direct, object:

El barbero **me** ha cortado el pelo.	The barber has cut my hair.
La madre corta las uñas **al** niño.	The mother cuts the child's nails.
El cirujano **le** ha compuesto el brazo.	The surgeon has set his arm.
Me apretó afectuosamente la mano.	He pressed my hand affectionately.
Le tomé la mano en la mía.	I took her hand in mine.
Me pisó el vestido.	He trod on my dress.
El viento **le** llevó el sombrero.	The wind carried off his hat.

6.6. When it is the owner or possessor of the part of the body or article of clothing who performs the action, the indirect object of the preceding paragraph is reflexive:

Me lavo las manos en la palangana.	I wash my hands in the basin.
Ella **se** corta las uñas con las tijeras.	She cuts her nails with the scissors.
El **se** ha cortado el dedo.	He has cut his finger.
Se desgarró la basquiña en un clavo.	She tore her basque on a nail.
Me he dislocado el hombro.	I have dislocated my shoulder.
Se ha roto el pescuezo.	He has broken his neck.
Se quita el sombrero.	He takes off his hat.

[1] This use of the indirect object may be regarded as a survival of an old and widely extended construction—the dative of possession.

El joven artista **se** mordió el labio y no dijo nada.	The young artist bit his lip and said nothing.
Don Ramiro **se** pasó la mano por la frente. (Baroja, **El mayorazgo de Labraz,** III, 2)	Don Ramiro passed his hand over his forehead.
Acababa de servirse un vaso de agua y **se** lo llevaba a los labios. (Gallegos, **Doña Bárbara,** I, 6)	She had just poured herself a glass of water and was lifting it to her lips.

The reflexive pronoun is required (cf. § 6.2) only when some external means or instrumentality (including another bodily organ) is necessary for the accomplishment of the act:

Muevo la cabeza.	I shake my head.
Me toco la cabeza.	I touch my head.
Extiendo las manos.	I stretch out my hands.
Me froto las manos.	I rub my hands.

6.7. When the part of the body is the subject of the sentence or clause, or, in most cases, object of a preposition, or even accompanied by an adjective, possession is expressed by a possessive adjective:

Sus ojos negros brillaron como chispas.	Her black eyes gleamed like sparks.
Eran de mediano grosor sus labios.	Her lips were of medium thickness.
Sus ojos eran grandes y negros, sus pestañas largas, y sus cejas de una delineación perfecta.	Her eyes were large and black, her lashes long, and her eyebrows of perfect form.
Mis pobres ojos no me sirven ya para gran cosa.	My poor old eyes are no longer good for very much.
Lucían sus ojos al través de sus lágrimas con desusado brillo.	Her eyes shone through her tears with unwonted brightness.
Su nariz recta, sobre la que se unían casi las cejas finas y bien arqueadas, aumentaba la animación de sus grandes ojos.	Her straight nose, over which her fine and well-arched brows almost joined, increased the vivacity of her large eyes.
Un inmenso gato negro se estregaba contra sus piernas.	An immense black cat was rubbing itself against his legs.

6.8. A person is sometimes singled out by naming some marked bodily or other characteristic, preceded by **de,** where in modern English *with* is used. In older English it was *of,* as in Spanish:

El soldado **de** la barba.	The soldier *with* the beard.
Aquel caballero **de** las grandes patillas es inglés.	That gentleman *with* the long side-whiskers is an Englishman.

¡Hola! Usted **del** sombrero de copa.	Hullo! You *with* the plug hat.
Prefiero la muchacha **del** traje azul.	I prefer the girl *with* the blue dress.
Aquella **de** pelo moreno es mi hermana.	That one *with* brown hair is my sister.
Vino a la puerta un hombre **de** cabeza calva y barba roja.	A man *with* a bald head and a red beard came to the door.

6.9. There is a usage in Spanish of applying an adjective as it were to the individual, and then restricting it to a particular part by the preposition **de**. The result is obtained in English in various ways, principally by a compound adjective:

Era un hombre de mediana edad, ancho de espaldas, agradable de facciones, resuelto de ademanes, firme de andadura, y de mirar osado y vivo.	He was a man of middle age, broad-shouldered, pleasant-featured, of determined bearing, firm step and with a quick, resolute glance.
El capitán mi tío es alto de estatura y robusto de temperamento.	My uncle the captain is tall in stature and of a robust constitution.

6.10. When describing the attitude or action of a person, the disposition of the parts of the body or things intimately connected therewith is usually given in an absolute clause without any connecting word, where in English it is introduced by *with* or *having*:

En eso entró mi hermano, los cabellos desordenados y la cara encendida, y me dijo...	At this juncture my brother came in with his hair in disorder and his face flushed, and told me...
Estaba en la esquina de la calle, las manos metidas en los bolsillos.	He was standing on the corner of the street with his hands thrust into his pockets.

This is a relic of the Latin ablative absolute; thus in the phrase *passis manibus milites implorabant* (with outstretched hands they implored the soldiers), the circumstance of the noun and adjective being in the ablative shows that they are merely explanatory; the Spaniards, not having any case endings, add the bare words, separating them from the main part of the sentence by commas.

6.11. The distinction between the definite and the indefinite article as applied to parts of the body, clothing, etc., is that the definite article applies to an habitual possession, a natural and expected feature; the indefinite article implies that the noun which it accompanies is unexpected or unusual. The indefinite article mentions a thing for the first time, and after it is associated with a person and becomes a known part of him, it takes the definite article:

Un oficial de marina estaba a la puerta con la espada desenvainada.	A naval officer stood at the door with his sword drawn.

(Navy officers usually carry swords.)

Mi padre entró con una espada en la mano.	My father entered with a sword in his hand.

(The old gentleman was not in the habit of carrying one.)

El teniente tenía un bigote poblado.	The lieutenant had a thick mustache.

(It was hitherto unknown that he had one.)

El teniente se retorcía el bigote.	The lieutenant twisted his mustache.

(The mustache has now become a recognized feature.)

VII

Plural and Feminine of Adjectives

7.1. Adjectives in Spanish, like articles, vary in form to indicate gender and number, taking those of the nouns to which they relate. This is called *agreeing* with a noun.

7.2. They form their plurals in both genders in the same manner as nouns. (See Chapter I.) The distinction of gender depends upon the following two principles:

1. The greater number of adjectives end in **o** in the masculine, and **a** in the feminine singular, adding **s** in the plural:

fresco, fresca; frescos, frescas	fresh, cool
claro, clara; claros, claras	clear, light

2. Those which do not end in **o** in the masculine singular, have the same ending for both genders:

cortés, corteses	courteous, polite
dulce, dulces	sweet, mild

útil, útiles	useful
belga, belgas	Belgian

7.3. The last principle has the following exceptions:

a. Adjectives which end in a consonant and signify geographical division, add **a** in the feminine:

inglés, inglesa	English
español, española	Spanish
andaluz, andaluza	Andalusian
vienés, vienesa	Viennese

b. Those ending in **án, ón** and diminutives in **-ín,** add **a** in the feminine:

holgazán, holgazana	idle, lazy
preguntón, preguntona	inquisitive
monín, monina	cute, cunning

c. Those ending in **or** which do not have a *comparative* value, add **a** in the feminine:

emprendedor, emprendedora	enterprising
hablador, habladora	talkative

REMARK. Such words as **exterior, inferior, superior, mejor** *(better),* **peor** *(worse),* **anterior, posterior, ulterior,** having a comparative value, are the same in both genders.

d. The augmentative and diminutive terminations[1] **ote** and **ete,** become **ota** and **eta** in the feminine.

APOCOPATION OF ADJECTIVES

7.4. Some adjectives assume a shortened form when standing immediately before certain nouns:

bueno, good	**grande,** great, large, big
malo, bad	**santo,** holy, blessed

REMARK. This shortening is called *apocopation,* and will be found to occur in several other words of the language (cf. § **12.15** for **primero, tercero, postrero;** § § **23.14-23.16** for **cualquiera, doquiera, siquiera).**

[1] Augmentative and diminutive terminations constitute one of the most marked peculiarities of Spanish. They assume many forms and embrace a variety of shades of meaning which cannot be mastered by a beginner. For their treatment, see Chapter XXXII.

7.5. **Bueno** and **malo** drop the final **o** when immediately preceding any noun in the masculine singular:

buen azúcar; buen café	good sugar; good coffee
mal tiempo; mal vino	bad weather; bad wine

REMARK. In the archaic phrases **en buen hora, en mal hora,** occasionally found in modern literary texts, the **a** of **buena** and **mala** has been absorbed by the stressed vowel standing at the beginning of the following word.

7.6. **Grande** drops the final **de** when placed immediately before a singular noun of either gender. In literary usage **de** is sometimes retained before a singular noun beginning with a vowel sound:

un gran general	a great general
un gran día; una gran cosa	a great day; a great thing
un gran amigo, *or* un grande amigo	a great friend
un grande hombre, *or* un gran hombre	a great man
una grande ocasión, *or* una gran ocasión	a great occasion, a grand affair

7.7. The full form is even sometimes used before consonants, when great emphasis is intended (the natural effect of emphasis being to give to a word its fullest form):

un grande sacrificio	an immense sacrifice
una grande desgracia	a tremendous misfortune

7.8. When used to express size, **grande** regularly stands after the noun to which it belongs (§ 33.12):

un hombre grande; una mujer grande	a large man; a large woman
una casa grande; un perro grande	a large house; a big dog

7.9. Strictly, these three adjectives do not assume the shortened forms if any word comes between them and their nouns:

un **bueno** y cariñoso padre un padre bueno y cariñoso	a *good* and loving father
un mozo malo e imprudente	a bad, imprudent young man
un **grande** y estimable amigo	a *great* and estimable friend

REMARK. No adjective is ever curtailed when it follows the noun or when the noun to which it refers is not expressed.

7.10. Both **alguno** and **ninguno** drop the final **o** when used as adjectives before masculine singular nouns. This occurs also when other adjectives intervene:

Ella tiene **algún** talento musical.	She has *some* musical talent.
Ella no tiene talento musical alguno.	She has no musical talent whatever.
¿Tiene V. **algún** buen café?	Have you *any* good coffee?
No tengo ninguno bueno.	I have none good.
No tenemos **ningún** buen tabaco.	We have *no* good tobacco.
No veo a **ningún** soldado.	I do not see *any* soldier.
No veo a ninguno de los soldados.	I do not see any of the soldiers.

REMARK. There is a popular tendency to drop the **a** of the feminine before a noun beginning with stressed **a** or **ha** (cf. § 2.3):

algún agua fresca *(for* **alguna** agua)	any cool water
ningún alma viviente	no living soul

7.11. The masculine singular **Santo,** as the title of a holy man, is abbreviated to **San,** unless the name of the saint begins with **To-** or **Do-.** In all other forms and uses of the word, it is left unabbreviated:

San Pedro, St. Peter	**San Pablo,** St. Paul
Santo Tomás, St. Thomas	**Santo Domingo,** St. Dominic

BUT:

El santo padre, the Holy Father	**Santa Ana,** St. Anne

REMARK. The name of the island of St. Thomas (West Indies) is written and pronounced **San Tomas,** out of deference to foreign usage, as it has always been held by others than Spaniards.

VIII

Comparison of Adjectives and Adverbs

8.1. The term *comparison* of adjectives and adverbs was invented by the early compilers of Latin grammars to denote the three forms assumed by adjectives and adverbs in Latin in making comparisons. These three forms were: *positive,* the original value; *comparative,* the value in a higher degree; *superlative,* the value in the highest degree.

a. In English we obtain these two higher degrees by adding respectively the terminations *er, est,* to the positive or simple form of the adjective or adverb *(long, longer, longest),* unless that would give rise to a clumsy word, in which case the same purpose is attained by employing the adverbs *more, most (more liberal, most liberal).*

b. The positive or simple form of the adjective does not in itself imply comparison.

8.2. There are, however, five possible degrees of comparison, three of which have been generally ignored by grammarians because they have no representative forms in Latin:

In comparing the quality of one thing with that of another, the result may be that the first is greater than the second, or is less than it, or that both are equal. Hence are produced the comparatives of superiority, inferiority and equality. Again, one quality compared with a number of others, may prove superior or inferior to *all* the rest thus making the superlatives of superiority and inferiority. The three additional degrees are obtained in English by the use of adverbs—*less, as, least.*

8.3. In Spanish all these degrees of comparison are expressed by adverbs, which do not affect the form of the adjective or adverb which they accompany; the only variations of form being in the following eight words:

Four adjectives, in addition to their regular comparatives, have other and preferred forms which were irregular in Latin and have descended as anomalies in Spanish:

POSITIVE	COMPARATIVE
bueno good	**mejor** (*rarely* **más bueno**) better[1]
malo bad, poor	**peor** (*seldom* **más malo**) worse, poorer[1]
grande great, large	**mayor** (*or* **más grande**) greater, larger[2]
pequeño little, small	**menor** (*or* **más pequeño**) littler, smaller

Four adverbs have independent comparatives derived from Latin, and have no others:[2]

POSITIVE	COMPARATIVE
mucho much	**más** more
poco little	**menos** less
bien well	**mejor** better
mal ill, badly	**peor** worse

REMARK. As the superlative does not differ from the comparative in form, it is omitted above.

In all other cases the comparative of superiority is obtained by the use of **más;** that of inferiority, by **menos:**

negro black	**más negro** blacker	**menos negro** less black
capaz capable	**más capaz** more capable	**menos capaz** less capable
temprano early	**más temprano** earlier	**menos temprano** less early
cuidadosamente carefully	**más cuidadosamente** more carefully	**menos cuidadosamente** less carefully

[1] E.g., **O eres el hombre más malo que hay en el mundo, o no sé lo que eres.** (Pérez Galdós, **Miau,** XIX) *Either you are the worst man that there is in the world, or I don't know what you are.* Cf. also **¡Pobre santo mío, es más bueno!...** (Benavente, **Rosas de otoño,** II, 4) *My poor saint, he is so good!* Cf. the common phrases **ser más bueno que el pan** *to be goodness itself;* **ser más malo que el diablo** *to be worse than the Devil himself,* etc.

[2] **Más bien,** although in use, is not employed in comparisons. It has the meaning of *rather,* in the sense of *more correctly,* and is used in such connections as the following:

La causa de su quiebra fué **más bien** mal manejo que mala suerte.	The cause of his failure (bankruptcy) was *rather* bad management than bad luck.
Su figura era seria **más bien que triste.**	His countenance was grave *rather* than sad.

Mayor is also used to indicate a considerable or excessive degree of, a sense inherited from Latin comparative forms: **Por ahora, la mar no les hace mayor daño.** (Palacio Valdés, **José,** VIII) *For the time being, the sea isn't doing them very great harm.* **Nuestro regalo no podrá ser cosa mayor, pero las felicitaciones serán cordialísimas.** (Benavente, **Por las nubes,** II, 5) *Our gift can't be anything very much, but the congratulations will be most heartfelt.*

COMPARISON OF INEQUALITY

8.4. **Más** and **menos** apply in the same way to any things or ideas susceptible of comparison. As the grammatical construction is the same for both, the two will be treated of together as the *comparison of inequality.*

In this comparison, the second member, or that with which the quality in question is compared, is introduced by **que** *than* when both members are of the same nature:[1]

La madre es más bonita que la hija.	The mother is prettier than the daughter.
Esta pluma es mejor que ésa.	This pen is better than that.
Es menos útil ahora que antes.	It is less useful now than before.
Don Eduardo me ha dicho que su hermana está peor.	Edward tells me his sister is worse.
Esta carta está mejor escrita que ésa.	This letter is better written than that one.
V. anda más aprisa que yo.	You walk faster than I.
Los eclipses de luna acaecen menos a menudo que los de sol.	Eclipses of the moon occur less often than those of the sun.
Tiene más dinero que juicio.	He has more money than sense.
Más es perdonar una injuria que vengarla.	It is more to pardon an injury than to avenge it.
Habla más que trabaja.	He talks more than he works.
La condesa fué más magnífica que elegantemente vestida.	The countess was more magnificently than elegantly dressed.
No apetezco más que el reposo de la vida privada.	I do not desire more than the quiet of private life.
No necesitamos nada más.	We do not need anything more.
Quedará tres días más.	He will remain three days more.
No aspira a menos que al poder ejecutivo.	He aspires to no less than the executive power.
Fué más que injusto, fué brutal.	He was more than unjust, he was brutal.
Una libra más o menos no importa.	A pound more or less does not matter.

8.5. When each member of the comparison contains a different verb, but the second member is elliptical in such a way that to fill

[1] **Que** may mean *than that* when the second member is a clause: **Nada más natural que las dos mujeres hubiesen pasado a cuchillo su huerto**...**para celebrar dignamente la primera misa del hijo de la siñá Pascuala.** (Blasco Ibáñez, **Cuentos Valencianos, Noche de bodas, I**) *Nothing more natural than that the two women should have devastated their garden... to celebrate properly the first mass of Siñá Pascuala's son.* Cf. § **11.32.**

the ellipsis the verb of the first member must be repeated, **que** is properly replaced by **de lo que:**

Es más rico **de lo que** V. cree.	He is richer *than* you believe [he is].
Tiene menos dinero **de lo que** dice.	He has less money *than* he says [he has].
El examen fué menos formidable **de lo que** habíamos temido.	The examination was less formidable *than* we had apprehended [it would be].
Me ha ayudado más **de lo que** prometió.	He aided me more *than* he promised [he would].
Averigüé que la yegua era más vieja **de lo que** me habían asegurado.	I ascertained that the mare was older *than* they had assured me [she was].
Ha cometido menos crímenes **de lo que** V. piensa.	He has committed less crimes *than* you think [he has].

REMARK. Occasionally in the language of literature and with greater frequency in colloquial practice **que** alone is used. **Veo que tienes aún mejor juicio que yo creía.** (Unamuno, **Nada menos que todo un hombre,** in **Tres novelas ejemplares**) *I see that you have even better judgment than I thought you had.* Rather rarely **que lo que** is used: **Las manos eran, en efecto, tan bellas, más bellas que lo que D. Luis había dicho en su cartas.** (Valera, **Pepita Jiménez, Paralipómenos,** third section) *Her hands were, indeed, as beautiful, more beautiful than Don Luis had said [they were] in his letters.*

8.6. If the point of comparison be a noun, the *object* of the first verb or of a preposition in the first member and elliptically omitted in the second member, the neuter **lo** is replaced by the proper objective pronoun **(el, la, los, las)** agreeing with said noun and taking its place:

Encontraron mayores **inconvenientes de los que** habían previsto.	They found greater difficulties *than* [the difficulties] they had foreseen.
Averigüé que la yegua tenía más **defectos de los que** habían nombrado.	I found out that the mare had more defects *than* [the defects] they had enumerated.
Ha cometido más **crímenes de los que** ha confesado.	He has committed more crimes *than* [the crimes] he has confessed.
Me ha traído menos **dinero del que** V. le dió.	He has brought me less money *than* [the money] you gave him.
Le resultó una huronera bastante capaz, con más **piezas de las que** él necesitaba. (Pérez Galdós, **Torquemada en la cruz,** VIII)	It turned into a retreat quite large enough for him, with more rooms than [the rooms] he needed.

REMARK. The original **que** may here be restored in place of **de,** although **de** is preferable, especially after the comparative forms in **–or.** Moreover, **que** alone is found (cf. § **8.5,** REMARK): **Clapés dió a Jaime más dinero que el que éste le pidió.** (Blasco Ibáñez, **Los muertos mandan,** I, 4) *Clapés gave James more money than the latter asked him for.* **Dios no nos envía más carga que la que podemos cargar** (Palacio Valdés, **Santa Rogelia,** III, 3) *God sends us no more burden than we can endure.* **Me lleva consumido este chico más paciencia y más dinero que él vale** (Palacio Valdés, **Maximina,** V) *This boy has used up more of my patience and money than he is worth.*

8.7. **De** alone is placed after **más** and **menos** when followed by numerals or any numerical expression, provided the sentence is affirmative; if it is in any way negative, either **que** or **de** may be used after **más,** the preference being for **que:**[1]

He perdido **más de mil** pesos.	I have lost *more than one thousand* pesos.
Quedan **menos de cuatro** días.	*Less than four* days remain.
No necesito **más que dos.**	I do *not* need *more than two.*
Le contesté **sin** escribir **más que cinco** renglones.	I answered him without writing *more than five* lines.
El almirante perdió **más de la mitad** de la flota.	The admiral lost *more than half* of the fleet.
Eran poco **más de las** once y nada tenía que hacer hasta las doce. (Pereda, **Nubes de estío,** XII)	It was little *more than eleven* o'clock, and he had nothing to do until twelve.
Quedará **más de mes y medio.**	He will remain *more than a month and a half.*
Gané en aquella especulación **más de la mitad** del dinero invertido.	I gained in that speculation *more than half* of the money invested.
Brindamos y bebimos por ella **más de una docena** de veces. (Palacio Valdés, **La hermana San Sulpicio,** X)	We offered toasts and drank to her health *more than a dozen* times.
Era más de media noche cuando llegó al Palmar. (Blasco Ibáñez, **Cañas y barro,** VIII)	It was *more than midnight* (after midnight) when he reached El Palmar.

[1] Theoretically, **no más que** means *only (the number stated)* and **no más de** means *not more than,* the number stated being the maximum in the circumstances. The former concept is the more frequent, as pointed out above, but the distinction is observed: **No necesito más que dos** means, strictly speaking, *I need only two.* **No necesito más de dos** equals *I do not need more than two* or *I need two at the most.*

REMARK I. It is to be observed that, regardless of whether the sentence is affirmative or negative, **que** is used, even before numerals or numerical expressions, if the meaning is not *a greater* or *less number than:* **Más vale un testigo de vista que ciento de oídas.** *One eye witness is better than one hundred hearsay witnesses.*

REMARK II. **De** is regularly used in phrases composed of **lo** + adjective: **más de lo justo** *more than what is (was) necessary.* **De** is frequently found in phrases composed of the definite article + adjective: **Tenía quince años y en aquella edad me indignaban muchas más cosas de las necesarias.** (Palacio Valdés, **La novela de un novelista,** XXXVI) *I was fifteen years old and at that age I was made indignant by many more things than the necessary ones.*

8.8. The adverb **no** is sometimes introduced as an expletive into the second member of a comparison of inequality, provided the sentence is neither interrogative nor negative:

Ella era más feliz entonces que no ahora.	She was happier then than now.

8.9. The only tangible distinction between **mayor, menor,** on the one hand and **más grande, más pequeño,** on the other, is that when applied to persons the former always signify respectively *older* and *younger.* In other cases the two forms are interchangeable. **Mayor** and **menor,** however, occur oftener in literary language than the other two; they are also occasionally used with a metaphorical meaning, denoting eminence or importance rather than actual size:

¿Es su hermano Juan **mayor** o **menor** que V.?	Is your brother John *older* or *younger than you?*
Diego es más grande que su hermano mayor.	James is larger than his older brother.
Esta mesa es menor que ésa. Esta mesa es más pequeña que ésa.	This table is smaller than that.
París es mayor que Madrid.	Paris is larger than Madrid.
El altar mayor; la Plaza Mayor; La Calle Mayor; el palo mayor.	The high altar; the principal square; Main Street; the mainmast.

8.10. When the measure of difference in a comparison is given, it precedes the comparative adjective as in English:

Esta grada es dos pies más ancha que aquélla.	This harrow is two feet wider than that one.

El es tres años mayor que yo. — He is three years older than I.

La Navidad es tres días más pronto de lo que yo creía. — Christmas is three days nearer than I thought.

COMPARISON OF EQUALITY

8.11. The comparison of equality is expressed by **tanto** *as much, so much, as, so,* the second member being introduced by **como** *as.* When **tanto** stands before or instead of a noun, it is to all intents an adjective, and is varied like adjectives in **o.** In most other cases it is an adverb, losing the final syllable before the positive forms of adjectives and adverbs, but otherwise usually invariable:[1]

Ya es tan rico como su padre. — He is now as rich as his father.

V. habla español tan bien como su maestro. — You speak Spanish as well as your teacher.

Yo estudio tanto como V., pero no adelanto tanto. — I study as much as you, but I do not advance as much.

Mi criado es tan testarudo como ignorante. — My servant is as obstinate as he is ignorant.

Es hombre de gran influencia, tanto con la clase trabajadora como con la gente rica. — He is a man of great influence, as much with the working classes as with the rich people.

Don José es tan amable como su hermano es malhumorado. — Joseph is as pleasant as his brother is ill-humored.

¿Está su habitación de V. tan bien amueblada como ésta? — Is your room as well furnished as this one?

¿Tiene V. tantas rosas como dalias? — Have you as many roses as dahlias?

Nunca he visto una carta tan mal escrita. — I have never seen a letter so badly written.

Mi padre posee cuatro casas. –Yo no creí que tenía tantas. — My father owns four houses. – I didn't think he had as many.

8.12. Although not with the universal approval of grammarians, **tan** is used before other parts of speech and before phrases and clauses:

Tan no nos reconocimos (continuó la señá Frasquita), que los dos nos — *To such an extent did we fail* to recognize each other (went on señá

[1] Though **tanto** is expected before comparative forms of adjectives and adverbs, **tan** is at times used before **mejor** and **peor** when these words refer to a state of health: **El enfermo está tan(to) mejor que quiere dejar la cama.** *The patient is so much better that he wants to leave his bed.* **A las nueve estaba tan(to) peor que mandaron traer el viático.** *At nine o'clock he was so much worse that they sent for the sacrament.*

asustamos. (Alarcón, **El sombrero de tres picos,** XXXIII)	Frasquita), that each one of us frightened the other.
Tan en las entrañas de aquella gente estaba la explotación inconsiderada del extraño, que hasta los mozos del hotel cobraban un tanto por ciento por cada viajero conducido a tiendas, cafés o casas de recreo. (Ramón y Cajal, **Mi infancia y juventud,** XXII)	*So imbedded in the nature of those people was* the selfish exploitation of the stranger that even the hotel servants collected a certain per cent for every traveller that they took to stores, cafés or places of recreation.
¿Sabías tú, José, que Donato es encantador?...Pues lo **es. Tan lo es,** que con enseñarles a estas palomitas una hogaza mágica, las ha convertido en panteras. (López Pinillos, **La tierra,** I)	Did you know, Joseph, that Donato is an enchanter?...Well, he *is. So much so,* that by showing these doves a magic loaf he has turned them into panthers.
Tan es así, que mi mesma madre lo sabe decir siempre... (Lynch, **El inglés de los güesos,** V)	*To such a degree* (or *So much so*) *is it true* that my very mother is accustomed to say so always.

8.13. When **tanto** is used absolutely after a verb, i.e. is not followed by a noun, adjective or adverb, **como** may be replaced in literary usage by **cuanto** (meaning literally *how much*):

Gasta **tanto cuanto** su hermano. Gasta **tanto como** su hermano.	He spends *as much as* his brother.
El tiene **tanto cuanto** quiere.	He has *as much as* he wants.
Tomó **tanto cuanto** le pareció necesario.	He took *as much as* seemed to him necessary.

8.14. When **tanto** merely denotes a high degree producing a certain result, its correlative is **que,** and not **como,** as there is no comparison:

Estaba tan oscuro que era imposible leer.	It was so dark that it was impossible to read.
Me dijo tanto sobre la belleza de aquella actriz que fuí a verla.	He told me so much about the beauty of that actress that I went to see her.

8.15. Tanto, used adverbially and followed by **que,** means *as well as:*

La construcción de este motor me costó muchos desvelos tanto que al sobrestante.	The construction of this motor cost me as well as the superintendent many sleepless nights.

8.16. In the formula **tan—como,** the first may be omitted, as may its English equivalent:

Negro como el ébano.	Black as ebony.
Redondo como una naranja.	Round as an orange.
Este pan es duro como una piedra.	This bread is hard as a rock.

8.17. In elevated style, when the first element of the formula **tan—como** has been omitted, **como** may be replaced by **cual.** In such cases the article is dropped:

blanco cual nieve *(or better:* cual la nieve blanco)	as white as snow, snow-white

8.18. In literary language **cual** may occasionally replace **como** in other constructions (cf. § **9.85**) :

Se arrojó sobre sus enemigos cual toro enfurecido.	He dashed upon his enemies like an enraged bull.
El conde contestaba a las preguntas con exquisita cortesía, cual si se hallase en una recepción palaciega.	The count answered their questions with exquisite courtesy, as if he were at a palace reception.

8.19. Before a comparative adjective in **-or, mucho, poco** and other indefinite words are by some authors treated as adjectives; some grammatical authorities consider that **mucho, poco,** etc., should agree only before **más** and **menos:**

—Para la casa de Meira no hay nada imposible— respondió el caballero con mucha mayor **solemnidad** (Palacio Valdés, **José,** XI)	"For the house of Meira there is nothing impossible," answered the gentleman with much greater solemnity.
Entonces Lucero se puso a caminar con alguna mayor **celeridad;** no mucha. (Palacio Valdés, **La novela de un novelista,** XXXVI)	Then Lucero began to go along with somewhat greater speed; not much.
Ya ve usted cuántos más elementos hay aquí que en Cumbrales para resistir, y cuánta mayor **responsabilidad** adquirimos ante la Historia. (Pereda, **El sabor de la tierruca,** XXVII)	Of course you see how many more elements there are here to resist than in Cumbrales and how much greater responsibility we acquire before History.
Añado que los proponentes se adhirieron a ella con tanta mayor **decisión** cuanto que, a fuer de se-	I add that the proponents adhered to it with so much the greater determination because, as gentlemen, it

ñores, nunca entró en sus ánimos bailar de otra manera. (Pereda, **Los bailes campestres,** in **Escenas montañesas**) — never entered their minds to dance in any other way.

8.20. **Cuanto—tanto,** followed by any comparatives, are used as correlatives to express ratio, corresponding to the English formula *the*. . .*the*. . .:[1]

Cuanto más gasta **tanto** menos ahorra. — *The* more he spends *the* less he saves.

Cuanto más viejo es el vino, **tanto** mejor es. — *The* older the wine *the* better it is.

Cuanto más largo es el día **tanto** más corta la noche. — *The* longer the day *the* shorter the night.

Cuanto más lo examino, **tanto** menos sentido encuentro en ello. — *The* more I examine it *the* less meaning I find in it.

8.21. In such sentences **tanto** may be, and usually is, elliptically omitted. Moreover, in the spoken language especially, **cuanto** is replaced by **mientras** (and even **entre** or **contra**):[2]

Cuanto más, mejor. — The more the better.

Claro era que cuantas más botellas de medicina tomaba, mis padecimientos eran mayores y más prolongados. — It was clear that the more bottles of medicine I took, the greater and more prolonged were my sufferings.

Cuanto más meditaba sobre su conjetura, más verosímil me parecía. — The more I meditated over his conjecture, the more likely it appeared to me.

Cuantas más horas pasaban más aumentaba el miedo de Adambis. (Alas, **Cuento futuro,** in **El señor; y lo demás son cuentos**) — The more hours passed, the more Adambis' fear increased.

El mundo es un valle de lágrimas y mientras más pronto salís de él, mejor. (Pérez Galdós, **Miau,** XL) — The world is a vale of tears, and the sooner you leave it, the better.

---

[1] The order may be reversed, as when what is logically the second member of the proportion is expressed first: **Un viaje de placer es para él tanto mejor cuanto dinero le ha costado.** (Camba, **La rana viajera, Variedades europeas,** V) *A pleasure trip is for him so much the better the more money it has cost him* (logically, *the more money it has cost him, the better is a pleasure trip for him*).

[2] E.g., **Contra más**. . .**contra más quiero olvidarlo, menos conseguirlo puedo.** (Alvarez Quintero, **El genio alegre,** II) *The more*. . .*the more I want to forget him, the less I can succeed in it.*

8.22. **Tanto**...**cuanto** are used adverbially as correlatives before two clauses which are considered equal in importance:

Me invitó a acompañarle, lo cual acepté con gusto, **tanto** por enterarle de mi proyecto **cuanto** por dar aquel grato paseo.	He invited me to accompany him and I accepted with pleasure, *as well* to inform him of my plan *as* to take that pleasant drive.
El príncipe era buen compañero, muy dado a los ejercicios corporales, y muy hábil **tanto** en la equitación **cuanto** en el manejo de las armas.	The prince was a good companion, much given to bodily exercise, and expert *both* in horsemanship *and* the use of arms.

8.23. In this connection **como** may be substituted for **cuanto,** being in fact the more usual at the present day:

Todas las repúblicas de Centro América, exceptuando el Salvador, tienen puertos **tanto** en el Mar Caribe **como** en el Océano Pacífico.	All the republics of Central America, except Salvador, have seaports on the Caribbean Sea *as* well *as* on the Pacific Ocean.

8.24. The formulae **tanto más**...**cuanto que, tanto menos**... **cuanto que,** correspond to the English *all the more*...*because, all the less*...*because:*

Esta reprensión era **tanto más** imperdonable **cuanto que** había sido merecida.	This rebuke was *all the more* unpardonable *because* it had been deserved.
Estoy **tanto menos** satisfecho de su conducta **cuanto que** me creía con más derechos a su amistad.	I am *all the less* satisfied with his conduct *because* I thought I had more rights to his friendship.
No temían que el árbol cediese al empuje de la corriente, pero la inundación creciente podía ganar sus ramas altas, **tanto más cuanto que** la depresión del suelo hacía de aquella parte de la llanura un punto el más a propósito para la acumulación de las aguas.	They did not fear that the tree would yield to the force of the current, but the rising flood might reach its upper limbs, *all the more because* the depression of the ground rendered that part of the plain most suitable for the water to collect in.

8.25. The **que** following **cuanto** is really superfluous and, although generally employed, may be omitted:

Adoptó por fin un plan de operaciones sobre el cual creyó poder contar, **tanto más cuanto** la ejecu-	He finally adopted a plan of action upon which he thought he could count, *the more so because* the

ción sólo dependía de él, y se sentía capaz de todo por la causa que había abrazado.	execution depended upon him alone and he felt himself capable of anything for the cause which he had embraced.

8.26. **Tanto,** in its invariable form, is used adverbially before comparative forms in **-or:**

¡Tanto mejor!	So much the better!
¡Tanto peor para V.!	So much the worse for you!

8.27. **Un tanto, algún tanto** or **un tanto cuanto,** form neuter phrases meaning *a little,* or *somewhat:*

Rosa, **un tanto** más consolada, regresaba a su casa.	Rosa was returning home *a little* more consoled.
Esta respuesta le satisfizo **algún tanto.**	This reply satisfied him *somewhat.*
La hija se retiró **un tanto** mortificada.	The daughter withdrew *rather* mortified.
La conversación era poco animada, y sólo crecía **un tanto cuanto** en interés cuando entraban nuevas visitas.	The conversation was not very animated, and only increased *a little* in interest whenever new callers came in.

8.28. **Entre tanto, mientras tanto** and also **en tanto** mean *in the meantime;* **por (lo) tanto** *consequently:*

Mientras tanto el partido revolucionario no había sido ocioso.	*In the meantime* the revolutionary party had not been idle.
Estoy en minoría, señores; **por lo tanto,** retiro mis palabras, mas no varío en mis ideas.	I am in the minority, gentlemen; *consequently* I retract my words, but I do not change my ideas.
Aguardemos, y **entre tanto,** vamos a votar los que estamos aquí. (Payró, **Pago Chico,** II)	Let us wait and *in the meantime* let those of us who are here go and vote.
En tanto la González procuraba aprender, progresar; quería subir mucho en el arte. (Alas, **La ronca,** in **El Señor; y lo demás son cuentos**)	*In the meantime,* González was trying to learn, to progress; she wanted to rise high in her art.

8.29. When the point of comparison in the second member is a personal pronoun, the object of a verb in the first member, it must be put in the terminal form (**a mí, a él,** etc.) :

Te admiro más que a **él.**	I admire you more than *him.*
Más quiere al artista que a **mí.**	She likes the artist better than *me.*

8.30. When several adjectives or adverbs with the same degree of comparison occur together, **más, menos** or **tan,** as the case may be, need only be placed before the first one; for greater emphasis, however, the adverb may be repeated before each:

Cicerón era más sabio, elocuente y patriótico que Catón.	Cicero was wiser, more eloquent and patriotic than Cato.
La vertiente oriental era menos escarpada, áspera y escabrosa que la que acababan de subir.	The eastern slope was less steep, rough and craggy than that which they had just ascended.

8.31. In the case of adverbial expressions made up of a noun and the preposition **con, más** or **menos** is placed immediately before the noun; with those composed of a noun and some other preposition, **más** or **menos** precedes the preposition:

con cuidado carefully	**con más cuidado** more carefully	**con menos cuidado** less carefully
de propósito purposely	**más de propósito** more purposely	**menos de propósito** less purposely
a fondo thoroughly	**más a fondo** more thoroughly	**menos a fondo** less thoroughly

8.32. When **tanto** is applied to such adverbial phrases, the usage is as follows:

con tanto cuidado as carefully	**tan de propósito** as purposely
con tanta diligencia as diligently	**tan a fondo** as thoroughly

8.33. The adverbs **más, menos, tan, muy** are placed immediately before nouns, with the same value which they have before adjectives; their English equivalents *more, less,* etc., require *of a* to connect them with a noun, or the idea is expressed in some different manner:

No le creí tan **niño.**	I did not think him such a *child.*
V. es menos **caballero** de lo que yo creía.	You are less of a *gentleman* than I thought.
Es muy **inglés.**	He is very much of an *Englishman.*
Es muy **hombre** de mundo.	He is a thorough *man* of the world.
Muy **señor** mío.	Dear *Sir.* *(In letters.)*

8.34. The force of these adverbs of comparison may, by means of other adverbs, be modified to any extent—made greater or less, or entirely negative—without affecting the grammatical construction:

La menor es aun más linda.	The younger one is even prettier.
Mucho mejor, mucho menos.	Much better, much less.
Bastante más difícil. Harto más difícil.	A good deal more difficult.
Considerablemente más útil.	Considerably more useful.
Poco más cómodo.	Little, scarcely more comfortable.
Un poco más cómodo.	A little more comfortable.
Todavía menos importante.	Still less important.
Ella no toca tan acertadamente como su hermana menor.	She does not play as accurately as her younger sister.
V. lo ha hecho mejor sin tener tantas ventajas como ellos.	You have done it better without having as many advantages as they.
El proyecto de V. no es más realizable que el mío.	Your plan is no more feasible than mine.
Ella no está menos adelantada que su hermano.	She is not less advanced than her brother.
Algo menos penoso.	Somewhat less laborious.

REMARK. Any of these modifying adverbs that are also used as adjectives. agree with a noun when followed by one:

Harta más paciencia.	A good deal more patience.
Poca más agua. Pocas más frutas.	Little more water. Few more fruit.
Muchos más ríos.	Many more rivers.
Tantas más dificultades.	As many more difficulties.

8.35. In Spanish **más is** applied to many adverbs which can not be preceded by *more* in English:

Para empezar no te daremos sueldo, pero **más adelante** lo doblaremos si estamos contentos de ti.	To begin with we won't give you any wages, but *later on* we'll double them if we're satisfied with you.
Más allá de la zona de escollos, el mar abierto resplandecía bajo los rayos del sol.	*Beyond* the belt of sunken rocks the open sea sparkled beneath the sun's rays.
Más allá del alcance ordinario de las mareas.	*Beyond* the ordinary reach of the tides.
Más acá del río.	*On this side of the* river.
Más arriba, el río estaba obstruido por altas yerbas que dificultaban la acción de los remos.	*Higher up,* the river was obstructed by high weeds which impeded the action of the oars.

REMARK. Other peculiar constructions with **más** are:

Este relato es tan verídico como el que más. *(I.e.,* como el que lo es más) — This account is as true as can be.

Ella es discreta hasta no más. — She is extremely discreet.

Estaba borracho hasta no más. — He was as drunk as could be.

Los dos alumnos son a cual más estudiosos *(or* estudioso). — The two scholars vie with each other in studiousness.

No vivimos en época estable. Los fenómenos sociales, a cual más inesperado y sorprendente, se suceden sin tregua. (Pérez Galdós, **El amigo Manso,** XLIV) — We do not live in a stable age. Social phenomena each one more unexpected and surprising than the preceding, succeed one another without respite.

Por un lado, doña Bárbara y por el otro una runfla de mayordomos, a cual más ladrones. (Gallegos, **Doña Bárbara,** V) — On one hand Doña Barbara and on the other a crowd of overseers, each more thievish than the rest.

THE SUPERLATIVE OF COMPARISON

8.36. There are two distinct forms in Spanish bearing the name of superlative: *a.* the true superlative, which regularly follows the comparative on the scale, and expresses the highest or lowest degree of a quality as compared with any other degrees of the same; *b.* the absolute superlative, which expresses a very high or the highest possible degree without reference to any other, and therefore does not belong to the comparative scale.

TRUE SUPERLATIVES OF ADJECTIVES

8.37. The superlative does not differ in form from the comparative of inequality, its meaning being determined entirely by the connection in which it is used. When followed by a noun, the superlative of adjectives is accompanied by the definite article or a possessive adjective:

El acusado contestaba a sus preguntas con **la** mayor calma posible. — The accused answered their questions with *the* greatest possible calmness.

El Nuevo Mundo, en que el Canadá ocupa **el** mayor territorio. — The New World, in which Canada occupies *the* largest territory.

Eso es mi menor cuidado. — That is my least concern.

Esta es su mejor obra. — This is his best work.

REMARK. There is thus no difference between a comparative preceded by a definite article or possessive adjective, and the superlative; but the context will seldom fail to decide which meaning is intended:

Los diplomáticos y cónsules de la Gran Bretaña unánimemente aseguran en sus informes oficiales, que sus paisanos son suplantados en los mercados hispanoamericanos por **los más frugales e industriosos** alemanes.	The diplomats and consuls of Great Britain affirm unanimously in their official reports that their countrymen are supplanted in the Spanish-American markets by the more (*or* most) frugal and industrious Germans.

8.38. The superlative of an adjective takes the same place before or after its noun that the positive would:

La más hermosa flor. La flor más hermosa.	The most beautiful flower.
Mi hermano mayor.	My oldest brother.
Su obra más larga.	His longest work.
Los cinco pasos más frecuentados en los Andes desde Chile hasta la República Argentina, son los de Doña Ana, Dehesa, Patos, Uspallata y Planchón.	The five most frequented passes in the Andes between Chile and the Argentine Republic are those of Doña Ana, Dehesa, Patos, Uspallata and Planchón.

8.39. When the superlative adjective follows the noun to which it belongs, the place of the definite article or possessive adjective is before the noun:

La cosa más fácil.	The easiest thing.
Es el libro menos interesante que en mi vida he leído.	It is the least interesting book I have read in my life.
Este barrio está habitado por la gente más mala de la ciudad.	This ward is inhabited by the worst people of the city.

8.40. When the noun qualified by the superlative adjective is in apposition to another noun, the article may immediately precede the superlative. The same is necessarily the case when the superlative is used absolutely (instead of a noun):

Tiahuatlán, ciudad la más antigua de América.	Tiahuatlan, the most ancient city of America.
La mordedura de la cobra, serpiente la más venenosa de la península india, es siempre mortal.	The bite of the cobra, the most venomous snake of the Indian peninsula, is always mortal.
Esta carta es la menos importante.	This letter is the least important [one].

8.41. When the superlative adjective is in the predicate, the article is omitted when reference is had to different degrees of a quality in the same person or thing. If the quality of the noun is compared with that of other nouns, named or understood, the article is required:

Esta mujer tiene la habilidad de llorar cuando está **menos** afligida.	This woman has the power of weeping when she is least afflicted.
De todas mis hermanas Pepita no lloró, aunque era **la más** afligida.	Of all my sisters, Josie did not cry, although she was *the* most afflicted [one].
Este era el procedimiento que nos pareció **más** realizable.	This was the procedure which seemed to us most feasible.
Este procedimiento nos pareció **el más** realizable.	This procedure seemed to us *the* most feasible [one].
Realizó que lo había perdido justamente en el momento en que su uso era **más** necesario.	He realized that he had lost it just at the moment that its use was most necessary.

REMARK. In the last example, **era el más necesario** would mean *when its use was the most necessary use,* and would not make sense.

8.42. The superlative, unaccompanied by a noun, may be used partitively by placing **de** before it; in rendering the construction into English, some such word as *kind, nature,* is to be supplied:

Tiene una pasión de las más exageradas por la música.	He has a passion of the most exaggerated kind for music.
Estoy sobre la pista de una conspiración de las más graves.	I am on the track of a conspiracy of the gravest nature.
Su vestido era carmesí del más vistoso.	Her dress was crimson of the most showy hue.

8.43. Superlatives are connected with the remainder of the sentence by the prepositions ***de*** *of* or **entre** *among.* The employment of **en** for this purpose, although met with, is a vulgarism to be avoided:

Era el catedrático más docto **del** país.	He was the most learned professor in the country.
¿Cuál es el río más largo **del** mundo?	Which is the longest river in the world?
La mayor fábrica **del** estado.	The largest factory in the state.
Soy de opinión que Tácito fué el más profundo **entre** los historiadores antiguos.	I am of the opinion that Tacitus was the most profound of ancient historians.

8.44. The English grammatical quibble whether we should say *the more learned* or *the most learned of the two,* is impossible in Spanish, as the form would be the same in either case:

¿Quién es más fuerte, V. o yo?	Which is the strongest, you or I?
La más plausible de las dos suposiciones era la presentada por el abogado.	The most plausible of the two suppositions was that presented by the lawyer.

8.45. Participles used as adjectives have the same degrees of comparison, formed in the same manner, as those of adjectives. Some of these participial adjectives need to be rendered into English by placing *well* before them; their comparatives and superlatives are then translated by *better* and *best* instead of *more* and *most:*

un hombre leído	a well read man
un hombre más leído	a better read man
el hombre más leído	the best read man
una ilustración conocida	a well-known illustration
una ilustración más conocida	a better-known illustration
la ilustración más conocida	the best-known illustration

8.46. It has already been shown at § 2.47 how the neuter article **lo** is used with the positives of adjectives and past participles; it is similarly employed, with great effect, before superlatives. The meaning may generally be rendered in English by adding *thing* or *part* to the adjective:

En **el más** apartado de los arrabales.	In the remotest of the suburbs.
En **lo más** apartado de los arrabales.	In the most remote part of the suburbs.
En **lo más** profundo del bosque.	In the depths of the wood.
El sueño profundo que se había apoderado del herido era **lo más** a propósito para reparar sus fuerzas.	The deep sleep which had overcome the wounded man was the most appropriate thing to restore his strength.

8.47. **Más,** although usually an adverb, sometimes serves as an adjective pronoun representing the majority or greatest number of any collective plural; with a singular noun the expression used is **la mayor parte:**

Los más de los indios se ocultaron detrás de las peñas.	The most of the Indians hid themselves behind the rocks.
Las más de las veces.	The greater number of times.

Ha perdido la mayor parte de su dinero. — He has lost the most of his money.

Pasó la mayor parte de la noche velando. — He passed the most of the night awake.

La cordillera marítima, dominando a la costa peruana, tiene una larga línea de montañas volcánicas, las más de ellas inactivas. — The Coast Chain, which overlooks the Peruvian coast, has a long line of volcanoes, the greater number of them inactive.

TRUE SUPERLATIVES OF ADVERBS

8.48. The true superlative of adverbs is formed in essentially the same manner as that of adjectives, but it is not preceded by a possessive adjective or definite article. It is therefore in no wise distinguished from the comparative:

Los mejores criados son los que hablan menos. — The best servants are those that talk least.

El río corre más aprisa justamente antes de la caída. — The river flows fastest just above the fall.

Acierto a comprenderle aun cuando habla más aprisa. — I manage to understand him even when he speaks fastest.

El alumno que había estudiado más diligentemente no logró ser aprobado en el examen. — The student who had studied most diligently failed to pass the examination.

Esa era la respuesta que menos esperaba oír. — That was the answer she least expected to hear.

Amo el mar cuando más alto suben las olas. — I love the sea when the waves run highest.

Remark. When the superlative adverb qualifies an adjective or participle used absolutely, it is preceded by the article — which is to be considered as applying to the adjective (§ 5.19):

Su casa es la más elegantemente amueblada. — His house is the most elegantly furnished.

8.49. When precision is required, the superlative use may be distinguished by a circumlocution with ser and the logical pronoun:

De todos los defectos el que más detesto es la afectación. — Of all foibles I hate affectation most.

La comisión informó que el fusil Lebel era el que más alargaba. — The Board reported that the Lebel rifle shot farthest.

Las historias cortas son las que escribe mejor. — Short stories are what he writes best.

Donde corre el río más aprisa es justamente antes de la caída. — The river flows fastest just above the fall.

De toda la compañía ella es la que canta más dulcemente. — She sings the sweetest of all the company.

8.50. An adverbial superlative is formed by placing the neuter article **lo** before a superlative adverb followed by any phrase expressing possibility. This is properly a superlative absolute and not a superlative of comparison:

Esta maniobra indicó que el capitán quiso **acercar** el bergantín **lo más posible** a la costa. — This maneuvre indicated that the captain wished to *bring* the brigantine *as near as possible* to the coast.

Me salvé lo mejor que pude de aquellos peligros. — I *escaped* from those dangers *as I best could.*

Echó a correr lo más aprisa que le pudieron llevar sus piernas. — He *set out on a run as fast as* his legs could carry him.

Los colonos se pusieron en marcha con intención de llegar **lo más pronto posible** a la costa occidental. — The colonists set out with the intention of *arriving as soon as possible* at the west coast.

ABSOLUTE SUPERLATIVE OF ADJECTIVES

8.51. The absolute superlative of adjectives, when formed regularly, is obtained by the addition of the termination **ísimo;** it is then varied like any adjective in **o.** This termination, although descended from the true superlative of the Latin, has in Spanish merely an augmentative value; its force may be rendered in English by placing *very* or *most* before the positive adjective.

REMARK. The principal stress of the absolute superlative is on the first syllable of the termination (whatever be its form). The syllable originally stressed then takes a secondary accent.

8.52. The original adjective sometimes requires modification before appending the termination **ísimo,** for the reason that, being a direct inheritance from the Latin, it is not derived from the modern Spanish adjectives.

8.53. The following distinctions are to be observed in the formation of the absolute superlative:

1. If the positive adjective ends in a consonant, it receives the termination **ísimo** without undergoing any change, unless the final consonant be **z**, which changes to **c** before **i** (§ 15):

hábil skilful	**habilísimo** very skilful
liberal liberal	**liberalísimo** very liberal
feliz happy	**felicísimo** very happy
feroz fierce	**ferocísimo** very fierce

2. A final vowel or diphthong is omitted before receiving the termination. If two terminal vowels form two syllables, only the last is omitted:

importante important	**importantísimo** very important
injusto unjust	**injustísimo** very unjust
simple simple	**simplísimo** very simple
duro hard	**durísimo** very hard
limpio clean	**limpísimo** very clean
sucio dirty	**sucísimo** very dirty
impío[1] impious, wicked	**impiísimo** very wicked
feo ugly	**feísimo** very ugly

3. If, after dropping a final **a** or **o**, the last remaining letter be **c**, it is changed to **qu**, and similarly **g** to **gu**, to preserve the hard sound (§ 15):

rico rich	**riquísimo,** very rich
fresco fresh, cool	**fresquísimo** very fresh
largo long	**larguísimo** very long

4. The expanded diphthongs **ie, ue,** occasionally, in literary Spanish, revert to their primitive vowels **e** and **o,** since the accent is transferred to the termination (§ 12):

bueno good	**bonísimo** very good
nuevo new	**novísimo** very new
fuerte strong	**fortísimo** very strong
ferviente fervent	**ferventísimo** very fervent

5. The termination **ble** reverts to the Latin *bil:*[2]

notable notable	**notabilísimo** very notable
voluble voluble	**volubilísimo** very voluble
terrible terrible	**terribilísimo** very terrible

[1] Many adjectives in **io** and **ío** do not admit the superlative termination; as, for example, **lacio, temerario, vario; sombrío, tardío, vacío,** etc.

[2] **Doble** *double;* **endeble** *frail;* **feble** *feeble,* are exceptions, since they are not Latin:

una dalia doblísima	a very double dahlia

6. Adjectives ending in **-fico, -volo** (from the Latin *-ficent, -volent*) substitute these latter before **ísimo:**

		LATIN
benéfico beneficent	**beneficentísimo**	*beneficentissimus*
benévolo benevolent	**benevolentísimo**	*benevolentissimus*
magnífico magnificent	**magnificentísimo**	*magnificentissimus*
munífico munificent	**munificentísimo**	*munificentissimus*

7. A few adjectives ending in **-ro** or **-re** (from Latin *-er*) may revert to the original Latin for the entire words:

			LATIN	
ACRE:	**acérrimo**	very bitter	*acer,*	*acerrimus*
ÁSPERO:	**aspérrimo**	very harsh	*asper,*	*asperrimus*
CÉLEBRE:	**celebérrimo**	very celebrated	*celeber,*	*celeberrimus*
ÍNTEGRO:	**integérrimo**	very upright	*integer,*	*integerrimus*
LIBRE:	**libérrimo**	very free	*liber,*	*liberrimus*
MÍSERO:	**misérrimo**	very wretched	*miser,*	*miserrimus*
POBRE:	**paupérrimo**	very poor	*pauper,*	*pauperrimus*
SALUBRE:	**salubérrimo**	very healthful	*saluber,*	*saluberrimus*
———	**ubérrimo**	very fertile	*uber,*	*uberrimus*

a. The forms **asperísimo** and **pobrísimo** are in commoner use.

b. **Ubérrimo** has no positive in Spanish, it place being supplied by **feraz** *fertile* (Lat. *ferax*). The positive *uber* was rare even among the Romans.

8. A few other adjectives, too various to be classified, may occasionally in literary language revert to the original Latin forms:

AMIGO*:	**amicísimo**	very friendly	*amicus,*	*amicissimus*
ANTIGUO*:	**antiquísimo**	very ancient	*antiquus,*	*antiquissimus*
CRUEL*:	**crudelísimo**	very cruel	*crudelis,*	*crudelissimus*
DIFÍCIL*:	**dificílimo**	very difficult	*difficilis,*	*difficillimus*
FÁCIL*:	**facílimo**	very easy	*facilis,*	*facillimus*
FIEL:	**fidelísimo**	very faithful	*fidelis,*	*fidelissimus*
FRÍO*:	**frigidísimo**	very cold	*frigidus,*	*frigidissimus*
PÍO: / PIADOSO*:	**pientísimo**	very devout	*pien[t]s,*[1]	*pientissimus*
SABIO:	**sapientísimo**	very wise	*sapien[t]s,*	*sapientissimus*
SACRO: / SAGRADO*:	**sacratísimo**	very sacred	*sacratus,*	*(wanting)*

NOTE. Those distinguished by an asterisk have regular superlatives which are more commonly met with.

8.54. A number of comparatives and superlatives have descended

[1] Rare.

from the Latin with little change of form, but retaining little of comparative or superlative force, and are to be considered as simple adjectives:

anterior previous, preceding	*(wanting)*
citerior hither	*(wanting)*
exterior external, outside	**extremo** extreme
inferior inferior, lower	**ínfimo** lowest
interior internal, inside	**íntimo** intimate
posterior posterior	**postremo** hindermost
(más cercano) nearer	**próximo** nearest, next
superior superior, upper	**supremo** / **sumo** } supreme, highest
ulterior ulterior, ultimate	**último** last

8.55. Instead of the regular absolute superlatives of **bueno, malo, grande** and **pequeño,** other forms are met with derived from the Latin superlatives, which were irregular. But these belong rather to the literary style than to everyday language:

BUENO:	**bonísimo**	*or*	**óptimo**	LATIN *optimus*
MALO:	**malísimo**	*or*	**pésimo**	*pessimus*
GRANDE:	**grandísimo**	*or*	**máximo**	*maximus*
PEQUEÑO:	**pequeñísimo**	*or*	**mínimo**	*minimus*

8.56. The above forms are occasionally used as simple adjectives, from which comparatives and superlatives may be formed:

Los mandó llevar a la estación más próxima del ferrocarril.	He had them taken to the nearest railway station.
Cuando más tarde atravesó aquellas calles, ya no encontró en ellas la más mínima señal de la confusión de la mañana.	When he went through those streets later on, he no longer found the least trace of the morning's confusion.
No lo quiero vender a precio tan ínfimo.	I do not wish to sell it at so low a price.
No me descompuse lo más mínimo por los insultos del enano.	I did not bother myself in the least about the dwarf's insults.
Hizo traición a su más íntimo amigo.	He betrayed his most intimate friend.

ABSOLUTE SUPERLATIVE OF ADVERBS

8.57. The absolute superlative of simple adverbs is formed in the same manner as that of adjectives; the distinctive ending **(-a)** of **cerca** *near* is transferred to the superlative termination:

pronto	soon	**prontísimo**	very soon
cerca	near	**cerquísima**	very near
lejos	far	**lejísimo(s)**	very far

8.58. In the case of derivative adverbs formed by adding **mente** to an adjective, the superlative termination is attached to the adjective; and as **mente** requires the adjective to be in the feminine, the termination assumes the form **ísima:**

noblemente	nobly	**nobilísimamente**	very nobly
ricamente	richly	**riquísimamente**	very richly
desproporcionadamente	disproportionately	**desproporcionadísimamente**	out of all proportion

8.59. The effect of the absolute superlative may also be obtained by placing before an adjective or adverb some such adverb or adverbial phrase as **muy** *very,* **sumamente** *highly,* **extremadamente** *extremely,* **en extremo** *to the extreme,* **en gran manera** *to a great degree,* **en alto grado** *to a high degree,* or by placing **además** after the word which is to convey the superlative idea. But the superlative termination has the most power, in addition to being much neater:

Las pruebas resultaron sumamente satisfactorias.	The tests proved highly satisfactory.
Sus esfuerzos nos parecían en alto grado ridículos.	His efforts seemed to be highly ridiculous.
La tentativa será peligrosa además.	The attempt will be fraught with great danger.
Muy pronto.	Very soon.

8.60. In popular language **re, rete** and **requete** are occasionally prefixed to adjectives, adverbs or even other parts of speech to add intensity; these intensified words may be accompanied by **muy, más,** etc.:

Es una tarea redifícil.	It is an awfully hard job.
Me saben muy rebién estas frambuesas.	These raspberries taste real good to me.
¡Jesús, y que no está Elena satisfecha viendo a la niña tan reteguapísima! (Martínez Sierra, **Primavera en otoño,** I)	Heavens, and isn't Helen satisfied to see the child so very handsome!
¡Ay, qué hijo más requetesimpático! (Martínez Sierra, **Mamá,** I)	Oh, what an extra fine son!

Foro ha hecho requetebién. Yo hubiera hecho otro tanto. (Palacio Valdés, **Sinfonía pastoral, Presto finale,** V)	Foro has done very, very well. I would have done the same.

NOTE. Many adjectives do not admit of comparison. The principal ones are those that involve the idea of infinity, or already express a superlative degree, or denote origin, material, shape or class:

supremo	metálico	principal	inmenso
italiano	circular	triangular	inmortal
infernal	militar	clerical	celestial

Some adjectives on account of their form do not admit the termination **–ísimo.** They are principally those which have an antepenultimate stress; those which end in **–eo, –ico, –imo, –fero;** those which end in **i** or **y;** and those which end in **–il** and refer to age, sex or condition:

sanguíneo	turquí	colérico	marítimo	juvenil	ignívomo
férreo	satírico	verdegay	legítimo	argentífero	senil

REMARK. Some adjectives of these forms may receive the termination **–ísimo** in burlesque style.

8.61. In conversational style intensification of adverbial and also adjectival expressions is not infrequently obtained by repetition of the expression:

Casi casi es preciso poner al contribuyente delante de una horca para que pague. (Pérez Galdós, **Miau,** XXII)	It is very, very nearly necessary to stand the taxpayer before a gallows so that he will pay.
Conque ya ven ustedes como así, a lo tonto a lo tonto, ha venido sobre mi Asilo el pan de cada día. (Pérez Galdós, **Fortunata y Jacinta,** I, 7, 1)	And so you see how in this way, without my seeming to be conscious of it, every day's bread has been provided for my Asylum.
En aquel momento, don Fernando se hubiera metamorfoseado de buena gana en ratón, y acaso acaso, en murciélago. (Palacio Valdés, **José,** X)	At that moment, Don Fernando would willingly have turned himself into a mouse, and perhaps into a bat.
Soy el hombre más infeliz más infeliz que hay bajo la capa del cielo. (Pardo Bazán, **La madre Naturaleza,** XXVIII)	I am positively the most unhappy man that there is under heaven.

IX
Adjective Pronouns

9.1. Adjective pronouns, as the name indicates, partake of the nature of both adjectives and pronouns. Their adjective quality is that they can be used with nouns; their pronominal quality, that they can be used instead of nouns, and that they express—not qualities, but relations; they can, moreover, be applied to any person or thing, whereas an adjective is applicable only to persons or things having the quality that it represents. Some of them are employed in their uninflected form as adverbs; some are varied like adjectives, and others invariable.

NOTE. The limits of the class are necessarily not well defined, and some of the members are of such an intermediate character that authorities may well differ in their classification; in most textbooks they will be found scattered among various denominations.

We will first treat of the following, in order:

todo, –a, –os, –as	every, all
entero, –a, –os, –as	whole, entire
cada *(invariable)*	each, every
mucho, –a, –os, –as	much, many
poco, –a, –os, –as	little, few
único, –a, –os, –as	only
solo, –a, –os, –as	alone, only

9.2. Todo, in the singular, followed by a definite article, possessive or demonstrative before a noun, signifies the entire quantity or amount of that noun; it may then be translated by *all:*

Leyó todo **el** día.	He read all day.
Bebió toda **la** cerveza.	He drank all the beer.
Ella gasta todo **su** dinero en frioleras.	She spends all her money in trifles.
Todo **aquel** terreno es baldío.	All that land is worthless.

REMARK. Without appreciable difference in meaning **todo** may follow the noun, the latter being preceded by the definite article or possessive adjective. Such usage is relatively infrequent: **mi vida toda, las naciones todas** *all my life, all nations.* (Unamuno, **Recuerdos de niñez y de mocedad,** II, 7; I, 5)

9.3. Todo, in the singular, when not followed by such defining word, indicates the entire class represented by the noun; it may then often be translated by *every:*

Todo hombre honrado lo rechaza.	Every honest man rejects it.
Toda obra importante requiere trabajo.	Every important work requires labor.
Toda tentativa para forzar la puerta fué infructuosa.	Every attempt to force the door was fruitless.
En toda ocasión; en todo caso; a toda costa.	On every occasion; at all events; at any cost.
A todo correr; a todo vapor; a toda prisa.	At full speed; under full steam; with all haste.

9.4. Todo, in the plural, and associated with one of the defining words above indicated, denotes the entire number of whatever it refers to:

Todas las clases le honran.	All classes honor him.
Todos estos huevos están hueros.	All these eggs are addled.
Todos nuestros esfuerzos fueron inútiles.	All our efforts were useless.
Por consiguiente todas esas explicaciones no explicaban nada.	Consequently all those explanations explained nothing.

REMARK. **Todos, –as,** before a definite article and a measure of time, is to be translated in English by *every,* with the noun in the singular:

El médico viene todas las horas.	The doctor comes every hour.
Sale todas las noches a las diez.	He goes out every night at ten.
Todos los lunes; todas las semanas; todos los quince días.	Every Monday; every week; every fortnight.

9.5. Todo seldom appears in the plural unaccompanied by one of the defining words above mentioned, except in certain indefinite phrases:

Huyeron los indios en todas direcciones.	The Indians fled in all directions.
En todas partes.	Everywhere *(rest).*

Por todas partes.	Everywhere *(motion).*
A todas horas del día.	At all hours of the day.
Tintas de imprimir de todas clases.	Printing inks of all kinds.
Mármoles de todos colores.	Marbles of all colors.
De todos modos no será preciso escribirle.	At all events it will not be necessary to write to him.

9.6. Used pronominally, **todo** appears in the singular as a neuter only, and has the meaning of *everything, all:*

Contiene un poco de todo.	It contains a little of everything.
Todo favorecía la fuga de los prisioneros.	Everything favored the escape of the prisoners.
Sobre todo; ante todo.	Above all; first of all.
Ante todo es preciso hacer provisión de combustible.	First of all it is necessary to get a supply of fuel.
Lo haré a pesar de todo.	I shall do it in spite of everything.
Estamos dispuestos a todo.	We are prepared for anything.
Esto es todo por ahora.	That is all for the present.

9.7. Used pronominally in the plural and not referring to a previous noun, it denotes persons only:

Todos admiten la justicia de su pretensión.	All concede the justice of his claim.
Esta es la opinión de todos.	This is the opinion of every one.

9.8. Standing for a noun in the plural, **todos, -as,** refers to either persons or things; when standing for persons, the preposition a is required when **todos, -as,** is the object of a verb, or is in apposition to an objective personal pronoun:

Seis hombres bajaron, todos armados con fusiles.	Six men descended, all armed with muskets.
Las he vendido todas *(houses).*	I have sold them all.
Las saludé a todas *(ladies).*	I greeted them all.
Nos ha convidado a todos.	He has invited us all.

9.9. When **todo** is connected by a relative with something following, an antecedent must be supplied, as **todo** alone is not used as such:

Todos **los** que han escrito sobre el asunto nos dan informes contradictorios sobre el estado político actual de Europa.	All who have written on the subject give us conflicting accounts of the present political status of Europe.

Interrogó a todos **los** que tomaron parte en el asalto.	He questioned all who took part in the assault.
Todo **el** que. Todo **aquel** que.	Everyone who.

9.10. In this manner the neuter **todo** followed by **lo que** forms a neuter phrase corresponding to the English *all that* (*that* being elidable):

Me ha referido **todo lo que** sucedió.	He has related to me all that happened.
Quitáronle los bandoleros la ropa que llevaba, que era **todo lo que** le quedaba en el mundo.	The robbers took from him the clothes he wore, which was all that he had in the world.
Tengo **todo lo que** quiero.	I have all I want.

9.11. In the case of the expression of similar meaning **todo cuanto** (**todos cuantos**) the antecedent is included in the relative:

Mataron a **todos cuantos** encontraron.	They killed all they found.
Ha vendido **todo cuanto** poseía para satisfacer su pasión por el juego.	He sold all he possessed to satisfy his passion for gambling.

9.12. The plural of **todo** may either precede or follow a plural personal pronoun. The English usage of placing *of* before a pronoun when *all* precedes has no parallel in Spanish:

nosotros todos *or* todos nosotros	we all *or* all of us
Vds. todos *or* todos Vds.	you all *or* all of you
ellos todos *or* todos ellos ellas todas *or* todas ellas	they all *or* all of them

9.13. **Todo** may precede an indefinite article and a noun, while its English equivalent would usually be placed between them:

Pasamos allí **todo un** invierno.	We spent a whole winter there.
Las aves marinas se arrojaron sobre el cadáver del cetáceo, lanzando graznidos capaces de ensordecer **a todo un** Congreso.	The seafowl pounced upon the body of the cetacean, uttering cries capable of deafening a whole Congress.
No dudaban que la isla estaba habitada y tenía quizá **toda una** colonia dispuesta a defenderla.	They did not doubt that the island was inhabited and perhaps had a whole colony prepared to defend it.
El tío Lucas era **todo un** hombre. (Alarcón, **El sombrero de tres picos**, VII)	Uncle Lucas was altogether a man (*or* quite a man).

9.14. **Todo,** as a neuter, may be applied to any neuter pronominal or adjective expressions:

Redundará todo eso en nuestro provecho.	All that will turn out to our advantage.
Todo lo demás no importa.	All the rest does not matter.
Todo lo cual es verdad.	All of which is true.
Ha gastado todo lo suyo.	He has squandered all his property.
Tiene todo lo necesario para su viaje.	He has everything necessary for his journey.
Eran aficionados a todo lo concerniente a la aerostática.	They were interested in everything concerning aerostatics.
Todo lo largo del río.	All along the river.
Todo lo largo de la calle.	All along the street.

9.15. When **todo,** used absolutely as a neuter, occurs as the object of a verb, but stands before it, the pronoun **lo** is added, showing that it is object (cf. § **4.17**) :

¿Qué nombre damos a este gran ser que **todo lo** ha creado y que es tan superior a todas sus criaturas?	What name do we give to this great being who has created *everything* and who is so superior to all his creatures?
No tenían ni una arma, ni un instrumento, ni siquiera un cortaplumas. **Todo lo** habían echado fuera de la barquilla para aligerar el globo.	They had not a weapon, nor an instrument, nor even a penknife. They had thrown *everything* out of the basket to lighten the balloon.
Anselmo partió al amanecer, y dos horas después el timbre eléctrico anunció que **todo lo** había encontrado en orden en la empalizada.	Anselmo started at daybreak, and two hours afterwards the electric bell announced that he had found *everything* in order at the stockade.
Para mí, contestó, el estudio es un apoyo, un aliciente, una diversión que **todo** me **lo** hace olvidar.	To me, he replied, study is a support, an attraction, a diversion, that makes me forget *everything*.

9.16. **Todo** is idiomatically used with the larger measures of time to denote some indefinite point within the period mentioned (cf. § **11.14**) :

En todo el otoño venidero.	During next autumn.
Lo haré construir en todo el mes de enero.	I shall have it built some time in January.

9.17. **Todos, -as,** requires the definite article before numerals:

Llegaron todos los cuatro a la misma hora.	All four arrived at the same time.
Todas las tres han ido al baile de máscaras.	All three have gone to the masked ball.

9.18. The expression **todo el mundo** is used as a stereotyped phrase meaning *everybody;* in society, *everyone of any consequence;* nautically, *all hands:*

Todo el mundo ha ido a los baños de mar.	Everybody has gone to the seashore.
Todo el mundo asistió.	Everybody was present.
¡Todo el mundo arriba!	All hands on deck!

9.19. The uninflected form **todo** is used adverbially with the meaning of *entirely, all;* this use of **todo** is generally rather colloquial:

El negocio ha salido todo al revés de lo que esperábamos.	The affair has turned out quite to the contrary of what we expected.
La inspiración no acude todo lo de prisa que él desearía. (Martínez Sierra, **Sueño de una noche de agosto,** II, end)	Inspiration does not come altogether so quickly as he would desire.

REMARK I. There are other cases apparently similar in appearance in which **todo** is an adjective agreeing with a noun or pronoun (cf. § **31.9,** REMARK):

Su biblioteca, que no es pequeña, es toda novelas y poesías.	Her library, which is not a small one, is all novels and poetry.
Este pez todo es espinas.	This fish is all bones.
El cielo era todo fuego; un relámpago no daba espera a otro.	The sky was all ablaze; there was no intermission between one flash of lightning and another.

REMARK II. In some authors **todo** is used invariably in this construction: **Y luego me retiene ver a mi madre, que es todo ternura para nosotros.** (Baroja, **La dama errante,** XX) *And then it holds me back to see my mother, who is all affection for us.* **Son fiestas todo vida y todo fuerza.** (Benavente, **Más fuerte que el amor,** III, 7) *They are entertainments all life, all force.*

9.20. **Todo** may be used as a noun with the meaning of *whole, total:*

¿Cuánto pide V. por **el todo?**	What do you ask for *the lot?*
El **todo** es mayor que cualquiera de sus partes.	*The whole* is greater than any of its parts.
No comprendemos más que una mínima parte **del gran todo.**	We do not understand more than a very small part of *the whole thing.*

9.21. **Entero** coincides in some respects with **todo**, meaning *whole, entire* or *all;* it always follows its noun:

Comió un pan entero.	He ate a whole loaf.
Empleó días enteros en copiarlo.	He spent whole days in copying it.
La noche entera; toda la noche.	All night.

9.22. **Cada** *each, every* is invariable in form and is used only before singular nouns:

Cada vez que viene trae un libro.	Every time he comes he brings a book.
Iba disminuyéndose sensiblemente el intervalo que separaba cada relámpago de cada trueno.	The interval which separated each lightning flash from each clap of thunder was sensibly diminishing.

9.23. In colloquial language **cada** is used in sentences of exclamatory value with the meaning of *all kinds of, one after another, so many, such,* etc.:

Después de llorar copiosamente en brazos de su madre, la cual daba cada gemido que partía el corazón, perdió el conocimiento. (Pérez Galdós, **El amigo Manso,** XXXI)	After weeping copiously in her mother's arms, each one of whose moans was enough to break the heart, she lost consciousness.
A mí me han jugado cada mala pasada. (Baroja, **La feria de los discretos,** I)	They have played me one bad trick after another.
Oye una cada historia. (Benavente, **Por las nubes,** I, 9)	One hears all sorts of stories.

9.24. **Cada,** however, may be associated with a plural noun preceded by a numeral and used as a collective expression:

Una tienda para cada doce soldados.	A tent for each twelve soldiers.
La luna cambia cada 28 días próximamente.	The moon changes about every 28 days.

9.25. **Cada** cannot stand in place of a noun; in order to be used pronominally it must be followed by **uno** or **cual,** the latter of which is not followed by **de** + noun:

Cada una de las señoritas tenía puesto un traje distinto.	Each of the young ladies had on a different toilet.
Cada uno llevó su mochila.	Each one carried his knapsack.
Di a cada cual lo que mereció.	I gave to each what he deserved.
Cada cual fué a tomar el puesto que le correspondía.	Each one went to assume the post which corresponded to him.

9.26. **Mucho,** as a declinable adjective pronoun, precedes nouns or stands in place of them; in the singular it is to be rendered by *much, a great deal of;* in the plural, by *many* or *a great many:*

Lo haré con mucho gusto.	I will do so with much pleasure.
No tenemos mucho tiempo.	We haven't much time.
He vendido mucha harina.	I have sold a great deal of flour.
Hemos recibido muchas cartas.	We have received a great many letters.

REMARK. **Mucho** and also **poco, tanto, cuanto** are idiomatically used with a singular noun though the meaning is plural. For a somewhat similar use of **alguno,** see § 9.46. The effect is not infrequently to disparage:

Hay mucha columna y mucha lápida de mármol blanco. (Baroja, **El mundo es ansí,** II, 3)	There are many columns and many white marble tablets.
¡Qué hombres hay, Señor! ¡Cuánta lengua venenosa! (Pérez de Ayala, **Luz de domingo,** VII)	What people there are, Lord! How many poisonous tongues!
No sé para qué queréis tanta flor. (Benavente, **Al natural,** II, 2)	I don't know what you want so many flowers for.

9.27. The uninflected form **mucho** is used with a neuter value, and occasionally as an adverb qualifying verbs:

Mucho quedaba aún por hacer.	Much still remained to be done.
Mucho dependía de su prudencia.	A great deal depended on his prudence.
Escribe mucho.	He writes a great deal.
Eso no me gusta mucho.	That does not please me much.

9.28. **Mucho** is intimately connected in meaning with the adverb **muy.** **Muy** qualifies the positive form of adjectives or adverbs,[1] but

[1] The comparative forms **mayor, menor, mejor, peor,** whether used as adjectives or adverbs, are nowadays qualified by **mucho,** not **muy: Yo estuve a tu edad mucho peor que tú; me quedé en puros huesos.** (Unamuno, **El espejo de la muerta, historia muy vulgar**) *At your age I was in much worse health than you; I was down to sheer bone.*

is never used with verbs. It is to be rendered in English by *very;* before past participles it means *much:*

muy bueno; muy bien; muy lejos	very good; very well; very far
Estoy muy molesto.	I am very annoyed.
BUT: Esta novela es **mucho más (menos) interesante.**	This novel is *much more (less) interesting.*
Este café era **muy** frecuentado por los artistas.	This café was *much* frequented by artists.
Las tierras altas no están **muy** cultivadas, aunque tienen un suelo fértil y bien regado.	The highlands are not *much* cultivated, although they have a fertile and well-watered soil.

9.29. **Muy** cannot stand alone, as may the English *very.* After a question or statement containing **muy** and requiring acquiescence, **mucho** is the word used:

¿Escribe bien el nuevo dependiente? —**Mucho.**	Does the new clerk write well?—*Very.*
Esta es una colección muy interesante. —Sí, **mucho.**	This is a very interesting collection. —Yes, *very.*

9.30. In modern Spanish **mucho** is not usually intensified by **muy,** although examples are encountered. **Muchísimo** *very much* is the customary expression in literary language:

Ella es **muchísimo** más agradable que su hermana.	She is *very much* more pleasant than her sister.
La cabeza me duele **muchísimo.**	My head aches *very much.*
Yo le miré **muy mucho** para ver si me columbraba. (Pérez Galdós, **El amigo Manso,** XXVIII)	I looked at you *a very great deal* to see if you recognized me.
Es cosa que debe meditarse **muy mucho.** (Alvarez Quintero, **El genio alegre,** III)	It is a matter which must be thought over *a very great deal.*

9.31. **Muy** before an adjective which is followed by **para** is equivalent to **demasiado** *too* or *too much.* **Mucho** alone or **mucho, -a** before a noun may be used in the same construction, in which case **mucho** takes on the same meaning as **muy:**

Estaba **muy** asustado para ofrecer resistencia.	He was *too* much frightened to offer resistance.
Mi marido es **muy** caballero **para** manifestar su enojo en presencia de ella.	My husband is *too* well-mannered to show his annoyance in her presence.

Vió que la distancia que separaba las rocas era **muy** larga **para** poder salvarse de un salto, y se arrojó al agua. — He saw that the distance that separated the rocks was *too* great to be cleared with a jump, and he threw himself into the water.

Don Félix nos quería **mucho para** fatigarnos con el estudio. (Unamuno, **Recuerdos de niñez y de mocedad,** II, 4) — Don Felix loved us *too much* to fatigue us with study.

9.32. The employment of **poco** is identical with that of **mucho.** In the singular it is to be rendered by *little;* in the plural, by *few:*

"**Poco** dinero, **pocos** amigos." — "*Little* money, *few* friends."

De esas maravillas he visto yo **pocas.** — I have seen *few* of those marvels.

Las siete plagas de Egipto parecían **poca cosa** a los de la huerta **para** arrojarlas sobre aquellos terrenos malditos. (Blasco Ibáñez, **La barraca,** I) — The seven *plagues* of Egypt seemed to the residents of the huerta *too small a thing* to hurl upon those cursed lands.

Las horas del día le parecían **pocas para** orar. (Palacio Valdés, **Marta y María,** V) — The hours of the day seemed to her *too few* for her prayers.

REMARK. It may be appropriate to observe that the concept of **too** + adjective or adverb is often expressed in Spanish by the use merely of the adjective or adverb:

Es **temprano.** — It is *too early.*

Es **tarde.** — It is *too late.*

Es **mucho.** — It is *too much.*

Es **poco.** — It is *too little.*

Con lo que tengo, que es **poco** para vivir de caballero, habría lo suficiente para adquirir la hacienda de un labrador acomodado. (Pereda, **La puchera,** XXVII) — With what I have, which is *too little* to live as a gentleman, there would be enough to acquire here the property of a rich farmer.

Yo soy ya **viejo** para competir contigo. (Baroja, **La leyenda de Jaun de Alzate,** II, 5) — I am already *too old* to compete with you.

9.33. The uninflected form **poco** is used as a neuter meaning *little,* and as an adverb with the signification of *little, not very.* In its adverbial use it is an exact counterpart of **muy** in meaning and has the same variety of application:

Queda **poco** que decir de esta materia. — *Little* remains to be said of this matter.

Vió que sus perseguidores **poco a poco** iban ganando terreno sobre él. — He saw that his pursuers were gaining ground on him *little* by *little.*

Un libro **poco** interesante. — A *not very* interesting book.

La noche era hermosa y tranquila, y la oscuridad **poco** profunda todavía. — The evening was fine and still, and the darkness *not* yet *very* intense.

Su padre era **poco** indulgente. — His father was *not very* indulgent.

El hijo de V. escribe **poco** bien.—Sí, **poco.** — Your son does *not* write *very* well.—No, *not very.*

9.34. Poco, in any of its acceptations, may be preceded by the indefinite article; the distinction is then the same as that exhibited in English between *little* and *a little:*

Hemos tomado **un poco** de vino. — We have taken *a little* wine.

Hemos bebido **poco vino.** — We have drunk *little* wine.

Me gusta **poco.** — It pleases me *little.*

Me gusta **un poco.** — It pleases me *a little.*

Habla **poco.** — He speaks *little.*

Hablo **un poco** el castellano. — I speak Spanish *a little.*

Tenemos **pocos** enemigos. — We have *few* enemies.

Tenemos **unos pocos** enemigos. — We have *a few* enemies.

REMARK. The use of **una poca (de)** + a feminine singular noun, instead of the invariable **un poco de,** is not rare in the spoken language, especially in America, though practically banished from literary Spanish:

Valerio se acomodó **una poca ropa** en su poncho. (Güiraldes, **Don Segundo Sombra,** VI) — Valerio placed *a little clothing* in his poncho.

Bebe **una poca agua.** (Benavente, **La malquerida,** III, 9) — Drink *a little water.*

Figueredo tiene más razón que un santo. —**Una poca,** sí. (Linares Rivas, **Cobardías,** I, 9) — Figueredo is more right than a saint. —*A little bit,* yes.

Antes que aquí se formen costumbres en armonía con el constitucionalismo, tiene que ir **una poca de agua** a su molino de usted. (Pardo Bazán, **La Madre Naturaleza,** X) — Before habits are formed here in harmony with constitutional government, *a little bit of water* has to go to your mill.

Hace bien en gastarse **una poca de plata** en eso. (Gallegos, **Doña Bárbara,** II, I)	He does well in spending *a little money* on that.

9.35. **Poco,** in any of its values, may be intensified by **muy,** or the absolute superlative form **poquísimo** may be used:

Tenemos **muy poca** luz.	We have *very little* light.
El sol ha lucido **poquísimo** durante la semana pasada.	The sun has shone *very little* during the past week.

9.36. **Solo** is used as an adjective with the meaning of *alone, sole, single, only, solitary.* As an adverb it is equivalent to **solamente** *only* for which it is a preferred shorter form. The adverbial employment of **solo** is signalized by an accent—**sólo.** Occasionally, **tan** is used before **sólo:**

Quedó **solo.**	He remained *alone.*
¿Ha venido V. **sola,** señorita?	Did you come *alone,* Miss?
Hoy la **sola** idea de marchar le producía el mismo efecto. (Pardo Bazán, **Los pazos de Ulloa,** XIX)	Today *only* the idea of departing produced the same effect on him.
Este mal tan grande no tiene una **sola** raíz sino muchas y diversas.	This great evil has not *one single* root but many and various.
Sólo tengo dos. Tengo dos **solamente.**	I have *only* two.
La noche era oscura; **sólo** algunos relámpagos de calor, reflejos de una tempestad lejana, iluminaban el horizonte.	The night was dark; *only* some heat-lightning, the reflection of a distant storm, illuminated the horizon.
Aun entonces, se las daré **tan sólo** a quien merezca oírlas. (Alarcón, **El sombrero de tres picos,** XXXIII)	Even then, I shall give them *only* to him who deserves to hear them.
No se trataba, como ustedes ven, de suprimir la fabricación ni la importación de alcohol, sino **tan sólo** de poner ambas cosas fuera de la ley. (Camba, **El pistolerismo,** IV, in **La ciudad automática**)	It was not a question, as you see, of suppressing the manufacture or the importing of alcohol but *only* of putting both things outside the law.

Remark. The addition of **tan,** which perhaps adds a degree of emphasis in the cases above, is found also with **siquiera:**

No hay que contar nada, ni **tan siquiera** mirarlo. (Benavente, **La honradez de la cerradura,** III, 3)	It is not necessary to count anything or *even* to look at it.

9.37. Único is not wholly synonymous with **solo.** It is used only adjectively, is not preceded ordinarily by the indefinite article, and has the meaning of *sole, single, only, unique:*

Un hijo **único.**	An *only* son.
Era el **único** sostén de su madre anciana.	He was the *only* support of his aged mother.
Es lo **único** que puedo responder a V.	It is the *only thing* that I can answer you.
Aquel eco lejano fué la **única** respuesta que obtuvieron sus gritos.	That distant echo was the *sole* answer that their shouts obtained.

REMARK. After **por, todo** is sometimes used interchangeably with **único:**

Anselmo **por toda** respuesta me indicó un paquete que reposaba sobre la mesa.	Anselmo *as his only* answer pointed out to me a package which lay upon the table.

We will now consider the following adjective pronouns:

otro, –a, –os, –as	other, another, others
algo	something
alguien	someone
alguno, –a	some
alguno que otro *(declinable)*	some . . . or other
uno, –a, –os, –as	one, some
unos, –as cuantos, –as	some, a few
uno y otro / **ambos** / **entrambos** *(declinable)*	both
varios, –as	various, several
el, la, lo, los, las demás	the rest, the others
mismo, –a, –os, –as	same; self, selves
propio, –a, –os, –as	own; self, selves
ajeno, –a, –os, –as	another's, somebody else's
cierto, –a, –os, –as	certain
sendos, –as	apiece
tal, –es	such
semejante, –es	similar, like, such
tamaño, –a, –os, –as	as much, as many

9.38. Otro, used adjectively or pronominally, applies to persons or things. When a particular person or thing is to be designated, **otro** is preceded by the definite article or demonstrative adjective. But it does not admit the indefinite article as in English *another* (*an + other*):

Otro tomo; **el otro tomo.** — *Another* volume; *the other* volume.

Busco **otro;** busco **el otro.** — I am looking for *another;* I am looking for *the other.*

Queremos **otros;** queremos **los otros.** — We want *some others;* we want *the others.*

Mi **otra** hija; sus **otras** fincas. — My *other* daughter; his *other* estates.

Estos otros grabados; **ese otro** lío. — *These other* engravings; *that other* bundle.

¿Dónde encontraré **otra** mujer igual? — Where will I find *another* woman like her?

De **otro** modo, de **otra** manera. — *Other*wise.

REMARK. **Otro** will occasionally be found appended to **este, ese—estotro** *this other;* **esotro** *that other*—although it is more usual nowadays to write them as separate words.

9.39. **Otra cosa** is a current phrase meaning *something else;* after an interrogative, *anything else;* with a negative, *nothing else:*

Otra cosa que el acaso ha producido el orden admirable del universo. — *Something else* than chance has produced the admirable order of the universe.

No piensa en **otra cosa** que en comer. — He doesn't think of *anything else* but eating.

No en **otra cosa** que en la justicia está cimentada la seguridad de las sociedades humanas. — The safety of human society is founded on *nothing else* but justice.

Yo no hago más que emitir una conjetura y no **otra cosa.** — I only express a conjecture and *nothing else.*

9.40. **Otro tanto** means *as much again, likewise* (repeating the idea of a previous expression), etc.; **otros tantos,** *as many more:*

Cerré los ojos. Creo que mis compañeros debieron hacer **otro tanto.** (Palacio Valdés, **Polifemo,** in **Aguas fuertes**) — I closed my eyes. I think that my companions must have done *likewise.*

Dieron la callada por respuesta y el interlocutor quedó corrido. **Otro tanto** le acaeció a don Raimundo Perejil. (Pérez de Ayala, **La caída de los Limones,** I) — They answered with silence and the speaker was abashed. *As much again* [*the same thing*] happened to Don Raimundo Perejil.

El resplandor de la luz eléctrica trasformaba las menores puntas de la — The brightness of the electric light transformed the minor points of

caverna en **otros tantos** carbunclos resplandecientes.	the cavern into *so many* glittering carbuncles.
De repente surcaron la oscuridad varios relámpagos, y luego estallaron **otras tantas** detonaciones.	Suddenly several flashes pierced the darkness and immediately afterwards an *equal number of* reports rang out.
La mitad y **otro tanto.** *(A slang phrase for the whole of anything.)*	As much again as half. *(Lit.* the half and as much more.)

9.41. Numerals and adjectives of quantity are preferably placed after the plural **otros, -as:**

Al norte **otros dos** cabos cerraban la bahía.	To the north *two other* capes shut in the bay.
Este distrito produce cobre, hierro, azogue, estaño, carbón y **otros muchos** minerales preciosos.	This district produces copper, iron, mercury, tin, coal and *many other* valuable minerals.
Y **otras muchas** cosas.	And *many other* things.
Desde su tiempo **otros varios** exploradores han intentado lo mismo.	Since his time *various other* explorers have attempted the same thing.
Citaremos a tres personas entre **otras mil.**	We will cite three persons among a *thousand others.*

9.42. Algo applies only to things. It may be used before an adjective just as *something* or *anything* is in English:

¿Busca V. **algo**?	Are you looking for *anything*?
Veo **algo** blanco.	I see *something* white.
¿Hace el muchacho **algo** útil?	Does the boy do *anything* useful?
¿Tiene V. **algo** bonito?	Have you *anything* pretty?

REMARK. An adjective following **algo** is often preceded by **de:**

Tengo **algo de** interesante.	I have *something* interesting.
¿Dicen **algo de** nuevo?	Do they say *anything* new?

9.43. Algo is also used as an adverb before adjectives or other adverbs in the sense of *somewhat, rather:*

Ella es **algo** preguntona.	She is *rather* inquisitive.
Mi padre está **algo** malhumorado hoy.	My father is *somewhat* ill-humored today.
Viene **algo** tarde, **algo** temprano.	He comes *rather* late, *rather* early.

9.44. Alguien applies to persons only. It may be preceded by any preposition. Since **alguien** denotes a person, it requires **a** when it is a direct object:

Alguien viene; **alguien** habla.	*Somebody* is coming; *someone* speaks.
¿Estudia V. con **alguien**?	Do you study with *anyone?*
¿Busca V. a **alguien**?	Are you looking for *someone?*
¿Ve V. a **alguien**?	Do you see *anybody?*

9.45. **Alguno** is used either alone or as an adjective, and applies to persons or things. It is varied like any adjective in **o**.

9.46. Referring to persons, **alguno** means *some, any, a few, an occasional, someone, anyone, somebody, anybody,* and requires the preposition **a** when it is the direct object:

Alguna niña; **algunos** soldados.	*Some* girl; *some* soldiers.
Vemos **a alguno** de los amigos de V.	We see *one* of your friends.
Voy a llamar **a alguno.**	I am going to call *one* (of them).
Pepita juega al tresillo con mi padre, con el señor Vicario y con **algún otro.** (Valera, **Pepita Jiménez, 7 de mayo**)	Pepita plays tresillo with my father, with the Vicar and with an *occasional* other man.
Una noche de invierno llovía en las calles de San Juan de Luz. **Algún** mechero de gas temblaba a impulsos del viento. (Baroja, **Zalacaín el aventurero,** II, 7)	One winter night it was raining in Saint-Jean de Luz. An *occasional* gas lamp (or A gas lamp *here and there)* flickered in the wind.

9.47. **Alguno,** used absolutely and denoting a person, is distinguished from **alguien** in this, that **alguno** applies to some one of a number already referred to or thought of; **alguien,** to somebody not previously considered. So **alguien** is not, like **alguno,** properly followed by **de,** to indicate some one of a number, although such usage is occasionally encountered:[1]

¿Ve V. a alguien?	Do you see anybody?
¿Ve V. a alguno?	Do you see any one (of those we are looking for)?
Alguien viene.	Someone *(unknown)* is coming.
Alguno viene.	Some one (of those we expect) is coming.
Alguno de mis amigos viene.	Some one of my friends is coming.

REMARK. Of course where a distinction of number or gender is required, the appropriate form of **alguno** takes the place of **alguien:**

[1] **Hablar...de lo que alguien de los presentes no puede entender.** (Benavente, **Titania,** I, 1) *To speak...of what some one of those present cannot understand.*

Veo a alguna.	I see somebody *(female).*
Algunos vienen.	Some folks are coming.

9.48. **Alguno,** when referring to things, has the meaning of *some, any, a few, an occasional.* It is oftener omitted before a noun than the corresponding English words (§ 9.49):

Voy a vender algunos de mis caballos.	I am going to sell some of my horses.
Quiero comprar algunos libros.	I want to buy a few books.
Yo también quiero comprar algunos.	I also wish to buy some.
¿Tiene V. tabaco?	Have you any tobacco?
Sí, tengo.	Yes, I have some.
Allí se pasaba largas horas, charlando, enterándose del expedienteo, fumando algún cigarrillo. (Pérez Galdós, **Miau, XXI**)	He spent long hours, there, chatting, informing himself of the business at hand, smoking an occasional cigarette.

9.49. It is not usual to employ a word corresponding to English *any* in such connections as the following:

¿Tiene V. azúcar?	Have you *any* sugar?
¿Tiene él cigarros?	Has he *any* cigars?
No tenemos tinta.	We haven't *any* ink.

9.50. The expression **alguno que otro,** when a noun follows **otro** or **alguno,** corresponds to English *some...or other, an occasional:*

El está buscando siempre **alguno que otro pretexto** para verla.	He is always seeking *some pretext or other* to see her.
La vereda, ensanchándose, se internaba por tierra montañosa, salpicada de manchones de robledal y **algún que otro castaño.** (Pardo Bazán, **Los pazos de Ulloa, I**)	The path, growing wider, entered mountainous country, spattered with patches of oak groves and *an occasional chestnut tree.*
Te hacía **alguna pregunta que otra.** (Pereda, **Nubes de estío, XI**)	I asked you *an occasional question.*

9.51. In this expression **uno** frequently takes the place of **alguno:**

Por entre esas ramas, flotantes y sombrías, pasan algunos rayos de luz, y **uno que otro** pájaro atraviesa esas ráfagas, volando perezoso.	A few rays of light penetrate among those dark and waving branches, and occasionally a bird, flying lazily, crosses those streaks of light.
Uno que otro chirrido, **uno que otro** canto interrumpe el silencio del bosque.	An occasional chirp, an occasional carol, interrupts the silence of the forest.

9.52. **Uno,** with which we are familiar as a numeral and indefinite article, is also an adjective pronoun of complete inflection, meaning *some:*

Un día veremos.	Some day we shall see.
Unas señoras están abajo y quieren verla a V.	Some ladies are down stairs and wish to see you, Ma'am.

9.53. The plural **unos, unas,** is weaker and more indefinite than **algunos** *some* and expresses a feeling of indifference as to the exact number. In some phrases it corresponds to *a pair of:*

Tenía unos cigarros por aquí, pero ya no los encuentro.	I had some cigarettes around here, but I don't find them any more.
Su pintura representaba un canasto con unas frutas.	His painting represented a basket with fruit.
Tenía unos bonitos ojos picarescos. (Palacio Valdés, **Sinfonía pastoral, Adagio cantábile,** V)	She had a pair of mischievous pretty eyes.

9.54. **Uno** may be used with a partitive effect, followed by the preposition **de** and a noun:

Uno de los puntos principales de interés en este lugar es la fábrica de seda.	One of the principal points of interest in this place is the silk factory.

9.55. The plural **unos,** however, is not so used; its place is taken by **algunos:**

Algunos de sus camaradas.	Some of his comrades (chums).
Algunas de las mujeres.	Some of the women.
Algunas de estas fresas (*not* unas).	Some of these strawberries.

REMARK. We may say **unos camaradas suyos** *some chums of his,* but preferably not **unos de sus camaradas.**

9.56. The combination **unos cuantos** is more definite than **unos,** and is interchangeable with **algunos** *some, a few:*

Allí vi a **unos cuantos** chicos jugando a la pelota.	I saw *a few* boys there playing ball.
Con excepción de **unas cuantas** personas cuyos negocios las obligaron a regresar a Barcelona, la partida llegó a la capital al día siguiente.	With the exception of *a few* persons whose business obliged them to return to Barcelona, the party arrived at the capital the next day.
Después de **unos cuantos** golpes de remo, la piragua tocó tierra.	After *a few* strokes of the oar, the boat touched land.

9.57. **Uno** is contrasted with **otro** in many ways. Contrary to the English usage, when employed absolutely it seldom takes the definite article:

Una cosa es el agradecimiento, y **otra** el amor.	Gratitude is *one* thing and love *another*.
La compañía mantiene dos casas de huéspedes para sus operarios, **una** para los hombres y **otra** para las mujeres.	The company keeps two boarding-houses for its operatives, *one* for the men, the *other* for the women.
Le dije que era imposible continuar de este modo—que era preciso resolver **una** cosa u **otra.**	I told her that it was impossible to go on in this way—that it was necessary to decide on *one* thing or the *other.*

9.58. **Uno y otro** is used with the meaning of *both* when we wish to preserve the separate identity of *each* of two nouns:

Uno y otro han contribuido materialmente al buen éxito del proyecto.	*Both* have contributed materially to the success of the scheme.
Será fácil abrir una carretera entre **uno y otro** punto.	It will be easy to cut a road between the *two* points.
Los cazadores, introduciendo sus venablos de **uno y otro** lado, lograron poner la tortuga patas arriba.	The hunters, introducing their spears from *each* side, succeeded in turning the tortoise over on his back.
Al ver allí a doña Tula y a don Oscar, hice dos profundas y consecutivas reverencias a **uno** y **otro.**	On seeing Doña Tula and Don Oscar there, I made them *two* profound and separate bows.

9.59. **Uno u otro** means *either* of two individuals; **unos u otros,** *either* of two groups. Their negative forms are **ni uno ni otro** *neither;* **ni unos ni otros,** *neither group*. Either, or each, member may assume the feminine form according as may be required:

¿Quiere V. el "Imparcial" o el "Globo"? —**Uno u otro,** no importa cuál.	Do you wish the "Impartial" or the "Globe"? —*Either;* it does not matter which.
¿Le mandaré libros franceses o españoles? —**Unos u otros;** lee ambos idiomas con facilidad.	Shall I send him French or Spanish books? —*Either;* he reads both languages with ease.
No voto **ni** por **el uno ni** por **el otro.**	I shall vote for *neither.*
Juana, si viene la señora Caldas o su hermano, no estoy en casa **ni** para **una ni** para **otro.** ¿Entiendes?	Jane, if Mrs. Caldas or her brother comes, I am not at home to *either* of them. Understand?

9.60. **Uno,** to avoid repetition, may take the place of a noun, and be qualified by an adjective or participle (cf. § 5.22):

La idea de V. es buena, pero creo tener una mejor.	Your idea is good, but I think I have a better one.
¿Quiere V. un cuello grande volteado o uno corto parado?	Will you have a deep turned-down collar or a small stand-up one?

9.61. **Uno + como** or a phrase of similar meaning, followed by a noun, has the meaning of *a sort of, something like,* etc.:

Una como oleada de vida iluminó entonces por un instante la cara morena de la muchacha. (Lynch, **El inglés de los güesos,** XXIII)	*Something like* a surge of life lighted up the girl's dark face for an instant.
Después vimos entrar **uno como** sacristán. (Pérez Galdós, **La familia de León Roch,** I, 2, 7)	Afterwards we saw a fellow *like a* sacristan come in.
Se puso en **uno a modo de** carro triunfal tirado por un jamelgo. (Valera, **Sobre el arte de escribir novelas,** I, toward end)	He got into *a sort of* triumphal chariot drawn by a sorry nag.
Allen dijo que podíamos hacer **unas a modo de** suelas para los pies. (Baroja, **Las inquietudes de Shanti Andía,** VII, 4)	Allen said that we could make *something like* wide soles for our feet.

9.62. **Ambos** *both* is one of the very few words that may be said to be of the dual number, applicable only to two:

Resultaron ambas proposiciones aprobadas por unanimidad.	Both propositions were unanimously adopted.
Ambos ríos son muy caudalosos.	Both rivers are very large.
Ambas orillas son altas y escabrosas.	Both banks are high and rugged.

REMARK. **Ambos** is usually replaced by **los dos** in colloquial language; thus we could also say:

Resultaron las dos proposiciones aprobadas por unanimidad.	Both propositions were unanimously adopted.
Los dos ríos; las dos orillas.	Both rivers; both banks.

9.63. **Entrambos,** in its present usage, is interchangeable with **ambos.** It originally signified *between two* (**entre ambos**). But this meaning is now expressed by **ambos a dos,** or **entrambos a dos** *between the two.* These are all literary or at least archaic nowadays:

Ella se quedó inmóvil, agarrada con entrambas manos a las rejas. — She remained motionless, clinging with both hands to the railings.

Consiguieron levantar la piedra entrambos a dos. — They succeeded between them in lifting the stone.

9.64. **Varios** *several, a good many* is employed either as an adjective or a noun; it has no singular:

Los operarios de la fábrica han formado varias sociedades de recreo e instrucción. — The factory hands have organized several societies of amusement and instruction.

Varias clases de lámparas de piano y de mesa. — Various styles of piano and table lamps.

Sacos de papel de varios tamaños. — Paper bags of various sizes.

9.65. A popular equivalent of **varios** is **una porción de** *several* although sometimes conveying the idea of considerable extent or numbers:

Ya se lo había dicho **una porción de** veces. — I had already told him so *several* times.

Atravesó **una porción de** calles sin apercibirse siquiera de lo que hacía. — He crossed *several* streets without even taking account of what he was doing.

Había citado **una porción de** casos semejantes.[1] — He had cited *quite a number of* similar cases.

9.66. **Demás** is invariable in form; preceded by the definite article, which serves to distinguish number and gender, it means *the rest, the others.* The neuter **lo demás** is equivalent to *everything else:*

Cada gobierno, en la forma admitida, puede dar independientemente de **los demás** su adhesión a los referidos tratados. — Each government may, in the prescribed form, give its adhesion, independently of the rest, to the treaties referred to.

Es bien conocido el principio legal de que la afirmación de una cosa implica la exclusión de todas **las demás.** — The legal maxim is well known to the effect that the expression of one thing implies the exclusion of all others.

Por **lo demás,** su observación era lógica. — Besides, his remark was logical.

Lo demás importa poco. — All else matters but little.

---

[1] In colloquial use **un porción (de)** is frequent: **Hay un porción de animales que no hacen daño ni a las personas ni a las casas.** (Baroja, **Aventuras, inventos y mixtificaciones de Silvestre Paradox,** I) *There are lots of animals that are not harmful to persons or to houses.*

REMARK. **De más** in the predicate, means *superfluous;* compare the analogous French *de trop:*

Abandonó bruscamente aquella sociedad donde se sentía estar de más.	He hastily left that society where he felt himself to be out of place.
En los tiempos tumultuosos actuales no está de más toda clase de precauciones.	In the present troublous times no kind of precaution is superfluous.

9.67. **Mismo** *same* when used adjectively, precedes its noun, and is itself preceded by some qualifying word — article, or demonstrative or an equivalent term. The neuter **lo mismo** is used absolutely and means *the same thing:*

También soy yo del **mismo** parecer.	I'm of the *same* opinion too.
Esta nueva tentativa obtuvo el **mismo** resultado.	This new attempt obtained the *same* result.
Será **lo mismo** que si él se lo hubiera dado a V.	It will be *the same thing* as if he had given it to you.

9.68. There is a distinction between the values of **el mismo** and **un mismo.** The former supposes a comparison, which the latter does not. The distinction is not carefully observed, however, the tendency being to use **el mismo** in either case:

Esta casa es **del mismo** dueño que la vecina.	This house belongs to *the same* owner as the one next door.
Eran solteros, mozos de **una misma** edad y unas mismas costumbres.	They were bachelors, young fellows of *one and the same* age and the same habits.
Ambos tenían **un mismo** odio a los ingleses, **una misma** astucia en concebir sus proyectos, **una misma** crueldad en ejecutarlos; eran una alma en dos cuerpos.	Both had *one and the same* hatred of the English, *one and the same* cunning in devising their plans, *one and the same* cruelty in executing them; they were one soul in two bodies.

9.69. **Mismo,** following a noun or the nominative or prepositional form of a personal pronoun, has an intensive or emphatic effect, which may be rendered by *self,*[1] *very* or *even:*

Habla demasiado de sí mismo.	He talks too much about himself.
Sus hijos saben más que ellos mismos.	Their children know more than they [do] themselves.

[1] **Mismo,** though frequently applied to reflexive pronouns, is never reflexive as the English *self* sometimes is. (See § § **3.51–3.53.**)

Vale más de lo que ella misma se figura. — It is worth more than she herself imagines.

El camino era aquí tan áspero y escarpado que las mulas mismas experimentaron suma dificultad en seguir adelante. — The road was here so rugged and steep that even the mules experienced extreme difficulty in going forward.

REMARK. The student should avoid confusing **el mismo, la misma,** with **él mismo, ella misma.** The former denote merely likeness or identity; the latter are emphatic:

Este hombre no es ya **el mismo** [que antes era]. *(Likeness)* — This man is no longer *the same* [as he was before].

Esta mujer no es **la misma** [que antes vimos]. *(Identity)* — This woman is not *the same one* [that we saw before].

El mismo salió a mi encuentro. — *He himself* came out to meet me.

Ella misma nos lo dijo. — She told us so *herself*.

9.70. In the case of nouns, **mismo** with the definite article or a possessive adjective may with the same effect be placed *before* a noun. The preposition **hasta** is occasionally used with similar emphasis either alone or in conjunction with **mismo:**

Los mismos verdugos temblaron al oír sus palabras. — *The very* executioners trembled on hearing his words.

Hasta **los mismos** cactos parecían encogerse bajo la influencia de los rayos abrasadores. — Even *the very* cactus plants seemed to shrivel under the influence of the scorching rays.

9.71. After adverbs of time and place, **mismo** is invariable with the meaning of *this* or *that very,* though in some cases it cannot be rendered in English:

Hoy mismo; ahora mismo. — This very day; this very moment.

Ayer mismo; mañana mismo. — Only yesterday; tomorrow.

Aquí mismo; allí mismo. — In this very place; that very place.

9.72. **Mismo** has a superlative form **mismísimo** *very same, self-same,* which is declinable and is used only before nouns:

Partió por casualidad en el **mismísimo** vapor que su rival. — He left by chance in the *very same* steamer as his rival.

Y allí vi los **mismísimos** versos. — And there I saw the *self-same* verses.

9.73. **Propio** emphasizes the word it accompanies. After a possessive adjective it is rendered *own;* in general it is interchangeable with **mismo** *self,* though not so widely used (cf. § **5.18**):

Cada estado hace por sí mismo sus **propias** leyes respecto a la herencia.	Each state makes for itself its *own* laws respecting inheritance.
Ellos propios han hecho la mismísima cosa.	*They* have done the very same thing *themselves.*

9.74. As a pure adjective, **propio** is followed by one of the prepositions **de, para** or **a.** With **de** it means *becoming, appropriate to;* with **para** or **a,** *suitable for,* with this distinction, that with **para propio** denotes immediate *suitableness* and with **a** future *adaptability:*

Su conducta no era **propia de** un oficial y caballero.	His conduct was *unbecoming* an officer and gentleman.
Me parece que su discurso no era **propio de** ocasión tan solemne.	It seems to me that his speech was not *appropriate to* so solemn an occasion.
Esta yerba no es **propia para** el ganado.	This grass is not *suitable for* stock.
Estas frutas son **propias a** hacer dulces.	This fruit is *suitable for* preserving.
Un hombre **propio para** todo.	A man *available for* anything.
Un hombre **propio a** todo.	A man *adaptable to* anything.

9.75. Ajeno (derived from Lat. *alienus,* but equivalent to Lat. *alterius)* serves as a possessive to **otro** with the pronominal signification of *somebody else's, other people's.* It is thus the opposite of **propio** *own:*

El hombre discreto percibe las **faltas ajenas,** pero no habla de ellas.	The discreet man notices the *faults of others,* but does not speak of them.
Así somos los hombres; hablamos de los **dolores ajenos** con una gran frialdad.	So it is with us men; we talk of *other people's sufferings* with great calmness.

9.76. Ajeno, as a pure adjective, means *foreign to* or *unaware of* and is followed by **de:**

La proposición me parece ser **ajena del** cometido de nuestra comisión.	The proposition appears to me to be *foreign to* the scope of our committee.
Entretanto el preso se hallaba muy	In the meantime the prisoner was

ajeno de la suerte que le aguardaba. — quite *unaware of* the fate that awaited him.

¡Qué **ajena** estaba **de** tenerle tan cerca! — How *oblivious* I was *of* his being so near!

9.77. **Cierto (a)** *certain* applies to persons or things which we wish to indicate, but about which we do not care to be explicit. It is then always followed by a noun, and is not infrequently accompanied by the indefinite article when it refers to degree:

El director de **cierta** revista literaria me había pedido un cuento para su naciente publicación. (Palacio Valdés, **Seducción**) — The director of *a certain* literary review had asked me for a story for his budding journal.

Hasta **cierto** punto era esto verdad. — To *a certain* point this was true.

Mostraba **cierta** superioridad que me humillaba. — He exhibited *a certain* superiority which humiliated me.

Lo dije así por **cierto** instinto dramático que todas las mujeres tenemos. — I said it so through *a certain* dramatic instinct which all of us women have.

Ciertos inviernos son muy rigurosos en España. — *Certain* winters in Spain are very severe.

Pero la contenía **un cierto** respeto que no acertaba a explicarse. (Pérez Galdós, **Fortunata y Jacinta,** III, 3, 2) — But she was restrained by *a certain* respect which she couldn't quite understand.

El trágico Tajo parece iniciar también **una cierta** tendencia a la lírica al internarse en tierras portuguesas. (Camba, **Aventuras de una peseta,** IV, 2) — The tragic Tagus also seems to begin *a certain* tendency toward lyricism on entering Portuguese territory.

9.78. **Cierto,** as a pure adjective, always following its noun, or standing in the predicate alone, has the literal meaning of *certain* in the sense of *reliable:*

Hemos recibido **noticias ciertas** de que la inundación reciente ha causado grandes perjuicios al trigo. — We have received *reliable information* that the recent flood has caused great damage to the grain.

Un **indicio cierto; pruebas ciertas;** una **muerte cierta.** — A *certain indication; sure proof;* a *certain death.*

No es **cierto** lo que dice. — What he says is not *reliable.*

9.79. **Tal** *such* when used adjectively, is not followed by the indefinite article, as is the case in English in the singular:

No quería arriesgar de **tal** modo su vida y la de sus compañeros.	He did not wish to risk in *such a* way his life and that of his companions.
Contra **tales** obstáculos es inútil luchar.	It is useless to struggle against *such* obstacles.
Por **tal** y **tal** causa.	For *such and such a* cause
Bajo **tales** y **tales** condiciones.	Under *such and such* conditions.

9.80. Used absolutely, **tal** is frequently followed by a further statement, which is introduced by either **como** or **que,** with this distinction, that **tal como** expresses a comparison, **tal que,** a result:

Bajo aquella bóveda de hojas la oscuridad era **tal que** no podían distinguir la vereda.	Under that vault of foliage the darkness was *such that* they could not distinguish the path.
Los estallidos del trueno eran continuos entonces, y su violencia **tal que** era imposible oír una palabra.	The peals of thunder were then continuous, and their violence *such that* it was impossible to hear a word.
El capitán había hablado con **tal** acento de convencimiento **que** sus compañeros no tuvieron objeción alguna que suscitar.	The captain had spoken with *such a* tone of conviction *that* his companions had no objection to raise.
No tengo papel **tal como** V. quiere.	I have no paper *such as* you want.
No encontramos a los indígenas **tales como** nos los habían descrito los libros de viajes.[1]	We did not find the natives *such as* the books of travels had described them to us.

9.81. **Tal** is used absolutely as an indeclinable neuter, meaning *such a thing:*

No quiero creer **tal** de su parte.	I won't believe *such a thing* of him.
Nunca he visto ni oído **tal.**	I have never seen or heard of *such a thing.*

REMARK. **Tal,** in the above connection, is now commonly replaced by **tal cosa:**

No permitiré **tal cosa.**	I will not allow *such a thing.*

[1] Though an adjective use might be expected, **tal** is also used by some writers as an adverb: **Las cosas ocurrían tal como él las anunciaba.** (Blasco Ibáñez, **Cañas y barro,** VII) *Things were happening just as he foretold them.* **Ese espacio y ese tiempo y ese principio de causalidad no existen fuera de nosotros tal como nosotros los vemos.** (Baroja, **El árbol de la ciencia,** IV, 1) *That space and that time and that principle of causality do not exist outside of us as we see them.*

9.82. **Tal** may be used adverbially to add emphasis to a statement or question:

¿Qué tal le parece a V. el resultado?	How does the result seem to you?
Sí tal; no tal.	Yes indeed; no indeed.
¿Y qué tal van tus amores con la hija del conde?	And how goes your love affair with the count's daughter?

9.83. **Tal** is preceded by the indefinite article only when used with the name of a person, in which case it has the meaning of *one, a certain.* Before other nouns the equivalent term is **cierto:**

Me lo dijo **un tal** Palomares.	*One* Palomares told me so.
Cierto joven turco, **un tal** Hassán, que anteriormente había vivido allí, y por consiguiente conocía el país, ofreció enseñarnos la vereda.	A certain Turkish youth, *one* Hassan, who had formerly lived there and consequently knew the country, offered to show us the path.

9.84. **El tal, la tal,** etc., applied to names of persons or things familiarly known, imparts an air of joviality:

Pero **el tal** criado no era tan tonto.	But the said servant wasn't such a fool.
Como **la tal** condesa era muy esclava de la moda, no podía obrar de otro modo.	As the countess was much a slave to fashion, she could not act otherwise.
El tal borrico no quiso ir ni adelante ni atrás.	The rascal of a donkey would neither go forwards nor backwards.
Era un hombre acreditado **el tal** Rodríguez.	He was a man of repute, this Rodriguez.

NOTE. Frequent in the spoken language is the expression **otro, -a (que) tal** meaning *another of the same kind, sort,* etc.:

Su padre era un bendito de Dios, y su madre **otra que tal.** (Pereda, La Montálvez, X, near end)	His father was a simple soul, and his mother *another of the same stripe.*

9.85. **Cual** is often used as a correlative to **tal** in comparisons of two similar persons, things or statements (cf. § **8.18**):

Según su doctrina, la vida futura será **tal cual** ha sido la de este mundo.	According to their belief, the future life will be *in accordance with what* that of this world has been.
Habían amueblado de nuevo algunas piezas; pero el resto de la casa lo habían dejado **tal cual** estaba antes.	They had refurnished a few rooms; but the rest of the house they had left *just as* it was before.

9.86. **Semejante** meaning *such, like, similar* is interchangeable with **tal** before nouns:

Semejante conducta merece el vituperio de todos.	Such conduct deserves the condemnation of all.
Los exploradores han hallado restos semejantes en todas partes de Asia.	Explorers have found similar remains in all parts of Asia.

9.87. **Sendos** has a distributive effect, being corrupted from the Latin *singulos,* and means *one apiece.* It is used only in the plural and is not often encountered in conversation:

Los jueces llevaban sendas pelucas.	The judges all had on wigs.
Regaló al duque sendas espadas de Damasco y de Toledo.	He gave the Duke two swords, of Damascus and Toledo respectively.
Los seis gitanos montados en sendos burros, cabalgaban detrás de los demás.	The six gypsies, mounted on as many donkeys, rode behind the rest.
La reina distribuyó entre los generales sendas medallas de esmalte y oro.	The queen distributed among the generals a medal apiece of gold and enamel.

9.88. **Uno, hombre, gente,** and with a negative, **persona,** are occasionally used pronominally, unaccompanied by an article, with the vague meaning of *someone, anyone;* a like effect may be obtained by placing the verb in the plural without a subject:[1]

No está uno siempre preparado a improvisar un discurso.	One is not always prepared to make an impromptu speech.
No vimos a persona con quien hablar.	We didn't see a person to talk to.
No quedó persona con vida.	No one was left alive.
No siempre es una dueña de sí misma.	One is not always mistress of one's self.
Llegar hombre a su casa y no encontrar escalera para subir a su cuarto, no es cosa de risa para gente cansada.	For a fellow to get home and not find any stairs to go up to his room by is not a laughing matter for tired folk.

9.89. **Cosa** *thing* is often used with a pronominal value, while

[1] **Uno,** contrary to English usage of *one,* has a more subjective value, and in colloquial style practically means *I.* Moreover, in familiar language **uno** may mean *a fellow, an individual:* **¿Tienes algo? —Es que he reñido con uno.** (Baroja, **El mundo es ansí,** III, 20) *Is something wrong? — The fact is that I have had a fight with a fellow.*

retaining its feminine gender. It is equivalent to *something, anything;* with a negative, *nothing:*

¿Qué le ha sucedido? Tiene V. la camisa toda ensangrentada. —Oh, no es **cosa**; un araño.	What has happened to you? Your shirt is all bloody. —Oh, it is *nothing;* a mere scratch.
¡Qué paisaje tan monótono! Ya hemos caminado veinte leguas sin ver **cosa** interesante.	What a monotonous landscape! We have already come sixty miles without seeing *anything* interesting.
El honorable delegado ha llevado su bondad hasta el extremo de intimar que yo sé muy **poca cosa** acerca del asunto.	The honorable delegate has been so kind as to intimate that I know *very little* about the subject.

9.90. **Alguna cosa** is a popular form of **algo,** with which it is interchangeable; in like manner **ninguna cosa** or **cosa alguna** is a substitute for **nada:**

Ya no se interesa en **cosa alguna.**	She no longer takes an interest in *anything.*
No encontraremos **ninguna cosa** más apropiada.	We shall not find *anything* more suitable.

9.91. **Tamaño** (from the Latin *tam magnus)* is used with exclamatory or relative force referring to size, either large or small:

Nunca había experimentado tamaña desvergüenza.	He never had experienced so great impudence.
Un brillante tamaño como una avellana.	A diamond as large as a hazel-nut.

REMARK. As a mere noun, **tamaño** is to be rendered by *size:*

¿Tiene V. una tuerca de este tamaño?	Have you a nut of this size?
Era un tiburón de gran tamaño.	It was a shark of large size.

X

Relative Pronouns

10.1. A relative pronoun connects two propositions having something in common. It belongs logically to the second of the two, and relates back to a person or thing mentioned in the first, which is called the *antecedent.* A relative is generally equivalent to a personal or demonstrative pronoun preceded by a conjunction:

Last winter my father bought two horses *which* died in the following spring.	Last winter my father bought two horses *and they* died in the following spring.

10.2. By far the most commonly used relative in Spanish is **que,** which is applicable alike as subject or object to persons or things of either gender or number.

Que follows close after its antecedent, so that, although it is invariable in form, we are at no loss to see what it refers to. A preposition may intervene when its relates to things; but when it relates to persons, no preposition is admissible:

Eligió en la playa un sitio despejado **que** el mar había nivelado perfectamente.	He selected on the beach a clear space *which* the sea had leveled perfectly.
Los asuntos **que** hemos sido invitados a considerar.	The matters *which* we have been invited to consider.
Los albañiles **que** hemos ajustado.	The bricklayers *whom* we have hired.
La yerba de **que** están alfombrados los prados.	The grass with *which* the meadows are carpeted.
Los estudios a **que** dedico mis horas desocupadas.	The studies to *which* I devote my leisure hours.

10.3. **Que** is invariable, having but one form for both genders and numbers; when used as subject or as direct object, it relates to persons or things of either gender or number. But it is normally preceded by a preposition only when it relates to things, though it is occasionally used of nouns referring to persons:

La señora que acaba de salir.	The lady who has just gone out.
Los soldados que he visto.	The soldiers whom I have seen.
La gramática que estudio.	The grammar that I am studying.
Las causas que determinan mis acciones.	The causes which determine my actions.
La facilidad con que escribe.	The facility which which he writes.
El asunto de que hablamos.	The matter of which we are speaking.
La casa en que vivo.	The house in which I live.
Trae a ese juez con que me amenazabas. (Pérez Galdós, **El amigo Manso,** XXXVI, end)	Bring that judge with whom you were threatening me.
Oye, ¿en qué piececilla trabaja esa muchacha de que me hablaste? (Benavente, **Rosas de otoño,** I, 2)	Listen, in what number is that girl of whom you spoke to me acting?
A mí ya me da sombra; a mi mujer flores para mi mesa...y para los santos en que ella cree. (Alvarez Quintero, **Doña Clarines,** II)	To me of course it gives shade, to my wife flowers for my table... and for the saints in whom she believes.

10.4. The relative pronoun is never suppressed in Spanish as it frequently is in English:

Las señoras **que** esperamos.	The ladies we expect.
El vino **que** hemos bebido	The wine we have drunk.
¿Dónde están los libros **que** acabo de comprar?	Where are the books I have just bought?

10.5. Que is preferable to **quien** as a direct object, and although referring to persons, it does not require the preposition **a:**

El hombre **que** (a quien) he visto.	The man I have seen.
Las señoras **que** (a quienes) esperamos.	The ladies whom we are expecting.

10.6. In Spanish the preposition must always precede the relative; the English construction of placing it last is inadmissible:

El error **en que** estamos.	The error *which* we are *in*.
Las leyes **a que** estamos sujetos.	The laws *which* we are subject *to*.
El hombre **de quien** he recibido el libro es un capitán del ejército turco.	The man I received the book *from* is a captain in the Turkish army.

10.7. Quien refers to persons or things personified. It is preceded by the preposition **a** when it is the direct object of a verb:

El arzobispo, a **quien** he visto hoy, me ha dicho...	The archbishop, *whom* I have seen today, told me...
Busco al hombre **a quien** V. busca.	I am looking for the man *whom* you are looking for.

REMARK. Although **quien** is properly used of things only when personified, the distinction between personification and non-personification is not always sharp:

Es el alma quien padece y no el cuerpo. (Palacio Valdés, **Marta y María,** IX)	It is the soul and not the body that suffers.
Allá lejos, sobre verde colina, a quien bañan por el norte el océano y por levante una tortuosa ría, está Ficóbriga. (Pérez Galdós, **Gloria,** I, 1)	There in the distance, on a green hill, which is bathed on the north by the ocean and on the east by a winding estuary, is Ficóbriga.

10.8. Quien is rarely used as subject in conversational style (cf. § **10.2** and § **10.3**), that duty being generally performed by **que. Quien** is invariable in form as regards gender, but it has a plural: **quienes.** (The older plural **quien** has, however, by no means disappeared from the language.[1]) It may be preceded by any preposition:

He recibido estas flores de una señora **a quien** he servido varias veces.	I have received these flowers from a lady whom I have aided several times.
Es un amigo **en quien** tengo confianza.	He is a friend in whom I have confidence.
Los oficiales **con quienes** he hablado sobre el suceso.	The officials with whom I have spoken about the occurrence.
Las mujeres **de quienes** hablamos.	The women of whom we speak.
Depende también de las personas **con quien** uno se junta. (Pérez Galdós, **Fortunata y Jacinta,** IV, 6, 12)	It depends also on the persons with whom one associates.
Después, [brindemos] por estos señoritos **a quien** no tengo el honor de conocer. (Benavente, **Las cigarras hormigas,** II, 18)	Afterwards, [let us drink a toast] to these young gentlemen whom I do not have the honor of knowing.

[1] The same is true of the interrogative use: **¿Pero quién son ellos para despreciar a mi hijo?** (Benavente, **Al fin, mujer,** III, 2, 3) *But who are they to spurn my son?*

10.9. As **que** governed by a preposition is not applied to persons, **quien** *who* is used in its place; just as in English we may say "the man *that*," but have to say "the man *from whom*." **Quien** is confined to persons, collective bodies of persons, and things personified:[1]

La persona a quien me recomendó V. ha prometido conseguirme un empleo.	The person to whom you recommended me has promised to get me a job.
Los autores de quienes he sacado estos ejemplos.	The authors from whom I have taken these examples.
Era hombre a quien nada significaban los medios si se consiguiera el fin.	He was a man to whom the means were of no consequence if the end was attained.
Pronto se mostraba la Aurora a quien saludaban los pájaros con alegres gorjeos.	Soon the dawn showed itself and the birds greeted it with joyous carols.

10.10. A peculiarity of **quien** either as subject or object is that it may, like **cuanto** (cf. § **10.25**), include its antecedent; it is then equivalent to *he who,* plural *those who:*

Quien no sabe esto es ignorante de veras.	*He who* does not know that is ignorant indeed.
La culpa no fué suya, sino **de quien** se lo aconsejó.	The fault was not his, but of *the person who* advised him [to do] it.
Afirman **quienes** presenciaron la erupción que la columna de cenizas fué proyectada hasta una altura de cinco millas.	*Those who* witnessed the eruption assert that the column of ashes was thrown to a height of five miles.
Quien más se distinguió en estas escaramuzas fué el teniente C.	*He who* most distinguished himself in these skirmishes was Lieut. C.
No teniendo **a quién** consultar, ideé una traza que me produjo el mejor resultado posible.	Not having *anyone* to consult, I devised a scheme which produced the best possible result.

REMARK. In English a like combination is presented by *what* = *that which,* rendered in Spanish, as we have seen, by **lo que.**

10.11. Used in this sense (meaning *he who, those who),* **quien** is not necessarily the first word of the clause:

[1] Some instances of the use of **quien** may be personifications or survivals of a more indiscriminate use: **No era el amor solamente quien le empujaba.** (Palacio Valdés, **Marta y María,** IV) *It was not love alone that impelled him.* Cf. § **10.7,** REMARK.

Soldados son quienes vienen. Quienes vienen son soldados.	Those who are coming are soldiers.
El corresponsal del Heraldo fué quien hizo esta pregunta.	It was the correspondent of the Herald who asked this question.
Francia fué en efecto quien fundó los primeros establecimientos extranjeros en la parte inferior del Plata.	It was indeed France who founded the first foreign settlements in the lower part of the Plata.
Hay quien envidia la suerte del escritor viajero. (Camba, **Aventuras de una peseta, Advertencia**)	There are those who envy the lot of the traveling journalist.
No había quien le quisiera mal en el pueblo ni en todos los del contorno. (Benavente, **La infanzona,** I, 4)	There was no one who bore him ill will in town or in all those roundabout.

10.12. When **quien** does not include its antecedent as above, it cannot be the subject of a sentence except when used as supplementary to an antecedent clause which is otherwise complete in itself:

El tiburón con un vigoroso aletazo se lanzó sobre el negro, **quien,** echándose diestramente a un lado, logró evitar el ataque del animal.	The shark, by a vigorous stroke, darted upon the Negro, who, throwing himself dextrously to one side, succeeded in avoiding the animal's attack.
No asistiré a la función de esta tarde; me quedaré en casa para escribir a mi esposa, **quien** está mala en San Francisco.	I shall not go to the play this evening. I shall stay at home and write to my wife, who is sick in San Francisco.
El primer europeo que tendió la vista por el inmenso piélago llamado, a causa de la tranquilidad de sus aguas, Océano Pacífico, fué Vasco Núñez de Balboa, **quien** tomó posesión de él a nombre del rey de España.	The first European who cast his gaze over the immense sea called, because of the stillness of its waters, Pacific Ocean, was Vasco Núñez de Balboa, who took possession of it in the name of the King of Spain.

10.13. The following contrasted examples illustrate the distinction in the usage and value of **que** and **quien** as subject of a relative clause. Both are permissible after a comma but **que** is the more colloquial, **quien** the more literary:

El rey confió esta misión a un diplomático **que** había vivido seis años en Constantinopla.	The king entrusted this mission to a diplomat *who* had lived six years in Constantinople.

El rey confió esta misión al conde Roberto, **quien** había vivido seis años en Constantinopla.	The king entrusted this mission to Count Robert, *who* had lived six years in Constantinople.
Este hermano Juan, **que** sólo contaba veinte años, vino a verle en la Pola. (Palacio Valdés, **Sinfonía pastoral, Andante con moto,** III)	This brother John, *who* was only twenty years old, came to see him in La Pola.
El dueño de la casa, **que** está muy deteriorada, me ha encargado de repararla.	The owner of the house, *which* is very dilapidated, has engaged me to repair it.
El dueño de la casa, **quien** está actualmente en el extranjero, me ha encargado de repararla.	The owner of the house, *who* is at present abroad, has engaged me to repair it.

EL CUAL[1] AND **EL QUE**

10.14. **Cual,** plural **cuales,** corresponds to the English *which,* as **que** does to *that.* **Cual** and **que,** preceded by the article **el, la, lo, los, las,** form relatives more precise than **quien** or **que** alone, as they have the advantage of inflection.

The two do not differ in meaning, and may be used as subject or object relating either to persons or things; but **el cual** belongs rather to a studied or oratorical, and **el que** to a more easy and off-hand, style—just the difference between *which* and *that* in English.

10.15. **El cual** or **el que** is substituted for **quien** and **que** (according as a person or thing is referred to) under the following circumstances:

1. When two or more nouns differing in gender or number in the antecedent clause require to be kept distinct. **El cual,** or **el que,** can then by means of its inflection point directly to the word intended:

Me dió unos apuntes sobre las costumbres del país, **los cuales** me fueron después muy útiles.	He gave me some points on the customs of the country *which* were very useful to me afterwards.
Le mando a V. la narración de los viajes de Dampier, **la que** hallará V. muy interesante.	I send you the narrative of Dampier's voyages, *which* you will find very interesting.

[1] The association of the definite article to **cual** was unknown in Spanish prior to the XIVth century. On account of its full inflection of gender and number, which facilitated the connection of clauses, it was universally adopted and had a marked influence upon the style of that period, as was evinced by the interminable sentences, pages in length, which soon became prevalent.

Mi abuelo nos contó unas anécdotas de Diógenes, **las que** nos divirtieron bastante. — My grandfather told us some anecdotes of Diogenes *which* amused us hugely.

Otras veces corría un arroyuelo al través de la espesura, **el que** atravesaban sin trabajo los exploradores. — At other times a brook ran through the undergrowth, which the explorers crossed without difficulty.

El barón de cuando en cuando daba batidas por aquellos bosques a **las cuales** convidaba a sus amigos. — The baron from time to time gave hunting parties in those woods, to *which* he invited his friends.

2. After a clause making sense by itself, and requiring a pause—more or less slight—in speech or a punctuation mark in writing, **el cual** or **el que** serves to resume the thread of discourse:

Los cazadores, apenas entraron en la espesura, vieron al perro luchando con un animal desconocido, **al cual** tenía asido por una oreja. — The hunters had scarcely entered the thicket when they saw the dog struggling with an unknown animal *which* he held fast by one ear.

Esta carta llegará a manos de V. por conducto de un criado que ha estado largo tiempo en mi servicio y **del cual** estoy seguro. — This letter will reach your hands through the medium of a servant who has been a long time in my service and *of whom* I am confident.

Pizarro acabó por hacer creer a sus compañeros que la empresa acometida era una empresa religiosa, en **la cual** tendrían siempre el poderoso y directo apoyo del cielo. — Pizarro eventually made his companions believe that the enterprise undertaken was a religious one, in *which* they would ever have the powerful and direct aid of heaven.

3. When the relative is preceded by one of the longer or less usual prepositions, or a prepositional phrase; in this case **el cual** is preferred in elegant style to **el que:**

El biombo **tras el cual** nos ocultábamos estaba entre el canapé y el rincón. — The screen *behind which* we were hiding was between the sofa and the corner.

El fin **hacia el que** caminamos está aún muy lejos. — The end *to which* we are advancing is still very far off.

Un minuto, que fué un siglo, trascurrió, **durante el cual** Núñez trató de sorprender algún latido del corazón del desgraciado. — A minute, which was a century, passed, *during which* Núñez tried to discover some pulsation of the unfortunate man's heart.

Los náufragos volvieron a la punta — The castaways returned to the rocky roqueña **cerca de la cual** había zozobrado la goleta.

point *near which* the schooner had capsized.

Pero la pared del fondo, **al través del cual** una puerta ancha comunicaba con la sala contigua, estaba adornada de un modo rústico pero pintoresco en alto grado.

But the farther wall, *through which* a wide door communicated with the adjacent hall, was adorned in a rustic but highly picturesque manner.

10.16. After any preposition **el que** nowadays encroaches upon the limits formerly assigned to **que**:

Arcelu tiene la manía del análisis y de las definiciones. Yo le digo que ésa es una enfermedad **de la que** debía curarse. (Baroja, **El mundo es ansí,** III, 14)

Arcelu has a mania for analysis and definitions. I say to him that that is a disease *of which* he should cure himself.

Algunas veces intentó resucitar en María el entusiasmo por la pasada vida, hablándola de aquella barraca **en la que** todos pensaban en ella. (Blasco Ibáñez, **El "femater",** III, in **Cuentos valencianos)**

Sometimes he tried to awaken in Mary enthusiasm for the old life, by talking to her about that cottage *in which* everybody thought of her.

10.17. When the antecedent denotes an idea or a statement and not a material reality, the relative assumes the neuter form **lo cual** or **lo que;** the simple relative **que** is then inadmissible:

Las aguas del arroyo eran dulces, lo que nos hacía suponer que las del lago lo eran también.

The water of the brook was fresh, which made us suppose that that of the lake was so likewise.

B— conocía al mozo y sabía que era muy capaz, por lo cual lo había recomendado al obispo.

B— knew the lad, and knew that he was very capable, for which [reason] he had recommended him to the bishop.

Al anochecer el horizonte occidental comenzó a cargarse de brumas espesas, lo que indicaba que el monzón iba a establecerse durante la noche.

At nightfall the western horizon began to fill with a dense haze, which [phenomenon] indicated that the monsoon was going to set in during the night.

10.18. So when the relative is of masculine or feminine form, it relates to some previous noun of that gender; but when it is neuter it refers to the entire statement embodied in the antecedent clause:

El coronel en su última carta habla en términos muy lisonjeros de la **obra** de V., **la que** le agrada muchísimo.
The colonel in his last letter speaks in very flattering terms of your *work, which* pleases him very much.

El coronel en su última carta habla en términos muy lisonjeros de la obra de V., lo que me agrada muchísimo.
The colonel in his last letter speaks in very flattering terms of your work, which pleases me very much.

Nuestro corresponsal nos envía **libros, informes** impresos y **recortes** de los periódicos del día, **que** nos proporcionan todos los datos que necesitamos.
Our correspondent sends us *books,* printed *reports* and *clippings* from the newspapers of the day, *which* give us all the information we need.

Nuestro corresponsal nos envía libros, informes impresos y recortes de los periódicos del día, lo que nos proporciona todos los datos que necesitamos.
Our correspondent sends us books, printed reports and clippings from the newspapers of the day, which gives us all the information we need.

Note. Thus, to analyze the last pair of examples, in the first one the relative refers to the articles sent, in the second to the action of the correspondent.

10.19. **El cual** may be followed by a noun, as may English *which:*

Trató de fraguar una explicación en **el cual esfuerzo,** no siendo hombre de imaginación acalorada, fracasó miserablemente.
He tried to invent an explanation, *in which effort,* not being a man of vivid imagination, he failed miserably.

El conde de Meneses entró y atravesando todo lo largo del salón, salió por la otra extremidad sin fijarse en nadie, **la cual conducta** sorprendió mucho al duque.
The count of Meneses entered and, crossing the entire length of the hall without noticing anybody, went out at the other end, *which conduct* very much surprised the duke.

10.20. Instead of this construction the noun (unaccompanied by an article) may be placed in apposition, the relative then following:

Trató de fraguar una explicación, **esfuerzo en que** fracasó miserablemente.
He tried to invent an explanation, *in which effort* he failed miserably.

Atravesó todo lo largo del salón sin fijarse en nadie, **conducta que**
He crossed the entire length of the hall without noticing anybody,

sorprendió mucho al duque. — *which conduct* very much surprised the duke.

Luego que terminó esta ceremonia el cura nos invitó a visitar el tesoro, **invitación que** fué inmediatamente aceptada. — As soon as this ceremony was over, the priest invited us to visit the treasure, *which invitation* was immediately accepted.

10.21. **Cuyo** is occasionally met with as a substitute for **el cual** in the construction shown above. Although objected to by grammarians, its use is nevertheless gaining acceptance:

El cóndor, adorado en otro tiempo por los incas, es el rey de los Andes meridionales, en **cuyas regiones** alcanza un desarrollo extraordinario. — The condor, worshipped in former times by the Incas, is the king of the southern Andes, in *which regions* it reaches an extraordinary size.

Toda la región de los contornos se inclina aquí por largas pendientes hacia un centro común, **cuya ancha depresión** está ocupada por el lago Salinas. — All the surrounding region converges here by long slopes toward a common center, *which wide depression* is occupied by Lake Salinas.

10.22. The possessive relative **cuyo, -a, -os, -as,** relates to either persons or things, and corresponds to English *whose, of which.* It agrees in gender and number with the things possessed and not with the possessor:

Un lago trasparente, **cuyas aguas** reflejan las formas de los árboles que lo asombran. — A transparent lake, *whose waters* reflect the forms of the trees which overshadow it.

Hermosos jardines **cuyas flores** perfuman el aire. — Beautiful gardens *whose flowers* perfume the air.

Es un soldado **cuyo valor** es incontestable. — He is a soldier *whose bravery* is unquestionable.

Un pequeño pueblo, **cuyo nombre** he olvidado. — A small village, the name of which *(whose name)* I have forgotten.

El comerciante **cuyos jardines** acabamos de visitar es excesivamente rico. — The merchant *whose gardens* we have just visited is exceedingly rich.

El caballero a **cuya hermana** le he presentado a V., es amigo de mi padre. — The gentleman to *whose sister* I presented you is a friend of my father's.

10.23. As the direct possessive is not invariably used in speaking of the parts of one's own person or clothing, **a quien** is at times employed in that connection instead of **cuyo:**

Mi esposa, **a quien** ya le empezaba a doler la cabeza, se retiró.	My wife, *whose* head was already beginning to ache, withdrew.
El sargento, **a quien** amputaron ayer la pierna, sigue bien esta mañana.	The sergeant *whose* leg they amputated yesterday is doing well this morning.

10.24. **Cuyo** naturally relates to an antecedent immediately preceding; reference may be made to an anterior word by means of **de quien** or **de quienes:**

Parmenio y Clito eran dos capitanes de Alejandro **de quienes** el espíritu y valor eran la admiración de la posteridad.	Parmenio and Clitus were two of Alexander's captains *whose* spirit and valor were the admiration of posterity.

(**Cuyo espíritu y valor** *would refer to* **Alejandro.**)

10.25. **Cuanto,** when used relatively, includes its antecedent, and is to be rendered *as many as, as much as, all that:*

Aquella desgracia inesperada llenó de espanto a **cuantas** personas se hallaban allí reunidas.	This unexpected calamity filled all who were there with terror.
Sus compañeros le dejaron decir **cuanto** quiso.	His companions let him say all he wanted to.
Respecto a comunicación telegráfica, posee Colombia **cuanto** puede necesitar actualmente.	With respect to telegraphic communication, Colombia has all it can need at present.
De **cuantas** personas veo no conozco a ninguna.	Of all the persons I see I do not know one.
Hasta hoy ha sido infructuoso **cuanto** he hecho.	Until now everything I have done has been fruitless.
Estas palabras causaron una impresión extraordinaria en **cuantos** las oyeron.	These words produced an extraordinary impression on all who heard them.

10.26. **Quien** and **cual** are repeated as correlatives either in the singular or in the plural, in which case they assume the accent for the purpose of distinction:

Se disfrazaron **quién** de una manera, y **quién** de otra.	They disguised themselves *some* one way, *some* another.
Tengo muchos libros, **cuáles** de inglés, **cuáles** de otros idiomas.	I have many books, *some* in English, *some* in other languages.

10.27. Another idiomatic use of **quién** is as a noun of depreciative value meaning *the proper person,* etc. **Qué** has a similar use as a kind of indefinite noun (cf. § **19.41** ff.):

Lo mando yo. —Usted no es **quién** para mandar eso. (Baroja, **César o nada,** II, 20)	I order it. —You are not *the proper person* to order that.
A su vez el gobierno rebelde no es **quién** para reprochar nada a nadie. (Madariaga, **España,** II, 2, 8)	In its turn the rebel government is not *the right one* to reproach anyone for anything.
La persona más severa y amiga de censurar no encontraría **qué.** (Pardo Bazán, **Los pazos de Ulloa,** XII)	The person who was most severe and fondest of finding fault wouldn't find *anything* (to criticize).

XI

Negatives

11.1. The usual Spanish negative is **no,** which in most cases applies to a verb. **No** regularly precedes the verb which it negatives; in the case of compound verbal forms in which **ser, estar** or **haber** is an element, it precedes the auxiliary, which is grammatically the verb:

Si nuestros amigos no llegan pronto, no conseguirán asientos.	If our friends do not arrive soon, they will not get seats.
Sus compañeros hasta entonces no habían querido interrogarle respecto del suceso.	His companions until then had not wished to question him about the occurrence.
No estamos dispuestos a negarlo.	We are not prepared to deny it.
Su informe no fué acogido con el interés que merecía.	His report was not received with the interest which it deserved.

11.2. To render a sentence negative, **no** is placed immediately before the verb; in the absence of a verb it usually follows the word which it negatives:

No tengo el azúcar.	I have not the sugar.
No tengo cigarros.	I have no / I haven't any } cigars.
El burro no quiere agua.	The donkey does not want water.
¿No tiene V. un revólver?	Have you not / Haven't you } a revolver?
Ahora no. Al presente no.	Not now. Not at present.
Yo no. El no.	Not I. Not he.
Bien te reirás algunas veces... –No siempre. (Benavente, **Pepa Doncel,** I, 6)	You must laugh loudly sometimes... –Not always.

11.3. The expression **¿no es verdad?** (frequently shortened to **¿verdad?** or merely **¿no?**) is used inquiringly with an expectation of assent, where in English we repeat the verb; thus:

V. quiere comprar mi caballo **¿no es verdad?**	You want to buy my horse, *don't you?*
V. tiene el dinero **¿verdad?**	You have the money, *haven't you?*
No necesitamos ir hoy al mercado **¿verdad?**	We don't need to go to market today, *do we?*
Las cortinas son de lana **¿no?**	The curtains are woolen, *aren't they?*
V. habla inglés **¿no?**	You speak English, *don't you?*

11.4. In conversational style **¿eh?** is often similarly used as a positive interrogation after a statement—not as a request for information, but with an implied scoff or threat:

Mi hijo aprende a fumar, **¿eh?**	My son is learning to smoke, *is he?*
No quieren venir **¿eh?**	They don't want to come, *don't they?*
Sí **¿eh?**	He does, *does he?* He is, *is he?* etc.
No **¿eh?**	He doesn't, *doesn't he?* etc., etc.

REMARK. The English usage of repeating the verb is not followed in either case in Spanish.

11.5. The order is not affected when the verb is omitted through having been previously expressed:

Somos simples leñadores y no espías disfrazados.	We are simple woodcutters, and not spies in disguise.
Nos trata como gente honrada y no como presidiarios.	He treats us like honest people and not like convicts.
Sabe tocar, aunque no mucho.	She can play, although not much.
Llegará mañana si no hoy.	He will arrive tomorrow if not today.

He corregido la mayor parte de las páginas, pero no todas.	I have corrected most of the pages, but not all.

11.6. When a verb governs one or more personal pronouns which necessarily precede it, these are placed between the verb and the negative. Otherwise no word should intervene (unless **no** negatives a phrase, as shown at § **11.7**):

Su proyecto no me parece realizable.	His plan does not seem feasible to me.
No se lo he conseguido todavía.	I have not obtained it for him yet.
Parecen distintos mas no lo son.	They seem different but are not.
Esta licencia no les fué otorgada.	This liberty was not granted them.

11.7. The influence of the negative is coextensive with that of the word which it precedes, since it equally affects whatever the action or influence of that word extends to. By means of its location, therefore, the negation may be restricted to a particular word or phrase, according to the shade of meaning desired (cf. § **26.25**):

La herida no puede ser mortal.	The wound cannot be mortal.
La herida puede no ser mortal.	It is possible that the wound is not mortal.
Hace bien en no perder el tiempo leyendo novelas.	She does well in not losing time reading novels.
No hace bien en perder el tiempo leyendo novelas.	She does not do well in losing time reading novels.
Se resolvieron a no abandonarle aunque estaba gravemente herido.	They resolved not to abandon him although he was seriously wounded.
No se resolvieron a abandonarle aunque estaba gravemente herido.	They did not decide to abandon him although he was seriously wounded.
De los candidatos no sirven todos para el destino.	Not all of the candidates are fit for the place.
De los candidatos todos no sirven para el destino.	All of the candidates are unfit for the place.
Procuraremos no pronunciar su nombre en presencia de su padre.	We will try not to pronounce his name in his father's presence.
No procuraremos pronunciar su nombre.	We will not try to pronounce his name.
No a todos es dado expresarse con facilidad y elegancia.	It is not given to all to express themselves easily and elegantly.

11.8. **No** is associated with other negative words, which come after it and do not, as in English, counteract the negation, but rather strengthen it:

No lo hallo en ninguna parte.	I don't find it anywhere.
No escogí ninguno de los tres.	I did not select any of the three.
No he visto nunca ningún espectáculo tan triste.	I have never seen so sad a sight.

11.9. From this it has often been supposed that in Spanish a number of negatives never counteract, but strengthen each other. But this is not strictly true. The general negative **no** neutralizes an adjective, adverb or proposition of negative value (except **nada, ni, ninguno, nunca, jamás**), and is itself neutralized by repetition:

"No sin" equivale a "con."	*Not without* is equivalent to *with.*
Se vió insultada la magistratura, no sin general escándalo.	The authorities were seen to be insulted, to the general disgrace.
Canta no sin cierta gracia.	Her singing is not without a certain grace.
Pero no le fué permitido no asistir.	But it was not permitted him not to attend *(i.e.* he was not allowed to be absent).
No podemos no admitir la justicia de sus observaciones.	We cannot fail to acknowledge the justice of his remarks.
Esta precaución no era inútil.	This precaution was not useless.
Se ocupa demasiado de detalles no importantes.	He occupies himself too much with unimportant details.

11.10. Otherwise, any number of negatives may be combined in the same sentence without destroying the negation; and, in fact, each adverb or pronoun of a negative clause assumes its negative form (when it has one):

No toleraba nunca ninguna intervención de nadie.	He never tolerated any interference from anyone.
Sin embargo no veían en ninguna parte nada que indicase que hubiese habido naufragio de ninguna especie.	Nevertheless they did not see anything anywhere to indicate that there had been a shipwreck of any kind.

11.11. One exception to the last statement is that **alguno,** when placed after a noun, is accepted as a negative interchangeable with **ninguno:**

Hasta esta hora no he recibido noticia alguna de ellos.	Up to this hour I have not received any tidings of them.
No toleraba de nadie broma alguna.	He used not to tolerate any levity from anyone.

11.12. All auxiliary negatives, when placed after the verb, require **no** before the verb to complete the negation. A few phrases violate the general rule (cf. § **11.22**). But they have full negative effect when they precede the verb, and **no** is then inadmissible:

En cuanto a indígenas, no vimos ningunos. (*more often* ninguno)	As for natives, we saw none.
En cuanto a indígenas, ningunos se mostraron. (or ninguno se mostró)	As for natives, none showed themselves.
Nunca emplea más tiempo que el estrictamente necesario. No emplea nunca más tiempo que el estrictamente necesario.	He never takes more time than what is strictly necessary.
¡Ahí es nada!	A mere trifle!
El cura comía nada más que regularmente. (Pereda, **Peñas arriba, IV**)	The priest ate only moderately.

11.13. Certain words and phrases, not in themselves negative, are used to emphasize or strengthen **no:**

No veo gota en este aposento.	I can't see at all in this room.
Por la calle no pasaba un alma.	Not a soul was passing in the street.
No entiendo palabra de lo que dice.	I do not understand a word of what he says.
No lo he hecho mejor en mi vida.	I have never done it better in my life.

11.14. A usage peculiar to Spanish is that many expressions of this kind, although having nothing negative in their nature, may be used with negative force and unaccompanied by **no** before a verb, in the same manner as the supplementary negatives above referred to (cf. § **9.16**):

En mi vida he visto tantas telarañas.	I have never seen so many cobwebs in my life.
En parte alguna la pudimos encontrar.	We could not find her anywhere.
En todo el año ha hecho tanto frío como hoy.	In the whole year it has not been so cold as today.
En toda la noche he podido dormir.	All night long I was unable to sleep.
En el mundo se hallará otra joven tan simpática.	You won't find another so charming a girl in the world.
En días de Dios ha sucedido tal cosa.	Never has such a thing happened before.

11.15. Three words which originally had nothing negative in their construction have come to be accepted as true negatives:

nadie *nobody* from Latin *natus* (born) with which *homo* (human being) is to be understood

nada *nothing* from Latin *nata* (born) with which *res* (thing) is to be understood

jamás *never* from a combination of Latin *iam* (now) and *magis* (more)

These are now employed as auxiliary to **no,** or as actual negatives before a verb:

Yo **no** le he ofendido **jamás.**	I have *never* offended him.
Yo **jamás** hago las cosas a medias.	I *never* do things by halves.
No ha ocurrido **nada de nuevo.**[1] **Nada de nuevo**[1] ha ocurrido.	*Nothing* new has occurred.
Aquella desgracia, **no** prevista por **nadie,** llenó de espanto a todas.	That misfortune, *not* foreseen by *anyone,* filled all with dismay.
Nadie había previsto semejante desenlace.	*No one* had foreseen such an outcome.

11.16. The distinctions drawn between **alguien, alguno** and **algo** (§§ **9.42** ff.) also apply for the most part to their corresponding negatives **nadie, ninguno** and **nada.** Thus these negatives require the addition of **no** to complete the negation when they stand after the verb, but not when they precede it or stand alone:

No veo a nadie.	I do not see anybody.
A nadie veo.	I see nobody.
Nadie de los seis sabe una palabra de esas cosas. (Pereda, **Peñas arriba,** XV, end)	Nobody of the six knows a word of those things.
No halla nada.	He does not find anything.
Nada halla.	He finds nothing.
¿Qué dice? —Nada.	What does he say? —Nothing.
¿Quién llama? —Nadie.	Who calls? —No one.
No viene ninguno de nuestros amigos. Ninguno de nuestros amigos viene.	None of our friends is coming.
¿No tiene V. tabaco?	Haven't you any tobacco?
No tengo ninguno.	I haven't any.
Ninguno tengo.	I have none.

[1] **De** may be omitted: **nada nuevo,** as with **algo** (§ **9.42**). If the adjective has an antecedent it may agree with it: **Representaba cierta novedad, que al mismo tiempo nada tenía de nueva.** (Blasco Ibáñez, **La reina Calafia, II**) *She represented a certain novelty, which at the same time had nothing new about it.* Another use of **nada de** is as the equivalent of **ninguno: Nada de prisa...Nada de ruido.** (Camba, **Un hotel,** in **La ciudad automática**) *No haste...no noise.*

REMARK. The construction with **no** is the common usage; the other is literary or rhetorical.

11.17. Any of these negatives may be combined in the same sentence:

El no dice nada a nadie.	He says nothing to anybody.
Nadie dice nada.	No one says anything.
Nadie quiere leer ninguno de mis poemas.	No one will read any of my poems.

11.18. The positive forms **alguien** and **algo** are never used with a negative meaning; in such a construction only **nadie** and **nada** are admissible:[1]

No escribo a nadie. (NOT: *No escribo a alguien.*)	I am not writing to anybody.
No quiero nada por ahora. (NOT: *No quiero algo.*)	I do not want anything at present.

11.19. Alguno, however, may be used in negation, but only when associated with and following a singular noun; in such a construction it is more forcible than **ninguno,** especially after **sin** *without:*

El nuevo president no hace cambio **alguno.**	The new president makes *no* changes.
No toma precaución **alguna.**	He takes *no* precaution *whatever.*
No tienen influencia **alguna.**	They have *no* influence *at all.*
Sin desgracia **alguna.**	*Without any* mishap.
Habla sin preparación **alguna.**	He speaks *without any* preparation.

11.20. But if the noun be understood, or placed at a distance, **ninguno** only can be used:

Habla de cambios sin hacer **ninguno.**	He talks of changes without making *any.*
Compra libros, pero no lee **ninguno.**	He buys books, but reads *none.*

11.21. After the prepositions **sin** *without* and **antes de** *before,* the negative forms **nadie, nada,** must be used, and not **alguien, algo:**

[1] But they may be used in negative sentences if the speaker's thought is affirmative: **¿Quién sabe si no hay algo de magia diabólica en este prestigio?** (Valera, **Pepita Jiménez, 14 de abril)** *Who knows whether there isn't something of devilish magic in this prestige?* **No dudo que mi tía Clara le dé algún buen consejo.** (Palacio Valdés, **La alegría del capitán Ribot, V)** *I do not doubt that my Aunt Clara gives him an occasional bit of good advice.*

Sin ver a nadie. — Without seeing anybody.

Antes de hacer nada. — Before doing anything.

Lee la carta sin decir nada. — He reads the letter without saying anything.

11.22. **Nada** is employed as an adverb with the meaning of *not at all, by no means.* When so used it sometimes discards the attendant negative **no:**

No adelanta **nada** en sus estudios. — He does *not* advance *at all* in his studies.

No es **nada** evidente. — It is *by no means* evident.

Ella es **nada** bonita. — She is *not at all* pretty.

Mi madre no sabe **nada** que he venido. (Benavente, **Por las nubes,** II, 11) — My mother has*n't the slightest idea* that I have come.

11.23. **Nada** may be followed directly by a qualifying adjective, which in that case is masculine. But if this qualifying adjective is preceded by **de** it may agree with the noun in question (cf. § **11.15,** note):

No tengo **nada bonito.** — I have *nothing pretty.*

No hace **nada útil.** — He does *nothing useful.*

No queremos hacer **nada imprudente.** — We don't want to do *anything imprudent.*

El paisaje portugués, en cambio, no tiene **nada de austero.** Es alegre, verde, húmedo y lírico. (Camba, **Aventuras de una peseta,** IV, 2) — The Portuguese landscape, on the other hand, has nothing austere about it. It is cheerful, green, damp and lyrical.

11.24. **Nada** may be employed as a feminine noun denoting the non-existence of everything, equivalent to the English *nothingness:*

Los millares de individuos que vivieron, pensaron, y cuyas vidas fueron para ellos de tanta importancia, mas cuyos nombres se han sumergido en **la nada.** — The thousands of beings who lived, thought, and whose lives were to them of so much importance, yet whose names have sunk into nothingness.

REMARK. There is also a feminine noun **nonada,** meaning *a thing of no consequence, a mere nothing;* this may be used in the plural:

Figúrese V. que esos dolores son **nonadas,** y dejará de padecerlos. — Imagine that those aches are *mere nothings* and you will cease to feel them.

Su don es una **nonada.** — His gift is a *mere nothing.*

11.25. **Nada** (or often **nada, nada**) is used with something of the effect of an exclamation to indicate emphatic dissent from a previous speech or the prevailing circumstances:

Por la mañana nos encontramos con un tiempo triste y lluvioso. —**Nada,** hasta que lleguemos a Sevilla no vamos a tener sol —ha dicho Juan. (Baroja, **El mundo es ansí,** III, 5)

In the morning we found the weather gloomy and rainy. *"There is no way out of it,* we are not going to have sun until we reach Seville," said John.

Pero considere usted... **¡Nada, nada!** Si insiste usted, se lo diré a la señora Marquesa. (Benavente, **Los malhechores del bien,** II, 1)

But consider... —*Certainly not.* If you insist, I'll tell the Marchioness.

11.26. **Para nada** not infrequently amounts to emphatic negation:

Observó que la curiosidad de todos estaba saciándose en lo que hacía y decía Sotileza, y que **para nada** se acordaba de él. (Pereda, **Sotileza,** XXIII)

He observed that everybody's curiosity was satisfying itself with what Sotileza was doing and saying, and did *not* recall him *in the slightest.*

Yo le aseguro que muy pronto no se notará **para nada** la falta de Fred. (Benavente, **La fuerza bruta,** III)

I assure you that very soon Fred's absence will *not* be noticed *at all.*

Hacía ya mucho tiempo que Machín no se ocupaba de Mary ni de mí **para nada.** (Baroja, **Las inquietudes de Shanti Andía,** V, 7)

For some time now Machín had *not* concerned himself *in any way* about Mary or me.

11.27. **Jamás** may be used as a mere expletive to strengthen **siempre** *ever,* or **nunca** *never:*

La amaré por **siempre jamás.**

I shall love her for *ever and ever.*

Nunca jamás consentiré en su unión.

I shall *never, never* consent to their union.

11.28. **Nadie, nada** and **jamás** are employed with their original positive values of *anybody, anything* and *ever* under the circumstances enumerated below (cf. § **11.18**). This usage is generally extended by analogy to **ninguno** and **nunca:**

a. In questions expecting negative answers:

¿Ha visto V. jamás nada que iguale a esto?

Have you ever seen *anything* to equal this?

¿Quién le exige a V. **nada** de eso? — Who is requiring of you *anything* of the kind?

¿Se le hubiese ocurrido a usted **nunca** comparar a Vigo con Pontevedra? (Camba, **La rana viajera, España,** X) — Would it *ever* have occurred to you to compare Vigo with Pontevedra?

b. In exclamations of interrogative form:

¡Hay **nada** más sublime! — Is there *anything* more sublime!

¡Se ha visto **jamás** tal cosa! — Did you *ever* see the like!

¡Ha sido **nadie** tan desgraciado como yo en perder todas mis notas de viaje! — Was anyone *ever* so unfortunate as I in losing all my travel notes!

c. After comparatives and in relative clauses following a superlative (cf. § **23.19,** REMARK):

Importa a V. más que a **nadie.** — It matters to you more than *anyone.*

Mis esperanzas renacieron ahora más frescas que **nunca.** — My hopes now sprang up again fresher than *ever.*

¿Ha olvidado V. que a mí más que a **ningún** hombre toca hacer justicia de ese asesino? — Have you forgotten that it belongs to me more than to *any* man to render justice to that assassin?

Alfonso y Alicia se entregaron con infantil alegría a la más fantástica y disparatada comedia que **nadie** pueda imaginarse. (Palacio Valdés, **Los cármenes de Granada,** II, 5) — Alphonso and Alice gave themselves over with childish glee to the most fantastic and nonsensical game that *anyone* can imagine.

Es el Conde Lucanor un "exemplario", pero el más bello que se haya escrito **nunca.** (Sánchez Cantón, prologue to edition of Juan Manuel, **El Conde Lucanor**) — The Conde Lucanor is a collection of moral tales, but the most beautiful one that has *ever* been written.

Esto dijo don César de las Matas, el hombre más docto que había producido **jamás** el valle de Laviana. (Palacio Valdés, **La aldea perdida,** IV) — So said Don César de las Matas, the most learned man that the Laviana valley had *ever* produced.

d. After expressions that embody a negative meaning:

Es imposible entender **nada.** — It is impossible to hear *anything.*

Me guardaré de hablar a **nadie** sobre lo sucedido. — I shall refrain from speaking to *anyone* about what has happened.

Era inútil hacer **ningún** esfuerzo para huir. — It was useless to make *any* effort to flee.

Malo es tener pensado ni previsto **nada** en la vida. (Benavente, **Rosas de otoño,** I, 3)	It is bad to plan or foresee *anything* in life.
Vivía en aquel lugar en la más pobre y miserable choza que **nadie** puede figurarse, una anciana llamada la tía María Alonso. (Palacio Valdés, **Sinfonía pastoral, Allegro ma non troppo,** III)	There lived in that village, in the poorest and most wretched hut that *anyone* can imagine an old woman called Aunt Mary Alonso.

e. In clauses beginning with **sin, antes de, apenas, ni** or **tampoco:**

Pero **antes de** emprender **nada,** convenía fijarse en el país.	But *before* undertaking *anything,* it was best to establish themselves in the country.
Prefiero tener arreglados todos los pormenores **antes de** avisar a **nadie.**	I prefer to have all the details arranged *before* informing *anyone.*
Ellas me dirigían mil preguntas **sin** aguardar **ninguna** respuesta.	They asked me a thousand questions *without* waiting for *any* answer.
La noche pasó **sin ningún** incidente.	The night passed *without any* incident.
Su marido **tampoco** dijo **nada.**	Her husband didn't say *anything either.*
Desde que estoy en Cenciella, **apenas** trabajo **ningún** día de labor. (Pérez de Ayala, **Luz de domingo,** IV)	Since I have been in Cenciella, I *scarcely* work *any* work day.
¡Ni tú **ni nadie** es capaz de quitarme lo que es mío! (Martínez Sierra, **Mamá,** III)	Neither you *nor anyone* is capable of taking away from me what is mine.

11.29. When no verb is expressed, the auxiliary negatives are sufficient, and **no** is not admissible in connection with them:

De ningún modo. De ninguna manera.	By no means, not by any means.
¿Consentirá V. en ello? —¡Nunca!	Will you consent to it? —Never!
A ningún precio, contestó el duque.	Not at any price, replied the duke.

11.30. A redundant and nonsensical use of the negative is common to both languages in exclamations of interrogative form:

¡Qué no daría yo para poseer una voz tan maravillosa!	What wouldn't I give to possess such a wonderful voice!
¡Qué no dirá Europa al oír tal escándalo!	What will Europe not say on hearing such a scandal!

11.31. **No** is sometimes used redundantly after **que** in the second term of a comparison:

Ella se lo sabrá decir a Vd. mejor que no yo.	She will know how to tell you better than I.
Me gustan más los jardines del Duque que no las Delicias.[1]	I like the Ducal gardens better than the Delicias.
Está más resuelto ahora que no entonces.	He is more resolute now than then.

11.32. But **no** is at times used (as is also **el: que el que**) between two **que's,** meaning *than that,* but does not alter the sense (cf. § **8.4,** note):

Más bien parecía que le llevaban que no que él andaba.	It seemed rather that they were carrying him than that he walked.
Es más probable que resigne su comisión que no que se someta a semejante injusticia.	It is more likely that he will resign his commission than that he will submit to such injustice.
No hay nada en el mundo que moleste más a un hombre que el que no se le tome en serio. (Palacio Valdés, **La hija de Natalia,** I, 4)	There is nothing in the world that annoys a man more than not being taken seriously *(lit.* than that he isn't taken seriously).

11.33. Another common redundant use of **no** is after **hasta (que)** *until,* **a menos que** and even other conjunctions, in a sentence of negative meaning:

El capitán no quería decidirse hasta no haber explorado la costa hasta el extremo de la península.	The captain did not wish to decide until he had explored the coast as far as the extremity of the peninsula.
No amé nunca hasta que no vi a V.	I never loved until I saw you.
Hasta que todo no esté arreglado quiero que ella lo ignore.	I do not want her to know it until everything is arranged.
Siempre que decís algo de fundamento... No dejáis de añadir, como dijo el sabio, a menos que no recordéis el nombre. Es mucha conciencia. (Benavente, **La escuela de las princesas,** I, 1)	Whenever you say something fundamental...you don't fail to add "as the sage said", unless you recall the name. That is too much conscientiousness.
No se pasaba día sin que por un motivo o por otro no sintiese los	Not a day passed without his feeling, for one reason or for another,

[1] Names of two extensive gardens in Seville, the former private the latter public.

estragos de la mano maternal. (Palacio Valdés, **José**, IV) — the ravages of his mother's hand.

Acampan en una población quince días, un mes, dos meses. Luego la dejan sin que no quede de ellos sino el recuerdo. (Arciniegas, **Los alemanes en la conquista de América**, XII) — They camp in a settlement two weeks, a month, two months. Then they leave it without there remaining anything except the memory of them.

REMARK. A redundant **no** is occasionally found in clauses dependent upon verbs which imply a negative thought:

Esto no impide que antes de decidirme al matrimonio no haya hecho una crítica fría y serena de mi situación. (Pérez Galdós, **Gloria**, I, 1, 7) — This doesn't prevent my having made a cold, calm analysis of my situation before deciding upon marriage.

11.34. No followed by a verb and **más que** or **sino** is equivalent to *not more than, not but,* or *only:*

Pero con eso **no** haremos **más que** retardar la inevitable catástrofe que nos espera. — But by that we will *only* retard the inevitable catastrophe that awaits us.

No tomaron **más** tiempo **que** el necesario para dar pequeños descansos a los caballos. — They took *only* what time was necessary to give short rests to the horses.

Durante el primer cuarto de hora de marcha el silencio **no** fué interrumpido **sino** por esta sola observación del guía. — During the first quarter of an hour's march, the silence was broken *only* by this single remark of the guide's.

A la verdad, hasta entonces **no** teníamos motivos **más que** para felicitarnos. — In fact until then we had *no* reason *except* to congratulate ourselves.

No les quedaba **más** remedio **que** rendirse. — They had *no* recourse *but* to surrender.

¿Qué tiene V.? **No** hace V. **sino** bostezar. — What's the matter with you? You *don't* do anything *but* yawn.

11.35. In the expressions **nada más que** and **nada menos que,** the meaning depends essentially upon what word the negative restricts (i.e. before which it is placed):

Nada más deseo que el reposo de la vida privada. — I desire nothing beyond the quiet of private life.

Nada deseo más que encontrarme con él cara a cara. — Nothing do I more desire than to meet him face to face.

En nada menos piensa que en ocupar un ministerio de Estado. — He thinks of nothing less than getting a cabinet office.

En nada piensa menos que en solicitar el cargo. — There is nothing that he thinks of less than applying for the position.

REMARK. In the first half of each of these pairs, **no más, no menos,** may be substituted for **nada más, nada menos,** respectively:

No deseo más que ir a reposar bajo el césped del viejo cementerio de mi pueblo. — I want nothing more than to be laid to rest 'neath the sod of the old cemetery in my village.

No aspira a menos que al mismo poder ejecutivo. — He aspires to no less than the executive power itself.

11.36. When **no** is limited by a following **sino** *but,* thus denying one thing and affirming another, these correlatives are placed immediately before the words or expressions which they contrast:

Los esclavos **no** corrieron **sino** más bien volaron. — The slaves did not run, *but* rather flew.

Era aquél, **no** el sueño de un volcán, **sino** su extinción completa. — That was not the sleep of a volcano, *but* its complete extinction.

El cuadro representaba un país iluminado **no** de frente por los rayos solares **sino** desde atrás por medio de su reflexión. — The picture represented a country not lighted from in front by the sun's rays, *but* from behind by means of their reflection.

Aplaudieron el discurso **no** porque les pareció elocuente **sino** porque era corto. — They applauded the speech, not because it seemed eloquent to them, *but* because it was short.

REMARK. To analyze the last example, for instance, if the order were **no aplaudieron el discurso porque,** etc., it would convey the meaning that they did not applaud the speech, for the reason that it seemed eloquent.

11.37. No sólo...sino también are placed before each of two clauses in the same manner as the English *not only...but also;* their location is governed by the principle given above:

No sólo mataron a los prisioneros sino también los cortaron en pedazos. — They not only killed the prisoners but also cut them in pieces.

Degollaron no sólo a los hombres sino también a las mujeres y a los niños. — They massacred not only the men but also the women and children.

Remark. In the first example the word restricted is **mataron;** in the second, **hombres.**

11.38. If two negative clauses are so contrasted, the formula is **no sólo** (or **solamente**)...**sino [que] tampoco:**

No solamente ninguna otra voz contestó a la suya, sino que tampoco ningún eco le devolvió el sonido de sus gritos.	Not only did no other voice reply to his own, but no echo returned the sound of his shouts.

11.39. Tampoco (lit. *as little*) negatives something in addition to a previous negation, and is equivalent to *neither, not...either;* it requires **no** or **ni** when it follows the verb, but not when it precedes:

Donde yo no he logrado pasar, el regimiento de V. no pasará tampoco.	Where I have not succeeded in passing, your regiment will not pass either.
Esta nueva tentativa tampoco obtuvo el resultado apetecido.	This new attempt likewise did not obtain the desired result.
Mientras no deseamos abusar de la debilidad de un vecino, no queremos tampoco someternos a su insolencia ni a sus caprichos.	While we do not desire to take advantage of a neighbor's weakness, just as little are we willing to submit to his insolence or caprices.
A decir verdad, no quiero ir.—Ni yo tampoco.	To tell the truth, I don't want to go. —Nor I either.

11.40. After an answer by simple **no,** a second similar answer is expressed by **tampoco:**

¿Sabe V. a dónde ha ido Paco? —No señor. —¿Ni qué comisión lleva? —Tampoco señor.	Do you know where Frank has gone? —No, Sir. —Or what errand he is on? —No, Sir.

11.41. Ni is a negative conjunction equivalent to a negative form of **y** *and.* Its English equivalent is *nor,* which is not equal to *not or* but to *and not:*

No veo el libro, **ni** tengo tiempo para buscarlo.	I do not see the book, *nor* have I time to look for it. I do not see the book *and* have *not* time to look for it.
La peste ha cesado, **ni** hay motivo para temer su nueva aparición.	The plague has ended, *and* there is *no* reason to fear its reappearance.
El presidente no ha leído aún la memoria de V., **ni** tiene tiempo hoy para examinarla.	The president has not read your memorial, *and* he has *not* time to look at it today.

11.42. **Ni** connects negative sentences in the same manner that **y** does affirmative ones:

No lo creo **ni** me lo persuadirá nadie.	I do not believe it *and* no one is going to persuade me of it.
Nunca recibí dinero de él **ni** pensé nunca en solicitárselo.	I never received any money from him *and* I never thought of asking him for any.
Muchas personas me califican de escéptico, y dicen que no creo en nada **ni** que en nada espero.	Many persons call me a skeptic, and say that I believe in nothing *and* hope for nothing.

11.43. After **ni** the negatives **nadie, ninguno, nada** must be used, and not **alguien, alguno, algo:**

No tengo vino ni quiero comprar ninguno.	I have no wine and do not wish to buy any.
Ni lo creo, ni me lo persuadirá nadie.	I do not believe it, nor will anyone persuade me to.
No encontraron en aquella vasta sábana de nieve ni leña, ni yerbas, ni musgo ni nada combustible.	They did not find in that vast expanse of snow any wood, or grass, or moss or anything combustible.

11.44. When repeated, **ni** has the meaning of *neither...nor* (or *not...either....or);* in this usage it requires the additional negative **no** when the phrase follows the verb, but not when preceding it:

No tengo **ni** tabacos **ni** pitillos. **Ni** tabacos **ni** pitillos tengo.	I have *neither* cigars *nor* cigarettes.
Mi Capitán, no he encontrado vestigios de él **ni** a la ida **ni** a la vuelta.	Captain, I have *not* found any trace of him *either* coming *or* going.
Ni el salvaje, **ni** el ave **ni** la fiera habitaban por entonces aquellas regiones de muerte.	*Neither* savage, *nor* bird *nor* wild beast then inhabited those regions of death.

11.45. **Ni** takes the place of **o** *or* after all negatives or clauses embodying a negative or restrictive meaning:

Los árboles formaban una cúpula impenetrable de muchas millas cuadradas de superficie, sin un claro **ni** una hendedura.	The trees formed an impenetrable dome many square miles in extent, without a clearing *or* a break.
Es difícil formarse una idea cabal de la enfermedad **ni** acertar con su curación.	It is difficult to form a correct idea of the disease *or* to devise a cure for it.

Será imposible atender tantas cosas a un tiempo, **ni** dar las órdenes oportunas.	It will be impossible to attend to so many things at once, *or* to give the proper orders.
Apenas podía respirar **ni** moverse.	He could scarcely breathe *or* move.
El buque seguía aquellas vueltas y recodos sin vacilar **ni** equivocarse nunca.	The vessel followed those turns and bends without hesitating *or* mistaking ever.
¿Quién será capaz de describir el encanto de este lugar pacífico; qué artista sabrá reproducir esos matices de luz, **ni** qué músico apuntar las notas del murmullo de las aguas cristalinas?	Who is able to describe the charm of this peaceful spot, what artist can reproduce those gradations of light, *or* what musician can write the notes of the murmur of the crystalline waters?

11.46. **Ni** is placed before a noun which we cite as evidence to a negation; it then corresponds to the English *not...even:*

No podría arrancarlo de sus manos **ni** el mismo Hércules.	*Not even* Hercules himself could wrest it from his hands.
La atmósfera estaba serena y tranquila; **ni** la más tenue nube se descubría por ningun lado.	The air was clear and motionless; *not even* the faintest cloud was to be seen anywhere.
No lo dudaban **ni** por un momento.	They did *not* doubt it *even* for a moment.
Observaba aquel espectáculo sin pronunciar **ni** una sola palabra.	He contemplated that spectacle without uttering a single word.

11.47. **Ni** may in this meaning be strengthened by **siquiera** *even.* **Siquiera** alone may be used in any negative sentence:

Lejos de dar toda la latitud debida a la defensa, ni siquiera dejó **hablar** al abogado.	So far from giving all necessary scope to the defense, he did not even allow the counsel to *speak.*
No le conozco ni siquiera de vista (*or* ni de vista siquiera).	I don't even know him by sight.
Nadie siquiera había oído hablar de él.	No one had even heard of him.
Jamás se le vió enfadarse ni dar siquiera señales de impaciencia. (Palacio Valdés, **La fe,** VII)	He was never seen to grow angry or even show signs of impatience.

11.48. But if a verb is interpolated between **siquiera** and the negative, the latter can also be **no:**

No dejó hablar siquiera al **abogado.**	He did not even allow the *counsel* to speak.

REMARK. Notice that in the first example of § **11.47** it is **hablar** that is restricted by **siquiera.** In the example of § **11.48** it is **abogado** that **siquiera** restricts.

11.49. Ni que followed by the past subjunctive has the effect of an exclamatory clause of concession for which a negative conclusion is to be understood:

Ni que fuéramos tontos. (Pérez Galdos, **Miau,** XXI) — Anybody would think that we were fools *(more literally:* Even if we were fools [we wouldn't believe such a statement]).

Ni que yo fuera alguna loca. (Martínez Sierra, **Primavera en otoño,** I) — Anybody would think that I was some crazy woman.

¡Ave María! ¡Ni que fuésemos algún par de tigres! *(Idem,* III, end) — Good heavens! Anybody would think that we were a couple of tigers!

Pero, hombre; ni que fuéramos gitanos y que estuviéramos en el mercado de caballos. (Benavente, **La honradez de la cerradura,** II, 3, 4) — But man alive; anybody would think that we were gypsies and that we were at the horse fair.

11.50. When a series of negative clauses or words are to be expressed, it is usual to employ **no** with the first one and **ni** with the rest when a verb follows the first negation; when a series of nouns or adjectives are to be negatived, it is preferable to place **ni** before each:

Sus investigaciones más minuciosas **no** revelaron **ni** el menor vestigio de campamento, **ni** cenizas de hoguera apagada **ni** huella de pie humano. — Their minutest investigations did *not* reveal the least trace of an encampment, *nor* the ashes of a burnt-out fire *nor* the print of a human foot.

Ni la templanza y benignidad del clima, **ni** la excelencia y fertilidad del suelo, **ni** su ventajosa posición para el comercio marítimo eran poderosas a superar los obstáculos que oponía a sus progresos la política coartatoria de los ingleses. — *Neither* the temperateness and mildness of the climate, *nor* the excellence and fertility of the soil *nor* its advantageous location for maritime commerce were sufficient to overcome the obstacles which the restrictive policy of the English opposed to its progress.

11.51. However, **no** may be repeated before a series of nouns under similar circumstances:

No la sed de la gloria, **no** una ambición noble, **no** el deseo de hacer feliz a la Gran Bretaña les empujaron a esta guerra, sino el deseo de borrar del mapa a un pueblo que había proclamado morir o mantener su independencia.	*Not* the thirst for glory, *nor* a noble ambition, *nor* the desire to make Great Britain prosperous incited them to this war, but the desire to wipe from the map a people who had proclaimed their intention to die or maintain their independence.

11.52. **Sino,** retaining its primary value—**si no** *if not*—is used in presenting an alternative in questions beginning with an interrogative pronoun or adverb and expecting a negative answer:

Pues ¿cuándo deberemos dar el golpe **sino** ahora?	Then when must we strike the blow *if not* now?
¿A quién he de acudir **sino** a mi propio hermano?	To whom am I to turn *if not* to my own brother?
¿Quién tiene el deber de velar sobre la moral pública **sino** la iglesia?	Whose duty is it to watch over the public morals *if not* that of the Church?

11.53. **No que** and **y no que** are nowadays used, with the equivalence of *whereas, when in fact,* etc., to imply opposition to a preceding statement:

Allí siquiera se hubiera educado; **no que** metida aquí desde pequeña, se ha hecho una salvaje. (Benavente, **El primo Román,** I, 4)	There at least she would have been educated; *whereas,* stuck away here from the time she was young, she has become a savage.
Y si te has cansado de mí, me lo debías haber dicho, **y no que me** estás haciendo hacer un papel feo. (Arniches, **El amigo Melquiades,** I, 3)	And if you have got tired of me, you should have told me so, *when in fact* you are making me appear ridiculous.

XII
Numerals And Numerical Values

12.1.

CARDINAL NUMERALS		ORDINAL NUMERALS	
uno, -a	1	**primero**	1st
dos	2	**segundo**	2nd
tres	3	**tercero**	3rd
cuatro	4	**cuarto**	4th
cinco	5	**quinto**	5th
seis	6	**sexto**	6th
siete	7	**séptimo** or **sétimo**	7th
ocho	8	**octavo**	8th
nueve	9	**noveno** or **nono**	9th
diez	10	**décimo**	10th
once	11	**undécimo**	11th
doce	12	**duodécimo**	12th
trece	13	**décimo tercio**[1]	13th
catorce	14	**décimo cuarto**[1]	14th
quince	15	**décimo quinto**[1]	15th
diez y seis	16	**décimo sexto**[1]	16th
diez y siete	17	**décimo séptimo**[1]	17th
diez y ocho	18	**décimo octavo**[1]	18th
diez y nueve	19	**décimo nono**[1]	19th
veinte	20	**vigésimo**	20th
veinte y uno	21	**vigésimo primo**	21st
veinte y dos	22	**vigésimo segundo**	22nd
veinte y tres, etc.	23	**vigésimo tercero**	23rd
treinta	30	**trigésimo**	30th
treinta y uno, etc.	31	**trigésimo primo**	31st
cuarenta	40	**cuadragésimo**	40th
cincuenta	50	**quincuagésimo**	50th
sesenta	60	**sexagésimo**	60th

[1] These forms are also written as one word, in which case the feminine form will be preferably **décimotercia,** etc. Cf. § **12.14.**

CARDINAL NUMERALS		ORDINAL NUMERALS	
setenta	70	**septuagésimo**	70th
ochenta	80	**octogésimo**	80th
noventa	90	**nonagésimo**	90th
ciento	100	**centésimo**	100th
ciento (y) uno	101	**centésimo primo**	101st
ciento (y) dos, etc.	102	**centésimo segundo**	102nd
doscientos, -as	200	**ducentésimo**	200th
trescientos, -as	300	**tricentésimo**	300th
cuatrocientos, -as	400	**cuadringentésimo**	400th
quinientos, -as	500	**quingentésimo**	500th
seiscientos, -as	600	**sexcentésimo**	600th
setecientos, -as	700	**septingentésimo**	700th
ochocientos, -as	800	**octingentésimo**	800th
novecientos, -as	900	**noningentésimo**	900th
mil	1000	**milésimo**	1,000th
dos mil	2000	**dos milésimo**	2,000th
doscientos, -as mil	200,000	**doscientos milésimo**	200,000th
quinientos, -as mil	500,000	**quinientos milésimo**	500,000th
un millón[1]	1,000,000	**millonésimo**	1,000,000th
diez millones	10,000,000	**diez millonésimo**	10,000,000th

CARDINAL NUMERALS

NOTE. The compounds **diez y seis, diez y siete, veinte y uno, veinte y dos, treinta y uno,** etc., are sometimes written as one word: **dieciséis, diecisiete, veintiuno, veintidós, treintaiuno,** etc.

12.2. The cardinal numerals are all invariable except **uno** and the compounds of **ciento:**

cuarenta caballos y cuatro mulas	forty horses and four mules
mil soldados	a thousand soldiers
veinte y cinco casas	twenty-five houses

12.3. **Uno** (which is the same word as the indefinite article) agrees in gender and number with the noun to which it refers, but drops the **o** when immediately preceding a masculine noun. In compounds it drops the final vowel before nouns of either gender (though it does not necessarily do so before a feminine noun) and no longer agrees with the noun:

[1] The system of numeration used in Spain differs from the American beginning with **billón** *billion.* From that point each higher number is a million times the smaller rather than a thousand.

un caballero; una señora	a gentleman; a lady
veintiún edificios	twenty-one buildings
veintiún casas	twenty-one houses
ciento y **un** sillas	a hundred and one chairs

REMARK. Still when such compounds follow the noun, as when used for ordinal numbers, **uno** may agree with the noun, but never loses the final vowel:

cápitulo veinte y **uno,** página ciento **una** *(or* uno)	chapter twenty-one, page one hundred and one

12.4. **Ciento** properly drops the final syllable when it comes immediately before a noun, or before **mil** *thousand.* An adjective may then intervene, but the full form **ciento** is required when followed by smaller numerals. The multiples of **ciento** agree in number and gender with the nouns to which they belong:

cien bocoyes de melote	one hundred hogsheads of molasses
cien valerosos hombres	a hundred brave men
cien mil almas	a hundred thousand souls
ciento cincuenta cigarros	one hundred and fifty cigars
quinientos libros; quinientas botellas de vino	five hundred books; five hundred bottles of wine
doscientas mil libras de tabaco	two hundred thousand pounds of tobacco
Posee un yate de recreo de trescientas toneladas.	He owns a pleasure yacht of three hundred tons
Tomaré ciento de esas acciones.	I will take a hundred of those shares.
a una distancia de ciento a doscientos pasos	at a distance of one or two hundred paces

REMARK. In modern usage **ciento** becomes **cien** in almost any position except before another numeral:

Uno solo, por ahora...; pero vale por **cien.** (Pardo Bazán, **La quimera,** II)	Only one, for now...; but it is worth a hundred.
A este grito contestaron otros **cien** que partieron de la muchedumbre. (Palacio Valdés, **La novela de un novelista,** XXII)	This shout was answered by a hundred others which rose from the crowd.
Cada diez pesetas se me convertían en **cien,** y cada cien en más de mil. (Camba, **Aventuras de una peseta,** I, 13)	Every ten pesetas turned into a hundred, and every hundred into more than a thousand.

Considérase que el presupuesto de Instrucción pública del Estado es insuficiente, lo menos en un **cien** por ciento. (Madariaga, **España,** II, 12)

It is considered that the Government budget for public instruction is insufficient, at least one hundred per cent.

12.5. In the formation of compound numbers, the same order is observed in Spanish as in English, except that the conjunction comes between tens, units and fractions; otherwise there is no conjunction:[1]

diez mil cuatrocientos setenta y cinco	ten thousand four hundred *and* seventy-five
ciento diez	a hundred and ten
quinientos veinte	five hundred and twenty
quinientos veinte y dos tercios	five hundred and twenty *and* two-thirds

BUT:

setenta y cinco y tres cuartos	seventy-five *and* three-fourths

12.6. Counting by hundreds is not carried above nine hundred in Spanish; beyond that it is by thousands, with any odd number of hundreds added:

dos mil quinientos	twenty-five hundred
mil ochocientos noventa y dos	eighteen hundred and ninety-two

12.7. **Millón** is considered as a noun and therefore takes the indefinite article and is followed by the preposition **de,** unless other numerals intervene:

un millón **de** millas	a million miles
El costo de construcción de las doscientas millas de ferrocarril ha sido de nueve millones **de** pesos.	The cost of the two hundred miles of railroad has been nine million dollars.
nueve millones, novecientos mil pesos	nine million, nine hundred thousand dollars

12.8. **Uno** is not used before **ciento** and **mil** unless its absence would cause ambiguity:

Mil ciento noventa y nueve, 1,199;

---

[1] Between hundreds (thousands, etc.) and units **y** is not infrequently used: **ciento y dos bonitos. . .¿Cuántos?. . .—ciento dos.** (Palacio Valdés, **José,** I) *One hundred and two tunnies. . .—How many?. . .—One hundred and two.*

BUT

Doscientos un mil ciento noventa y nueve, 201,199,

BECAUSE

Doscientos mil ciento noventa y nueve *would be* 200,199.

12.9. **Uno, una,** when expressing *unity,* has no plural; it may have a plural under the following circumstances:

1. When it is employed as the indefinite article to denote an undetermined number:

unos bollos; unas frambuesas	some cakes; some raspberries

2. When used as a noun denoting the numeral "1":

Once se escribe con dos **unos.**	Eleven is written with two *1's.*

3. When used in the predicate to denote identity or similarity, it agrees in number (and gender) with its noun:

El **mundo** siempre es **uno.**	The world is ever one.
Los **corazones** de mis partidarios son **unos.**	The hearts of my followers are one.

12.10. The remaining numerals are necessarily plurals; however, when employed as nouns they are considered as singular, and as such may be made plural in the same manner as nouns:

255 se escribe con un dos y dos **cincos.**	255 is written with one 2 and two *5's.*
el siete de infantería ligera	the 7th Light Infantry
Tiré un par de **sietes.**	I drew a pair of *sevens.*

12.11. **Ciento** and **mil,** when used as collective nouns, may be made plural:

Tenemos muchos cientos, muchos miles de documentos.	We have many hundreds, many thousands of documents.
Una brisa fresca que viene de la cordillera a algunos cientos de leguas de aquí.	A cool breeze which comes from the mountains some hundreds of leagues from here.

12.12. After the verb **ser,** numerals denoting prices, dimensions, etc., are preceded by the preposition **de:**

El precio de este solar es **de** $2 por pie cuadrado.	The price of this building lot is $2 per square foot.
La distancia es **de** veinte millas.	The distance is twenty miles.

La cosecha será probablemente **de** 20.000 arrobas.[1]	The crop will probably be 5,000 hundredweight.

12.13. The arithmetical signs +, ×, −, ÷, =, are read respectively **más, por, menos, dividido por, igual a:**

Veintiocho más siete menos doce igual a veintitrés.	28 + 7 − 12 = 23.
Siete y ocho, quince; asiento cinco y llevo uno.	7 and 8 are 15; I put down 5 and carry 1.
Siete por ocho, cincuenta y seis, y nueve hacen sesenta y cinco.	7 times 8 are 56, and 9 makes 65.
Dos por dos son cuatro.	Twice two is four.
Uno en seis no alcanza; trece en seis, toca dos, y queda uno, *etc.*	6 into 1, no times; 6 into 13, twice and 1 over, *etc.*

ORDINAL NUMERALS

12.14. The ordinal numbers are to all intents adjectives, and, whether single or compound, agree with their nouns in gender and number:

los cinco primeros capítulos[2]	the first five chapters
la página vigésima séptima	the twenty-seventh page

NOTE. The compound forms of the ordinals are written by some grammarians as one word; as: **cuadragésimoséptimo** *(fem.* **cuadragésimaséptima).** But it is preferable to write them separately.

12.15. Primero and **tercero** invariably drop the final **o** when they immediately precede a masculine noun in the singular or when they are separated from it only by an adjective. **Primera** and **tercera** occasionally drop the final **a** before feminine singular nouns. The apocopation of **postrero, -a** is similar to that of **primero, -a** and **tercero, -a:**

el **primer día;** el **tercer tomo**	the first day; the third volume
el **primer** buen **ejemplo**	the first good example
Pero lo más sorprendente fué que antes de pronunciar la **primer**	But the most surprising thing was that before pronouncing the first

[1] The **arroba** is the weight of twenty-five pounds and is used both as a dry and a liquid measure.

[2] The cardinal numerals usually precede the ordinal when both modify a noun, as they also do ordinarily before other adjectives: **los tres últimos capítulos,** *the last three chapters.* Cf. § **9.41.**

palabra, el Señor alargó hacia él la diestra. (Pérez Galdós, **Miau,** IX)	word the Lord stretched out his hand toward him.
A la **tercer dedalada** de licor, me decido. ¡Pecho al agua! (Pardo Bazán, **La sirena negra,** VII)	At the third thimble-full of liqueur I make up my mind. Here goes!
¿Cuándo descansaré, Dios mío? ¿Cuál será mi **postrer anhelo?** (Unamuno, **Recuerdos de niñez y de mocedad,** II, 7)	When shall I rest, my Lord? What will be my last aspiration?
Pero en el momento...en que se abrían las bocas para la **postrer despedida**...la voz de don Juan, resonando recia, detuvo bruscamente a todos. (Lynch, **El inglés de los güesos,** XXXI)	But at the moment...in which mouths were opening for the last farewell...Don Juan's voice, echoing loudly, brusquely stopped everybody.

12.16. The ordinals are not so frequently used in Spanish as in English; indeed, with the exception of **primero,** they are not infrequently replaced by the cardinal numbers, except in grave, religious or antique style:

libro dieciséis, página ciento veinte	book sixteen, page one hundred and twenty
el siglo diez y nueve	the nineteenth century
el décimo aniversario	the tenth anniversary
el salmo centésimo séptimo	the hundred and seventh psalm
al estilo del siglo décimo sexto	in sixteenth-century style

REMARK. When the cardinal numbers are used as ordinals, they regularly follow the noun if it be expressed. The simple ordinals usually follow the noun, the compound ones always do.

12.17. In naming a succession of sovereigns, the ordinal numbers are regularly employed up to **décimo** or **undécimo;** above that the cardinals are substituted. The name and number of the potentate are not connected by the definite article as in English:

Pedro segundo; Carlos quinto	Pedro the Second; Charles the Fifth
Pío nono; León trece	Pius the Ninth; Leo the Thirteenth
Alfonso doce; Luis catorce	Alphonso the Twelfth; Louis the Fourteenth

12.18. The ordinal numbers are abbreviated by adding the final syllable to the appropriate Arabic numeral, the termination varying according to gender. Occasionally the abbreviation is made by the addition of merely **o, a, os, as,** in smaller type:

el 1ro de noviembre	the 1st of November
la 2da cláusula	the 2nd clause
3ro, 4to, 5to, 6to, 7mo, *etc.*	3rd, 4th, 5th, 6th, 7th, *etc.*
1°, 2^{a}, 3°, 21os, 66as, *etc.*	1st, 2^{d}, 3^{d}, 21st, 66th, *etc.*

COLLECTIVE NUMERALS

12.19. Collective numerals are nouns representing a number as a unity:

par pair, couple	**cuarentena** two score; quarantine
decena ten, half a score	**centena** *or* **centenar** hundred
docena dozen	**gruesa** gross
quincena fifteen	**millar** thousand
veintena twenty, score	**millón** million
treintena thirty	**cuento** *(ant.)*, million

REMARK. **Ciento** and **mil** may be used as collectives.

12.20. **Centenar** is preferred to **ciento** as a collective noun except when employed to express rate:

centenares de aves marinas	hundreds of sea fowl
a cuatro pesetas el ciento	at four pesetas per hundred

12.21. **Millar** is generally interchangeable with **mil** as a collective noun; but in expressing rate **millar** alone is admissible:

millares *or* miles de animálculas	thousands of animalcula
a diez pesos el millar	at ten pesos per thousand

REMARK. In mercantile language the article is usually omitted:

35.000 ladrillos, a $12,00 millar	35,000 bricks, at $12.00 per 1,000
Estos tabacos se venden a $6,00 ciento.	These cigars sell at $6.00 a hundred.
buñuelos a real uno	fritters 25 céntimos apiece
¡a perro chico! ¡a perro chico![1]	only 5 céntimos apiece!

[1] In Spain the 5-céntimo coin is called familiarly **perro chico** or **perra chica** *little dog* and the 10-céntimo piece, **perro grande** or **perra grande** because of the rather indefinite figure of the lion on the reverse.

PARTITIVE OR FRACTIONAL NUMBERS

12.22. Fractional numbers from $1/2$ to $1/10$ inclusive correspond more or less to the ordinal numbers:

un medio	$1/2$	un cuarto	$1/4$	un octavo *or*	$1/8$
uno y medio	$1\,1/2$	un quinto	$1/5$	un ochavo	$1/8$
una y media	$1\,1/2$	un sexto	$1/6$	un noveno	$1/9$
un tercio	$1/3$	un séptimo	$1/7$	un décimo	$1/10$

12.23. From $1/11$ onwards they are, in technical language, formed from the cardinals by adding the termination **-avo.** If the denominator is a numeral of simple form, this termination is usually appended to it so as to form one word. If the denominator is a compound numeral, the various component parts should be connected by hyphens:

un onzavo *or* once-avo	$1/11$	un veintavo *or* veinte-avo	$1/20$
un dozavo *or* doce-avo	$1/12$	un veintiunavo *or* veinte-y-unavo, *etc.*	$1/21$
un trezavo *or* trece-avo	$1/13$	un treintavo	$1/30$
un catorzavo *or* catorce-avo	$1/14$	un cuarentavo	$1/40$
un quinzavo *or* quince-avo	$1/15$	un cincuentavo	$1/50$
Un dieciseisavo *or* diez-y-seis-avo	$1/16$	un sesentavo	$1/60$
un diecisiete-avo *or* diez-y-siete-avo	$1/17$	un setentavo	$1/70$
un dieciocho-avo *or* diez-y-ocho-avo	$1/18$	un ochentavo	$1/80$
un diecinueve-avo *or* diez-y-nueve-avo	$1/19$	un noventavo	$1/90$
		un centavo *or* centésimo	$1/100$
		un milésimo	$1/1000$

12.24. The denominator of course assumes the plural form when the numerator is greater than one:

dos tercios	$2/3$	treinta y tres centavos	$33/100$
tres cuartos	$3/4$	cincuenta y cinco doscientos-cuarenta-y-cuatro-avos	$55/244$
cuatro quintos	$4/5$	novecientos ochenta y tres milcuatrocientos-cincuenta-y-cinco-avos	$983/1455$
cinco octavos	$5/8$		
once dieciseisavos	$11/16$		
veintitrés quincuagésimos novenos	$23/59$		

12.25. Fractions above $1/12$ are more commonly expressed by the appropriate ordinal numeral preceding and agreeing with the feminine noun **parte** *part,*[1] especially when the thing divided follows or is understood. The same is applicable to fractions between ⅓ and 1/10 inclusive, when the thing divided follows or is understood:

la duodécima parte una duodécima parte	1/12	las dos terceras partes	⅔
las treinta y tres centésimas partes	33/100	las tres cuartas partes	¾
las veintitrés quincuagésimas novenas partes	23/59	la diez milésima parte	1/10,000

NOTE. There are a few irregularly formed partitive numerals which are restricted in their application to particular objects. Thus, **una tercia, una cuarta** and **una sesma,** are respectively *a third, a quarter* and *a sixth of a yard;* **un cuarterón,** *a quarter of a pound;* **una cuarterola,** *a keg or quarter cask;* **un cuartal,** *a peck* (quarter of a **fanega**); **una arroba** (from the Arabic for ¼), *25 pounds* or ¼ *cwt.,* applied to liquid as well as dry measure in Spain. **Un quinto,** *a fifth, a fifth man,* hence *a conscript soldier;* **la quinta,** *the military conscription.* **Un diezmo,** *a tithe, 10% tax;* from which is made **diezmar,** *to decimate.*

12.26. Partitive numerals are employed as follows in Spanish to designate the size of a book; i.e. the number of leaves in a signature or of pages to a form:

un tomo en folio (f°)	a folio volume
un tomo en cuarto (4°)	a 4to volume
un tomo en octavo (8°)	an 8vo volume
un tomo en 8° mayor	a royal 8vo volume
un tomo en dozavo (12°)	a 12mo volume
un tomo en diez-y-seis-avo (16°)	a 16mo volume
un tomo en veinte-y-cuatro-avo (24°)	a 24mo volume

12.27. The noun **un medio** means *a half* in arithmetical calculations; otherwise it signifies *a means* or *middle.* In other cases the noun **la mitad** is used. **Medio, -a,** is the adjective meaning half:[2]

la mitad de su caudal	half of his property
Le daré la mitad.	I will give him half.
en el medio de la estancia	in the middle of the room

[1] **Parte(s)** is not infrequently omitted: **dos décimas** *two tenths,* **tres centésimas** *three hundredths,* etc.

[2] As in the case of the English equivalent the indefinite article is sometimes used with **medio: Del lugar al molino habrá... Yo creo que habrá una media legua.** (Alarcón, **El sombrero de tres picos,** XIV) *From the village to the mill it must be... I think it must be a half league.*

medio luto	half mourning
media docena	half a dozen
media hora, una hora y media	half an hour, an hour and a half
un mes y medio	a month and a half
por término medio	on an average
La temperatura media del año en la Martinica es de 81° (ochenta y un grados).	The mean annual temperature of Martinique is 81° (eighty-one degrees).

12.28. **Medio** may be employed indeclinably as an adverb:

El cura bajó **medio** dormido **medio** despierto.	The priest came downstairs *half* asleep, *half* awake.
Quedamos **medio** muertos de espanto.	We were *half* dead with fright.
Los malteses hablan una lengua **medio** árabe **medio** italiana.	The Maltese speak a language *half* Arabic, *half* Italian.
Aquella noche, entre bromas y veras, **medio** hicimos las paces. (Benavente, **Al natural,** II, 7)	That night, joking one moment and serious the next, we *half* made peace.
El artista, loco de contento, quería comunicárselo al atribulado padre, y **medio** se echó de la cama. (Pérez Galdós, **Torquemada en la hoguera,** VIII)	The artist, mad with joy, wished to communicate it to the grieving father, and *half* jumped out of bed.

REMARK. The noun **mitad** is similarly used before nouns:

La sirena es una ninfa marina fabulosa, **mitad** mujer, **mitad** pez.	The mermaid is a fabulous sea nymph, *half* woman, *half* fish.

MULTIPLE NUMERALS

12.29. Multiple numerals answer the question *how many fold?* They comprise adjectives and nouns as follows:

simple *single*	**quintuplo** *or* **quintuplicado** fivefold
doble *or* **duplicado** double	**séxtuplo** sixfold
triple *or* **triplicado** triple	**décuplo** *or* **decuplado** tenfold
cuádruplo *or* **cuadruplicado** quadruple	**céntuplo** *or* **centuplicado** a hundredfold

These are used in the same manner as their English equivalents:

movimiento simple, partida doble	single motion, double entry
una máquina de simple efecto, de doble acción	a single-acting, a double-acting engine
triple expansión, *or* expansión triplicada	triple expansion

doble fuerza, *or* fuerza duplicada	double power
ritmo cuádruplo, *or* cuadruplicado	quadruple rhythm

12.30. The multiple forms not ending in **ado** may be employed as masculine nouns:

Yo apuesto el doble.	I bet twice as much.
Le devolveré el décuplo.	I will return him tenfold.

12.31. Multiple numerals may be made from the cardinals from **tres** to **diez** inclusive, by the addition of **tanto:**

Es verdad que el valor de esta industria supera en el **cuatrotanto** el valor de las materias primas que les damos.	It is true that the value of this industry exceeds *fourfold* the value of the raw materials we give them.

12.32. The termination **-eno,** added to cardinals, forms a series of adjectives with the value of ordinal numerals but also applied to cloth and signifying the number of threads in the warp.

Veinteno, treinteno, cuarenteno, *etc.*	Twentieth, thirtieth, fortieth, *etc.*
Dieciseiseno, dieciocheno, veinteno, veintidoseno, veinticuatreno, *etc.*	1600, 1800, 2000, 2200, 2400, *etc.*

NUMERAL ADVERBS

12.33. Numeral adverbs expressing the number of times of an occurrence are formed by a cardinal numeral and the feminine noun **vez** *a time:*

una vez once	**diez veces** ten times
dos veces twice	**cien veces** a hundred times
tres veces three times	**mil veces** a thousand times
Le he escrito dos veces, si no tres.	I have written him twice, if not three times.

12.34. Numeral adverbs expressing order of procedure are made by the addition of **mente** to the feminine form of the ordinal numerals:

primeramente firstly	**décimamente** tenthly
segundamente secondly	**décima sexta y últimamente** sixteenthly and lastly
terceramente thirdly	

INDEFINITE NUMERAL EXPRESSIONS

12.35. The most usual way of expressing a number approximately is by placing before it the plural of **uno,** which is then generally to be rendered *some:*

Guayacán, notable por sus extensas obras de fundición de cobre, tiene **unos** 2.000 habitantes.	Guayacan, noted for its extensive copper-smelting works, has *some* 2,000 inhabitants.
Unas diez de las baterías del enemigo se han colocado a lo largo de aquel cerro.	*Some* ten of the enemy's batteries have planted themselves along yonder ridge.
La cantidad de lluvia que cae anualmente en la isla de la Trinidad es de **unas** 65 pulgadas.	The mean annual rainfall in the island of Trinidad is *about* 65 inches.

12.36. The following expressions also are frequently used:

El faro está situado **como** a seis millas del promontorio.	The lighthouse is situated at *about* six miles from the point.
De aquí el pico parece tener una altura de 3.000 metros, **poco más o menos.**	From here the peak appears to have an altitude of 10,000 feet, *more or less.*
Este lago tiene una superficie **como de unas** doscientas millas cuadradas.	This lake has an area of *some* two hundred square miles.
El diámetro total es **cosa de** 80 centímetros.	The total diameter is *about* 80 centimeters.
A **cosa de** seis leguas de la costa.	At *about* 15 miles from the coast.
600 pies **o cosa así.**	600 feet *or thereabouts.*
La cosecha total monta a **cerca de** 2.900 fanegas.	The total crop amounts to *about* 2,900 bushels.

12.37. The collective numerals in **-ena** have frequently an indefinite value:

una decena de libras	about ten pounds
una centena de varas de terciopelo negro	some hundred yards of black velvet

TIME AND ITS DESIGNATIONS

12.38.

DIVISIONS OF TIME

el siglo the century

el año the year

el anochecer (the) dusk, nightfall

la hora the hour

el año bisiesto the leap year
el mes the month
la quincena / **quince días** } the fortnight
la semana / **ocho días** } the week
el día the day
la noche the night
mediodía midday, noon
medianoche midnight
el amanecer the dawn, daybreak
media hora half an hour
un cuarto de hora a quarter of an hour
tres cuartos de hora three quarters of an hour
una hora y media an hour and a half
una hora y tres cuartos an hour and three quarters
el minuto the minute
el segundo the second

THE SEASONS OF THE YEAR

la primavera the spring
el verano the summer
el otoño the autumn
el invierno the winter

THE MONTHS

enero January
febrero February
marzo March
abril April
mayo May
junio June
julio July
agosto August
septiembre September
octubre October
noviembre November
diciembre December

THE DAYS OF THE WEEK

el domingo Sunday
el lunes Monday
el martes Tuesday
el miércoles Wednesday
el jueves Thursday
el viernes Friday
el sábado Saturday

ADVERBIAL EXPRESSIONS OF TIME

ayer yesterday
antes de ayer / **anteayer** / **antier** } the day before yesterday
mañana tomorrow
pasado mañana the day after tomorrow
mañana y pasado tomorrow and the next day
anteanteayer three days ago
ayer por la mañana yesterday morning
hoy (en) día at the present day, nowadays
anoche last night
antes de anoche / **ante(a)noche** } the night before last
de día by day, in the daytime
de noche by night, in the night
a la madrugada before sunrise, at an early hour
a la noche at night
anteantenoche three nights ago
por la mañana in the morning

ayer (por la) tarde yesterday afternoon
ayer (por la) noche yesterday evening
mañana por la mañana tomorrow morning
mañana por la tarde tomorrow afternoon
mañana por la noche tomorrow evening *or* night
al amanecer at dawn
en el día at the present day
por la tarde in the afternoon
por la noche in the evening
por la mañana temprano early in the morning
por la tarde temprano early in the afternoon
a una hora avanzada de la noche late at night
a la caída de la noche at nightfall
al anochecer at dusk
al otro día on the following day

12.39.

VARIOUS KINDS OF DAYS

día adiado *or* día diado	appointed day
día aplazado, señalado *or* convenido	day agreed upon
día de campo	field day
día festivo, feriado, de asueto	holiday
día de entre semana	weekday
día de gala	gala day
día de hacienda, de trabajo, laborable, de labor	work day
día de hueco, de descanso	day of rest
día de huelga	day off *(among working men)*
días	saint's day, birthday
días de gracia *or* de cortesía	days of grace *(commercial)*
días caniculares	dog days
día de ayuno	fast day
día de pescado	fish day
el día de año nuevo	New Year's Day
el día de Navidad	Christmas Day
pascuas de Navidad	Christmas, yuletide
la noche buena	Christmas Eve
el día de noche buena	the day before Christmas
¡Felices Pascuas!	Merry Christmas!

12.40. The days of the month, with the exception of the first, are counted in Spanish by the cardinal numerals, preceded by the definite article. In dating letters, however, the article is omitted. The month and year, when expressed, are connected with the date by the preposition **de:**

el primero de mayo	the first of May

el cuatro de julio	the fourth of July
el siete de agosto de mil ochocientos noventa	August seventh, eighteen hundred and ninety
Lima, 26 de Abril de 1891	Lima, April 26th, 1891
viernes, diez y ocho de agosto de mil ochocientos noventa y tres	Friday, August the eighteenth, eighteen ninety-three

12.41. When the month is not expressed, it is usual to place the word **día** *day* before the numeral; this is occasionally done when the month is given:

Le espero el día treinta.	I expect him the thirtieth.
Partiremos el día quince.	We shall start on the fifteenth.
el día catorce de marzo el catorce de marzo	the fourteenth of March

12.42. There are several formulæ for inquiring the day of the month, among which there is no preference; the only restriction is that the answer should conform to the terms of the question:

¿A cómo estamos? ¿A cuántos estamos? ¿Qué día del mes tenemos? ¿Qué fecha tenemos? ¿Cuál es la fecha?	What day of the month is it?
Estamos a diez y seis. Tenemos el diez y seis.	It is the sixteenth.
¿A cómo estamos hoy?	What day of the month is today?
a veinticinco	the twenty-fifth
¿A cómo estaremos mañana? ¿A cuántos estaremos mañana? ¿Qué día del mes tendremos mañana?	What day of the month will it be tomorrow?
a veintiséis el veintiséis	the twenty-sixth

12.43. In addition to the division of time into *day* (**día** = *sunrise to sunset*) and *night* (**noche** = *sunset to sunrise*), the Spaniards further subdivide these into four portions, which are:

la madrugada the morning *(midnight to sunrise)*
la mañana the morning, forenoon *(sunrise to noon)*
la tarde the afternoon *(noon to sunset)*
la noche the evening *(sunset to midnight)*[1]

[1] In popular usage these limits are not strictly adhered to, the point or division being often a little later than that prescribed above.

12.44. In salutations, these divisions of the day are put in the plural:

> **¡buenos días!** good morning! good day!
> **¡buenas tardes!** good afternoon!
> **¡buenas noches!** good evening! good night!

REMARK. **Buenas mañanas** is not used, and **buenas madrugadas** appears only in the well-worn joke on the young lover who loiters so long that he can no longer properly say **buenas noches. Buenos días** is the salutation used in the forenoon. As **buenas noches** is applicable any time after sunset, it is employed as a greeting as well as an adieu.

12.45. The days of the week are usually preceded by the definite article, except when used in the dating of letters and the like. No preposition corresponding to the English *on* is then employed:

Quedaré hasta el lunes.	I will stay until Monday.
El domingo es día de descanso.	Sunday is a day of rest.
El sábado es el último día de la semana.	Saturday is the last day of the week.
Tendré el dinero el lunes.	I shall have the money Monday.
Comemos pescado los viernes.	We eat fish on Fridays.
Toma lecciones de francés los lunes, miércoles y viernes, y de música los martes y jueves.	She takes French lessons Mondays, Wednesdays and Fridays, and music lessons Tuesdays and Thursdays.

12.46. The day of the month, when unaccompanied by the day of the week, may be expressed by a cardinal numeral without an article, but preceded by **a** which is to be rendered *on:*

a uno de mayo	on the first of May
a dos de junio	on the second of June
a quince de octubre	on the fifteenth of October

12.47. The hour or time of day is expressed by the cardinal numbers, preceded by the feminine article (to agree with **hora, horas,** understood). The verb *to be,* when needed, is then singular or plural as may be required by the number of hours:

¿Qué hora es?	What time is it?
¿Qué hora tiene V.?	What time have you?
Es la una.	It is one o'clock.
Son las dos; son las cuatro.	It is two o'clock; it is four.
A la una; a las cinco.	At one o'clock; at five o'clock.
Lo haré antes de las doce.	I shall do it before twelve.

Estaré en mi despacho a las nueve en punto.	I shall be at my office at exactly nine.
Entre la una y las dos.	Between one and two o'clock.
¿Son las ocho ya?	Is it eight o'clock yet?
Sólo son las siete.	It is only seven.
Son cerca de las once.	It is nearly eleven.

12.48. Portions of time before or after the hour named are placed after it, connected by **y** *and* or **menos** *less;* the word **minutos** *minutes* is often omitted. Portions of time before the hour named are also indicated by **faltar** *be lacking:*

Es la una y media.	It is half *past* one.
Es la una **menos** cuarto.	It is a quarter *to* one.
Faltan quince minutos para la una.	It is a quarter *to* one.
Son las dos y diez minutos.	It is ten minutes *past* two.
Me ha prometido venir a las diez **menos** veinte.	He promised me to come at twenty minutes *to* ten.
Estará aquí a las cuatro y pico.	He will be here at a little *after* four.
Le espero a las once y cuarto.	I expect him at quarter *past* eleven.
Quedará hasta la una y diez minutos.	He will stay until ten minutes *past* one.

12.49. The particular hour of any of the larger divisions of the day is connected with it by the preposition **de,** where in English *in* or *at* is used:

A las tres **de** la madrugada.	At three o'clock *in* the morning.
A las siete **de** la mañana.	At seven o'clock *in* the morning.
A las cinco **de** la tarde.	At five o'clock *in* the evening.
Hasta las diez **de** la noche.	Until ten o'clock *at* night.
Son las doce del día.	It is twelve noon.
Son cerca de las doce **de** la noche.	It is nearly twelve *at* night.

12.50. *To strike,* in speaking of the hour, is **dar,** used intransitively, the verb then agreeing in number with the hour:

La una va a dar.	It is going to strike one.
Las dos van a dar. Van a dar las dos.	} It is going to strike two.
¿Han dado las doce ya?	Has it struck twelve yet?
Han dado las cinco. Son las cinco dadas.	} It has struck five.
Este reloj da las medias horas.	This clock strikes the half hours.

12.51. The divison of time in the immediate future is expressed by **próximo** *next* or **que viene** (in literary style, **venidero**) *coming;* the present time is represented by **actual** or **presente** *present* or **corriente** *current;* and that past by **pasado, último** *last* or **próximo pasado** *lately past.* Thus:

El siglo pasado; el siglo venidero.	The last century; the next century.
El año pasado; el año que viene.	Last year; next year.
El mes pasado; el mes que viene.	Last month; next month.
De otro modo quedaremos empatados hasta el otoño venidero.	Otherwise we shall remain in a deadlock until next autumn.
La comitiva partirá en el mes que viene.	The retinue will start next month.
Iré el viernes próximo.	I will go next Friday.
En el mes de julio próximo pasado.	In the month of July just past.
Desde el jueves de la semana pasada.	Since Thursday of last week.
El lunes de la semana que viene.	On Monday of next week.
El día treinta y uno del mes corriente recibiré mil pesos.	The thirty-first of the current month I shall receive 1000 pesos.

12.52. In business style, when the month is qualified by one of the above expressions, the word **mes** is frequently omitted:

El día veinte del próximo pasado.	The twentieth of the month just past.
El cinco del actual; el doce del último.	The fifth instant; the twelfth ultimo.

12.53. The expressions **quince días, ocho días,** are more frequently employed than the general terms **quincena** and **semana:**

De hoy en quince días.	Two weeks from today.
De hoy en ocho días.	A week from today.
De mañana en ocho días.	A week from tomorrow.
Llegará dentro de ocho días.	He will arrive within a week.

12.54. Expressions for the beginning, middle or end of any period of time are made more indefinite by being put in the plural:

a primero del mes que viene	on the first of next month
a primeros del mes que viene	in the early part of next month
a principios del siglo actual	along at the beginning of the present century
a fin del año	at the end of the year
a fines del año	in the latter part of the year
a mediados del año pasado	about the middle of last year
a últimos del mes	toward the end of the month

NOUNS EXPRESSING TIME IN ITS VARIOUS ASPECTS

There are in Spanish a number of nouns which correspond to some value of the English *time,* but which are distinct in their usages.

12.55. **Tiempo** is *time* in its widest and most general sense, and is the term for time in philosophy and science:

El tiempo es el oro del sabio y el juguete del necio.	Time is the wise man's gold and the fool's plaything.
Tiempo sideral, tiempo medio.	Sidereal time, mean time.
No tenemos tiempo ahora.	We have not time now.
No llegará a tiempo.	He will not arrive in time.

REMARK. **Tiempo** means also *weather:*

Tiempo variable, tiempo borrascoso, tiempo apacible, tiempo cubierto, *etc.*	Changeable weather, stormy weather, pleasant weather, cloudy weather, *etc.*

12.56. **Plazo** is a period of time appointed or agreed upon:

Señalar un plazo.	To appoint a time, set a time.
Acortar, alargar el plazo.	To shorten, extend the time.
El plazo se ha cumplido.	The time has expired.
A plazos cortos.	On short instalments.
Al plazo y en el lugar convenidos.	At the time and place agreed on.

12.57. **Rato** is an undetermined, generally short, space of time, equivalent to the English *while.* It is also used when reference is had to the quality of an occasion:

Al cabo de rato.	After a while.
Después de un buen rato.	After a good while.
Estuvo largo rato pensando.	He stood a long while thinking.
¿No quiere V. esperarle un rato?	Won't you wait for him a while?
¿Qué rato han llevado Vds.?	What kind of a time did you have?
Hemos llevado mal rato.	We had a poor time.
Al poco rato.	In a little while *or* soon *or* shortly thereafter.

12.58. **Espacio** is often used when especial reference is had to duration:

Permaneció silencioso durante un espacio considerable.	He remained silent for a considerable length of time.

12.59. **Epoca** is a fixed point of time:

En aquella época estaba de cónsul en Valparaíso.	At that time he was consul at Valparaiso.

12.60. **Vez** is a point of time considered as part of a series, an occasion:

Esta vez te lo perdono.	This time I forgive you.
Es la primera vez que ha hecho tal cosa.	It is the first time he has done such a thing.
algunas veces; rara vez *or* raras veces; repetidas veces	sometimes; rarely; repeatedly
alguna vez	on some occasion, occasionally

MANNER OF EXPRESSING DIMENSIONS

12.61. The principal nouns and adjectives used are the following:

NOUNS	ADJECTIVES
la altura *or* **elevación** height	**alto** high *or* tall
la longitud *or* **extensión** length	**largo** long
la anchura width *or* breadth	**ancho** wide *or* broad
la profundidad depth	**profundo** *or* **hondo** deep
el espesor thickness	**grueso** thick

12.62. When the dimension stands in the predicate after the object described, the connecting verb is **tener** in Spanish, while in English it is the verb *to be*. **Tener** is followed by a noun of dimension connected with the numeral by **de.** The adjectives **alto, largo** and **ancho,** however, are used in the same manner as their corresponding nouns, and are, in fact, more usual:

El interior de la catedral de Milán tiene 449 pies de largo y 275 de ancho en la nave del centro, y 238 pies de alto debajo de la cúpula.	The interior of the Milan cathedral is 449 feet long and 275 wide in the central nave, and 238 feet high under the dome.
El río tiene aquí una anchura de media milla, y una profundidad de cuatro brazas.	The river is here half a mile wide and four fathoms deep.
El foso que lo rodea tiene tres metros de ancho y cuatro de profundidad.	The ditch which surrounds it is three yards wide and thirteen feet deep.

El Itata es un vapor de hélice, de 1.200 toneladas. Tiene 300 pies de largo, 45 de ancho, y un calado medio de 18½ pies,[1] y desaloja 3.730 toneladas. Su velocidad pasa de 18 nudos por hora.	The Itata is a screw steamer of 1,200 tons. She is 300 feet long, 45 wide and has an average draft of 18½ feet and 3,730 tons displacement. Her speed exceeds 18 knots per hour.
La rada de adentro tiene 1½ millas de largo con una anchura como de 3 cables. La rada de afuera tiene de tres a 4 millas de largo, con una anchura de media milla y una profundidad de 4 brazas.	The inner harbor [at Buenos Aires] is 1½ miles long with a width of about three cable-lengths. The outer harbor is from three to four miles long with a width of half a mile and a depth of four fathoms.
La cúpula de la iglesia de S. Pedro en Roma tiene 450 pies de elevación y 130 de diámetro por dentro.	The dome of St. Peter's at Rome is 450 ft. high and 130 in diameter inside.
El pedestal tiene diez pies en cuadro y quince de altura.	The pedestal is ten feet square and fifteen feet high.
Este pozo artesiano tiene una profundidad de 1.000 pies. El tubo tiene seis pulgadas de diámetro, y la presión del agua es de 150 libras por pulgada cuadrada.	This artesian well is 1,000 feet deep. The tube is six inches in diameter and the pressure of the water is 150 lbs. to the square inch.
La mesa de alimentación es de acero colado y tiene media pulgada de espesor.	The feed-table is of cast steel, half an inch thick.

REMARK. There are cases where a noun of dimension is required as a leading word in the sentence, and the adjectives **alto, largo** and **ancho** are not admissible:

El valle de Quito tiene una altura media de 9.540 pies.	The valley of Quito has a mean altitude of 9,540 feet.
El grueso de la tapia es de cuatro ladrillos.	The thickness of the wall is four bricks.

12.63. When the word denoting dimension is used attributively without a connecting verb, the following modes of expression are in use:

La línea de ferrocarril atraviesa aquí una cañada **de 500 pies de ancho y 120 de profundidad.**	The railroad here crosses a ravine *500 feet wide* and *120 feet deep.*

[1] Or, in technical terms, **300 pies de eslora, 45 de manga y 18½ de puntal.**

La faja de rocas fosfatadas al oeste constituye mantos de gran extensión, a veces **de 6 a 9 metros de espesor.** — The stratum of phosphated rocks to the west forms veins of great extent, at times *from 6* to *9 meters thick.*

Una vara de acero, **larga de 6 metros.** — A steel rod *6 meters long.*

El corral está rodeado de una fuerte empalizada, alta **de dos metros** *(or* **de dos metros de alto).** — The stockyard is surrounded by a stout fence, *6½ feet high.*

La fachada tiene cinco puertas situadas debajo de un pórtico **448 pies de longitud** y **39 de ancho.** — The façade has five doors situated under a portico *448 feet long* and *39 wide.*

He comprado una alfombra turca, **de veinte pies por catorce.** — I have bought a Turkish carpet, *twenty feet by fourteen.*

El tamaño de los torpedos es **de 14 pulgadas de diámetro** y **de 14 pies 6 pulgadas de largo.** — The size of the torpedoes is *14 inches in diameter* and *14 feet 6 inches in length.*

El edificio tendrá una **área de 250 pies** próximamente. — The building will have an *area of* about *250 feet.*

La segunda parte, de la misma altura, es una continuación de la rotonda central, **de 175 pies cuadrados,** rodeada por todas partes por una columnata abierta **de 20 pies de ancho** y **40 de alto** con columnas **de 4 pies de diámetro.** — The second part, of the same height, is a continuation of the central rotunda, *measuring 175 square feet,* surrounded on all sides by an open colonnade *20 feet wide and 40 high,* with columns *4 feet in diameter.*

12.64. Weight is expressed in the same manner as in English:

El cañón con su cureña pesa 261.000 libras. — The cannon with its carriage weighs 261,000 lbs.

Esta grúa levanta con facilidad un peso de doscientas toneladas. — This crane raises with ease a weight of 200 tons.

415 billetes nuevos de a dólar, de los Estados Unidos, según prueba verificada, equivalen en peso a una libra. — 415 new U. S. dollar bills are, according to actual experiment, equal in weight to one pound.

MANNER OF EXPRESSING AGE

12.65. Age is expressed by **tener**, followed by a cardinal denoting the number of years:

¿Cuántos años tiene V.?
¿Qué edad tiene V.? } How old are you?

Yo tengo veintitrés años y mi hermano tiene veinte.	I am twenty-three years old and my brother twenty.
Tiene treinta años cumplidos.	He is just thirty years old.

12.66. The birthday is not celebrated in Spanish countries, but the day of the saint after whom the person is named. When mention is made of the anniversary of one's birth it is called **el día de su cumpleaños, el día de sus años,** or **su cumpleaños.** One's saint's-day is spoken of as **el día de su santo,** or simply **sus días:**

Mañana son los días de don Agapito.	Tomorrow is Don Agapito's saint's-day.

12.67. The following adjective and adverbial expressions relating to age are the same in both languages:

No representa su edad.	He does not look his age.
Somos de la misma edad.	We are of the same age.
A la edad de 30.	At the age of 30.
Ha entrado en su sexagésimo año.	He has entered his sixtieth year.

XIII

INFLECTION OF MODEL VERBS

13.1. Spanish verbs are inflected by means of a series of terminations, expressing distinctions of person, number, tense and mood, added to a basis, called the *stem,* which embodies the meaning of the verb.

a. All Spanish verbs in the infinitive end in **-ar, -er** or **ir,** and are classified into conjugations according to these terminations:

-ar:	1st conjugation
-er:	2nd conjugation
-ir:	3rd conjugation

b. By removing the infinitive ending of a verb we obtain the stem.

c. In regular verbs, the terminations of the future indicative and conditional are added to the full infinitive; all other terminations are applied to the unchanged stem.

13.2. With the exception of the infinitive and those forms constructed upon it, the inflections of the second and third conjugations differ only in the 1st and 2nd persons plural of the indicative present and in the 2nd person plural of the imperative. The two conjugations are combined in the following table when their terminations are identical:

INFLECTIONAL ENDINGS OF THE THREE CONJUGATIONS

INFINITIVE			PAST PARTICIPLE		PRESENT PARTICIPLE	
1	2	3	1	2 and 3	1	2 and 3
-ar	-er	-ir	-ado	-ido	-ando	-iendo

INDICATIVE MOOD			SUBJUNCTIVE MOOD	
PRESENT			PRESENT	
1	2	3	1	2 and 3
-o	-o	-o	-e	-a
-as	-es	-es	-es	-as
-a	-e	-e	-e	-a
-amos	-emos	-imos	-emos	-amos
-áis	-éis	-ís	-éis	-áis
-an	-en	-en	-en	-an

INDICATIVE MOOD		SUBJUNCTIVE MOOD	
IMPERFECT		IMPERFECT	
1	2 and 3	1	2 and 3
-aba	-ía	-ara	-iera
-abas	-ías	-aras	-ieras
-aba	-ía	-ara	-iera
-ábamos	-íamos	-áramos	-iéramos
-abais	-íais	-arais	-ierais
-aban	-ían	-aran	-ieran
PRETERITE		IMPERFECT	
1	2 and 3	1	2 and 3
-é	-í	-ase	-iese
-aste	-iste	-ases	-ieses
-ó	-ió	-ase	-iese
-amos	-imos	-ásemos	-iésemos
-asteis	-isteis	-aseis	-ieseis
-aron	-ieron	-asen	-iesen

Indicative Mood	Subjunctive Mood		
FUTURE	FUTURE		
1, 2 and 3	1		2 and 3
-é	-are		-iere
-ás	-ares		-ieres
-á	-are		-iere
-emos	-áremos		-iéremos
-éis	-areis		-iereis
-án	-aren		-ieren
CONDITIONAL	IMPERATIVE MOOD		
1, 2 and 3	1	2	3
-ía	—	—	—
-ías	-a	-e	-e
-ía	—	—	—
-íamos	—	—	—
-íais	-ad	-ed	-id
-ían	—	—	—

13.3. These terminations are applied as follows to the three model verbs, like which all other regular verbs are to be inflected, according to conjugation:

PARADIGMS OF THE THREE MODEL VERBS

	1st Conjugation	2nd Conjugation	3rd Conjugation
Infinitive	compr-ar	vend-er	viv-ir
Present Participle	compr-ando	vend-iendo	viv-iendo
Past Participle	compr-ado	vend-ido	viv-ido
	Indicative Mood		
Present	compr-o	vend-o	viv-o
	compr-as	vend-es	viv-es
	compr-a	vend-e	viv-e
	compr-amos	vend-emos	viv-imos
	compr-áis	vend-éis	viv-ís
	compr-an	vend-en	viv-en

	1st Conjugation	2nd Conjugation	3rd Conjugation
	Indicative Mood		
Imperfect	compr-aba compr-abas compr-aba compr-ábamos compr-abais compr-aban	vend-ía vend-ías vend-ía vend-íamos vend-íais vend-ían	viv-ía viv-ías viv-ía viv-íamos viv-íais viv-ían
Preterite	compr-é compr-aste compr-ó compr-amos compr-asteis compr-aron	vend-í vend-iste vend-ió vend-imos vend-isteis vend-ieron	viv-í viv-iste viv-ió viv-imos viv-isteis viv-ieron
Future	compr-ar-é compr-ar-ás compr-ar-á compr-ar-emos compr-ar-éis compr-ar-án	vend-er-é vend-er-ás vend-er-á vend-er-emos vend-er-éis vend-er-án	viv-ir-é viv-ir-ás viv-ir-á viv-ir-emos viv-ir-éis viv-ir-án

	Subjunctive Mood		
Present	compr-e compr-es compr-e compr-emos compr-éis compr-en	vend-a vend-as vend-a vend-amos vend-áis vend-an	viv-a viv-as viv-a viv-amos viv-áis viv-an
Imperfect	compr-ara compr-aras compr-ara compr-áramos compr-arais compr-aran	vend-iera vend-ieras vend-iera vend-iéramos vend-ierais vend-ieran	viv-iera viv-ieras viv-iera viv-iéramos viv-ierais viv-ieran

	1st Conjugation	2nd Conjugation	3rd Conjugation
	Subjunctive Mood		
Imperfect	compr-ase compr-ases compr-ase compr-ásemos compr-aseis compr-asen	vend-iese vend-ieses vend-iese vend-iésemos vend-ieseis vend-iesen	viv-iese viv-ieses viv-iese viv-iésemos viv-ieseis viv-iesen
Future	compr-are compr-ares compr-are compr-áremos compr-areis compr-aren	vend-iere vend-ieres vend-iere vend-iéremos vend-iereis vend-ieren	viv-iere viv-ieres viv-iere viv-iéremos viv-iereis viv-ieren

Conditional Mood		
compr-ar-ía compr-ar-ías compr-ar-ía compr-ar-íamos compr-ar-íais compr-ar-ían	vend-er-ía vend-er-ías vend-er-ía vend-er-íamos vend-er-íais vend-er-ían	viv-ir-ía viv-ir-ías viv-ir-ía viv-ir-íamos viv-ir-íais viv-ir-ían
Imperative Mood		
compr-a compr-ad	vend-e vend-ed	viv-e viv-id

REMARKS ON THE INFLECTION OF VERBS

13.4. When an inflectional ending is unlike any other, or when it is not likely to be mistaken for another of the same form, it may serve the purpose of a personal pronoun as subject; in that case the personal pronoun is dispensed with unless required by way of emphasis or contrast.

13.5. It will be seen by the paradigms that the endings of the first and third persons singular are alike in the conditional, the imperfect indicative and all the tenses of the subjunctive; with these the pronoun subject is often expressed when ambiguity would result from its omission:

Imp. Ind.:	yo, él, ella, Vd.	compraba	vendía	vivía
Pres. Subj.:	yo, él, ella, Vd.	compre	venda	viva
Imp. Subj.:	yo, él, ella, Vd.	comprara	vendiera	viviera
Imp. Subj.:	yo, él, ella, Vd.	comprase	vendiese	viviese
Fut. Subj.:	yo, él, ella, Vd.	comprare	vendiere	viviere
Cond.:	yo, él, ella, Vd.	compraría	vendería	viviría

These persons became identical by the dropping of the original Latin terminations *m* and *t,* since no Spanish words end in these letters. It may be interesting to note the simplification undergone by the Latin inflectional endings, as exemplified by the imperfect indicative:

Latin	Spanish
ama-ba-*m*	ama-ba-
ama-ba-s	ama-ba-s
ama-ba-*t*	ama-ba-
ama-ba-mus	ama-ba-mos
ama-ba-*tis*	ama-ba-is
ama-ba-n*t*	ama-ba-n

13.6. The first person plural is the same in the present and preterite indicative of the first and third conjugations, and is only distinguishable by the context:

Compramos, vendemos, vivimos.	We buy, we sell, we live.
Compramos, vendimos, vivimos.	We bought, we sold, we lived.

13.7. The singular of the imperative is identical with the third person singular of the indicative present in all three conjugations:

Compra, vende, vive.	Buy, sell, live.
Compra, vende, vive.	Buys, sells, lives.

13.8. All other forms that are composed of the same letters are distinguished by the accent both in pronunciation and writing:

compre	compré	compro	compró
comprare	compraré	comprara	comprará
compraras	comprarás	comprareis	compraréis
compráremos	compraremos	compraran	comprarán

Remark I. There are no such pairs or homonymous forms in the second and third conjugations.

In popular language the preterite terminations of the second person—**aste, asteis** and **iste, isteis**—are very generally assimilated into the forms **astes** and **istes**:

tú *or* vos	**comprastes** **vendistes** **vivistes**	*for*	tú compraste *or* vos comprasteis tú vendiste " vos vendisteis tú viviste " vos vivisteis

In familar style the **d** of the past participle of the first conjugation is very generally omitted in pronunciation; it is pronounced in careful speaking:

he **comprao, negao, tomao** *for* he comprado, negado, tomado

NOTE. Many other tense, mood and voice forms may be compounded from the infinitive, present participle or past participle by means of the auxiliaries **haber, ser** and **estar,** and various other verbs. These constructions are explained under the heads of "Compound Tenses," "The Passive Voice" and "Periphrastic Verbal Expressions."

REMARK II. In Argentina, Uruguay and Paraguay, in which countries its use is most widespread, **vos** (§ 3.3) is used, in the tenses named below, with verb forms which derive from the second person plural form of Castilian: present indicative **comprás, vendés, vivís;** present subjunctive **comprés, vendás, vivás;** preterite **compraste(s), vendiste(s), viviste(s).** The imperative forms are **comprá, vendé, viví.** In the remaining tenses the **tú** form of Castilian is used with vos, as it sometimes is in the tenses above named. Moreover, **os** is, in this usage, replaced by **te,** Castilian **compraos un libro** becoming **comprάte un libro.** The accent mark is often omitted **(comprate).**

REMARK III. In non-literary language everywhere **n** of plural verb forms of command is often transferred to a following object pronoun or even repeated after it. Thus, for example **denme** becomes **demen, denle** becomes **delen, dénmelo** becomes **démelon, dense** becomes **desen, densen,** etc.

ORTHOGRAPHIC CHANGES

13.9. An irregular verb is, strictly speaking, one which in its inflection varies in any way from that of the model verb of its conjugation. If this definition were rigorously adhered to, the number of irregular verbs in Spanish would be very large; but in the greater number the deviations are so uniform as to constitute a kind of secondary regularity, and may be grouped into several general classes.

13.10. The majority of the deviations are purely orthographic, and should not be considered as irregularities, as they are mere changes of spelling for the sake of preserving the sound of the stem as pronounced in the infinitive.

In stamping a verb as irregular, we are not to consider the letters with which it is written, but the sound it has when pronounced. As the spoken word is the original of which the written is but a copy, there is no irregularity in changes of letters necessary to maintain uniformity of sound.

13.11. The inflectional endings of verbs begin only with **a, o, e** and **i** *(or* its substitute **y**), although **i** or **y** occurs only in the 2nd and 3rd conjugations. Therefore, since certain consonantal sounds are variously expressed according to the vowel which follows (§ **15**), the following changes are necessary for uniformity in pronunciation:

a. Verbs whose infinitives end in **-car** and **-gar**, change the **c** and **g** to **qu** and **gu** respectively before **e**, in order to preserve the hard sound:

Tocar to touch

PRET. IND.	**toqué**	tocaste	tocó	tocamos	tocasteis	tocaron
PRES. SUBJ.	**toque**	**toques**	**toque**	**toquemos**	**toquéis**	**toquen**

Pagar to pay

PRET. IND.	**pagué**	pagaste	pagó	pagamos	pagasteis	pagaron
PRES. SUBJ.	**pague**	**pagues**	**pague**	**paguemos**	**paguéis**	**paguen**

b. Verbs in **-guar** require the diæresis over the **u (gu)** before **e**, in order to prevent it from becoming mute:

Averiguar to ascertain

PRET. IND.	**averigüé**	averiguaste	averiguó	-guamos	-guasteis	-guaron
PRES. SUBJ.	**averigüe**	**averigües**	**averigüe**	**-güemos**	**-güéis**	**-güen**

c. Verbs in **-ger** and **-gir** change the **g** into **j** before **o** and **a**:

Escoger to choose, select

PRES. IND.	**escojo**	escoges	escoge	escogemos	escogéis	escogen
PRES. SUBJ.	**escoja**	**escojas**	**escoja**	**escojamos**	**escojáis**	**escojan**

d. Verbs in **-guir** and **-quir** discard the orthographic **u** and revert to simple **g** and **c** before **o** and **a**:

Distinguir to distinguish

PRES. IND.	**distingo**	distingues	distingue	-tinguimos	-tinguís	-tinguen
PRES. SUBJ.	**distinga**	**distingas**	**distinga**	**-tingamos**	**-tingáis**	**-tingan**

Delinquir to transgress

PRES. IND.	**delinco**	delinques	delinque	delinquimos	delinquís	delinquen
PRES. SUBJ.	**delinca**	**delincas**	**delinca**	**delincamos**	**delincáis**	**delincan**

REMARK. There are no infinitives in **-guer** and **-quer**; and **delinquir** is the only example in **-quir.**

e. Verbs ending in **-cer** or **-cir** *preceded by a consonant,* change the **c** to **z** before **o** and **a:**

Vencer to conquer

PRES. IND.	**venzo**	vences	vence	vencemos	vencéis	vencen
PRES. SUBJ.	**venza**	**venzas**	**venza**	**venzamos**	**venzáis**	**venzan**

Esparcir to scatter

PRES. IND.	**esparzo**	esparces	esparce	esparcimos	esparcís	esparcen
PRES. SUBJ.	**esparza**	**esparzas**	**esparza**	**esparzamos**	**esparzáis**	**esparzan**

f. Verbs ending in **-cer** or **-cir** *preceded by a vowel,* interpolate **z** before the **c,** when followed by **o** or **a:**

Crecer to grow

PRES. IND.	**crezco**	creces	crece	crecemos	crecéis	crecen
PRES. SUBJ.	**crezca**	**crezcas**	**crezca**	**crezcamos**	**crezcáis**	**crezcan**

Lucir to shine

PRES. IND.	**luzco**	luces	luce	lucimos	lucís	lucen
PRES. SUBJ.	**luzca**	**luzcas**	**luzca**	**luzcamos**	**luzcáis**	**luzcan**

EXCEPTIONS. **Mecer** *to rock, stir,* and its derivative **remecer** *to rock, swing;* **cocer** *to boil,* and its derivatives **recocer** *to over-boil,* and **escocer** *to smart,* are exceptions and change the **c** to **z** before **o** and **a.** The irregular verbs **decir, hacer** and **yacer,** moreover, do not undergo this change.

13.12. The following changes do not affect the pronunciation, but are required by the laws of Spanish orthography:

a. Verbs in **-zar** change the **z** to **c** before **e,** as **z** should not be written before **e** or **i** (§ 14):

Rezar to pray

PRET. IND.	**recé**	rezaste	rezó	rezamos	rezasteis	rezaron
PRES. SUBJ.	**rece**	**reces**	**rece**	**recemos**	**recéis**	**recen**

b. The palatalized consonants **ll** and **ñ,** when coming before the diphthongs **ie** and **io,** absorb the **i,** as being no longer necessary:

Bullir to boil, seethe

PRES. PART.	**bullendo**					
PRET. IND.	bullí	bulliste	**bulló**	bullimos	bullisteis	**bulleron**
IMP. SUBJ.	**bullera**	**bulleras**	**bullera**	**bulléramos**	**bullerais**	**bulleran**
IMP. SUBJ.	**bullese**	**bulleses**	**bullese**	**bullésemos**	**bulleseis**	**bullesen**
FUT. SUBJ.	**bullere**	**bulleres**	**bullere**	**bulleremos**	**bullereis**	**bulleren**

Tañer to play (a stringed instrument)

Pres. Part.	**tañendo**					
Pret. Ind.	tañí	tañiste	**tañó**	tañimos	tañisteis	**tañeron**
Imp. Subj.	**tañera**	**tañeras**	**tañera**	**tañéramos**	**tañerais**	**tañeran**
Imp. Subj.	**tañese**	**tañeses**	**tañese**	**tañésemos**	**tañeseis**	**tañesen**
Fut. Subj.	**tañere**	**tañeres**	**tañere**	**tañéremos**	**tañereis**	**tañeren**

Bruñir to burnish

Pres. Part.	**bruñendo**					
Pret. Ind.	bruñí	bruñiste	**bruñó**	bruñimos	bruñisteis	**bruñeron**
Imp. Subj.	**bruñera**	**bruñeras**	**bruñera**	**bruñéramos**	**bruñerais**	**bruñeran**
Imp. Subj.	**bruñese**	**bruñeses**	**bruñese**	**bruñésemos**	**bruñeseis**	**bruñesen**
Fut. Subj.	**bruñere**	**bruñeres**	**bruñere**	**bruñéremos**	**bruñereis**	**bruñeren**

Remark. This usage is now usually extended to **ch: hinchó, hincheron, hinchendo,** etc., from **henchir** (§§ 14.32-14.33).

13.13. Where the stem of the verb ends in a vowel, the **i** of the diphthongal endings **ie** and **io** must be changed to **y**, since Spanish orthography does not allow unstressed **i** to come between vowels:

Caer to fall

Pres. Part.	**cayendo**					
Pret. Ind.	caí	caíste	**cayó**	caímos	caísteis	**cayeron**
Imp. Subj.	**cayera**	**cayeras**	**cayera**	**cayéramos**	**cayerais**	**cayeran**
Imp. Subj.	**cayese**	**cayeses**	**cayese**	**cayésemos**	**cayeseis**	**cayesen**
Fut. Subj.	**cayere**	**cayeres**	**cayere**	**cayéremos**	**cayereis**	**cayeren**

Creer to believe

Pres. Part.	**creyendo**					
Pret. Ind.	creí	creíste	**creyó**	creímos	creísteis	**creyeron**
Imp. Subj.	**creyera**	**creyeras**	**creyera**	**creyéramos**	**creyerais**	**creyeran**
Imp. Subj.	**creyese**	**creyeses**	**creyese**	**creyésemos**	**creyeseis**	**creyesen**
Fut. Subj.	**creyere**	**creyeres**	**creyere**	**creyéremos**	**creyereis**	**creyeren**

Huir to flee

Pres. Part.	**huyendo**					
Pret. Ind.	huí	huiste	**huyó**	huimos	huisteis	**huyeron**
Imp. Subj.	**huyera**	**huyeras**	**huyera**	**huyéramos**	**huyerais**	**huyeran**
Imp. Subj.	**huyese**	**huyeses**	**huyese**	**huyésemos**	**huyeseis**	**huyesen**
Fut. Subj.	**huyere**	**huyeres**	**huyere**	**huyéremos**	**huyereis**	**huyeren**

Argüir to argue

Pres. Part.	**arguyendo**					
Pret. Ind.	argüí	argüiste	**-guyó**	-güimos	-güisteis	**-guyeron**
Imp. Subj.	**arguyera**	**-guyeras**	**arguyera**	**-guyéramos**	**-guyerais**	**-guyeran**
Imp. Subj.	**arguyese**	**-guyeses**	**arguyese**	**-guyésemos**	**-guyeseis**	**-guyesen**
Fut. Subj.	**arguyere**	**-guyeres**	**arguyere**	**-guyéremos**	**-guyereis**	**-guyeren**

REMARK. When the termination begins with stressed **i** followed by a vowel, it does not constitute a diphthong and the above does not apply:

CAER	caía	caías	caía	caíamos	caíais	caían
CREER	creía	creías	creía	creíamos	creíais	creían
HUIR	huía	huías	huía	huíamos	huíais	huían
ARGÜIR	argüía	argüías	argüía	argüíamos	argüíais	argüían

13.14. In the case of verbs ending in **-guir** and **-quir**, since the **u** of the stem is a mere orthographic expedient to preserve the hard sound of the preceding consonant, it does not count as a vowel, and the above principle does not apply:

Distinguir to distinguish

PRES. PART.	distinguiendo					
PRET. IND.	distinguí	-guiste	-guió	-guimos	-guisteis	-guieron
IMP. SUBJ.	distinguiera	-guieras	-guiera	-guiéramos	-guierais	-guieran
IMP. SUBJ.	distinguiese	-guieses	-guiese	-guiésemos	-guieseis	-guiesen
FUT. SUBJ.	distinguiere	-guieres	-guiere	-guiéremos	-guiereis	-guieren

Delinquir to transgress

PRES. PART.	delinquiendo					
PRET. IND.	delinquí	-quiste	-quió	-quimos	-quisteis	-quieron
IMP. SUBJ.	delinquiera	-quieras	-quiera	-quiéramos	-quierais	-quieran
IMP. SUBJ.	delinquiese	-quieses	-quiese	-quiésemos	-quieseis	-quiesen
FUT. SUBJ.	delinquiere	-quieres	-quiere	-quiéremos	-quiereis	-quieren

13.15. When the stem of a verb of the first conjugation ends in a weak vowel, this vowel in many cases bears the stress and consequently the written accent before unstressed terminations beginning with a vowel:

Variar to vary

PRES. IND.	varío	varías	varía	variamos	variáis	varían
PRES. SUBJ.	varíe	varíes	varíe	variemos	variéis	varíen
IMPER.	—	varía	—	—	variad	—

Continuar to continue

PRES. IND.	continúo	continúas	-núa	-nuamos	-nuáis	-núan
PRES. SUBJ.	continúe	continúes	-núe	-nuemos	-nuéis	-núen
IMPER.	—	continúa	—	—	-nuad	—

13.16. Some of the verbs which are conjugated like **variar** are **agriar** (usually), **aliar, amnistiar, ampliar, ansiar** (usually), **arriar, averiar, aviar, cariar, confiar, contrariar, criar, chirriar, desafiar, desca-**

rriar, desviar, enfriar, enviar, espiar, estriar, expatriar, expiar, extasiar, extraviar, fiar, filiar, fotografiar, gloriarse, guiar, hastiar, historiar, inventariar, liar, obviar, paliar, piar, porfiar, repatriar, resfriar, rociar, telegrafiar, vaciar, vanagloriarse, zurriar (usually). There is much vacillation in actual use and a few of the verbs in the preceding list are at times pronounced with the stress upon the vowel of the syllable which comes before **-iar,** that is, conjugated like **cambiar: cambio, cambias, cambia,** etc.

In general, verbs whose infinitive ends in **-uar** are conjugated like **continuar,** with the exception of those few whose infinitive ends in **guar: averiguar (averiguo, averiguas, averigua,** etc.). Here again the language often shows both forms, the preference being for stressing the **u: evacúa** as against **evacua,** etc.

XIV
IRREGULAR VERBS

14.1. We have seen that in regular verbs the stem, as obtained by removing the infinitive ending, is the same throughout the conjugation, except for those changes of letters necessary to maintain uniformity of sound or required by the laws of orthography. The only deviation from this is that the terminations of the future indicative and conditional are added to the full infinitive form.

14.2. In irregular verbs, with a few isolated exceptions, the irregularity is entirely in the stem, which may change several times in the conjugation.

14.3. Irregular verbs, primarily, are inflected on three stems—present, preterite and future—as bases. The groups of tenses formed from these stems are as follows:

I. PRESENT STEM	II. PRETERITE STEM
Infinitive	Present Participle (*occasionally*)
Past Participle	Preterite Indicative
Present Participle (*usually*)	Imperfect Subjunctive
Present Indicative	Future Subjunctive
Imperfect Indicative	III. FUTURE STEM
Present Subjunctive	Future Indicative
Imperative	Conditional

REMARK. Some one or two of these may be regular. The present and preterite stems may contain internal irregularities which depend upon the form or stress of the termination. The future stem, when irregular, retains the same irregularity throughout.

PRESENT STEM

14.4. The present stem of irregular verbs is never irregular throughout; its regular and irregular forms are distributed according to the following conditions:

1. The stem is either stressed or unstressed.
2. The stem begins either with a strong vowel (a, o) or a weak vowel (e, i).

14.5. One of each of these alternatives is present in every verbal form. The combinations are therefore limited to four:

a. stressed stem, weak termination (**dices, sienten**)
b. stressed stem, strong termination (**digo, sientas**)
c. unstressed stem, weak termination (**decimos, sentís**)
d. unstressed stem, strong termination (**digáis, sintamos**)

14.6. The unstressed stem followed by a weak termination is always regular; any or all of the remaining combinations may be irregular.

NOTE. The form of the stem that is peculiar to any of the above combinations is always the same wherever that combination occurs.

IRREGULARITIES

14.7. The irregularities of the present stem are methods of strengthening it either when stressed or followed by a strong vowel.

This strengthening is effected by adding to or changing either the stem vowel, stem consonant, or both:

PERDER:	pierd-*a*	pierd-*as*	pierd-*a*	perd-*amos*	perd-*áis*	pierd-*an*
VESTIR:	vist-*a*	vist-*as*	vist-*a*	vist-*amos*	vist-*áis*	vist-*an*
SALIR:	salg-*a*	salg-*as*	salg-*a*	salg-*amos*	salg-*áis*	salg-*an*
ASIR:	asg-*a*	asg-*as*	asg-*a*	asg-*amos*	asg-*áis*	asg-*an*
CAER:	caig-*a*	caig-*as*	caig-*a*	caig-*amos*	caig-*áis*	caig-*an*
HACER:	hag-*a*	hag-*as*	hag-*a*	hag-*amos*	hag-*áis*	hag-*an*

14.8. Four verbs add **y** to the original **o** of the first person singular of the present indicative:

SER	*to be:*	ancient	*so*	modern	**soy**	*I am*
ESTAR	*to be:*	"	*estó*	"	**estoy**	*I am*
DAR	*to give:*	"	*do*	"	**doy**	*I give*
IR	*to go:*	"	*vo*	"	**voy**	*I go*

14.9. The imperfect indicative is irregular only in the three following verbs (and a compound of **ver: prever**):

IR:	iba	ibas	iba	íbamos	ibais	iban
VER:	veía	veías	veía	veíamos	veíais	veían
SER:	era	eras	era	éramos	erais	eran

PRETERITE STEM

14.10. The preterite stem may be irregular throughout or only in part.

14.11. When only *partially* irregular, the preterite stem is irregular only when followed by a diphthong:

SENTIR:	sentí	sentiste	sintió	sentimos	sentisteis	sintieron
DORMIR:	dormí	dormiste	durmió	dormimos	dormisteis	durmieron

14.12. The verbs whose preterite stems are irregular *throughout* are seventeen in number, which have retained more or less distinctly the form of the Latin irregular perfects as they must have been popularly used in the Iberian peninsula.

a. Fourteen of these, in addition to the stem irregularity, agree in having the first and third persons singular of the preterite indicative end in **e** and **o** respectively, the stress falling on the penultimate instead of the final vowel:

			HABER		
hube	**hub**-iste	**hubo**	**hub**-imos	**hub**-isteis	**hub**-ieron
			TENER		
tuve	**tuv**-iste	**tuvo**	**tuv**-imos	**tuv**-isteis	**tuv**-ieron
			ESTAR		
estuve	**estuv**-iste	**estuvo**	**estuv**-imos	**estuv**-isteis	**estuv**-ieron
			ANDAR		
anduve	**anduv**-iste	**anduvo**	**anduv**-imos	**anduv**-isteis	**anduv**-ieron
			CABER		
cupe	**cup**-iste	**cupo**	**cup**-imos	**cup**-isteis	**cup**-ieron
			SABER		
supe	**sup**-iste	**supo**	**sup**-imos	**sup**-isteis	**sup**-ieron
			PODER		
pude	**pud**-iste	**pudo**	**pud**-imos	**pud**-isteis	**pud**-ieron
			PONER		
puse	**pus**-iste	**puso**	**pus**-imos	**pus**-isteis	**pus**-ieron
			VENIR		
vine	**vin**-iste	**vino**	**vin**-imos	**vin**-isteis	**vin**-ieron
			HACER		
hice	**hic**-iste	**hizo**	**hic**-imos	**hic**-isteis	**hic**-ieron
			QUERER		
quise	**quis**-iste	**quiso**	**quis**-imos	**quis**-isteis	**quis**-ieron
			DECIR		
dije	**dij**-iste	**dijo**	**dij**-imos	**dij**-isteis	**dij**-eron[1]
			TRAER		
traje	**traj**-iste	**trajo**	**traj**-imos	**traj**-isteis	**traj**-eron[1]
			Compounds in -DUCIR		
deduje	**deduj**-iste	**dedujo**	**deduj**-imos	**deduj**-isteis	**deduj**-eron[1]

b. In the remaining three, **ser** and **ir** form the preterite upon the Latin root *fu,* while **dar,** though of the first conjugation, takes the terminations of the second conjugation in all the tenses made from the preterite stem:

SER:	**fu**-í	**fu**-iste	**fué**	**fu**-imos	**fu**-isteis	**fu**-eron
IR:	**fu**-í	**fu**-iste	**fué**	**fu**-imos	**fu**-isteis	**fu**-eron
DAR:	**d**-i	**d**-iste	**d**-ió	**d**-imos	**d**-isteis	**d**-ieron

FUTURE STEM

14.13. Five verbs form the future stem by eliding the vowel of the infinitive ending; five others replace this vowel by a phonetic **d:**

[1] The **i** of the termination is omitted after **j.** Cf. § **13.12** *b.*

CABER:	**cabr-é**	**cabr-ía**	PONER:	**pondr-é**	**pondr-ía**
HABER:	**habr-é**	**habr-ía**	SALIR:	**saldr-é**	**saldr-ía**
PODER:	**podr-é**	**podr-ía**	TENER:	**tendr-é**	**tendr-ía**
QUERER:	**querr-é**	**querr-ía**	VALER:	**valdr-é**	**valdr-ía**
SABER:	**sabr-é**	**sabr-ía**	VENIR:	**vendr-é**	**vendr-ía**

14.14. Finally, two verbs form the future stem from older infinitives which are now obsolete:

DECIR *(dir):*	**dir-é**	**dir-ía**	HACER *(far):*	**har-é**	**har-ía**

PARADIGMS OF THE IRREGULAR VERBS

14.15. The addition of a prefix to a verb rarely alters the manner of its inflection; hence derivatives will be understood to be inflected like their primitives. The few exceptions to this will be noted in each case.

14.16. It usually happens that the irregularities of a given verb are also found in other verbs which present the same conditions. Consequently most of the irregular verbs may be grouped into classes, a representative verb then sufficing to exhibit the irregularities of its class.

a. By counting obsolete and very rare words, and repetitions of the same simple stems with different prefixes, the number of irregular verbs may be raised to nearly 900. By omitting those additions, the number is reduced to 416. The greater part of these belong to two or three classes so regular in their departure from the normal models as to present no difficulty. The other classes, although more irregular, are smaller; and finally a few are so erratic that they have to be treated singly.

b. There are irregularities affecting only the past participle that will be treated of separately.

NOTE. In the following paradigms the irregularities are printed in bold-faced type.

FIRST CLASS

14.17. This class is composed of verbs of the 1st and 2nd conjugations only. Their irregularity consists in the expansion of the stem vowels **e** and **o** into **ie** and **ue** respectively whenever they receive the stress in pronunciation. When the stress is transferred to another syllable, the original vowel resumes its place.

This irregularity occurs only in the 1st, 2nd and 3rd persons of the singular and the 3rd person plural of the present indicative and present subjunctive, and in the 2nd person singular of the imperative, for in all other forms of the verbs the stress falls on the inflectional ending and not on the stem.

E STEM: FIRST CONJUGATION

14.18. **Cerrar**, cerrando, cerrado *to shut*

	PRESENT STEM: *stressed,* **cierr**; *unstressed,* cerr					
PRES. IND.	**cierr**-o	**cierr**-as	**cierr**-a	cerr-amos	cerr-áis	**cierr**-an
PRES. SUBJ.	**cierr**-e	**cierr**-es	**cierr**-e	cerr-emos	cerr-éis	**cierr**-en
IMPER.	—	**cierr**-a	—	—	cerr-ad	—
IMP.	cerr-aba	cerr-abas	-aba	-ábamos	-abais	-aban

	PRETERITE STEM: REGULAR					
PRET. IND.	cerr-é	-aste	-ó	-amos	-asteis	-aron
IMP. SUBJ.	cerr-ara	-aras	-ara	-áramos	-arais	-aran
IMP. SUBJ.	cerr-ase	-ases	-ase	-ásemos	-aseis	-asen
FUT. SUBJ.	cerr-are	-ares	-are	-áremos	-areis	-aren

	FUTURE STEM: REGULAR					
FUT. IND.	cerrar-é	-ás	-á	-emos	-éis	-án
COND.	cerrar-ía	-ías	-ía	-íamos	-íais	-ían

14.19. **Perder**, perdiendo, perdido *to lose*

	PRESENT STEM: *stressed,* **pierd**; *unstressed,* perd					
PRES. IND.	**pierd**-o	**pierd**-es	**pierd**-e	perd-emos	perd-éis	**pierd**-en
PRES. SUBJ.	**pierd**-a	**pierd**-as	**pierd**-a	perd-amos	perd-áis	**pierd**-an
IMPER.	—	**pierd**-e	—	—	perd-ed	—
IMP.	perd-ía	perd-ías	perd-ía	perd-íamos	perd-íais	perd-ían

	PRETERITE STEM: REGULAR					
PRET. IND.	perd-í	-iste	-ió	-imos	-isteis	-ieron
IMP. SUBJ.	perd-iera	-ieras	-iera	-iéramos	-ierais	-ieran
IMP. SUBJ.	perd-iese	-ieses	-iese	-iésemos	-ieseis	-iesen
FUT. SUBJ.	perd-iere	-ieres	-iere	-iéremos	-iereis	-ieren

	FUTURE STEM: REGULAR					
FUT. IND.	perder-é	-ás	-á	-emos	-éis	-án
COND.	perder-ía	-ías	-ía	-íamos	-íais	-ían

O STEM: FIRST CONJUGATION

14.20. Costar, costando, costado *to cost*

PRESENT STEM: *stressed,* **cuest**; *unstressed,* cost

PRES. IND.	**cuest**-o	**cuest**-as	**cuest**-a	cost-amos	cost-áis	**cuest**-an
PRES. SUBJ.	**cuest**-e	**cuest**-es	**cuest**-e	cost-emos	cost-éis	**cuest**-en
IMPER.	—	**cuest**-a	—	—	cost-ad	—
IMP.	cost-aba	-abas	-aba	-ábamos	-abais	-aban

PRETERITE STEM: REGULAR

PRET. IND.	cost-é	-aste	-ó	-amos	-asteis	-aron
IMP. SUBJ.	cost-ara	-aras	-ara	-áramos	-arais	-aran
IMP. SUBJ.	cost-ase	-ases	-ase	-ásemos	-aseis	-asen
FUT. SUBJ.	cost-are	-ares	-are	-áremos	-areis	-aren

FUTURE STEM: REGULAR

FUT. IND.	costar-é	-ás	-á	-emos	-éis	-án
COND.	costar-ía	-ías	-ía	-íamos	-íais	-ían

O STEM: SECOND CONJUGATION

14.21. Morder, mordiendo, mordido *to bite*

PRESENT STEM: *stressed,* **muerd**; *unstressed,* mord

PRES. IND.	**muerd**-o	**muerd**-es	**muerd**-e	mord-emos	mord-éis	**muerd**-en
PRES. SUBJ.	**muerd**-a	**muerd**-as	**muerd**-a	mord-amos	mord-áis	**muerd**-an
IMPER.	—	**muerd**-e	—	—	mord-ed	—
IMP.	mord-ía	-ías	-ía	-íamos	-íais	-ían

PRETERITE STEM: REGULAR

PRET. IND.	mord-í	-iste	-ió	-imos	-isteis	-ieron
IMP. SUBJ.	mord-iera	-ieras	-iera	-iéramos	-ierais	-ieran
IMP. SUBJ.	mord-iese	-ieses	-iese	-iésemos	-ieseis	-iesen
FUT. SUBJ.	mord-iere	-ieres	-iere	-iéremos	-iereis	-ieren

FUTURE STEM: REGULAR

FUT. IND.	morder-é	-ás	-á	-emos	-éis	-án
COND.	morder-ía	-ías	-ía	-íamos	-íais	-ían

EUPHONIC AND ORTHOGRAPHIC CHANGES

14.22. When the expansion of **e** takes place at the beginning of a verb, the initial **i** of the diphthong **ie** is changed to **y**, since no word may begin with **ie** (§ **8**):

Errar, errando, errado *to err*

PRES. IND.	yerro	yerras	**yerra**	erramos	erráis	**yerran**
PRES. SUBJ.	yerre	yerres	**yerre**	erremos	erréis	**yerren**
IMPER.	—	yerra	—	—	errad	—

erraba; erré, errara, errase, errare; erraré, erraría

14.23. In like manner when the stem vowel **o** is initial, the resultant diphthong **ue** is preceded by **h,** since no word may begin with **ue** (§ 8):

Oler, oliendo, olido *to smell (emit an odor)*

PRES. IND.	**huelo**	**hueles**	**huele**	olemos	oléis	**huelen**
PRES. SUBJ.	**huela**	**huelas**	**huela**	olamos	oláis	**huelan**
IMPER.	—	**huele**	—	—	oled	—

olía; olí, oliera, oliese, oliere; oleré, olería

14.24. Desosar *to bone (remove the bones from meat)* and **desovar** *to spawn* introduce an **h** before the diphthong **ue,** as they are derived from **hueso,** *bone,* and **huevo,** *egg,* respectively:

Desosar, desosando, desosado *to bone*

PRES. IND.	**deshueso**	deshuesas	**deshuesa**	-osamos	-osáis	**deshuesan**
PRES. SUBJ.	**deshuese**	**deshueses**	**deshuese**	-osemos	-oséis	**deshuesen**
IMPER.	—	**deshuesa**	—	—	-osad	—

desosaba; desosé, desosara, -ase, -are; desosaré, -ía

14.25. The orthographic changes laid down in § **13.11** are also to be observed:

Plegar, plegando, plegado *to fold*

PRES. IND.	pliego	pliegas	pliega	plegamos	plegáis	pliegan
PRES. SUBJ.	**pliegue**	**pliegues**	**pliegue**	**pleguemos**	**pleguéis**	**plieguen**
IMPER.	—	pliega	—	—	plegad	—

plegaba; **plegué,** plegara, -ase, -are; plegaré, -ía

Empezar, empezando, empezado *to begin*

PRES. IND.	empiezo	empiezas	empieza	-pezamos	-pezáis	-piezan
PRES. SUBJ.	**empiece**	**empieces**	**empiece**	**-pecemos**	**-pecéis**	**-piecen**
IMPER.	—	empieza	—	—	-pezad	—

empezaba; **empecé,** empezara, -ase, -are; empezaré, -ía

Trocar, trocando, trocado *to barter*

PRES. IND.	trueco	truecas	trueca	trocamos	trocáis	truecan
PRES. SUBJ.	**trueque**	**trueques**	**trueque**	**troquemos**	**troquéis**	**truequen**
IMPER.	—	trueca	—	—	trocad	—

trocaba; **troqué,** trocara, -ase, -are; trocaré, -ía

Colgar, colgando, colgado *to hang*

PRES. IND.	cuelgo	cuelgas	cuelga	colgamos	colgáis	cuelgan
PRES. SUBJ.	**cuelgue**	**cuelgues**	**cuelgue**	**colguemos**	**colguéis**	**cuelguen**
IMPER.	—	cuelga	—	—	colgad	—
	colgaba; **colgué,** colgara, -ase, -are; colgaré, -ía					

In this place belongs the verb **jugar** (Lat. *jocari),* as its stem vowel was originally **o,** but has degenerated to **u** when not stressed:

Jugar, jugando, jugado *to play, gamble*

PRES. IND.	**juego**	**juegas**	**juega**	**jugamos**	**jugáis**	**juegan**
PRES. SUBJ.	**juegue**	**juegues**	**juegue**	**juguemos**	**juguéis**	**jueguen**
IMPER.	—	**juega**	—	—	**jugad**	—
	jugaba; **jugué,** jugara, -ase, -are; jugaré, jugaría					

Forzar, forzando, forzado *to force*

PRES. IND.	fuerzo	fuerzas	fuerza	forzamos	forzáis	fuerzan
PRES. SUBJ.	**fuerce**	**fuerces**	**fuerce**	**forcemos**	**forcéis**	**fuercen**
IMPER.	—	fuerza	—	—	forzad	—
	forzaba; **forcé,** forzara, -ase, -are; forzaré, -ía					

Agorar, agorando, agorado *to divine, augur*

PRES. IND.	**agüero**	**agüeras**	**agüera**	agoramos	agoráis	**agüeran**
PRES. SUBJ.	**agüere**	**agüeres**	**agüere**	agoremos	agoréis	**agüeren**
IMPER.	—	**agüera**	—	—	agorad	—
	agoraba; agoré, agorara, -ase, -are; agoraré, -ía					

Torcer, torciendo, torcido *to twist*

PRES. IND.	**tuerzo**	tuerces	tuerce	torcemos	torcéis	tuercen
PRES. SUBJ.	**tuerza**	**tuerzas**	**tuerza**	**torzamos**	**torzáis**	**tuerzan**
IMPER.	—	tuerce	—	—	torced	—
	torcía, torcí, torciera, -iese, -iere; torceré, -ía					

14.26. One verb of the third conjugation, **discernir**[1] (originally *discerner),* belongs to this class. Although the change of the last vowel has placed it in the third conjugation, it still retains the irregularities of its primitive **cerner:**

Discernir, discerniendo, discernido *to discern*

PRES. IND.	**discierno**	**-ciernes**	**-cierne**	discernimos	-cernís	**-ciernen**
PRES. SUBJ.	**discierna**	**-ciernas**	**-cierna**	discernamos	-cernaís	**-ciernan**
IMPER.	—	**discierne**	—	—	discernid	—
	discernía; -cerní, -cerniera, -iese, -iere; cerniré, -ía					

[1] So also the defective verb **concernir** (§ 15.8).

SECOND CLASS

14.27. This class is composed of verbs of the third conjugation only whose stem vowels are **e** or **o.** In the present stem these vowels are expanded to **ie** and **ue** respectively in the same places as the verbs of the preceding class, and in addition subside into **i** and **u** respectively when unstressed and followed by a strong termination.

In the preterite stem the vowels **e** and **o** become **i** and **u** respectively when the termination begins with a diphthong.

The present participle in this class belongs uniformly to the preterite system.

E STEM

14.28. Sentir, sentido *to feel, perceive*

PRESENT STEM: *stressed,* **sient;** *unstressed weak,* **sent;** *unstressed strong,* **sint**

PRES. IND.	**sient**-o	**sient**-es	**sient**-e	sent-imos	sent-ís	**sient**-en
PRES. SUBJ.	**sient**-a	**sient**-as	**sient**-a	**sint**-amos	**sint**-áis	**sient**-an
IMPER.	—	**sient**-e	—	—	sent-id	—
IMP.	sent-ía	sent-ías	sent-ía	sent-íamos	sent-íais	sent-ían

PRETERITE STEM: *before diphthong,* **sint;** *otherwise,* sent

PRET. IND.	sent-í	-iste	**sint**-ió	sent-imos	-isteis	**sint**-ieron
IMP. SUBJ.	**sint**-iera	-ieras	-iera	-iéramos	-ierais	-ieran
IMP. SUBJ.	**sint**-iese	-ieses	-iese	-iésemos	-ieseis	-iesen
FUT. SUBJ.	**sint**-iere	-ieres	-iere	-iéremos	-iereis	-ieren
PRES. PART.	**sint**-iendo					

FUTURE STEM: REGULAR

FUT. IND.	sentir-é	-ás	-á	-emos	-éis	-án
COND.	sentir-ía	-ías	-ía	-íamos	-íais	-ían

O STEM

14.29. Dormir, dormido *to sleep*

PRESENT STEM: *stressed,* **duerm;** *unstressed weak,* dorm; *unstressed strong,* **durm**

PRES. IND.	**duerm**-o	**duerm**-es	**duerm**-e	dorm-imos	dorm-ís	**duerm**-en
PRES. SUBJ.	**duerm**-a	**duerm**-as	**duerm**-a	**durm**-amos	**durm**-áis	**duerm**-an
IMPER.	—	**duerm**-e	—	—	dorm-id	—
IMP.	dorm-ía	dorm-ías	dorm-ía	dorm-íamos	dorm-íais	dorm-ían

PRETERITE STEM: *before diphthongs,* **durm**; *otherwise,* dorm

PRET. IND.	dorm-í	-iste	**durm**-ió	dorm-imos	-isteis	**durm**-ieron
IMP. SUBJ.	**durm**-iera	-ieras	-iera	-iéramos	-ierais	-ieran
IMP. SUBJ.	**durm**-iese	-ieses	-iese	-iésemos	-ieseis	-iesen
FUT. SUBJ.	**durm**-iere	-ieres	-iere	-iéremos	-iereis	-ieren
PRES. PART.	**durm**-iendo					

FUTURE STEM: REGULAR

FUT. IND.	dormir-é	-ás	-á	-émos	-éis	-án
COND.	dormir-ía	-ías	-ía	-íamos	-íais	-ían

14.30. **Adquirir** and **inquirir,** being derived from a primitive root **quer** (Lat. *quærere),* still have the diphthong **ie** in the present stem when stressed; otherwise the stem is **i** throughout:

Adquirir, adquiriendo, adquirido *to acquire*

PRES. IND.	**adquiero**	**adquieres**	**adquiere**	-quirimos	-quirís	**-quieren**
PRES. SUBJ.	**adquiera**	**adquieras**	**adquiera**	-quiramos	-quiráis	**-quieran**
IMPER.	—	**adquiere**	—	—	adquirid	—

adquiría; adquirí, adquiriera, -iese, -iere; adquiriré, -ía

14.31. **Podrir** *or* **pudrir,** pudriendo, podrido *to decay.* The stem vowel of this verb formerly changed to **u** when stressed or followed by a strong vowel or diphthong; it has now been fixed as **u** throughout, except in the past participle (and the infinitive, where it is optional).

THIRD CLASS

14.32. This class is composed exclusively of verbs of the third conjugation with the stem vowel **e.**

In the present stem the stem vowel e becomes **i** where in the two preceding classes it became a diphthong, namely when stressed. In addition to this it becomes **i** whenever the termination begins with a strong vowel. Consequently it is regular only when the stem is unstressed and the termination begins with a weak vowel.

In the preterite stem (as in the preceding class) the stem vowel becomes **i** whenever the termination begins with a diphthong.

The present participle in this class belongs uniformly to the preterite stem.

14.33. Servir, servido *to serve*

PRESENT STEM: *stressed,* **sirv**; *unstressed strong,* **sirv**; *unstressed weak,* serv

PRES. IND.	**sirv**-o	**sirv**-es	**sirv**-e	serv-imos	serv-ís	**sirv**-en
PRES. SUBJ.	**sirv**-a	**sirv**-as	**sirv**-a	**sirv**-amos	**sirv**-áis	**sirv**-an
IMPER.	—	**sirv**-e	—	—	serv-id	—
IMP.	serv-ía	serv-ías	serv-ía	serv-íamos	serv-íais	serv-ían

PRETERITE STEM: *before diphthongs,* **sirv**; *otherwise,* serv

PRET. IND.	serv-í	-iste	**sirv**-ió	serv-imos	-isteis	**sirv**-ieron
IMP. SUBJ.	**sirv**-iera	-ieras	-iera	-iéramos	-ierais	-ieran
IMP. SUBJ.	**sirv**-iese	-ieses	-iese	-iésemos	-ieseis	-iesen
FUT. SUBJ.	**sirv**-iere	-ieres	-iere	-iéremos	-iereis	-ieren
PRES. PART.	**sirv**-iendo					

FUTURE STEM: REGULAR

FUT. IND.	servir-é	-ás	-á	-emos	-éis	-án
COND.	servir-ía	-ías	-ía	-íamos	-íais	-ían

14.34. The verb **erguir** is conjugated either as of the third class or of the second; in the latter case the diphthong **ie,** being initial, is changed to **ye.** The two styles are united below:

The **u** following the **g** is merely orthographic and disappears before a strong vowel.

Erguir, erguido *to raise, erect*

PRES. IND.	**yergo** **irgo**	**yergues** **irgues**	**yergue** **irgue**	erguimos	erguís	**yerguen** **irguen**
PRES. SUBJ.	**yerga** **irga**	**yergas** **irgas**	**yerga** **irga**	**irgamos**	**irgáis**	**yergan** **irgan**
IMPER.	—	**yergue** **irgue**	—	—	erguid	—
IMP.	erguía	-ías	-ía	-íamos	-íais	-ían
PRES. PART.	**irguiendo**					
PRET. IND.	erguí	erguiste	**irguió**	erguimos	erguisteis	**irguieron**
IMP. SUBJ.	**irguiera**	-ieras	-iera	-iéramos	-ierais	-ieran
IMP. SUBJ.	**irguiese**	-ieses	-iese	-iésemos	-ieseis	-iesen
FUT. SUBJ.	**irguiere**	-ieres	-iere	-iéremos	-iereis	-ieren
FUT. IND.	erguiré	-ás	-á	-emos	-éis	-án
COND.	erguiría	-ías	-ía	-íamos	-íais	-ían

14.35. Five verbs ending in **-eír** (**desleír** *to dissolve;* **engreír** *to make conceited;* **freír** *to fry;* **sonreír** *to smile),* on changing the stem

e to **i**, lose the **i** of terminations beginning with diphthongs **ie** and **io** throughout the preterite stem:

Reír, reído *to laugh*

PRES. IND.	**rí**-o	**rí**-es	**rí**-e	re-ímos	re-ís	**rí**-en
PRES. SUBJ.	**rí**-a	**rí**-as	**rí**-a	**ri**-amos	**ri**-áis	**rí**-an
IMPER.	——	**rí**-e	——	——	reíd	——
IMP.	re-ía	re-ías	re-ía	re-íamos	re-íais	re-ían
PRES. PART.	**ri-endo**					
PRET. IND.	re-í	re-íste	**ri-ó**	re-ímos	re-ísteis	**ri-eron**
IMP. SUBJ.	**ri-era**	**ri-eras**	**ri-era**	**ri-éramos**	**ri-erais**	**ri-eran**
IMP. SUBJ.	**ri-ese**	**ri-eses**	**ri-ese**	**ri-ésemos**	**ri-eseis**	**ri-esen**
FUT. SUBJ.	**ri-ere**	**ri-eres**	**ri-ere**	**ri-éremos**	**ri-ereis**	**ri-eren**
FUT. IND.	reir-é	reir-ás	reir-á	reir-emos	reir-éis	reir-án
COND.	reir-ía	-ías	-ía	-íamos	-íais	-ían

ORTHOGRAPHIC CHANGES

14.36. The orthographic changes laid down in § 13.11 are also to be observed:

Regir, regido *to rule*

PRES. IND.	**rijo**	riges	rige	regimos	regís	rigen
PRES. SUBJ.	**rija**	**rijas**	**rija**	**rijamos**	**rijáis**	**rijan**
IMPER.	——	rige	——	——	regid	——
IMP.	regía	regías	regía	regíamos	regíais	regían
PRES. PART.	rigiendo					
PRET. IND.	regí	registe	rigió	regimos	registeis	rigieron
IMP. SUBJ.	rigiera	-ieras	-iera	-iéramos	-ierais	-ieran
IMP. SUBJ.	rigiese	-ieses	-iese	-iésemos	-ieseis	-iesen
FUT. SUBJ.	rigiere	-ieres	-iere	-iéremos	-iereis	-ieren
FUT. IND.	regiré	-ás	-á	-emos	-éis	-án
COND.	regiría	-ías	-ía	-íamos	-íais	-ían

Seguir, seguido *to follow*

PRES. IND.	**sigo**	sigues	sigue	seguimos	seguís	siguen
PRES. SUBJ.	**siga**	**sigas**	**siga**	**sigamos**	**sigáis**	**sigan**
IMPER.	——	sigue	——	——	seguid	——
IMP.	seguía	seguías	seguía	seguíamos	seguíais	seguían
PRES. PART.	siguiendo					
PRET. IND.	seguí	-iste	siguió	seguimos	-isteis	siguieron
IMP. SUBJ.	siguiera	-ieras	-iera	-iéramos	-ierais	-ieran
IMP. SUBJ.	siguiese	-ieses	-iese	-iésemos	-ieseis	-iesen
FUT. SUBJ.	siguiere	-ieres	-iere	-iéremos	-iereis	-ieren
FUT. IND.	seguiré	-ás	-á	-emos	-éis	-án
COND.	seguiría	-ías	-ía	-íamos	-íais	-ían

Verbs of this class ending in **-ñir,** in addition to modifying the stem vowel **e** into **i,** absorb the initial **i** of the diphthongal endings **ie, io,** as prescribed in § 13.12 *b:*

Reñir, reñido *to quarrel*

PRES. IND.	**riño**	**riñes**	**riñe**	reñimos	reñís	**riñen**
PRES. SUBJ.	**riña**	**riñas**	**riña**	**riñamos**	**riñáis**	**riñan**
IMPER.	——	**riñe**	——	——	reñid	——
IMP.	reñía	reñías	reñía	reñíamos	reñíais	reñían
PRES. PART.	**riñendo**					
PRET. IND.	reñí	reñiste	**riñó**	reñimos	reñisteis	**riñeron**
IMP. SUBJ.	**riñera**	**riñeras**	**riñera**	**riñéramos**	**riñerais**	**riñeran**
IMP. SUBJ.	**riñese**	**riñeses**	**riñese**	**riñésemos**	**riñeseis**	**riñesen**
FUT. SUBJ.	**riñere**	**riñeres**	**riñere**	**riñéremos**	**riñereis**	**riñeren**
FUT. IND.	reñiré	reñirás	reñirá	reñiremos	reñiréis	reñirán
COND.	reñiría	-ías	-ía	-íamos	-íais	-ían

FOURTH CLASS

14.37. This class is composed of verbs of the second and third conjugations ending in **-cer** or **-cir** preceded by a vowel. Their irregularity consists in strengthening the stem by interpolating **z** before the **c** when followed by a strong termination.

Verbs of this class generally are what are called *inceptives,* which will be treated in Chapter XXI. The Latin pattern upon which these are formed was characterized by an intruded *sc,* which becomes **zc** in Spanish:

SECOND CONJUGATION

14.38. Crecer, creciendo, crecido *to grow*

PRESENT STEM: *weak,* crec; *strong,* **crezc**

PRES. IND.	**crezc**-o	crec-es	crec-e	crec-emos	crec-éis	crec-en
PRES. SUBJ.	**crezc**-a	**crezc**-as	**crezc**-a	**crezc**-amos	**crezc**-áis	**crezc**-an
IMPER.	——	crec-e	——	——	crec-ed	——
IMP.	crec-ía	crec-ías	crec-ía	crec-íamos	crec-íais	crec-ían

PRETERITE STEM: REGULAR

PRET. IND.	crec-í	-iste	-ió	-imos	-isteis	-ieron
IMP. SUBJ.	crec-iera	-ieras	-iera	-iéramos	-ierais	-ieran
IMP. SUBJ.	crec-iese	-ieses	-iese	-iésemos	-ieseis	-iesen
FUT. SUBJ.	crec-iere	-ieres	-iere	-iéremos	-iereis	-ieren

FUTURE STEM: REGULAR

FUT. IND.	crecer-é	-ás	-á	-emos	-éis	-án
COND.	crecer-ía	-ías	-ía	-íamos	-íais	-ían

14.39. Lucir, luciendo, lucido *to shine*

PRES. IND.	**luzc**-o	luc-es	luc-e	luc-imos	luc-ís	luc-en
PRES. SUBJ.	**luzc**-a	**luzc**-as	**luzc**-a	**luzc**-amos	**luzc**-áis	**luzc**-an
IMPER.	——	luc-e	——	——	luc-id	——
IMP.	luc-ía	luc-ías	luc-ía	luc-íamos	luc-íais	luc-ían

NOTE. The preterite and future stems are regular (as above).

FIFTH CLASS

14.40. This class is composed of those verbs terminating in **-uir** in which both vowels are sounded (excluding therefore those in **-guir, -quir,** but including **-güir**). Their irregularity consists in strengthening the stem by the addition of y when stressed or followed by a strong vowel.

The preterite stem is regular, but the initial **i** of the diphthongal terminations **ie, io,** is changed to y since it comes between two vowels (§ 13.13).

The present participle in this class belongs uniformly to the preterite system.

14.41. Huir, huido *to flee*

PRESENT STEM: *stressed,* **huy**; *unstressed strong,* **huy**; *unstressed weak,* hu

PRES. IND.	**huy**-o	**huy**-es	**huy**-e	hu-imos	hu-is	**huy**-en
PRES. SUBJ.	**huy**-a	**huy**-as	**huy**-a	**huy**-amos	**huy**-áis	**huy**-an
IMPER.	——	**huy**-e	——	——	hu-id	——
IMP.	hu-ía	hu-ías	hu-ía	hu-íamos	hu-íais	hu-ían

PRETERITE STEM: REGULAR (**i** of diphthongs becomes y)

PRET. IND.	hu-í	hu-iste	hu-yó	hu-imos	hu-isteis	**-yeron**
IMP. SUBJ.	**hu-yera**	**hu-yeras**	**hu-yera**	**-yéramos**	**-yerais**	**-yeran**
IMP. SUBJ.	**hu-yese**	**hu-yeses**	**hu-yese**	**-yésemos**	**-yeseis**	**-yesen**
FUT. SUBJ.	**hu-yere**	**hu-yeres**	**hu-yere**	**-yéremos**	**-yereis**	**-yeren**
PRES. PART.	**hu-yendo**					

FUTURE STEM: REGULAR

FUT. IND.	huir-é	-ás	-á	-emos	-éis	-án
COND.	huir-ía	-ías	-ía	-íamos	-íais	-ían

14.42. Verbs in **-güir** necessarily discard the diæresis upon the insertion of the y:

Argüir, argüido *to argue*

PRES. IND.	**arguyo**	**arguyes**	**arguye**	argüimos	argüís	**-guyen**
PRES. SUBJ.	**arguya**	**arguyas**	**arguya**	**-guyamos**	**-guyáis**	**-guyan**
IMPER.	—	**arguye**	—	—	argüid	—
IMP.	argüía	argüías	argüía	-güíamos	-güíais	-güían
PRES. PART.	**arguyendo**					
PRET. IND.	argüí	argüiste	**arguyó**	argüimos	-isteis	**-guyeron**
IMP. SUBJ.	**arguyera**	-yeras	-yera	yéramos	-yerais	-yeran
IMP. SUBJ.	**arguyese**	-yeses	-yese	-yésemos	-yeseis	-yesen
FUT. SUBJ.	**arguyere**	-yeres	-yere	-yéremos	-yereis	-yeren
FUT. IND.	argüiré	-ás	-á	-emos	-éis	-án
COND.	argüiría	-ías	-ía	-íamos	-íais	-ían

SIXTH CLASS

14.43. This class is composed of verbs that have irregular preterite systems which are more or less close imitations of the Latin and have the spoken accent on the stem in the first and third persons singular of the preterite indicative.

NOTE. As the present and future stems present various irregularities, each verb of the class will be given separately and in full.

14.44. HABER (Lat. *habere*)

The **b** has disappeared wholly from the present subjunctive, and in the present indicative remains only in the second person plural. The present subjunctive is from the Latin *habeam,* etc., by dropping *b* and parts of some of the personal endings; the *e,* which is properly a part of the termination, becomes **y.**

The preterite stem is **hub.** The future stem drops the **e** of the infinitive ending: **habr.**

Haber, habiendo, habido *to have*

PRESENT STEM: *strong,* **hay;** *weak,* hab, **he** *and* **h**

PRES. IND.	**he**	**has**	**ha**	**hemos**[1]	hab-éis	**han**
PRES. SUBJ.	**hay**-a	**hay**-as	**hay**-a	**hay**-amos	**hay**-áis	**hay**-an
IMPER.	—	**he**	—	—	hab-ed	—
IMP.	hab-ía	hab-ías	hab-ía	hab-íamos	hab-íais	hab-ían

[1] Occasionally **habemos.**

			Preterite Stem: **hub**			
Pret. Ind.	**hube**	**hub**-iste	**hubo**	**hub**-imos	-isteis	-ieron
Imp. Subj.	**hub**-iera	-ieras	-iera	-iéramos	-ierais	-ieran
Imp. Subj.	**hub**-iese	-ieses	-iese	-iésemos	-ieseis	-iesen
Fut. Subj.	**hub**-iere	-ieres	-iere	-iéremos	-iereis	-ieren

			Future Stem: **habr**			
Fut. Ind.	**habr**-é	-ás	-á	-emos	-éis	-án
Cond.	**habr**-ía	-ías	-ía	-íamos	-íais	-ían

14.45. ANDAR

Andar is irregular only in the preterite stem.

Andar, andando, andado *to go*

			Present Stem: Regular			
Pres. Ind.	and-o	and-as	and-a	and-amos	and-áis	and-an
Pres. Subj.	and-e	and-es	and-e	and-emos	and-éis	and-en
Imper.	—	anda	—	—	and-ad	—
Imp.	and-aba	and-abas	and-aba	and-ábamos	and-abais	and-aban

			Preterite Stem: **anduv**			
Pret. Ind.	**anduve**	**anduv**-iste	**anduvo**	-imos	-isteis	-ieron
Imp. Subj.	**anduv**-iera	-ieras	-iera	-iéramos	-ierais	-ieran
Imp. Subj.	**anduv**-iese	-ieses	-iese	-iésemos	-ieseis	-iesen
Fut. Subj.	**anduv**-iere	-ieres	-iere	-iéremos	-iereis	-ieren

			Future Stem: Regular			
Fut. Ind.	andar-é	-ás	-á	-emos	-éis	-án
Cond.	andar-ía	-ías	-ía	-íamos	-íais	-ían

14.46. TENER (Lat. *tenere*)

The present stem is strengthened by the addition of **g** before a strong vowel. When accented, the stem vowel is expanded to **ie** before a weak termination. The singular imperative has the shortened form **ten.**

The preterite stem is **tuv;** the future, **tendr.**

Tener, teniendo, tenido *to have, possess*

			Present Stem: *strong,* **teng;** *stressed weak,* **tien;** *unstressed weak,* ten			
Pres. Ind.	**teng**-o	**tien**-es	**tien**-e	ten-emos	ten-éis	**tien**-en
Pres. Subj.	**teng**-a	**teng**-as	**teng**-a	**teng**-amos	**teng**-áis	**teng**-an
Imper.	—	**ten**	—	—	ten-ed	—
Imp.	ten-ía	ten-ías	ten-ía	ten-íamos	ten-íais	ten-ían

			PRETERITE STEM: **tuv**			
PRET. IND.	**tuve**	**tuv**-iste	**tuvo**	tuv-imos	**tuv**-isteis	**tuv-ieron**
IMP. SUBJ.	**tuv**-iera	-ieras	-iera	-iéramos	-ierais	-ieran
IMP. SUBJ.	**tuv**-iese	-ieses	-iese	-iésemos	-ieseis	-iesen
FUT. SUBJ.	**tuv**-iere	-ieres	-iere	-iéremos	-iereis	-ieren
			FUTURE STEM: **tendr**			
FUT. IND.	**tendr**-é	-ás	-á	-emos	-éis	-án
COND.	**tendr**-ía	-ías	-ía	-íamos	-íais	-ían

14.47. ESTAR (Lat. *stare)*

This verb adds **y** to the first person present indicative; the monosyllabic terminations of the indicative and subjunctive, and the singular imperative are stressed. The preterite stem is **estuv.** In other respects it is regular.

Estar, estando, estado *to be*

			PRESENT STEM: est			
PRES. IND.	**estoy**	est-**ás**	est-**á**	est-amos	est-áis	est-**án**
PRES. SUBJ.	est-**é**	est-**és**	est-**é**	est-emos	est-éis	est-**én**
IMPER.	—	est-**á**	—	—	est-ad	—
IMP.	est-aba	est-abas	est-aba	est-ábamos	est-abais	est-aban
			PRETERITE STEM: **estuv**			
PRET. IND.	**estuve**	**estuv**-iste	**estuvo**	**estuv**-imos	-isteis	**estuv**-ieron
IMP. SUBJ.	**estuv**-iera	-ieras	-iera	-iéramos	-ierais	ieran
IMP. SUBJ.	**estuv**-iese	-ieses	-iese	-iésemos	-ieseis	-iesen
FUT. SUBJ.	**estuv**-iere	-ieres	-iere	-iéremos	-iereis	-ieren
			FUTURE STEM: REGULAR			
FUT. IND.	estar-é	-ás	-á	-emos	-éis	-án
COND.	estar-ía	-ías	-ía	-íamos	-íais	-ían

14.48. CABER (Lat. *capere)*

The present stem is changed to **quep** before a strong vowel. The preterite stem is **cup;** the future, **cabr.**

Caber, cabiendo, cabido *to be contained in*

			PRESENT STEM: *strong,* **quep**; *weak,* cab			
PRES. IND.	**quep**-o	cab-es	cab-e	cab-emos	cab-éis	cab-en
PRES. SUBJ.	**quep**-a	**quep**-as	**quep**-a	**quep**-amos	**quep**-áis	**quep**-an
IMPER.	—	cab-e	—	—	cab-ed	—
IMP.	cab-ía	cab-ías	cab-ía	cab-íamos	cab-íais	cab-ían

PRETERITE STEM: **cup**

PRET. IND.	**cupe**	**cup**-iste	**cupo**	**cup**-imos	**cup**-isteis	**cup**-ieron
IMP. SUBJ.	**cup**-iera	-ieras	-iera	-iéramos	-ierais	-ieran
IMP. SUBJ.	**cup**-iese	-ieses	-iese	-iésemos	-ieseis	-iesen
FUT. SUBJ.	**cup**-iere	-ieres	-iere	-iéremos	-iereis	-ieren

FUTURE STEM: **cabr**

FUT. IND.	**cabr**-é	-ás	-á	-emos	-éis	-án
COND.	**cabr**-ía	-ías	-ía	-íamos	-íais	-ían

14.49. SABER (Lat. *sapere)*

The present stem is changed to **sep** before a strong vowel. The first person present indicative is shortened to **se.** The preterite stem is **sup;** the future, **sabr.**

Saber, sabiendo, sabido *to know*

PRESENT STEM: *strong,* **sep;** *weak,* sab

PRES. IND.	**sé**	sab-es	sab-e	sab-emos	sab-éis	sab-en
PRES. SUBJ.	**sep**-a	**sep**-as	**sep**-a	**sep**-amos	**sep**-áis	**sep**-an
IMPER.	—	sab-e	—	—	sab-ed	—
IMP.	sab-ía	sab-ías	sab-ía	sab-íamos	sab-íais	sab-ían

PRETERITE STEM: **sup**

PRET. IND.	**supe**	**sup**-iste	**supo**	**sup**-imos	**sup**-isteis	**sup**-ieron
IMP. SUBJ.	**sup**-iera	-ieras	-iera	-iéramos	-ierais	-ieran
IMP. SUBJ.	**sup**-iese	-ieses	-iese	-iésemos	-ieseis	-iesen
FUT. SUBJ.	**sup**-iere	-ieres	-iere	-iéremos	-iereis	-ieren

FUTURE STEM: **sabr**

FUT. IND.	sabr-é	-ás	-á	-emos	-éis	-án
COND.	sabr-ía	-ías	-ía	-íamos	-íais	-ían

14.50. PODER (Lat. *posse* [*pot-esse*])

The vowel of the present stem is expanded to **ue** when stressed. The preterite stem is **pud;** the present participle is formed on this stem. The future stem is **podr.**

Poder, podido *to be able*

PRESENT STEM: *stressed,* **pued;** *unstressed,* pod

PRES. IND.	**pued**-o	**pued**-es	**pued**-e	pod-emos	pod-éis	**pued**-en
PRES. SUBJ.	**pued**-a	**pued**-as	**pued**-a	pod-amos	pod-áis	**pued**-an
IMPER.	—	—	—	—	—	—
IMP.	pod-ía	pod-ías	pod-ía	pod-íamos	pod-íais	pod-ían

PRETERITE STEM: **pud**

PRES. PART.	**pud**-iendo					
PRET. IND.	**pude**	**pud**-iste	**pudo**	**pud**-imos	**pud**-isteis	**pud**-ieron
IMP. SUBJ.	**pud**-iera	-ieras	-iera	-iéramos	-ierais	-ieran
IMP. SUBJ.	**pud**-iese	-ieses	-iese	-iésemos	-ieseis	-iesen
FUT. SUBJ.	**pud**-iere	-ieres	-iere	-iéremos	-iereis	-ieren

FUTURE STEM: **podr**

FUT. IND.	**podr**-é	-ás	-á	-emos	-éis	-án
COND.	**podr**-ía	-ías	-ía	-íamos	-íais	-ían

14.51. PONER (Lat. *ponere*)

The present stem is strengthened by the addition of **g** before a strong vowel. The singular imperative has the shortened form **pon.** The preterite stem is **pus**; the future, **pondr.**

Poner, poniendo, puesto *to put, place*

PRESENT STEM: *strong,* **pong**; *weak,* pon

PRES. IND.	**pong**-o	pon-es	pon-e	pon-emos	pon-éis	pon-en
PRES. SUBJ.	**pong**-a	**pong**-as	**pong**-a	**pong**-amos	**pong**-áis	**pong**-an
IMPER.	—	**pon**	—	—	pon-ed	—
IMP.	pon-ía	pon-ías	pon-ías	pon-íamos	pon-íais	pon-ían

PRETERITE STEM: **pus**

PRET. IND.	**puse**	**pus**-iste	**puso**	**pus**-imos	**pus**-isteis	**pus**-ieron
IMP. SUBJ.	**pus**-iera	-ieras	-iera	-iéramos	-ierais	-ieran
IMP. SUBJ.	**pus**-iese	-ieses	-iese	-iésemos	-ieseis	-iesen
FUT. SUBJ.	**pus**-iere	-ieres	-iere	-iéremos	-iereis	-ieren

FUTURE STEM: **pondr**

FUT. IND.	**pondr**-é	-ás	-á	-emos	-éis	-án
COND.	**pondr**-ía	-ías	-ía	-íamos	-íais	-ían

14.52. VENIR (Lat. *venire*)

The present stem is strengthened by the addition of **g** before a strong vowel; before a weak vowel it is expanded to **vien** when stressed. The singular imperative has the shortened form **ven.**

The preterite stem is **vin**; the present participle is formed on this stem. The future stem is **vendr.**

Venir, venido *to come*

	PRESENT STEM: *strong,* **veng**; *stressed weak,* **vien**; *unstressed weak,* ven					
PRES. IND.	**veng**-o	**vien**-es	**vien**-e	ven-imos	ven-ís	**vien**-en
PRES. SUBJ.	**veng**-a	**veng**-as	**veng**-a	**veng**-amos	**veng**-áis	**veng**-an
IMPER.	—	**ven**	—	—	ven-id	—
IMP.	ven-ía	ven-ías	ven-ía	ven-íamos	ven-íais	ven-ían
			PRETERITE STEM: **vin**			
PRES. PART.	**vin**-iendo					
PRET. IND.	**vine**	**vin**-iste	**vino**	**vin**-imos	**vin**-isteis	**vin**-ieron
IMP. SUBJ.	**vin**-iera	-ieras	-iera	-iéramos	-ierais	-ieran
IMP. SUBJ.	**vin**-iese	-ieses	-iese	-iésemos	-ieseis	-iesen
FUT. SUBJ.	**vin**-iere	-ieres	-iere	-iéremos	-iereis	-ieren
			FUTURE STEM: **vendr**			
FUT. IND.	**vendr**-é	-ás	-á	-emos	-éis	-án
COND.	**vendr**-ía	-ías	-ía	-íamos	-íais	-ían

14.53. HACER (Lat. *facere*)

The **c** of the present stem is changed to **g** before a strong vowel. The past participle is irregular, **hecho.**

The preterite stem is **hic,** changing to **hiz** before a strong vowel to preserve the sound.

The future stem is **har.**

Hacer, haciendo, **hecho** *to do, make*

		PRESENT STEM: *strong,* **hag**; *weak,* hac				
PRES. IND.	**hag**-o	hac-es	hac-e	hac-emos	hac-éis	hac-en
PRES. SUBJ.	**hag**-a	**hag**-as	**hag**-a	**hag**-amos	**hag**-áis	**hag**-an
IMPER.	—	**haz**	—	—	hac-ed	—
IMP.	hac-ía	hac-ías	hac-ía	hac-íamos	hac-íais	hac-ían
			PRETERITE STEM: **hic**			
PRET. IND.	**hice**	**hic**-iste	**hizo**	**hic**-imos	**hic**-isteis	**hic**-ieron
IMP. SUBJ.	**hic**-iera	-ieras	-iera	-iéramos	-ierais	-ieran
IMP. SUBJ.	**hic**-iese	-ieses	-iese	-iésemos	-ieseis	-iesen
FUT. SUBJ.	**hic**-iere	-ieres	-iere	-iéremos	-iereis	-ieren
			FUTURE STEM: **har**			
FUT. IND.	**har**-é	-ás	-á	-emos	-éis	-án
COND.	**har**-ía	-ías	-ía	-íamos	-íais	-ían

Three of the compounds of **hacer, liquefacer, rarefacer** and **satisfacer,** have not changed the original Latin *f* to **h. Satisfacer** has the duplicate imperative forms **satisfaz** and **satisface.**

14.54. Satisfacer, satisfaciendo, **satisfecho** *to satisfy*

	satis-	*satis-*	*satis-*	*satis-*	*satis-*	*satis-*
PRES. IND.	**fago**	faces	face	facemos	facéis	facen
PRES. SUBJ.	**faga**	**fagas**	**faga**	fagamos	**fagáis**	**fagan**
IMPER.	—	**faz** *or* face	—	—	faced	—
IMP.	facía	facías	facía	facíamos	facíais	facían
PRET. IND.	**fice**	**ficiste**	**fizo**	**ficimos**	**ficisteis**	**ficieron**
IMP. SUBJ.	**ficiera**	-ieras	-iera	-iéramos	-ierais	-ieran
IMP. SUBJ.	**ficiese**	-ieses	-iese	-iésemos	-ieseis	-iesen
FUT. SUBJ.	**ficiere**	-ieres	-iere	-iéremos	-iereis	-ieren
FUT. IND.	**faré**	-ás	-á	-emos	-éis	-án
COND.	**faría**	-ías	-ía	-íamos	-íais	-ían

14.55. QUERER (Lat. *quærere*)

The present stem is expanded to **quier** when stressed. The preterite stem is **quis.** The future stem, by elision of the **e** of the infinitive ending, becomes **querr.**

Querer, queriendo, querido *to want, wish*

	PRESENT STEM: *stressed,* **quier**; *unstressed,* quer					
PRES. IND.	**quier**-o	**quier**-es	**quier**-e	quer-emos	quer-éis	**quier**-en
PRES. SUBJ.	**quier**-a	**quier**-as	**quier**-a	quer-amos	quer-áis	**quier**-an
IMPER.	—	**quier**-e	—	—	quer-ed	—
IMP.	quer-ía	quer-ías	quer-ía	quer-íamos	quer-íais	quer-ían
	PRETERITE STEM: **quis**					
PRET. IND.	**quise**	**quis**-iste	**quiso**	**quis**-imos	**quis**-isteis	**quis**-ieron
IMP. SUBJ.	**quis**-iera	-ieras	-iera	-iéramos	-ierais	-ieran
IMP. SUBJ.	**quis**-iese	-ieses	-iese	-iésemos	-ieseis	-iesen
FUT. SUBJ.	**quis**-iere	-ieres	-iere	-iéremos	-iereis	-ieren
	FUTURE STEM: **querr**					
FUT. IND.	**querr**-é	-ás	-á	-emos	-éis	-án
COND.	**querr**-ía	-ías	-ía	-íamos	-íais	-ían

14.56. DECIR (Lat. *dicere*)

The vowel of the present stem changes to **i** when stressed; before a strong vowel this vowel change takes place also, and the **c** is changed to **g.** The imperative singular has the shortened form **di.** The past participle is irregular, **dicho.**

The preterite stem is **dij**; the **j** represents an original *x* of Latin and early Spanish, before which (as in the case of **ll** and **ñ**) the **i** of the diphthong **ie** is absorbed.

The future is formed upon the stem **dir.**

There is a special form **diz,** used occasionally and familiarly as the equivalent of **se dice** (Lat. *dicitur) they say.*

Decir, diciendo, dicho *to say, tell*

	PRESENT STEM: *strong,* **dig**; *stressed weak,* **dic**; *unstressed weak,* dec					
PRES. IND.	**dig**-o	**dic**-es	**dic**-e	dec-imos	dec-ís	**dic**-en
PRES. SUBJ.	**dig**-a	**dig**-as	**dig**-a	**dig**-amos	**dig**-áis	**dig**-an
IMPER.	—	di	—	—	dec-id	—
IMP.	dec-ía	dec-ías	dec-ía	dec-íamos	dec-íais	dec-ían
			PRETERITE STEM: **dij**			
PRET. IND.	**dije**	**dij**-iste	**dijo**	**dij**-imos	**dij**-isteis	**dij**-eron
IMP. SUBJ.	**dij**-era	-eras	-era	-éramos	-erais	-eran
IMP. SUBJ.	**dij**-ese	-eses	-ese	-ésemos	-eseis	-esen
FUT. SUBJ.	**dij**-ere	-eres	-ere	-éremos	-ereis	-eren
			FUTURE STEM: **dir**			
FUT. IND.	**dir**-é	-ás	-á	-emos	-éis	-án
COND.	**dir**-ía	-ías	-ía	-íamos	-íais	-ían

14.57. The compounds of **decir** are inflected like their primitive except in the following particulars:

All the compounds have the singular imperative **dice** instead of **di.**

Bendecir *to bless* and **maldecir** *to curse* have the future stem regular, **decir** instead of **dir.** The Academy is in favor of **decir** for all the compounds, but it is not very generally adopted: **me desdiré** from **desdecirse** *to retract,* etc.

The archaic participles **bendito** and **maldito** are still in use, but are employed only adjectively.

Bendecir, bendiciendo, bendecido *or* **bendito** *to bless*

	ben-	*ben-*	*ben-*	*ben-*	*ben-*	*ben-*
PRES. IND.	**digo**	**dices**	**dice**	decimos	decís	**dicen**
PRES. SUBJ.	**diga**	**digas**	**diga**	**digamos**	**digáis**	**digan**
IMPER.	—	dice	—	—	decid	—
IMP.	decía	decías	decía	decíamos	decíais	decían
PRET. IND.	**dije**	**dijiste**	**dijo**	**dijimos**	**dijisteis**	**dijeron**
IMP. SUBJ.	**dijera**	-eras	-era	-éramos	-erais	-eran

IMP. SUBJ.	**dijese**	-eses	-ese	-ésemos	-eseis	-esen
FUT. SUBJ.	**dijere**	-eres	-ere	-éremos	-ereis	-eren
FUT. IND.	decir-é	-ás	-á	-emos	-éis	-án
COND.	decir-ía	-ías	-ía	-íamos	-íais	-ían

14.58. TRAER (Lat. *trahere*—compare Eng. *drag)*

The present stem is strengthened to **traig** before a strong vowel. The present participle belongs to the present stem, but the **i** of the termination is changed to **y** since it comes between two vowels.

The preterite stem is **traj** (Lat. *trax),* after which the **i** of the diphthong **ie** is absorbed, as shown above under **decir.** The future stem is regular.

Traer, trayendo, **traído** *to bring*

PRESENT STEM: *strong,* **traig;** *weak,* tra

PRES. IND.	**traig**-o	tra-es	tra-e	tra-emos	tra-éis	tra-en
PRES. SUBJ.	**traig**-a	**traig**-as	**traig**-a	**traig**-amos	**traig**-áis	**traig**-an
IMPER.	—	tra-e	—	—	tra-ed	—
IMP.	tra-ía	tra-ías	tra-ía	tra-íamos	tra-íais	tra-ían

PRETERITE STEM: **traj**

PRET. IND.	**traje**[1]	**traj**-iste	**trajo**	**traj**-imos	**traj**-isteis	**traj**-eron
IMP. SUBJ.	**traj**-era	-eras	-era	-éramos	-erais	-eran
IMP. SUBJ.	**traj**-ese	-eses	-ese	-ésemos	-eseis	-esen
FUT. SUBJ.	**traj**-ere	-eres	-ere	-éremos	-ereis	-eren

FUTURE STEM: REGULAR

FUT. IND.	traer-é	-ás	-á	-emos	-éis	-án
COND.	traer-ía	-ías	-ía	-íamos	-íais	-ían

14.59. Compounds of DUCIR (Lat. *ducere*)

Ducir *to lead* is now obsolete; its compounds have the following irregularities in common:

The present stem is strengthened to **duzc** before a strong vowel.

The preterite stem is **duj** (Lat. *dux),* after which the **i** of the diphthong **ie** is absorbed, as shown under **decir.**

The future stem is regular.

Deducir, deduciendo, deducido *to deduce*

---

[1] Occasionally still encountered in the spoken language are the preterite forms **truje, –iste, –o, –imos, –isteis, –eron.**

PRESENT STEM: *strong,* **deduzc;** *weak,* deduc

PRES. IND.	**deduzc-o**	-duc-es	-duc-e	-duc-imos	-duc-ís	-duc-en
PRES. SUBJ.	deduzc-a	**-duzc-as**	**-duzc-a**	**-duzc-amos**	**-duzc-áis**	**-duzc-an**
IMPER.	—	-duc-e	—	—	-duc-id	—
IMP.	deduc-ía	-duc-ías	-duc-ía	-duc-íamos	-duc-íais	-duc-ían

PRETERITE STEM: **deduj**

PRET. IND.	**deduje**	**deduj**-iste	**dedujo**	**deduj**-imos	-isteis	**deduj**-eron
IMP. SUBJ.	**deduj**-era	-eras	-era	-éramos	-erais	-eran
IMP. SUBJ.	**deduj**-ese	-eses	-ese	-ésemos	-eseis	-esen
FUT. SUBJ.	**deduj**-ere	-eres	-ere	-éremos	-ereis	-eren

FUTURE STEM: REGULAR

FUT. IND.	deducir-é	-ás	-á	-emos	-éis	-án
COND.	deducir-ía	-ías	-ía	-íamos	-íais	-ían

SEVENTH CLASS

14.60. This class is composed of miscellaneous verbs whose irregularities are not reducible to any of the previous classes.

14.61. DAR (Lat. *dare*)

Dar has irregularities of two kinds. It is one of those that add **y** to the first person singular of the present indicative. If the infinitive ending **ar** be removed, there remains as a stem only **d**; taking this **d** as the present stem, it is conjugated regularly in the first conjugation with the exception of the added **y.**

The same **d,** as the preterite stem, is conjugated regularly as of the *second or third conjugation.*

The future stem is regular.

Dar, dando, dado *to give*

PRESENT STEM: d *(1st Conj.)*

PRES. IND.	**doy**	d-as	d-a	d-amos	d-ais	d-an
PRES. SUBJ.	d-é	d-es	d-é	d-emos	d-eis	d-en
IMPER.	—	d-a	—	—	d-ad	—
IMP.	d-aba	d-abas	d-aba	d-ábamos	d-abais	d-aban

PRETERITE STEM: d *(2nd Conj.)*

PRET. IND.	d-**i**	d-**iste**	d-**ió**	d-**imos**	d-**isteis**	d-**ieron**
IMP. SUBJ.	d-**iera**	d-**ieras**	d-**iera**	d-**iéramos**	d-**ierais**	d-**ieran**
IMP. SUBJ.	d-**iese**	d-**ieses**	d-**iese**	d-**iésemos**	d-**ieseis**	d-**iesen**
FUT. SUBJ.	d-**iere**	d-**ieres**	d-**iere**	d-**iéremos**	d-**iereis**	d-**ieren**

FUTURE STEM: REGULAR

FUT. IND.	dar-é	-ás	-á	-emos	-éis	-án
COND.	dar-ía	-ías	-ía	-íamos	-íais	-ían

14.62. SER (Lat. *esse*)

This verb is made from two distinct roots, **es** and **fu,** the first of which is in some places so transformed as to be scarcely recognizable. The parts formed on the present stem are so erratic that they are not reducible to any principle.

The preterite is regularly formed on the stem **fu,** except that the third person singular of the preterite indicative is **fué,** and that the **i** of the diphthong **ie** is everywhere lost.

The future stem is regular.

Ser, siendo, sido *to be*

PRESENT STEM: *phases of* **es**

PRES. IND.	**soy**	**eres**	**es**	**somos**	**sois**	**son**
PRES. SUBJ.	se-a	se-as	se-a	se-amos	se-áis	se-an
IMPER.	—	sé	—	—	s-ed	—
IMP.	**era**	**eras**	**era**	**éramos**	**erais**	**eran**

PRETERITE STEM: **fu**

PRET. IND.	**fu-í**	fu-iste	**fué**	fu-imos	fu-isteis	**fu-eron**
IMP. SUBJ.	fu-era	**fu-eras**	**fu-era**	**fu-éramos**	**fu-erais**	**fu-eran**
IMP. SUBJ.	fu-ese	**fu-eses**	**fu-ese**	**fu-ésemos**	**fu-eseis**	**fu-esen**
FUT. SUBJ.	fu-ere	**fu-eres**	**fu-ere**	**fu-éremos**	**fu-ereis**	**fu-eren**

FUTURE STEM: REGULAR

FUT. IND.	ser-é	-ás	-á	-emos	-éis	-án
COND.	ser-ía	-ías	-ía	-íamos	-íais	-ían

14.63. IR (Lat. *ire*)

This verb is extremely irregular. At first sight there seems to be nothing of it but a termination; but it is known that the root is *i,* which is found in Sanskrit and in the Latin imperative. But as a whole it is made up of fragments from different sources.

We may reckon three distinct roots: **i, va** or **ve** and **fu.** The tenses usually formed on the present stem are in part from the first and in part from the second of these roots. The imperfect indicative, present participle and past participle are from the root **i.** In the present participle, **i** is changed to **y** since it is initial before **e.**

Instead of **vayamos,** the first person plural of the present subjunctive, **vamos** is usually used as an affirmative imperative, though **no vayamos** serves as the corresponding negative. Of the affirmative forms **vamos** is colloquial, **vayamos** literary in effect.

The preterite stem **fu** is the same as the corresponding part of **ser** *to be,* and the forms constructed upon it are identical with those of **ser.** The future stem is regular: **ir.**

Ir, yendo, ido *to go*

	PRESENT STEMS: *strong,* **vay;** *weak,* **v,** *and phases of* **i**					
PRES. IND.	**voy**	**vas**	**va**	**vamos**	**vais**	**van**
PRES. SUBJ.	vay-a	vay-as	vay-a	vay-amos	vay-áis	vay-an
IMPER.	—	v-e[1]	—	**vamos**	id	—
IMP.	**iba**	**ibas**	**iba**	**íbamos**	**ibais**	**iban**
	PRETERITE STEM: **fu**					
PRET. IND.	fu-í	fu-iste	**fué**	fu-imos	fu-isteis	**fu-eron**
IMP. SUBJ.	**fu-era**	**fu-eras**	**fu-era**	**fu-éramos**	**fu-erais**	**fu-eran**
IMP. SUBJ.	**fu-ese**	**fu-eses**	**fu-ese**	**fu-ésemos**	**fu-eseis**	**fu-esen**
FUT. SUBJ.	**fu-ere**	**fu-eres**	**fu-ere**	**fu-éremos**	**fu-ereis**	**fu-eren**
	FUTURE STEM: REGULAR					
FUT. IND.	ir-é	-ás	-á	-emos	-éis	-án
COND.	ir-ía	-ías	-ía	-íamos	-íais	-ían

14.64. VER[2] (Lat. *videre*)

Ver was originally *veer,* and the irregularities of the forms made upon the present stem are relics of a former regularity. The past participle is irregular, **visto.**

The preterite stem is **v,** and is conjugated regularly. The future stem is regular.

Ver, viendo, **visto** *to see*

	PRESENT STEM: *strong,* **ve;** *weak,* **v**					
PRES. IND.	**ve-o**	v-es	v-e	v-emos	v-eis	v-en
PRES. SUBJ.	**ve-a**	**ve-as**	**ve-a**	**ve-amos**	**ve-áis**	**ve-an**
IMPER.	—	v-e	—	—	v-ed	—
IMP.	**ve-ía**	**ve-ías**	**ve-ía**	**ve-íamos**	**ve-íais**	**ve-ían**

[1] In non-literary Spanish **ves,** of debatable origin, is found as the equivalent of **ve: ¡Anda, pícara, ves a reunirte otra vez con la sacristana.** (Palacio Valdés, **José,** III) *Go on, you sly woman, go and join the sacristan's wife again!*

[2] **Dar, ser, ir** and **ver** are the only monosyllabic infinitives in the language.

PRETERITE STEM: REGULAR

PRET. IND.	v-i[1]	v-iste	v-ió[1]	v-imos	v-isteis	v-ieron
IMP. SUB.	v-iera	v-ieras	v-iera	v-iéramos	v-ierais	v-ieran
IMP. SUB.	v-iese	v-ieses	v-iese	v-iésemos	v-ieseis	v-iesen
FUT. SUBJ.	v-iere	v-ieres	v-iere	v-iéremos	v-iereis	v-ieren

FUTURE STEM: REGULAR

FUT. IND.	ver-é	-ás	-á	-emos	-éis	-án
COND.	ver-ía	-ías	-ía	-íamos	-íais	-ían

14.65. Authorities are not agreed as to the most correct way to conjugate the compounds of this verb, whether the original vowel should, as above, be omitted in most places, or should be retained throughout. The preference is for the latter mode, in which case the **i** of the diphthongs **ie** and **io** in the terminations of the present participle and the preterite stem, is changed to **y**, as required by the laws of Spanish orthography.

Proveer, proveyendo, proveído *or* **provisto** *to provide*

PRES. IND.	proveo	provees	provee	proveemos	proveéis	proveen
PRES. SUBJ.	provea	proveas	provea	proveamos	proveáis	provean
IMPER.	—	provee	—	—	proveed	—
IMP.	proveía	proveías	proveía	proveíamos	proveíais	proveían
PRET. IND.	prove-í	-íste	-yó	-ímos	-ísteis	-yeron
IMP. SUB.	prove-yera	-yeras	-yera	-yéramos	-yerais	-yeran
IMP. SUB.	prove-yese	-yeses	-yese	-yésemos	-yeseis	-yesen
FUT. SUBJ.	prove-yere	-yeres	-yere	-yéremos	-yereis	-yeren
FUT. IND.	proveer-é	-ás	-á	-emos	-éis	-án
COND.	proveer-ía	-ías	-ía	-íamos	-íais	-ían

14.66. CAER (Lat. *cadere)*

The present stem is strengthened to **caig** before a strong vowel.

The remainder of the verb is conjugated regularly, except that in the terminations of the present participle and the preterite stem, the **i** of the diphthongs **ie** and **io** is changed to **y.**

Caer, cayendo, caído *to fall*

[1] The antiquated forms **vide** (first person) and **vido** (third person) are **occasionally** encountered.

PRESENT STEM: *strong,* **caig**; *weak,* ca

PRES. IND.	**caig**-o	ca-es	ca-e	ca-emos	ca-éis	ca-en
PRES. SUBJ.	**caig**-a	**caig**-as	**caig**-a	**caig**-amos	**caig**-áis	**caig**-an
IMPER.	—	ca-e	—	—	ca-ed	—
IMP.	ca-ía	ca-ías	ca-ía	ca-íamos	ca-íais	ca-ían

PRETERITE STEM: REGULAR

PRET. IND.	ca-í	ca-íste	ca-yó	ca-ímos	ca-ísteis	ca-yeron
IMP. SUB.	ca-yera	-yeras	-yera	-yéramos	-yerais	-yeran
IMP. SUB.	ca-yese	-yeses	-yese	-yésemos	-yeseis	-yesen
FUT. SUBJ.	ca-yere	-yeres	-yere	yéremos	-yereis	-yeren

FUTURE STEM: REGULAR

FUT. IND.	caer-é	-ás	-á	-emos	-éis	-án
COND.	caer-ía	-ías	-ía	-íamos	-íais	-ían

14.67. OÍR (Lat. *audire*)

The present stem is strengthened to **oig** before a strong vowel; it is, moreover, changed to **oy** when stressed before a weak vowel.

The remainder of the verb is regular, except that in the terminations of the present participle and the preterite stem, the **i** of the diphthongs **ie, io,** is changed to **y.**

Oír, oyendo, oído *to hear*

PRESENT STEM: *strong,* **oig**; *stressed weak,* **oy**; *unstressed weak,* o

PRES. IND.	**oig**-o	**oy**-es	**oy**-e	o-ímos	o-ís	**oy**-en
PRES. SUBJ.	**oig**-a	**oig**-as	**oig**-a	**oig**-amos	**oig**-áis	**oig**-an
IMPER.	—	**oy**-e	—	—	o-íd	—
IMP.	o-ía	o-ías	o-ía	o-íamos	o-íais	o-ían

PRETERITE STEM: REGULAR

PRET. IND.	o-í	o-íste	o-yó	o-ímos	o-ísteis	o-yeron
IMP. SUB.	o-yera	o-yeras	o-yera	o-yéramos	o-yerais	o-yeran
IMP. SUB.	o-yese	o-yeses	o-yese	o-yésemos	o-yeseis	o-yesen
FUT. SUBJ.	o-yere	o-yeres	o-yere	o-yéremos	o-yereis	o-yeren

FUTURE STEM: REGULAR

FUT. IND.	oir-é	-ás	-á	-emos	-éis	-án
COND.	oir-ía	-ías	-ía	-íamos	-íais	-ían

14.68. ASIR

The present stem is strengthened by the addition of **g** before a strong vowel.[1] The remainder of the verb is regular.

Asir, asiendo, asido *to seize, lay hold of*

PRESENT STEM: *strong,* **asg;** *weak,* as

PRES. IND.	**asg**-o	as-es	as-e	as-imos	as-ís	as-en
PRES. SUBJ.	**asg**-a	**asg**-as	**asg**-a	**asg**-amos	**asg**-áis	**asg**-an
IMPER.	—	as-e	—	—	as-id	—
IMP.	as-ía	as-ías	as-ía	as-íamos	as-íais	as-ían

PRETERITE STEM: REGULAR

PRET. IND.	as-í	as-iste	as-ió	as-imos	as-isteis	as-ieron
IMP. SUB.	as-iera	-ieras	-iera	-iéramos	-ierais	-ieran
IMP. SUB.	as-iese	-ieses	-iese	-iésemos	-ieseis	-iesen
FUT. SUBJ.	as-iere	-ieres	-iere	-iéremos	-iereis	-ieren

FUTURE STEM: REGULAR

FUT. IND.	asir-é	-ás	-á	-emos	-éis	-án
COND.	asir-ía	-ías	-ía	-íamos	-íais	-ían

14.69. VALER AND SALIR

Valer and **salir** have the following irregularities in common:

The present stem is strengthened by the addition of **g** before a strong vowel. The imperative singular is the unmodified stem; **valer** has also the regular imperative **vale.** The preterite stem is regular. The future stem drops the last vowel and inserts **d.**

Valer, valiendo, valido *to be worth*

PRESENT STEM: *strong,* **valg;** *weak,* val

PRES. IND.	**valg**-o	val-es	val-e	val-emos	val-éis	val-en
PRES. SUBJ.	**valg**-a	**valg**-as	**valg**-a	**valg**-amos	**valg**-áis	**valg**-an
IMPER.	—	**val** *or* vale	—	—	val-ed	—
IMP.	val-ía	-ías	-ía	-íamos	-íais	-ían

PRETERITE STEM: REGULAR

PRET. IND.	val-í	val-iste	val-ió	val-imos	val-isteis	val-ieron
IMP. SUB.	val-iera	-ieras	-iera	-iéramos	-ierais	-ieran
IMP. SUB.	val-iese	-ieses	-iese	-iésemos	-ieseis	-iesen
FUT. SUBJ.	val-iere	-ieres	-iere	-iéremos	-iereis	-ieren

[1] The irregular forms are rarely used.

FUTURE STEM: **valdr**

FUT. IND.	**valdr-é**	-ás	-á	-emos	-éis	-án
COND.	**valdr-ía**	-ías	-ía	-íamos	-íais	-ían

Salir, saliendo, salido *to go* or *come out*

PRESENT STEM: *strong,* **salg**; *weak,* sal

PRES. IND.	**salg-o**	sal-es	sal-e	sal-imos	sal-ís	sal-en
PRES. SUBJ.	**salg-a**	**salg-as**	salg-a	salg-amos	**salg-áis**	**salg-an**
IMPER.	—	**sal**	—	—	sal-id	—

salía; salí, saliera, saliese, saliere; **saldré, saldría**

XV

Defective Verbs Past Participles

15.1. Verbs are called defective when they are employed only in certain tenses or persons. This limited use may be to avoid cacophony, or it may result from the meaning of the respective verbs. The latter class comprises the impersonal verbs, which will be considered in Chapter XXI.

15.2. Of the following ten verbs the only forms in use are those in which the inflectional endings begin with **i**, including, however, the forms made from the future stem:

abolir to abolish *(regular)*
aguerrir to inure to war *(regular)*
arrecirse to grow numb *(regular)*
aterirse to grow numb *(regular)*
desmarrirse to grow sad *(regular)*
despavorir to take fright *(regular)*
embaír to impose upon *(regular)*
empedernir[1] to harden *(regular)*
garantir[2] to guarantee *(regular)*
manir to become tender *(regular)*

---

[1] The missing forms may be supplied from **empedernecer.**
[2] The missing forms may be supplied from **garantizar.**

15.3. The following paradigm will serve as a model:

PRES. IND.	—	—	—	abol-imos	abol-ís	—
PRES. SUBJ.	—	—	—	—	—	—
IMPER.	—	—	—	—	abol-id	—
IMP.	abol-ía	-ías	-ía	-íamos	-íais	-ían
PRET.	abol-í	-iste	-ió	-imos	-isteis	-ieron
IMP. SUB.	abol-iera	-ieras	-iera	-iéramos	-ierais	-ieran
IMP. SUB.	abol-iese	-ieses	-iese	-iésemos	-ieseis	-iesen
FUT. SUBJ.	abol-iere	-ieres	-iere	-iéremos	-iereis	-ieren
FUT. IND.	abolir-é	-ás	-á	-emos	-éis	-án
COND.	abolir-ía	-ías	-ía	-íamos	-íais	-ían

REMARK. **Blandir** originally belonged to this class, but the forms **blande** and **blanden** are now coming into use.

15.4. **Antojarse** *to long for* is limited to the third persons, singular and plural, of the several tenses.

15.5. **Atañer** *to appertain* is nearly obsolete, and appears only in the infinitive and the third persons, singular and plural, of the present and imperfect indicative:

PRES. IND.	atañe	atañen	IMP.	atañía	atañían

15.6. **Balbucir** *to stammer* uses only forms that have inflectional endings which begin with **i** and occasionally **e.**

15.7. **Cocer** is rarely employed in those forms of which the termination begins with a strong vowel: **cuezo; cueza, cuezas,** etc.

Mecer, regular but little used, was formerly conjugated like **crecer** (§ 14.38).

15.8. **Concernir** *to concern* is little used and is limited to the third persons, singular and plural, of the several tenses:

PRES. IND.	**concierne**	**-ciernen**	IMP. SUB.	concerniera	-cernieran
PRES. SUBJ.	**concierna**	**-ciernan**	IMP. SUB.	concerniese	-cerniesen
IMP.	concernía	-cernían	FUT. SUBJ.	concerniere	-cernieren
PRET. IND.	concernió	-cernieron	COND.	concerniría	-cernirián
FUT. IND.	concernirá	-cernirán	PRES. PART.	concerniendo	

15.9. **Nacer** *to be born* on account of its meaning is not often employed in the first person singular[1] of the present indicative or in the singular of the imperative.

15.10. **Pacer** *to graze* is not used in those forms where the stem would be strengthened by the addition of **z** before a strong vowel: **pazco; pazca, pazcas,** etc.

15.11. **Placer** *to please* (impersonal, Lat. *placet)* is rarely, if ever, used at the present time, except in certain phrases. Being impersonal, it is restricted to the third person singular. It is used in the following persons and tenses:

PRES. IND.	place	PRET. IND.	**plugo**
PRES. SUBJ.	**plazca, plega** or **plegue**	IMP. SUBJ.	**pluguiera**
IMP.	placía	IMP. SUBJ.	**pluguiese**
		FUT. SUBJ.	**pluguiere**

REMARK. The compounds of **placer, aplacer, complacer, desplacer,** are conjugated throughout like irregular verbs of Class IV.

15.12. **Raer** *to erase* is in a great measure replaced by **borrar** and **raspar;** but when found, it is generally inflected like **caer:**

PRES. IND.	**raigo** / **rayo**	raes	rae	raemos	raéis	raen
PRES. SUBJ.	**raiga** / **raya**	**raigas** / **rayas**	**raiga** / **raya**	**raigamos** / **rayamos**	**raigáis** / **rayáis**	**raigan** / **rayan**
IMP. IND.	raía	raías	raía	raíamos	raíais	raían
PRET. IND.	raí	raíste	**rayó**	raímos	raísteis	**rayeron**

rayera, rayese, rayere; raeré, raería; **rayendo**

15.13. **Reponer,** when it has the meaning of *to reply,* is restricted to the preterite indicative; **repuse, repusiste, repuso,** etc.

15.14. **Roer** *to gnaw* has three forms of the present stem before a strong vowel:

[1] There are many verbs which, on account of their meaning, do not take a personal object, and therefore occur only in the third person. These need not be enumerated, since the circumstance in question will be evident from their meaning.

PRES. IND.	ro-o **roig**-o **roy**-o	roes	roe	roemos	roéis	roen
PRES. SUBJ.	ro-a	ro-as	ro-a	ro-amos	ro-áis	ro-an
	roig-a	**roig**-as	**roig**-a	**roig**-amos	**roig**-áis	**roig**-an
	roy-a	**roy**-as	**roy**-a	**roy**-amos	**roy**-áis	**roy**-an

REMARK. **Corroer** *to corrode* makes **corroe, corroen,** in the present indicative, and **corroa, corroan,** in the subjunctive.

15.15. **Soler** *to be in the habit of* is used only in present, imperfect and perfect (**he solido,** etc.) of the indicative:

PRESENT		IMPERFECT	
suelo	I am wont, accustomed	solía	I was wont, I used to
sueles	you are wont	solías	you were wont
suele	he is wont	solía	he was wont
solemos	we are wont	solíamos	we were wont
soléis	you are wont	solíais	you were wont
suelen	they are wont	solián	they were wont

15.16. **Usucapir** *to acquire by right of possession* occurs only in the infinitive, as a legal term.

15.17. **Yacer** *to lie* (Lat. *jacere*) is now rarely used except in epitaphs, for which only the third persons, singular and plural, of the present and imperfect indicative are required:

Aquí yace *or* yacen.	Here lieth, or lie.
Aquí yacía *or* yacían.	Here lay.

REMARK. Formerly it was used in the sense of *to repose, to rest,* and was conjugated throughout. Its only irregularity was in the present stem, variously strengthened to **yazc, yazg** or **yag** before a strong vowel. The singular imperative, in addition to the regular form **yace,** had the shortened form **yaz:**

PRES. IND.	**yazc**-o **yazg**-o **yag**-o	yaces	yace	yacemos	yacéis	yacen
PRES. SUBJ.	**yazc**-a	**yazc**-as	**yazc**-a	**yazc**-amos	**yazc**-áis	**yazc**-an
	yazg-a	**yazg**-as	**yazg**-a	**yazg**-amos	**yazg**-áis	**yazg**-an
	yag-a	**yag**-as	**yag**-a	**yag**-amos	**yag**-áis	**yag**-an
IMPER.		yace **yaz**				

IRREGULAR PAST PARTICIPLES

15.18. Participles in the first conjugation end in **ado,** in the other two conjugations in **ido: comprar, comprado; vender, vendido; vivir, vivido.** Those having any other endings are said to be irregular, and have been in part exhibited among the irregular verbs. The irregularities are generally due to a closer adherence to the original Latin form of the participle, whether classic or post-classic.

15.19. The following verbs, which are otherwise regular, have an irregular past participle:

abrir to open	*pp.* **abierto**	LATIN, *apertus*
cubrir to cover	**cubierto**	*co-opertus*
escribir to write	**escrito**	*scriptus*
imprimir to impress, print	**impreso**	*impressus*

REMARK. The compounds of **abrir, cubrir** and **escribir** form their past participles in the same manner.

15.20. The following irregular verbs, together with their compounds, have an irregular past participle:

decir to say, tell	*pp.* **dicho**	LATIN, *dictus*
hacer *(facer)* to do, make	**hecho**	*factus*
morir to die	**muerto**	*mortuus*
poner to put, place	**puesto**	*positus*
solver to loosen	**suelto**	*solutus*
ver to see	**visto**	*vistus*
volver to turn, return	**vuelto**	*volutus*

15.21. In the cases given above, the irregular past participle is the only one in use. There are, however, a considerable number of verbs which have two past participles: one regular in form and usage; and the other, a closer imitation of the Latin, irregular. The list need not be given in full, since the irregular forms are usually restricted to use as adjectives, and are to be found as such in the dictionaries. The regular forms are used in the formation of the compound tenses and the passive voice. The following will serve as examples:

INFINITIVE	REGULAR	IRREGULAR	LATIN
abstraer	abstraído	abstracto	*abstractus*
atender	atendido	atento	*attentus*
bendecir	bendecido	bendito	*benedictus*

INFINITIVE	REGULAR	IRREGULAR	LATIN
comprimir	comprimido	compreso	*compressus*
confundir	confundido	confuso	*confusus*
desertar	desertado	desierto	*desertus*
distinguir	distinguido	distinto	*distinctus*
elegir	elegido	electo	*electus*
excluir	excluido	excluso	*exclusus*
fijar	fijado	fijo	*fixus*
invertir	invertido	inverso	*inversus*
juntar	juntado	junto	*junctus*
maldecir	maldecido	maldito	*maledictus*
manifestar	manifestado	manifiesto	*manifestus*
ocultar	ocultado	oculto	*occultus*
pervertir	pervertido	perverso	*perversus*
requerir	requerido	requisito	*requisitus*
soltar	soltado	suelto	*solutus*
torcer	torcido	tuerto	*tortus*

15.22. There are a few verbs, having two participial forms, which require more particular notice:

INFINITIVE	REGULAR	IRREGULAR	LATIN
bienquerer	bienquerido	bienquisto	
freír	freído	frito	*frictus*
ingerir *or* injerir	ingerido *or* injerido	ingerto *or* injerto	*insertus*
malquerer	malquerido	malquisto	
oprimir	oprimido	opreso	*oppressus*
prender	prendido	preso	*prensus*
romper	rompido	roto	*ruptus*
suprimir	suprimido	supreso	*suppressus*

15.23. **Bienquerer** and **malquerer** preserve the usual distinction between the regular forms in **-querido** and the irregular in **-quisto,**[1] though the latter is no longer current. Even in the past participles, these two verbs are oftener used as separable:

Queremos bien a todo el mundo.	We wish well to everybody.
Me dijo que me quería bien, que no me quería mal.	He told me he wished me well, that he did not wish me ill.
Mi madre era bienquista de cuantos la conocían.	My mother was liked by all who knew her.
Es un hombre malquisto de todos.	He is a man disliked by everybody.

[1] See also § **14.55.**

15.24. Nowadays the past participle of **freír** *to fry* is almost invariably **frito:**

¿Han frito o asado el escombro?	Have they fried or baked the mackerel?
Ya está frito.	It is already fried.
Media docena de ostiones fritos.	Half a dozen fried oysters.

15.25. Injerir *to graft* has **injerido** and **injerto.** This is the spelling favored by the Spanish Academy, although **ingerir** is also found. **Injerido** is used both after **haber** and **estar, injerto** as an adjective only:

Los ramos han sido quebrados para que yo sea ingerido.	The branches were broken off, that I might be grafted in. *(Romans,* xi, 19)
Un peral ingerto en membrillo.	A pear tree grafted on a quince.

REMARK. The regular verb **injertar** is now more frequently used than **injerir.**

15.26. Muerto, although from **morir,** an entirely different word, is occasionally used as a euphemism for **matado,** past participle of **matar** *to kill, slaughter.* **Matado** is the only form used with figurative meaning. **Muerto,** when intransitive, has its primary meaning—*dead:*

El herido ha muerto.	The wounded man is dead *(lit.* has died).
Hemos muerto al salteador.	We have killed the robber.
Se ha muerto de tristeza.	He died broken-hearted.
Se ha matado.	He has killed himself.
El aguacero ha matado el polvo.	The shower has laid the dust.
Este caballo está matado.	This horse is saddle-galled.
Este caballo está muerto.	This horse is dead.
Hay tan grande escasez de forraje que los hacendados han matado gran parte de su ganado.	Fodder is so scarce that the farmers have killed many of their cattle.
Me ha matado con su palabrería.	He has worn me out with his long talk.

REMARK. In speaking of the casualties of battles and accidents it is customary to use the active **morir** instead of the passive **ser muerto** (contrary to the English usage):

De los nuestros 43 murieron y 152 fueron heridos.	On our side 43 were killed and 152 were wounded.
Trece obreras murieron debajo de los escombros.	Thirteen work girls were killed under the ruins.

15.27. **Oprimir** *to oppress* and **suprimir** *to suppress* prefer the regular participle, **oprimido** and **suprimido,** even after **ser** and **estar,** but **imprimir** *to print* prefers **impreso** in all cases, though **imprimido** survives especially in Spanish America, at least with **haber** and **ser:**

Todas las loterías han sido suprimidas.	All the lotteries have been suppressed.
Su testimonio fué suprimido.	His testimony was suppressed.
La clase obrera es muy oprimida.	The working classes are much oppressed.

15.28. With **prender** the usual distinction holds good generally between **prendido** and **preso,** the latter being used as an adjective; but in the sense of *to arrest,* **prendido** is preferred after **haber:**

Dos de los ladrones han sido presos.	Two of the robbers have been arrested.
Los civiles han prendido *(or* preso) a otros dos.	The police have arrested two others.
El fuego ha prendido en la bodega de popa.	Fire has broken out in the after-hold.

REMARK. The participles of the compounds of **prender—aprender** *to learn,* **comprender** *to understand,* **emprender** *to undertake*—are regular.

15.29. **Romper** *to break* has **rompido** and **roto;** but the latter is preferred even after **haber** whenever the meaning is transitive:

La granizada ha roto muchos vidrios del invernadero.	The hail has broken many panes of glass in the greenhouse.
La cuerda de mi reloj está rota.	The mainspring of my watch is broken.
¡Ya que he roto a hablar! (Pereda, **Sotileza,** XX)	Now that I have begun to speak!
Tan pronto desaparecía de la casa, haciendo suponer que había roto con Fina, como se presentaba sin previo anuncio. (Pérez de Ayala, **La pata de la raposa,** p. 72 of **Obras Completas** edition)	At one moment he would disappear from the house, causing it to be supposed that he had broken with Fina, at the next he would present himself without warning.

Ella ha rompido con su novio.	She has broken with her lover.
Ha rompido un día de principios nuevos.	A day of new dispensation has dawned.

REMARK. The compounds of **romper** form their past participles regularly: **corrompido** *corrupted;* **interrumpido** *interrupted;* etc.

15.30. There are a few participles which, although passive in form, are employed as designations of the person who manifests (generally in an active manner) the action of the verb. They are then to all intents true adjectives:

agradecido grateful
almorzado who has breakfasted
atrevido daring
bebido having drunk plenty; **bien bebido** drunk
callado silent
cansado tiresome
cenado who has eaten supper
comedido polite
comido having eaten enough
considerado considerate, prudent
desconfiado distrustful
descreído unbelieving
desesperado without hope, desperate
disimulado dissembling
emigrado an emigrant
encogido spiritless, timid
esforzado stout, brave
fingido dissembling
leído well-read
medido cautious, moderate
mirado circumspect, precise
moderado moderate
osado fearless, bold
[**bien**] **parecido** [good-]looking
porfiado opinionated, disputatious
precavido cautious
preciado self-important
presumido presuming, boastful
recatado modest, circumspect
resuelto resolute, determined
sabido knowing
sacudido a rough customer
sentido sensitive
valido influential

ALPHABETICAL INDEX OF THE IRREGULAR AND DEFECTIVE VERBS

15.31. In the list of irregular verbs to be presented, those compounded with prefixes are "indented" (i.e. *set in* from the margin) when their primary verbs are conjugated in the same manner. When the primary verb is inflected differently, or is no longer in use, the first compound, reckoned alphabetically, is "flush" with the margin. It will be seen that the number of verbs not indented is 415 as compared with 461 derivatives. The apportionment of these 876 verbs among the several classes is as follows:

Class 1	342
Class 2	53

Class 3	54
Class 4	208
Class 5	37
Class 6	102
Class 7	27
Defective	21
Orthographic and Miscellaneous	32

NOTE. In the following list the verbs belonging to the first five classes are indexed accordingly. Of the miscellaneous verbs remaining, each is followed by the number of the section in which that particular verb, or the model upon which it is conjugated, is to be found.

Abastecer	IV
Abnegar	I
Abolir	§ 15.2
Aborrecer	IV
Absolver	I
Absonar	I
Abstenerse	§ 14.46
Abstraer	§ 14.58
Abuñolar	I
Acaecer	IV
Acertar	I
Aclocar	I
Acollar	I
Acontecer	IV
Acordar[1]	I
Acornar	I
Acostar	I
Acrecentar	I
Acrecer	IV
Adecentar	I
Adestrar	I
Adherir	II
Adolecer	IV
Adormecer	IV
Adormir	II
Adquirir (§ 14.30)	II
Aducir	§ 14.59
Advertir	II
Afollar	I
Aforar[2]	I
Agorar	I
Agradecer	IV
Aguerrir	§ 15.2
Alebrarse	I
Alentar	I
Aliquebrar	I
Almorzar	I
Alongar	I
Amanecer	IV
Amoblar	I
Amolar	I
Amollecer	IV
Amorecer	IV
Amortecerse	IV
Amover	I
Andar	§ 14.45
Anochecer	IV
Antedecir	§ 14.56
Anteponer	§ 14.51
Antever	§ 14.64
Apacentar	I
Aparecer	IV
Apercollar	I
Apernar	I

[1] Regular when meaning *to tune* a musical instrument.

[2] Regular when meaning *to gauge* or *appraise*.

Apetecer	IV
Aplacer	§ 15.11
Apostar[1]	I
Apretar	I
Aprobar	I
Argüir	V
Arrecirse	§ 15.2
Arrendar	I
Arrepentirse	II
Ascender	I
Asentar	I
Asentir	II
Aserrar	I
Asir	§ 14.68
Asolar	I
Asoldar	I
Asonar	I
Asosegar	I
Atañer	§ 15.5
Atender	I
Atenerse	§ 14.46
Atentar[2]	I
Aterirse	§ 15.2
Aterrar[3]	I
Atestar[4]	I
Atraer	§ 14.58
Atravesar	I
Atribuir	V
Atronar	I
Avalentar	I
Avanecerse	IV
Avenir	§ 14.52
Aventar	I
Avergonzar	I
Azolar	I
Balbucir	§ 15.6
Bendecir	§ 14.57
Bienquerer	§ 14.55
Blanquecer	IV
Bregar	I
Bruñir	§ 13.12
Bullir	§ 13.12
Caber	§ 14.48
Caer	§ 14.66
Calentar	I
Canecer	IV
Carecer	IV
Cegar	I
Ceñir	III
Cerner	I
Cerrar	I
Cimentar	I
Circuir	V
Clarecer	IV
Clocar	I
Cocer	I
Colar	I
Colegir	III
Colgar	I
Comedir	III
Comenzar	I
Compadecer	IV
Comparecer	IV
Competir	III
Complacer	IV
Complañir	§ 13.12
Componer	§ 14.51
Comprobar	I
Concebir	III
Concernir	§ 15.8
Concertar	I
Concluir	V
Concordar	I
Condescender	I
Condolerse	I
Conducir	§ 14.59
Conferir	II

[1] Regular when meaning *to post* troops, guards, etc.

[2] Regular with the more usual modern meaning of *to attempt* a crime.

[3] **Aterrar** (from **terror**) *to terrify* is regular; **aterrar** (from **tierra**) *to fell to the ground* is irregular.

[4] Regular when meaning *to testify*.

Confesar	I
Confluir	V
Conmover	I
Conocer	IV
Conseguir	III
Consentir	II
Consolar	I
Consonar	I
Constituir	V
Constreñir	III
Construir	V
Contar	I
Contender	I
Contener	§ 14.46
Contorcerse	I
Contracordar	I
Contradecir	§ 14.56
Contraer	§ 14.58
Contrahacer	§ 14.53
Contraponer	§ 14.51
Contravenir	§ 14.52
Contribuir	V
Controvertir	II
Convalecer	IV
Convenir	§ 14.52
Convertir	II
Corregir	III
Corroer	§ 15.14
Costar	I
Crecer	IV
Creer	§ 13.13
Dar	§ 14.61
Decaer	§ 14.66
Decentar	I
Decir	§ 14.56
Decrecer	IV
Deducir	§ 14.59
Defender	I
Defenecer	IV
Deferir	II
Degollar	I
Demoler	I
Demostrar	I
Denegar	I
Denegrecer	IV
Denostar	I
Dentar	I
Deponer	§ 14.51
Derrenegar	I
Derrengar	I
Derretir	III
Derrocar	I
Derruir	V
Desabastecer	IV
Desacertar	I
Desacollar	I
Desacordar	I
Desadormecer	IV
Desadvertir	II
Desaferrar	I
Desaforar	I
Desagradecer	IV
Desalentar	I
Desamoblar	I
Desandar	§ 14.45
Desaparecer	IV
Desapretar	I
Desaprobar	I
Desarrendar	I
Desasentar	I
Desasir	§ 14.68
Desasosegar	I
Desatender	I
Desatentar	I
Desaterrar	I
Desatraer	§ 14.58
Desatravesar	I
Desavenir	§ 14.52
Desaventar	I
Desbastecer	IV
Desbravecer	IV
Descabullirse	§ 13.12
Descaecer	IV
Descender	I
Desceñir	III
Descolgar	I

Descollar	I
Descomedirse	III
Descomponer	§ 14.51
Desconcertar	I
Desconocer	IV
Desconsentir	II
Desconsolar	I
Descontar	I
Desconvenir	§ 14.52
Descordar	I
Descornar	I
Descrecer	IV
Desdar	§ 14.61
Desdecir	§ 14.56
Desdentar	I
Desembebecerse	IV
Desembellecer	IV
Desembravecer	IV
Desempedrar	I
Desempobrecer	IV
Desencarecer	IV
Desencerrar	I
Desencordar	I
Desencrudecer	IV
Desencruelecer	IV
Desenfurecerse	IV
Desengrosar	I
Desenmohecer	IV
Desenmudecer	IV
Desensoberbecer	IV
Desentenderse	I
Desenterrar	I
Desentorpecer	IV
Desentristecer	IV
Desentumecer	IV
Desenvolver	I
Deservir	III
Desfallecer	IV
Desfavorecer	IV
Desferrar	I
Desflaquecerse	IV
Desflocar	I
Desflorecer	IV
Desfortalecer	IV
Desgobernar	I
Desguarnecer	IV
Deshacer	§ 14.53
Deshelar	I
Desherbar	I
Desherrar	I
Deshombrecerse	IV
Deshumedecer	IV
Desimponer	§ 14.51
Desinvernar	I
Desleír	III
Deslendrar	I
Deslucir	IV
Desmajolar	I
Desmarrirse	§ 15.2
Desmedirse	III
Desmelar	I
Desmembrar	I
Desmentir	II
Desmerecer	IV
Desmullir	§ 13.12
Desnegar	I
Desnevar	I
Desobedecer	IV
Desoír	§ 14.67
Desolar	I
Desoldar	I
Desollar	I
Desobstruir	V
Desosar[1] (§ 14.24)	I
Desovar (§ 14.24)	I
Desparecer	IV
Despavorir	§ 15.2
Despedir	III
Despedrar	I
Desperecer	IV
Despernar	I
Despertar	I

[1] **Desosar** *not to dare* (derived from **osar**) is regular. When irregular, **desosar** is from **hueso.**

Despezar[1]	I
Desplacer	IV
Desplegar	I
Despoblar	I
Desproveer	§ 14.65
Destentar	I
Desteñir	III
Desterrar	I
Destituir	V
Destorcer	I
Destrocar	I
Destruir	V
Desvanecer	IV
Desventar	I
Desverdecer	IV
Desvergonzarse	I
Desvolver	I
Detener	§ 14.46
Detraer	§ 14.58
Devolver	I
Dezmar	I
Diferir	II
Difluir	V
Digerir	II
Diluir	V
Discerner	I
Discernir (§ 14.26)	I
Disconvenir	§ 14.52
Discordar	I
Disentir	II
Disminuir	V
Disolver	I
Disonar	I
Dispertar	I
Displacer	IV
Disponer	§ 14.51
Distender	I
Distraer	§ 14.58
Distribuir	V
Divertir	II
Dolar	I
Doler	I
Dormir	II
Educir	§14.59
Elegir	III
Embaír	§ 15.2
Embarbecer	IV
Embastecer	IV
Embebecer	IV
Embellecer	IV
Embermejecer	IV
Embestir	III
Emblandecer	IV
Emblanquecer	IV
Embobecer	IV
Embosquecer	IV
Embravecer	IV
Embrutecer	IV
Emparentar	I
Empecer[2]	IV
Empedernir	§ 15.2
Empedrar	I
Empellar	I
Empequeñecer	IV
Empezar	I
Emplastecer	IV
Emplumecer	IV
Empobrecer	IV
Empodrecer	IV
Empoltronecerse	IV
Emporcar	I
Enaltecer	IV
Enardecer	IV
Encabellecerse	IV
Encalvecer	IV
Encallecer	IV

[1] Regular when it means to taper the end of a tube so that it will fit into another.

[2] Vicente Salvá (Gramática 10th Ed., p. 65) considers **empecer** as regular, in which he disagrees with the majority of classic authors. The verb is little used. Since it did not take a person as subject, the present subjunctive was the only form in which the irregularity could occur.

Encandecer	IV
Encanecer	IV
Encarecer	IV
Encarnecer	IV
Encender	I
Encentar	I
Encerrar	I
Enclocar	I
Encloquecer	IV
Encomendar	I
Encontrar	I
Encorar	I
Encordar	I
Encorecer	IV
Encornar	I
Encovar	I
Encrudecer	IV
Encruelecer	IV
Encubertar	I
Endentar	I
Endentecer	IV
Endurecer	IV
Enfierecerse	IV
Enflaquecer	IV
Enfranquecer	IV
Enfurecer	IV
Engorar	I
Engrandecer	IV
Engreír	III
Engrosar	I
Engrumecerse	IV
Engullir	§ 13.12
Enhambrecer	IV
Enhambrentar	I
Enhestar	I
Enlenzar	I
Enloquecer	IV
Enlucir	IV
Enllentecer	IV
Enmagrecer	IV
Enmalecer	IV
Enmarillecerse	IV
Enmelar	I
Enmendar	I
Enmohecer	IV
Enmollecer	IV
Enmudecer	IV
Ennegrecer	IV
Ennoblecer	IV
Ennudecer	IV
Enorgullecer	IV
Enrarecer	IV
Enriquecer	IV
Enrobustecer	IV
Enrodar	I
Enrojecer	IV
Enronquecer	IV
Enroñecer	IV
Enruinecerse	IV
Ensalmorar	I
Ensandecer	IV
Ensangrentar	I
Ensoberbecer	IV
Ensoñar	I
Ensordecer	IV
Entallecer	IV
Entender	I
Entenebrecer	IV
Enternecer	IV
Enterrar	I
Entigrecerse	IV
Entontecer	IV
Entorpecer	IV
Entortar	I
Entredecir	§ 14.56
Entregerir	II
Entrelucir	IV
Entremorir	II
Entreoír	§ 14.67
Entreparecerse	IV
Entrepernar	I
Entreponer	§ 14.51
Entretener	§14.46
Entrever	§ 14.64
Entristecer	IV
Entullecer	IV

Entumecer	IV
Envanecer	IV
Envejecer	IV
Enverdecer	IV
Envestir	III
Envilecer	IV
Envolver	I
Enzurdecer	IV
Equivaler	§ 14.69
Erguir (§ 14.34)	III
Errar (§ 14.22)	I
Escabullirse	§ 13.12
Escandecer	IV
Escarmentar	I
Escarnecer	IV
Esclarecer	IV
Escocer	I
Escolar	I
Esforzar	I
Establecer	IV
Estar	§ 14.47
Estatuir	V
Estregar	I
Estremecer	IV
Estreñir	III
Excluir	V
Expedir	III
Exponer	§ 14.51
Extender	I
Extraer	§ 14.58
Fallecer	IV
Favorecer	IV
Fenecer	IV
Ferrar	I
Florecer	IV
Fluir	V
Follar[1]	I
Fortalecer	IV
Forzar	I
Fregar	I
Freír	III
Gañir	§ 13.12
Garantir	§ 15.2
Gemecer	IV
Gemir	III
Gobernar	I
Gruir	V
Gruñir	§ 13.12
Guañir	§ 13.12
Guarecer	IV
Guarnecer	IV
Haber	§ 14.44
Hacendar	I
Hacer	§ 14.53
Heder	I
Helar	I
Henchir	III
Hender	I
Heñir	III
Herbar	I
Herbecer	IV
Herir	II
Herrar	I
Hervir	II
Holgar	I
Hollar	I
Huir	V
Humedecer	IV
Imbuir	V
Impedir	III
Imponer	§ 14.51
Improbar	I
Incensar	I
Incluir	V
Indisponer	§ 14.51
Inducir	§ 14.59
Inferir	II
Infernar	I
Influir	V
Ingerir (*or* injerir)	II
Inhestar	I
Inquirir (§ 14.30)	II

[1] Regular with the meaning *to shape into leaves.* (When irregular it is derived from fuelle, *a bellows*).

Inseguir	III
Instituir	V
Instruir	V
Interdecir	§ 14.56
Interponer	§ 14.51
Intervenir	§ 14.52
Introducir	§ 14.59
Invernar	I
Invertir	II
Investir	III
Ir	§ 14.63
Jimenzar (*or* simenzar)	I
Jugar (§ 14.25)	I
Languidecer	IV
Leer	§ 13.13
Liquefacer	§ 14.54
Lobreguecer	IV
Lucir	IV
Luir	V
Llover	I
Maldecir	§ 14.57
Malherir	II
Malquerer	§ 14.55
Malsonar	I
Maltraer	§ 14.58
Mancornar	I
Manifestar	I
Manir	§ 15.2
Mantener	§ 14.46
Mecer	§ 15.7
Medir	III
Melar	I
Mentar[1]	I
Mentir	II
Merecer	IV
Merendar	I
Moblar	I
Mohecer	IV
Moler	I
Morder	I
Morir	II
Mostrar	I
Mover	I
Muir	V
Mullir	§ 13.12
Muñir	§ 13.12
Nacer	IV
Negar	I
Negrecer	IV
Nevar	I
Obedecer	IV
Oscurecer	IV
Obstruir	V
Obtener	§ 14.46
Ofrecer	IV
Oír	§ 14.67
Oler (§ 14.23)	I
Oponer	§ 14.51
Pacer	IV
Padecer	IV
Palidecer	IV
Parecer	IV
Pedir	III
Pensar[2]	I
Perder	I
Perecer	IV
Permanecer	IV
Perniquebrar	I
Perseguir	III
Pertenecer	IV
Pervertir	II
Pimpollecer	IV
Placer	§ 15.11
Plañir	§ 13.12
Plastecer	IV
Plegar	I
Poblar	I
Poder	§ 14.50
Podrecer	IV
Podrir (*or* pudrir)	§ 14.31
Poner	§ 14.51
Poseer	§ 13.13

[1] The derivatives **comentar** and **dementar** are regular.
[2] The derivatives **compensar, recompensar,** are regular.

Posponer	§ 14.51
Preconocer	IV
Predecir	§ 14.56
Predisponer	§ 14.51
Preferir	II
Prelucir	IV
Premorir	II
Preponer	§ 14.51
Presentir	II
Presuponer	§ 14.51
Prevalecer	IV
Prevaler	§ 14.69
Prevenir	§ 14.52
Prever	§ 14.64
Probar	I
Producir	§ 14.59
Proferir	II
Promover	I
Proponer	§ 14.51
Proseguir	III
Prostituir	V
Proveer	§ 14.65
Provenir	§ 14.52
Quebrar	I
Querer	§ 14.55
Raer	§ 15.12
Rarefacer	§ 14.54
Reagradecer	IV
Reaparecer	IV
Reapretar	I
Reaventar	I
Rebendecir	§ 14.57
Reblandecer	IV
Rebullirse	§ 13.12
Recaer	§ 14.66
Recalentar	I
Recentar	I
Receñir	III
Recluir	V
Recocer	I
Recolar	I
Recolegir	III
Recomendar	I
Recomponer	§ 14.51
Reconducir	§ 14.59
Reconocer	IV
Reconstruir	V
Recontar	I
Reconvalecer	IV
Reconvenir	§ 14.52
Recordar	I
Recostar	I
Recrecer	IV
Recrudecer	IV
Redargüir	V
Redoler	I
Reducir	§ 14.59
Reelegir	III
Reencomendar	I
Referir	II
Reflorecer	IV
Refluir	V
Reforzar	I
Refregar	I
Refreír	III
Regañir	§ 13.12
Regar	I
Regimentar	I
Regir	III
Regoldar	I
Regruñir	§ 13.12
Rehacer	§ 14.53
Rehenchir	III
Reherir	II
Reherrar	I
Rehervir	II
Rehollar	I
Rehuir	V
Rehumedecer	IV
Reír	III
Rejuvenecer	IV
Relentecer	IV
Relucir	IV
Remendar	I
Rementir	II
Remolar	I
Remoler	I
Remorder	I

Remover	I
Remullir	§ 13.12
Renacer	IV
Rendir	III
Renegar	I
Renovar	I
Reñir	III
Repacer	IV
Repadecer	IV
Repedir	III
Repensar	I
Repetir	III
Replegar[1]	I
Repoblar	I
Repodrir	II
Reponer	§ 14.51
Reprobar	I
Reproducir	§ 14.59
Repudrir	§ 14.31
Requebrar	I
Requerer	§ 14.55
Requerir	II
Resaber	§ 14.49
Resalir	§ 14.69
Resegar	I
Resembrar	I
Resentirse	II
Resolver	I
Resollar	I
Resonar	I
Resplandecer	IV
Resquebrar	I
Restablecer	IV
Restituir	V
Restregar	I
Restreñir	§ 13.12
Retallecer	IV
Retemblar	I
Retener	§ 14.46
Retentar	I
Reteñir	III
Retiñir	§ 13.12
Retoñecer	IV
Retorcer	I
Retostar	I
Retraer	§ 14.58
Retribuir	V
Retronar	I
Retrotraer	§ 14.58
Revejecer	IV
Revenirse	§ 14.52
Reventar	I
Rever	§ 14.64
Reverdecer	IV
Reverter	I
Revestir	III
Revolar	I
Revolcarse	I
Revolver	II
Robustecer	IV
Rodar	I
Roer	§ 15.14
Rogar[2]	I
Saber	§ 14.49
Salir	§ 14.69
Salpimentar	I
Salpullir	§ 13.12
Sarmentar	I
Sarpullir	§ 13.12
Satisfacer	§ 14.54
Segar	I
Seguir	III
Sembrar	I
Sementar	I
Sentar	I
Sentir	II
Ser	§ 14.62
Serrar	I
Servir	III
Simenzar (*see* jimenzar)	I
Sobrecrecer	IV
Sobrentender	I

1 Regular when meaning *to fold again.*
2 All the derivatives of **rogar** are regular.

Verb	Reference
Sobreponer	§ 14.51
Sobresalir	§ 14.69
Sobresembrar	I
Sobresolar	I
Sobrevenir	§ 14.52
Sobreventar	I
Sobreverterse	I
Sobrevestir	III
Sofreír	III
Solar	I
Soldar	I
Soler	§ 15.15
Soltar	I
Solver	I
Sollar	I
Somover	I
Sonar	I
Sonreír	III
Sonrodarse	I
Soñar	I
Sorregar	I
Sosegar	I
Sostener	§ 14.46
Soterrar	I
Subarrendar	I
Subentender	I
Subseguir	III
Subtender	I
Subvenir	§ 14.52
Subvertir	II
Sugerir	II
Superponer	§ 14.51
Supervenir	§ 14.52
Suponer	§ 14.51
Sustituir	V
Sustraer	§ 14.58
Tallecer	IV
Tañer	§ 13.12
Temblar	I
Tender[1]	I
Tener	§ 14.46
Tentar[2]	I
Teñir	III
Torcer	I
Tostar	I
Traducir	§ 14.59
Traer	§ 14.58
Trascender	I
Trascolar	I
Trascordarse	I
Trasegar	I
Trasferir	II
Trasfregar	I
Traslucirse	IV
Trasoír	§ 14.67
Trasoñar	I
Trasponer	§ 14.51
Trastrocar	I
Trasverter	I
Trasvolar	I
Travesar	I
Trocar	I
Tronar	I
Tropezar	I
Tullir	§ 13.12
Tumefacerse	§ 14.54
Usucapir	§ 15.16
Valer	§ 14.69
Venir	§ 14.52
Ventar	I
Ver	§ 14.64
Verdecer	IV
Verter	I
Vestir	III
Volar	I
Volcar	I
Volver	I
Yacer	§ 15.17
Yuxtaponer	§ 14.51
Zabullir	§ 13.12
Zaherir	II
Zambullirse	§ 13.12

[1] The derivative **pretender** is regular.

[2] The derivatives **contentar, detentar, intentar,** are regular.

XVI

Uses Of Ser And Estar

16.1. There are in Spanish two verbs, **ser** and **estar**, corresponding to the English verb *to be*. They are not employed interchangeably, but each has its distinct province.

16.2. When the predicate is a noun, **ser** is the verb to be used:

Colombia es una república.	Colombia is a republic.
La Paz y Potosí son departamentos de Bolivia.	La Paz and Potosi are departments of Bolivia.
El perro es un animal dócil e inteligente.	The dog is a docile and intelligent animal.
¿Cuál es la distancia de Cárdenas a Júcaro?	What is the distance from Cardenas to Jucaro?

REMARK I. In certain exclamatory phrases, usually ironical in value, **estar** is used:

¡Valiente hipócrita estás tú...! (Pérez Galdós, **Fortunata y Jacinta,** II, 1, 3)	A fine hypocrite you are!
¡Buena hidalguía está la de Pepito! (Valera, **Juanita la larga,** XVII)	A pretty nobility Pepito's is!
¡Buen par de tarabillas estáis tu primo y tú! (Alvarez Quintero, **El genio alegre,** II)	A nice couple of chatterboxes you and your cousin are!

REMARK II. As a consequence of their similarity to another type of sentence (**El día está muy hermoso.**), **estar** is sometimes used in sentences like:

¡Está un día tan hermoso! (Benavente, **Lo cursi,** I, 8)	It is such a fine day!

16.3. Ser is to be used to express the origin of a person or thing, and the ownership of a thing or the material of which it is composed:

Mi criada es de Valencia.	My servant girl is from Valencia.
El vino es de Málaga.	The wine is from Malaga.

El violín es de mi padre.	The violin is my father's.
La taza es de plata.	The cup is of silver.

16.4. A predicate noun, used with a temporary value and preceded by **de,** may follow **estar** as an adverbial phrase, in which case **de** is equivalent to *as:*

Mi hermano está ahora de cónsul en Bogotá.	My brother is at present (as) consul at Bogota.

16.5. Ser a + infinitive or **a** + infinitive alone is used in descriptions to indicate that an act is in progress and often that it is performed with a certain intensity:[1]

Yo rabiaba y pataleaba, y por consolarme, todos eran a comprarme dulces, a contentarme de todas maneras. (Benavente, **Campo de armiño,** I, 7)	I would scream and kick, and to console me, everybody was a-buying me candy, a-gratifying me by all means.
Paco tiene mucho amor propio... Todos son a encelarlo, y temo que, por no dejarse quitar las palmas, haga alguna barbaridad. (Reyles, **El embrujo de Sevilla,** IV)	Frank has a great deal of self-esteem ...Everybody is engaged in making him jealous and I am afraid that, so as not to let himself be outdone, he will do something rash.
Cada edad tiene sus emociones. Los jóvenes a desesperarnos, porque los viejos no nos dejan hacer lo que nos da la gana, y los viejos a desatinarse, porque los jóvenes no queremos hacer lo que a ellos les parece. (Martínez Sierra, **El reino de Dios,** I)	Every age has its feelings. We young people despairing because old people won't let us do what we feel like, and old people talking nonsense because we young people don't want to do what they think best.

16.6. Estar, being derived from the Latin *stare, to stand,* is used to denote the location of a person or thing, even though it be a permanent one:

Mi cuñado está en Venezuela.	My brother-in-law is in Venezuela.
Su casa está alta.	His house is high up *(located high).*
Mi casa está en el campo.	My house is in the country.

[1] The energy accompanying an act is also suggested by **venga a** (or **de**) + infinitive: **El vestido ya se descosía por un lado, ya por otro..., y yo venga a dar puntadas y clavar alfileres.** (Benavente, **La honradez de la cerradura,** II, 1) *The dress would rip first on one side, then on another...and I kept taking stitches and fastening pins.*

REMARK I. Especially with **a** + infinitive, **estar,** though with a basic meaning of location, comes to have practically the meaning of **ir** *to go* or **venir** *to come:*

Ayer nos lo mandaron a decir, y ahora está mi madre a ver al notario. (Martínez Sierra, **Madame Pepita,** II, near beginning)	Yesterday they sent us word and now my mother has gone to see the notary.
Una mañana, después de oír misa con don Valentín, estuvo doña Blanca a visitar a doña Antonia y a felicitarla. (Valera, **El comendador Mendoza,** X)	One morning, after hearing mass with Don Valentine, Doña Blanca went to visit Doña Antonia and to congratulate her.
A las seis menos cuarto estoy a buscaros. (Linares Rivas, **Cobardías,** I, 6)	At a quarter to six I shall come and get you.

REMARK II. The phrase **soy (seré) con usted,** etc., does not emphasize location but rather means "I'll attend to," "I'll look after," etc.:

Soy con usted al instante. (Pérez Galdós, **La familia de León Roch,** I, 3, 3)	I'll be with you in a moment.

16.7. **Ser** is used to mean *take place,* the subject being in this case an intangible thing:

Y apenas estallada la bomba, si era en nuestra calle, salíamos a recoger los cascos. (Unamuno, **Recuerdos de niñez y de mocedad,** I, 15)	And scarcely had the bomb burst, if it [that is, the explosion] was in our street, we would go out to gather up the fragments.
Genoveva viene conmigo a Madrid; allí será su boda. (Benavente, **Pepa Doncel,** III, 12)	Genevieve is coming to Madrid with me; her wedding will take place there.

Similar in form, though related in structure to those of § **16.2,** are sentences like:

Aquí fué donde Marco Antonio pronunció aquella arenga. (Camba, **Aventuras de una peseta,** III, 7)	Here was where Mark Anthony pronounced that speech.
Salieron a una vasta playa de arena: allí era donde José tenía cifrada principalmente su esperanza. (Palacio Valdés, **José,** VI)	They came out upon a broad sandy beach: it was there (*or* it was upon that spot) that Joseph had fixed his hope principally.
Uno de mis alojamientos fué en los altos de un despacho de vinos situado cerca del puerto. (Blasco Ibáñez, **La barraca, Al lector**)	One of my lodging places was in the upper story of a wine shop near the harbor.

REMARK. The use of **ser** in some expressions seemingly of location is perhaps an extension or at least an association with the use treated above:

Aquí es —dijo Guillermina, después de andar un trecho por la calle. (Pérez Galdós, **Fortunata y Jacinta,** I, 9, 1)	"Here is the place [that we are looking for]," said Wilhelmina, after walking a short distance along the street.
Señalándome con la mano una casita que había en el fondo de él, me dijo: Allí es. Llame usted fuerte. (Palacio Valdés, **La hermana San Sulpicio,** VI)	Indicating to me with his hand a little house that there was at the back of it, he said to me, "There's the place. Knock loud."
[Llévelos] Al almacén de ultramarinos que hay allá. ¿Sabe usted dónde es? (Baroja, **La feria de los discretos,** I, 1)	[Take them] to the grocery store that there is there. Do you know where it is?

16.8. The use of **ser** with an adjective implies that the speaker considers the subject as belonging to the class of persons or things indicated by the adjective (§ **16.2**):

Estas manzanas son agrias.	These apples are (the) sour (kind).
El agua de esta fuente es fría.	The water from this spring is (the) cold (kind).
Mi hermano es callado.	My brother is close-mouthed (*or* taciturn).
Juan es borracho.	John is a drunkard.
Siempre era pálida. (Pérez Galdós, **El amigo Manso,** XIII)	She was always pale (-complexioned).

16.9. The use of **estar** with an adjective implies that the speaker considers the subject as being in the state indicated by the adjective:

Estas manzanas están agrias.	These apples are sour [because they haven't ripened yet].
El agua del baño está fría.	The bath water is cold [because it has been allowed to cool].
Mi hermano está callado.	My brother is silent [he isn't talking].
Juan está borracho.	John is drunk.
El hotel está siempre lleno. (Benavente, **Las cigarras hormigas,** II, 3)	The hotel is always full.

Frequently the use of **estar** emphasizes that the state is different from the normal or expected. Thus it often comes to mean *to have* *become* and moreover not infrequently conveys some emotional reaction:

Hija mía, no sabes lo guapa que estás con ese pañolín colorado. (Palacio Valdés, **Sinfonía pastoral, Adagio cantábile,** IV)	My child, you don't know how [unusually] attractive you are with that red kerchief.
Estoy muy viejo, hijos míos. Mi vida toca ya su término. (Pérez de Ayala, **La caída de los Limones,** VII)	I have greatly aged *(or* I have become *or* I feel very old), my children. My life is now touching its end.
Entramos en el cuarto de mi madre que, al ver a Machín, quedó sorprendida no sé por qué: Machín estuvo con ella muy amable. (Baroja, **Las inquietudes de Shanti Andía,** V, 7)	We entered my mother's room, who, on seeing Machín, was greatly surprised for some reason: Machín was very (unusually) kind to her.
Tú no has pensado... Estuviste mortificante, cruel. (Benavente, **La escuela de las princesas,** III, 6)	You didn't think. You were mortifying, cruel [*more so than would have been expected*].
La noche está muy hermosa... El mes de septiembre no le ha ido en zaga al de agosto. (Palacio Valdés, **La alegría del capitán Ribot,** XIV)	The night is very beautiful [*more so than the average*]...The month of September has not been surpassed by August.
La noche de diciembre estaba fría, cruel. El vaho se congelaba en los cristales de las ventanillas y el viento helado se metía por entre las rendijas de la portezuela. (Baroja, **El árbol de la ciencia,** III, I)	The December night was [abnormally] cold, cruel. Vapor congealed on the window panes and the icy wind slipped between the cracks around the door.
Están muy buenos estos sandwichs. (Benavente, **De cerca,** III)	These sandwiches are *(or* taste) very good. [exceptionally so]
Si esas botas están estallando.—Pero mamá, si me están anchas. (Frontaura, **Las tiendas,** V)	Why those shoes are bursting! — But mother, they are too wide on me. [wider than my proper size]
Fermín, prueba este helado; ¡está riquísimo! (Benavente, **La comida de las fieras,** II, 2)	Fermín, try this ice cream; it is *(or* tastes) delicious. [more so than I expected]
Su madre, abrázandole, le hizo pasar a un cuarto y le acercó al balcón. —¡Qué alto estás, hijo mío! (Baroja, **La feria de los discretos,** I)	His mother, embracing him, made him enter a room and drew him to the balcony window. — How tall you are *(or* have grown), my boy!

De veras que estuve muy imprudente. No se debe hablar mal de nadie sin tener seguridad de lo que se dice. (Pérez Galdós, **Fortunata y Jacinta,** IV, 3, 1)	Indeed I was very imprudent [more so than is my habit]. One must not speak ill of anybody without being sure of what he says.

REMARK. It is therefore to be kept in mind that the use of **estar** with an adjective rather often conveys a thought additional to that expressed by **ser: El tiempo era triste y lluvioso: estábamos en el corazón del invierno.** (Palacio Valdés, **Santa Rogelia,** III, 8) *The weather was gloomy and rainy: we were in the dead of winter.* **Corría el mes de enero: era ya la hora del oscurecer. El tiempo estaba tan triste y sucio como en Algeciras. (idem,** second paragraph following) *It was in January, at nightfall. The weather was as gloomy and dirty as in Algeciras* [something better in the way of weather is to be expected in Madrid, even in winter].

16.10. Further illustrations of the use of **ser** *to be by nature, inwardly, absolutely* and **estar** *to be by condition, outwardly, relatively,* when introducing an adjective, are:

No hay allí nadie que no haya sido rico una vez y nadie que lo sea siempre. (Benavente, **La comida de las fieras,** I, 4)	There is no one there who hasn't been rich once and no one who is always so.
Ahora que está rico no se acuerda de cuando empezaba a ganarlo. (Pérez Galdós, **Torquemada en la hoguera,** VIII)	Now that you are rich you don't remember when you were beginning to earn it.
Ahora que es pobre abomina de la riqueza. (León, **Alcalá de los Zegríes,** II, 12)	Now that he is poor, he abominates wealth.
Pues debe estar ahora más pobre que una rata. (Pérez Galdós, **Misericordia,** X)	Well, he must be poorer than a church mouse now.
Unas veces soy alegre; otras, triste. (Unamuno, **Bonifacio, in El espejo de la muerte)**	Sometimes I am cheerful *(or* a cheerful fellow); sometimes sad *(or* a sad one).
Algunos días estaba tan alegre que, francamente, me parecía que había conseguido sacarse del pozo. **(idem)**	Some days he was so cheerful that, frankly, it seemed to me that he had succeeded in getting out of his difficulty.
¿Hago mal en estar siempre alegre? (Benavente, **Los malhechores del bien,** I, 6)	Do I do wrongly in aways being cheerful?

Pepita tendrá veinte años; es viuda; sólo tres años estuvo casada. (Valera, **Pepita Jiménez, 22 de marzo**)[1]	Pepita must be twenty; she is a widow; she was married only three years.
Manuel era casado, como sabes, y tenía un hijo de cuatro años. (Pérez Galdós, **Zaragoza,** XXV)	Manuel was married *(or* a married man), as you know, and he had a four-year-old child.
No tengo señora. Estoy soltero. (Palacio Valdés, **La alegría del capitán Ribot,** II)	I have no wife. I am [still] a bachelor.
Dicen que está muy guapa; siempre fué guapa. (Pérez Galdós, **La familia de León Roch,** I, 1, 6)	They say that she is [still] attractive; she always was attractive *(or* an attractive person).

Ser not infrequently takes on the connotation of *act* = *behave* = *bear* or *conduct oneself* with the quality named:

Yo le aconsejo que sea muy amable con todos, muy fina, muy cortés. (Pérez Galdós, **Misericordia,** XVIII)	I advise you to be very nice to everybody, very polite, very courteous.
Espero que, en un día próximo, podré ser menos cruel que he sido esta noche. (Pérez Galdós, **Mariucha,** II, 2)	I hope that, on a future day, I shall act less cruelly than I have acted tonight.
En este momento eres sincero, como lo eres siempre. (Benavente, **Campo de armiño,** I, 6)	At this moment you are conducting yourself with sincerity, as you always do.
El caso es que yo fuí bien prudente. (Pardo Bazán, **El tesoro de Gastón,** I)	The fact is that I behaved very prudently.

16.11. **Bueno** and **malo,** when construed with **ser,** apply to the quality of persons or things; with **estar** they refer to the state of one's health:

Su hermano de V. es bueno.	Your brother is good.
Su hermano de V. está bueno.	Your brother is well (in good health).
Mi hijo es malo.	My son is bad.
Mi hijo está malo.	My son is ill.

16.12. Depending on whether they are used with **ser** or **estar,**

[1] The distinction between **ser** and **estar** can not be said to be carefully observed with **casado, soltero** and **viudo.** Possibly on their model, **estar** is often used with **prisionero** (usually classed as a noun only, cf. § 16.2): **En ese castillo hacía años que estaba prisionero el ex rey de Lérida.** (Menéndez Pidal, **La España del Cid,** III, 8, 2) *In that castle the ex-king of Lerida had been prisoner for years.*

some adjectives have varying meanings, which often call for different translations:

	WITH **ser**	WITH **estar**
aburrido	boring	bored
alto	tall, high	in a high location
bajo	short, low	in a low location
bueno	good *(by nature)*	well, in good health
callado	close-mouthed, taciturn	silent
cansado	tiresome	tired
cierto	true	assured
despierto	alert, wide-awake	awake
divertido	amusing	amused
enfermo	sickly	sick
feliz	happy, fortunate	felicitous, apt, opportune
interesado	mercenary, self-interested	interested
libre	free	free, exempt
limpio	cleanly	clean
listo	smart, clever	ready
loco	silly, crazy *(by nature)*	crazy *(by state),* frantic
malo	bad *(by nature)*	sick, in poor health
nuevo	newly made	unused
seguro	reliable, safe	assured, confident, protected, safe
triste	dull	gloomy, sad
verde	green *(in color)*	green *(unripe)*
vivo	lively, keen	alive

16.13. Both **ser** and **estar** can be used before past participles, but the choice of the verb must depend on the nature of the idea to be expressed (cf. § 21.32). **Estar** is oftener so employed, as Spanish prefers to view the state attained rather than the act producing it. Indeed when **ser** is used with the past participle, the latter often has the value of a noun or an adjective:

Juan está empleado.	John is (at present) employed.
Juan es empleado.	John is an employee, a clerk.
Juanita era muy distraída e iba además pensando en sus travesuras de muchacha. (Valera, **Juanita la larga,** VII)	Juanita was very absent-minded and besides she was thinking of her girlish pranks.

Lo cierto es que si no eran fundadas mis sospechas, debían serlo. (Pereda, **Peñas arriba,** X, end)	The truth is that if my suspicions weren't reasonable, they should have been.
Si las teorías de ese mediquillo están bien fundadas, alguien ha de empezar esa obra. (**idem,** XXXIII, end)	If the theories of that insignificant doctor are well-grounded, someone must begin that work.
¿De cuándo acá es permitido que te burles de mí? (Pérez Galdós, **Miau,** XXIII)	Since when is it permissible that you make fun of me?
¿Se va usted a quedar aquí? — Sí — Pero no está permitido. (Baroja, **La feria de los discretos,** XXXI)	Are you going to stay here? — Yes. — But it isn't allowed.
A la hora de recreo también hablaban. Fuera de estas horas estaba prohibido comunicarse. (Palacio Valdés, **La hermana San Sulpicio,** X)	At recess hour also they would talk. Outside of these hours it was forbidden to communicate with one another.
La comida de la noche estuvo mejor atendida. (Pérez de Ayala, **La caída de los Limones,** XI)	Dinner at night was better attended.

XVII

Imperfect And Preterite

17.1. In addition to the perfect tense (described in Chapter XVIII), which is a compound tense, the Spanish verb has two past tenses of simple form: the *imperfect* and the *preterite*[1] (or *past*

[1] There were in Greek three past tenses—imperfect, aorist and perfect—corresponding generally to those in Spanish. The distinction between aorist and perfect was lost in Latin, where one tense, called *perfect,* served both purposes; and as grammar has been modeled from Latin, the term *aorist* has disappeared.

definite). In regular verbs these are obtained by adding the following terminations to the stem:

	IMPERFECT			PRETERITE	
	1st Conj.	2d and 3d Conj.		1st Conj.	2d and 3d Conj.
1.	**-aba**	**-ía**	1.	**-é**	**-í**
2.	**-abas**	**-ías**	2.	**-aste**	**-iste**
3.	**-aba**	**-ía**	3.	**-ó**	**-ió**
1.	**-ábamos**	**-íamos**	1.	**-amos**	**-imos**
2.	**-abais**	**-íais**	2.	**-asteis**	**-isteis**
3.	**-aban**	**-ían**	3.	**-aron**	**-ieron**

IMPERFECT TENSE OF THE MODEL VERBS

Sing.	1 p.	compraba	vendía	vivía
	2 p.	comprabas	vendías	vivías
	3 p.	compraba	vendía	vivía
Plur.	1 p.	comprábamos	vendíamos	vivíamos
	2 p.	comprabais	vendíais	vivíais
	3 p.	compraban	vendían	vivían

PRETERITE TENSE OF THE MODEL VERBS

Sing.	1 p.	compré	vendí	viví
	2 p.	compraste	vendiste	viviste
	3 p.	compró	vendió	vivió
Plur.	1 p.	compramos	vendimos	vivimos
	2 p.	comprasteis	vendisteis	vivisteis
	3 p.	compraron	vendieron	vivieron

Note. It will be seen that the first person plural of the preterite and that of the present indicative are identical in verbs of the first and third conjugations.

17.2. The imperfect tense is formed irregularly in three verbs only: **ser** *to be* forms its imperfect from a different root; the imperfect of **ir** *to go* resembles those of the first conjugation; and **ver** *to see* restores the original **e** of the stem in forming the imperfect:

Ser:	era	eras	era	éramos	erais	eran
Ir:	iba	ibas	iba	íbamos	ibais	iban
Ver:	veía	veías	veía	veíamos	veíais	veían

17.3. Tener, estar, haber, querer, hacer, venir and **decir** form the preterite tense upon stems entirely different from those of their infinitives; they all have this point in common, that the first and third persons singular are stressed on the penultimate, instead of the last syllable as in the regular verbs. **Ser** forms the preterite from a different root (as does the Latin *esse, to be*). **Ir** has no preterite of its own, and borrows that of **ser. Dar** forms the preterite like verbs of the second or third conjugations:

TENER **(tuv):**	tuve	tuviste	tuvo	tuvimos	tuvisteis	tuvieron
ESTAR **(estuv):**	estuve	estuviste	estuvo	estuvimos	estuvisteis	estuvieron
HABER **(hub):**	hube	hubiste	hubo	hubimos	hubisteis	hubieron
QUERER **(quis):**	quise	quisiste	quiso	quisimos	quisisteis	quisieron
HACER **(hic):**	hice	hiciste	hizo[1]	hicimos	hicisteis	hicieron
VENIR **(vin):**	vine	viniste	vino	vinimos	vinisteis	vinieron
DECIR **(dij):**	dije	dijiste	dijo	dijimos	dijisteis	dijeron[2]
SER / IR } **(fu):**	fuí	fuiste	fué	fuimos	fuisteis	fueron[2]
DAR **(d):**	di	diste	dió	dimos	disteis	dieron

17.4. The fundamental value of the imperfect is to express continuance. It is the tense used to express what was habitual or customary, and to describe the qualities of persons or things, and the place or condition in which they were, in the past:

En los tiempos de los bucaneros, los colonos españoles construían sus ciudades a distancia de la costa.	In the times of the buccaneers, the Spanish colonists built their towns at a distance from the coast.
Anteriormente esta isla era una posesión inglesa.	Formerly this island was an English possession.
El señor Garcés era un caballero muy agradable, pero tenía un defecto —el de hablar demasiado.	Mr. Garces was a very agreeable gentleman, but he had one fault—that of talking too much.
Creíamos que estaba V. en Chicago.	We thought you were in Chicago.
El tiempo estaba tempestuoso y sobre todo lluvioso, pero los caminos todavía no estaban malos y resistían bien a las ruedas de las carretas, aunque éstas eran bastante pesadas.	The weather was stormy and above all rainy, but the roads were not yet bad and resisted the wheels of the wagons well, although they were pretty heavy.
Este convento estaba situado sobre un contrafuerte elevado de la montaña, y dominaba la ciudad y sus cercanías.	This convent was situated on a high spur of the mountain, and overlooked the city and its environs.

[1] The **c** is changed to **z** to preserve the sound.
[2] Observe that the **i** of the diphthong **ie** is lost.

17.5. The preterite expresses a past action as occurring at some particular time, understood or designated, of which no part is continued to the present. It is the historical tense of Spanish, corresponding to the Greek aorist in all cases not implying duration, which is the distinctive characteristic of the imperfect:

El pueblo de Chile, en Julio de 1810, proclamó su independencia, derrocó al presidente español, y el 18 de setiembre puso la autoridad suprema a cargo de una comisión de siete individuos.	The people of Chile in July, 1810, proclaimed their independence, deposed the Spanish president, and on the 18th of September placed the supreme authority in the hands of a commission of seven persons.
Cuando Aníbal vió a los embajadores romanos, tomó veneno.	When Hannibal saw the Roman ambassadors, he took poison.
Ayer me hallé un peso en la calle.	I found a peso in the street yesterday.
El general presentó al príncipe los oficiales de su plana mayor.	The general presented the officers of his staff to the prince.
El primer síntoma de guerra fué una disputa ocurrida en el Club del Progreso... Casi hubo cachetadas, y quizá hubiera sido mejor, porque la venganza de Machado fué terrible. (Payró, **Pago Chico,** I)	The first symptom of war was a dispute which took place in the Progress Club... People almost came to blows, and perhaps it would have been better, because Machado took a terrible revenge.
Fué en San Fernando donde por primera vez la oyó. La segunda vez fué en una de las posadas del camino. (Gallegos, **Doña Bárbara,** I, 1)	It was in San Fernando where he heard it for the first time. The second was in one of the lodging places on the road.

17.6. Thus the preterite serves to indicate that an act came to an end or that it began:

Hasta los diez y ocho o diez y nueve años, el joven Leguía estuvo empleado en un almacén de San Sebastián. (Baroja, **El aprendiz de conspirador,** I, 4)	Until the age of eighteen or nineteen young Leguía was employed in a store in San Sebastian.
Mientras duró aquella conversación, pensaba Moreno si iría o no a despedirse de los de Santa Cruz. (Pérez Galdós, **Fortunata y Jacinta,** IV, 2, 5)	While that conversation lasted, Moreno was thinking whether or not he would go and say good-bye to the members of the Santa Cruz family.

Son dos pesetas. —¡Ah! Yo creí... Tome usted. Creí que no se vendía. (Benavente, **La comida de las fieras,** I, 1)	The price is two pesetas. —Oh! I thought... Here. I thought it was not for sale.
Nunca fuí aficionado a viajes. (Benavente, **Lo cursi,** I, 4)	I was never [*in the period ending now*] fond of trips.
De niñas las dos eran rollizas y altas; en cambio, yo siempre fuí pequeño y encanijado. (Baroja, **El aprendiz de conspirador,** VI, 2)	As children both were plump and tall; on the other hand, I was always [*in the period ending now*] small and sickly.
Ciudades que un tiempo fueron heroicas, esforzadas, activas, abundantes, hoy sólo tienen una existencia imaginaria y soporífera. (Pérez de Ayala, **La caída de los Limones,** III)	Cities that once were heroic, courageous, active and abundant today have only an imaginary and sleepy existence.
Desde entonces, y por largos años, Navarra estuvo gobernada por reyes de procedencia francesa. (Altamira, **Manual de historia de España, VII (El reino de Navarra)**	From that time on, and for long years, Navarre was governed by kings of French origin.
Bueno —dijo Antonio a su hermano cuando estuvieron solos. (Palacio Valdés, **Sinfonía pastoral, Adagio cantábile,** I)	"Well," said Anthony to his brother when they were [left] alone.
La expedición estuvo lista al acabar el estío de 1082. (Menéndez Pidal, **La España del Cid,** III, 8, 2)	The expedition was [= became, began to be] ready at the end of the summer of 1082.
Me fuí poniendo cada vez más sombrío. (Palacio Valdés, **La hermana San Sulpicio,** XI)	I began to grow more and more melancholy.
Ni entonces supe ni sabré jamás definir las complejas impresiones que me produjo la súbita aparición de aquel espectáculo. (Pereda, **Peñas arriba,** II)	Neither then did I know how *(or* become able to) nor shall I ever know how to define the complex impressions which the sudden appearance of that spectacle inspired in me.
La fisiología, cursándola así, parecía una cosa estólida y deslavazada, sin problemas de interés ni ningún atractivo. Hurtado tuvo una verdadera decepción. (Baroja, **El árbol de la ciencia,** I, 7)	Physiology, when studied in that way, seemed a dull and insipid affair, without interesting problems or attractiveness. Hurtado had *(or* suffered) a real deception.

Al fin, haciendo un esfuerzo supremo para serenarme, pude leer la sección de gacetillas. (Palacio Valdés, **El crimen de la calle de la Perseguida,** in **Aguas fuertes**)

Finally, making a supreme effort to calm myself, I became able to read (*or* managed to read) the local news section.

Montando las llaves se aproximó cautelosamente a dicho sitio. Nadie... Unicamente a alguna distancia le pareció que las plantas ondulaban en la obscuridad. (Blasco Ibáñez, **La barraca,** X)

Cocking his gun, he approached the aforesaid spot cautiously. Nobody ... Only at some distance it seemed to him that the shrubbery was moving in the darkness.

Cuando estuve en la playa de Ugoibea tuve el gusto de verla. (Pérez Galdós, **La familia de León Roch,** I, 1, 6)

When I was at Ugoibea Beach [my stay has ended], I had the pleasure of seeing her.

17.7. Consequently the preterite of some verbs (**conocer, poder, querer, saber, ser, tener**) often has a special translation:

Allí conoció y se enamoró de una hija de los dueños de la fonda donde se alojaba. (Palacio Valdés, **Sinfonía pastoral, Andante con moto,** III)

There he **met** (*or* became acquainted with) and fell in love with the daughter of the proprietors of the hotel where he was living.

Preso por la policía, pudo huir con una audacia extraordinaria cuando lo conducían deportado a Siberia. (Baroja, **El mundo es ansí,** I, 6)

Having been arrested by the police, he **managed to** flee with extraordinary boldness when they were deporting him to Siberia.

De pronto se puso lívido. Quiso hablar y le faltó la voz. (Pérez de Ayala, **Luz de domingo,** VI)

Suddenly he turned pale. He **tried to** speak and his voice failed him.

No pudimos hablar más, porque llegamos a la puerta de salida y era preciso montar en carruaje. Yo no quise hacerlo, aunque me invitaron con insistencia. (Palacio Valdés, **La hermana San Sulpicio,** XII)

We couldn't talk any more, because we reached the exit and it was necessary to get into the carriage. I **refused to** do so, although they urgently invited me.

Yo también hubiera venido anoche en cuanto supe la noticia; pero temí ser indiscreta. (Benavente, **La propia estimación,** II, 2)

I too would have come last night as soon as I **learned**[1] the news; but I was afraid that I would be indiscreet.

---

[1] **Saber** may have this translation in almost any tense. It is merely the usual one in the preterite. In any tense **conocer** may mean *recognize, perceive.*

Rómulo fué el primer rey de Roma.	Romulus **became** the first king of Rome.
Viera no tuvo aviso esta vez y se retardó en la redacción de "La Pampa" hasta mucho después de anochecido. (Payró, **Pago Chico,** II)	Viera **received** no warning this time and lingered in the offices of "The Pampa" until much after nightfall.

17.8. If the occurrence in question took place within a space of time not yet expired, as this day, month, year, etc., or an indefinite time *in any way* connected with the present, the perfect tense is employed. Still, the preterite is used in speaking even of today, if the hour is given, for in that case the time specified is wholly past:

He aprendido el castellano este año.	I have learned Spanish this year.
He leído hoy en el periódico que el monumento naval ha sido derribado por el viento.	I read in the paper today that the naval monument has been blown down by the wind.
He visto a menudo a aquel hombre, pero no recuerdo dónde.	I have often seen that man, but do not recollect where.
He escrito seis cartas esta mañana.	I have written six letters this morning.
¿Ha escrito Vd. hoy a su señor tío?	Have you written to your uncle today?
Sí; le escribí a las diez, y le mandé la esquela a las diez y media.	Yes, I wrote to him at ten o'clock and sent him the note at half past.

Remark. Doubtless through imitation of French, the perfect is often used, especially in Madrid, where the preterite might be expected: **Encarnación, la doncella, se ha casado el lunes de la semana pasada. No os podéis imaginar cómo está la casa desde que ella salió** (Palacio Valdés, **Maximina,** XVIII) *Encarnación, the maid, got married Monday of last week. You can't imagine the state the house is in since she left.* **He llegado de París hace unos días... Estudié la carrera en Madrid, pero me fuí a París donde he permanecido cinco años.** (Palacio Valdés, **Santa Rogelia,** II, 2) *I arrived from Paris a few days ago. I studied for my profession in Madrid, but I went off to Paris, where I remained five years.* **Te digo que he visto el cielo abierto cuando he comprendido que tu tío no se disgusta** (Benavente, **Al fin, mujer,** III, 2, 1) *I tell you that I saw the heavens open when I understood that your uncle is not displeased.*

17.9. The following may serve further to distinguish the preterite and perfect tenses:

a. A specified time wholly past calls for the preterite.

b. A specified time connected with the present requires the perfect.

c. An unspecified time is, necessarily, not connected with either past or present, except in the mind of the speaker. If he has only the past in view, he uses the preterite tense; if the present be in his mind, he makes use of the perfect tense.[1]

NOTE. The boundary line here, as in all questions of rhetoric and style, is not clearly defined, and is subject to joint-occupancy and the exercise of individual taste. In ordinary conversational style the perfect tense, when admissible, is preferred to the preterite, which latter is the more usual in literary language.

COMPARATIVE EXAMPLES OF THE PERFECT AND PRETERITE TENSES

He escrito hoy a mi padre.	I wrote to my father today.
(Includes present time.)	
Escribí a mi padre el sábado.	I wrote to my father Saturday.
(Excludes present time.)	
Grecia **produjo** grandes oradores y poetas.	Greece produced great orators and poets.
(Here we speak of ancient Greece, now past and gone.)	
Francia **ha producido** muchos autores eminentes.	France has produced many eminent authors.
(Her ability to produce them extends to the present.)	
Francia **produjo** muchos autores eminentes en el reinado de Luis Catorce.	France produced many eminent authors in the reign of Louis XIV.
(Here the time is restricted to a period entirely past.)	
Ha dejado a su familia sin sustento.	He has left his family without support.
Ha dejado un ejemplo insigne a la posteridad.	He has left a notable example to posterity.
(In the last two the influence of the deceased extends to the present.)	
No **he ido** a los baños de mar este verano, pero **estuve** allí el verano pasado.	I did not go to the sea-shore this summer, but I was there last summer.

[1] If we say *mi padre* **perdió** *$1.000 en esa especulación,* we consider the occurrence as entirely past and gone; but if we say *mi padre* **ha perdido** *$1.000 en esta especulación,* we speak of a comparatively recent occurrence, the effects of which are still felt, thus connecting it with the present time. Note, also, the change of demonstrative adjectives.

DISTINCTION BETWEEN PRETERITE AND IMPERFECT

17.10. The Spanish imperfect can generally be represented in English by either *used to* followed by an infinitive, or by the past tense of the verb *to be* and a present participle; the preterite cannot ordinarily be so represented. The English rendering does not necessarily assume one of these forms, but they are exact equivalents of the Spanish in meaning:

Los griegos **consideraban** a todas las demás naciones como bárbaras.	The Greeks *used to consider all* other nations as barbarians.
Los tribunos **tenían** su asiento en la puerta del senado romano.	The tribunes *used to have* their seat at the door of the Roman senate.
Fumaba mucho en el colegio, pero más tarde abandoné la costumbre.	I *used to smoke* a great deal in college, but later gave up the habit.
Iba a la pesca todas las mañanas cuando **vivía** en el campo.	I *used to go* fishing every morning when *I was living* in the country.
Tenía una casa de huéspedes en Lima cuando estalló la revolución.	He *was keeping* a boarding house in Lima when the revolution broke out.
El herido **dormía** profundamente y no le despertaron sus camaradas.	The wounded man *was sleeping* soundly and his comrades did not wake him.
Como **apuntaba** el alba del siguiente día, los expedicionarios salieron de la aldea.	Just as the dawn of the following day *was appearing*, the members of the expedition set out from the village.
Llegaron al muelle donde el vapor "Cuzco" **aguardaba** a sus pasajeros.	They reached the wharf where the steamer "Cuzco" *was awaiting* its passengers.
El pescador **remendaba** sus redes mientras que su mujer **preparaba** la cena.	The fisherman *was mending* his nets while his wife *was getting* supper.
El viento **soplaba** con violencia, pero por fortuna ya no **llovía.**	The wind *was blowing* with violence, but fortunately it *was* no longer *raining.*
Luchaba con valor contra las olas, pero una corriente fuerte le cogió y le arrastró hacia el norte.	He *was struggling* bravely against the waves, but a strong current caught him and swept him northward.

17.11. In narration, where the events are wholly past the preterite applies to actions of some and any duration, provided we have no especial reference to the fact of their continuance. It is as if the area over which the action extends were by the perspective of time reduced to a mere point:

Estuvo muchas veces a punto de hacer fortuna, lo que no consiguió por indiferencia. (Baroja, **Elizabide el vagabundo, in Fantasías vascas**) — He was many times on the point of making a fortune, which he didn't achieve through indifference.

Se enredó de nuevo la disputa sobre el percance de la tarde. Poco a poco todos los marineros fueron tomando parte en ella. (Palacio Valdés, **José**, VIII) — The dispute about the afternoon's incident started up again. Little by little all the sailors began to take part in it.

No ya esta vez en la iglesia de la Soledad sino en la nueva parroquia Juanita estuvo rezando fervorosamente, durante mucho tiempo. (Valera, **Juanita la larga**, XLI) — Not this time in the church of la Soledad but in the new parish church Juanita continued to pray with fervor for a long time.

Vera se colgó al cuello de Sacha y la abrazó y la besó repetidas veces. (Baroja, **El mundo es ansí**, I, 16) — Vera clung to Sacha's neck and hugged her and kissed her repeatedly.

Sacha fué con frecuencia a ver a su madre. (**idem**, I, 2) — Sacha went frequently to see her mother.

COMPARATIVE EXAMPLES OF THE IMPERFECT AND PRETERITE TENSES

¿Qué le **decía** a V. su señor padre? — What *was* your father *saying* to you?

¿Qué le **dijo** a V. su señor padre? — What *did* your father *say* to you?

¿Cuáles **eran** los deberes de su señor hermano cuando **estaba** empleado en el Banco Nacional? — What *were* your brother's duties when he *was* employed in the National Bank?

Escribía las cartas extranjeras. Una vez **escribió** al Sr. presidente de Méjico. — He *wrote* the foreign letters. One time he *wrote* to the President of Mexico.

Mi padre **tenía** dos hermosos caballos, pero los **vendió**. — My father *had* two fine horses, but he *sold* them.

Cuando **vi** al cuñado de V., **tenía** en la mano una escopeta de dos cañones. — When I *saw* your brother-in-law, he *had (was holding)* a double-barreled gun in his hand.

Yo **atizaba** la lumbre cuando ella **entró**. — I *was poking* the fire when she *came* in.

¿**Visitó** V. la Biblioteca Nacional en Quito? — *Did* you *visit* the National Library in Quito?

Sí, en efecto, **leí** y **estudié** allí con frecuencia. — Yes indeed, I *read* and *studied* there frequently.

¿A dónde **iba** V. cuando yo le **encontré?** —**Venía** del teatro.

Where *were* you going when I *met* you? —I *was coming* from the theater.

¿Ha venido alguien? —**Vino** su señor padre, pero como **estaba** de prisa y V. **estaba** fuera, **no** le **aguardó.**

Did any one come? —Your father *came,* but as he *was* in a hurry and you *were out,* he *did not wait* for you.

17.12. In narrations the preterite tells the occurrences which furnish the thread of the story; the imperfect describes the scene in which they occurred:

Los exploradores **salieron** de la choza. **Eran** las seis de la tarde, y el sol con sus últimos rayos se **despedía** de los enhiestos picos de los cerros andinos. El frío, a pesar de la absoluta calma de la atmósfera, se **dejaba** sentir vivamente. Pablo **consultó** el barómetro y **vió** que el mercurio se **mantenía** a 0,423 milímetros, lo que **correspondía** a una elevación de 11.700 pies. El ingeniero y Pablo **llegaron** a una loma desde la cual **pasearon** sus miradas por todo el horizonte. **Ocupaban** entonces la cima de los nevados de la cordillera, y **dominaban** un espacio de cuarenta millas. Hacia el sur el volcán de Antuco **rugía** como un monstruo enorme y **vomitaba** ardientes humaredas mezcladas con torrentes de llamas fuliginosas. El circo de montañas que lo **rodeaba parecía** incendiado; un resplandor inmenso, que por instantes **adquiría** intensidad, una deflagración deslumbradora **llenaba** aquel vasto circuito con sus esplendentes reverberaciones. Del cráter del volcán **salían** cohetes de lava que **formaban** haces centelleantes; nubes de vapores rojizos **coronaban** su cumbre, y granizadas de piedras candentes **caían** sobre sus lados.

The explorers *came out* of the cabin. It *was* six o'clock in the evening, and the sun *was* with his last rays *taking leave of* the sharp peaks of the Andine chains. The cold, in spite of the absolute stillness of the air, *made itself* keenly *felt.* Paul *consulted* the barometer and *saw* that the mercury *stood* at 423 millimeters, which *corresponded* to an altitude of 11,700 feet. The engineer and Paul *reached* an eminence from which they *swept* their gaze over the entire horizon. They *were* then *occupying* the summit of the snow-fields of the cordillera, and *overlooked* a range of forty miles. Towards the south the volcano of Antuco *roared* like an enormous monster and *vomited* glowing clouds of smoke mixed with torrents of sooty flames. The circle of mountains that *surrounded* it *appeared* on fire; an immense glare which every instant *gained* intensity, a dazzling deflagration *filled* that vast circuit with its vivid flashes. From the crater of the volcano *issued* jets of lava which *formed* sheaves of sparks; clouds of reddish vapor *crowned* its apex and showers of glowing stones *fell* upon its sides. In the distance the glaciers and snow-fields

A lo lejos **deslumbraban** los ventisqueros y capas de nieve sumergidos en aquella irradiación, mientras que las eminencias, las crestas, los picos, **reflejaban** la luz cobriza que **adornaba** sus contornos.

submerged in that irradiance *were* perfectly dazzling, whilst the eminences, crests and peaks *reflected* the coppery light which tinged their outlines.

Después de pasar mucho tiempo contemplando aquella magnífica lucha de los fuegos de la tierra con los del cielo, Pablo **rompió** el silencio, etc.

After remaining a long time contemplating that magnificent contest of the fires of earth with those of the sky, Paul *broke* the silence, etc.

Thus the speaker or writer is free to use the tense which suits his purpose of the moment, which may be either to continue the sequence of events by naming an incident or to detail the circumstances which accompany an incident. In a given sentence several combinations are usually possible, according as the context in which they lie:

Mientras **estuvieron** solos, Bringas y su mujer apenas **hablaron.** (Pérez Galdós, **La de Bringas,** XX)

While they *remained* alone, Bringas and his wife scarcely *spoke.*

(The writer is relating what happened after someone had gone for the doctor.)

Mientras **duró** la cena, las graciosas espectadoras **no cesaban** en su charla picotera. (**idem,** VIII)

So long as the dinner *lasted,* the gracious spectators *did not stop* their prattling talk.

(The writer is describing the witnesses of a ceremony: the feeding of the poor.)

Mientras **llegaban,** el joven Bernal **asistía** todas las tardes al te. (Palacio Valdés, **La hija de Natalia,** IV, 13)

While they *were coming,* young Bernal *attended* the tea every afternoon.

(The writer is describing the circumstances incidental to a request that certain documents be forwarded.)

17.13. It is a stylistic device of literary Spanish to build up, however briefly, the picture of the circumstances with the imperfect, then, as a sort of climax, indicating with a preterite the act that took place. Thus the contrast between description and incident is heightened and events become the more vivid as they appear to unfold before us. There is also the opposite procedure of beginning a passage or paragraph, however short, with a preterite, thus condensing the story in a word at the outset, then with the imperfect relating the circumstances which describe the background of the act:

¡Pum! ... ¡Pum! ... ¡Pum! ... Y ¡nada! ¡No **respondía** nadie! **¡No abrían!** ¡No **se movía** una mosca! Sólo **se oía** el claro rumor de los caños de una fuente que **había** en el patio de la casa. Y de esta manera **transcurrían** minutos, largos como eternidades. Al fin, cerca de la una, **abrióse** un ventanillo del piso segundo. (Alarcón, **El sombrero de tres picos,** XXVIII)

Bang! ... Bang! ... Bang! ... And not a sound! Nobody *answered!* They *didn't open* the door! Not a fly *moved!* There *was* only to be heard the sharp sound of the jets of a fountain that there *was* in the patio of the house. And in this wise there *passed* minutes, each one as long as eternity. Finally, near one o'clock, a small window on the second floor *was opened.*

"Tú sabrás lo que has hecho con el dinero, que **no era** poco. Me pides más, de nuevo; imposible, hijo, imposible..." Aquella misma noche **se suicidaba**... Esto **acontecía** a los dos años de enviudar la italiana. A los pocos días del suicidio, huyendo de lenguas ociosas, la Cioretti **salió** de Pilares y **fué** a refugiarse en Cenciella. (Pérez de Ayala, **La pata de la raposa,** p. 58 of **Obras completas** edition, Madrid, 1923)

"You will know what you have done with the money, which *wasn't* little. You ask me for more, again; impossible, my boy, impossible..." That same night he *committed suicide.* This *took place* two years after the Italian's husband died. A few days after the suicide, fleeing from idle tongues, the Cioretti woman *left* Pilares and *took refuge* in Cenciella.

Al día siguiente mi abuela **cerró** la casa, y **nos pusimos** en camino para San Clemente de Brandeso. Ya **estaba** yo en la calle montado en la mula de un montañés que me **llevaba** delante en el arzón, y **oía** en la casa batir las puertas, y gritar buscando a mi hermana Antonia. **No** la **encontraban,** y con los rostros demudados **salían** a los balcones, y **tornaban** a entrarse y a correr las estancias vacías, donde

On the following day my grandmother *closed* the house and we *set out* for San Clemente de Brandeso. I *was* already in the street on the mule of a mountaineer who *was taking* me in front of him on the saddle and I *heard* the doors slam in the house and the shouts as they looked for my sister Antonia. They *didn't find* her, and with disturbed faces *came out* on the balconies and *went in* again

andaba el viento a batir las puertas, y las voces gritando por mi hermana. Desde la puerta de la catedral una beata la **descubrió** desmayada en el tejado. (Valle-Inclán, **Mi hermana Antonia,** XXII, in **Jardín umbrío**)

to search through the empty rooms, where the wind *was slamming* the doors and the voices shouting for my sister. From the cathedral door a devout old woman *discovered* her in a faint on the roof.

Míster Harvey se **levantó** y **comenzó** a declamar con muchos gestos. Su hija **traducía.** A mí me **hacía** mucha gracia el ver que **se utilizaba** un idioma tan difícil como el inglés para explicar el esperanto. (Camba, **Una escuela de esperanto,** in **Londres**)

Mr. Harvey *got up* and *began* to declaim with many gestures. His daughter *translated.* It *amused* me greatly to see that a language as difficult as English *was used* to explain Esperanto.

XVIII

Compound Tenses Imperative Mood

18.1. Besides the simple tenses—present, imperfect, preterite and future, already discussed—grammarians, out of deference to their Latin models, have usually reckoned an equal number of *compound* tenses. These are formed in Spanish by adding an invariable past participle to the various forms of the verb **haber** *to have.* In such a position **haber** is called an auxiliary or helping verb, and retains no idea of possession. It is varied like any other verb to express mood, tense, person and number.

Remark. So far, then, as grammatical construction goes, **haber** is the principal verb in these compound tenses; and it is getting to be so considered by the most eminent philologists. It is only necessary to learn once for all the inflections of **haber** in order to dispense with the repetition of numerous diagrams of compound tenses which needlessly occupy the pages of grammars.

18.2. The Spanish verb has 7 moods, 2 of which have 4 tenses each; the others exhibiting no distinctions of tense. These 13 heads, with their various distinctions for person, number and gender, include all the inflectional forms of the Spanish conjugation:

SCHEME OF INFLECTION OF VERBS

MOOD	NO. OF TENSES	DESIGNATION	NATURE OF SECONDARY INFLECTION	NO. OF FORMS
Indicative	4	Present	Person and Number	6
		Imperfect	" "	6
		Preterite	" "	6
		Future	" "	6
Subjunctive	4	Present	" "	6
		Imperfect	" "	6
		Imperfect	" "	6
		Future	" "	6
Conditional	1	Conditional	" "	6
Imperative	1	—	2nd person, sing. and plur.	2
Infinitive	1	—	Invariable	1
Past Participle[1]	1	—	Gender and Number	4
Present Participle[1]	1	—	Invariable	1
				62

Thus the maximum number of forms of a Spanish verb is 62; but as many of them are identical, and are only distinguished grammatically, the actual number is considerably less. One of the principal Spanish grammars has, by combination with **haber**, by counting **usted** as a separate number, and by other repetitions, made the number of forms mount up to 179.

It remains now only to discuss the application of the several forms of **haber** to a past participle, and the subject may then be dismissed.

18.3. Although **haber** was originally an independent active verb meaning to possess (cf. § 22.1), it is no longer used as such except in a few phrases which are relics of its former usage, and occasionally in poetic or archaic style. Its present usage is as an auxiliary before a past participle, to form the compound tenses of all verbs.

[1] Although the past participle and present participle are not usually called moods, yet they differ from the other moods in the same manner as these moods do from each other.

18.4. The past participle when conjugated with **haber** never agrees with its object, as it does, for instance, in French. With any other verb, or when no verb is expressed, the participle agrees with its object in gender and number, in the same manner as an adjective:

He abierto la ventana.	I have opened the window.
Ella ha escrito la carta.	She has written the letter.
Ella tiene escrit**a** la carta.	She has the *letter written.*
Tenemos pagad**os** a los soldad**os**.	We have got the *soldiers paid off.*
Ella ha dejado abiert**a** la ventan**a**.	She has left the *window open.*
Las cart**as** están mal escrit**as**.	The *letters* are badly *written.*
cart**as** recibid**as**; visit**as** hech**as**	*letters received; visits made*

18.5. When possession or ownership is to be indicated, **tener** is the verb used. **Tener** is, indeed, sometimes used before a past participle. Basically **tener** thus employed denotes the actual possession of an object upon which the action of the participle has been performed. In practice this construction more often denotes the subsistence of the state produced by the action. In some cases such usage may be dialectal:

Tenemos contado el dinero.	We have the money counted.
Tengo arado el campo.	I have got the field plowed.
El traje que tengo comprado...	The dress that I have bought...
Los padres en el colegio nos tenían prohibido que leyéramos cuentos. (Benavente, **Campo de armiño,** II, 8)	The priests at the school had in force the rule that we must not read stories.
Si tienes llorado alguna vez en tu vida, han sido lágrimas de administración. (Benavente, **Al fin, mujer,** I, 2, 1)	If you have wept at any time in your life, it has been administrative tears.
Si me has entendido, ya puedes figurarte lo que tengo pensado. **(ibid.)**	If you have understood me, you can imagine what my thoughts are.
Pues ten entendido que si no llegas a hacer lo que te encargo, voy a hacerlo yo. (Pereda, **Sotileza,** XXVII)	Well, keep in mind that if you don't do what I direct you to, I am going to do it myself.
Alguna vez se le tienen escapado esta y otras exclamaciones semejantes. (Palacio Valdés, **La hermana San Sulpicio,** XV)	At one time or another this and other exclamations of the sort have escaped her.

REMARK. **Tener** is usually applicable as an auxiliary only to past participles which take a direct object. Thus it would be impossible to say:

Tenemos estado ausentes.	We have been absent.

18.6. The present indicative of **haber,** with a past participle, forms the *perfect tense,* or *past indefinite,* used in speaking of a past event without reference to any particular time; it then sometimes corresponds to the English *past.* It more generally conveys an allusion to the present time, and denotes an action or occurrence of the present day, month, year or age; in this respect it corresponds to the English *perfect* tense:

Hasta ahora no ha contestado a nuestra petición.	Thus far he has not answered our request.
En cambio de la sangre que he derramado ¿qué me han hecho el rey y la patria? ¡Nada!	What have the king and country done for me in payment for the blood I have lost? Nothing!
He aprendido el español en España.	I learned Spanish in Spain.
He pasado un mes en Egipto.	I spent a month in Egypt.
¿Ha copiado V. el informe?	Did you copy / Have you copied } the report?
He leído la carta de V.	I have read your letter.
Mi hermano ha llegado hoy.	My brother has arrived today.

18.7. The auxiliary **haber** is usually not separated from the participle by another word, though occasionally a subject or object pronoun or adverb is placed between them. In a question, the subject usually follows the participle:

No he vendido mi casa.	I have not sold my house.
He evitado siempre las discusiones inútiles.	I have always avoided useless discussions.
¿Ha estudiado **V.** la lección?	Have you studied the lesson?
¿Han llegado los amigos de V.?	Have your friends arrived?
¿Habría **Caballero** adivinado algo? (Pérez Galdós, **Tormento,** XXIII)	Could Caballero have guessed something?
Usted no habrá **nunca** pensado de mí que podía ser tan cobarde. (Benavente, **La propia estimación,** III, 4)	You must never have thought of me that I could be so cowardly.
Creí que había **usted** estornudado. (Benavente, **Al natural,** I, 3)	I thought you sneezed.

18.8. The imperfect of **haber** with a past participle forms what is usually called the PLUPERFECT tense. The pluperfect represents an action or event as not only past but prior to another event also past; this latter is expressed by the preterite or imperfect but not by the perfect. The usage is thus the same in both languages:

Todo esto me lo dijo no creyendo que yo mismo había presenciado lo que había pasado en la huerta.	She told me all this not knowing that I had witnessed what had happened in the orchard.
Llegó a mi noticia que el rey había nombrado ya un almirante.	I learned that the king had already appointed an admiral.
Abrieron, no sin trabajo, camino entre aquella espesura y aquellas malezas que jamás habían sido apartadas por mano de hombre.	They opened for themselves, not without labor, a road through that thicket and that undergrowth which had never been separated by human hand.
Di al cochero las señas de una casa de huéspedes que mi tío me había recomendado.	I gave the driver the address of a boarding house that my uncle had recommended to me.

18.9. The preterite of **haber** with a past participle forms the PRETERITE PERFECT. This tense, the use of which is literary, is always preceded by a conjunction of time:

luego que		**apenas** *hardly, scarcely*
en cuanto		**cuando** *when*
así que	*as soon as*	**después que** *after*
tan pronto como		**no bien** *no sooner*
al momento (*or* **punto**) **que**		

En cuanto hube acabado mi obra, se la llevé.	As soon as I had finished my work, I took it to him.
Así que hubo salido al balcón el presidente, la turba se calló.	As soon as the president had stepped out on the balcony, the crowd became silent.
Luego que los convidados hubieron tomado sus puestos, empezó el banquete.	After the guests had taken their places, the banquet began.
Cuando la madre hubo concluido su relación, o al menos cuando yo creí que la había concluido, tomé la palabra.	When the mother had concluded her narration, or at least when I thought she had concluded, I took the floor.
Después que hubieron discutido un rato, el catedrático intervino sonriendo con superioridad.	After they had argued awhile, the professor interposed, smiling with superiority.

Apenas hubo pronunciado estas palabras cuando un gran golpe de agua cayó encima del puente.	He had scarcely uttered these words when a large volume of water fell upon the deck.

18.10. The preterite perfect is little used in colloquial style, not only because it always appears after a conjunction of time, but because its place may even then be taken by the simple preterite:

No bien me vió que me conoció.	No sooner did he see me than he knew me.
En cuanto empezó a hablar le perdí el respeto que le había tenido.	As soon as he commenced to speak I lost the respect which I had had for him.
Luego que el tumulto **cesó** completamente, Pizarro congregó a todos los reclutas sobre cubierta.	*When* the uproar *had ceased* completely, Pizarro assembled all the recruits on deck.

18.11. When a customary occurrence is to be expressed after these conjunctions, the pluperfect takes the place of that of the preterite:

En cuanto había acabado una página, yo se la llevaba.	As soon as I had finished a page, I used to take it to him.
No bien habíamos matado a un antílope o cualquier caza mayor que los buitres aparecían cerniéndose en el aire.	We had no sooner shot an antelope or any large game than the vultures appeared hovering in the air.
Apenas se había levantado algún miembro del partido nacional para tomar la palabra, cuando la oposición ahogaba su voz tosiendo, silbando, pateando y voceando.	Scarcely had any member of the Government party risen to take the floor, when the Opposition drowned his voice by coughing, whistling, stamping and shouting.

18.12. The combination of the future of **haber** with a past participle is called FUTURE PERFECT. This tense expresses an event or action which *will be* past before some future event or action takes place:

Los plomeros habrán terminado su trabajo para las seis.	The plumbers will have finished their work by six o'clock.
Según las indicaciones actuales habrá desaparecido cada vestigio de la institución antes de la mitad del siglo venidero.	According to the present indications, every vestige of the institution will have disappeared before the middle of the next century.

NOTE. Four corresponding compound tenses are formed from the four tenses of the subjunctive mood; these will be dealt with when that mood is discussed.

18.13. The infinitive and present participle of **haber,** in combination with a past participle, form a PERFECT INFINITIVE and PERFECT PARTICIPLE not differing in usage from the simple forms:

No recuerdo haber visto nada semejante a lo que V. describe.	I do not recollect having seen anything similar to what you describe.
Leibnitz dice que más vale haber aprendido las matemáticas y haberlas olvidado que nunca haberlas aprendido, pues su estudio habrá efectuado en la mente un cambio que no se borrará jamás.	Leibnitz says that it is better to have learned mathematics and forgotten it than never to have learned it at all, for the study of it will have wrought a change in the mind which will never be effaced.
Habiéndole causado estas heridas, como era natural, un copioso derrame de sangre, pronto sintió que la tierra huía bajo sus pies, se le anubló la vista, y vino al suelo abrumado por el peso de la armadura.	These wounds having caused him, as was natural, a profuse loss of blood, he soon felt that the ground was sinking beneath his feet, his sight became dim, and he fell to the ground borne down by the weight of his armor.

THE IMPERATIVE

18.14. The IMPERATIVE in Spanish is limited to the second person, and is employed only in direct, positive commands. It has only two forms, a singular and a plural.

18.15. The singular form is identical with the third person singular of the indicative present, whether that be regular or not; the plural form is obtained by changing the final **r** of the infinitive to **d,** and is therefore always regular:

	SINGULAR	PLURAL	
abrir *to open*	**abre**	**abrid**	*open*
copiar *to copy*	**copia**	**copiad**	*copy*
correr *to run*	**corre**	**corred**	*run*
dar *to give*	**da**	**dad**	*give*
leer *to read*	**lee**	**leed**	*read*

18.16. Nine verbs make the second person singular of the imperative in abbreviated or irregular forms, the plural being regular:

	SINGULAR	PLURAL	
decir *to say, tell*	**di**	**decid**	*say, tell*
hacer *to do, make*	**haz**	**haced**	*do, make*
ir *to go*	**ve**	**id**	*go*
poner *to put*	**pon**	**poned**	*put*
salir *to go out*	**sal**	**salid**	*go out*
ser *to be*	**sé**	**sed**	*be*
tener *to have*	**ten**	**tened**	*have*
valer *to avail*	**val** and **vale**	**valed**	*help*
venir *to come*	**ven**	**venid**	*come*

18.17. As the Spanish imperative relates only to the second person, it is only applicable in the cases where that mode of address is used.

REMARK. In polite language where **usted** is used, and in all negative commands, the imperative is replaced by the subjunctive, as will be explained when that mood is treated (§§ 23.49 ff.). The substitutes for imperatives of the first and third persons are also subjunctives.

18.18. In cases where it is applicable, the use of the imperative in Spanish is the same as in English:

Juan, abre la puerta.	John, open the door.
Toma lo que quieres.	Take what you want.
Da una silla a esta señora.	Give this lady a chair.
Niño, ven acá.	Boy, come here.

18.19. When the pronoun subject of the imperative is expressed, it usually follows, although in conversational style it may occasionally precede, the imperative:

Págame tú lo que me debes.	Pay me what you owe me.
Desechad vosotros el miedo.	Dismiss all fear.
Tú déjamelo gobernar.	Let me manage it.

18.20. A COMPOUND IMPERATIVE, made by associating the imperative of **haber** with a past participle, is met with, though it is of rare occurrence. This applies only to the plural:

Habed aderezado la comida para cuando yo vuelva.	Have the dinner prepared by the time I return.

18.21. When the imperative of **tener** is substituted for that of **haber** there is both a singular and a plural form:

Tenme preparado el desayuno.	Have breakfast ready for me.
Tenedme barrida la alcoba.	Have the alcove swept out.

XIX
Particular Uses of the Tenses

NOTE. This chapter is designed to explain minor peculiarities, not yet touched upon, in the usage of certain tenses, and to treat more fully the application of the infinitive and past participle than has been done hitherto.

19.1. The present tense is frequently substituted in Spanish for the imperfect and preterite in narrations, and thus by bringing the occurrence to the present time, we represent it as if it were passing before our eyes, giving more animation to the recital. The pluperfect is then changed to perfect, and the conditional to future indicative:

El prisionero corre hacia la playa, y después de dar algunos saltos, alcanza las primeras olas del mar. Siente tras sí a los guardias civiles, y oye el estampido de sus armas, cuyas balas, disparadas al azar, le rozan a veces la cabeza. Salva los charcos de agua, saltando de roca en roca; pero entonces su silueta se destaca más visiblemente sobre el fondo menos oscuro del horizonte, los guardias le divisan, y se lanzan todos a su persecución. Hasta ahora el fugitivo ha logrado conservar su delantera, pero el terreno sólido le faltará bien pronto. En efecto, llega a las últimas rocas del arrecife, y ve que los guardias están tan sólo a unos cien pasos de él. Lanza entonces un último grito, grito de adiós dirigido

The prisoner dashed towards the beach, and with a few bounds reached the first waves of the sea. He heard the police behind him, heard the crack of their rifles; and their bullets, fired at random, at times grazed his head. He cleared the pools of water, leaping from rock to rock; but then his profile was more clearly outlined against the lighter background of the horizon, the police descried him, and they all dashed on in pursuit. So far the fugitive had managed to keep the lead, but the solid ground was soon to fail him. In fact, he reached the last rocks of the reef and saw that the police were only about a hundred paces from him. He gave a last cry, a cry of adieu directed to heaven, and at the moment when

al cielo, y en el momento en que una nueva descarga le envuelve en una granizada de balas, se precipita al mar.	a fresh volley enveloped him in a shower of bullets, he threw himself into the sea.

REMARK. The same usage is found in English, although not so extensively.

19.2. The present tense is also substituted (especially if an adverbial or conjunctive expression of time is present) for the future, giving more vivacity and color to the statement, as well as expressing greater certainty of its occurrence:

El baile empezará a las diez.	The ball will commence at ten.
El baile empieza a las diez.	The ball commences at ten.
El buque se hará a la vela mañana.	The vessel will set sail tomorrow.
El buque se hace a la vela mañana.	The vessel sets sail tomorrow.
El mes que viene habrá un eclipse anular de sol.	Next month there will be an annular eclipse of the sun.
El mes que viene hay un eclipse anular de sol.	Next month there is to be an annular eclipse of the sun.

19.3. Future contingencies may be expressed with greater energy and certainty of result by means of the present indicative; and by making this present apply graphically to a past time, it may take the place of the conditional perfect and the pluperfect subjunctive:

Si abres la boca, estás muerto.	If you open your mouth you are a dead man.
Si da un paso más, se precipita al abismo.	If he had taken another step he would have pitched headlong into the abyss.
Si no acudo tan pronto, sucede un desastre.	If I hadn't got there so soon, there would have been an accident.

19.4. The present indicative is also used as a sort of imperative, presenting the act commanded as an accomplished fact:

Tú, Cantarote, te callas. (Baroja, **La feria de los discretos,** VI)	You, Cantarote, hush up.
Tú, Aragonés, y tú, Segura, os ponéis en aquel almear. (**idem,** VIII)	You, Aragonés, and you, Segura, station yourselves in that haystack.
Ustedes no me hagan caso. Usted sigue con sus labores; usted con sus papeles. (Benavente, **La honradez de la cerradura,** I, 1, 3)	Don't pay any attention to me. You go ahead with your handwork, you with your papers.

19.5. Both **ir** and **venir** and indeed any verb (cf. § **19.10**) are used in the present tense with a reference to the near future, thus corresponding to the English mode of expression:

Voy a la ciudad mañana.	*I am going* to the city tomorrow.
Mi padre no **viene** hoy.	My father *is* not *coming* today.

19.6. **Ir,** with an infinitive, has the same meaning of intention or purpose which is expressed by *going to* or *about to* in English:

¿Qué va V. a hacer?	What are you going to do?
Voy a escribir una carta ahora.	I am going to write a letter now.

19.7. The imperative, often in combination with the future indicative, makes up a verbal formula which suggests the tenacity with which an act is performed:

Si usted no tiene gana, dígalo; pero no nos tenga tanto tiempo **espera que te espera.** (Pérez Galdós, **Miau,** VIII)	If you don't feel like it, say so; but don't keep us *waiting patiently* so long.
Entre las dos hermanitas me han tenido a mí lo mejor de mi vida con un dogal al cuello, **aprieta que te apretarás. (idem,** XLIII)	Between the two dear sisters they had me the best part of my life with a noose around my neck, *tightening away at it.*
Mientras el agua me cae encima, yo estoy **canta que canta.** (Gallegos, **Doña Bárbara,** VII)	While the water falls on me, *I sing away at it.*

19.8. The use of the future is practically the same in Spanish as in English:

Yo no diré nada.	I shall not say anything.
¿No tomará V. un vaso de vino?	Won't you take a glass of wine?
Será preciso obrar con prudencia.	It will be necessary to act prudently.
Pasaremos un mes en el campo.	We will spend a month in the country.
Partiremos mañana.	We will set out tomorrow.
¿A qué teatro iremos?	What theater shall we go to?

19.9. **Querer,** used with an infinitive in asking a favor, corresponds to the English *will,* which must not be confounded with the true future:

¿Quiere V. abrir la ventana?	Will you open the window?
¿Quiere V. tomar una taza de te?	Will you take a cup of tea?

REMARK. Such an expression as *will you be at home tomorrow?* requires the future tense.

19.10. In short emphatic declarations and in brief requests for instructions, the present indicative replaces the future tense in familiar language, especially in the first person:

Voy a su casa luego.	I shall go to his house soon.
No pago la cuenta.	I shan't pay the bill.
No emprendo ningún proyecto semejante.	I won't undertake any such project.
¿Dónde pongo el quinqué?	Where shall I put the lamp?
¿Quito el mantel o no?	Shall I take off the table-cloth or not?
¿Qué digo? ¿Qué hago?	What shall I say? What shall I do?
¿Me hace V. el favor de abrir la ventana?	Will you do me the favor of opening the window?

19.11. The future perfect is formed as in English by the association of the future of **haber** and a past participle. Its usage does not differ materially in the two languages:

Habremos terminado la obra mañana.	We shall have finished the work tomorrow.
¿Habrá copiado V. el informe antes de mi vuelta?	Will you have copied the report before my return?

REMARK. The use of **tener** with a past participle contrasts well with that of **haber** in the above examples (cf. § **18.5**):

Tendremos terminada la obra mañana.	We shall have the work finished tomorrow.
¿Tendrá copiado V. el informe antes de mi vuelta?	Will you have the report copied before my return?

19.12. In the same manner as the present expresses positively a future occurrence, the imperfect expresses the same relation with regard to some point in the past:

Yo iba ayer al campo, pero amanecí indispuesto y tuve que diferir el paseo.	I was going to the country yesterday, but I got up feeling badly and had to postpone the trip.

19.13. The future is frequently used in place of the present tense to convey an idea of conjecture, or of probability in which we do not place implicit confidence:

¿Qué hora es? —Son las tres.	What time is it? —It is three o'clock.
¿Qué hora es? —**Serán** las tres.	What time is it? —It *is probably* three o'clock.
Resolví cinco años ha retirarme de los negocios.	Five years ago I decided to retire from business.
Resolví, **hará** cinco años, retirarme de los negocios.	I decided *some* five years ago to retire from business.

19.14. The future and future perfect are used in this manner to express surprise in interrogative sentences:

¿Será posible que yo, hasta ahora el juguete de la fortuna, haya heredado tan inmenso caudal?	Is it possible that I, until now the sport of fortune, have inherited such an immense property?
Pero ¿qué interés habrá tenido Mendoza en ello?	But what interest can Mendoza have had in it?

19.15. The conditional in like manner expresses a conjecture about a past event:

Su madre **tendría** entonces treinta años.	His mother *was* then *probably* thirty years old.
Casi todos los convidados **estarían** entre los treinta y los cuarenta años.	Nearly all the guests *were probably* between thirty and forty years of age.
Una anciana regordeta entró; presumí que **sería** la madre de Gloria.	A stout old lady entered; I supposed she *was* Gloria's mother.

19.16. The same degree of conjecture or probability is indicated by the future perfect indicative and conditional perfect forms, about an action regarded as completed at the present, or a past time, respectively:

¿Dónde ha cogido ese hombre tantos peces? —Los **habrá comprado** en el mercado.	Where did that man catch so many fish? —He *probably bought* them at the market.
¿Cómo ha sabido V. eso? —Lo **habré leído** en alguno que otro periódico.	How did you learn that? —I *probably read* it in some newspaper or other.
Les **habrá parecido** inverosímil el relato.	The account *must have seemed* improbable to them.

Todavía se descubría en sus facciones que en su mocedad **habría hecho** puntear a sus rejas[1] bastantes guitarras.	One could still see from her features that in her youth she *had caused* many a guitar to be thrummed at her window.
De joven la madre **habría sido** una mujer muy linda.	As a girl the mother *had probably been* a very beautiful woman.

REMARK. A particular application of the conditional and conditional perfect for the expression of conjecture in journalistic use, especially in Argentina, is to mean "It is reported that, etc.":

Moscú **estaría decidido** a aflojar presión en Europa.	*It is reported* that Moscow *has decided* to relax the pressure in Europe.
Estados Unidos **habría expresado** deseos de no suscribir resolución alguna sobre la cuestión colonial.	*It is reported* that the United States *has expressed* the wish not to subscribe to any resolution on the question of colonies.

19.17. The future indicative, in Spanish as well as in English, is used as an imperative in orders which are to be carried out at a future time:

Me harás ahora una naranjada cargadita de azúcar. (Pérez Galdós, **Realidad**, II, 8)	You will now make me an orangeade with plenty of sugar.
Se formará la parada a las diez.	The parade will be formed at ten o'clock.
No matarás; no hurtarás.	Thou shalt not kill; thou shalt not steal.

19.18. The preterite will occasionally be found, especially with **ya**, where the perfect would naturally be expected:

Ya **di** con lo que me conviene.	Now I *have found* what I want.
Se **acabó** todo.	*It's* all *over.*
¡Adiós! Retiraos, no me incomodéis más. Ya **pronuncié** la última palabra que se oirá salir de mi boca.	Adieu! Go, do not molest me more. I *have spoken* the last word that will ever be heard to issue from my mouth.

19.19. After **por poco** and **a poco** meaning *within a little, almost,*

[1] **Rejas** are the iron bars with which all accessible windows are provided, in order to maintain the seclusion of the womanfolk—an inheritance from the Moors.

nearly, etc., the present is used where a past tense would naturally be expected. Sometimes **más** or **no** is added, without changing the meaning:

Por poco le **matan.**	They *came near* killing him.
Por poco pierdo la vida.	I *came near* losing my life.
Por poco se **cae.**	He *came near* falling.
Por poco no nos **arrastra** a los escollos. (Baroja, **Las inquietudes de Shanti Andía,** II, 1)	It *almost drew* us upon the reefs.
Mi papá se puso furioso y **a poco** me pega. (Pérez Galdós, **Miau,** XXXVII)	My father became furious and *almost struck* me.

19.20. The form in **-ra** is met with in literary language in both Spain and Spanish America as an indicative tense, chiefly the pluperfect but occasionally with the value of other past tenses.[1] As an indicative only its use in relative clauses is generally considered proper, though it is sometimes found in principal clauses as a reflection of dialectal usage in the northwestern quarter of Spain or as a mere trick of style on the part of modern Spanish American writers:

No tuvo Magallanes motivo para arrepentirse de la buena acción que **ejecutara.**	Magellan did not have occasion to regret the good action that he *had performed.*
Pero pronto un revés de fortuna debía nublar aquel cielo de esperanza que hasta entonces le **sonriera.**	But soon a reverse of fortune was to cloud the sky of hope which until then *had smiled* upon him.
Apoyada la joven en aquel mismo ajimez, quizá, donde algunos siglos antes la sultana granadina se **apoyara** pensativa, soñando con los recuerdos de algún amor perdido, contemplaba la pintoresca vega que se extendía a sus pies.	The young girl, leaning against the very same window, perhaps, where, a few centuries before, the sultana of Granada *had leaned* in thought, dreaming of the memories of some lost love, was watching the picturesque valley stretched out at her feet.

[1] The explanation of this usage is that the form in **-ra,** which now functions chiefly as an imperfect subjunctive, is derived from the Latin pluperfect indicative. The original pluperfect use has finally become nearly obsolete; in Portuguese, however, it is still quite common.

La pobre Concha **enojárase** conmigo porque oía sonriendo el relato de una celeste aparición. (Valle-Inclán, **Sonata de otoño,** p. 136 of **Opera Omnia** edition)

Poor Concha *had grown angry* with me because I smiled at the account of a celestial apparition.

Había oído hablar de él; pero nunca **cayera** en sus manos hasta entonces. (Palacio Valdés, **La fe,** VIII)

He had heard of it but it *had* never *fallen* into his hands until then.

THE INFINITIVE

19.21. The infinitive represents the abstract action of the verb, without distinction of time, number, person or determining circumstance. It partakes of the nature of both a verb and a noun. It is with its substantive use that we are principally to deal here.

19.22. Like a noun, it may be preceded by an article or governed by a preposition, and may be the subject or object of another verb. When an article precedes it, it is always **el.** But the infinitive lacks noun traits in its rare admission of plural and of making distinction of gender, and in being rarely qualified by an adjective or adjective pronoun:

Hacer desaparecer en todo el país los obstáculos que se opongan al crecimiento del comercio; **derramar** a torrentes la instrucción general, sobre todo la instrucción profesional; **establecer** relaciones cada vez más íntimas entre el agricultor y el manufacturero; **hacer** de fácil acceso, por medio de la construcción de ferrocarriles y de canales navegables, todas estas tierras ricas y vírgenes que no aguardan sino los brazos del hombre para producir riquezas incalculables; y **disminuir** así los gastos de trasporte, que forman el más poderoso obstáculo que se opone al progreso de las sociedades humanas: tal es, señores, la resolución del problema económico que ofrezco a la consideración de los hombres de estado de la América latina.

To cause to disappear throughout the entire country all obstacles which may oppose the growth of trade; *to diffuse* general and, above all, technical instruction; *to establish* ever closer relations between the farmer and the manufacturer; *to open* up, by the construction of railways and canals, all those rich, virgin lands which only await the hand of man in order to produce incalculable riches; and thus *diminish* the cost of transportation, which is the most formidable obstacle that opposes the progress of human society: such is, Gentlemen, the solution of the economic problem which I offer for the consideration of the statesmen of Latin America.

19.23. The infinitive in Spanish is used as a verbal noun corresponding to the English verbal in *-ing*. Hence the infinitive stands after prepositions:

No habla **sin decir** una mentira.	He does not speak *without telling* a lie.
Con enseñar también aprendo.	*By teaching* I learn also.
Además de ser rica, es amable y bonita.	*Besides being* rich, she is pleasant and pretty.
Necesito buscar mis botas **antes de ir** a la ciudad.	I need to look for my boots *before going* to the city.

19.24. It is like a verb in that, even when used as a noun, it may have a subject and it may also retain its original power of governing an object. When the infinitive is replaced by a true noun, this must be connected with the subject or object by means of a preposition:

Informado el general de estar ya a poca distancia el enemigo, mandó reforzar las avanzadas.	The general, being informed of the enemy's being at a short distance, ordered the advance guard to be reinforced.
Informado el general de la **aproximación del** enemigo, ordenó el **refuerzo de** las avanzadas.	The general, being informed of the *nearness of the enemy,* gave orders for the *reinforcement of the* advance guard.
Al comenzar la carrera Andrés, Margarita tenía unos veinte años. (Baroja, **El árbol de la ciencia,** I, 3)	When Andrew began his course, Marguerite was some twenty years old.

Remark. Either subject or object may be a pronoun:

Sentíase avergonzado de vivir él, tan viejo y tan feo, muriendo su mujer, joven y hermosa.	He felt ashamed that he, so old and ugly, was still alive while his young and beautiful wife had died.
El concedérsele a él semejante privilegio sería señal para que todos los demás pidiesen otro tanto.	The granting of such a privilege to him would be a signal for all the rest to ask as much.
El resultado de haber tomado yo tu defensa ha sido nulo.	The effect of my having spoken in your behalf has been nil.
Enrique me ha dado ánimos sin él saberlo. (Valera, **Doña Luz,** X)	Henry has encouraged me without his knowing it.
Murió mi padre en 1870, antes de haber yo cumplido los seis años. (Unamuno, **Recuerdos de niñez y de mocedad,** I, 1)	My father died in 1870 before I reached the age of six.

19.25. Still, in poetic style, the infinitive occasionally loses its verbal character and is used as a pure noun, which may be connected with another noun by means of a preposition:

El trabajar (*or* trabajo) suyo (*noun*). El trabajar ellos (*verbal noun*).	Their labor.
Escuchábamos el pacífico murmurar (*or* murmullo) de las fuentes.	We listened to the bubbling of the springs.
La agria amonestación del señor Vélez fué un doloroso despertar (*or* despertamiento) de sus ilusiones.	The sharp warning of Mr. Velez was a painful awakening from his illusions.

REMARK. Hence the infinitives of certain verbs have come to be accepted as pure nouns:

La conocí por su **andar** gracioso.	I recognized her by her graceful *gait*.
Es mi **parecer** sincero.	It is my candid *opinion*.
Debemos cumplir con nuestro **deber.**	We must do our *duty*.

19.26. Furthermore the infinitive differs from a pure noun in that it may be qualified by adverbs of manner, which become adjectives if the infinitives be replaced by pure nouns:

Para administrar bien los intereses de la sociedad, es preciso conocerlos perfectamente.	In order to manage well the interests of society, it is necessary to be perfectly acquainted with them.
Para la **buena administración** de los intereses sociales, es necesario el conocimiento perfecto de ellos.	A perfect acquaintance with the interests of society is necessary for their *proper management*.
El obedecer implícitamente es el primer deber del soldado.	To obey implicitly is the first duty of a soldier.
La **obediencia implícita** es el primer deber del soldado.	*Implicit obedience* is the first duty of a soldier.

REMARK. Nevertheless, nouns may occasionally be explained by means of adverbs of time or place:

Su regreso mañana sorprendería a su familia.	His return tomorrow would surprise his family.
Mi permanencia allí fué muy agradable.	My stay there was very pleasant.

19.27. When the infinitive is subject or object it may or may not be accompanied by the definite article: omission rather than use is perhaps commoner when the infinitive is subject, use rather than omission is commoner if the infinitive is object of a verb not widely used with a following infinitive or if its substantive value needs to be distinguished:

(El) leer y (el) observar son las fuentes de la sabiduría, (el) escribir aumenta la exactitud, y la fluidez proviene de(l) hablar. — Reading and observing are the sources of knowledge, writing promotes accuracy, and fluency comes from speaking.

¿Ha visto V. qué efecto ha causado a los dos (el) volverse a ver? — Did you see what effect their seeing each other again had on both of them?

No podría perdonarme nunca el haberle ocasionado un solo día de retraso. — I could never forgive myself for having caused you a single day's delay.

Evitaba el dirigirme la palabra. (Pérez Galdós, **El amigo Manso,** XXXI) — He avoided speaking to me.

Le había costado dos días de cama el descalzarse, e ir a la Maruca para no descalzarse era como no ir. (Pereda, **Sotileza,** X) — Going barefoot had cost him two days in bed, and going to la Maruca without going barefoot was like not going.

Verlo, y haber caído sobre él, y tenerlo entre sus garras fué todo cosa de un segundo. (Alarcón, **El sombrero de tres picos,** XX) — To see it, to have fallen on it, and to hold it in one's "hands", was all a matter of a second.

BUT

Procura serenarte; prometimos ser juiciosos. — Try to calm yourself; we promised to be good.

19.28. The infinitive preceded by **al** is to be rendered into English by a finite verb introduced by *when, as,* or by a participle preceded by *on* or *in:*

Al asomar el día, la tempestad se desencadenaba todavía con extraordinario furor. — When day appeared, the storm was still raging with extraordinary violence.

Al pasar por el tambo de Ginés, y al reparar en el desorden en que había quedado el famoso establecimiento, no supo qué pensar. — On passing the Gines Tavern, and noticing the disorder which reigned in that famous establishment, he knew not what to think.

Al abrir la carta, vi con asombro un giro de cien pesos. — On opening the letter, I was astonished to see a draft for 100 pesos.

Al cerrar la noche, cesó la lluvia, y el viento saltó al noroeste. — At nightfall the rain ceased, and the wind swung around to the northwest.

REMARK. When so used, the infinitive applies to any time, past, present or future, according as determined by the immediate context:

Al oír las campanas, salí.	On hearing the bells I went out.
Al oír las campanas, saldré.	On hearing the bells, I shall go out.

19.29. The infinitive preceded by a and nowadays perhaps more often by **de,** may take the place of the if-clause in a conditional sentence—generally of implied negation:

A conocer yo (si hubiese conocido) su carácter, no le hubiera ajustado.	If I had known his character I should not have hired him.
A no estar tan lejos de la población, me convendría la quinta de todos modos.	If it were not so far from the town, the country house would suit me in every respect.
A tomar su genio más elevado vuelo, no dejara de alcanzar algún importante destino.	If he had higher aspirations he would not fail to rise to some important position.
De haberme dicho Aurelio que le acompañara, te hubiera avisado. (Benavente, **La propia estimación,** II, 2)	If Aurelio had told me to go with him, I would have sent you word.
Iba a contarme un cuento que indudablemente sería un sucedido, pues de no ser así, no se lo habría contado a él su padre. (Blasco Ibáñez, **La apuesta del "Esparrelló", in Cuentos valencianos)**	He was going to tell me a story which doubtless must have been a real event, for, if it weren't so, his father wouldn't have told it to him.

REMARK. In parts of South America especially **de no,** possibly representing an original **de no** + infinitive, means *if not, otherwise,* etc.:

¡Haga que güelva m'hija!... ¡O, **de no,** atraquelé una multa a ese bandido! (Payró, **Pago Chico,** IV)	Bring my daughter back! Or *otherwise,* fine that wretch!
De no se hubiese tenido que pasar toda la noche sin pitar. (Lynch, **Palo verde,** III)	*Otherwise* (or *If it hadn't been for that)* he would have had to pass the whole evening without smoking.

19.30. When a noun, the object of a verb of seeing or hearing, is the subject of an infinitive, the latter preferably precedes the noun:

He visto **morir** a mis dos **hermanos** en la terrible lucha civil; he visto **bajar** a la tumba en la flor de su vida a mi querida **madre**; y por último he visto **extinguirse** a mi **padre** en el destierro sin que cerrasen sus ojos las manos de un amigo. — I have seen my two *brothers killed* (*lit.* die) in the terrible civil strife; I have seen my beloved *mother go down* to the grave in the flower of her years; and finally I have seen my *father perish* in exile without a friendly hand to close his eyes.

Vió entonces el jefe **entrar** en su tienda a un **mozo** alto y bien parecido. — The chieftain then saw a tall and good-looking *youth enter* his tent.

Oyéronse a lo lejos **retumbar** los **truenos.** — The *thunder* was heard *rumbling* in the distance.

19.31. Verbs expressing acts of perception may take the infinitive of an impersonal verb as object:

Se veía relampaguear. — It was seen to lighten.

¿No oyen Vds. tronar? — Don't you hear it thunder?

19.32. The infinitive of a transitive verb, accompanied by its subject or object or both, may stand as the object of these verbs of perception; when the infinitive has both pronoun subject and object, its subject becomes, in the usage of some writers, the indirect object of the governing verb:

Vi fusilar **a** los desertores. — I saw *the deserters* shot.

Anoche oí cantar un dúo **a** las señoritas hermanas de V. — Last night I heard *your sisters* sing a duet.

Les *or* **Los** vimos rechazar al enemigo. — We saw *them* repulse the enemy.

Los vimos rechazar por el enemigo. — We saw *them* repulsed by the enemy.

Era delicioso oír**le** pronunciar el francés. (Palacio Valdés, **La hermana San Sulpicio,** X) — It was delightful to hear *her* pronounce French.

REMARK. Both the subject and the object of the infinitive may be represented by pronouns, both of which may precede the main verb:

Los vi fusilar *or* Vi fusilarlos. — I saw them shot.

Se lo oí cantar *or* Las oí cantarlo. — I heard them sing it.

Se los vimos rechazar *or* Los vimos rechazarlos. — We saw them repulse them.

19.33. These verbs expressing the action of the perceptive faculties, may take as objects the infinitive of an intransitive verb together with the latter's subject—which may be a pronoun:

Oigo repicar las campanas.	I hear the bells chime.
Las oigo repicar.	I hear them chime.
Vimos arder el bosque.	We saw the forest burn.
Lo vimos arder.	We saw it burn.

19.34. Such constructions would be expressed by the reflexive substitute for passive as follows:

Se vió arder el bosque.	The forest was seen burning *or* to burn.
Se vió arder.	It was seen burning *or* to burn.
Se oyeron repicar las campanas.	The bells were heard chiming.
Se oyeron repicar.	They were heard chiming.
Se le oyeron cantar dos arias.	He was heard to sing two airs.
Se le oyeron cantar.	He was heard to sing them.
Se les oyó cantar un dúo.	They were heard to sing a duet.
Se les oyó cantar.	They were heard to sing it.

REMARK. Such constructions are not expressed by the true passive (the verb **ser** and a past participle). Hence the following would be inadmissible:

Las flores **fueron vistas marchitarse.**	The flowers were seen to wither.
El reloj **fué oído dar** las doce.	The clock was heard to strike twelve.

19.35. Dejar *to allow;* **hacer** *to cause, to have;* **impedir** *to prevent;* **mandar** *to order;* **permitir** *to permit;* **prohibir** *to forbid* and a few other verbs of similar meaning may be construed similarly to the above verbs which express acts of perception. (For their use with the subjunctive mood see § **23.6**.) When the dependent infinitive has an object only, the English construction is passive; if it has a noun subject, this becomes the indirect object of the main verb, but in this case the subjunctive construction is more common:

Entonces los otros lo dejaron irse. (Payró, **Pago Chico,** II)	Then the others allowed him to leave.
Detúvose Minia: su instinto femenil la impedía continuar. (Pardo Bazán, **La quimera,** I, near end)	Minia stopped: her feminine instinct prevented her from continuing.
Las listas de verbos irregulares eran mi mayor tormento. Nos las hacía aprender de memoria. (Unamuno, **Recuerdos de niñez y de mocedad,** II, 1)	The lists of irregular verbs were my greatest torment. He made us learn them by heart.
No le permito hablar así de España. (Baroja, **El árbol de la ciencia,** II, 1)	I do not permit you to speak in that way of Spain.

Su tío le prohibió volver a poner allí los pies. (Pereda, **Sotileza,** XXI)	His uncle forbade him to set foot there again.
Pero la menguada luz no permitía al anciano descifrar el rostro de su hija. (Pérez Galdós, **Miau,** XXX)	But the weak light did not allow the old man to make out his daughter's face.
Marina, que retozaba como una niña, impedía a su hermana trabajar. (Baroja, **El mayorazgo de Labraz,** I, 3)	Marina, who was as frolicsome as a child, prevented her sister from working.
El general mandó evacuar las plazas.	The general ordered the towns to be evacuated.
El general mandó a los vencidos {evacuar las plazas. {que evacuasen las plazas.	The general ordered the vanquished to evacuate the towns.
Josué mandó {al sol detenerse. {que el sol se detuviese.	Joshua ordered the sun to stand still.

REMARK I. The objective nouns in the above sentences would be reproduced by pronouns, or the sentences expressed by the reflexive substitute for passive, as follows:

El general las mandó evacuar.	The general ordered them to be evacuated.
El general se las mandó evacuar.	The general ordered them to evacuate them.
Josué le mandó detenerse.	Joshua ordered it to stand still.
Josué se lo mandó.	Joshua ordered it [to do so].
Las plazas se mandaron evacuar.	The towns were ordered to be evacuated.
Se mandó detenerse al sol.	The sun was ordered to stand still.

REMARK II. If the second of two pronouns refers to the same person or thing as the first, it is often omitted, especially when reflexive:

Torquemada, echándoselas de bondadoso, la hizo sentar a su lado. (Pérez Galdós, **Torquemada en la hoguera,** VII)	Torquemada, assuming the role of a kind-hearted man, made her sit down at his side.
Déjame sentar, tomar aliento. (Pérez Galdós, **Miau,** XVIII)	Let me sit down, get my breath.
Sosténme, no me dejes hundir. (Gallegos, **Doña Bárbara,** III, 11)	Hold me, don't let me sink.

19.36. We should note the double construction of which this use of the infinitive is susceptible, according as we consider the subject or object of the dependent infinitive:

Speaking of the executioner, we say:

Le *(dat.)* mandaron azotar a los malhechores.	They ordered him to scourge the offenders.
Le hicieron azotar a los malhechores.	They had him scourge the offenders.

Speaking of the criminals, we say:

Los *(acc.)* mandaron azotar por mano del verdugo.	They ordered them to be scourged by the hand of the executioner.
Los hicieron azotar por mano del verdugo.	They had them scourged by the hand of the executioner.

Speaking of a wolf, we say:

El pastor le *(dat.)* dejó devorar al cordero.	The shepherd let him devour the lamb.

Speaking of the lamb, we say:

El pastor lo *(acc.)* dejó devorar por el lobo.	The shepherd let it be devoured by the wolf.

REMARK. The use of the dative form of a personal pronoun object of the main verb, when the infinitive has an object too (cf. § **19.32**), is most usual with **hacer,** but usage varies from author to author with all the verbs listed in §§ **19.35, 19.36:**

Acudió muy de mañana a casa de Juanita la larga y **le** mandó hacer seis hermosas camisas. (Valera, **Juanita la larga,** VIII)	He went very early in the morning to Juanita la larga's house and ordered *her* to make six fine shirts.
El acento acalorado, la expresión sincera con que pronuncié estas palabras **le** hicieron levantar la cabeza. (Palacio Valdés, **La alegría del capitán Ribot,** XIV)	The heated tone, the sincere expression with which I pronounced these words made *her* raise her head.
En vena de esplendidez las convidó con tabletas de mazapán y rosquillas bañadas. Además **les** hizo beber vasos de agua con azucarillos y aguardiente. (Palacio Valdés, **Santa Rogelia,** I, 3)	In a liberal fit he treated them to cakes of marchpane and iced buns. In addition he made *them* drink glasses of water with sugar wafers and brandy.

19.37. In the above construction (§§ **19.35-19.36**) the infinitive often may have a passive translation in English, as it does also in other constructions (e.g., § **19.32**):

Don Enrique y Fernanda se dejaron **convencer.** (Pérez de Ayala, **La caída de los Limones,** IX)	Henry and Fernanda allowed themselves *to be convinced.*

Don Guillermo se dejó **arrebatar** el papel. (Gallegos, **Doña Bárbara,** III, 6) — William allowed the paper *to be snatched* away from him.

Se hizo **temer.** (Pérez de Ayala, **Prometeo,** V) — He made himself *feared.*

Se hizo **atar** una cuerda a la cintura. (Blasco Ibáñez, **La tumba de Alí-Bellús,** in **Cuentos valencianos**) — He caused a rope *to be tied* (or He had a rope tied) around his waist.

Trajo después un saco al hombro, **a medio llenar,** que vació en el arca. (Baroja, **La feria de los discretos,** VII) — Afterwards he carried in on his shoulder a *half-filled* sack, which he emptied into the bin.

Todas las barreras están a **componer** en la carpintería. (Benavente, **La fuerza bruta,** I, 1)[1] — All the hurdles are in the carpenter's shop *to be repaired.*

En suma, la procesión no dejó nada que **desear.** (Valera, **Juanita la larga,** XV, end) — All in all, the procession left nothing *to be desired.*

19.38. The infinitive (like the present participle) naturally refers to the immediate subject of the sentence (cf. § **20.7**); when it has any other subject, that should be repeated, or represented by a pronoun, after the infinitive:

No logró derribar a su adversario por ser **éste** el más fuerte. — He did not succeed in downing his opponent on account of *the latter* being the stronger.

El rey despidió al ministro a causa de haber aceptado **éste** un soborno. — The king dismissed the minister for having accepted (. . . because *the latter* had accepted) a bribe.

19.39. The infinitive has a passive value after the verb **ser** used impersonally (cf. § **23.10**):

No es de **olvidar** (*or* olvidarse). — It is not *to be forgotten.*

Es de **sentir** que no tengamos datos más fidedignos. — It is *to be regretted* that we do not have more reliable data.

19.40. Infinitives connected by the preposition **de** with a preceding adjective, have a passive value in the active form; or they may be made passive by being made reflexive:

[1] The use of **a** in this sense instead of **por,** etc., especially when an act remains to be performed, is considered an imitation of French usage.

Bueno de comer—de comerse.	Good to eat.
Digno de notar—notarse.	Worthy of note.
Fácil de hacer—hacerse.	Easy to do.

19.41. The infinitive may, as in English, follow an interrogative used after a verb expressing an act of the perception or understanding:

No sabía qué pensar—cuándo callar —cómo apagar el gas—a quién acudir—por dónde dirigirse.	He did not know what to think—when to keep silent—how to put out the gas—whom to apply to—which way to go.

19.42. It is frequently convenient to suppose an ellipsis of some verb such as **poder** or **deber** before an infinitive preceded by a relative:

No tengo vestido que (pueda) ponerme.	I have no clothes to put on.
No conocíamos persona alguna de quien (pudiésemos) valernos.	We did not know anyone that we could make use of.
Hay mucho que (se debe) hacer.	There is a great deal to do.

19.43. If there is no expressed antecedent, the seeming relative (some scholars consider the interrogative use to be the original one; if so, there was no antecedent) is correctly written with an accent mark, though it is not always so written and almost never in certain phrases. The construction is essentially that of § **19.41**:

No tengo (nada) qué ponerme.	I have nothing to put on.
No veíamos (persona) de quién fiarnos.	We saw no one that we could trust.
Buscábamos (lugar) dónde guarecernos de la lluvia.	We were looking for a place to shelter us from the rain.
Al fin hallaron (camino) por dónde escapar.	They finally found a way to escape.
No hay (motivo) por qué diferir la partida.	There is no reason for postponing the departure.
Vamos, hija, come, que a Dios gracias no nos falta de qué. (Unamuno, **El espejo de la muerte, historia muy vulgar)**	Come, child, eat, for, thank God, we do not lack something (to eat).
Le haré comprender que ya basta de ponernos en ridículo y de dar que hablar a la gente. (Benavente, **Lo cursi,** III, 3)	I will make her understand that there has been enough of making us ridiculous and causing people talk.

REMARK. These phrases must not be confused with those in which the verb **haber** or **tener** is followed by an infinitive preceded by **que** (§ **21.70**):

No hay que avergonzarse.	You must not feel ashamed.
Tengo que escribir varias cartas.	I have to write several letters.

19.44. So we see that **haber que** or **tener que,** followed by an infinitive, is at times an apparently elliptical phrase and at others it is not. The meaning of **haber que** and **tener que,** followed by an infinitive, varies according as the **que** is stressed in speaking or bears an accent mark in writing:

Hay que escribir.	It is necessary to write.
Hay **qué** escribir.	There is *something* to write.
Tengo que comer.	I have got to eat.
Tengo **qué** comer.	I have *something* to eat.

REMARK. This twofold meaning is only possible when the **que** can be the object of the infinitive. The use of the accent mark is not always adhered to.

19.45. The infinitive may be used as an imperative in sudden exclamations or short directions, as in notices to the public, or as an interrogative exclamation of surprise. Lacking person and number, it is less peremptory than an imperative or a subjunctive:

¡Callar! ¡No correr![1]	Hush! Don't run!
Adiós, hija, conservarse. (Pérez Galdós, **Fortunata y Jacinta,** III, 6, 11)	Good-bye, child. Take care of yourself.
No empujar, no atropellarse, señores —dijo Manuela riendo. (Pérez Galdós, **Zaragoza,** XXI)	"Don't push, don't crowd, gentlemen," said Manuela, laughing.
Dirigirse dentro.	Apply within.
¿Casarme yo?	I get married?
¿Abandonarle? ¡Nunca!	Abandon him? Never!

19.46. The perfect infinitive is used with the effect of a reproof:

¡Cómo erré la vocación! — Pues haberlo pensado antes. (Pérez Galdós, **Tormento,** XVIII)	How I mistook my calling! — Well, you might have thought it over beforehand.
No lo sé, que la Blanca no me lo dijo — Habérselo preguntado, animal. (Grau, **Don Juan de Carillana,** I, 10)	I don't know, for la Blanca didn't tell me — You could have asked her, idiot.

[1] In the expression of a command the infinitive is at times preceded by **a,** there being possibly an ellipse of some form of **ir: ¡A callar!** (Pérez Galdós, **Fortunata y Jacinta,** II, 6, 6) *Hush!*

19.47. An infinitive especially (but also any noun or adjective), with or without **como** or **por,** may be used to anticipate a verbal (or other) idea:

Yo le acompaño algunas veces... ¡Eso sí, tirar, nunca tiro! (Benavente, **Al natural,** II, 10)	I go with him sometimes... One thing is sure: as far as shooting goes, I never shoot.
Digo, como saberlo, lo sabe... (Pérez Galdós, **Torquemada en la hoguera,** V)	I say, as for knowing it, he knows it.
No hubo influencia para declarar inútil a Pinín, que, por ser, era como un roble. (Alas, **¡Adiós, "Cordera"!**)	There was no influence to declare Pinín ineligible, who, as far as that went, was as strong as an oak.
Y como pesado ¡vaya si era pesado! (Unamuno, **Recuerdos de niñez y de mocedad,** I, 12)	And as foı being a bore, he certainly was!

PAST PARTICIPLE

19.48. The past participle represents the action of the verb as completed. It has the properties either of an adjective or a verb, but does not combine the two. In its leading use in forming compound tenses in connection with the auxiliary verb **haber,** it is invariable in form; it then has all the effect of a verb and has no adjective quality:

El chaparrón que ha caído ha matado el polvo.	The shower that has fallen has laid the dust.
He leído con gran interés todos los artículos que él ha dado a luz respecto de la cuestión de industrias y salarios.	I have read with much interest all the articles that he has published on the question of labor and wages.

19.49. In all other applications it is an adjective, agreeing in number and gender with whatever noun it applies to, and has no verbal power. Although an adjective, and thus expressing a quality, that quality is the result of the action of a verb:

Libros **impresos;** una taza **rota.**	*Printed* books; a *broken* cup.
Una casa nuevamente **pintada.**	A newly *painted* house.
En 1793 dos funcionarios públicos de un nombre muy **conocido** en León, **acusados** de federalismo, fueron **entregados** al furor de una multitud **empeñada** en su pérdida.	In 1793 two public functionaries of well-*known* reputation in Leon, who were *accused* of federalism, were *turned over* to the fury of a mob bent upon their destruction.

La escalera que de la sala baja subía al primer piso, desembocaba en un corredor **compuesto** de tablones mal **unidos** y **alumbrado** por un farolillo de aceite **colgado** del techo.

The stair which led from the lower hall to the second floor opened upon a passage-way *formed* of boards badly *joined* and *lighted* by a little oil-lamp *suspended* from the ceiling.

19.50. In detached clauses the past participle is used without being connected with a verb. Such participles may relate to the subject of the sentence, or may be wholly unconnected with it:

1. The participle relates to the subject of the sentence:

Puesta a votación la propuesta del señor B., resultó adoptada por unanimidad.

The proposition of Mr. B. having been put to a vote, it was unanimously adopted.

Su mujer, acostumbrada al regalo, no pudo sufrir largo tiempo tantas privaciones.

His wife, having been accustomed to every comfort, could not long suffer so many privations.

2. When the participle does not relate to the subject of the sentence, the clause in which it stands is called an *absolute clause,*[1] and corresponds to the frequent Latin construction known as the "ablative absolute":

Agotada la orden del día, se levantó la sesión.

The order of the day being exhausted, the meeting was adjourned.

Determinada la ruta que habían de seguir, partieron los expedicionarios al rayar el alba.

The route which they were to follow having been decided upon, the members of the expedition set out at daybreak.

Idas ellas, el lugar ya no tenía atractivos para mí.

After they had gone, the place no longer had any attractions for me.

REMARK. Adjectives may be used in absolute clauses in the same way as participles:

El 8 de agosto del mismo año, libre ya la capital de franceses, volvió a publicarse el Diario.

On the 8th of August of the same year [1808], the capital being now free of the French, the publication of the Daily was resumed.

19.51. These absolute clauses are susceptible of three renderings: when a participle of a transitive verb is used, *having been* (or *being)*

[1] It will be seen that in an absolute clause, the participle usually precedes its subject, especially when the absolute clause is at the beginning of the sentence or clause (cf. § **20.6**).

is to be supplied in the English translation; with a participle of an intransitive verb, *having;* with an adjective, *being:*

Zanjado este asunto.	This affair *having been* settled.
Visto esto por los soldados, no pensaron ya sino en ponerse en cobro.	This *being seen* by the soldiers, they no longer thought of anything but getting under cover.
Llegada la trama a noticias de D. Alvaro.	The plot *having* reached the ears of Don Alvaro.
Impotente el rey para apaciguar la tempestad que amenazaba al trono.	The king *being* powerless to calm the tempest that threatened the throne.

REMARK. The subject of an absolute clause may be an entire phrase introduced by **que:**

El rey, visto que no podía tomar por fuerza la villa, mandóla escalar una noche con gran silencio.	It being evident that he could not take the city by assault, the king one night ordered an escalade to be made with great silence.

19.52. The subject of an absolute clause is occasionally omitted, to avoid repetition, when it has been previously expressed at a short distance:

Se decidió amueblar el palacio, y amueblado, se trasladaron a él los tribunales.	It was decided to furnish the palace, and when it was furnished, the courts were removed thither.
Mandó que se dividiese el botín en veinte partes iguales, y hecho, que se repartiese entre la tripulación.	He ordered the booty to be divided into twenty equal parts, and this done, that it be distributed among the crew.

19.53. A past participle in an absolute clause does not receive enclitic personal pronouns (although they would be applicable to the present participle were *it* expressed) (cf. § **4.15**). When there is no present participle, the prepositional form of the pronouns must be employed:

Comunicado a ellos *(not* comunicádoles) el suceso, partimos.	Having informed them of the occurrence, we departed.
Admitidos los diputados y asignados a ellos *(not* asignádosles) los asientos que debían ocupar, invocó el obispo la bendición divina sobre la asamblea.	The deputies having been admitted, and the seats which they were to occupy assigned to them, the bishop invoked the divine blessing upon the assembly.

19.54. The past participle of an absolute clause may be followed by **que** and an auxiliary (**haber, tener, ser** or **estar**). When **haber** is thus employed, the participle is invariable:

Leído que hubo la carta, se retiraron los circunstantes.	When he had read the letter, the bystanders withdrew.
Compuesto que hubo los versos, los ofreció el poeta a la duquesa.	When he had composed the verses, the poet offered them to the duchess.
Concluida que tuvieron la obra.	When they had finished the work.
Examinados que tuviese los autos.	When he should have examined the decrees.
Prestados que fueron los oportunos juramentos.	When the proper oaths were taken.
Leído que fué el diario de los procedimientos del día anterior.	When the journal of the proceedings of the previous day had been read.
Encarcelados que estén los reos.	When the criminals have been jailed.
Asentados que estuvieron por fin los visigodos en la península.	When the Visigoths were finally established in the peninsula.

19.55. These detached participial clauses may be preceded by **antes de, después de,** and occasionally **luego de,** to express relation of time:

Antes de dada la seña.	Before the signal was given.
Luego de terminada la ceremonia.	As soon as the ceremony was over.
Después de muerto yo.	After I am dead.
Después de tantas veces contada, la historia llegó a ser muy fastidiosa.	After being told so many times, the story became very tiresome.
Después de discutido el punto, se puso a votación, y resultó desechada la enmienda por un voto de quince contra doce.	After this point had been discussed, it was put to a vote, and the amendment was defeated by a vote of fifteen to twelve.
Recogióse, pues, gran cantidad de estas algas, y después de secas fueron quemadas en hoyos al aire libre.	A large quantity of these algae were collected, and after they were dried, they were burned in pits in the open air.

19.56. The following phrases in Spanish and English respectively are equivalents:

Es asunto para tratado a solas entre los dos. (Pereda, **Sotileza,** XVIII)	It is a matter to be discussed privately between us two.
No es para negado.	It is not to be denied.
No es para tolerado.	It is not to be tolerated.

No es para imitado.	It is inimitable.
No es para creído.	It is incredible.

These phrases are applicable to things that *ought not* as well as to things that *cannot* be done:

Oferta tan generosa no es para rechazada.	So generous an offer is not to be rejected.
Los principios pequeños no son para despreciados.	Small beginnings are not to be despised.
La cuestión que aquí se presenta no es para decidida sin un estudio cuidadoso.	The question here presented is not to be decided without careful consideration.
Este punto no es para descuidado.	This point is not to be overlooked.

REMARK. This usage is applicable only to the past participles of transitive verbs which do not require a preposition to connect them with their objects.

XX
The Present Participle

20.1. The true present participle ending in **ante, ente** or **iente,** derived from the Latin participle in *an[t]s, antis, en[t]s, entis,* is no longer in use in Spanish as a part of the verb. Some of these obsolete participles are now employed as adjectives, others only as nouns, while a few do duty as prepositions, adverbs or conjunctions; but the greater number have disappeared from the language:

causar to cause	**causante** causative
distar to be distant	**distante** distant
perseverar to persevere	**perseverante** persevering
diferir to differ	**diferente** different
depender to depend	**dependiente** dependent
estudiar to study	**el estudiante** the student
residir to reside	**el residente** the resident
habitar to inhabit	**el habitante** the inhabitant

escribir to write	**el escribiente** the amanuensis
romper to break	**los rompientes** the breakers
amar to love	**el amante** the lover
presidir to preside	**el presidente** the president
bastar to suffice	**bastante** sufficient, enough
durar to last	**durante** during
obstar to stand in the way	**no obstante que** notwithstanding that

20.2. The place of the true present participle, as a part of the verb, has been taken by a form adopted almost unchanged from the Latin. In regular verbs of the first conjugation this is formed by adding **ando** to the stem; in verbs of the second and third conjugations, by the addition of **iendo:**

comprar: **comprando**	to buy: *buying*
vender: **vendiendo**	to sell: *selling*
vivir: **viviendo**	to live: *living*

This is also the case in most of the irregular verbs:

estar: **estando**	querer: **queriendo**	dar: **dando**
haber: **habiendo**	tener: **teniendo**	ver: **viendo**
ser: **siendo**	hacer: **haciendo**	salir: **saliendo**

20.3. In the 2nd and 3rd conjugations, the **i** of the termination **iendo** is changed to **y** in the following cases: (1) when the stem of the verb ends in a vowel, because unstressed **i** does not occur between vowels; (2) the present participle of **ir** *to go* is **yendo,** because initial **i** followed by **e** is changed to **y:**

caer: **cayendo**	construir: **construyendo**	ir: **yendo**

20.4. There is a *perfect* of the present participle made up of a past participle governed by the present participle of **haber:**

habiendo comprado having bought	**habiendo vivido** having lived
habiendo vendido having sold	**habiendo visto** having seen

20.5. The present participle is invariable in form and has the same regimen as the verb from which it is derived. It is always subordinate to some other verb and relates to either past, present, or future, according to the connection in which it is employed. Its leading use is in parenthetic, explanatory clauses:

Su discusión será además trabajo para muchos meses, porque, **siendo** tan complicada la materia y **teniendo** tan estrechas relaciones con la legislación interior de cada país, no será posible conciliar de momento sus diversos intereses.	Its discussion, furthermore, will be a work of many months, because, the subject *being* so complex and *having* such close relations with the internal legislation of each country, it will not be possible to adjust off-hand their several interests.
Pasando ayer por la plaza, encontré a doña Carmen.	*Going* through the square yesterday, I met Doña Carmen.
Abriendo los ojos, vió a su esposa sentada cerca de la cabecera.	*Opening* his eyes, he saw his wife seated near the head of the bed.

20.6. In descriptions and narrations the present participle is regularly placed at the beginning of the sentence or clause, even when the subject is a noun:

Habiendo el general ganado la victoria, expidió una orden agradeciendo a las tropas.	The general, having gained the victory, issued an order thanking the troops.
Llegando tarde a la fonda los demás, no hallaron habitación vacía.	The rest arriving late at the hotel, did not find a room empty.
Viajando un derviś por la Tartaria, llegó a la capital del reino y por equivocación tomó el palacio del rey por una posada pública.	A dervish, travelling through Tartary, arrived at the capital of the kingdom and by mistake took the king's palace for a public tavern.
No podía conciliar el sueño, no siendo extraña a este fenómeno la dureza del banco en que reposaba. (Pérez Galdós, **Miau,** XI)	He couldn't go to sleep, the hardness of the bench on which he was resting having something to do with this phenomenon, too.

20.7. In clauses where it would otherwise be difficult to determine which of several nouns is the subject of the present participle, the appropriate personal pronoun is inserted immediately after the present participle:

La encontré **volviendo yo** de la caza.	I met her as I was returning from hunting.
Temí que mi hermano, no **estando yo** presente, cometiera algún disparate.	I feared that my brother, I not being present, would commit some blunder.
Toda su felicidad estaba circunscrita en aquel niño, y **faltándoles él,** parecía la casa solitaria.	All their happiness was centered in that child, and when he was absent from them the house seemed desolate.

20.8. In all the above examples the present participle is explanatory of the subject of the sentence; it may equally apply to the object:

Veo a los niños jugando en la plaza.	I see the children playing in the square.
Oyeron el reloj de la Puerta del Sol dando las diez. (Pérez Galdós, **Fortunata y Jacinta,** III, 7, 2)	They heard the clock in the Puerta del Sol striking ten.
Hallé a mi hermano escribiendo una carta a su esposa.	I found my brother writing a letter to his wife.
Aquí tengo su carta anunciando su intención de partir.	I have his letter here announcing his intention to leave.

20.9. The present participle serves also to describe the action of a verb which it accompanies:

El muchacho viene corriendo.	The boy comes running.
Van cantando por las calles.	They go singing through the streets.
Ella entró llorando.	She came in weeping.
Continúa hablando.	He continues speaking.
El general pasó la noche estudiando los mapas de la comarca y marcando en ellos las posiciones que consideraba ventajosas.	The general spent the night studying the maps of the territory and marking on them the positions which he considered advantageous.

20.10. The present participle is used with **estar** *to be* to express the action of the verb as continuing at the time in question. This usage is parallel with the English mode of expression:

Ella está tocando el piano.	She is playing the piano.
¿De qué están Vds. hablando?	Of what are you talking?
¿Qué ha estado V. haciendo hoy?	What have you been doing today?
Estaba yo escribiendo cuando entró.	I was writing when he entered.
¿Qué estaban haciendo los muchachos en el patio?	What were the boys doing in the court yard?
Mañana a estas horas estaremos viajando.	This time tomorrow we will be travelling.
Toda la tarde estuvieron entrando visitas. (Pérez Galdós, **Fortunata y Jacinta,** III, 6, 7)	All afternoon visitors continued to come in.

REMARK. The verb **ser** *to be* is never employed with the present participle, since the latter denotes only a temporary duration.

20.11. The present participles of **estar, ir, venir, andar** and, to a less extent, other verbs of motion, are not ordinarily used with any tense of **estar** to express continuance; the verb is more often placed in the tense proper to the time in question, or the idea is expressed by some different construction. The use of the present participle of **ser,** though not uncommon, is condemned by some authorities:

Mis tres hermanas vienen esta tarde para tocar el piano.	My three sisters are coming this evening to play the piano.
Iba allí cuando V. me vió.	I was going there when you saw me.
El actual gobierno está siendo un instrumento del de Suavia. (Benavente, **La escuela de las princesas,** II, 7)	The present government is being the instrument of that of Suavia.

Remark. Almost any verb may be and occasionally is used with the present participle, especially in a figurative sense:

Ya estamos andando. (Pereda, **La puchera,** XXVI)	We are already on our way.
Págame lo mío que ya me estoy yendo. (Gallegos, **Canaima,** XXVII: **Contaban los caucheros**)	Pay me what is due me, for I am already leaving.
Por eso he estado yendo en casa de Juanita todas las noches. (Valera, **Juanita la larga,** XVIII)	For that reason I have been going to Juanita's house every night.

20.12. With the verbs **ir** and **andar,** both meaning *to go,* the present participle expresses continuance, indicating that the action of the present participle goes on increasing. More specifically, **ir** indicates the beginning of the action; **andar** suggests the idea of "here and there," often implying a degree of disparagement on the part of the speaker:

Voy comprendiendo su significado.	I am getting to understand its meaning.
El aspecto del mar iba siendo peor. (Baroja, **Las inquietudes de Shanti Andía,** V, 5)	The appearance of the sea was growing worse.
¡Oh, excelente amiga!, ya vas estando un poco carcamal. (Pérez de Ayala, **Prometeo,** I)	Oh excellent friend, you are beginning to be a bit decrepit!
En la parte exterior, y conforme avanzaba la noche, la tempestad iba tomando proporciones formidables.	Outside, the storm, as the night advanced, was assuming formidable proportions.
Anda haciendo disparates.	He goes about making blunders.

Si la llamaban de pronto, mientras estaba ensimismada, se ruborizaba y se confundía. –No sé lo que anda maquinando cuando está así. (Baroja, **El árbol de la ciencia,** II, 4)

If people called her when she was absorbed, she blushed and became embarrassed. –I don't know what she is scheming when she is like that.

With **venir** the present participle emphasizes that an act began in the past and continued toward the present:

Se entrega a la tarea de atar los botines a su patrón, servicio que viene desempeñando a conciencia desde hace largos años. (Lynch, **Los caranchos de la Florida,** I)

He devotes himself to the task of tieing his employer's shoe laces, a service that he has been conscientiously performing for long years.

Su situación viene siendo muy triste hace tiempo. (Pérez Galdós, **Miau,** XII)

His situation has been very unfortunate for some time.

Desistieron por consejo de su tío y gracias a una cesión que yo les hice de unas fincas que ellos venían disfrutando por condescendencia de mi marido. (Benavente, **Pepa Doncel,** I, 6)

They stopped through the advice of their uncle and thanks to my yielding to them some pieces of property that they had been having the returns from through my husband's kindness.

20.13. The present participles of **estar, ir,** etc., may be used as auxiliaries to other present participles:

Yendo haraganeando de esta manera, atravesó un puente y llegó a una plaza espaciosa.

Going strolling along in this way, he crossed a bridge and came to a spacious square.

Estando escribiendo el coronel, no quiso molestarle su ayudante.

As the colonel was writing, his adjutant did not wish to disturb him.

20.14. When the present participle governs one or more personal pronouns of simple objective form, they are appended to it so as to form one word:

Encontrándola; viéndose.

Meeting her; seeing himself.

Dándomelo; prestándonoslos.

Giving me it; lending us them.

Encontrándose tan inesperadamente privados de luz,...

Finding themselves so suddenly deprived of light,...

El único caballo que nos quedó, faltándole un ojo, no servía.

The only horse we had left was of no use, as he lacked an eye.

20.15. But if the present participle be governed by **estar, ir, andar,** or **venir** (expressing continuance, as shown above), the pronouns may precede the verb or be joined to the present participle, the former being the usual arrangement:

Le estoy escribiendo ahora. Estoy escribiéndole ahora.	I am writing to him now.
Me estaba afeitando cuando llamó a la puerta. Estaba afeitándome cuando llamó a la puerta.	I was shaving myself when he knocked at the door.
Le voy comprendiendo a V.	I am getting to understand you.
Ella se va americanizando.	She is becoming Americanized.

REMARK. The objective pronouns, as we have seen, are similarly appended to the infinitive. Cf. §§ 3.57; 4.12; 19.32, REMARK.

20.16. If the personal pronoun is governed by the perfect participle (formed of **habiendo** and the past participle of another verb), it is attached to **habiendo,** and does not follow the past participle:

El marinero sacó de su bolsillo una pipa corta y ennegrecida, y **habiéndola llenado** de tabaco ordinario, la encendió con una brasa.	The sailor drew from his pocket a short blackened pipe, and *having filled it* with coarse tobacco, lit it with a coal.
El juez limpió sus espejuelos, y **habiéndoselos puesto,** escudriñó al testigo.	The judge wiped his glasses, and *having put them on,* scrutinized the witness.

20.17. The present participle is used to express the cause, manner or means of an action, without being introduced by any connecting word. In English some such word as *by, as, since, when* or *while* would be needed, or the present participle would be replaced by some other tense:

El comercio no debemos buscarlo **combatiendo** los artículos de producción barata sino **abaratando** los de producción cara, para que ellos aumenten el consumo **poniéndose** al alcance del mayor número y consultando así el interés de la colectividad.	We must not seek trade *by* fighting against articles of cheap production, but *by* cheapening those of dear production, so as to increase their consumption *by* placing them within the reach of the greater number and consulting in this way the interests of the people at large.
Los hombres se hacen infelices **deseando** lo que no necesitan.	Men make themselves unhappy *by* desiring what they do not need.
No **teniendo** dinero, empeñó su reloj.	As he *had* no money he pawned his watch.

Siendo tan tarde, no iré.	Since it *is* so late I shall not go.
Siendo capitán el almirante Blake, fué mandado con una pequeña escuadra contra las posesiones españolas.	While Admiral Blake *was* a captain, he was sent with a small squadron against the Spanish possessions.

REMARK. The greater number of such sentences might also be rendered as in English:

Como no tenía dinero...	As he had no money...
Puesto que es tan tarde...	Since it is so late...
Mientras que era capitán...	While he was captain...

20.18. The present participle is never preceded by any preposition except (and then not very frequently) by **en**, which construction is used principally when something happens after the completion of the action expressed by the present participle; an expression of like value is formed in English by *on* before a present participle. The construction may also express condition:

En acabando mi cigarro, le acompañaré a V.	When I have finished (on finishing) my cigar, I will go with you.
En regresando del teatro, fuí a mi habitación.	On returning from the theater I went to my room.
De filosofía habla, en queriendo, y no habla mal, toda persona de imaginación y viveza. (Valera, **El comendador Mendoza,** XXX)	If (or when) he wants to, any imaginative and keen person can talk about philosophy and he won't talk badly.

BUT

Regresando del teatro perdí mi cartera.	In returning from the theater I lost my wallet.

20.19. In all other cases it is the infinitive which in Spanish is governed by a preposition, while in English it is uniformly the present participle:

No soy capaz **de distinguirlos** entre sí.	I am incapable *of distinguishing* between them.
Está adicto **a beber.**	He is addicted *to drinking.*
No tardará **en venir.**	He will not delay *in coming.*
La dificultad consiste **en hallarle** en casa.	The difficulty consists *in finding* him at home.
Después de comer fuma su cigarro de sobremesa.	*After eating* he smokes his after-dinner cigar.
Además **de** no **pagarme,** me insulta.	*Besides* not *paying* me he insults me.

20.20. After verbs of *seeing* and *hearing*, the infinitive is more usual than the present participle[1] (cf. § **20.8**):

La vimos bailar.	We saw her dance.
Los veo venir.	I see them coming.
La oímos tocar el piano.	We heard her playing the piano.

20.21. The Spanish present participle cannot be used as a verbal noun, as is the English present participle; in Spanish it is the infinitive which is so employed. When not governed by a preposition, the verbal noun often takes the definite article (cf. § **19.27**):

El perfecto **tocar** de este músico me encanta.	*The* perfect *playing* of this musician delights me.
(El) leer con luz insuficiente perjudica los ojos.	*Reading* with insufficient light injures the eyes.
No es cosa fácil **(el) escribir** un buen poema.	*Writing* a good poem is no easy thing.
Esta señorita aborrece **el fumar.**	This young lady abhors *smoking.*

20.22. Nor can the present participle be used as an adjective to qualify a noun; the meaning must be expressed by a participial adjective in **ante, ente, iente** (cf. § **20.1**) or some adjective of equal value. As it is sometimes difficult to determine whether the meaning requires the present participle or not, more copious examples are here given to aid the student in distinguishing between it and a participial adjective:

Un libro interesante.	An interesting book.
Una cesta colgante.	A hanging basket.
Agua **corriente.**	*Running* water.
Esta inmensa cantidad de agua **corriendo** al mar, se pierde para ser levantada después por la acción de los rayos solares.	This immense body of water *running* to the sea, loses itself to be afterwards drawn up by the action of the solar rays.
Un blanco **flotante.**	A *floating* target.
Los marineros vieron un objeto informe **flotando** en el agua.	The sailors saw a shapeless object *floating* in the water.
La colonia **creciente.**	The *growing* colony.
El niño, **creciendo** diariamente, llegará a ser hombre.	The child, *growing* daily, will get to be a man.

[1] An alternative construction is the use of a clause with **que: Yo les he visto que tomaban por este camino.** (Baroja, **La dama errante,** XX) *I saw you start up this road.* **Acabo de verla que marchaba orilla de la presa.** (Palacio Valdés, **Sinfonía pastoral,** Scherzo, V) *I just saw her walking along beside the mill race.*

El gladiador **moribundo.**	The *dying* gladiator.
Le encontramos **muriendo** de hambre.	We found him *dying* of hunger.
Un Fauno **danzante.**	A *dancing* Faun.
El fresco representaba al dios Pan con un grupo de Sátiros y Faunos **danzando** al son de la flauta.	The fresco represented the god Pan with a group of Satyrs and Fauns *dancing* to the sound of the flute.

20.23. Still, the present participle of **arder** *to burn* and of **hervir** *to boil* and occasionally of some other verbs is by exception used after a noun with the value of an adjective:

Moisés ante la zarza **ardiendo.** (Alas, **Cambio de luz,** in **El Señor; y lo demás son cuentos**)	Moses before the *burning* bush.
Ordenó que la señora María se encargase de preparar la bizma de pez **hirviendo.** (Pardo Bazán, **La Madre Naturaleza,** II)	He ordered that Mary prepare the poultice of *boiling pitch.*
Y ahora, por si alguien duda todavía de que yo sea la cordura andando, voy a dar a todos la última prueba de ello. (Pérez Galdós, **Fortunata y Jacinta,** IV, 5, 3)	And now, in case anyone doubts that I am discretion personified, I am going to give everybody the last proof of it.

20.24. Some traces of the Latin future passive participle or gerundive in *-ndus* are still to be found in Spanish, but they are now used as substantives or adjectives only:

los ordenandos	the candidates for ordination
el graduando	the person about to graduate
palabras a la clase graduanda	words to the graduating class
un anciano venerando	a venerable old man
el dividendo	that which is to be divided, dividend
un curso vitando	a course to be avoided
las examinandas	the young ladies to be examined
el educando	the pupil, the student
el poeta laureando	the poet about to be crowned
	BUT
el poeta laureado	the poet laureate (who has been crowned)

REMARK. Of the Latin future active participle in *-rus* there is scarcely a trace, except the adjectives **futuro** *future;* **venturo** *coming, future;* **vacaturo** *about to cease.*

XXI
Classes of Verbs

21.1. Verbs have, for convenience of treatment, been divided into several classes, with reference to the manner in which their action is represented. These classes are:

1. Transitive or Active
2. Reflexive and Reciprocal
3. Intransitive or Neuter
4. Impersonal
5. Inceptive, Inchoative or Continuative
6. Periphrastic Verbal Expressions

These classes will now be taken up in order and their definitions and applications considered.

TRANSITIVE VERBS

21.2. A transitive verb is one that has a subject and an object—an actor who (or which) acts directly upon some person or thing. This object must be expressed, or the verb ceases to be transitive. Most verbs, either in English or Spanish, belong to this class; and the student is already familiar with their characteristics:

El tábano pica al caballo.	The horsefly bites the horse.
No quiero plegar el papel.	I do not want to fold the paper.
Apagaron su sed con agua.	They quenched their thirst with water.

REFLEXIVE VERBS

21.3. A transitive verb is called *reflexive* when its action returns upon the actor—when its subject and object are identical. Whatever the form of the subject and whether expressed or not, the object is always a pronoun, always expressed, and always agrees in person with the subject and verb. It also agrees with them in number, with this proviso, that the reflexive pronoun of the third person, **se,** is without distinction of number.

21.4. The usual position of the pronominal object is immediately before the verb, and before the auxiliary in compound tenses—in short, immediately before the finite verb. The following paradigm will serve for all tenses and combinations:

yo	me disfrazo	yo	me he disfrazado
tú	te disfrazas	tú	te has disfrazado
él / ella / usted	se disfraza	él / ella / usted	se ha disfrazado
nosotros / nosotras	nos disfrazamos	nosotros / nosotras	nos hemos disfrazado
vosotros / vosotras	os disfrazáis	vosotros / vosotras	os habéis disfrazado
ellos / ellas / ustedes	se disfrazan	ellos / ellas / ustedes	se han disfrazado

21.5. When the subject is a pronoun, it is usually omitted unless required for emphasis or contrast. When expressed, it either precedes or follows the entire verbal and pronominal phrase. In interrogations it is more frequently placed last:

Ella se presenta. Se presenta ella.	She presents herself.
Nosotros no nos degradaremos. No nos degradaremos nosotros.	We will not degrade ourselves.
Aunque ellos se habían disfrazado. Aunque se habían disfrazado ellos.	Although they had disguised themselves.
¿Se ha cortado V.?	Have you cut yourself?

21.6. The reflexive object is regularly attached to the infinitive or the present participle, forming one word with it; if the subject pronoun is then expressed, it is usually placed after these forms:

Disfrazándome pasaré desapercibido.	By disguising myself I shall pass unobserved.
Quiere disfrazarse.	He wishes to disguise himself.

Habiéndose disfrazado él.	He having disguised himself.
Habiéndome disfrazado yo.	I having disguised myself.
No habiéndose disfrazado ellas.	They not having disguised themselves.
No disfrazarme yo.	For me not to disguise myself.
Haberse disfrazado él.	For him to have disguised himself.
No haberse disfrazado usted.	For you not to have disguised yourself.
Creyéndose fuera del alcance de sus tiros, se expuso temerariamente por encima del parapeto.	Believing himself out of reach of their shots, he exposed himself rashly above the parapet.

21.7. The reflexive object is in like manner appended to the imperative, and to the subjunctive used imperatively, provided the verb be not negatived. In doing this two elisions take place: 1. the second person plural of the imperative loses the final **d**; 2. the first person plural of the subjunctive loses the final **s**, as do the present indicative, preterite, and even other tenses, in the rare event that **nos** follows them:

consolaos	*for* consola*d*os	**consolémonos**	*for* consolémo*s*nos
defendeos	" defende*d*os	**defendámonos**	" defendámo*s*nos
cubríos	" cubri*d*os	**cubrámonos**	" cubrámo*s*nos

Cerré la puerta de mi gabinete, sentámonos los dos con la mesita entre ambos, y comencé a hablarle. (Pereda, **Peñas arriba**, XXXI)	I closed my sitting room door. We both sat down with the little table between us, and I began to speak to him.

Exception. The imperative of **irse (ir-se)** retains the **d: idos** *go away.*

21.8. In literary or elevated style, the reflexive object may be appended to the verb in the simple tenses, and to the auxiliary in compound tenses, provided the verb stands at the beginning of the phrase. If the subject be then expressed, it follows the entire verbal expression:[1]

Entregóse en manos de nuestros piquetes.	He gave himself into the hands of our pickets.
Heme equivocado yo sin duda.	I have doubtless made a mistake.
Viéronse forzados a pernoctar allí.	They saw themselves forced to pass the night there.
Habíanse provisto los rebeldes de varios cañones de campaña.	The rebels had provided themselves with several field-pieces.

[1] The conditions under which this location is applicable are set forth at length in Chapter IV.

21.9. The location, with regard to the verb, of two or more pronominal objects of the same verb is the same as for a single pronoun, they being placed in immediate sequence, and if one be appended to the verb, all are:

Procurándoselo.	Procuring it for himself.
Después de habérselo procurado.	After having procured it for himself.

21.10. What one does to another he may do to himself; and so any transitive verb may be used reflexively if its meaning permits:

Le culpo; se culpa.	I blame him; he blames himself.
La miré; se miró en el espejo.	I looked at her; she looked at herself in the mirror.
Me defenderá; me defenderé.	He will defend me; I will defend myself.
Nos lisonjean; nos lisonjeamos.	They flatter us; we flatter ourselves.

21.11. When the verb is one that usually takes as its objects the dative of a person and the accusative of a thing, the pronominal or reflexive object is dative:

No se permite diversión alguna.	He does not allow himself any recreation.
Se apropió el único asiento cómodo.	He appropriated to himself the only comfortable seat.
Me he comprado un bastón nuevo.	I have bought myself a new stick.
Nos hemos encontrado una casa de huéspedes.	We have found ourselves a boarding house.

REMARK. Unfortunately there is no distinction of form between a dative and an accusative reflexive object.

21.12. This use of the dative reflexive is extended further in Spanish than in English, imparting a slight degree of energy to the expression which can seldom be rendered into the latter language, though an idea of willfulness is often added (cf. § 21.26):

Yo sé lo que me digo: quiere a otro... (Benavente, **Lo cursi,** escena última)	I know what I am saying: she is in love with somebody else.
¿Qué enredos se traerán éstos dos? (Baroja, **El aprendiz de conspirador,** III, 2)	What schemes are these two up to?

Nos pasamos lo más del bombardeo metidos en la lonja de una confitería. (Unamuno, **Recuerdos de niñez y de mocedad,** I, 15)	We spent most of the bombardment in the storeroom of a confectioner's shop.
Ya les habían despedido de su barraca. Los hombres negros la habían cerrado, llevándose las llaves. (Blasco Ibáñez, **La barraca,** II)	They had already put them out of their dwelling. The black men had closed it, carrying away the keys.
Se reclama el primer puesto.	He claims the first place (for himself.)
Me propongo hacer un viaje a las Islas de Barlovento.	I propose to take a trip to the Windward Islands.
Se arrogó el mando.	He usurped the command.
Se pidió un vaso de agua.	He asked for a glass of water (for himself).
Se guardó la carta.	He kept the letter.
Los ratones se han comido el queso.	The mice have eaten up the cheese.
Me lo bebí.	I drank it up.
Me hallé un peso en la calle.	I found (me) a peso in the street.
Tú te lo sabes todo.	Oh you think you know everything!
Me tomé la libertad de entrar.	I took the liberty of entering.
Los tiburones se tragan a los hombres.	Sharks swallow men.
Háblate primero con Vellorini. (Gallegos, **Canaima,** III: **Vellorini Hermanos)**	Just speak first with Vellorini.

REMARK. There is occasionally a chance for confusion between **se** as reflexive dative and **se** as a substitute for the objective third person, before another objective pronoun of the third person:

A Enriqueta se le cayó el pañuelo y un oficial que iba tras ella lo recogió y **se lo llevó.**	Henrietta dropped her handkerchief, and an officer who was walking behind her picked it up and carried it off *(or* carried it to her).

NOTE. The meaning would be made clear by saying **se lo llevó consigo, or se lo llevó a ella,** according to which were intended.

21.13. Many verbs in Spanish are essentially reflexive, and have no meaning without the reflexive pronoun:

abstenerse de to abstain from
acurrucarse to huddle up
arrepentirse de to repent of
atreverse a to dare to
dignarse to deign
gloriarse to boast
jactarse to boast, vaunt
preciarse to boast
quejarse de to complain of
vanagloriarse to boast

REMARK. In English only two verbs, *betake* and *bethink,* are essentially reflexive; in all other cases the reflexive verbs are merely employed reflexively in a particular meaning.

RECIPROCAL VERBS

21.14. If of several actors each acts on another, the verb is called reciprocal. It does not differ in form from the reflexive use, although necessarily the verb is always plural; consequently, when not specified, the expression is susceptible of two renderings (if the meaning permits):

Se engañan.	They deceive themselves. They deceive each other.
Se felicitaban.	They were congratulating themselves. They were congratulating each other.
Se mostraron por encima de las murallas *(reflex.).*	They showed themselves over the ramparts.
Se mostraban sus condecoraciones *(recip.).*	They were showing each other their decorations.
Se vieron pero no se hablaron.	They saw each other but did not speak to each other.
Los lobos se *(dative)* disputaban los trozos del rengífero.	The wolves were wrangling with one another over the pieces of the reindeer.
Nos quedamos inmóviles y confusos, mirándonos con estupor.	We stood motionless and confused, looking at one another stupidly.
Ellas se parecen como dos gotas de agua.	They resemble each other like two drops of water.
Nosotras no nos parecemos en nada.	We do not resemble each other at all.

REMARK. As in the case of the reflexive use (§ 3.30), **él, ella,** etc. tend to be used instead of **sí:**

Dos monjas de toca blanca han estado mirándome y hablando entre **ellas.** (Baroja, **Las inquietudes de Shanti Andía,** III, I)	Two nuns in white hoods have been looking at me and talking to *one another.*

21.15. When, for emphasis or to prevent ambiguity, it is desired to show unmistakably that the action of each of several actors falls upon himself, the pronoun is repeated in the prepositional form strengthened by the appropriate form of **mismo** or **propio.** This may be done solely for emphasis in the case of a singular verb:

Los bribones se engañaron a sí mismos.	The rogues deceived themselves.
Se burlan de sí mismos.	They make fun of themselves.
El día vendrá en que nos llamaremos borricos a nosotros mismos por no haberlo aprovechado.	The day will come when we will call ourselves asses for not having taken advantage of it.

REMARK. **Mismo** is sometimes associated with the subject of a reflexive verb (cf. § **3.51**).

Se educó él mismo.	He educated himself.
Ordinariamente me afeito yo mismo.	Ordinarily I shave myself.

21.16. When it is desired to show beyond question that the action is mutual among several actors, accuracy is secured by the use of the appropriate forms of **uno...otro,** equivalent to the English *each other:*

Los bribones se engañaron el uno al otro.	The rogues deceived each other.
Los aeronautas, ayudándose unos a otros, lograron desprenderse de las mallas de la red.	The aeronauts, assisting one another, succeeded in freeing themselves from the meshes of the net.

REMARK. The same effect may be produced by the adverbs **mutuamente** or **recíprocamente:**

Se detestan mutuamente.	They detest each other.
Debemos ayudarnos recíprocamente.	We must help each other.

21.17. With regard to the inflection of **uno** and **otro,** the following distinctions are theoretically to be observed:

1. With two males...................... **uno ...otro**
2. With two females..................... **una ...otra**
3. With one male and one female......... **uno ...otra**
4. With two or more males............... **unos...otros**
5. With two or more females............. **unas...otras**
6. A group of males only, contrasted with one composed entirely of females..... **unos...otras**
7. With any other mixed companies there is no distinction of gender.......... **unos...otros**

EXAMPLES

En el minué los caballeros y las señoras se hacen frente los unos a las otras.	In the minuet the ladies and gentlemen face one another.
Se querían entrañablemente y se escribían muchas cartas la una a la otra.	They loved each other fondly and wrote many letters to each other.
Se aborrecen uno a otra.	They hate each other.

REMARK. Where the objects are of both sexes, the distinction of feminine is generally disregarded in colloquial and even literary style.

Así lo creían ambos, Ramiro y Rosa, al atraerse el uno al otro. (Unamuno, **La tía Tula,** I)	So both Ramiro and Rosa thought when they were attracted to each other.
Pedro y Manuela se aproximaron el uno al otro. (Pardo Bazán, **La Madre Naturaleza,** IV)	Peter and Manuela drew near to each other.
Perfecta y Juan dejaron de verse desde que uno y otro se casaron. (Pérez Galdós, **Doña Perfecta,** III)	Perfecta and John stopped seeing each other after both were married.

21.18. **Uno** may be thus contrasted with **otro** when the verb has not the reciprocal form, the reciprocal effect being imparted by means of a preposition governing **otro:**

Los bailadores avanzan los unos hacia las otras.	The dancers advance toward one another.
Los novios parecen haber nacido el uno para la otra.	The lovers appear to have been born for each other.
Estas dos jóvenes son muy íntimas; no puede vivir la una sin la otra.	These two young girls are very intimate; they cannot live without each other.
Disputaban unos con otros.	They disputed with one another.
El padre Iñigo y el joven caminaban uno junto a otro sin hablar.	Father Ignatius and the young man walked along beside each other without speaking.
Será preciso no alejarnos unos de otros.	We must not separate from one another.
Estas dos cordilleras corren casi paralelamente una a otra.	These two mountain chains run almost parallel to each other.

REMARK. Here, too, the distinction of feminine is generally disregarded:

El comendador y Lucía, a pesar de la diferencia de edad, estaban perdidamente enamorados el uno del otro. (Valera, **El comendador Mendoza,** XXX)
The commander and Lucy, in spite of the difference of age, were desperately in love with each other.

Cástor y Balbina se dejaron morir dulcemente, abrazados el uno al otro. (Pérez de Ayala, **Luz de domingo,** VIII)
Castor and Balbina allowed themselves to die peacefully clinging to each other.

INTRANSITIVE VERBS

21.19. An intransitive verb is one whose action is complete in itself; it has a subject, but no object:

El sol brilla; la yerba crece. The sun shines; the grass grows.
El caballo relincha; el burro cojea. The horse neighs; the donkey limps.
El criado no titubeó. The servant did not hesitate.
Los niños están nadando. The boys are swimming.

21.20. The action of an intransitive verb may, in both languages, be further extended by means of adverbial expressions of manner, time or place, but this does not amount to supplying it with an object:

Los niños nadan en el lago. The boys swim in the lake.
Quieren salir de la casa. They want to go out of the house.
El sol brilla sobre la tierra. The sun shines on the earth.

21.21. This class is in Spanish relatively—indeed inconveniently—small. Moreover, in English most verbs may be used either transitively or intransitively; but in Spanish they less often oscillate from the one class to the other:

Thus in English we may say *the horses trot,* and also that *the driver trots the horses;* in Spanish, **trotar** is intransitive only, and could apply in the first meaning but not in the second. Conversely, we may say in English that *the man opens the door,* and also that *the door opens easily;* but in Spanish **abrir** is purely transitive, and would ordinarily be used only in the first value. A Spaniard could by no stretch of imagination suppose that the door could, of its own action, *open* anything. It must be admitted, however, that the language of the present day tends to use more and more verbs as either transitive or intransitive: **El balcón abría sobre un corredor.** (Palacio Valdés, **La novela de un novelista,** I) *The balcony window opened upon a passage way.* Older usage would have allowed only **se abría.** In addition to **abrir, cerrar** *close;* **cansar** *tire;* **derretir** *melt;* **encoger** *shrink;* **estirar** *stretch;* **retirar** *withdraw;* **romper** *break,* etc., etc., ordinarily demand the expression of an object: **El museo se cierra a las cuatro.** *The museum closes at four o'clock.* **Me canso muy pronto.** *I tire very soon.* **El hielo se derrite en el sol.** *Ice melts in the sun,* etc., etc. See also §§ 21.25, 21.28. Conspicuous examples of verbs which may be used with or without an expressed object are **acabar, concluir, terminar** *end;* **despertar** *wake up.*

21.22. In Spanish a few transitive verbs such as the following, whose objects are not very essential to the meaning, may be used intransitively:

Ella va a cantar una copla.	She is going to sing a couplet.
Ella va a cantar.	She is going to sing.
Vi que escribía una carta.	I saw he was writing a letter.
Vi que escribía.	I saw he was writing.
El niño quiere beber agua.	The child wants to drink water.
El niño quiere beber.	The child wants to drink.
Este camino nos conducirá al castillo.	This road will take us to the castle.
Este camino conduce al castillo.	This road leads to the castle.

21.23. Certain intransitive verbs may take an object expressing in substantive form the action, or a variety of the action, signified by the verb itself. This is called a *cognate* object, i.e. one allied or related in meaning to the verb:

Vive una **vida** miserable.	He *lives* a miserable *life.*
Murió una **muerte** horrible.	He *died* a horrible *death.*
"Yo he **peleado** buena **batalla,** he acabado mi carrera, he guardado la fe."	"I have *fought* a good *fight,* I have finished my course, I have kept the faith."
Llorar lágrimas de gozo.	To *weep tears* of joy.
Dormir un **sueño** profundo.	To *sleep* a deep *sleep.*

NOTE. Otherwise verbs can not always be used interchangeably as transitive or intransitive; resort must often be had to either one of the expedients given below, or else a different verb must be chosen.

21.24. A transitive sense may be imparted to an intransitive verb by placing a verb of causing before its infinitive:

Al chocar el proyectil contra un obstáculo, la varilla por razón de la inercia es llevada hacia adelante hasta caer sobre el fulminante, el cual se enciende, y comunicando una chispa a la carga, **hace estallar** la granada.	When the projectile strikes an obstacle, the plunger is by reason of its inertia thrown forward upon the fulminate, which ignites, and communicating a spark to the charge, *bursts* the shell.

Dejó caer el libro.	He *dropped* the book.
El centinela le **hizo parar.**	The sentinel *halted* him.

21.25. Transitive verbs may often be used intransitively by making them reflexive, so that although their action has an object, yet as that object is the actor, the action passes to no second person or thing. A comparison of the transitive and the intransitive use of each of the following verbs should make this distinction sufficiently clear:

TRANSITIVE VALUE	INTRANSITIVE VALUE
acostar to put to bed	**acostarse** to go to bed
levantar to raise, lift up	**levantarse** to rise, get up
enfadar to anger	**enfadarse** to become angry
desmayar to dismay, discourage	**desmayarse** to faint, swoon
sentar to seat, cause to sit down	**sentarse** to sit down
alegrar to gladden	**alegrarse** to be glad
avergonzar to shame, make ashamed	**avergonzarse** to be ashamed
helar to freeze	**helarse** to freeze, become frozen
desatar to untie	**desatarse** to become untied
marchitar to wither, cause to fade	**marchitarse** to wither, fade
acercar to approach, bring near to	**acercarse** to approach, come near
alejar to move away	**alejarse** to move away
estremecer to shake, make tremble	**estremecerse** to tremble, shudder
fundir to melt	**fundirse** to melt
extender to extend	**extenderse** to extend
mejorar to improve	**mejorarse** to improve
mojar to wet	**mojarse** to become wet, get wet
secar to dry	**secarse** to dry
desgarrar to tear	**desgarrarse** to tear
hender to split, crack	**henderse** to split, crack

COMPARATIVE EXAMPLES

No debo **acostarme** antes de **acostar** a los niños.	I must not *go to bed* before *putting* the children *to bed.*
El fuego **funde** el plomo.	The fire *melts* the lead.
El plomo **se funde** fácilmente.	Lead *melts* easily.
El sol ha **marchitado** las flores.	The sun *has faded* the flowers.
Las rosas **se marchitan** pronto.	Roses *fade* quickly.
Acercó una silla a la lumbre.	He *placed* a chair near the fire.
Se acercó a la lumbre.	He *approached* the fire.
Ella me **enfadó.**	She *angered* me.
Ella se **enfadó.**	She *became angry.*
Ellos nos **horrorizaron.**	They *horrified* us.
Ellos **se horrorizaron.**	They *were horrified.*

Las aves me **regocijan.**	The birds *gladden* me.
Las aves **se regocijan.**	The birds *rejoice.*
Su mujer le **irrita.**	His wife *provokes* him.
Su mujer **se irrita.**	His wife *is (gets) provoked.*
Le **avergüenzo.**	I *put* him *to shame.*
Me avergüenzo.	I *am ashamed.*
Vende vino y licores.	He *sells* wine and liquors.
El vino **se vende** bien este año.	Wine *sells* well this year.
Decidiré la cuestión.	I *will decide* the question.
Me he decidido a partir.	I *have decided* to set out.
El generalísimo **opuso** un ejército de 10.000 hombres a su avance.	The commanding general *opposed* an army of 10,000 men to their advance.
El presidente de la comisión **se opuso** a la medida.	The chairman of the committee *opposed* the measure.

21.26. Verbs naturally intransitive are often made reflexive, an idiomatic usage which has no parallel in English. In reality this pleonasm is intended to emphasize the actor's interest, volition or free will and accord in the case, sometimes implying that the accomplishment of the act calls for a special effort:

Estuvo escondido.	He was hidden.
Se estuvo escondido.	He *was* in *voluntary* concealment.
La gente entraba.	The people were going in.
A pesar de las guardias apostadas a la puerta, la gente **se** entraba.	In spite of the guards stationed at the gate, the people *kept getting in.*
Los presos salieron.	The prisoners went out.
Los presos **se** salieron.	The prisoners *got* out.
Aquí **me** espero hasta que salga. (Benavente, **La comida de las fieras,** III, 7)	*Right* here I wait until she comes out.

21.27. In some cases the meaning of an intransitive verb is so changed by being made reflexive as to amount to a new word, while in others the effect of the reflexive is so slight as not perceptibly to affect the meaning. Careful observation is the only means of determining this usage:

caer to fall, to lose one's balance, to become loose	**caerse** to tumble down
correr to run	**correrse** to be ashamed or embarrassed
dormir to sleep	**dormirse** to fall asleep

entrar to go in	**entrarse** to slip in, to get in
escapar to escape	**escaparse** to run away, to get clear
estar to be	**estarse** to stay, to remain
ir to go	**irse** to go away
llegar to arrive	**llegarse** to approach
marchar to march (usually)	**marcharse** to leave, to depart
morir to die	**morirse** to be at the point of death, to be dying, *but also* to die
parar to stop, to come to end at, to lodge	**pararse** to stop, to come to a stop *(in Spanish America,* to stand up, to rear up)
salir to go out	**salirse** to slip out, to get out; to leak
venir to come	**venirse** to come along
volver to return	**volverse** to turn around *(usually,* cf. 21.26)

21.28. The following verbs may ordinarily be used optionally (but cf. §§ 21.12, 21.26) with or without the reflexive pronoun in the *meaning given here:*

acabar *or* **acabarse**	to end (come to an end)
bajar *or* **bajarse**	to get off
callar *or* **callarse**	to become silent
concluir *or* **concluirse**	to end (come to an end)
desayunar *or preferably* **desayunarse**	to breakfast
desembarcar *or* **desembarcarse**	to disembark, get off a ship
despertar *or* **despertarse**	to wake up
embarcar *or* **embarcarse**	to embark, get on a ship
enfermar *or* **enfermarse** *(especially in Spanish America)*	to grow sick
parar *or* **pararse**	to stop (come to a stop)
parecer *or* **parecerse**	to resemble
pasar *or* **pasarse**	to spend
pasear *or* **pasearse**	to stroll, take a walk
quedar *or* **quedarse**	to remain
regresar *or* **regresarse** *(especially in Spanish America)*	to return
reír *or* **reírse**	to laugh
sonreír *or* **sonreírse**	to smile
subir *or* **subirse**	to get on
tardar *or* **tardarse** *(especially in Spanish America)*	to delay, tarry
terminar *or* **terminarse**	to end (come to an end)
volver *or* **volverse**	to return

THE PASSIVE VOICE

21.29. The passive voice is a variation in the manner of expressing the action of an active transitive verb, in which the object of the active verb becomes the subject of the passive, and the subject of the active verb (if expressed) is connected with the passive by a preposition:

ACTIVE: **El alguacil persigue a los ladrones** *the sheriff is pursuing the thieves.*

PASSIVE: **Los ladrones son perseguidos por el alguacil** *the thieves are pursued by the sheriff.*

21.30. The regular passive is formed in Spanish by associating the past participle of any transitive verb with the various forms of the verb **ser,** in which case the participle agrees with the subject in gender and number:

Soy respetado. Soy respetada.	I am respected.
Hemos sido insultados.	We have been insulted.
Ella no será convidada.	She will not be invited.
El salteador fué ahorcado.	The road agent was hanged.
Habiendo sido derrotados los insurgentes,...	The insurgents having been routed,...
La máquina necesitaba ser recorrida y limpiada tanto interior como exteriormente.	The engine needed to be gone over and cleaned both inside and out.
Mi familia es muy conocida en Madrid. (Benavente, **Campo de armiño,** II, 12)	My family is very well known in Madrid.
Machín sabía que entre los pescadores era odiado. (Baroja, **Las inquietudes de Shanti Andía,** V, 5)	Machín knew that among the fishermen he was hated.

21.31. When the active agent is introduced, it is connected with the passive verb by **por** when the action is a physical or bodily one, and by **de** when it is one of thought or feeling. **De** is more usual with **acompañado, precedido, rodeado, seguido** but **por** tends to displace **de** in all cases nowadays:

No eran flojos los trabajos que sufría don Joaquín para hacerse **entender de** sus discípulos. (Blasco Ibáñez, **La barraca,** VI)	The trials that Don Joaquín endured to make himself *understood by* his pupils were not light.

Era envidiada de todos.
She was *envied by* all.

Fueron ahorcados **por** el verdugo.
They were *hanged by* the hangman.

Las órdenes del ingeniero fueron ejecutadas inmediatamente **por** sus compañeros.
The orders of the engineer were immediately *carried out by* his companions.

Subió la escalera **precedida por** el tendero. (Palacio Valdés, **Santa Rogelia,** I, 6)
She went up the stairs, *preceded by* the shopkeeper.

Doña Bárbara comía **acompañada de** Balbino Paiva. (Gallegos, **Doña Bárbara,** I, 6)
Doña Barbara was eating, *accompanied by* Balbino Paiva.

El espectáculo de esta madre **rodeada de** sus hijos...enterneció todavía más a Ricardo. (Palacio Valdés, **Marta y María,** IV)
The spectacle of this mother *surrounded by* her children...touched Richard even more.

Remark. Indeed, **de** is not infrequently used with any verb to introduce the agent dependent upon a past participle in a phrase without **ser** or **estar:**

La mujer, **ayudada de** su compañero, bajó penosamente de su cabalgadura. (Baroja, **El mayorazgo de Labraz,** I, 1)
The woman, *aided by* her companion, got off her mount with difficulty.

Se creía usted **abandonado de** todos. (Benavente, **La fuerza bruta,** II, 7)
You thought yourself *abandoned by* everybody.

21.32. **Estar** is used instead of **ser** when the state or condition of the subject is described without reference to any action. The past participle is then merely an adjective:

El aposento **está** imperfectamente alumbrado.
The apartment is imperfectly lighted.

El informe **estaba** mal redactado.
The report was badly prepared.

Era evidente que el informe **había sido** redactado con precipitación.
It was evident that the report had been hastily prepared.

El palacio **fué** destruido por el terremoto reciente.
The palace was destroyed by the recent earthquake *(an occurrence).*

El palacio, cuando yo lo visité, **estaba** destruido.
The palace, when I visited it, was destroyed [in a destroyed condition].

Las olas **eran** agitadas por el viento.
The waves were agitated by the wind *(action).*

Las olas **estaban** todavía agitadas por el viento.
The waves were still agitated by the wind *(condition).*

Este artículo **está** escrito por una persona indocta.	This article is written by an uneducated person.
Este artículo **ha sido** escrito por una persona indocta.	

21.33. Under such circumstances the expression may be varied by substituting for **estar** one of the following verbs:

ir, andar to go	**quedar, quedarse** to remain
verse to see one's self	**sentirse** to feel one's self
hallarse, encontrarse to find one's self	**presentarse** to present one's self
	mostrarse to show one's self

These all may be translated in English by the verb *to be:*

La entrada de la cueva **se hallaba** obstruida por una cortina de arbustos espesos.	The entrance of the cave was obstructed by a curtain of thick shrubbery.
En las cercanías de Arequipa el país **se presenta** más accidentado.	In the neighborhood of Arequipa the country is more uneven.
El interior de la república del Uruguay **se ve** atravesado por cerros poblados de árboles.	The interior of the Republic of Uruguay is crossed by mountains covered with trees.
Se halla enfermo.	He is sick.
Se encontraba desprovisto de todo.	He was destitute of everything.
Quedaron asombrados al oír la noticia.	They were astounded on hearing the news.
Se quedó callado.	He was silent.
Se siente perplejo.	He is perplexed.
Anda muy distraído.	He is very absent-minded.
Los gauchos **iban** vestidos de pieles de guanacos, y llevaban, a más de los acostumbrados lazos y bolas, unas lanzas que tenían quince pies de longitud.	The Gauchos were dressed in guanaco skins, and carried in addition to the customary lassos and bolas, lances fifteen feet in length.

REMARK. It is to be observed that **sido** and **estado** are invariable when preceded by any form of **haber,** while a following past participle of a transitive verb agrees in number and gender with its noun. This is because **sido** and **estado** are governed by **haber,** while the other past participle depends upon **ser** or **estar:**

La casa había sido nuevamente pintada.	The house had been newly painted.
Habiendo sido limpiados y dorados los marcos,...	The frames having been cleaned and gilded,...

Era evidente que aquella botella había sido arrojada al mar desde un buque náufrago. — It was evident that that bottle had been thrown into the sea from some shipwrecked vessel.

REFLEXIVE SUBSTITUTE FOR PASSIVE

21.34. In modern Spanish the formal passive is relatively less used, because of the number of equivalent constructions. Its place is often taken by the much overworked reflexive form of the verb. This, however, occurs only with the verb in the third person.

The reflexive may be applied in two ways as a substitute for the passive: (1) personally; (2) impersonally. In the first case the verb can be transitive only; in the second, either transitive or intransitive.

21.35. (1) When employed personally the subject is an expressed noun or pronoun (referring to a thing) with which the verb agrees in number, taking the reflexive **se** as its object.[1] The reflexive force disappears, and the meaning conveyed is purely passive:

Eso se hará fácilmente. — That will be easily done.

La cena se despachó pronto. — The supper was quickly dispatched.

Por fortuna sus temores no se realizaron. — Fortunately their fears were not realized.

El bosque se componía en aquellos parajes de árboles coníferos semejantes a los que se habían observado en las inmediaciones del lago. — The forest in this region was composed of coniferous trees similar to those which had been noticed in the neighborhood of the lake.

Su crédito se ha agotado. — His credit has been exhausted.

Se dejó a babor el célebre pico de Tenerife. — The celebrated peak of Teneriffe was left to port (larboard).

Se aplazó la construcción del almacén para el verano siguiente. — The building of the warehouse was postponed until the following summer.

En Centro América por lo general no son los hoteles dignos de llamarse así. — In Central America the hotels are generally not worthy of being so called.

Los demás puntos no merecen la pena de visitarse. — The other points are not worth being visited.

---

[1] Failure to make the verb plural to agree with its subject, in which case **se** becomes a kind of indefinite subject (cf. § 21.41), is probably more frequent in the spoken language than in the written, where it is not lacking: **Era don Quijote amigo de la caza, en cuyo ejercicio se aprende astucias y engaños de guerra.** (Unamuno, **Vida de don Quijote y Sancho, I**) *Don Quixote was fond of hunting, in the exercise of which one learns tricks and deceits of war.*

21.36. (2) When employed impersonally the verb is in the third person *singular,* with the reflexive **se** as its object, but *no subject* is expressed and none is understood; the verb is connected by a conjunction, adverb, or equivalent word, with the remainder of the sentence:

Se dice que las fuerzas del gobierno se han sublevado.	It is said that the government forces have revolted.
No se explica cómo salió del apuro.	It is not explained how he extricated himself from the difficulty.
Se sabe bien que este peso disminuirá en razón inversa del cuadrado de la distancia.	It is well known that this weight will decrease in an inverse ratio to the square of the distance.
Se penetraba en aquella torre de metal por una abertura estrecha practicada en las paredes de la base.	Entrance was effected into the metal turret by means of a narrow aperture cut in the walls of the base.
Se asegura que el pueblo está más enterado sobre la vida de los santos que sobre la geografía de su propio país.	It is asserted that the people are better informed about the lives of the saints than about the geography of their own country.
Se comprenderá fácilmente cuánto impacientaba a ambos esta tardanza inesperada.	It will be easily understood how much this unexpected delay irritated them both.

REMARK. Nevertheless this construction is sometimes used in familiar style to refer to a person definitely understood.

Se me **dijo** anoche en el baile que se **estaría** en el paseo a eso de las seis.	*Somebody* told me at the ball last night that *somebody* was going to be on the promenade about six o'clock.

(A friendly matron is giving the young man a pointer.)

¡Conque! ¿**Se ha estado** juiciosa durante mi ausencia? —Sí, papá.	Well, has my little girl been good while I was away? —Yes, Papa.

21.37. If the subject represents a person capable of performing the action expressed by the verb, the latter will naturally be understood to be reflexive or reciprocal and not passive in meaning:[1]

Se envenenó el duque.	The duke poisoned himself. *(not* The duke was poisoned.)

[1] But occasionally the meaning is passive: **Tú bien sabes que en las minas se matan algunas veces los hombres.** (Palacio Valdés, **La alegría perdida,** VI) *You know very well that men are sometimes killed in mines.*

Se miraban los reyes como superiores a la ley.	The kings regarded themselves *(or* each other) as above the law. *(not* The kings were regarded, etc.)
La joven se lisonjea.	The young girl flatters herself.
Los fugitivos caminaban de noche, y se escondían en los matorrales o entre los helechos altos durante el día.	The fugitives traveled at night, and hid themselves in the thickets or among the tall ferns by day.
Se ataron uno a otro.	They tied themselves together.
Los intendentes se amenazaban.	The overseers threatened each other.

21.38. When there is a desire to render the meaning of such phrases unmistakably passive, the impersonal construction (cf. §§ **21.34, 21.36**) is employed and the noun is made the object:

Se envenenó al duque.	The duke was poisoned *or* They poisoned the duke.
Se miraba a los reyes como superiores a la ley.	The kings were regarded as above the law *or* They regarded the kings as above the law.
Se lisonjea a la joven.	The young girl is flattered.
Se escondió a los fugitivos entre los helechos altos.	The fugitives were concealed among the tall ferns.
Se les ató uno a otro.	They were tied together.
Se amenazaba a los intendentes.	The overseers were threatened.
Se les señaló doble pago.	They were given double pay.

21.39. The same distinction exists when the subject in the English equivalent is of the first or second person:

Se me rechazó.	I was blackballed.

(**Me rechacé** would mean *I blackballed myself.)*

Cuando las llamas me chamuscaron la ropa, **me arrojé** por la ventana.	When the flames scorched my clothing, *I threw myself* from the window.
En un abrir y cerrar de ojos **se me arrojó** por la ventana.	In the twinkling of an eye *I was thrown* out of the window.
Nos privábamos de todos los lujos, y aun de muchas cosas necesarias para la comodidad.	We *deprived ourselves* of all luxuries and even of many things necessary to comfort.
Se nos privaba de todos los lujos, y aun de muchas cosas necesarias para la comodidad.	*They deprived us* of all luxuries and even of many things necessary to comfort.

REMARK. This is equally applicable with the redundant construction of personal pronouns:

A él se le mató a pedradas.	They stoned him to death.
No se nos dejó entrar a nosotros.	They did not allow us to enter.

21.40. It is customary to use the dative form **les** instead of the accusative **los,** when the objective pronoun is masculine plural; otherwise the accusative form is used:

Se les (*not* los) desterró.	They were banished.
Se les condenó a muerte.	They were condemned to death.
Se las ayudó a bajar.	They were assisted to alight (were aided in alighting).
Cuando menos se la esperaba, entró Cándida turbadísima. (Pérez Galdós, **La de Bringas,** XLIX)	When she was least expected Candida came in very disturbed.

21.41. These passives of reflexive form (both the personal and impersonal constructions) are often equivalent in meaning to the English indefinite *they, you, we, one,* used as subject:

De este modo **se** ganará tiempo y **se** ahorrará trabajo.	In this way *we* will gain time and save work.
Se caminó durante toda la mañana.	*They* journeyed all the forenoon.
¿A dónde **se** nos va a conducir?	Where are *they* going to take us?
El pueblo es pequeñísimo; al instante **se** sale de él.	The village is very small; *you* get outside of it in no time.
¡Jardinero! ¿Cómo **se** sale de estos jardines?	Gardener! How do *you* get out of these gardens?
¿Qué **se** debe hacer?	What's *one* to do?
Alemania era un país exclusivamente militar; parecía que no **se** vivía más que para la guerra.	Germany was an exclusively military country; it seemed that *they* did not live for anything but war.
En el patio vecino **se** tocaba la guitarra y **se** cantaban sentidas peteneras de notas prolongadas.	In the patio next door *they* were playing the guitar and singing sentimental "peteneras" with long-drawn-out notes.
¿**Se** puede entrar? ¿**Se** puede pasar?	May *I (we)* go in? May *I (we)* come in?
¿**Se** puede subir?	May *I (we)* come up?

(These requests are more modest than if put in the first person.)

Cuando **se** es mal ciudadano, **se** es mal hombre. (Baroja, **El aprendiz de conspirador,** V, 3)	When *one* is a poor citizen, *he* is a poor man.

Erase que se era...*(at the beginning of fairy stories and folk tales)*	Once upon a time there was...

REMARK I. In Latin the verb often assumed the passive form, in the third person singular, with an indefinite meaning:

Sic itur ad astra.	So one goes to the stars.
Ei resistetur.	They will oppose him.
Nuntiatum est adesse Scipionem.	They reported that Scipio was near.
Diu et acriter pugnatum est.	They fought long and sharply.

REMARK II. In French and German there are expressions precisely equivalent in meaning to the Spanish, but different in form:

On peut le voir à son bureau.	You can see him at his office.
On a doublé la garde.	They have doubled the guard.
Où prend-on les crevettes?	Where do they catch shrimps?
Man hat mich versichert.	They assured me.
Man ist glücklich wenn man zufrieden ist.	We are happy when we are contented.

21.42. In Spanish also the verb may be used impersonally in the third person plural with the same indefinite meaning as that conveyed by the reflexive:

¿A dónde nos van a conducir?	Where are they going to take us?
¿Me han traído las botas?	Have they brought my boots?
Hacen muy buenos quesos allí.	They make very good cheeses there.
¿Qué dicen de la elección?	What do they say of the election?
Producen mejor vino que éste en mi país.	They produce better wine than this in my country.
Tocáronle en el hombro. Era doña Predestinación. (Pérez de Ayala, **Prometeo, II**)	Someone touched him on the shoulder. It was Doña Predestinación.

REMARK. **Diz,** as the equivalent of **se dice** or **dicen,** survives only to an extent in Spain; in Spanish America it is very much in use in the original and in a number of variant forms which are often combined with **que** in writing (**izque, isque, i que, quizque, quesque,** etc.). The word belongs to the colloquial rather than the literary language:

Los dinerales que diz que tenemos en el banco, ¿eh? (Pérez Galdós, **Mariucha, I, 1**)	The big sums of money that people say we have in the bank, what?

21.43. In placards and similar notices in which the reflexive is employed in Spanish, the meaning is usually expressed in English by the past participle alone, with elision of the verb *to be:*

Se necesita un jardinero.	Wanted, a gardener.
Aquí se habla español.	Spanish spoken here.
Se garantiza el trabajo.	Work warranted.
Se cierra los domingos.	Closed on Sundays.
Se compran y venden libros de lance.	Second-hand books bought and sold.
Se confeccionan tarjetas y facturas en el acto.	Cards and billheads made up without delay.

REMARK. The reflexive form of the present subjunctive is often used in giving directions (cf. § **19.45**):

Tómese de media a una cucharadita disuelta en un vaso de agua.	Take from a half to one teaspoonful dissolved in a glass of water.
Córtese por el borde.	Cut along the edge.

21.44. When the personal construction is used, the active agent may be introduced by **por** or **de** just as with the true passive:

Las pirámides se edificaron por esclavos.	The pyramids were built by slaves.
Estas obras se venden por todos los libreros.	These works are sold by all booksellers.
¿Para qué quiere aquí a Vespasiano? —Para aconsejarme de él y solicitar su valimiento. (Pérez de Ayala, **Tigre Juan,** p. 98 of **Obras completas** edition)	What do you want Vespasian here for? —To be advised by him and to request his support.

21.45. In many cases it does not matter whether we construe a reflexive verb as truly reflexive or as passive in meaning, and in like manner whether it shall be considered intransitive or passive, the meaning being about the same either way:

Este obrero se llama Paco.	This workman calls himself Frank. This workman is called Frank.
La porcelana se rompe fácilmente.	Porcelain breaks easily. Porcelain is easily broken.

21.46. A verb that requires a preposition to complete its meaning cannot be used passively. It therefore takes the impersonal construction, the preposition being retained:

Se jugó al ajedrez y chaquete. *(Not* se jugaron ajedrez y chaquete.)	They played chess and backgammon.

Se habló de varias cosas. (*Not* varias cosas se hablaron.)	Various things were talked of.
Se trata de un asunto importantísimo.	A very important matter is being dealt with.

21.47. If the verb is essentially reflexive, the impersonal construction is not admissible. Thus the following must always refer to a subject, either expressed or understood:

Se arrepiente.	He repents.
No se atreve a emprenderlo.	He does not dare to undertake it.
Se ausentó.	He absented himself.
Se acordó de la apuesta.	He remembered the bet.
Se ocupaba poco de aquellos rumores.	He concerned himself but little about those rumors.

21.48. Those verbs which may take the reflexive pronoun to modify their meaning (as when transitive verbs are made intransitive, or intransitives are made vivacious), are susceptible of two acceptations when they appear in the third person singular without an expressed subject. They may be considered either as having the modified meaning and referring to some singular subject, or as being indefinite with the unmodified meaning of the verb:

Se entró.	He "got in." People entered. (Fr. *on entra.*)
Se marcha.	He "goes away." They march. (Fr. *on marche.*)
Se durmió.	He "fell asleep." They slept. (Fr. *on dormit.*)

21.49. When it is desired to retain the modifying force conveyed by the reflexive, and at the same time to render the phrase impersonal, the only way is to supply an indefinite subject—**uno** or **gente**—or place the verb in the third person plural (as explained in § 21.42 of this chapter):

Se burlan de sus amenazas.	They scoff at his menaces. (Fr. *on se fiche de ses menaces.*)
Cuanto más se acerca uno a la cumbre de una alta montaña, menor es la densidad del aire y más difícil la respiración.	The more one approaches the summit (Fr. *plus on s'approche du sommet*) of a high mountain, the less is the density of the air and the more difficult is respiration.

Se abriga uno para no sentir el frío.	A person wraps himself up so as not to feel the cold. (Ger. *man verhüllt sich, um die Kälte nicht zu fühlen.)*
Se acordaron de la apuesta.	They remembered the bet. (Fr. *on se souvint du pari.)*
La gente se ocupaba poco de aquellos rumores.	They concerned themselves but little about those rumors. (Fr. *on s'occupait peu de ces rumeurs.)*

REMARK. The idea is that **se** either renders the verb passive, or modifies its meaning; but it cannot usually perform both duties at the same time:[1]

IMPERSONAL VERBS

21.50. Impersonal verbs have neither subject nor object. Whatever they may represent as being or as going on, nothing is suggested as taking any active part in it. There is no perfect example of such a verb in use in the English language; but Spanish has many that are either always or occasionally employed without a subject, expressed or understood:

Ha llovido mucho durante la noche.	It rained a great deal during the night.
Relampaguea por el lado del norte.	It lightens towards the north.
Parece que vamos a tener un temporal.	It seems that we are going to have a storm.

REMARK. The English pronoun *it* is a mere form of expression due to the habit of our language, and in nowise represents the actor. The corresponding neuter pronoun **ello** is sometimes employed in Spanish when emphasis is required, but never in representing natural phenomena:

Ello importa mucho.	It matters a great deal.
¿Ha oído V. tronar?	Did you hear *it* thunder?
¿Ha visto V. relampaguear?	Did you see *it* lighten?
Me gusta ver nevar.	I like to see *it* snow.

NOTE. We will first consider those verbs which are strictly impersonal, and then discuss those of occasional impersonal use.

21.51. The only verbs restricted to the impersonal construction are those which express the phenomena of nature. They are limited

[1] This can best be illustrated by comparison with the French and German. **Se lisonjea** may mean on the one hand *he flatters himself, il se flatte, er schmeichelt sich,* or on the other *they flatter, on flatte, man schmeichelt;* but could not mean *they flatter themselves, on se flatte, man schmeichelt sich.*

in form to the infinitive, present participle, past participle and the third person singular of all other tenses; but within these limits their conjugational forms do not differ from those of other similar verbs. The following are the principal ones in use:

ALBOREAR:	**alborea** it dawns.
AMANECER:	**amanece** it is getting to be morning.
ANOCHECER:	**anochece** it is getting to be night.
DILUVIAR:	**diluvia** it is pouring.
ESCAMPAR:	**escampa** it stops raining.
ESCARCHAR:	**escarcha** there is hoarfrost.
GRANIZAR:	**graniza** it is hailing.
HELAR:	**hiela** it is freezing.
LLOVER:	**llueve** it is raining.
LLOVIZNAR:	**llovizna** } it is drizzling.
MOLLIZNAR:	**mollizna** } it is drizzling.
MOLLIZNEAR:	**molliznea** } it is drizzling.
NEVAR:	**nieva** it is snowing.
RELAMPAGUEAR:	**relampaguea** it is lightning.
TRONAR:	**truena** it is thundering.
VENTEAR:	**ventea** it is blowing.
VENTISCAR:	**ventisca** it is snowing and blowing.

REMARK. Even some of these verbs may occasionally be supplied with a subject by figure of speech, and examples are to be found with an object:

Tronaba la artillería por todos lados.	The artillery thundered on all sides.
Sus ojos relampagueaban.	His eyes flashed.
Amaneció el día claro y frío.	The day dawned clear and cold.
Los indígenas acudieron a Cortés, clamando sobre que no llovían sus dioses. (Solís)	The natives came to Cortes, complaining that their gods did not rain.
No hicieron caso del pedrisco que llovía sobre ellos. (Cervantes)	They paid no attention to the shower of stones which rained upon them.
Comenzaron los galeotes a llover piedras sobre Don Quijote. *(Ibid.)*	The galley slaves began to shower stones upon Don Quixote.

21.52. **Amanecer** and **anochecer** are at times, used as verbs of full inflection, with the meaning of *to arrive* or *be present at daybreak* or *nightfall:*

¿Anocheceremos en Cienfuegos?	Shall we get to Cienfuegos by nightfall?
Amanecimos a vista de tierra.	When day dawned we were in sight of land.

21.53. The infinitives and present participles of impersonal verbs communicate their impersonal effect to whatever verbs they depend upon. The same is true of verbs of occasional impersonal use:

Parece que va a llover.	It looks as if it were going to rain.
Comienza a nevar.	It is beginning to snow.
Acaba de tronar a lo lejos.	It has just thundered in the distance.
Seguía diluviando.	It continued pouring.
Eran entonces las cinco de la mañana, y empezaba a amanecer.	It was five o'clock in the morning, and it was beginning to dawn.

21.54. The verbs of occasional impersonal use are intransitive and correspond very closely to their English equivalents, used impersonally:

acaecer to happen
acontecer to happen
bastar to suffice
constar to be evident
convenir to suit, behoove
importar to be important, to matter
parecer to appear, seem
precisar to be necessary

EXAMPLES

Precisa, señores, poner término a esas crueles hecatombes, que han venido presenciándose en el nuevo mundo con vilipendio y escarnio de la humanidad y de la civilización.	It is necessary, gentlemen, to put an end to these cruel sacrifices, which have been witnessed in the new world to the shame and horror of humanity and civilization.
Conviene aquí decir que en las playas asiáticas esta especie de algas entra por mucho en la alimentación de los indígenas.	It should be mentioned here that on the Asiatic coasts this species of algae is extensively used as food by the natives.
Constaba por las acciones de aquellos animales que no habían visto nunca al hombre.	It was evident from the actions of those animals that they had never seen a human being.
Acaeció que su marido se hallaba ausente por algunos días.	It happened that her husband was absent for a few days.

21.55. The verbs **ser** and **estar** are used with especial frequency impersonally, followed by nouns or adjectives:

Es lástima. Es maravilla.	It is a pity. It is a wonder.
Está claro.	It is clear.
Es necesario partir al instante.	It is necessary to start at once.
Estaba todavía oscuro cuando me levanté.	It was still dark when I got up.
Está muy nublado.	It is very cloudy.

Era demasiado tarde para ver la campiña.	It was too late to see the landscape.

REMARK. There is an impersonal expression, usually of active form (cf. § **23.10**) but of passive value, formed by the verb **ser** and an infinitive, the two being connected by **de**:[1]

Es de esperar.	It is to be hoped.
Es de desear.	It is to be desired.

21.56. A reflexive impersonal construction is applicable to a few verbs naturally reflexive, by which they are made reflexive in a second degree, so to speak, the meaning remaining the same:

Me figuro.	I imagine *(I figure to myself).*
Se me figura.	I imagine *(it figures itself to me).*
Me olvidé de hacerlo.	I forgot to do it.
Se me olvidó hacerlo.	I forgot to do it *(it forgot itself to me).*
Me permito.	I allow myself.
Se me permite.	It is allowed me.

21.57. There are many cases where in English a verb would be used impersonally, governing an infinitive, while in Spanish the infinitive is the subject of the verb:

Nos costó algún trabajo mantener el trineo en el camino, a causa de las muchas vueltas que fué preciso dar.	It cost us some trouble to keep the sleigh in the road, on account of the many turns it was necessary to make. (I.e., keeping the sleigh in the road cost us some trouble.)
Me tocó sentarme a su lado en la mesa.	It happened to me to be seated beside her at table.

21.58. Es menester is not an impersonal phrase, since it always has a subject, expressed or understood:

Es menester mucha paciencia.	Much patience is necessary.
Eran menester muchas reparaciones.	Many repairs were necesarry.
Era menester haberlo visto.	It was necessary to have seen it.

---

[1] When **ser** has a subject the meaning is that the latter is worthy of the act of the infinitive: **Eran de ver las precauciones que una astucia recelosa hacía adoptar a la pobre gente.** (Blasco Ibáñez, **Cañas y barro**, IV, toward end) *The precautions which a sly cunning made the poor people adopt were worthy of being seen* (or *you should have seen the precautions,* etc.).

But the more literary **ha menester** *there is need of* is a true impersonal expression:

Ha menester cien duros para completar la suma.	There is need of 100 duros to complete the sum.
Había menester largos rodeos para ganar la cumbre.	Long detours were necessary to gain the summit.

INCEPTIVE VERBS

21.59. Verbs of this class, when intransitive, signify *to become* of a certain character or condition. They are formed from nouns or adjectives, and have the infinitive termination **-ecer,** in imitation of the corresponding class of Latin verbs ending in *-scere* (generally *-escere*).

A few inceptive verbs are intransitive; but the greater number are active, meaning *to make* of the character or condition expressed by the radical word. These become intransitive by being made reflexive.

21.60. The following are intransitive:

envejecer to grow old	**florecer** to bloom
encanecer to grow gray	**enruinecer** to become vile
encarnecer to grow fleshy	**convalecer** to get better
palidecer to grow pale	**verdecer** to turn green

21.61. The following are transitive, unless used reflexively:

TRANSITIVE USE	INTRANSITIVE USE
desvanecer to cause to vanish	**desvanecerse** to vanish
endurecer to harden	**endurecerse** to become hard
empobrecer to impoverish	**empobrecer(se)** to become poor
enaltecer to exalt	**enaltecerse** to exalt oneself
enflaquecer to make thin	**enflaquecer(se)** to become thin
ennegrecer to blacken	**ennegrecerse** to become black
enorgullecer to make proud	**enorgullercerse** to become proud
enriquecer to enrich	**enriquecerse** to become rich
enrojecer to redden	**enrojecerse** to become red
entristecer to sadden	**entristecerse** to grow sad
esclarecer to make clear	**esclarecerse** to become clear
fortalecer to strengthen	**fortalecerse** to become strong
humedecer to moisten	**humedecerse** to become moist
oscurecer to darken	**oscurecer(se)** to grow dark

21.62. The same meaning may be expressed by **hacerse, ponerse, volverse, llegar a ser, venir a ser,** or **venir a parar,** all equivalent to the English *become,*[1] followed by an appropriate noun or adjective:

¿Qué se ha hecho de su hermano menor? —Se ha hecho médico; se ha trasladado a Nueva York, y a juzgar de las noticias que tengo de él, pronto se hará rico.	What has become of your youngest brother? —He has become a doctor; he has located in New York, and, to judge from the reports I have of him, he will soon become rich.
V. se pondrá malo si come más de esa ensalada de langosta.	You will make yourself sick if you eat any more of that lobster salad.
Se puso como una cereza, y bajó la mirada.	She became [as red] as a cherry, and looked down.
¡Qué caballerete se ha vuelto el nieto de V.!	What a dude your grandson has become!
No es imposible que Alahabad llegue a ser un día la capital de la India inglesa.	It is not impossible that Allahabad may one day become the capital of British India.
Llegó a ser decano de la universidad.	He became dean of the university.
Si su señor hermano sigue así, vendrá a parar en loco.	If your brother keeps on so, he will go crazy.

21.63. The expressions **ir siendo, irse haciendo,** and **irse poniendo,** have a cumulative value, equivalent to the English *getting to be:*

Este diálogo va siendo monótono.	This dialogue is getting monotonous.
La conducta del indio iba siendo sospechosa.	The conduct of the Indian was getting to be suspicious.
Al acercarnos a la frontera del Ecuador el aspecto del país iba siendo más agreste.	As we approached the frontier of Ecuador the aspect of the country kept getting wilder.
Me voy poniendo gordo.	I am getting fat.
Este calor se va haciendo insoportable.	This heat is getting to be insupportable.

21.64. The same progressive value may be obtained by making a transitive verb reflexive (i.e. intransitive), and employing its present participle in connection with **ir:**

La temperatura se va elevando.	The temperature is rising.
El orador, según avanzaba en el discurso, se iba animando.	The orator, as he progressed in his speech, became more and more animated.

---

[1] *Become* is also often expressed by reflexive verbs: **enfadarse, enojarse,** etc. *to become angry;* **impacientarse** *to become impatient;* **cansarse** *to become tired;* etc.

Las sombras se iban espesando. — The shadows were growing deeper and deeper.

Notamos que el terreno se iba elevando poco a poco. — We noticed that the ground was becoming gradually higher.

PERIPHRASTIC VERBAL EXPRESSIONS

21.65. By a *periphrastic verbal expression* is meant, primarily, a combination of two or more words to express a single verbal action; the term is here applied to a number of phrases which govern the infinitive, modifying its meaning in various ways, and are sometimes nearly equivalent to additional tense forms. Let us consider these in detail.

21.66. **Ir a,** governing an infinitive, forms a future expression with its starting point either at the present or at a past time, according to the tense assumed by **ir:**

No **vamos a acrecentar** las pesadumbres de nuestro honrado jefe, participándole la defección de aquellos hombres. — *We are* not *going to augment* the cares of our worthy chief by telling him of the defection of those men.

El cazador apuntaba con mano segura al tigre, que **iba a lanzarse** sobre él. — The hunter aimed with a steady hand at the tiger which *was about to spring* upon him.

21.67. **Acabar de,** governing an infinitive, usually expresses an action immediately past and prior either to the present or a past time, according as **acabar** is present or imperfect:

Se anuncia en los periódicos que dos nuevos cruceros acorazados **acaban de botarse.** — It is reported in the papers that two new armored cruisers *have just been launched.*

Me dejó para ir a dar la bienvenida a un señor gordiflón y mofletudo que **acababa de entrar.** — She left me to welcome a corpulent gentleman with pendulous cheeks, who *had just come in.*

Se veía también que el edificio apenas **acababa de terminarse.** — It was plain, also, that the building *had* but *just been completed.*

REMARK. In any of its tenses **acabar de** + infinitive may have the meaning of completing the act of the infinitive, at times in an idiomatic sense: **Acabo de** trabajar a las cuatro. *I finish working at four o'clock.* Juan no **acababa de** convencerse. *John wasn't completely convinced.* Esta idea **acabó de** desconcertarnos. *This idea completely upset us.*

21.68. **Haber de,** with an infinitive, expresses a probable futurity, denoting what is to (was to, etc.) happen in the ordinary course of events. In the spoken language it not infrequently is the equivalent of the future tense form:

La dirección de los negocios **ha de confiarse** a una comisión de siete accionistas.	The direction of affairs *is to be entrusted* to a board of seven stockholders.
Y entonces ¿qué **ha de hacer** una?	Then, what *is one to do?*
¿Y por qué **hemos de rehusar** los goces que se hallan esparcidos en el difícil camino de la vida? Siendo ellos tan raros, tan escasos, ¿por qué no **hemos de detenernos** y hasta **separarnos** un poco del escabroso sendero para coger todos los que se hallen a nuestro alcance?	And why *are* we *to refuse* the pleasures which are scattered along life's difficult road? Since they are so rare, so scarce, why *should* we not *stop* and even *step aside* a little from the rugged path to gather all that happen to be within our reach?
¿Cómo **había** yo **de imaginar** que había de topar contigo y con tu compañero y que me **habíais de traer** por fuerza a este lugar? (Valera, **Juanita la larga,** XXXI)	How *was I* to *imagine* that I was to run into you and your companion and that you *were to bring* me to this place by force?
El médico que con ellos venía le hizo la primera cura, le transportaron al coche, y **hubo de permanecer** en la cama algunos días. (Palacio Valdés, **Sinfonía pastoral, Andante con moto,** VI)	The physician that came with them gave him first aid, they took him to the carriage and he *was obliged to stay* in bed for several days.

21.69. Haber de is also used with reference to the present, expressing then the belief of the speaker in the truth of the following statement:

Ha de ser muy rico.	He must be very rich.
He de haberle visto en alguna parte.	I am sure I have seen him somewhere.
La palabra ha de estar en el diccionario.	The word must be in the dictionary.

21.70. Tener que denotes obligation or necessity to perform the action expressed by the following infinitive:

Tengo que marcharme.	{ I have got to go. I must be off.
Tengo que copiar cinco páginas.	I have to copy five pages.
Tengo cinco páginas que copiar.	I have five pages to copy.
Su conducta fué tal que tuve que despedirle.	His conduct was such that I had to dismiss him.

El agente tuvo que contentarse con estos insignificantes detalles. — The agent had to be contented with these insignificant details.

Me desagrada sobre manera tener que comprar el silencio de ese hombre. — I dislike extremely having to buy that man's silence.

21.71. **Tener que** also denotes provision without implying obligation:

Tengo mucho que hacer. — I have a great deal to do.

No teníamos nada que comer. — We had nothing to eat.

¿Qué tiene V. que fumar? — What have you got to smoke?

REMARK. But should a noun expressive of any sentiment, feeling or duty intervene between the two verbs, then **de** is used instead of **que**:

Tengo la honra **de avisar** a V. que... — I have the honor *to inform* you that...

V. tendrá el gusto **de presenciarlo.** — You shall have the pleasure *of witnessing it.*

Tuve la satisfacción **de verla.** — I had the satisfaction *of seeing her.*

21.72. **Tener de,** a survival from the older language, is occasionally encountered:

¿Tú no te acuerdas de él? —¿No tengo de acordarme? (Alvarez Quintero, **El genio alegre,** I) — You do not remember him? —Do I not have to remember?

XXII

HABER and HACER Used Impersonally

HABER

22.1. We have seen that **haber** has practically lost all its original meaning of possession, and that its principal value is that of an auxiliary verb to build up compound tenses in connection with a past participle. It has also one other wide acceptation not yet spoken of, namely, when it is used impersonally.

NOTE. In a few phrases, remnants of the value which it had in the past, **haber** still has the meaning of *to possess:*

El ladrón no pudo ser habido.	The thief could not be taken.
Tendrá que habérselas conmigo.	He will have to have it out with me.
El difunto, cuya ánima Dios haya.	The deceased, may God have his soul.
Más vale saber que haber. *(Proverb)*	Knowledge is better than riches. *(Lit.* it is worth more to know than to have.)

22.2. The form **he,** followed by one of the adverbs **aquí** *here,* **ahí** and **allí** *there,* has been generally associated in the popular mind with **haber.** It is probably of Arabic origin. The object, if a noun, is placed last; if a pronoun, affixed to the verb. The expression can usually be rendered *Here (There) is (are), behold,* etc. Its use is now practically limited to the written language:

He aquí las razones.	These are the reasons *(indicating what follows).*
He ahí las razones.	These are the reasons *(indicating what precedes).*
¿Dónde está mi raspador?—Helo aquí.	Where is my eraser? —Here it is.
No veo mis babuchas en ninguna parte. —Helas ahí, debajo de su butaca.	I don't see my slippers anywhere.—There they are under your easy-chair.

REMARK. In the Bible **he aquí** corresponds to the English *lo* or *behold:*

He aquí yo estableceré mi pacto con vosotros.	Behold I will establish my covenant with you.

22.3. Only the third person singular, the infinitive, past participle and present participle of **haber** are used impersonally. The compound tenses are built up in the usual manner. One irregularity is that the present indicative is not **ha** but **hay.**

IMPERSONAL CONJUGATION OF **HABER**

SIMPLE TENSES

INFINITIVE	PRESENT PARTICIPLE	PAST PARTICIPLE
haber there...to be	**habiendo** there being	**habido** there having been

INDICATIVE MOOD	SUBJUNCTIVE MOOD
PRESENT	PRESENT
hay there is, there are	**haya** there may be

INDICATIVE MOOD	SUBJUNCTIVE MOOD
IMPERFECT **había** there was, there were	IMPERFECT **hubiera** there might be
PRETERITE **hubo** there was, there were	IMPERFECT **hubiese** there might be
FUTURE **habrá** there will be	FUTURE **hubiere** there should be

CONDITIONAL

habría there would bc

COMPOUND TENSES

PAST INFINITIVE	PERFECT PARTICIPLE
haber habido there...to have been	**habiendo habido** there having been

INDICATIVE MOOD	SUBJUNCTIVE MOOD
PERFECT **ha habido** there has been, there have been	PERFECT **haya habido** there may have been
PLUPERFECT **había habido** there had been	PLUPERFECT **hubiera habido** there might have been
FUTURE PERFECT **habrá habido** there will have been	FUTURE PERFECT **hubiere habido** there should have been

CONDITIONAL PERFECT

habría habido there would have been

NOTE. The peculiar form **hay** is a combination of **ha** with the now obsolete *y, there,* from Latin *ibi, i'i, i, y.* **Ha** y is therefore homologous to the French *il y a, it has there = there is, there are.*

22.4. These forms denote the existence of what follows, and are to be rendered in English by the appropriate forms of the verb *to be* preceded by *there.* In English the verb agrees in number with the following noun or nouns, while in Spanish the verb is singular throughout:[1]

Habrá mucha fruta este año.	*There will be* much fruit this year.
Hubo un rato de silencio.	*There was* a moment of silence.
Ha habido terremotos e inundaciones.	*There have been* earthquakes and floods.
Por este lado no **había** ni arrecifes ni escollos.	On this side *there were* neither reefs nor submerged rocks.
Hay manantiales termales y alcalinos en varias provincias.	*There are* thermal and alkaline springs in several provinces.
No **hay** volcanes activos, pero existen señales de algunos ya extinguidos.	*There are* no active volcanoes, but traces exist of some now extinct.
En las regiones cubiertas de bosques de estas mirtáceas no **hay** fiebres intermitentes.	In the regions covered with forests of these myrtaceae, *there are* no intermittent fevers.
Antes de esta época **había habido** ligeras vibraciones del suelo.	Prior to this time *there had been* slight vibrations of the ground.
La región que se halla situada entre la latitud 42° y la de 56° posee un clima notablemente saludable, no **habiendo** grandes extremos de calor ni de frío.	The region which is situated between latitudes 42° and 56° has an especially healthful climate, *there being* no great extremes of heat or cold.

22.5. If the noun governed by **haber** has been previously expressed, its place may be taken by a personal pronoun, to avoid repetition:

Se creyó que habría frutas en abundancia y **las hubo.**	They thought there would be an abundance of fruit and *there was.*
Hay magníficas perspectivas en la cordillera, y no **las hay** menos hermosas y variadas en los valles.	There are magnificent views in the mountains, and *there are* no less beautiful and varied ones in the valleys.
Yo estaba temiendo un conflicto pero no **lo hubo.**	I was fearing a conflict, but *there was* none.

[1] The use of the plural form (even **hain** for **hay**) is a very general error, especially in Spanish America: **Antes, por dondequiera habían casas.** (Gallegos, **Doña Bárbara,** I, 12) *Previously, there were houses everywhere.* **En lo de Sandalio hain doña Rosa, Jacinto y Pedro.** (Lynch, **Los caranchos de la Florida,** III) *At Sandalio's there are Doña Rosa, Jacinto and Peter.*

Hay humorismo de varias clases; **lo hay** que consiste en mofarse de todo lo creado, poniendo una negación constante al lado de cualquier sentimiento humano. — There are several kinds of humor; *there is* that which consists in scoffing at all creation, placing a constant negation against every human feeling.

22.6. The infinitives **haber** and **haber habido** can be used impersonally:

Para ustedes no **puede haber** secretos en esta casa. (Benavente, **Pepa Doncel**, III, 3) — For you *there can be* no secrets in this house.

Puede haber habido ocasión. — *There may have been* an opportunity.

Solía haber un castillo en esta loma. — *There used to be* a castle on this hill.

Debe haber habido un lago aquí en otros tiempos. — *There must have been* a lake here at some time (in the past).

Si seguimos así, no **va a haber** camas en este hospital. (Baroja, **Paradox Rey**, III, 11) — If we go on like this, *there are not going to be* enough beds in this hospital.

22.7. Hay is used elliptically to denote distance:

¿Cuánto hay de aquí a Londres? — How far is it from here to London?

¿Hay mucho de aquí a Cádiz? — Is it far from here to Cádiz?

¿Cuántas millas hay de París a Berlín? — How many miles is it from Paris to Berlin?

Hay próximamente quinientas millas. — It is about 500 miles.

Hay más de A a B que de C a D. — It is farther from A to B than from C to D.

22.8. Haber used impersonally and followed by **que** and the infinitive of some other verb, denotes necessity or obligation, and may be rendered by *to be necessary:*

Había que perdonarle esta injusticia por lo que el pobre padecía. — It was necessary to forgive him this injustice on account of what the poor fellow suffered.

¿Qué hay que hacer? — What is to be done?

Hay que matarlos como se mata a los perros rabiosos. — They should be killed like mad dogs.

No había que pensar en ello. — That was not to be thought of.

Hay que tomar en cuenta, además, que la mayor parte de las ventas de mercancías importadas se hacen a plazo, concediendo los ingleses a los comerciantes sudamericanos condiciones más favorables que los norteamericanos. — It must be borne in mind, moreover, that the greater part of sales of imported goods are made on credit, the English offering the South American tradesmen more favorable terms than do the merchants of the United States.

22.9. When a noun (or equivalent word) intervenes between **haber** and **que**, the meaning of obligation or necessity is more or less modified:

Había muchos puntos de interés que visitar, pero no teníamos tiempo para todo. — There were many points of interest to visit, but we did not have time for everything.

No habiendo otro asunto que tratar, se suspendió la sesión. — There being no other business to consider, the meeting was adjourned.

Habrá más de una dificultad que vencer. — There will be more than one difficulty to overcome.

No había ningún peligro que temer por aquel lado. — There was no danger to be feared on that side.

22.10. With similar value **haber** may take a subject, the following infinitive being then introduced by **de** (cf. § 21.68):

¿Qué hemos de hacer? — What are we to do?

El gobernador ha de comer con nosotros esta tarde. — The governor is to dine with us this evening.

Mañana han de principiar las elecciones municipales. — Tomorrow the municipal elections are to begin.

¡Qué disparate! —¿Y por qué había de ser disparate? (Valera, **El comendador Mendoza,** VII) — What nonsense! —And why should it be nonsense?

22.11. The perfect **ha habido** closely approaches **ha estado** in meaning, but the two are not interchangeable. The former is impersonal and takes an object; the latter is personal and has a subject, with which it agrees in number. **Ha habido** covers the entire existence of its object, which may be but short; **ha estado** relates only to the time when its subject was in a certain place or condition:

Ha habido un incendio en la casa. — There has been a fire in the house.

(It did not exist before or after being in the house.)

Ha estado un ladrón en la casa. — There has been a thief in the house.

(His presence there was but a part of his existence.)

Ha habido durante los últimos tres días gran aglomeración de gente en la ciudad.	During the last three days there has been a great crowd of people in town.

(The crowd did not exist as a crowd before or after being in the city.)

Han estado durante los últimos tres días cuatro gobernadores en la ciudad.	During the last three days there have been four governors in town.

(Their official existence did not begin or end with that visit.)

Ha habido un cambio de administración. (*Not* ha estado.[1])	There has been a change of administration.

HACER

22.12. **Hacer** is used impersonally with two values, in reckoning time and in expressing the state of the weather. In either case only the third person singular, the infinitive, present participle and past participle are used. The object of **hacer** is either a measure of time or a noun expressing the state of the weather, and in either case to be rendered in English by the verb *to be* used impersonally:

Hace todo un año.	It is a whole year.
Hace frío, hace viento.	It is cold, it is windy.

APPLIED TO TIME

22.13. The expression of time containing **hacer** is followed by a date from which this time is reckoned; when this second clause contains a verb, it is connected with **hacer** by the conjunction **que,** equivalent to the English *since;* when it is expressed by a noun, it is introduced by the preposition **desde,** *since:*

Hace más de seis años que le vi.	It is more than six years since I saw him.
No hace más de cuatro días desde el último día de pagos.	It is not more than four days since last pay day.

22.14. **Hacer** expresses the length of time between two points. The initial point is always past; the terminal point may be past, present or future. **Hacer** corresponds to the terminal point, and is past, present or future accordingly:

Hacía diez años que...	It was ten years since...
Hace diez años que...	It is ten years since...
Hará diez años que...	It will be ten years since...

[1] The distinction between **ha habido** and **ha estado** applies to the remaining tenses of **haber** and **estar: había habido** vs. **había estado,** etc.

22.15. The verb following **hacer** corresponds to the initial point. If the initial point is a completed occurrence, the verb is pluperfect when the terminal point is past and preterite when the terminal point is present or future:

Hacía entonces seis meses que había llegado.	It was then six months since he had arrived.
Hoy hace seis meses que llegó.	It is six months today since he arrived.
Mañana hará seis meses que llegó.	It will be six months tomorrow since he arrived.
Eran entonces las siete y media; hacía veinte minutos que el sol se había ocultado detrás de las cumbres occidentales.	It was then half-past seven, and it was twenty minutes since the sun had set behind the western peaks.
Hace sólo una hora que almorcé.	It is only an hour since I breakfasted.
Hacía siete meses, día por día, que los náufragos habían sido arrojados a la isla.	It was seven months to a day since the castaways had been thrown on the island.
Hace poco tiempo que salió.	It is a short time since he went out.

22.16. When the second verb covers the entire time between the two points it is ordinarily of the same tense as **hacer**. In English the second verb is one tense anterior to the terminal point:

Hacía dos años que vivíamos en aquella casa.	We had been living for two years in that house.
Hace dos años que vivimos en esta casa.	We have been living two years in this house.
No hacía más que media hora que estaba subiendo la marea.	The tide had been rising only half an hour.
Hace más de una hora que la aguardo aquí.	I have been waiting for her here for more than an hour.
Es un secreto que hace mucho tiempo guardo en mi corazón.	It is a secret which I have been keeping for a long time in my heart.

Remark I. If the principal verb is negative, the perfect and pluperfect tenses may be used as in English:

Hacía dos años que no habíamos vivido en aquella casa.	We had not been living in that house for two years.
Hace dos años que no hemos vivido en esta casa.	We have not been living in this house for two years.

REMARK II. The form of **hacer** is at times preceded by **desde,** in which case the clauses are not connected by **que:**

Desde hacía dos años vivíamos (no habíamos vivido) en aquella casa.	We had been living (had not been living) in that house for two years.
Desde hace dos años vivimos (no hemos vivido) en esta casa.	We have been living (have not been living) in this house for two years.

22.17. The following examples show the contrast between the two usages:

Hace dos años que **estoy** en Arica.	*I have been* in Arica for two years.
Hace dos años que **estuve** en Arica.	It is two years since *I was* in Arica.
Hace más de un año que **oí** hablar de él.	It is more than a year since *I heard* of him.
Hace más de un año que **no oigo** hablar de él.	*I have* not *heard* of him for more than a year.

22.18. *Ago* or the equivalent is expressed by **hace** or some other tense of **hacer.**

(a) If the clause containing **hace,** etc., stands second, **que** is not used:

Era usted de nuestra opinión no hace mucho tiempo.	You were of our opinion not long ago.
Yo lo sabía hace dos meses.	I knew it two months ago.
El tren salió hace solamente tres minutos.	The train left only three minutes ago.
Había habido un terremoto hacía unas semanas.	There had been an earthquake some weeks before *(or* previously).
Los bramanes vienen sustituyendo a los sacerdotes de Buda desde hace muchos siglos.	The Brahmins have supplanted the priests of Buddha for some centuries past.
El niño no había comido desde hacía muchas horas.	The child had not eaten for many hours past.

(b) If the clause containing the form of **hacer** stands first, **que** will ordinarily be used (except as stated in § 22.16, REMARK II) and there will usually be an alternate translation with *since* (§ 22.13):

No hace mucho tiempo que era Vd. de nuestra opinión.	Not long ago you were of our opinion *or* It is not long since you were of our opinion.
Hace solamente tres minutos que el tren salió.	Only three minutes ago the train left *or* It is only three minutes since the train left.

Hacía unas semanas que había habido un terremoto. — Some weeks before there had been an earthquake *or* It was some weeks since there had been an earthquake.

22.19. As a special case of the preceding paragraph **hace** + imperfect indicative often implies that the act has lately ended:

Hace diez minutos que estábamos de acuerdo...pero en la primera dificultad se fué tu convencimiento. (Linares Rivas, **Cobardías,** II, 9) — Ten minutes ago we were in agreement...but at the first difficulty your conviction vanished.

¡Jesús, los años que hace que yo no lloraba! —Otros tantos hace que no vivías. (Martínez Sierra, **Primavera en otoño,** III, near end) — Heavens! The years it is since I have wept! —The same number that you haven't lived.

¿Cómo se encuentran? ¡Caramba! La verdad es que hace tiempo que no nos veíamos. (Azorín, **La fiesta,** in **Los pueblos)** — How are you? The deuce! The truth is that we haven't seen one another for a long time.

22.20. Haber also may be used impersonally to express time, in which case it usually follows the measure of time, especially in the present indicative which is then **ha** and not **hay.** This use is at present literary only, being practically obsolete in daily speech:

Dos horas ha; quince días ha. — Two hours ago; a fortnight ago.

Años ha; poco ha. — Years ago; a little while ago.

Vi al alcalde hora y media ha. — I saw the mayor an hour and a half ago.

Algunos meses ha estaba en B. — A few months ago I was in B.

Don Cipriano Lourido había más de cuatro años que no vivía en el castillo. (Pardo Bazán, **El tesoro de Gastón,** V) — Don Cipriano Lourido had not lived in the castle for more than four years.

22.21. Length of time is also idiomatically expressed by **llevar** *to carry;* colloquially by **ir** and in America by **tener:**[1]

¿Cuánto tiempo lleva V. en América? — How long have you been in America?

[1] In a few phrases **de** + a noun indicative of the passage of time serves the same purpose: **La conocían de años atrás.** (Pérez Galdós, **Misericordia,** XXIX) *They had known her for many years back.*

Encendí el cigarro y saboreé sus primeras aspiraciones con el deleite de un aficionado que llevaba dos días sin fumar.	I lit the cigar and enjoyed the first whiffs with the relish of a devotee who had gone two days without smoking.
La luna, que apenas llevaba dos días, se perdía todavía entre los rayos solares.	The moon, which was hardly two days old, was still lost within the sun's rays.
La primavera llevaba entonces dos meses de fecha.	The spring was then two months advanced.
Es que irá lo menos para los diez o doce años que dejamos de vernos. (Benavente, **Pepa Doncel,** I, 6)	The fact is that it must be going on ten or twelve years since we stopped seeing one another.
Ya van cuatro meses que no escribe. (Espina, **La esfinge maragata,** VII)	It is four months now that he hasn't written.
El viejo dice que la tribu no tiene muchos años aquí. Sus abuelos, que eran poderosos, vivieron en el valle. (Lopéz y Fuentes, **El indio, I: El oro)**	The old man says that the tribe has not been here many years. Their ancestors, who were very powerful, lived in the valley.

APPLIED TO WEATHER

22.22. In speaking of the state of the weather, **hacer** takes as its object a noun expressing the phase desired:

Hace mucho sol.	The sun shines brightly.
Ha hecho buen tiempo hoy por la mañana pero ahora lo hace malo.	It was fine this morning, but now it is bad weather.
¿Qué tiempo hace?	What kind of weather is it?
Hace un tiempo muy malsano.	The weather is very unhealthy.
¿Qué tiempo hizo ayer?	What kind of weather was it yesterday?
¿Qué tal tiempo hacía cuando V. entró?	What kind of weather was it when you came in?
Hacía mucho viento.	It was very windy.
Hacía un tiempo magnífico para viajar.	It was magnificent weather for travelling.
Se había abandonado el patio por hacer ya demasiado sol.	The courtyard had been deserted on account of being too sunny.
Hace fresco en la sombra.	It is cool in the shade.

Hacía niebla. (Baroja, **El mayorazgo de Labraz,** II, 4)	It was foggy.

REMARK. The use of **hacer** in speaking of the weather is so general that it encroaches on territory belonging also to **ser:**

Hace una mañana tan hermosa. (Benavente, **Lo cursi,** I, 8)	*It is* such a fine morning.
Hacía un día espléndido, el cielo estaba claro, el lago azul. (Baroja, **El mundo es ansí,** I, 14)	*It was* a splendid day, the sky was clear, the lake blue.

22.23. In expressing temperature, the Spanish verb corresponding to the English *to be* varies according to what is its subject. In speaking of the weather, the verb is **hacer;** of a person, or anything animate, **tener;** and of a thing, **ser** or **estar** according as the quality is inherent or accidental:

Hace calor, hace frío.	It is hot, it is cold.
Hacía un calor insoportable.	It was unbearably hot.
Me acerco a la lumbre porque tengo frío.	I approach the fire because I am cold.
Teníamos calor, por haber andado aprisa.	We were warm from having walked rapidly.
El hielo es frío.	Ice is cold.
Esta sopa está fría.	This soup is cold.
El agua no está todavía caliente.	The water is not yet hot.
La pimienta es cálida.	Pepper is hot (pungent).

REMARK. **Frío,** after **hacer** and **tener,** is a noun, and is intensified by **mucho;** after **ser** or **estar,** it is an adjective and requires **muy. Calor,** being a noun, requires **mucho:**

Tengo mucho (muchísimo) frío.	I am very cold.
Hace mucho (muchísimo) frío.	It is very cold.
Esta cama está muy fría.	This bed is very cold.
Tengo mucho (muchísimo) calor.	I am very warm.
Hace mucho (muchísimo) calor.	It is very warm.

22.24. Haber, used impersonally, also applies to certain natural phenomena, especially the visible ones. Even in these cases, however, **hacer** appears to be gradually taking the place of **haber** (cf. § 22.22):

Hay luna, hay claridad de luna.	It is moonlight.
Hay neblina; hay niebla.	It is foggy, misty.
Hay humedad; hay mucho polvo.	It is damp; it is very dusty.
Hay tempestad; hay mucho lodo.	It is stormy; it is very muddy.

NOTE. As the weather is so frequent a subject of conversation, some miscellaneous expressions may not be out of place here:

Corre mucho aire.	There is a good breeze.
El viento se refresca.	The wind freshens.
El tiempo es húmedo y caluroso, y creo que vamos a tener un temporal.	The weather is hot and damp, and I think we are going to have a storm.
En efecto, ya acabo de sentir unas gotas.	Yes indeed, I just then felt a few drops.
¿Cuándo le parece a V. que escampará?	When do you think it will stop raining?
El tiempo se ha aclarado un poco.	It has cleared up a little.
El cielo se está poniendo despejado.	The sky is getting clearer.
El tiempo se asegura.	The weather is becoming settled.
Ayer fuí sorprendido por un aguacero que me caló hasta los huesos.	Yesterday I was overtaken by a shower which drenched me to the bones.
El tiempo está pesado, el calor es muy molesto, y se ven en el cielo esas nubes cobrizas que anuncian la tempestad.	The weather is close, the heat is very oppressive, and in the sky are seen those coppery clouds which presage a storm.
Opino que el tiempo está para cambiar; los calores continúan siendo excesivos, y se conoce que la atmósfera está cargada de humedad; es realmente de temerse un período de tiempo tempestuoso.	I think the weather is about to change; the heat continues intense, and it is evident that the air is charged with moisture; it is really to be feared that we will have a spell of stormy weather.
El viento se levanta; el cielo se está cubriendo de nubes espesas.	The wind is rising; the sky is becoming covered with dense clouds.
Aquellos nubarrones amenazan resolverse en lluvias tempestuosas.	Those storm clouds threaten to turn into pouring rain.
Llueve a cántaros, y los truenos retumban con gran violencia.	It is raining pitchforks, and the thunder rolls with great violence.
Las nubes se disipan y aparece de nuevo el sol.	The clouds break and the sun comes out again.
La tormenta ha pasado.	The storm has passed.
Tenemos quince grados bajo cero.	It is fifteen degrees below zero.
Hiela de una manera atroz. Las aceras están muy resbaladizas.	It is freezing fearfully. The sidewalks are very slippery.
El tiempo se ha dulcificado algo.	The weather has moderated somewhat.

XXIII
The Subjunctive Mood

23.1. The subjunctive mood derives its name from the circumstance that it is always *subjoined* to or subservient to some leading or governing idea.

The indicative mood is based upon knowledge or certainty; the subjunctive upon doubt, desire or some emotion or mental inquietude. The indicative is employed in principal and leading clauses, and states positive certainties—things that actually are or are not—or asks direct questions. The subjunctive never makes a direct statement nor asks a direct question; it is secondary and dependent for existence either upon some finite verb or upon an uncertainty implied in some other way.

This is the fundamental distinction, pervading the various uses of the subjunctive, which must be expounded separately and step by step.

The student should bear in mind that: *a.* The subjunctive is not the only means for expressing contingence or dependence, which may be shown also by the infinitive and indicative. *b.* In many cases where the subjunctive would be adopted in a formal or elevated style, or to emphasize the feature of contingency, it would be deemed affected in more free or colloquial speech. *c.* The line of demarcation is often faint, and not susceptible of clear definition. *d.* In Spanish, as in other modern languages, the use of the subjunctive is decreasing; so that many of the delicate distinctions of the last century would appear strained in writings of the present day.

NOTE. The subjunctive mood has the same complement of tenses as the indicative; viz., present, imperfect and future, and the corresponding compound tenses formed by **haber** and a past participle.

23.2. The present subjunctive is formed in regular verbs by joining the following terminations to the stem of the verb:

		1st Conjugation	2nd and 3rd Conjugation
Sing.	1 pers.	**-e**	**-a**
	2 pers.	**-es**	**-as**
	3 pers.	**-e**	**-a**
Plur.	1 pers.	**-emos**	**-amos**
	2 pers.	**-éis**	**-áis**
	3 pers.	**-en**	**-an**

Remark. In the present indicative the characteristic vowel of the first conjugation is **a**, of the second and third, **e**. They change places in the present subjunctive.

PRESENT SUBJUNCTIVE OF THE MODEL VERBS

Sing.	1 pers.	compre	venda	viva
	2 pers.	compres	vendas	vivas
	3 pers.	compre	venda	viva
Plur.	1 pers.	compremos	vendamos	vivamos
	2 pers.	compréis	vendáis	viváis
	3 pers.	compren	vendan	vivan

23.3. The subjunctive present of irregular verbs generally follows the irregularity of the indicative. The subjunctive present of those already introduced is given below—that of **dar** being regular, and that of **estar** being irregular only in its accentuation:[1]

Querer:	quiera	quieras	quiera	queramos	queráis	quieran
Tener:	tenga	tengas	tenga	tengamos	tengáis	tengan
Venir:	venga	vengas	venga	vengamos	vengáis	vengan
Haber:	haya	hayas	haya	hayamos	hayáis	hayan
Hacer:	haga	hagas	haga	hagamos	hagáis	hagan
Ser:	sea	seas	sea	seamos	seáis	sean
Salir:	salga	salgas	salga	salgamos	salgáis	salgan
Decir:	diga	digas	diga	digamos	digáis	digan
Ir:	vaya	vayas	vaya	vayamos	vayáis	vayan
Ver:	vea	veas	vea	veamos	veáis	vean
Estar:	esté[1]	estés	esté	estemos	estéis	estén
Dar:	dé[2]	des	dé	demos	deis	den

[1] **Estar** is accented on the last syllable because that is the essential part of the verb. The root is *sta* (Latin and Italian *stare*), and the initial *e* is prefixed in Spanish because that language does not tolerate an initial *s* followed by a consonant.

[2] The accent on **dé** is merely diacritic—to distinguish it from the preposition **de.**

23.4. The present subjunctive of **haber** followed by a past participle forms the perfect subjunctive, the two tenses bearing the same relation to each other as in the indicative mood:

SING.	haya	ido,	dicho,	visto,	etc.	PLUR.	hayamos	ido,	dicho,	etc.
	hayas	"	"	"	"		hayáis	"	"	"
	haya	"	"	"	"		hayan	"	"	"

THE SUBJUNCTIVE IN SUBORDINATE CLAUSES

23.5. The application of the subjunctive mood may be divided into two heads according as the idea which requires it is expressed or not. We will first consider the various cases where it is expressed.

AFTER VERBS OF CAUSING

23.6. The principal use of the subjunctive is after verbs expressing an action calculated to cause another person or thing to act. The force of the governing verb varies from an authoritative command to a mere request or preference. What is true of the above is equally applicable to verbs of opposite effect, tending to prevent another from doing something:

COMMAND

El general ha mandado que se **fusile** a los desertores. — The general has ordered that the deserters *be shot.*

El tribunal decreta que se le **restituya** la propiedad. — The court has decreed that the property *be restored* to him.

Diré al gaitero que se **vaya** en seguida. — I will tell the bagpiper *to be off* at once.

Se resuelve: Que se **nombre** por el Señor Presidente una Comisión sobre Comisiones, con el objeto de indicar e informar al Congreso el número de comisiones que a su juicio deban establecerse. — Resolved, That there *be appointed* by the President a Committee on Committees, whose duty it shall be to designate and report to the Congress the number of committees which, in its judgment, should be appointed.

DEMAND, REQUEST

Nuestro deber exige que lo **intentemos.** — Our duty demands that we *attempt* it.

Le ruego a V. que me **ayude.** — I beg you *to aid* me.

Suplico a Vds. que no se **enfaden.** — I entreat you not *to be angry.*

El conde de Meneses está en la antecámara, y pide que Vuestra Majestad **se digne** acordarle la gracia de una corta audiencia.	Count Meneses is in the anteroom, and asks that Your Majesty *deign* to grant him the favor of a short audience.

PROPOSAL, SUGGESTION

Propongo que, resultando empate en la votación, la cuestión **se considere** resuelta negativamente.	I propose that in case of a tie vote the question *be considered* as decided in the negative.
Me permito sugerir a la Mesa que **declare** un receso de quince minutos para el cambio de opiniones acerca de esta materia.	I beg to suggest that the Chair *declare* a recess of fifteen minutes for an exchange of opinions on this matter.

DESIRE

Yo sólo deseo que **seas** venturosa. (Pérez de Ayala, **La caída de los Limones,** VII)	I only want you *to be* happy.
Una cosa es decirle no más a un hombre: "El patrón no quiere que **pase.**" (Lynch, **Palo verde,** I)	It is one thing just to say to a man: "The boss doesn't want you *to pass* through."

PERMISSION, DISPOSITION

Permitiré que **se ausente** por dos días.	I will permit him *to be absent* for two days.
Deja que Rufo me acompañe. (Payró, **Pago Chico,** X)	Let Rufus go with me.
He dispuesto que los empleados **tengan** un día festivo.	I have arranged for the clerks *to have* a holiday.

APPROVAL, PREFERENCE

Apruebo que lo **hagan.**	I approve of *their doing* it.
Prefiero que no **se lea** la carta ahora.	I prefer that the letter *be* not *read* now.
¿Tendrá V. a bien que yo no **vaya** allí?	Will you approve of *my* not *going* there?

PROHIBITION, HINDRANCE

Prohibo que **entren.**	I forbid *their coming* in.
Esto impedirá que **salga** el agua.	This will prevent the water *from getting out.*
Desapruebo que lo **hagan.**	I disapprove of *their doing* it.
No permito que los niños **jueguen** con armas de fuego.	I do not permit the children *to play* with firearms.
El objeto de las leyes es impedir que se **cometan** injusticias.	It is the object of the law to prevent injustice from *being committed.*

REMARK. **Hacer, mandar, dejar, permitir, prohibir** and a few other verbs may have the infinitive instead of the subjunctive. See §§ **19.35-19.36.**

AFTER EXPRESSIONS OF EMOTION AND FEELING

23.7. By extension of the foregoing usage the subjunctive is required after verbs expressing a feeling about an action of some other person or thing:

Extraño que V. **haya necesitado** tanto tiempo.	I am surprised that you *have needed* so much time.
Celebro que le **haya salido** tan bien su empresa.	I rejoice that his undertaking *has turned out* so well for him.
Temo que se lo **diga** a ella.	I am afraid he *will tell* it to her.
Tememos que este retardo **sea** fatal para nuestros proyectos.	We fear that this delay *may be* fatal to our plans.
Siento que Vds. se **hayan** visto precisados a aguardarme.	I am sorry you *have been obliged* to wait for me.

REMARK. When affirmative, **esperar** *to hope, to expect* and **temer** *to fear* are quite often followed by the indicative, especially the future indicative instead of the present subjunctive, conditional instead of imperfect subjunctive and also perfect indicative instead of perfect subjunctive:

Mañana espero que **podremos** hablar con tus padres con más tranquilidad. (Benavente, **Rosas de otoño,** II, 9)	Tomorrow I hope that we *shall be able* to speak more calmly with your parents.
Ya temí que **no vendríais.** (Benavente, **Los intereses creados,** I, 2, 6)	Of course I feared that you *wouldn't come.*
Temo con sobrado motivo que **ha llegado** el momento. (Martínez Sierra, **Madame Pepita,** II)	I fear with more than enough reason that the moment *has come.*

AFTER IMPERSONAL VERBS AND EXPRESSIONS

23.8. When impersonal verbs that do not state a certainty characterize the action of a following verb with an expressed subject, that verb is subjunctive:

Conviene que V. se lo **avise.**	It is proper for you *to inform* him of it.
Importa que **lleguen** a tiempo.	It is important for them *to arrive* in time.
Bastará que yo **recoja** algo más las costuras debajo del brazo.	It will do if *I take in* the seams under the arms a little more.
Precisa que nos **mantengamos** preparados.	It is necessary that *we hold* ourselves in readiness.

23.9. The subjunctive is likewise used when **ser** (or **estar**), used impersonally, is followed by an adjective not stating a certainty—or noun having the value of such adjective:

Es lástima que **tenga** V. tanta prisa.	It is a pity that you *are* in such a hurry.
Es cosa singular que no **se haya tratado** nunca de este asunto.	It is a singular thing that this subject *has* never *been treated* of.
Es muy raro que **se encuentren** ballenas en esta latitud.	It is very rare that whales *are met* with in this latitude.
Es dudoso que **hallen** un coche a una hora tan avanzada.	It is doubtful if they *find* a hack at so late an hour.
No es conveniente que V. mismo lo **haga.**	It is not proper for you *to do* it yourself.
Es tiempo de que **partamos.**	It is time for us *to start.*
Es triste que **haya visto** fracasar todas sus tentativas.	It is sad that he *has seen* all his attempts fail.
Es muy probable que, dentro de unos días, los de Bu-Tata nos **ataquen.** (Baroja, **Paradox Rey,** II, 9)	It is very probable that, within a few days, the Bu-Tatans *will attack* us.
Es posible que ya **se haya roto** el encanto para siempre. (Camba, **Aventuras de una peseta,** I, 15)	It is possible that the charm *has* now *been broken* forever.

REMARK. A verb modified by **acaso, quizá(s), tal vez** and even by other adverbs or adverbial phrases of similar meaning, may be in the subjunctive, in which case these adverbs have the effect of an expression of possibility. The meaning is not appreciably different when the indicative is used:

Acaso **haya tenido** demasiada confianza en la indulgencia de usted. (Palacio Valdés, **Sinfonía pastoral, Andante con moto,** VI)	Perhaps I *have had* too much confidence in your forbearance.
Volverá al sur, y quizás entonces sí **llegue** al reino del Dorado. (Arciniegas, **Los alemanes en la conquista de América,** XI)	He will turn to the south and perhaps then indeed he *may reach* the kingdom of El Dorado.
Tal vez esa recámara **comunique** con la sala y por ella **pueda** entrar. (Azuela, **Los de abajo,** II, 4)	Perhaps that room *leads* to the parlor and I *can* enter through it.

23.10. The impersonal expression of passive value (§ **21.55,** REMARK), composed of **ser** connected with a following infinitive by **de,** likewise has the subjunctive if the infinitive is a verb of causing, emotion or feeling, or uncertainty:

Es de esperar(se) que la noche nos **permita** evadir sus pesquisas.	It is to be hoped that the night *will permit* us to elude their search.
Es de temer(se) que el gasto **exceda** a los ingresos.	It is to be feared that the expenditure *will exceed* the receipts.
Es de desear(se) que, a fin de disminuir el costo de la obra, **se aprovechen** en cuanto sea posible las vías férreas existentes.	It is desirable that, in order to diminish the cost of the work, existing railroad lines *be utilized* as far as possible.

AFTER EXPRESSIONS OF DENIAL OR DOUBT

23.11. When the verb of the principal clause denies, or expresses uncertainty, doubt or disbelief about the action of another person or thing, the verb expressing that action is subjunctive:

Niego que el ebanista **tenga** la intención de devolver el cepillo.	I deny that the cabinetmaker *intends* to return the plane.
Dudo que **sea** culpable.	I doubt *his being* guilty.
Apenas puedo creer que ella **haya dicho** tal cosa.	I can hardly believe that she *has said* such a thing.
¿Puede ser verdad que **trate** de engañarnos?	Can it be true that he *is trying* to deceive us?
No me imagino ni por un momento que **abrigue** la menor sospecha acerca de nuestros proyectos.	I do not suppose even for an instant that he *entertains* the least suspicion with regard to our plans.
No creo que mi padre **se alegre** mucho de este descubrimiento.	I do not think my father *will be* very *glad* of this discovery.
¿Cree V. que **se haya rechazado** el proyecto de ley para el aumento de mi pensión?	Do you believe the bill for the increase of my pension *has been rejected?*

REMARK I. In questions, if the dependent verb relates to the future, it is usually put in the future indicative:

¿Cree V. que llegaremos a tiempo?	Do you think we will arrive in time?
¿Suponen Vds. que se publicará mi novela?	Do you suppose my novel will be published?

REMARK II. **Parecer, suponer** and **sospechar,** though ordinarily indicating certainty, may function as expressions of uncertainty and occasionally have their dependent verb in the subjunctive even in the affirmative sentence:

Ese muchacho parece que me **odie,** que nos **persiga** como si sintiera celos. (Blasco Ibáñez, **El "femater", in Cuentos valencianos)**	That boy seems *to* (*or* It seems that, etc.) *hate* me, *to pursue* us as if he were jealous.

Supongo que ésta **sea** la única noche en que le tengamos en nuestra compañía. (Pérez de Ayala, **La pata de la raposa, Obras Completas** edition, 1923, page 172)	I suppose that this *may be* the last night that we shall have you among us.
Sospecho que **haya sido** Manolo Lasso. (Palacio Valdés, **La hija de Natalia,** II, 3)	I suspect that it *may have been* Manolo Lasso.

REMARK III. **Comprender, explicar** and verbs of equivalent value may function as expressions of approval (or disapproval) and preference (cf. § 23.6) and will then introduce a subjunctive:

Comprendo que hasta ahora **no estuviera** usted muy satisfecho a mi lado. (Benavente, **La propia estimación,** II, 4)	I understand *(or* find natural) that you *shouldn't be* very satisfied at my side.
¿Cómo se explica que desde entonces acá no **haya** usted **dado** paso alguno? (Pereda, **La puchera,** IX)	How is it explainable *(or* justifiable) that up to now you *have taken* no step?

AFTER A RELATIVE

23.12. After a relative pronoun referring to a person, thing or idea which is either unknown or not definitely known, the verb of the dependent clause is subjunctive:[1]

Quiero un guía que **hable** inglés.	I want a guide who *speaks* English.
No tardaremos en encontrar algún aldeano que nos **enseñe** el camino.	We shall not be long in meeting some peasant who *will show* us the road.
Debemos hacer cuanto **esté** de nuestra parte para ocultar nuestra presencia en la vecindad.	We must do all that *is* in our power to hide our presence in the neighborhood.
El capitán ha prometido una recompensa al primero de la tripulación que **aborde** un buque enemigo.	The captain has promised a reward to the first one of the crew who *boards* a vessel of the enemy.
Si V. quiere una hoja cuyo temple **sea** bueno, yo podré proporcionársela.	If you want a blade whose temper *shall be* good, I can furnish you with one.

[1] A clause with **que,** seemingly relative, occasionally has the effect of a condition in English: **Ciertas cosas acabarían con la paciencia del santo Job que resucitase.** (Pardo Bazán, **Los pazos de Ulloa,** VII) *Certain things would end the patience of saintly Job if he were to come to life.*

Haré construir por este lado una torre tan alta que **domine** a todas las cercanías. — I will have a tower built on this side so high as *to overlook* all the surrounding country.

Trate V. de hablar de tal modo que nadie **se ofenda.** — Try to speak in such wise that no one *will be offended.*

23.13. In the same manner a subjunctive follows a relative adverb of manner or place when the manner or place is not definitely known:

La pieza se amueblará como V. **quiera.** — The room will be furnished as you *may wish.*

Iré a donde V. me **mande.** — I will go where you *may send* me.

23.14. Hence the indefinite expressions formed by appending the termination **quiera** to relative pronouns and adverbs are followed by a subjunctive if uncertainty is implied (cf. § 25.30). The **quiera** is itself the subjunctive present of **querer,** and corresponds to the English appended *ever* or *soever,* meaning *what you will:*

Quienquiera que **sea.** — Whoever he *may be.*

Dondequiera[1] que se **encuentre** Vd. — Wherever you *may find* yourself.

Cuandoquiera que **vuelvan.** — Whenever they *return.*

Comoquiera que **obremos.** — However we *manage.*

Cualquiera disculpa que **ofrezca.** — Whatever excuse he *offers.*

23.15. Cualquiera and its plural **cualesquiera** may drop the final **a** when immediately preceding a noun, but not otherwise. The apocopation of the other words is now antiquated:

Cualesquier noticias que nos traigan. — Whatever news they *bring* us.

Cualesquier esfuerzos que V. haga. — Whatever efforts you *make.*

REMARK. **Quequiera** is not in use; its place is taken by **cualquier[a] cosa** *whatever:*

Cualquier cosa que **digan.** — Whatever they *say.*

Cualquiera cosa que V. **haya hecho** por mi hermano. — Whatever you *may have done* for my brother.

Apuesto cualquier cosa a que **no** lo **intenta.** — I'll bet anything that he *won't attempt* it.

23.16. Cualquiera may be employed as an adjective before a noun of either number, or after a singular noun preceded by the indefinite article; it is also used as a pronoun:

---

[1] **Dondequiera** has an alternate form **doquiera** or **doquier,** found in poetic style. **Siquiera** *at least, even* may become **siquier** in similar circumstances.

Cualquier día; cualesquier criadas.	Any day at all; any servants at all.
Un defecto cualquiera.	Any fault at all.
Cualquiera de los buques.	Whichever of the vessels.
Aquel hijo no era un hijo cualquiera. (Pérez Galdós, **Torquemada en la hoguera,** III)	That son was not an ordinary son.

REMARK I. As a result of being used ironically, **cualquiera** has in colloquial usage and particularly in exclamatory sentences, the value of *no* or *nobody:*

¡Anda! ¡Cualquiera diría que es usted gallego! Con esas palabritas gitanas, más parece usted un gaditano. (Palacio Valdés, **La hermana San Sulpicio,** III)	Go on! Nobody would say that you are a Galician! With that gypsy-like talk you seem a native of Cádiz rather.

REMARK II. *Whatever* may also be expressed by **sea el que quiera,** the demonstrative **el** agreeing with a following noun. The phrase is followed by a subjunctive preceded by **que:**

Sean las que quiera las escalas que **haga** el vapor, no por eso tendremos ocasión de ver mucho del país.	Whatever be the landings that the steamer *makes* we will not necessarily have a chance to see much of the country.
Sean los que quiera los obstáculos que **se opongan** a nuestro progreso, no dejaremos de conseguir el fin apetecido.	Whatever obstacles *may oppose* our advance, we shall not fail to reach the desired goal.

23.17. The subjunctive, if uncertainty is implied (cf. 25.31), is found with the formula of similar value, **por**. . .**que,** the interval being filled by an adjective or adverb. The construction is to be rendered in English by *however,* followed by an adjective or adverb:

Por atrevidos que **sean** sus proyectos.	However daring his plans *may be.*
Por cuerdamente que **obren.**	However prudently they *act.*
Por mucho que V. **diga,** no la convencerá.	However much you *say,* you will not convince her.
Por muy sencilla que **parezca** a primera vista aquella pregunta.	However simple that question *may appear* at first sight.

23.18. When the intervening word is a noun, it is preceded by **mucho** or **más,** the formula being then translated by *whatever:*

Por muchas riquezas que **tenga,** bien pronto les verá el fin.	Whatever riches he *has,* he will soon see the end of them.

Por más dinero que **gane**, nunca se hará rico. — Whatever money he *earns* he will never get rich.

Por muchos disparates que V. **haga**, no me reiré de V. — Whatever blunders you *make* I shall not laugh at you.

23.19. The dependent verb is also subjunctive after a relative when the antecedent clause is negative, restrictive, or interrogative requiring a negative answer:

No conozco a nadie que **pueda** igualarle. — I know no one who *can* equal him.

No puede hallar ningún criado que **quiera** servirle. — He cannot find any servant who *is willing* to serve him.

Aquí no hay cosa que **merezca** nuestra atención. — There is nothing here which *deserves* our attention.

Los dos hermanos gemelos son tan parecidos en todo que viéndolos juntos no hay quien los **distinga.** — The twin brothers are so much alike in every respect that there is no one who *can distinguish* them on seeing them together.

¿Acaso existe otra nación a cuya vista **se despliegue** el espectáculo de un porvenir tan grande e inspirador; otro pueblo, digo, que **tenga** como éste, territorios tan amplios, habitantes tan adelantados, leyes tan justas y una libertad tan asegurada? — Does any other nation exist before whose gaze *is unfolded* the prospect of so grand and inspiring a future; any other people, I say, which *possesses,* as this does, such extensive territories, such enlightened inhabitants, such just laws and such a firmly-founded liberty?

Remark. The subjunctive may be employed after a relative preceded by a superlative or word of superlative value (**primero, último, único**). This, when used, serves to modify the force of the superlative or to suggest that the statement is merely an opinion:

Esta es la mejor presentación del asunto que yo **haya visto.** — This is the best presentation of the subject that I *have seen.*

Es el médico más hábil que yo **haya conocido.** — He is the most able physician that I *have known.*

Este es el amor que nos ennoblece, el único digno del ser humano y que **merezca** tal nombre. (Palacio Valdés, **La fe,** XI) — This is the love that ennobles us, the only one worthy of the man, the only one that *deserves* such a name.

AFTER CONJUNCTIVE EXPRESSIONS

23.20. The theory has been advanced by some that certain conjunctions govern the subjunctive mood. A more correct view is that these conjunctions are themselves required by a previous idea which requires also the subjunctive. This is evidenced by the fact that often the same conjunction may be followed by a subjunctive or an indicative according to the leading idea of the sentence.

The most important of these conjunctions and conjunctive expressions are given in detail below; it is to be borne in mind that the subjunctive is employed after them only when the leading verb or idea expresses *causation,* or when the dependent verb implies *negation* or *uncertainty.*

PURPOSE

23.21. The subjunctive is normally used after the following conjunctions, to express the purpose or intention of an action:

a que *(only after an introductory expression implying movement)* in order that

a fin de que in order that

de manera que so as, so that

de modo que so as, so that

para que in order that

porque (por que) so that, in order that

que so that, in order that *(after an expression of command)*

no sea (fuera, fuese) que lest, in order that not

EXAMPLES

Me ha llevado mi marido a San Sebastián a que **vea** una corrida de toros. (Baroja, **El mundo es ansí,** III, 1)	My husband has taken me to San Sebastian in order that I *might see* a bull fight.
Las muestras se hallan rotuladas con el mayor esmero, a fin de que los visitantes **sepan** a que atenerse.	The specimens are labelled with the greatest care in order that the visitors *may know* what they are looking at.
Colocaré el reverbero de manera que su luz **se derrame** sobre el libro de V.	I will place the lamp so that its light *shall be shed* on your book.
Lo pongo aquí de modo que no lo **vea** nadie.	I put it here so that no one *shall see* it.
De noche ponen linternas sobre los montones de morrillos para que los transeúntes no **tropiecen** con ellos.	At night they put lanterns on the heaps of rubble so that the passers-by *shall* not *stumble* against them.

Para todo esto que le he dicho, necesitamos tres mil reales, y no digo cuatro porque **no se asuste.** (Pérez Galdós, **Torquemada en la hoguera,** VII) — For all this that I have told you we need three thousand reals, and I don't say four so that you *won't take alarm.*

Ven que te **abrace.** — Come, that I *may embrace* you.

Colóquese V. aquí que no le **vean.** — Place yourself here so that they *may* not *see* you.

Importúnele V. tanto que se **vea** forzado a pagarle. — Dun him so much that he *will have* to pay you.

Pero no me atrevo a tener esperanzas, no sea que las **perdamos** esta tarde. (Pérez Galdós, **Torquemada en la hoguera,** VIII) — But I don't dare to have hopes, lest we *lose* them this afternoon.

23.22. NEGATIVE RESULT

sin que without — **que...no** that...not, without

EXAMPLES

No podremos pasar las líneas sin que los piquetes **hagan** fuego sobre nosotros. — We cannot pass the lines without the pickets *firing* on us.

La oscuridad no era tanta que no **consintiese** distinguir los bultos. (Palacio Valdés, **José,** VI) — The darkness was not so great that it *did* not *allow* objects to be made out.

23.23. Que no, after a negative, when introducing a subjunctive clause is often equivalent to *without:*

Nadie oía el relato **que no** virtiese lágrimas. — No one heard the story *without* shedding tears.

Nunca dió una promesa **que no** la cumpliese. — He never made a promise *without* fulfilling it.

A ninguna parte se volvían los ojos **que no** se presentasen objetos de horror. — One could not turn his eyes in any direction *without* meeting objects of horror.

REMARK. The same result may be obtained by **sin** with an infinitive, or **sin que** with a subjunctive (when there is a change of subject, cf. § 25.24):

Nadie oía el relato sin verter lágrimas. — No one heard the story without shedding tears.

Nunca dió una promesa sin cumplirla. — He never made a promise without fulfilling it.

A ninguna parte se volvían los ojos sin que se presentasen objetos de horror. — One could not turn his eyes in any direction without meeting objects of horror.

SUPPOSITION

23.24. The subjunctive is employed after the following conjunctive expressions indicating supposition:

dado que, **dado caso que** — in case, supposing that
en caso de que, **para el caso de que** — in case
sea que, **ya sea que** — if, whether
supóngase que, **suponiendo que**, **supuesto que** — supposing

EXAMPLES

Dado que él **haya divulgado** el proyecto, como se dice, no veo que tengamos por qué desesperarnos. — Supposing he *has divulged* the plan, as they say, I do not see that we have reason to give up.

En caso de que **venga** el alcalde, ¿qué le diremos? — In case the mayor *comes,* what shall we tell him?

Será conveniente apartarnos todos del sitio para el caso de que la pieza **reviente.** — It will be advisable for all of us to get out of the way lest the piece *should burst.*

Ella tiene necesidad de nuestro auxilio, sea que lo **merezca** o no. — She needs our assistance, whether she *deserves* it or not.

Aun suponiendo que **sea** un ciervo, no es posible que nuestras balas le alcancen a una distancia de media milla. — Even supposing that it *be* a deer, it is not possible for our bullets to hit him at a distance of half a mile.

23.25. PROVISO

como[1], **con tal (de) que**, **siempre que** — provided that
a condición (de) que — on condition that

EXAMPLES

Como no le **echen** a perder con elogios tontos y malos ejemplos, ese chico tal vez sea una maravilla. (Alas, **El Señor; y lo demás son cuentos**) — Provided that they don't (*or* Unless they) *spoil* him with silly praise and bad examples, that boy may perhaps be a wonder.

[1] In formal composition the subjunctive, almost solely in a past tense nowadays, is also used with **como** meaning *as, since:* **Como tardasen en arbolar la bandera negra, signo de que ya estaban muertos, la muchedumbre se amotinó.** (Pérez de Ayala, **La caída de los Limones,** XI) *As they were a long time in hoisting the black flag, a sign that they were already dead, the throng became rebellious.*

Terminaré este capítulo a eso de las nueve, con tal que no **vengan** visitas que me interrumpan. — I shall finish this chapter about nine o'clock provided no visitors *come* to interrupt me.

Consentiremos en asegurar su casa con tal de que **mande** demoler las barracas contiguas. — We are willing to insure his house provided he *will have* the adjoining sheds torn down.

Consiento en comprar la casa por el precio mencionado, siempre que su dueño **mande** reparar los establos. — I am willing to buy the house at the price named, provided the owner *has* the stables repaired.

Mandaré hacer el apeo a condición de que V. **pague** la mitad de los gastos. — I will have the survey made on condition that you *pay* half of the expense.

23.26. EXCEPTION

a menos que, **a no ser que** — unless

excepto que except that

salvo que save that, unless

EXAMPLES

No saldré a menos que V. me **acompañe.** — I shall not go out unless you *accompany* me.

Es decir, a no ser que **se me avise** lo contrario. — That is to say, unless *I am informed* to the contrary.

Partiré mañana a menos que **haga** mal tiempo. — I shall start tomorrow unless the weather *be* bad.

Nada impedirá que lleguemos a San Francisco en cuatro días excepto que **acontezca** un choque o un descarrilamiento. — Nothing will prevent us from arriving in San Francisco in four days unless *there is* a collision or the train runs off the track.

Salvo que los precios **bajen** de un modo inesperado, ganaré por lo menos el ochenta por ciento. — Unless prices *fall* unexpectedly I shall gain at least eighty per cent.

23.27. CONCESSION (cf. § 25.32)

aunque, **así** — although, though

bien que although

mas que[1] although

por más que although

aun cuando even though, even if

a pesar de que, **a despecho de que** — in spite of

no obstante que, **sin embargo de que** — notwithstanding that

[1] **Mas que,** not infrequent in colloquial Spanish, at least in Spanish America, is not often encountered in the literary language: **[Es] buen revolucionario, digo, mas que antes haya sido catrín.** (Guzmán, **La sombra del caudillo,** III, 4) *He is a good rebel, I say, although he may have been a fop before.*

EXAMPLES

No acabará V. el traje para la hora prometida aunque **trabaje** toda la noche.	You will not finish the gown by the hour promised, although you *work* all night.
No faltaré a la cita, así **tenga** que pasar el río a nado.	I shall not break my appointment, though I *have* to swim the river.
Es un joven que, a pesar de que al principio **tenga** muchos obstáculos que vencer, no tardará en cobrar fama.	He is a young man who, in spite of (the fact) that he *may have* many obstacles to overcome at first, will not fail to make a name for himself.
Aun cuando la rapidez de su marcha **exceda** quince nudos, no nos alcanzarán con la delantera que les llevamos.	Even if their speed *be over* fifteen knots, they will not overtake us with the start we have on them.
Lo que se llama "la Sociedad" a menudo rechazará a un hombre sin embargo de que su carácter **sea** intachable, sus modales distinguidos y sus sentimientos elevados.	What is called "Society" will often reject a man notwithstanding that his character *may be* without fault, his manners refined and his sentiments elevated.
La marquesa, bien que no **hubiera entendido,** aprobó con vehemencia. (Pérez de Ayala, **Prometeo,** IV)	Although the marchioness *might* not *have understood,* she approved vehemently.
Supongo en esta vida que vivimos, por más que **sirva** para ganar la otra, un fin y un propósito en sí. (Valera, **El comendador Mendoza,** V)	I suppose in this life that we live, although it *may serve* to gain the next, an end and a purpose in itself.

23.28. DENIAL

lejos de que so far from

Lejos de que la adversidad **sea** un mal, es a menudo un remedio, un contraveneno de la prosperidad.	So far from adversity *being* an evil, it is often a cure, an antidote to prosperity.

23.29. TEMPORAL CLAUSES

After the following and other conjunctive expressions of time or extent, the subjunctive is required when futurity is implied:

a medida que according as
antes (de) que before (cf. § 25.36)
así que as soon as
como as, whenever

cuando when
después (de) que after
en cuanto as soon as; as far as
hasta donde as far as
hasta el momento en que until the time when
hasta que until[1]
luego que as soon as
mientras (que)[2] while
para cuando by the time when
siempre que whenever
tan pronto como as soon as

EXAMPLES

Me encargo de corregir las pruebas a medida que **lleguen** de la imprenta.	I will take care to correct the proof according as it *comes* from the printer's.
Hay que estar en Arequipa antes de que **salga** el sol.	We must be in Arequipa before the sun *rises.*
Le mandaré a V. los fondos como V. los **necesite.**	I will send you the funds as you *need* them.
Se lo diré cuando **venga.**	I will tell him when he *comes.*
Después que **haya hecho** visar mi pasaporte, estaré a la disposición de V.	After I *have had* my passport viséed I shall be at your disposal.
En cuanto V. la **conozca** mejor, la hallará simpática e instruida.	As soon as you *get* better *acquainted with* her, you will find her congenial and intelligent.
Trataré de complacer a V. en cuanto me **sea** posible.	I shall endeavor to oblige you as far as *may be* possible for me.
Viajaremos en coche hasta donde el camino **sea** practicable.	We shall travel in a carriage as far as the road *is* passable.
Juzgo prudente el echar el cerrojo hasta el momento en que no **haya** que temer tan mala visita.	I deem it prudent to bolt the door until the time when there *will be* no *need* to fear such an unpleasant visit.
Quedaremos al abrigo de esta choza hasta que la tempestad **se modere.**	We will remain under the shelter of this cabin until the storm *moderates.*
Luego que V. los **vea,** admitirá que no he exagerado su tamaño.	As soon as you *see* them you will admit that I have not exaggerated their size.
Seguiré la pista del asesino mientras que me **sostengan** las piernas.	I shall follow the trail of the murderer while my legs *sustain* me.

[1] With **esperar** and **aguardar a que** is very often used instead of **hasta que,** provided the subjunctive is called for: **Esperemos a que te entiendas y nos entendamos.** (Pérez de Ayala, **Prometeo,** II) *Let us wait until you know your own mind and we know each other's mind.*

[2] The omission of **que** is usual nowadays, except in the sense of *whereas.*

Los españoles no nos incorporaremos por completo a Europa mientras no nos **desarrimemos** de los faroles y **echemos** a andar. (Camba, **La rana viajera, España,** VI) — We Spaniards shall not be completely incorporated into Europe until we *separate* ourselves from lampposts and start walking.

Estaremos listos para la partida para cuando **salga** la luna. — We will be ready for the start by the time the moon *rises.*

Siempre que V. **necesite** al portero, no tendrá V. que hacer más que tocar el botón del timbre eléctrico. — Whenever you *need* the messenger, you will have but to touch the button of the electric bell.

Cuanto más **achiquemos** nuestro mundo, más dueños seremos de él. (Benavente, **Titania,** III, 13) — The more we *reduce* the size of our world, the more we shall be masters of it.

REMARK. With **mientras (que)** both indicative and subjunctive (cf. § 25.36) are used, the latter conveying an idea of proviso, when the act continues into the future (cf. § 25.36):

Hazme de almorzar mientras yo voy a echar al correo esta carta. (Alarcón, **Moros y cristianos,** IV) — Make breakfast for me while I go to mail this letter.

Mientras Esteban **esté** vivo, la expedición desafiará todos los peligros. (Arciniegas, **Los alemanes en la conquista de América,** X) — So long as Stephen *is* alive, the expedition will defy all dangers.

PERFECT SUBJUNCTIVE

23.30. The perfect subjunctive occurs only in connection with an independent verb in the present or future tense and represents an action as completed before the time indicated by that verb:

Es un milagro que no se **haya roto** el pescuezo. — It is a wonder that he *has* not *broken* his neck.

Le prestaré a V. este libro cuando lo **haya leído** yo mismo. — I will lend you this book when I *have read* it myself.

Se habrá ganado mucho cuando se **haya llegado a adquirir** aquella común confianza sobre la que debe descansar toda amistad internacional. — Great will have been the gain when we *have acquired* that common confidence upon which all international friendship must rest.

GENERAL REMARKS

23.31. Certain verbs, mostly intransitive, require a preposition both in English and Spanish to connect their meaning with a noun object. But while in English this preposition is omitted before a dependent verb, it is retained in Spanish, the conjunction **que** following it:

Todo contribuye a la felicidad de Vds.	Everything contributes to your happiness.
Todo contribuye a que sean Vds. felices.	Everything contributes to your being happy.
Me alegro del restablecimiento de la Srta. hermana de V.	I am glad of your sister's recovery.
Me alegro **de que** la Srta. hermana de V. esté restablecida.	I am glad *that* your sister has recovered.
Se admira **de que** hayamos logrado aprender el ruso.	He wonders *that* we have succeeded in learning Russian.
Señores, la Mesa insiste **en que** las actas sean suscritas por cada uno de los miembros.	Gentlemen, the Chair insists *that* the minutes be signed by each of the members.

REMARK. Omission of the preposition is occasionally encountered, especially after adjectives (**estar seguro que** *to be sure that;* cf. § 23.32) in conversational speech: **Me alegro que me encuentre aquí.** (Pérez Galdós, **La familia de León Roch,** II, 3, 19) *I am glad that he should find me here.* **Me acuerdo que la sangre seguía golpeándome las sienes.** (Cela, **La familia de Pascual Duarte,** p. 91 of 1946 edition) *I remember that my temples continued to throb.*

23.32. The preposition is in like manner retained after an adjective, participle or noun, when followed by **que** and a dependent verb:

Estamos muy contentos **con que** no se haya perdido el original.	We are very glad *that* the original has not been lost.
Estoy sorprendido **de que** el trabajo haya exigido tanto tiempo.	I am surprised *that* the work has taken so much time.
Tengo el más sincero deseo **de que** se adopten lo más pronto posible esas medidas.	I have the most sincere wish *that* those measures be adopted as soon as possible.
Hemos tenido sumo cuidado **en que** la doctrina de los modelos sea ejemplarísima y moral.	We have taken great care *that* the teaching of the examples may be most exemplary and moral.

23.33. The idea which causes the dependent verb to be subjunctive is not necessarily expressed by a verb. The ideas of causation and emotion require either a verb or an equivalent noun; but those of negation and uncertainty may be conveyed by a noun, pronoun, adverb or conjunction:

Su objeción a que **emprendamos** el negocio nos tiene con poco cuidado.	His objection to *our undertaking* the business gives us little concern.
Sólo el temor de que su padre le **castigue** le hace observar buena conducta.	Only the fear that his father *will punish* him makes him observe good behavior.
No hay peligro de que los equipajes se **extravíen.**	There is no danger *of* the baggage *going astray.*
La sentencia es que **pague** una multa de cien pesos, o a falta de esto, que **sufra** tres meses de prisión.	The sentence is that he *pay* a fine of 100 pesos, or, in default thereof, that he *receive* three months' imprisonment.

23.34. Although such usage is relatively rare outside of business letters, **que** may be omitted before a noun clause (§§ **23.6-23.11**). On the other hand, it is quite frequently omitted if the sentence contains another clause beginning with **que**:

Me permito suplicar a V. se sirva enviarme, a vuelta de correo, dos ejemplares del mapa de Méjico levantado por usted.	I beg to request you to be so kind as to send me, by return mail, two copies of the map of Mexico prepared by you.
Tememos sean socorridos los enemigos.	We are afraid the enemy will be reinforced.
Es de esperarse no tarden mucho en presentarse.	It is to be hoped they will not be long in presenting themselves.
Espero se digne V. recordar que yo no he abusado nunca de esta autoridad.	I hope that you will be good enough to remember that I have never abused this authority.
Me dijo que me agradecía la noticia y que sentía no se la hubiese dado primero. (Palacio Valdés, **La hermana San Sulpicio,** XI)	He told me that he was grateful to me for the information and that he was sorry that I hadn't given it to him before.
Le encargó le dijese que una señora deseaba verla *(idem,* XVI)	She directed her to say to her that a lady wanted to see her.
Lo he llevado y traído por tantos lugares absurdos, que temo se niegue a hacer nuevas exploraciones. (Camba, **La ciudad automática,** I, 12)	I have led him this way and that about so many ridiculous places that I fear he may refuse to make new explorations.

TENSES OF THE SUBJUNCTIVE FORMED FROM THE PRETERITE STEM

NOTE. In the preceding portions of this chapter have been set forth the principal cases in which the subjunctive mood is required. The illustrations have been confined to the present and perfect tenses. In treating the remaining tenses it is to be understood that we are dealing with cases in which the subjunctive mood is required, and that we have only to consider what tense of that mood is to be adopted.

23.35. The imperfect (both forms) and future tenses are made in all cases by adding the terminations in the table below to the stem of the preterite as found by removing the termination of the first person singular. If that is irregular, the same irregularity pervades the tenses of the subjunctive. In regular verbs, this is the same thing as adding the termination to the stem of the verb as obtained by removing the infinitive ending.

TABLE OF TERMINATIONS

IMPERFECT -ra Form		IMPERFECT -se Form		FUTURE	
1 CONJ.	2 AND 3 CONJ.	1 CONJ.	2 AND 3 CONJ.	1 CONJ.	2 AND 3 CONJ.
-ara	**-iera**	**-ase**	**-iese**	**-are**	**-iere**
-aras	**-ieras**	**-ases**	**-ieses**	**-ares**	**-ieres**
-ara	**-iera**	**-ase**	**-iese**	**-are**	**-iere**
-áramos	**-iéramos**	**-ásemos**	**-iésemos**	**-áremos**	**-iéremos**
-arais	**-ierais**	**-aseis**	**-ieseis**	**-areis**	**-iereis**
-aran	**-ieran**	**-asen**	**-iesen**	**-aren**	**-ieren**

IMPERFECT AND PLUPERFECT SUBJUNCTIVE

23.36. The imperfect tense forms are interchangeable (except in expressing conditions, as shown in Chapter XXIV).[1] It is found, however, that the **-ra** form is the more frequently used.

23.37. The imperfect subjunctive is used after a governing verb in the present or future tense when the action of the subjunctive verb is wholly past:

Es muy dudoso que Marco Antonio **fuese** un hombre tan disoluto y abandonado como Cicerón le pinta.	It is quite doubtful whether Mark Antony *was* as dissolute and abandoned a man as Cicero paints him.

[1] The use of a past tense of the subjunctive as a substitute for the conditional is not amenable to the ordinary rules of the subjunctive, and will be treated of separately.

Algún día bendecirás a Dios de que tu padre **tuviese** la previsión de inculcarte la importancia de fijarte cuidadosamente en los pormenores.

Some day you will praise God that your father *had* the foresight to inculcate in you the importance of attending carefully to minor details.

23.38. The imperfect subjunctive is also used after a governing verb in any past tense, when the action of the subjunctive verb is simultaneous or subsequent to (but not prior to) the governing verb:

El muro era acantilado sin puntos salientes; y parecía imposible que un hombre **bajara** por aquel sitio.

The wall was vertical without projecting points; and it seemed impossible for a man *to descend* at that place.

Le dije a la niña que se **alejase** del pozo, porque temía que cayese dentro.

I told the child *to go away* from the well, for I was afraid she would fall in.

Solón mandó que a su muerte **se llevasen** sus restos mortales a Salamis, que allí **se quemasen** y que las cenizas **se esparciesen** por el campo.

Solon ordered that on his death his remains *be carried* to Salamis and *burned* there, and that the ashes *be scattered* over the country.

Comisionó a un muchacho que le **trajese** un ejemplar de dicho periódico.

He paid a boy *to bring* him a copy of the paper in question.

Se había mandado que los soldados **economizasen** las municiones.

It had been ordered that the men *were to economize* their ammunition.

23.39. The pluperfect subjunctive is required after a governing verb in any past tense, when the action of the subjunctive verb is prior to that of the governing verb:

Cuanto más reflexionaba, se admiraba más de que no se le **hubieran ocurrido** las objeciones que el agricultor acababa de hacerle.

The more he reflected the more he wondered why the objections which the farmer had just made to him *had* never *occurred* to him.

Antes de leer aquel tratado, siempre había dudado que los noruegos **hubiesen desembarcado** en el continente americano.

Before reading that treatise I had always doubted whether the Norsemen *landed* on the American continent.

23.40. The pluperfect subjunctive is also used after a governing verb in any past tense when the action of the subjunctive verb is subsequent to that of the governing verb, but completed before another action now also past:

El indio esperó a que **se hubiera apaciguado** la agitación de las aguas, antes de dejar aquel sitio.	The Indian waited until the disturbance of the waters *had subsided* before leaving that place.
Preferíamos aguardar a que se **hubiese marchado.**	We preferred to wait until he *had left.*

23.41. When the subjunctive is preceded by a conjunction, or relative adverb or pronoun (in clauses implying causation, negation or uncertainty) and no governing verb occurs, the tense of the subjunctive is determined by the time of its action with relation to the context:

Todos se desearon una buena noche sin que nadie la **esperase.**	All wished each other a good night without anyone's *expecting* it.
Me prometió que cuando su secretario **hubiese copiado** el informe, me lo devolvería.	He promised me that when his clerk *had copied* the report, he would return it to me.
Lo dije en voz alta, a fin de que lo **oyesen** los transeúntes.	I said it in a loud tone, so that the passers-by *should hear* it.
Estaba resuelta a no quedarme en el convento, aunque **tuviese** que saltar por la ventana.	I was determined not to stay in the convent, even though I *should have* to jump out at the window.
Vi que se preparaban a someterme a un examen, y me disponía yo a contestar como Dios me **sugiriese.**	I saw that they were preparing to subject me to an examination, and I got ready to answer as God *might suggest* to me.

23.42. So when the subjunctive depends upon an infinitive or a present participle, its tense is determined by that of the leading finite verb of the sentence:

Me costó trabajo impedir que se **pusiese** de rodillas.	It cost me some trouble to prevent him from *falling* on his knees.
Temiendo que se **advirtiese** mi distracción, me despedí de las damas con afectada efusión, y me marché.	Fearing that they *would notice* my preoccupation, I took leave of the ladies with affected effusiveness, and departed.

23.43. SYNOPSIS

a. The present subjunctive may relate to a time either coexistent with, or subsequent to, the time of the governing verb:

Es dudoso que lo sepa.	It is doubtful whether he knows it.
Merece que le castiguen.	He deserves to be punished.

b. When the governing verb is in the present tense, an imperfect subjunctive relates usually to a prior time but cf. § 24.23, last example.

Es improbable que los fenicios conociesen la brújula.	It is improbable that the Phoenicians knew of the compass.

c. When the governing verb is imperfect or preterite, the imperfect subjunctive can refer only to a coexistent or subsequent time:

No percibí que nadie hablase en el cuarto vecino.	I did not notice whether any one was talking in the next room.
Temíamos todos que el buque fuese a pique.	We all feared the vessel would go down.

d. After a governing verb in the imperfect, a subjunctive referring to a prior time must be put in the pluperfect:

En el siglo pasado se dudaba que Troya hubiese existido jamás; pero hoy día se acepta como un hecho histórico.	In the last century they doubted whether Troy ever existed; but nowadays it is accepted as an historic fact.

e. So we see that although the simple forms of the imperfect subjunctive may relate to a time prior to the present time, they cannot refer to a time prior to a past time:

Se teme que los refuerzos no partiesen ayer.	It is feared that the reinforcements did not start yesterday.
Se temía que los refuerzos no hubiesen partido (*not* partiesen) el día anterior.	It was feared that the reinforcements had not started the day before.

FUTURE SUBJUNCTIVE

23.44. The future subjunctive applies only to future contingencies depending upon doubt or uncertainty; it is never dependent upon causation or emotion:

Devolveré todo cuanto me **dieren.**	I shall return all they *may give* me.
Le escribiré a V. lo que **decidieren.**	I will write you what they *may decide.*

23.45. The future subjunctive is never governed by a verb, but is introduced by a conjunction, or a relative pronoun or adverb:

En lo que **tocare** a defender mi persona, no tendré mucha cuenta con esas leyes, pues las divinas y humanas permiten que cada uno se defienda de quien **quisiere** agraviarle.
As far as *may concern* the defense of my person, I shall not take much account of those laws, for both human and divine ones permit everybody to defend himself against whoever *tries* to attack him.

Si el próximo invierno **fuere** tan riguroso como el último, los pobres padecerán muchísimo.
If next winter *be* as severe as the last, the poor will suffer greatly.

Los demás Estados que **tomaren** parte en la Conferencia serán representados por el número de Delegados que cada uno **designare.**
The other States which *may participate* in the Conference shall be represented by as many Delegates as each *may elect.*

23.46. The future subjunctive, although once frequent, is now little used, except in certain phrases or formulas, often judicial or proverbial, handed down from the past. Its place is ordinarily taken by the present subjunctive or, in conditional sentences, by the present indicative:

¿Qué tiene que hacer Valentín en el cielo? Nada, digan lo que **dijeren.** (Pérez Galdós, **Torquemada en la hoguera,** IX)
What need is there of Valentine in Heaven? None, let people say what they *will.*

Vaya, salga lo que **saliere** —dijo Aracil. —Agárrate a mí, María. (Baroja, **La dama errante,** XXVII)
"Come, let happen what *may,*" said Aracil. "Catch hold of me, Mary."

Sea de ello lo que **fuere,** la preocupación unitaria de la reina Isabel se manifiesta francamente en años posteriores. (Madariaga, **España,** I, 2, 18)
Be that as it *may,* Queen Isabel's concern with unification manifests itself clearly in later years.

23.47. It may be remarked here that **si** *if* is not usually followed by a present or perfect subjunctive, as is the case in English:

Si hace viento propicio.
If there *be* a fair wind.

23.48. The equally disused future perfect subjunctive (formed from the future subjunctive of **haber** and a past participle) indicates that the action of the verb is regarded as completed prior to a certain future time:

Si para fines del mes la comisión **hubiere terminado** sus deliberaciones.
If by the end of the month the Committee *has concluded* its deliberations.

Dado caso que, a la expiración de dicho plazo, no se **hubieren ofrecido** posturas.	In case, at the expiration of said time, no bids *shall have been presented.*

REMARK. There is practically no difference in meaning, either in Spanish or English, among the following expressions:

Cuando algún error se descubra.	When any error is discovered.
Cuando algún error se descubriere.	When any error shall be discovered.
Cuando algún error se haya descubierto.	When any error has been discovered.
Cuando algún error se hubiere descubierto.	When any error shall have been discovered.

THE SUBJUNCTIVE IN INDEPENDENT CLAUSES

23.49. The subjunctive without any governing word expressed, is of limited application. Expressions of this character may be considered elliptical, as a governing word or clause can easily be supplied, and are referable to the two general principles of causation and uncertainty. Under the first of these the subjunctive expresses a wish or command, and is equivalent to an imperative; under the second, it expresses an alternative or presents the statement as a possibility.

THE SUBJUNCTIVE USED AS IMPERATIVE

23.50. The principal use of the subjunctive when no governing word is expressed, is as a substitute for an imperative. It may either take the place of an existing imperative, or supply the place of forms that are wanting. As the direct imperative is confined to the second person, and is never employed negatively, as in forbidding, its use is extremely limited. The present subjunctive is used for all other purposes of an imperative, and from its indirectness is more courteous.

23.51. There are various degrees of indirectness:

1. When a wish or command is conveyed as a message through one person to another, the subjunctive is preceded by **que**, and a verb of wishing or commanding may be understood:

Que suban la comida.	Let them bring up the dinner.
Que no entre nadie.	Let no one come in.
Que pase a mediodía.	Let him call at noon.
Que se les despida.	Let them be dismissed.
Que todo esté listo para cuando volvamos.	Let everything be ready by the time we return.

¡Volver a casa después de haberle echado de ella su padre tan sin motivo ni razón! ¡Que penara, que penara un poco por su dureza inoportuna! (Pereda, **Sotileza,** XXVI)	Return home after his father had thrown him out so without cause or reason! Let him suffer, let him suffer a little for his unseasonable severity!
Si otros querían callar, que callasen. (Blasco Ibáñez, **Guapeza valenciana,** II, in **Cuentos valencianos**)	If others wanted to be silent, let them be silent.

2. When the wish or command is not delivered as a message, but is merely expressed indefinitely about some person or thing not present, the employment of **que** is not uniform; its absence, however, pertains rather to an antique or elevated style:

Que me ahorquen si lo hago.	May I be hanged if I do.
Que te caigan los cielos.	May the heavens fall on you.
Que el diablo se vuele con él y sus antojos.	May the D—l take him and his fancies.
Séale la tierra leve.	May the earth rest lightly upon him.
Dios le ampare a V.	God protect you.
Cúmplase la voluntad de Dios.	God's will be done.
Padre nuestro, que estás en los cielos, santificado sea tu nombre.	Our Father, who art in heaven, hallowed be thy name.
¡Viva la República!	Long live the Republic!
Húndase el mundo y vamos adelante.	Let the world sink and let us go forward.
Cierre usted pronto ese balcón, no se constipe el niño. (Blasco Ibáñez, **La caperuza,** in **Cuentos valencianos**)	Close that balcony window quickly, lest *(Lit.* may the baby not) the baby catch cold.

REMARK I. Certain stereotype expressions of a passive or impersonal nature, regularly discard the conjunction:

Baste decir que llegó a su destino sin ser molestado.	*Suffice* it to say that he reached his journey's end without being molested.
Figúrense mis pensamientos, **figúrese** mi asombro, al verle vivo.	*Imagine* my thoughts, *imagine* my dismay, on seeing him alive.
No se crea que yo participaba de sus ideas pesimistas.	Let it not *be believed* that I shared his pessimistic ideas.

REMARK II. The use of the past subjunctive (which implies that it is less likely that the wish be attained) without introductory particle is no longer very frequent in literary Spanish, where it inclines toward the rhetorical and old-fashioned, but is by no means unusual in colloquial language:

¡Supiera al menos cómo se compone el blasón de la noble casa de Bradomín! (Valle-Inclán, **Sonata de otoño,** p. 131 of **Opera Omnia** edition)	I wish I knew at least how the escutcheon of the noble house of Bradomín is made up!
¡Viera[1] cómo se quedan comiendo unas sopicas de ajo...! (Valle-Inclán, **Sonata de invierno,** p. 180 of **Opera Omnia** edition)	I wish you could see how they look eating garlic soup!
¡Vamos, hubiera venido yo solo! (Benavente, **La comida de las fieras,** III, 4)	Now, now; I wish I had come alone!
¡Nunca hubiera tomado sobre sí este cargo! (Palacio Valdés, **La novela de un novelista,** XV)	Would that he had never taken this duty upon himself!
¡Dijéranlo de una vez! (Benavente, **Alfilerazos,** II, 2)	I wish they had said so at once!
Marchaba ligero con la frente baja mirando a hurtadillas en todas direcciones. No fuera a encontrarse con algún acreedor. (Prieto, **El socio,** XXIX)	He walked along quickly with his head down glancing furtively in every direction. He didn't want to *(Lit.,* Would that he didn't) meet some creditor.

3. When the command is addressed to a person who is present, **que** is omitted, and the subjunctive is immediately followed by **V.** or **Vds.,**[2] as the case may require:

Hable V. más alto.	Speak louder.
Ponga V. la maleta sobre el baúl.	Put the valise on the trunk.
Vuelva V. cerca de las dos.	Come back about two o'clock.
Suban Vds. un piso más.	Come up another flight.
No abran Vds. las ventanas.	Don't open the windows.

[1] The use of **viera,** with wide extension of its meaning, is frequent in Spanish America: **Pero si todo el mundo lo sabe...Vieras los escándalos que ha dado mi tío por esa muchacha.** (Lynch, **Los caranchos de la Florida,** XIV) *But everybody knows it...I wish you had seen the scandals that my uncle has caused over that girl.*

[2] Or, in ceremonious style when titles are used, by the latter: **Siéntese el señor conde.** *Sit down, count (literally,* may the count sit down).

4. A somewhat stiffly ceremonious form is obtained by applying the above to some such verb as **servirse** *to please;* **dignarse** *to deign;* or some other circumlocution:

Sírvase V. tomar un asiento.	Please take a seat.
Dígnense Vds. pasar adelante.	Please go first.
Tenga V. la bondad de alargarme el apio.	Kindly reach me the celery.

23.52. The subjunctive is substituted for the true imperative in negative commands addressed in the second person:

Haz lo que te digo.	Do what I tell you.
No hagas lo que te prohibo.	*Do not do* what I forbid you.
Haced lo que os digo.	Do what I tell you.
No hagáis lo que os prohibo.	*Do not do* what I forbid you.

23.53. When the subjunctive used imperatively has for object one or more personal pronouns, they are appended to it, forming one word, when the command is affirmative; when negative, or when the subjunctive is not the first word in the clause (§ **4.10**), they are placed before it. The accent, being on the stem of the verb, must be written if the stem thus stands two or more syllables before the last:

Váyase V. Acérquese V.	Go away. Come near.
No se vaya V. No se acerque V.	Don't go away. Don't come near.
Dénmelos Vds.	Give me them.
No me los den Vds.	Do not give them to me.
Enséñeselo V. a ella.	Show it to her.
No se lo enseñe V. a ella.	Do not show it to her.
Préstennoslos Vds. a nosotros.	Lend them to us.
Quítenmele Vds.	Take him off of me.
Echemelos V.	Toss them to me.
¡La Virgen me ampare!	May the Virgin protect me!
¡Allá se las componga Vd!	That's your worry!

REMARK. In an affirmative alternative expression (§§ **23.60** ff.) the pronouns may precede: **Mala o buena, te repugne o no, en ella tengo que seguir.** (Alvarez Quintero, **Pepita Reyes,** toward end) *Good [life] or bad, whether it be repugnant to you or not, in it I must continue.*

23.54. The subjunctive also supplies the want of an imperative of the first person. When so used it is to be rendered in English by *let* or *may;* a personal pronoun, when subject, is then not expressed except for emphasis:

Salgamos a dar un paseo. — Let us go out and take a walk.
Entremos en la casa. — Let us go into the house.
Ocultémonos aquí, detrás de esta peña. — Let us conceal ourselves here, behind this rock.
Ande yo caliente y ríase la gente. (Góngora, **Letrilla**) — Let me go warm and the people may scoff.

REMARK. The verb **ir,** *to go,* has a variant form, **vamos,** usually used in the affirmative (cf. § **14.63**) instead of the expected form of the first person plural subjunctive present, **vayamos:**

Vamos a la corrida de toros. — Let us go to the bullfight.
Vamos a ver lo que haya. — Let's go see what there is.
Vámonos *(from* irse). — Let us go, let us be off.
Vayamos al comedor y allí os contaré. (Pérez de Ayala, **El profesor auxiliar,** in **El ombligo del mundo)** — Let us go to the dining room and I'll tell you there.

23.55. The subjunctive is used after **ojalá,** with or without **que,**[1] in exclamatory wishes; but this is merely a seeming independent use of the subjunctive, as **ojalá** has all the force of a verb, being derived from the Arabic *in sha'llah, Allah grant that:*

¡Ojalá que venga pronto! — Oh that he may come soon!
¡Ojalá que semejante desgracia no le suceda a V. nunca! — May heaven grant that such a misfortune may never happen to you!

23.56. Ojalá may be followed by the past tense of the subjunctive, the imperfect relating to the present, and the pluperfect to a past time:

¡Ojalá que mi hermano estuviese aquí! — Would that my brother were here!
¡Ojalá que mi hermano hubiese estado allí! — Would that my brother had been there!

23.57. With a past subjunctive **quién** is used to express a wish usually in the first person:

¡Quién tuviera su distinción y su atrevimiento! (Benavente, **Lo cursi,** I, 1) — I wish I had their distinction and their daring!

[1] **Ojalá y** is used also: **¡Ojalá y fuera eso!** (Benavente, **Los malhechores del bien, I,** 17) *I wish it would be that!*

¡Quién se volviera a los veinte años! (Palacio Valdés, **La aldea perdida,** II) — I wish I were twenty years old again!

¡Ay, Madrí!... ¡Quién se fuera!... ¿Se atreve usté a yevarme en er baú? (Alvarez Quintero, **Las flores,** I) — Oh, Madrid! I wish I could go! Do you dare to take me in your trunk?

REMARK. Occasionally the value of **quién** is indefinite: *someone.* This may have been the original use:

¡Ah, quién me volviera a aquellos hermosos días de mi infancia! ¡Quién me diera vivir otra vez entre vosotros! (Palacio Valdés, **La novela de un novelista,** XXVI) — Oh, I wish that someone might return me *(practically,* I wish I might return) to those fine days of my childhood! I wish that someone would make it possible for me to live *(practically,* I wish that I might live) among you again.

23.58. Another way of expressing an exclamatory wish is by the use of **así** + subjunctive:

¡Así se hunda la casa! (Valle-Inclán, **El rey de la máscara, in Jardín umbrío)** — I wish the house would collapse!

Así Dios me castigue si le miento. (Pereda, **Peñas arriba,** XXIX) — So may God punish me if I lie to you.

Dicen que le ha roto una costilla. ¡Así se las hubiese roto todas! (Palacio Valdés, **Sinfonía pastoral, Presto finale,** V) — They say that he has broken a rib for him. I wish that he had broken them all.

23.59. The use of the subjunctive of the irregular verb **placer,** chiefly in the expression **pluguiera** or **pluguiese a Dios** *would to God,* is now limited to elevated style:

¡Plegue a Dios que no salga así! — God grant it may not turn out so!

¡Pluguiera a Dios que yo fuera muerto! — Would to God I were dead!

¡Pluguiese a Dios que no hubiera ido! — Would to God I had not gone!

ALTERNATIVE EXPRESSIONS

23.60. The alternative expressions made by the subjunctive used independently, may be regarded as modifications of the imperative, in which the thing commanded is so indeterminate that they are mere general permissions:

Hagan lo que se les antoje.	*Let them do* what they please.
Digan lo que quieran, no por eso alteraré mi conducta.	*Let them say* what they will, I shall not alter my conduct on that account.
Será preciso intentar la fuga, **cueste** lo que cueste.	It will be necessary to attempt an escape, *cost* what it may.
Venga lo que viniere, le sostendré hasta el último extremo.	*Come* what may, I will stand by him to the last.

REMARK. The subjunctive in these clauses is required by the idea of uncertainty, after a relative.

23.61. A further deviation from the imperative force is found in such alternative expressions as the following:

Tendrá que pagarme, que quiera o que no quiera.	He will have to pay me, whether he be willing or not.
Que llueva o que no llueva, iré.	I shall go whether it rain or not.
Que lo consiga o no, su intención es laudable.	Whether he succeed or not, his intention is laudable.

23.62. The **que** before the first subjunctive of an alternative clause may be omitted; and when the clause forms part of a sentence whose leading time is past, both subjunctives are put in the appropriate past tense:

Sea hombre o **sea** demonio, no me dejaré amedrentar.	*Be he* man or *be he* demon, I will not let myself be frightened.
Mañana, **hayan llegado** o no los refuerzos, intentaremos una surtida.	Tomorrow, whether the reinforcements *have arrived* or not, we will attempt a sortie.
Nos decidimos a que al día siguiente, **hubiesen llegado** o no los refuerzos, intentaríamos una surtida.	We decided that on the next day, whether the reinforcements *had arrived* or not, we would attempt a sortie.
Declaró que, **viniese** lo que **viniese**, me sostendría hasta el último extremo.	He declared that, *come* what *might*, he would stand by me to the last.
Nos prometimos fidelidad hasta la muerte, **sucediese** lo que **sucediese**.	We promised each other fidelity until death, no matter what *might happen*.

Era un hombre sin fe ni ley, aventurero de oficio, a la disposición del primero que le pagase bien, o del segundo que le pagase mejor, **fuese** cual **fuese** la clase del trabajo.

He was a faithless and lawless man, adventurer by trade, at the disposal of the first person who would pay him well, or of the second who would pay him better, no matter what the class of work *might be.*

23.63. The subjunctive of **saber** *to know,* **recordar** *to remember* and **ver** *to see* may be employed with **que** to modify a preceding negation or question:[1]

No ha entrado nadie, **que yo sepa.**	No one has entered, *so far as I know.*
No existen otros ejemplares, **que sepamos.**	No other copies exist, *to our knowledge.*
¿Se ha expedido jamás tal orden, **que V. sepa?**	Has any such order ever been issued, *so far as you know?*
No lo he leído jamás, **que yo recuerde.**	I have never read it, *so far as I remember.*
No demuestra el menor remordimiento, **que yo vea.**	He doesn't show the slightest remorse, *so far as I see.*
No había padecido, **que él supiera,** menoscabo alguno. (Pereda, **El sabor de la tierruca,** XV)	It had suffered, *so far as he knew,* no damage whatever.

23.64. A clause with the subjunctive, regularly exclamatory in value and usually introduced by **que,** may indicate doubt of the possibility of the act stated:

¡Que viva aquí un hombre tan rico!	To think that so rich a man lives here!
¡Que sea tan corta la memoria de Vd!	Is it possible that your memory is so short!
Buscaba gentes que lo hicieran por mí... ¡No las buscara hoy, paño, ya que he roto a hablar! (Pereda, **Sotileza,** XX)	I was looking for people to do it for me... To think that I didn't look (*or* I wish I had looked) for them today, what the deuce, now that I have begun to speak!

[1] Compare the Latin *quod sciam, quod noverim, quod meminerim.* Though perhaps most frequent after expressed or implied negation, the use of **que yo sepa,** etc., is not restricted to such situation: **Este es el único lazo, que yo sepa, que a este distrito le une.** (Valera, **Doña Luz,** XI) *This is the only bond, so far as I know, that holds him to this district.*

¡Allá van! ¡Allá van! ¡No les llevaran los demonios! (Benavente, **De cerca,** I) — There they go! There they go! To think that the devil wouldn't (*or* I wish that the devil would) take them!

¡Oh, que no te hubiese conocido antes, Eleuteria! (Unamuno, **El amor que asalta,** in **El espejo de la muerte**) — Oh, to think that I shouldn't have (*or* I wish I had) known you before, Eleutheria!

23.65. As subject especially a clause with **el que** or **que** is frequently used to mean that the statement is presented as something merely conceived of:

El que volviese Pepita a su retiro habitual era naturalísimo. (Valera, **Pepita Jiménez, Paralipómenos**) — That Pepita should return to her habitual seclusion was most natural.

Ramona y Ricardo no pueden ver con tranquilidad el que Petra venga a nuestra casa. (Benavente, **Gente conocida,** I, 4) — Ramona and Richard can't endure calmly that Petra should come to our house.

Que esté amable con el Príncipe nada tiene de particular. (Benavente, **La escuela de las princesas,** III, 2) — That she should be agreeable to the Prince has nothing strange about it.

No ha de sorprenderles el que no hayas querido recibirlas. (Martínez Sierra, **Primavera en otoño,** II) — It will not surprise them that you have not wanted to receive them.

El se empeñó en que es mucho más artístico y más conforme con la naturaleza humana el que un pintor rico engañe a una florista pobre que el que la adore y se case con ella. (Martínez Sierra, **Sueño de una noche de agosto,** II) — He insisted that it is much more artistic and in greater conformity with human nature that a rich painter should deceive a poor flower-seller than that he should worship her and marry her.

¡Cuánto mejor es que vuestro amor se pierda y se evapore ahora... que no[1] el que muera...a manos del hastío. (Valera, **Pepita Jiménez, Paralipómenos**) — How much better it is that your love should be lost and disappear now ...than that it should die...at the hands of loathing.

[1] For the presence of **no** see § **11.32.**

XXIV
The Conditional

24.1. There has been much disagreement among grammarians where to class this form of the verb, some having considered it a tense of the indicative, some making it a part of the subjunctive, others leaving it unattached to any mood. But *(a)* as its principal use is in conditions it differs from the indicative, and *(b)* as it cannot be governed by an expression requiring the subjunctive it is not subject to the restrictions of this latter mood, it differs from these moods quite as much as they differ from each other. It will be found convenient, therefore, to consider it as a sporadic mood, just as the imperative is.[1]

If its mood be conditional its tense is future, both in form and usage. When formed regularly, its terminations are added to the full forms of the infinitive, just as is the case with the indicative future. Both are regularly future with reference to the principal verb of the sentence or to the time in the mind of the speaker.

24.2. The terminations of the conditional are as follows:

SING.	1	-ía	*E.g.:*	compraría	vendería	viviría
	2	-ías		comprarías	venderías	vivirías
	3	-ía		compraría	vendería	viviría
PLUR.	1	-íamos		compraríamos	venderíamos	viviríamos
	2	-íais		compraríais	venderíais	viviríais
	3	-ían		comprarían	venderían	vivirían

24.3. Those verbs which form the indicative future irregularly, present the same irregularity in the conditional. Five elide the

[1] Andrés Bello, one of the most learned writers upon Spanish grammar also considers this as a separate *mood,* although he does not call it conditional but "hypothetic." (*Gramática,* p. 394, 14th Ed., Madrid, 1887.) The most appropriate name would be "consequential," as it does not express a condition, but the consequence of a condition; but as the majority of grammarians agree in calling the form "conditional," this term has been adopted here.

vowel of the infinitive ending, five elide this vowel and interpolate **d**, and two form the futures from obsolete stems. So that in all cases the two tenses have the same stem:

CABER:	cabr-é	—	cabr-ía	PONER:	pondr-é	—	pondr-ía
HABER:	habr-é	—	habr-ía	SALIR:	saldr-é	—	saldr-ía
PODER:	podr-é	—	podr-ía	TENER:	tendr-é	—	tendr-ía
QUERER:	querr-é	—	querr-ía	VALER:	valdr-é	—	valdr-ía
SABER:	sabr-é	—	sabr-ía	VENIR:	vendr-é	—	vendr-ía

DECIR:	dir-é	—	dir-ía
HACER:	har-é	—	har-ía

A further similarity between these two tenses is their identity of origin. They are not forms descended from literary Latin, but were made at a later time by appending certain forms of the auxiliary **haber** to an infinitive:

dar-he	dar-has	dar-ha	dar-hemos	dar-heis	dar-han
dar-hia	dar-hias	dar-hia	dar-hiamos	dar-hiais	dar-hian

Formerly in Spanish, as is still the case in Portuguese, these appended forms of the auxiliary were separable to allow an objective personal pronoun to be interpolated:

OLD SPANISH:	esforçar-me-he	dezir-se-hia
PORTUGUESE:	esforçar-me-hei	dir-se-hia
OLD SPANISH:	limitar-nos-hemos	escrivir-les-hiamos
PORTUGUESE:	limitar-nos-hemos	escrever-lhes-hiamos

24.4. The conditional is always dependent upon a past tense, expressed or understood. Its primary and leading value is to express futurity dating from a past time—thus bearing the same relation to a past tense that the future indicative does to the present or future:

Me aseguran que guardarán silencio.	They assure me they will keep silent.
Me aseguraban que **guardarían** silencio.	They assured me they *would keep* silent.
Le preguntaré si tardará en llegar.	I will ask him if he will be long getting there.
Le pregunté si **tardaría** en llegar.	I asked him if he *would be long* getting there.
Pensamos que lloverá.	We think it will rain.
Pensábamos que **llovería.**	We thought it *would rain.*
Este desagüe sin duda forma una cascada cuya fuerza mecánica será posible utilizar.	This outlet doubtless forms a fall whose mechanical power it will be possible to utilize.

Aquel desagüe sin duda formaba una cascada cuya fuerza mecánica **sería** posible utilizar.

That outlet doubtless formed a fall whose mechanical power it *would be* possible to utilize.

24.5. In this manner it is extended to apply as a future after any past tense, whether indicative or subjunctive, or an infinitive or present participle applied to a past time:

He estado pensando que tal vez le **encontraría** por aquí.

I have been thinking that perhaps I *should meet* him around here.

Negó que su criado nos hubiese preguntado si **asistiríamos** a la función.

He denied that his servant had asked us if we *would attend* the performance.

Suponiendo que **llegaría** en el tren directo de las 7, me dirigí inmediatamente a la estación.

Supposing that he *would arrive* on the seven o'clock express, I started at once for the station.

Era natural creer que lo **haría** despues de haberse expresado así.

It was natural to believe that he *would do* it after having expressed himself in that way.

24.6. The conditional is inadmissible in such cases if the meaning of the leading verb or clause is such as to require the subjunctive:

Temíamos todos que se **precipitase** (*not* precipitaría) al abismo.

We all feared he *would fall* into the abyss.

Era dudoso que este río **proporcionase** (*not* proporcionaría) a los colonos una cantidad suficiente de agua potable.

It was doubtful whether this river *would supply* the colonists with a sufficient quantity of drinking water.

Con piedras, ramas entrelazadas y barro se taparon las hendeduras entre las rocas, dejando abierto un solo agujero estrecho y sinuoso para que **se condujese** el humo al exterior y **tuviese** tiro el hogar.

With stones, interlaced branches and clay they stopped up the rifts between the rocks, leaving a single narrow and winding hole open so that the smoke *would be carried* outside and the fireplace *would have* a draught.

En su carta suplicaba a su padre que no juzgase a su Guillermo (según ella llamaba a su marido) por lo que oyese decir a los demás; sino que aguardase a hacerlo cuando le **conociese**[1] personalmente.

In her letter she entreated her father not to judge her William (as she called her husband) by what he might hear others say; but to delay doing so until he *should know* him personally.

[1] The subjunctive is here required by the idea of uncertainty when preceded by a relative adverb of time or place; cf. §§ **23.13, 23.29.**

CONDITIONS WITH IMPLIED NEGATION

24.7. The most frequent application of the conditional is in conditions with an implied negation, which are grammatically expressed in a past tense although relating to either past, present or future.

24.8. It is a function of the preterite and imperfect to suggest a negation with respect to the present. To say that a thing **fué** is to imply that it is not. Hence a negation is implied in conditional clauses by using the past tenses of the subjunctive after **si**, although speaking of the present time. The following are the possible arrangements for conditions:

PRESENT

Si él tiene poderosos valedores, conseguirá sin duda el empleo.	If he has powerful backers, he will no doubt get the place.
Si él tuviera poderosos valedores, conseguiría sin duda el empleo.	If he had powerful backers, he would no doubt get the place.

PAST

Si él tenía poderosos valedores, no les empleó, porque no obtuvo el empleo.	If he had powerful backers, he did not make use of them, for he did not get the place.
Si él hubiera tenido poderosos valedores, sin duda habría conseguido el empleo.	If he had had powerful backers, he would no doubt have got the place.

FUTURE

Si él tiene poderosos valedores, conseguirá sin duda el empleo.	If he has powerful backers, he will no doubt get the place.

24.9. The clause stating the condition supposed may be called the if-clause; the corresponding clause stating the consequence may be called the conclusion. The place of the conditional is in the conclusion:

Si yo fuera rico, no trabajaría en nada.	If I were rich, I would not work at all.
Si V. le hubiese dado dinero, él habría comprado ron.	If you had given him money, he would have bought rum.

24.10. By conditions with an implied negation is meant those in which the if-clause supposes a state of affairs not existing now or likely to exist in the future. On account of this implied negation the verb of the if-clause is subjunctive:[1]

Si no fuese soldado inválido, le despediría.	If he were not an invalid soldier (but he is), I would discharge him.
Si fuese soldado inválido, le daría el empleo.	If he were an invalid soldier (but he is not), I would give him the place.

24.11. In the if-clause, as in the cases stated in the preceding chapter, the imperfect forms of the subjunctive are interchangeable:

Si tuviese *(or* tuviera) tiempo, iría esta noche al teatro.	If I had time, I would go to the theater this evening.
Si hubiésemos *(or* hubiéramos) sabido eso, no habríamos dicho lo que dijimos.	If we had known that, we would not have said what we did.
Si hubiese *(or* hubiera) harina, haría pan.	If there were any flour, I would make some bread.

24.12. It is unimportant whether the if-clause or the conclusion be placed first:

Se lo daría si lo tuviese.	I would give it to him if I had it.
Si lo tuviese, se lo daría.	If I had it I would give it to him.
¿Iría V. al campo si escampase?	Would you go to the country if it stopped raining?
Si escampase, ¿iría V. al campo?	If it stopped raining would you go to the country?

24.13. The if-clause is usually introduced by **si** *if,* but the result may be obtained by any mode of expression of similar value:

Aunque viniera (aun si viniera), no le recibiría.	Although he should come (even if he came), I would not receive him.

---

[1] For this reason the verb introduced by **como si** or the more literary **cual si** *as if,* **mismo. . .que si** *same. . .as if,* etc., will be subjunctive:

Le trató como si en la noche anterior por arte mágico la sangre roja del doctor se hubiese tornado azul. (Palacio Valdés, **Santa Rogelia,** II, 3)	He treated him as if during the previous night by magic art the doctor's red blood had turned blue.
Cargó el fusil y la pistola con el mismo cuidado y minuciosidad que si estuviera en una escuela de tiro. (Baroja, **El aprendiz de conspirador,** IV, 4)	He loaded the rifle and the pistol with the same care and thoroughness as if he were at the shooting gallery.

En otras circunstancias (si las circunstancias fuesen otras), no tendría inconveniente en ello.	Under other circumstances (if the circumstances were different), I should have no objection to it.
No lo habría logrado sin su ayuda (si él no me hubiese ayudado).	I would not have succeeded without his aid (if he had not aided me).
Una perdigonada habría producido una hecatombe en aquella volatería, pero por desgracia no teníamos ninguna arma de fuego.	A shower of bird shot would have killed a hundred of those birds, but unfortunately we had no firearms.

24.14. The conditional may appear in sentences without a preceding supposition. Such usages are elliptical, the wanting if-clause being easily supplied:

Vd. haría mal en despedirle (si le despidiese).	You would do wrong in discharging him (if you discharged him).
No colgaría el cuadro ahí (si yo fuese Vd.).	I would not hang the picture there (if I were you).
Dice que no haría cavar la bodega tan cerca de la calle (si a él le tocara dirigir el trabajo).	He says he would not have the cellar dug so near the street (if he had charge of the work).
La razón que V. acaba de dar nunca se me habría ocurrido.	The reason you have just given would never have occurred to me.

24.15. The use of the conditional in expressing a wish in a modest manner is explainable by supplying an if-clause as follows:

Desearía hablar dos palabras con Vd. (si eso no le molestase).	I should like to say a few words to you (if it would not inconvenience you).
Yo también gustaría de tener una biblioteca (si las circunstancias me lo permitiesen).	I would like to have a library too (if circumstances would permit me).

24.16. A single exception to the principles stated with regard to the past tenses of the subjunctive is that the **-ra** form (but not properly the **-se** form) may take the place of the conditional in all types of conditional sentences. This substitution of the **-ra** form for the conditional, except in literary style, is more common in the compound than in the simple tenses. The conditional, however, cannot be substituted for the imperfect subjunctive, and cannot, therefore, stand in the if-clause:

Si V. no hubiera acudido generosamente en mi ayuda, ya habría *(or* hubiera) muerto de hambre.	If you had not generously come to my aid, I should have starved to death. *(Lit.* I should already have died of hunger.)
Si la casualidad permitiera el encuentro de esos dos buques de guerra, habría *(or* hubiera) probabilidades de un combate naval que el valor reconocido de chilenos y norteamericanos y lo equilibrado de sus fuerzas haría *(or* hiciera) reñidísimo.	If chance were to permit the encounter of those two war-vessels, there would be a likelihood of a naval combat which the recognized valor of the Chileans and U. S. seaman, and the equality of their forces, would make a very hard-contested one.

24.17. Therefore a condition with implied negation has the following latitude of expression:

Si tuviese dinero Si tuviera dinero	lo compraría.	If I had money, I would buy it.
Si tuviese dinero Si tuviera dinero	lo comprara.	
Si hubiese tenido dinero Si hubiera tenido dinero	lo habría comprado.	If I had had money, I would have bought it.
Si hubiese tenido dinero Si hubiera tenido dinero	lo hubiera comprado.	

REMARK I. As stated in § **24.16** the substitution of the **-ra** form for the **-ría** is not usual, in the style of the spoken language, when it is a matter of a simple tense. Yet **debiera, pudiera** (§§ **26.19, 26.27**) and **quisiera** (§ **24.20**) are altogether current. Moreover, **creyera, dijérase, pensara, valiera,** are not infrequent in the style of literature.

REMARK II. Though not enjoying the approval of grammarians, the use of the **-se** form, in compound tenses only, is quite common in the conclusion: **Si hubiese tenido alas, me hubiese lanzado al infinito luminoso.** (Palacio Valdés, **La hermana San Sulpicio,** XII) *If I had had wings, I would have hurled myself into luminous space.* **La casa era tal y tan cómoda y señoril, que si la hubiera alquilado don Paco, no hubiese faltado quien le diese por ella 400 reales al año.** (Valera, **Juanita la larga,** I) *The house was such and so comfortable and aristocratic that if Don Paco had rented it, there would have been somebody who would have given him 400 reals a year for it.* **María, que no hubiese sido cruel con otro cualquiera, pensando que Brull se había reído de su padre, le devolvió la carta.** (Baroja, **La dama errante,** VI) *Mary, who wouldn't have been cruel to anyone else, thinking that Brull had laughed at her father, returned the letter to him.*

REMARK III. **Por si (acaso)** *in case* ordinarily has its verb in the indicative but with past tenses the subjunctive is occasionally found (cf. § **23.9**, REMARK): **He venido antes por si tenías que hacerme alguna advertencia.** (Benavente, **Al natural**, I, 5) *I have come beforehand in case you had to make some remark to me.* **Por si nadie supiese el destino de ellos, advirtió muy oportuna la copla...** (Espina, **La esfinge maragata**, XXI) *In case no one knew the use of them, the verses suggested very opportunely...*

24.18. The conditional perfect, formed by the conditional of **haber** and a past participle, is used only when the verb of the if-clause is pluperfect. That occurs when the action of both verbs is anterior to the time of uttering the sentence:

Imagino que si en vez de dos pesetas hubiera tenido ánimo para ofrecerle cinco duros, no me lo **habría rehusado.**	I imagine that if instead of two pesetas I had had the courage to offer him five duros, he *would* not *have refused* me.
Si el camino no hubiera estado sombreado por grandes árboles, creo que **habríamos sido** abrasados.	If the road had not been shaded by large trees, I believe we *should have been* roasted.
Si me hubiese dicho tal cosa le **habría pegado** un puñetazo.	If he had said such a thing to me I *should have struck* him with my fist.

24.19. The conditional and conditional perfect may govern a subjunctive, in which case they are treated as the imperfect and pluperfect respectively and usually require the subjunctive to be in the past tense (cf. § 25.12):

Sería bueno que V. **tuviese** tiempo para dar este paseo.	It *would be* nice if you *had* time to take this outing.
Preferiríamos que **lloviese** a que **hiciese** tanto polvo.	We *would rather* have *it rain* than *be* so dusty.
Habríamos mandado que se **preparase** la comida antes, si hubiéramos sabido que Vds. tenían tanta prisa.	We *would have ordered* dinner *to be prepared* earlier if we had known you were in such a hurry.

24.20. The **-ra** form of the subjunctive of **querer, quisiera,** is very often substituted for the conditional **querría. Quisiera** is a standard mode of expressing a request politely:

Quisiera que V. viese mi colección de fotografías.	I should like you to see my collection of photographs.
Quisiéramos visitar la galería de pinturas.	We should like to visit the picture gallery.

Vengo de parte de mi hermano, quien está indispuesto y quisiera pedirle prestado su ejemplar ilustrado del Quijote.	I come on behalf of my brother, who is under the weather and would like to borrow your illustrated copy of "Don Quixote."
Quisiera que V. me enseñase su biblioteca.	I should like you to show me your study.

REMARK. The present indicative, **quiero que V. me enseñe,** *etc.,* would be tantamount to a peremptory order.

24.21. **Quisiera** is also equivalent to the present indicative of the English *wish,* which is likewise followed by a past tense:

Quisiera que viniesen.	I wish they would come.
Quisiera tener un alfiler.	I wish I had a pin.
Quisiéramos que sucediese como V. desea.	We wish it may turn out as you desire.
En cuanto a mí, quisiera que no hubiéramos venido.	As for me I wish we hadn't come.
Quisiera que hubiese medio de ahorrarnos esta pérdida de tiempo.	I wish there were some way of saving ourselves this loss of time.

24.22. In expressing a wish about a past event, there is a distinction in Spanish which is not so strictly maintained in English, between the conditional perfect and the conditional followed by the infinitive of **haber** and a past participle. The former (the most usual construction) expresses a wish entertained in the past; the latter a wish entertained at present about the past:

Hubiera querido presenciar aquella escena.	I should have liked (at that time) to witness that scene.
Quisiera haber presenciado aquella escena.	I should like (now) to have witnessed that scene. *(I.e.* I wish I had witnessed it.)
Hubiera querido que V. me acompañase.	I should have liked you to accompany me.
Quisiera que V. me hubiese acompañado.	I should like you to have accompanied me. I wish you had accompanied me.
Hubiera querido que mi hijo aprendiese el castellano durante su permanencia en California, pero no tenía inclinación para ello.	I should have liked my son to learn Spanish during his stay in California, but he had no inclination towards it.
Hubiéramos querido que los músicos hubiesen llegado un poco antes.	We should have liked the musicians to have come a little earlier.

24.23. When the conclusion is governed by a verb which requires a subjunctive, the conditional and the conditional perfect are inadmissible, and they are replaced by the imperfect and the pluperfect subjunctive respectively:

No creo que los otros señores de esta aldea, si se hubieran hallado en el caso de V., **hubiesen** *(or* **hubieran,** *but not* habrían) obrado tan honradamente.	I do not believe that the other gentlemen of this village, if they had found themselves in your position, *would have* acted so honestly.
Si el Sr. profesor hubiese sabido que V. había hecho un estudio tan profundo de las lenguas muertas, dudo que se **hubiese** *(not* habría) atrevido a expresar sus opiniones delante de V., por temor de que V. las confutara.	If the professor had known that you had made such a profound study of the dead languages, I doubt whether he *would have* dared to express his ideas before you, for fear you might disprove them.
Es probable que el General **no aceptase** este sacrificio. (Palacio Valdés, **Años de juventud del doctor Angélico,** XII)	It is probable that the General *wouldn't accept* this sacrifice [if he were asked].

24.24. The conditional and the conditional perfect are equally inadmissible when the conclusion is dependent upon any idea of doubt, denial, uncertainty, or negation not expressed by a verb:

Se le veía sorbiendo su chocolate, sin que nada indicara que aquel hombre de trazas tan pacíficas **se convirtiese** *(not* convertiría) en tigre furibundo si le contrariase algo.	He was sipping his chocolate without anything to indicate that that man with such a placid expression *would become* a raging tiger if anything should cross him.
El criado ocultó las pistolas, no sea que su amo, si las viera, **sintiese** *(not* sentiría) la tentación de acabar con la vida.	The servant hid the pistols, lest his master, if he saw them, *should feel* a temptation to put an end to his life.

24.25. When introduced by **si,** the verb of the if-clause may be imperfect or pluperfect indicative if the statement represents the quotation, expressed or implied, of an original thought calling for the use of the indicative (§ **24.8**):

El ventor parecía estar cazando por su propia cuenta, y era probable que si alguna pieza de caza le **caía** entre los dientes, no quedara a los cazadores la menor parte de ella.

The pointer seemed to be hunting on his own account, and it was probable that if any game *got* between his teeth, there would not be the least bit of it left for the hunters.

Pensó que si el casero **se conformaba** a hacer algunas reparaciones, no quedaría mal. (Pérez Galdós, **Fortunata y Jacinta,** IV, 3, 7)

She thought that if the landlord *agreed* to make some repairs, it wouldn't be bad.

El cura le dijo que si **bebía** un vaso de vino cobraría ánimo. (Valle-Inclán, **El rey de la máscara,** in **Jardín umbrío)**

The priest said to her that if she *drank* a glass of wine she would gather strength.

24.26. In constructions like the following, however, the imperfect indicative is the only form admissible, since it relates to a fact:

Si este razonamiento no **era** lógico, parecía sin embargo conformado al genio de sus oyentes, puesto que consiguió el efecto apetecido.

If this reasoning *was* illogical, it seemed nevertheless suited to the humor of his hearers, since it obtained the desired effect.

Si **estaban** mojados, atormentados por el hambre y rendidos de la fatiga, al menos tendrían aquí un abrigo donde guarecerse y fuego con que secar su ropa y estirar sus miembros.

If they *were* wet, famished with hunger and exhausted with fatigue, at least they would have here a shelter to take refuge in and a fire to dry their clothes and thaw out their limbs.

24.27. In elevated style, the **si** of the if-clause may be omitted, in which case the conclusion begins with **que** or **y**:

Tuviesen todos los países la misma base para su moneda, **que** entonces sería exacto el argumento alegado por mi ilustrado amigo.

If all the countries had the same standard for their coinage, then the argument adduced by my learned friend would be correct.

Pidiesen mi consentimiento abiertamente **y** no se lo negara a ellos.

If they asked my consent openly I would not refuse it to them.

XXV
Correspondence of Tenses

25.1. The tense of the leading verbs of a sentence depends upon the date of their action with reference to the present time (i.e., the date of speaking or writing the sentence). The leading verbs may be of any tense whatever; but the tense of a dependent verb is more or less restricted by that of the leading verb. The term *correspondence of tenses* relates to the extent of this control.

REMARK. The extent of the control exercised by a leading verb depends, in a considerable degree, on its lexical meaning. Some verbs have inherently a prospective or a retrospective reference, whatever their tense may be. We *remember* or *regret* the past; *foresee* and *anticipate* the future. All verbs of causing or influencing are prospective, since causes precede their effects.

25.2. So far as one verb can influence the tense of another, the preterite and imperfect are alike. Whatever influences the one would influence the other in the same way.

25.3. The order of the tenses with relation to time may be aptly represented by a railroad diagram, in which the present is the central station:

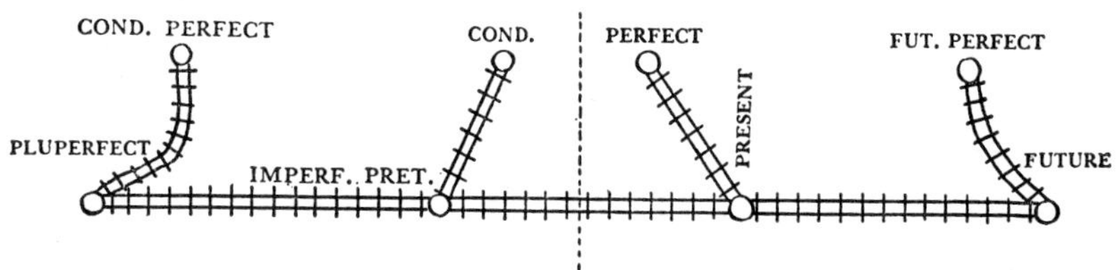

The roads to the left of the central station are assigned to the past, and those on the right to the future. The branch roads run to the dependent tenses, and the direction in which these lie shows whether they are anterior or subsequent to the tenses on which they depend. The various tenses have intercommunication only through existing lines: thus from the present the pluperfect can be reached only through the imperfect or preterite, and the future perfect only through the future.

25.4. A line may be drawn between the perfect and the imperfect or preterite, dividing the whole into two groups of tenses—the past tenses on the left, and the perfect, present and the futures on the right. We may in this case call them collectively the *past* and *non-past* tenses. Very generally the dependent verbs must belong to the same group with the leading verb, and will change their tense when it changes:

Le preguntaré si ha considerado el asunto.	I will ask him if he has considered the matter.
Le pregunté si había considerado el asunto.	I asked him if he had considered the matter.

REMARK. In the first sentence, the leading verb being future, the dependent verb is perfect, because it relates to an action prior to the time of *asking*. When the asking is thrown into the past, the considering is thrown still farther back so as to retain its relative priority.

25.5. The influence of a governing verb is seen in the indicative as well as in the subjunctive mood. The infinitive and present and past participles, having no distinction of tense, are of the same time as the immediate governing verb:

Opinamos que la Comisión no excedió los límites de sus facultades **proponiendo** que se incluyese en el tratado la cláusula respecto a procedimientos judiciales.	We consider that the Committee did not overstep the limits of its functions in *proposing* that the clause relative to judicial procedure be included in the treaty.
Apresuraron su marcha, pero **tomando** más precauciones con el objeto de sorprender y no exponerse a ser sorprendidos.	They quickened their step, *taking* additional precautions, however, so as to surprise without exposing themselves to being surprised.
El agua estaba excesivamente profunda, pues al **sondear** cerca de la orilla no se encontró fondo con veinte brazas de sonda.	The water was extremely deep, for on *sounding* near the shore, they did not touch bottom with twenty fathoms of line.

25.6. The perfect infinitive and participle (formed respectively of the infinitive and present participle of **haber** and a past participle), however, always date one tense prior to the governing verb:

Me alegro de **verlo.**	I am glad *to see it.*
Me alegro de **haberlo visto.**	I am glad *to have seen it.*
Wilkes, oyendo decir que d'Urville había descubierto la tierra el 19 de enero, pretendió **haberla descubierto** el día anterior.	Wilkes, hearing that d'Urville had discovered land on the 19th of January, claimed *to have discovered* it on the day preceding.
La borrasca duró treinta y seis horas; y **habiéndonos librado** muchas veces de estrellarnos contra las rocas, nos encontramos al fin a 60 millas a sotavento del cabo.	The squall lasted thirty-six hours; and *having saved* ourselves many times from being dashed to pieces on the rocks, we found ourselves finally 60 miles to leeward of the cape.

25.7. The perfect tense is dependent upon the present, the future perfect upon the future, the pluperfect on the imperfect or preterite, and the two conditionals on the imperfect or preterite and pluperfect respectively. These secondary tenses have always an expressed or implied reference to their respective primary tenses. When the primary tenses change, the dependent verbs, in preserving the same relation, change according to the following proportions:

Present	:	Non-past	: :	Imperfect-Preterite	:	Past
Future	:	Non-past	: :	Conditional	:	Past
Future Perfect	:	Non-past	: :	Conditional Perfect	:	Past
Perfect	:	Non-past	: :	Pluperfect	:	Past
Imperfect-Preterite	:	Non-past	: :	Pluperfect	:	Past

25.8. A governing verb in the non-past tenses may be followed by a dependent verb in any one of these tenses or in the imperfect-preterite, provided the meaning of the particular verb admits of its being so employed:

He sabido que la cosecha de naranjas **será** abundantísima.	I have learned that the crop of oranges *will be* most abundant.
He sabido que el Sr. tío de V. **está** enfermo.	I have learned that your uncle *is* ill.
He sabido que el banco **ha quebrado.**	I have learned that the bank *has failed.*
He sabido que nuestros amigos **llegaron** sin novedad a su destino.	I have learned that our friends *reached* their journey's end without mishap.
Es dudoso que **logre** convencer al jurado de la inocencia de su cliente.	It is doubtful whether he *will succeed* in convincing the jury of his client's innocence.

Es dudoso que dicho libro se **encuentre** en la Biblioteca Nacional. — It is doubtful whether the book in question *is* in the National Library.

Es dudoso que el buque se **haya hecho** a la mar todavía. — It is doubtful whether the ship *has put* to sea yet.

Es dudoso que Parry **llegase** más allá de los 78° de latitud norte. — It is doubtful whether Parry *went* beyond the 78th degree of north latitude.

(These examples might be varied and extended to great length.)

25.9. A past tense cannot have a non-past tense dependent upon it.[1] Hence when a leading verb is made past, all its dependent tenses become past. This is best shown by taking a sentence whose leading verb is present, and, in changing it to past or future, observing the consequent changes of the dependent verbs:

Quiero saber si el arquitecto ha prometido que la casa estará terminada antes que nosotros volvamos de Europa. — I wish to know if the architect has promised that the house will be ready before we return from Europe.

Preguntaré al arquitecto si ha prometido que la casa estará terminada antes que nosotros volvamos de Europa. — I will ask the architect if he has promised that the house will be ready before we return from Europe.

Pregunté al arquitecto si había prometido que la casa estaría terminada antes que nosotros volviésemos de Europa. — I asked the architect if he had promised that the house would be finished before we should return from Europe.

Propongo que se manden imprimir las recomendaciones que hemos escuchado, como también las que se presenten en lo sucesivo. — I propose that we authorize the printing of the recommendations which we have heard, as well as of those which may be presented in future.

Propondré que se manden imprimir las recomendaciones que hemos escuchado, como también las que se presenten en lo sucesivo. — I shall propose that we authorize the printing of the recommendations which we have heard, as well as of those which may be presented in future.

Propuse que se mandaran imprimir las recomendaciones que habíamos escuchado, como también las que se presentaran en lo sucesivo. — I proposed that we should authorize the printing of the recommendations which we had heard, as well as of those which might be subsequently presented.

---

[1] But cf. § **25.11 ff.**

25.10. In cases where a leading verb in a non-past tense would be followed by a present subjunctive, a leading verb in a past tense takes an imperfect subjunctive. In like manner a perfect subjunctive becomes pluperfect subjunctive:

El general {mandará / manda / ha mandado} que todos los que **deserten sean** fusilados.	The general {will order / orders / has ordered} that all who *desert be* shot.
El general {mandó / había mandado} que todos los que **desertasen fuesen** fusilados.	The general {ordered / had ordered} that all who *deserted should be* shot.
El comandante declara que, **obtenga** o no condiciones favorables del enemigo, si para mañana no ha **llegado** el socorro que se **espera, será** preciso capitular la plaza.	The commandant declares that, whether he *obtain* favorable terms from the enemy or not, if the *expected* reinforcements *have* not *arrived* by tomorrow, it *will be* necessary to surrender the position.
El comandante declaró que, **obtuviese** o no condiciones favorables del enemigo, si para el día siguiente no **hubiese llegado** el socorro que se **esperaba, sería** preciso capitular la plaza.	The commandant declared that whether he *obtained* favorable terms from the enemy or not, if the *expected* reinforcements *did* not *arrive* by the following day, it *would be* necessary to surrender the position.

25.11. The past tenses may be followed by a dependent verb in the present tense when it expresses something that is always true:

El doctor Kane descubrió que Groenlandia **es** una isla.	Doctor Kane discovered that Greenland *is* an island.
El autor del Libro de Job sabía que la tierra **está** sin apoyo.	The author of the Book of Job was aware that the earth *is* unsupported.

25.12. The conditional may be followed by a present or a perfect subjunctive expressing something represented as taking place at the time of speaking (cf. § 24.19):

Podría creerse que esté dormido, mas no lo está.	One might think he is asleep, but he is not.

Se supondría por la manera como habla que tenga la oreja del príncipe, pero no es así.	One would imagine from the way he talks that he has the ear of the prince, but it is not so.
Parecería que haya profundizado el asunto.	It would seem that he has thoroughly investigated the subject.

25.13. The perfect is followed by present or imperfect (or the corresponding compound tenses) according as it has, in the mind of the speaker, some relation to present or past time respectively:

¿Ya sabes que Rafael quiere hablar contigo? Me **ha pedido** que le **acompañe.** (Benavente, **Al fin, mujer,** III, 1, 6)	You already know that Raphael wants to talk with you? He has asked me to come with him. *(the person hasn't come yet)*
Yo le he dicho a Juan que la niña se va a constipar aquí, y él **ha mandado** que **traigan** un brasero. (Baroja, **El mundo es ansí,** III, 2)	I told John that the child is going to catch cold here, and he asked them to bring a brasier. *(it has not yet been brought)*
Después de comer, el pintor Briones **ha propuesto** que **fuéramos** al Museo. (Baroja, **idem,** III, 10)	After dinner the painter Briones proposed that we go to the Museum. *(we went; many things have happened since)*
He dicho que nos **preparasen** una merienda en el comedor. (Benavente, **Al fin, mujer,** II, 6)	I told them to prepare a lunch for us in the dining room. *(the meal was at once prepared)*

25.14. After a leading verb in a past tense, a dependent subjunctive is in the present tense if its action applies to all time or relates the act of the dependent verb to the time of making the statement:

Dios nos dió la razón para que **distingamos** lo bueno de lo malo.	God gave us reason in order that we *may distinguish* good from evil.
El primer día pasó sin incidentes que **merezcan** la pena de mencionarse.	The first day was passed without any occurrences which *are worth* being mentioned.
Le escribí que **esté** aquí a las ocho.	I wrote him *to be* here at eight o'clock. *(it is not yet eight)*
Le escribí que **estuviera** aquí a las ocho.	I wrote him *to be* here at eight o'clock. *(it is now eight or later)*

25.15. So far as dependence of tenses is concerned, a relative clause is excluded, being in effect an independent sentence, having any tense required by the date of the action, irrespective of the tense of the leading verb in the sentence:

Discutíamos si convendría comprar el cuadro que el artista había pintado, pintaba, está pintando, pinte, está para pintar, *etc.*	We were discussing if it would be desirable to buy the picture which the artist had painted, was painting, is painting, may paint, is about to paint, *etc.*
No hay rango a que él no aspire, haya aspirado, aspirase, hubiese aspirado, *etc.*	There is no rank to which he does not aspire, *or* will not aspire, has not aspired, would not aspire, would not have aspired, *etc.*

25.16. The leading time of a sentence may sometimes be indicated and the tenses of dependent verbs determined without a leading verb; still the time must be indicated in some way:

Había mostrado evidentes indicios de talento antes de su décimoquinto año.	He had shown evident marks of genius before his fifteenth year.
Para el fin del mes próximo habré terminado el segundo tomo de mi novela.	By the end of next month I shall have finished the second volume of my novel.

TENSE EQUIVALENTS

25.17. A peculiarity of the subjunctive mood is that each tense, besides covering its own appropriate time, extends to subsequent time.

This will be made clear by taking sentences containing dependent verbs in the various tenses of the indicative, and changing the construction so as to require these verbs to become subjunctives. One tense of the subjunctive will be seen throughout to correspond to two of the indicative:

1. Present and future indicative become alike present subjunctive:

Es claro que se engaña.	It is clear that he is mistaken.
Es posible que se engañe.	It is possible that he is mistaken.
Estoy seguro de que vendrá.	I am sure he will come.
No estoy seguro de que venga.	I am not sure he will come.

2. Perfect and future perfect indicative become perfect subjunctive:

Afirma que V. lo ha escrito.	He declares you have written it.
Niega que V. lo haya escrito.	He denies that you have written it.

Es indudable que para la puesta del sol se habrá moderado la tempestad.	It is certain that by sunset the storm will have moderated.
Es dudoso que para la puesta del sol se haya moderado la tempestad.	It is doubtful whether the storm will have moderated by sunset.

3. Imperfect or preterite indicative and conditional become imperfect subjunctive:

El gobernador estaba seguro de que las noticias eran exactas.	The governor was certain the news was authentic.
El gobernador dudaba que las noticias fuesen exactas.	The governor doubted whether the news was authentic.
Los periódicos aseguraban que al día siguiente llegarían las tropas.	The newspapers declared that on the next day the troops would arrive.
La guarnición no creía que al día siguiente llegasen las tropas.	The garrison did not believe that the troops would arrive on the next day.

4. Pluperfect indicative and conditional perfect become pluperfect subjunctive:

Era evidente que por allí había pasado un ejército grande.	It was evident that a large army had passed by there.
Era dudoso que por allí hubiese pasado un ejército grande.	It was doubtful if a large army had passed by there.
Me dijo que para cuando yo volviese, su secretario habría copiado la carta.	He said that by the time I got back, his clerk would have copied the letter.
Dispuso que para cuando yo volviese, su secretario hubiese copiado la carta.	He arranged it so that by the time I got back, his clerk would have copied the letter.

THE SUBJUNCTIVE CONTRASTED WITH THE INDICATIVE AND INFINITIVE

25.18. It may be seen from the foregoing lessons that the subjunctive depends essentially upon two principles; viz.:

1. It depends upon a preceding verb (or equivalent word) which influences, or expresses an emotion or opinion about, the action of some person or thing *other than the subject of that preceding verb.*

2. The verb which is put in the subjunctive is dependent upon an idea implying *negation, doubt* or *future uncertainty.*

(The words italicized show the reason for the subjunctive.)

25.19. Under the first of these principles, the dependent verb is subjunctive when its subject is different from that of the principal verb; if the subject of both be the same; the dependent verb is *infinitive.*[1]

Under the second principle, the dependent verb is subjunctive when it relates to something unknown, uncertain or future; when it relates to what is regarded by the speaker as certain, it is *indicative.*

NOTE. These two principles underlie the distinction in the contrasted usages given below.

SUBJUNCTIVE AND INFINITIVE

25.20. Verbs of command do not apply to the action of the speaker. But verbs expressing a desire or preference, etc., expect a dependent verb to be subjunctive when its subject is different from that of the principal verb; when there is no change of subject, the dependent verb is infinitive:

Quiero borrar una palabra.	I want to rub out a word.
Quiero que se **borre** esta palabra.	*I* want this *word* to be rubbed out.
Preferimos ir a la biblioteca.	We prefer to go to the library.
Preferimos que V. **vaya** a la biblioteca.	*We* prefer that *you* go to the library.
Me permito llamar la atención de V. sobre lo que sigue.	I take the liberty of calling your attention to what follows.
Le permito que **juegue** en la huerta.	*I* permit *him* to play in the orchard.
Me propongo ir a las Bermudas.	I propose to go to Bermuda.
Propongo que se **trate** de indagar su paradero.	*I* propose that *someone* endeavor to find out his abode.

25.21. So verbs expressing a feeling or emotion about an occurrence require the subjunctive when there is a change of subject, but the infinitive when there is no change:

Siento no haber presenciado la pelea.	I am sorry not to have witnessed the combat.
Siento que V. no **presenciase** la pelea.	*I* am sorry *you* did not witness the combat.

[1] If the subjects are the same, and also with some verbs used impersonally, the dependent verb may be infinitive after a principal verb which usually has the indicative, the use of the infinitive being rather less colloquial than that of a **que** clause with the indicative: **Creo haber hecho un descubrimiento.** (Benavente, **¡No quiero, no quiero!**, II, 12) *I think that I have made a discovery.* **Me parecía caer en una red.** (Pardo Bazán, **Doña Milagros**, XV) *It seemed to me that I was falling into a trap.*

Temen no llegar a tiempo.	They are afraid they will not arrive in time.
Temen que no **lleguemos** a tiempo.	*They* are afraid *we* will not arrive in time.
Celebro conocerla a V., señora.	I am pleased to make your acquaintance, Madam.
Celebro que V. **tenga** tan buen semblante.	*I* am pleased that *you* are looking so well.

25.22. After impersonal expressions not indicative of certainty, when the dependent verb also has no subject, it is infinitive; but if the dependent verb has a subject, it is equivalent to a change of subject, and the dependent verb is subjunctive:

Es menester ganar la delantera.	It is necessary to gain the advance.
Es menester que los exploradores **ganen** la delantera.	*It* is necessary for the *scouts* to gain the advance.
Convendrá hacer la escalera menos empinada.	It will be advisable to make the staircase less steep.
Convendrá que V. **haga** la escalera menos empinada.	*It* will be advisable for *you* to make the staircase less steep.
Bastaría mandarle una tarjeta postal.	It would be sufficient to send him a postal card.
Bastaría que ella le **mandase** una tarjeta postal.	*It* would be sufficient for *her* to send him a postal card.

25.23. A verb denying or expressing doubt or disbelief about the action of another, requires the verb expressing that action to be subjunctive. If the negation or doubt applies to the action of the speaker, the dependent verb is preferably infinitive:

Niego haber redactado aquel documento.	I deny that I prepared that document.
Niego que mi secretario **redactase** aquel documento.	*I* deny that my *clerk* prepared that document.
Dudo poder lograrlo.	I doubt whether I will be able to accomplish it.
Dudo que nuestro agente **pueda** lograrlo.	*I* doubt whether our *agent* will be able to accomplish it.
¿Cree V. tener los medios?	Do you believe you have the means?
¿Cree V. que **tenga** los medios?	Do *you* believe *he* has the means?

25.24. Clauses stating purpose, proviso, exception and time preferably have the infinitive when the subject of the principal and of the dependent verb is one and the same. If the subjects are different, the dependent verb is subjunctive or, in the case of expressions of time, indicative if certainty is implied (cf. §§ **23.29** and **25.36**):

Construyeron un puente para pasar el río.	They made a bridge to cross the river on.
Construyeron un puente para que el ejército pasase el río.	*They* made a bridge for the *army* to cross the river on.
He hecho esto a fin de obtener el ascenso.	I have done this in order to obtain the promotion.
He hecho esto a fin de que V. **obtenga** el ascenso.	*I* have done this in order that *you* may obtain the promotion.
No entablaré el negocio ahora, a menos de recibir informes sobre la condición actual de la mina.	I shall not undertake the business unless I receive information of the present status of the mine.
No entablaré el negocio ahora, a menos que mi agente me **dé** informes satisfactorios de la condición actual de la mina.	*I* shall not undertake the business now unless my *agent* gives me a satisfactory account of the present status of the mine.

SUBJUNCTIVE AND INDICATIVE

25.25. Verbs expressing the action of the perceptive faculties, and those with the value of declaring or affirming, are followed by an indicative when used affirmatively, and by a subjunctive when employed negatively, interrogatively or in a condition:

Preví que encontraría grandes obstáculos.	I foresaw that I would meet with great obstacles.
No preví que **encontrara** tan grandes obstáculos.	I did not foresee that I would meet with such great obstacles.
Se ve por sus ojos que ha llorado.	It is apparent from her eyes that she has been weeping.
¿Se ve por sus ojos que **haya** llorado?	Is it apparent from her eyes that she has been weeping?
Me imagino que se atreverán a acometerle.	I imagine that they will dare to attack him.
Si V. se imagina que se **atrevan** a acometerle, yo mismo le escoltaré.	If you imagine that they will dare to attack him I myself will be his escort.
Estoy persuadido de que es su intención el engañarnos.	I am persuaded that it is his intention to deceive us.
No estoy persuadido de que **sea** su intención el engañarnos.	I am not persuaded that it is his intention to deceive us.

25.26. Nevertheless, when the leading verb is negative, interrogative or in a condition, the dependent verb is indicative if there is no doubt in the mind of the speaker or he wishes to make a fact prominent:

Ese hombre es un ateísta; no cree que existe un ser supremo. *(An undoubted fact, thinks the speaker, hence the indicative.)*	That man is an atheist; he does not believe that there exists a Supreme Being.
No cree que **existan** aparecidos.	He does not believe that there are ghosts.
¿Cree V. que su hermano ha jurado matarle?	Do you believe your brother has sworn to kill you? *(I.e.* he has sworn to kill you; do you believe it?)
¿Cree V. que su hermano **haya** jurado matarle?	Do you believe [this unlikely story that] your brother has sworn to kill you?
Si nuestro jefe averigua que V. ha hablado así, le reprenderá severamente.	If our chief learns that you have spoken thus, he will censure you severely.
Si averiguo que **quiera** venir, se lo mandaré decir a V.	If I learn that she wants to come, I will send you word.

25.27. Some verbs take the subjunctive or indicative according as their meaning directs something to be done, implies emotion or merely makes a statement:

Diré al criado que es un borrico.	I will tell the servant that he is an ass.
Diré al criado que **barra** el suelo.	I will tell the servant to sweep the floor.
Mi hermano me ha escrito que no lo cree.	My brother has written me that he does not believe it.
Mi hermano me ha escrito que no lo **crea.**	My brother has written me not to believe it.
Isabel me hizo una mueca para indicarme que no tenía miedo.	Isabel made me a gesture to indicate to me that she was not afraid.
Isabel me hizo una mueca para indicarme que no **tuviese** miedo.	Isabel made me a gesture to indicate to me not to be afraid.

25.28. Impersonal expressions bearing upon the certainty or truth of what follows, take the indicative in affirmative sentences, but the subjunctive when used negatively or interrogatively:

Se sigue que es incorrecto.	It follows that it is incorrect.
¿Se sigue que **sea** incorrecto?	Does it follow that it is incorrect?
No se sigue que **sea** incorrecto.	It does not follow that it is incorrect.
Es cierto que volverá.	It is certain he will return.
¿Es cierto que **vuelva?**	Is it certain that he will return?
No es cierto que **vuelva.**	It is not certain he will return.

REMARK. Though expressions of probability normally introduce a subjunctive, there are sporadic instances of the indicative, the expression then functioning as one of certainty:

Es muy probable que de este proceso educativo habría salido un régimen parlamentario. (Madariaga, **España,** I, 3, 26)	It is very probable that out of this educative process there would have come a parliamentary regime.

25.29. A dependent verb in a relative clause is subjunctive when it refers to what is unknown or uncertain; if it refers to what is regarded as certain, it is indicative:

La próxima vez que la **vea.**	The next time I see her.
La primera vez que la vi.	The first time I saw her.
Quiero una criada que **sepa** guisar.	I want a servant who knows how to cook.
Tengo una criada que sabe guisar.	I have a servant who knows how to cook.
Haré lo que V. me **diga.**	I will do what you may say.
Haré lo que V. me dice.	I will do what you say.
El cuadro se colgará como V. **sugiera.**	The picture shall be hung as you may suggest.
El cuadro se colgará como V. sugiere.	The picture shall be hung as you suggest.
Le mandaré a V. alguno de mis batidores que **conozca** el terreno. *(The man is yet to be found.)*	I will send you one of my scouts who knows the country.
Le mandaré a V. uno de mis batidores que conoce el terreno. *(The man is known.)*	I will send you one of my scouts who knows the country.

25.30. The indefinite relative expressions made by the addition of **-quiera** to a relative are followed by the indicative if referring to something known (cf. §§ **23.14** ff.):

Dondequiera que iba María, el tal cordero no dejaba de seguirla. — Everywhere that Mary went the lamb was sure to go.

Los tigres se encontraban en gran número dondequiera que la llanura les ofrecía altas yerbas. — The tigers were found in great numbers wherever the plain was covered with tall grass.

A cualquiera parte que he ido, le he encontrado siempre. — Wherever I have gone, I have always met him.

25.31. The formula **por...que** is followed by the indicative if no uncertainty is felt by the speaker (cf. § **23.17**):

No me valieron excusas, por más que **ponderé** lo largo de la jornada que tenía que hacer. (Pereda, **Peñas arriba,** XII) — Excuses didn't avail me, no matter how I *dwelt* on the length of the trip I had to make.

Por más esfuerzos que **hacía** por aparecer alegre, no lo alcanzaba. (Palacio Valdés, **La hermana San Sulpicio,** VIII) — No matter how many efforts I *made* to appear cheerful, I didn't succeed.

Por pronto que **acudieron,** ya era tarde. (Blasco Ibáñez, **¡Cosas de hombres!,** in **Cuentos valencianos**) — No matter how quickly they *came,* it was too late.

25.32. Conjunctive phrases implying concession are followed by the subjunctive, unless the dependent verb expresses a statement which the speaker grants to be a certainty, in which case the indicative is used:

Aunque será severa la lección que yo dé, no pasará a ser tragedia, y quedará en sainete. (Valera, **Juanita la larga,** XLII) — Although the lesson that I give will be severe, it will not get to be a tragedy but will remain at the farcical stage.

Aunque me lo jura, no lo creo. — Although he does swear to it, I do not believe it.

BUT

Aunque me lo jure manaña, no lo creeré. — Even if he swears to it tomorrow, I will not believe it.

Mis primeras impresiones no son de Entralgo, aunque haya nacido allí como he dicho. (Palacio Valdés, **La novela de un novelista,** IX) — My earliest impressions are not of Entralgo, even if I was born there as I have said.

Pero la calle polvorienta, abrasada por un sol de fuego aunque ya estuviesen en el final del mes de marzo...estaba desierta. (Payró, **Pago Chico,** V) — But the dusty street, burned by a fiery sun although they were at the end of the month of March, was deserted.

25.33. Porque meaning *because* will have its verb in the subjunctive only if the reason is regarded as insufficient, especially when the sentence is negative:

Anita no le convenía de ningún modo. No es **porque sea** mi sobrina, pero está muy mal educada. (Benavente, **Al natural,** I, 2) — Anita wasn't the proper one for him at all. It isn't *because she is* my niece, but she is badly brought up.

¿A que usted tampoco puede repetir lo que he dicho ahora? —También es cierto. Pero no **porque no te haya prestado** atención. (Gallegos, **Doña Bárbara,** II, 11) — What do you bet that neither can you repeat what I have said now? —That's true too. But not *because I haven't paid* attention to you.

No se incomodará usted **porque** el otro **testigo** de nuestra boda **sea** el mozo del hotel, ¿verdad? (Baroja, **El mundo es ansí, Prólogo**) — You won't be put out just *because* the other *witness* to our wedding *is* the hotel servant, will you?

25.34. Siempre que invariably has its verb in the subjunctive when it means *provided that;* if it means *whenever = every time that,* its verb follows the usual rules for conjunctive expressions of time. (§§ 23.29, 25.36):

Vamos, yo le voy a decir todo... **siempre que prometa** tener valor. (Pardo Bazán, **Doña Milagros,** XII) — Well, I will tell you everything, *provided you promise* to be brave.

Había quien se avergonzaba de confesar que era de Bilbao, y decía ser del pueblo de alguno de sus padres o abuelos, **siempre que fuese** pueblo más genuina y exclusivamente vascongado. (Unamuno, **Recuerdos de niñez y de mocedad, Estrambote,** V) — There were those who were ashamed to confess that they were from Bilbao, and said they were from the town of some one of their parents or grandparents, *provided it was* a town more genuinely and exclusively Basque.

Por eso no le colocan... Yo se lo digo siempre que pasa por aquí. (Pérez Galdós, **Miau,** II) — That's why they don't give him a job... I tell him so whenever he passes by here.

Siempre que sentía pasos en la escalera, iba a la puerta para abrirla antes de que llamase. (Pérez Galdós, **Fortunata y Jacinta,** IV, 3, 2) — Whenever she heard steps on the stairs, she went to the door to open it before she knocked.

Ya sabes que con alma y vida le serviría **siempre que** me **necesitara.** (Benavente, **La propia estimación,** II, 2) — Of course you know that I would aid him with heart and soul *whenever he needed* me.

25.35. **Ya que** *now, since* is used with either indicative or subjunctive without noticeable difference of meaning, the former being more frequent:

Ya que no me recibes, no te vayas de la reja y háblame un rato. (Valera, **Juanita la larga,** XII) — Since you don't receive me, don't go away from the grating but talk to me a little.

Ya que vengas sin que nadie te llame, que sea para servir de algo y no de estorbo. (Pereda, **La puchera,** XVII) — Since you come without anyone's calling you, let it be to be of some use and not a hindrance.

Consideraba luego don Paco que Juanita, ya que no le amase, se deleitaba en su conversación. (Valera, **Juanita la larga,** XVIII) — Don Paco considered then that, since Juanita didn't love him, (at least) she took pleasure in his conversation.

25.36. The temporal conjunctions already mentioned require the subjunctive when they relate to a subsequent time, since what is future is uncertain:

Nos embarcaremos en cuanto nuestros equipajes **estén** a bordo. — We shall go aboard as soon as our baggage *is* on board.

Nos embarcamos en cuanto nuestros equipajes estuvieron a bordo. — We went aboard as soon as our baggage was on board.

Teníamos la intención de embarcarnos en cuanto nuestros equipajes **estuviesen** a bordo. — We intended to go aboard as soon as our baggage *was* on board.

Mientras que estaba en mi empleo era muy laborioso. — While he was in my employ he was very industrious.

Mientras **quede** en mi empleo será bien pagado. — While he *remains* in my employ he shall be well paid.

REMARK I. **Antes (de) que** *before* normally has its verb in the subjunctive in all cases where order of events is implied:

En 1063 el papa Alejandro II promovió una expedición a España, treinta años antes que se predicase la primera cruzada a Palestina. (Menéndez Pidal, **La España del Cid,** II, 3, 4)[1]

In 1063 Pope Alexander II promoted an expedition to Spain, thirty years before the first crusade to Palestine was preached.

REMARK II. Except for **antes (de) que,** conjunctive expressions of time will have their verb in the indicative, provided a general truth is intended, even if the act extends into the future:

Un hombre no es verdaderamente mundano y no alcanza una perfecta distinción mientras no envejece un poco y no adquiere un aire algo cansado y algo escéptico. (Camba, **La rana viajera, Alemania,** I)

A man isn't really worldly and does not attain genuine distinction until he ages a little and acquires a rather tired and skeptical air.

25.37. Verbs expressing a doubt or something unknown take the indicative if the dependent verb is introduced by **si,** but the subjunctive if **que** is employed:

No sé si vendrá.[2]	I do not know whether he will come.
No sé que venga.	I do not know that he will come.
No sabía si vendría.	I didn't know whether he would come.
Dudo si lo obtendrá. Dudo que lo obtenga.	I doubt whether he will obtain it.
Dudaba si lo obtendría. Dudaba que lo obtuviese.	I doubted whether he would obtain it.

[1] Such a passage as the following is obviously beside the point as the speaker does not mean to say that the act of arriving will precede that of imagining: **¿Crees tú que llegará ese momento? —Sí, Laura, y antes que imaginas.** (Martínez de la Rosa, **La conjuración de Venecia,** II, 3) *Do you think that that moment will come? —Yes, Laura, and sooner than you imagine.*

[2] The use of the present subjunctive with **si** meaning *whether* is infrequent and, when found, increases the degree of uncertainty: **Quién sabe si la necesidad, que ya se sabe que tiene la cara de hereje, me obligue a echar mano de lo que aprendí en la sacristía.** (Gallegos, **Canaima,** IX: **Las carcajadas de Apolonio)** *Who knows whether necessity, who, as is well known, has the face of a heretic, may oblige me to make use of what I learned in the sacristy.* As the equivalent of the English infinitive, the subjunctive is found in sentences like **Soy de otra raza, no sé si diga exquisita o gastada y vieja.** (Pardo Bazán, **La sirena negra,** VIII) *I am of another race, I don't know whether to say fastidious or spent and old.*

XXVI

The Auxiliary Verbs DEBER and PODER

DEBER

26.1. **Deber** is conjugated regularly throughout. Its primary meaning, which it still has before a noun, is *to owe:*

Llegó a mi noticia que mi hijo debía grandes sumas de dinero.	I learned that my son owed large sums of money.
Debe su puesto al favor del general B.	He owes his position to the favor of General B.

26.2. The infinitive is used as a noun meaning *duty:*

Es nuestro **deber** ayudarlos.	It is our *duty* to aid them.
Ha hecho su **deber.**	He has done his *duty.*

26.3. Placed as an auxiliary verb before an infinitive, **deber** has the two following values:

1. It expresses the ideas of duty, obligation or undefined necessity which are represented in English by the defective verbals *ought, should, must:*

V. **debe** contestar a su esquela.	You ought to reply to his note.
Este hecho **debe** tomarse en consideración.	This fact should be taken into consideration.
Debo ir al correo ahora.	I must go to the post office now.

2. It expresses an inference from circumstantial evidence, represented in English by one acceptation of *must:*

Debe haber viajado mucho.	He *must* have traveled a great deal.
Esa gente **debe** tener ideas muy extrañas acerca de la América del Sur.	Those people *must* have very strange ideas about South America.

REMARK I. With the latter meaning it may be connected with the following infinitive by the preposition **de**; but generally it governs the infinitive directly without a preposition:

Su casa **debe de estar,** me parece, en la manzana vecina.	It seems to me their house *must be* in the next block.

REMARK II. Misuse of **deber de,** i.e., employing it with the sense of *duty, obligation* or *undefined necessity,* is widespread in speaking and is not rare in standard writers:

Debía de haberle dado a usted dos millones de gracias, y soy tan burro que no le he dicho a usted nada; pero nada. (Benavente, **Pepa Doncel,** II, 2, 2)	I should have given you two million thanks, and I am so asinine that I have said nothing to you, absolutely nothing.
Alfonso opinaba que debíamos de venir cada año a ver a nuestros papás: yo creía que debíamos de venir cada seis meses. (Palacio Valdés, **La novela de un novelista,** XII)	Alphonso thought that we should come to see our parents every year; I thought that we should come every six months.
En fin, que me quedo con la carta, porque debo de quedarme con ella. (Pereda, **Nubes de estío,** XXIV)	In short, I am keeping the letter because I have the obligation of keeping it.

26.4. When **deber,** expressing an inference or conjecture, is preceded by a negative, it is rendered in English by *cannot* or *ought not,* as well as by *must not:*

Este bosque **no debe** ser interminable; debemos hallar salida en esta dirección.	This forest *cannot* be endless; we must surely find an outlet in this direction.
No debe ser difícil hallar un hombre tal como V. lo necesita.	It *ought not* to be difficult to find a man such as you need.

26.5. As the manner in which **deber** is to be rendered in English varies considerably according as it expresses a past, present or future obligation or probability, the various moods and tenses will be illustrated separately.

NOTE. As the English words *ought, should* and *must,* which correspond most nearly to **deber,** are practically invariable, the full inflectional forms of **deber** can, in cases of difficulty, be more adequately represented in English by some expression equally capable of inflection, as *to be obliged to.*

PRESENT INDICATIVE

26.6. Expresses an obligation or probability existing at the present time:

OBLIGATION

La luna **debe salir** dentro de diez minutos.	The moon *ought to be up* in ten minutes.
Mi hija **debe quedarse** en Marsella hasta fines del mes de mayo.	My daughter *is to stay* in Marseilles till the latter part of May.
Consideraciones de esta especie **deben inspirar** a los americanos el más vivo presentimiento del poder y de la grandeza que les espera.	Considerations of this character *should inspire* Americans with the liveliest expectations of future grandeur and power.

INFERENCE

Debe haber algún medio de lograrlo.	*There must be* some way of attaining it.
V. **debe estar** cansada después de andar tanto.	You *must be* tired after walking so much.
La extensión de este contrabando **no debe ser** desconocida a las autoridades fiscales.	The extent of this smuggling *cannot be* unknown to the fiscal authorities.
El tren **debe haber llegado.**	The train *must have arrived.*

IMPERFECT INDICATIVE

26.7. Expresses, without regard to its completion, an obligation or a probability which existed during the past or, as the equivalent of **debería** (cf. § 26.16), advice concerning present or future conduct:

OBLIGATION

Debían encontrarnos aquí.	They *were to meet us* here.
Allí se detuvieron para examinar el sitio donde **debía construirse** el puente.	They halted there to examine the location where the bridge *was to be built.*
Como la cantera estaba expuesta directamente al sol levante, **no debía tardar** en estar alumbrada por las luces del alba.	As the quarry was exposed directly to the rising sun, it *ought soon* to have been illuminated by the light of the dawn.
Al pasar cerca del farol lo rompió, y todo quedó sumergido en una oscuridad profunda que **debía favorecer** su fuga.	In passing by the lantern he broke it, and everything was thrown into profound darkness *calculated to favor* (or which *should have favored)* his flight.

En vista del éxito obtenido allí, **no debía** usted **haber preguntado** aquí nada. (Benavente, **Lo cursi,** III, 2)	In view of the success achieved there, you *shouldn't have asked* anything here.

INFERENCE

Según ese viejo retrato la abuela de V. **debía ser** hermosa a la edad de veinte años.	According to that old portrait, your grandmother *must have been* a beauty at the age of twenty.
El médico era un buen hombre, pero **no debía de saber** gran cosa.	The doctor was a good man, but *it was not likely that he knew* much.
Adelantóse con precaución hacia popa para llegar bajo la toldilla del bergantín, donde **debía estar** la Santa Bárbara.	He advanced carefully towards the stern so as to get under the quarterdeck of the brigantine, where the powder magazine *was likely to be.*
Mi hermano creyó que el tren **debía haber llegado.**	My brother believed that the train *must have arrived.*
La baja de los fondos públicos por aquella época en las principales plazas de Europa **debía haberle afectado** seriamente.	The fall in state stocks about that time in the principal markets of Europe *must have affected* him seriously.

AS EQUIVALENT OF **debería**

No creo que dé jamás tan mal paso. De todos modos, aunque tan mal paso fuese posible, **no se debía apelar** a él. (Valera, **El comendador Mendoza,** XII)	I don't believe she will ever take such a bad step. Anyway, even if such a bad step were possible, recourse *should not be had* to it.
Si cuando se admira a un artista, **no debía** una **conocerle** personalmente. (Benavente, **Lo cursi,** II, 7)	Why, when one admires an artist, one *shouldn't know him* personally!
Eso, que debiera acercarme más, es lo que me separa; eso, que **debía darme** valor, es lo que me acobarda. (Benavente, **La propia estimación,** II, 7)	That, which should draw me closer, is what holds me at a distance; that, which *should give me* courage, is what makes me afraid.
Lo que **debías hacer** es no andar más con Brull. (Baroja, **La dama errante,** VI)	What you *should do* is not go around with Brull any more.
José, ¿por qué no cortejas a la hija de la maestra?. . . José, tú **debías casarte** con la hija de la maestra. (Palacio Valdés, **José,** IV)	Joseph, why don't you court the schoolteacher's daughter? . . . Joseph, you *should marry* the schoolteacher's daughter.

PRETERITE INDICATIVE

26.8. Expresses a past obligation to perform an act, or an inference that an act took place, the act being considered as completed:

OBLIGATION

Ocho días después **debimos salir** para Londres.	Eight days afterwards we *were obliged to start* for London.
La criada robaba tanto que **debí despedirla.**	The servant girl stole so much that I *had to discharge her.*
Me sentí tan mareado que **debí subir** sobre cubierta.	I felt so seasick that I *had to go up* on deck.
¡Y estabas aquí!...**Debí figurármelo.** (Benavente, **Al natural,** I, 15)	And you were here! I *should have imagined it.*
Debemos irnos... No **debimos haber venido.** (Benavente, **Al fin, mujer,** II, 1)	We must go... We *shouldn't have come.*
El reparto de cuarenta reales, que **debió haberse hecho** en la semana anterior, no se hizo en ocasión oportuna. (Pereda, **Sotileza,** VI)	The distribution of forty reals, which *should have been made* during the previous week, was not made at the proper time.

INFERENCE

Imaginé yo que la fuga de las jóvenes **debió de ser** causada por la indiscreción y necedad de D. Nemesio.	I imagined that the flight of the young ladies *must have been* caused by the indiscretion and stupidity of Don Nemesio.
La buena mujer **debió de observar** mi turbación, porque al levantar los ojos vi una sonrisa en sus labios.	The good woman *must have noticed* my confusion, for on raising my eyes I saw a smile on her lips.

REMARK. The line separating the preterite from the imperfect of **deber** is so fine that it is not consistently maintained. The distinction, naturally, is the usual one between imperfect and preterite. In cases of doubt, the preference is for the imperfect (cf. §§ **17.4** ff.).

PERFECT INDICATIVE

26.9. Expresses an obligation of the recent past or one whose effects extend to the present time, or a conjecture about the past judging from evidence of the present time:

OBLIGATION

He debido salir inmediatamente para Londres.	I *have been obliged* to start at once for London.

He debido sufrir muchos desaires.	I *have had* to bear many affronts.
Mi General, nuestra ala izquierda **ha debido** abandonar las obras avanzadas.	General, our left wing *has been obliged* to abandon the outworks.
Creí que no querría usted recibirme. —¿Por qué? —Porque **he debido** venir mucho antes. (Benavente, **Pepa Doncel,** III, 6).	I thought that you wouldn't want to receive me. —Why? —Because I *should have* come long before.

INFERENCE

Esa señora **ha debido** ser muy guapa durante su juventud.	That lady *must have* been very pretty during her youth *(judging from what she is now).*
Ha debido haber un desbordamiento considerable en este punto.	*There must have* been a considerable overflow at this point *(judging from appearances).*

26.10. There is often not much (if any) distinction between the present tense of **deber** followed by perfect infinitive **(El tren debe haber llegado)** and the perfect tense of **deber** followed by simple infinitive **(El tren ha debido llegar).** The same is true of other tenses of **deber (El tren debía haber llegado, El tren había debido llegar),** the preference in conversational style being for the use of simple tense of **deber** plus perfect infinitive. Furthermore, with past tenses the simple infinitive and the perfect infinitive are used almost interchangeably **(El tren debió llegar, El tren debió haber llegado).**

The same considerations apply to the use of **poder** (§ **26.27**).

PLUPERFECT INDICATIVE

26.11. Expresses an obligation or conjecture that had existed prior to some past event:

El marinero **había debido** renunciar a aquel trabajo que le crispaba horrorosamente los nervios.	The sailor *had been obliged* to give up that work, which made him terribly nervous.
Habían debido de terminar el trabajo, porque, al cabo de poco tiempo, se levantaron todos. (Baroja, **El mayorazgo de Labraz,** II, 7)	They *must have* finished the work, because shortly after everybody got up.
Al principio **habían debido** creer que Paco, sorprendido en la garita, había sido muerto.	At first they *had been obliged* to think that Frank, surprised in the sentry box, had been killed.

FUTURE INDICATIVE

26.12. Expresses a duty or obligation which will exist in the future, or an inference about a future occurrence:

OBLIGATION

Deberemos levantarnos muy de mañana.	We *shall have* to get up very early in the morning.
Se resuelve: Que se nombre una comisión de diez y siete delegados, la cual **deberá** examinar y presentar informe acerca de la comunicación por ferrocarril entre los diferentes países representados en esta Conferencia.	Resolved, That a committee of seventeen delegates be appointed, whose duty it *shall be* to consider and report upon the subject of railway communication between the several countries represented in this Conference.
Pa esto ya **deberás** haber arreglado antes la cosa. (Lynch, **El inglés de los güesos,** XXIX)	For this of course you *must have* arranged the thing beforehand.

INFERENCE

El proyecto de V. presenta muchas y grandes ventajas, pero los gastos **deberán** ser inmensos.	Your scheme offers many and great advantages, but the expense *will necessarily be* enormous.
Si tratamos ahora de pasar este canal, correremos el riesgo de que la corriente nos arrastre hasta el mar, porque es muy rauda; pero **deberá** comenzar el reflujo dentro de poco, y teniendo paciencia, en la marea baja será probable[1] que encontremos un paso vadeable.	If we try at present to cross this channel we will run the risk of being carried out to sea by the current, for it is very swift; but the tide *will most likely* turn within a little, and if we have patience we will probably find a ford at low water.
La familia **deberá** haberse acostado antes de que nosotros lleguemos.	The family *will probably* have gone to bed before we get there.

FUTURE PERFECT

26.13. Expresses a future obligation to have done something or an inference that something has been done recently:

Antes de que los socorros puedan llegar, **habremos debido** rendirnos por falta de víveres.	Before the reinforcements can arrive, we *will have been obliged* to surrender for want of provisions.

[1] It would be equally proper to say **en la marea baja deberemos encontrar un paso vadeable**, were it not that it would allow less variety of expression, in view of the preceding **deberá.**

CONDITIONAL

26.14. The value of the conditional of **deber** is further subdivided according as it expresses a future dating from a past time, or stands in the if-clause of a condition of implied negation.

As a past future:

OBLIGATION

Nos previno que **deberíamos** levantarnos muy de mañana.	He informed us that *we would have* to get up very early in the morning.
Colocóse a un criado en la puerta de la galería, quien **debería** impedir la entrada a las personas que no tuviesen billetes.	A servant was stationed at the door of the gallery, whose *duty it was* to prevent persons from entering who had not tickets.

INFERENCE

Conocimos que el choque **debería** de ser espantoso.	We knew that the shock would most likely be frightful.
Según los nuevos síntomas que se habían presentado, la calentura no **debería** durar sino dos días más.	According to the new symptoms which had appeared, the fever ought not to last more than two days longer.
Los isleños creían que de esta manera haciendo fuego en los piratas desde cuatro puntos diferentes, **deberían** éstos pensar que la isla estaba suficientemente poblada y al mismo tiempo bien defendida.	The islanders thought that by firing on the pirates in this manner from four different points, the latter would naturally think that the island was sufficiently populated and at the same time well defended.

26.15. In conditions of implied negation the meaning of probability disappears and only that of obligation remains:

Si aquella casa quebrase, **deberíamos** suspender el crédito.	If that house were to fail *we should have* to suspend payments.
Si llegara su señor tío esta noche, **debería** V. cederle su aposento.	If your uncle should arrive tonight you *would have* to give up your room to him.
Si aconteciera que V descubriese el autor del robo, **debería** avisar a las autoridades civiles.	If you should happen to discover the author of the robbery, it *would be your duty* to inform the authorities.

26.16. The most frequent use of the conditional of **deber** is when the if-clause is wanting; in which case it expresses a present obligation to perform something that is not being done—or the contrary. Nowadays **debía** and **debiera** (a customary equivalent of the conditional) have the same use (cf. §§ **24.20, 26.7, 26.19, 26.22**):

V. **debería** manejarse mejor con su hermano.	You *ought to* (or *should*) behave better towards your brother.
No **deberíamos** permanecer más tiempo aquí.	We *ought* not *to* (or *should* not) stay here any longer.
V. **debería** contentarse con esta suma, porque excede al valor del trabajo.	You *ought to* (or *should*) be content with this sum, for it is more than the work is worth.

CONDITIONAL PERFECT

26.17. Is employed principally to express a past obligation to perform something which was not done—or the contrary:

V. **habría debido** mostrarle más indulgencia.	You *ought to have* (or *should have*) shown him more indulgence.
V. **no habría debido** romper el sello de una carta dirigida a mí.	You *ought* not *to have* (or *shouldn't have*) broken the seal of a letter addressed to me.
Confieso que **no habría debido** hacerlo.	I confess that I *ought not to have* (or *shouldn't have*) done so.

26.18. The conditional followed by a past infinitive expresses a present obligation to have performed, in the past, something which was not done—or the contrary—and is scarcely distinguishable from the preceding usage:

V. **debería haberse preparado** para este examen.	You *ought to have* (or *should have*) *prepared yourself* for this examination.

REMARK. For the expression of an obligation to have performed an act in the past there are many practically equivalent forms of **deber,** bearing in mind that the distinction between imperfect and preterite of this verb is not carefully observed and that the distinction between perfect and preterite is at times slight for any verb. Thus *You should have studied* might be rendered **Vd. debió estudiar, debió haber estudiado, debía** or **debiera** or **debería haber estudiado, ha debido estudiar, había** or **hubiera** or **habría debido estudiar,** and also **debía** or **debiera estudiar.** See §§ **26.7, 26.10, 26.16, 26.18.**

26.19. The values of the remaining forms of **deber** follow in such regular sequence those which have been given, that their usages will be sufficiently apparent from the examples without further explanation:

PRESENT SUBJUNCTIVE

OBLIGATION

Siento que **deba** V. marcharse tan temprano.	I am sorry you *have to* go so early.
Este libro no contiene nada **que** la Srta. hija de V. no **deba** leer.	This book contains nothing which your daughter *should* not *read.*

INFERENCE[1]

No creo que el error de observación **deba** pasar de unos cuantos segundos en latitud.	I do not think the error of observation *ought to* exceed a few seconds in latitude.
No me imagino que ella **deba** divertirse mucho allí.	I don't imagine she *can be* very much entertained there.

PERFECT SUBJUNCTIVE

OBLIGATION

Es lástima que **haya debido** V. sacrificar su biblioteca.	It is a pity you *have had to* sacrifice your library.

INFERENCE

No creo que él **haya debido** aprender gran cosa en el colegio.	I don't believe it *likely that he has* learned much at college.

IMPERFECT SUBJUNCTIVE

OBLIGATION

El coronel mandó destruir el puente, de modo que los enemigos, al llegar, **debieran** hacer un rodeo.	The colonel ordered the bridge to be destroyed, so that the enemy, on coming up, *should be obliged* to make a detour.
Si hubiéramos sabido que V. **debiese** venir, habríamos mandado preparar una comida mejor.	If we had known that you *were to come* we should have had a better dinner prepared.

INFERENCE

No creo que **debiese** de entender lo que yo dije, porque siguió leyendo.	I do not believe he *could have* heard what I said, for he kept on reading.

---

[1] The value of **deber** as expressing an inference is of extremely limited application in the dependent tenses.

No nos imaginábamos que el ruido **debiera significar** nada. — We did not suppose that the noise *meant* anything.

Ra FORM AS SUBSTITUTE FOR CONDITIONAL

Si el camino estuviese en buen estado, **debiera** V. recorrer la distancia en tres horas. — If the road were in good condition, you *ought to* walk the distance in three hours.

El enamorado Montesinos no puso obstáculos a este deseo, aunque **debiera** ponerlos. (Palacio Valdés, **La fe,** V) — The smitten Montesinos presented no obstacles to this wish, although he *should* have.

FUTURE SUBJUNCTIVE

Dejo este punto para los que **debieren** resolver los enigmas políticos de lo futuro. — I leave this point for those whose *duty it may be* to solve the political riddles of the future.

PLUPERFECT SUBJUNCTIVE

Era de sentirse que **hubiera debido** renunciar a su proyecto. — It was to be regretted that he *had been obliged to* give up his project.

Hubiera debido ir allí, como jefe de la expedición. (Arciniegas, **Los alemanes en la conquista de América,** V, toward end) — *He should have* gone along there as leader of the expedition.

INFINITIVE

Había cedido a sus deseos sin **deber** hacerlo. — He had yielded to his impulses when he *ought* not *to* have done so.

Creemos **deber** añadir que la sociedad que frecuenta estas termas y la belleza de las perspectivas que se presentan a la vista, igualan por completo a las ventajas sanitarias que acaban de exponerse. — We think *we ought* to add that the society and the scenery at these springs are fully equal to the sanitary advantages which have just been set forth.

PAST INFINITIVE

Siento **haber debido** despedirlo. — I am sorry to *have been obliged to* discharge him.

Don Ramón se jacta de no **haber debido** nunca reconocer una derrota. — Mr. Ramón boasts that he *has* never *been obliged to* acknowledge a defeat.

PAST PARTICIPLE

When not employed with **haber** in the formation of the compound tenses, the past participle is used only as an adjective with the original value of *due:*

Para espantar a los cuervos, se pusieron maniquíes grotescos, **debidos** a la imaginación fantástica de Ruiz, los que bastaron para ahuyentarlos.

To frighten the crows, grotesque effigies were erected, *due* to the fantastic imagination of Ruiz, which were sufficient to scare them away.

PRESENT PARTICIPLE

Debiendo leer esta noche un ensayo delante de la Sociedad Filológica, suplico a V. se sirva recibir mis excusas con la expresión de mi agradecimiento por su atento convite.

As I am to read an essay before the Philological Society this evening I beg you to accept my regrets with the expression of my thanks for your kind invitation.

PERFECT PARTICIPLE

Habiendo debido enviar últimamente una remesa a mi hijo, quien está haciendo sus estudios en Europa, siento deber manifestar que no tengo disponible la suma que V. dice.

Having been lately *obliged to* send a remittance to my son who is studying in Europe, I am sorry to have to say that I have not at my disposal the sum you name.

26.20. CORRESPONDENCE OF TENSES OF **DEBER**

Necesitábamos tiempo para juzgar lo que **debíamos** hacer en aquel asunto.

We needed time to consider what we *ought to* do in the matter.

Necesitamos tiempo para juzgar lo que **debemos** hacer en este asunto.

We need time to consider what we *ought to* do in the matter.

Necesitaremos tiempo para juzgar lo que **deberemos** hacer en este asunto.

We will need time to consider what we *will need to* do in the matter.

En este caso necesitaríamos tiempo para juzgar lo que **deberíamos** hacer en este asunto.

In that case we would need time to consider what we *ought to* do in the matter.

En ese caso habríamos necesitado tiempo para juzgar lo que **hubiéramos debido** hacer en aquel asunto.

In that case we should have needed time to consider what it *would have been our duty to* do in the matter.

PODER

26.21. **Poder** is quite irregular in its inflection; its complete conjugation will be found in § **14.50.** For convenience, however, each tense will be conjugated here as it is presented.

26.22. The infinitive is used as a noun meaning *power*:[1]

Nos tiene en su **poder.**	He has us in his *power.*
El **poder** ejecutivo.	The executive *power.*
El fuego tiene el **poder** de calcinar todos los cuerpos.	Fire has the *power* of calcining all bodies.

26.23. **Poder** is a true auxiliary, as it always applies either to a following infinitive, or relates to a foregoing infinitive which does not need to be repeated. It has the following values:

1. It corresponds to the English *be able,* and expresses physical power or ability, generally represented in English by the defective verb *can:*

El niño ya **puede** andar.	The child *can* walk now.
Puedo probar que es verdad.	I *can* prove that it is true.

2. By extension of the above, it is used like the English *may* to express permissibility:

Se **puede** también emplear la gasa yodoformizada.	Iodoform gauze *may* also be employed.
Vds. **pueden** salir si quieren.	You *may* go out if you want to.

3. It expresses the liability of an occurrence, or the possibility of the truth of a statement or supposition which the speaker is not

[1] Mechanical *power* is **fuerza;** *power* in mathematics and when it relates to the authority of states, is **potencia:**

Fuerza motriz; fuerza de tracción; fuerza hidráulica; fuerza propulsora.	Motive power; power of traction; water power; propelling power.
Elevar un guarismo a la décima potencia.	To raise a figure to the tenth power.
Estas dos potencias han celebrado un tratado de reciprocidad.	These two powers have ratified a treaty of reciprocity.
Las potencias del cielo; las potencias de las tinieblas.	The powers on high; the powers of darkness.
Un torno mecánico; un telar mecánico; una prensa mecánica de rotación.	A power lathe; a power loom; a rotary power press.

prepared to deny; this value is represented in English by *may,* in interrogations by *can:*

El niño **puede** caerse.	The child *may* fall.
Puede ser verdad.	It *may* be true.
¿**Puede** ser posible que haya descubierto la clave?	*Can* it be possible that he has discovered the clue?

26.24. For the sake of clearness, usage 3 may be distinguished from the others by employing the third person singular of **poder** impersonally before **ser;** the whole being followed by the subjunctive of the dependent verb:

Puede hacerse.	It *can* be done.
Puede ser que se haga.	It *may* be done.

26.25. Moreover when **poder** is used in a negation, the negative **no** is placed before **poder** when it denotes power or ability; but when mere liability or possibility is intended, the negative is restricted to the infinitive by being placed between it and **poder** (cf. § **11.7**):

El espejo **no puede** caerse.	The mirror *cannot* fall.
El espejo **puede no** caerse.	The mirror *may not* fall.

26.26. **Poder** may be used before an indefinite pronoun, expressed or understood, without relating to a previous infinitive, in which case **hacer** *to do* may be considered to be understood. With the meaning of *be able to stand up to, dominate,* **poder** takes an object:

Contra tales adversarios no **podemos** nada.	Against such adversaries we can [do] nothing.
No **puedo** con él.	I cannot [do anything] with him.
Estoy agotado; no **puedo** más.	I am exhausted; I can [do] no more.
Ninguno de su edad, de los que andaban con él, le había podido. (Unamuno, **Recuerdos de niñez y de mocedad,** I, 12)	No one of his age, of those who went about with him, had been able to stand up to him.

NOTE. As the English auxiliaries *may, might,* and *can, could,* which correspond most nearly to **poder,** are fragmentary and have but two forms respectively, the full inflectional forms of **poder** can often be better rendered by some expression equally capable of inflection, as *to be able to, to be possible that.*

26.27. In the exposition of **deber** the student has seen the effects of the several moods and tenses in expressing an obligation or inference. Their varying effects upon **poder**, in expressing ability or possibility, are precisely similar, and will be sufficiently apparent from the examples without need of further explanation. The various moods and tenses will be treated separately (as was done with **deber**):

PRESENT INDICATIVE

[*puedo, puedes, puede; podemos, podéis, pueden*]

Aquellos batidores son gente escogida, hombres disciplinados y diestros, con los cuales **se puede contar** con seguridad.	Those scouts are picked men, expert and well disciplined, who *may be* safely *counted on*.
Los buques de mayor calado **pueden atracarse** a los muelles.	Vessels of the largest draught *can come alongside* of the wharves.
No se **puede repicar** y **andar** en la procesión.	One *cannot do* two things at once.
La exportación anual de productos naturales del Istmo **puede estimarse** en $1.200.000.	The annual export of natural products from the Isthmus *may be estimated* at $1,200,000.

FOLLOWED BY PAST INFINITIVE

La escuadra todavía **no puede haber doblado** el cabo de Hornos.	The fleet *cannot* yet *have doubled* Cape Horn.
La escuadra **puede no haber doblado** todavía el cabo de Hornos.	The fleet *may not have doubled* Cape Horn yet.
Las corrientes **pueden haberlos llevado** más lejos de la costa.	The currents *may have carried them* farther from the coast.

PERFECT INDICATIVE

[*he, has, ha podido; hemos, habéis, han podido*]

La escuadra todavía no **ha podido** doblar el cabo de Hornos.	The fleet *has* not yet *been able to* double Cape Horn.
Le hemos buscado por todas partes, pero no le **hemos podido** encontrar.	We have looked for him everywhere, but *have* not *been able to* find him.
Los jurados no **han podido** ponerse de acuerdo.	The jurors *have* not *been able to* agree.

IMPERFECT INDICATIVE

[*podía, podías, podía; podíamos, podíais, podían*]

Se preguntaba lo que **podía** haber de cierto en la noticia, dada la	It was asked what certainty there *could* be in the report, considering

poca confianza que debía tenerse en aquel que la refería. — the little confidence to which the narrator was entitled.

Escuchaban ávidamente todos los rumores que **podían** llegar del exterior. — They listened eagerly to every noise that *could* reach them from without.

Su proyecto era atrevido, pero **podía** tener buen éxito gracias a la oscuridad de la noche. — Their project was daring, but *might* succeed through favor of the darkness of the night.

Aquí **podíamos** pasar la noche. —¿Y si hay algún perro de esos de ganado? (Baroja, **El mayorazgo de Labraz, I, 1**) — We *could* pass the night here. —And what if there is one of those cattle dogs?

Si después volviera a llover unos días, todavía **podía** arreglarse la cosecha. (Benavente, **Al natural,** II, 2)[1] — If afterwards it would rain again for a few days, the crop *could* still be managed.

FOLLOWED BY PAST INFINITIVE[2]

Claro era que ninguno de ellos **podía haber sido** visto, porque ellos mismos no distinguían el buque al través de la niebla. — It was clear that none of them *could have been* seen, for they themselves did not distinguish the ship through the fog.

El torpedero no **podía haberse alejado** mucho, por rápida que hubiera sido su marcha. — The torpedo boat *could not* have *got* very *far away,* however great might have been her speed.

Si usted las ha contado... —Yo, sí, muchas veces, pero **podía haberme equivocado**... (Benavente, **La honradez de la cerradura,** I, 3) — If you have counted them...—Indeed, I have, many times, but I *might have made a mistake.*

PRETERITE INDICATIVE

[*pude, pudiste, pudo; pudimos, pudisteis, pudieron*]

Cada cual trató de acomodarse para dormir, como mejor **pudo.** — Each one tried to accommodate himself, as best he *could,* to sleep.

Hablaban los piratas en alta voz, refiriendo sus proezas mientras bebían desmesuradamente, y Ramírez **pudo** oír la siguiente relación:... — The pirates were talking in a loud voice, recounting their exploits, while they kept on drinking immoderately, and Ramírez *was able* to hear the following recital:...

[1] For the use of **podía** instead of **podría,** cf. § **26.16.** For the expression of the possibility of performing an act in the past (*could have, might have*) there exists the same variety of forms as for *should have.* (Cf. § **26.18,** REMARK.)

[2] **Poder** followed by a past infinitive most often expresses not power but probability or possibility. It usually does not correspond to "be able," but to "may" or "can."

Carlos no **pudo** contener un suspiro de satisfacción al oír aquella respuesta. — Charles *could* not restrain a sigh of relief on hearing this answer.

FOLLOWED BY PAST INFINITIVE

Pues, querida, en manos peores **pudiste haber caído.** (Palacio Valdés, **Sinfonía pastoral, Adagio Cantábile,** III) — Well, dear, you *could have fallen* into worse hands.

Bien **pudo haber sido** un poco menos terco con su padre. (Pereda, **Sotileza,** XXVIII) — He *might* well *have been* a little less obstinate with his father.

PLUPERFECT INDICATIVE

[*había, habías, había podido; habíamos, habíais, habían podido*]

Los pasajeros habían hecho todo lo que **habían podido** para apagar las llamas. — The passengers had done all they *could* to extinguish the flames.

Los toros habían tratado de romper la empalizada, pero **no habían podido** lograrlo. — The bulls had tried to break through the palisade, but *had* not *been able* to effect it.

Estos síntomas no **habían podido** escapar a la penetración del médico. — These symptoms *had* not *been able to* escape the doctor's penetration.

FUTURE INDICATIVE

[*podré, podrás, podrá; podremos, podréis, podrán*]

Desde la cima de aquel cerro **podremos** obtener, sin duda, un conocimiento exacto de la isla. — From the top of that ridge we *shall* no doubt *be able* to obtain a correct understanding of the island.

Aquel oficial **podrá** sin duda proporcionar a V. todos los informes que V. desee. — That officer *will* doubtless *be able* to furnish you with all the information which you may desire.

Tú **podrás** haber perdido parte de la fe; pero toda no se pierde nunca. (Pérez Galdós, **Fortunata y Jacinta,** IV, 2, 5) — You *may* have lost part of your faith, but it is never lost altogether.

FUTURE PERFECT INDICATIVE

Para entonces **habré podido** enterarme de todos los pormenores de la fábrica. — By that time I *shall have been able* to acquaint myself with all the details of the manufacture.

Estoy seguro de que antes del viernes próximo la comisión **habrá podido** terminar sus presupuestos. — I am positive that the committee *will have been able* to complete its estimates before next Friday.

CONDITIONAL

[*podría, podrías, podría; podríamos, podríais, podrían*]

AS A PAST FUTURE

Se acordó pasar la noche en la choza abandonada, la cual **podría** calentarse suficientemente por medio de la provisión de leña que se hallaba en un rincón. — It was agreed to pass the night in the deserted hut, which *could* be sufficiently warmed with the stock of wood that was found in one corner.

Como les separaba media milla de la costa, a tal distancia sus tiros **podrían** no ser muy dañosos. — As they were half a mile from the shore, their shots *might* not be very dangerous at that distance.

IN CONDITIONS

¿**Podría** V., sin inconveniente, prestarme cinco pesos? — *Could* you without inconvenience lend me five dollars?

Si la brisa no se dirigiese ahora hacia la catarata, creo que **podríamos** oír el susurro a esta distancia. — If the breeze were not now blowing towards the falls, I think we *would be able* to hear their roaring at this distance.

Si estuviéramos en uno de los balcones, **podríamos** ver mejor los fuegos artificiales. — If we were in one of the balconies we *could* see the fireworks better.

FOLLOWED BY PAST INFINITIVE

Por otra parte, los indígenas **podrían haber dificultado** mucho la operación proyectada. — Besides, the natives *might have* seriously *interfered with* the projected operation.

La joven se quitó la boina, y al sacudir la cabeza a uno y otro lado, comenzaron a desprenderse y esparcirse sobre sus hombros unos cabellos que **podrían** los del sol **haberles tenido** envidia. — The young girl took off her tam-o'shanter, and shaking her head from side to side, her hair, which the sun's rays *might have envied,* began to escape and fall down over her shoulders.

CONDITIONAL PERFECT

[*habría, habrías, habría podido; habríamos, habríais, habrían podido*]

El centinela **habría podido** ver que le espiaban y hasta que era seguido de cerca, pero no **habría** — The sentinel *might have* seen that he was watched and even that he was closely followed, but he *could* not

podido oír los pasos del indio, porque éste, con los pies descalzos, más bien se deslizaba que andaba, y ningún ruido daba indicio de su presencia.

have heard the Indian's footsteps, for the latter, with bare feet, glided rather than walked, and no sound betrayed his presence.

Los marineros fácilmente **habrían podido** matar con sus remos algunos de los pingüinos pero no pensaron en entregarse a aquella matanza inútil.

The sailors *could* easily *have* killed some of the penguins with their oars, but they did not think of devoting themselves to that useless slaughter.

PRESENT SUBJUNCTIVE

[*pueda, puedas, pueda; podamos, podáis, puedan*]

Es dudoso que **podamos** escaparnos de la tormenta, puesto que las tempestades de los trópicos se declaran con rapidez asombrosa.

It is doubtful whether we *can* escape the storm, for these tropical tornadoes come up with frightful rapidity.

Es imposible predecir lo que se **pueda** hacer antes de hacer una tentativa.

It is impossible to say what *can* be done before making an attempt.

¡Ojalá **podamos** salvar la vida de nuestro compañero!

God grant we *may be able* to save the life of our companion!

Esta isla no ofrece ni siquiera un puerto que **pueda** servir de abrigo a buques de calado medio.

This island does not even offer a port which *can* accommodate vessels of medium draught.

PERFECT SUBJUNCTIVE

[*haya, hayas, haya podido; hayamos, hayáis, hayan podido*]

Es de sentir que el asunto no se **haya podido** arreglar amigablemente.

It is to be regretted that it *has* not *been possible* to arrange the matter amicably.

No creo que ninguno de estos tunantes **haya podido** irse lejos.

I do not believe any of the rascals *can have* gone far.

Nos alegramos de que **haya podido** probar su inocencia.

We are delighted that he *has been able* to prove his innocence.

IMPERFECT SUBJUNCTIVE

[*pudiera, pudieras, pudiera; pudiéramos, pudierais, pudieran*]

La embarcación fué amarrada sólidamente para que el reflujo **no pudiera** llevársela.

The boat was firmly moored in order that the ebb tide *might* not carry it away.

Tomó un puñado de yerbas secas, y lo puso bajo los leños y astillas dispuestas de manera que el aire **pudiese** circular fácilmente e inflamar con rapidez la leña seca.

He took a handful of dry grass and put it under the sticks and twigs arranged so that the air *would be able* to circulate freely and rapidly ignite the dry wood.

El perro, antes de que su amo **pudiese** contenerlo, se precipitó sobre la garganta del desconocido.

The dog, before his master *could* restrain him, leaped at the stranger's throat.

Ra FORM AS SUBSTITUTE FOR CONDITIONAL

Si V. me permitiese emplear el éter, **pudiera** extraer esta muela sin ocasionarle dolor.

If you would permit me to employ ether I *could* extract this tooth without causing you pain.

En efecto él supo tan bien fingir la necesidad de su ausencia que nadie **pudiera** entender que era fingida.

In fact he knew so well how to feign the necessity for his absence that no one *could* know that it was a pretense.

PLUPERFECT SUBJUNCTIVE

[*hubiera, hubieras, hubiera podido; hubiéramos, hubierais, hubieran podido*]
[*hubiese, hubieses, hubiese podido; hubiésemos, hubieseis, hubiesen podido*]

No creo que **hubiesen podido** evadirse por este lado del muro.

I do not think they *could have* escaped on this side of the wall.

Si **hubiese podido** pasar la puerta de Perona y llegar adonde dejé a mi caballo, no me hallaría en el apuro en que me veo.

If I *had been able* to pass through the Perona gate and reach the place where I left my horse, I should not find myself in the fix I am in now.

AS SUBSTITUTE FOR CONDITIONAL PERFECT

Sin embargo, **hubiera podido** hacerme el más dichoso de los mortales si me hubiera dirigido una sola palabra cariñosa.

Still, she *could have* made me the happiest of mortals if she had addressed to me a single affectionate word.

La corriente marchaba hacia alta mar, y aun cuando hubiera querido, no **hubiera podido** volver a tierra.

The current was running out to the open sea, and even if I had wanted to I *could* not *have* returned to land.

FUTURE SUBJUNCTIVE

[*pudiere, pudieres, pudiere; pudiéremos, pudiereis, pudieren*]

El que **pudiere** recoger y almacenar para su uso los recursos no uti-

Whoever *shall be able* to gather and store for his use the waste re-

lizados de la Naturaleza, que los mandare trabajar en su taller, calentar y alumbrar su domicilio y fertilizar sus campos, alcanzará una soberanía desconocida para los Césares y más singular que todas las fábulas del Oriente.

sources of Nature, who will make them work in his shop, warm and light his dwelling and fertilize his fields, will acquire a sovereignty unknown to the Caesars and stranger than all the fables of the East.

INFINITIVE

[*poder*]

Al mismo tiempo se dispusieron las municiones y las armas para **poder** utilizarlas en el primer instante en caso de una agresión repentina.

At the same time the arms and ammunition were disposed so as *to be* available on the first instant in case of a sudden attack.

Sí señor, debo; pero deber no es **poder.**

Yes, Sir, I ought; but ought is not *can.*

Quisiera **poder** hacerlo.

I should like *to be able* to do it.

Espero **poder** hacerlo mañana.

I hope *to be able* to do it tomorrow.

PAST INFINITIVE

[*haber podido*]

Ellos se quedarán sorprendidos de **haber podido** pensar un solo instante en semejante proyecto.

They will be astonished at *having* ever *been able* to think for a single instant of such a scheme.

Napoleón se vanagloriaba de **haber podido** dictar a Europa la paz o la guerra a su albedrío.

Napoleon boasted of *having been able* to dictate peace or war to Europe at his will.

PRESENT PARTICIPLE

[*pudiendo*]

Desde esta altura la mirada, **pudiendo** extenderse sin límites, abarca todos los detalles de un panorama que se extiende por un horizonte de sesenta millas.

The sight *being able,* from this elevation, to extend itself without limits, takes in all the details of a panorama stretching out to a horizon sixty miles distant.

Me refugié entre las niaras, y **pudiendo** más la fatiga que el hambre, me dormí.

I crept in among the hayricks, and fatigue *being* more *potent* than hunger, I fell asleep.

PERFECT PARTICIPLE

[*habiendo podido*]

No comprendía el buen sacerdote los malos corazones, no **habiendo podido** nunca despedir a un desgraciado sin darle socorro. — The good priest did not understand hard hearts, never *having been able* himself to turn away an unfortunate without aiding him.

NO PODER MENOS DE[1]

26.28. This expression, in its various moods and tenses, may be rendered by some form of the English *cannot help,* followed by a present participle, or *cannot fail to,* followed by an infinitive:

No puedo menos de temer un desenlace funesto. — I *cannot help* fearing a disastrous outcome.

No podrá menos de querernos, porque seremos buenos para él. — He *cannot fail* to like us, for we will be good to him.

No podían menos de sentir grande ansiedad por saber la importancia del nuevo incidente. — They *could not help* feeling great anxiety to know the importance of the new occurrence.

No pudo menos de sentir una especie de secreta satisfacción. — He *could not help* feeling a kind of secret satisfaction.

No pudieron menos de advertir que algo extraordinario acontecía. — They *could not help* noticing that something unusual was going on.

Atrevidas y felices especulaciones de bolsa, gran número de negocios de importación, importantes empréstitos cuya emisión le había sido confiada, **no habían podido menos** de llevar mucho dinero a su caja. — Bold and successful speculations on the Exchange, a large amount of importing trade, important loans whose issue had been entrusted to him, *had not failed* to net him large sums.

[1] In America particularly but occasionally in Spain also **de** is replaced by **que: Míster James, que la escuchaba serio y atento, no pudo menos que admirarse al oírla.** (Lynch, **El inglés de los güesos,** XV) *Mr. James, who was listening to her seriously and attentively, could not help being astonished on hearing her.* **Esta mujer...no podía menos que estorbar.** (Valera, **Pepita Jiménez, Epílogo)** *This woman...couldn't help being in the way.*

XXVII

Idiomatic Uses Of Some Verbs

27.1. The English usage of specifying particular meanings of verbs by the addition of adverbs is not common in Spanish, where the idea is usually conveyed in a single word. This is well exhibited in the following verbs of motion:

bajar		down	*(to descend)*
subir		up	*(to rise, ascend)*
partir	to go *or* come	away	*(to depart, set out, start)*
entrar		in	*(to enter)*
salir		out	*(to appear, turn out)*

REMARK. Although **salir** is an irregular verb, its present indicative exhibits no irregularity except the interpolation of a **g** in the first person singular: **salgo** *I go* or *come out.*

27.2. These verbs merely express the nature of a motion up, down, out, etc. and make no distinction between direction TOWARD and AWAY FROM the speaker, as is the case with their English equivalents:

Los soldados han bajado al agua con sus caballos.	The soldiers have gone down to the water with their horses.
¿Cuándo va V. a bajar?	When are you coming down?
Salen inmediatamente después de entrar.	They go out immediately after coming in.
Salgo ahora.	I am going out now.
Cuando entra, sube a su habitación.	When he comes in, he goes up to his room.
Parto mañana en el autobús.	I set out tomorrow in the bus.
Nuestros negocios han salido mal.	Our affairs have turned out badly.
Los precios han subido.	The prices have gone up.

27.3. The following are regular verbs of common occurrence which are usually rendered in English by a different construction:

aguantar to put up with

escuchar to listen to

aprovechar to profit by	**esperar** to wait for, to hope for
apuntar to note down, to make a note of	**ignorar** to be unaware of, not to know
averiguar to find out	**incendiar** to set fire to
bastar to be enough, sufficient	**meter** to put, put in
sobrar to be over, remain over	**sacar** to take out, pull out
faltar to be wanting, missing	**quitar** to take away, take off
callar to be silent, keep silent	**presenciar** to be present at
cuidar to take care of	**mirar** to look at
distar to be distant	**repasar** to look over, go over

REMARK. There is really nothing unusual about these Spanish verbs; they are simple and direct. Whatever peculiarity there may be is in their present English renderings, and direct equivalents for many of them may be found in English words of Latin origin:

aguantar to tolerate	**esperar** to expect
averiguar to ascertain	**sacar** to extract
bastar to suffice	**quitar** to remove
presenciar to attend	**repasar** to review

EXAMPLES

No es posible aguantar su insolencia.	It is not possible to put up with his insolence.
Hemos aprovechado la ocasión.	We have profited by the occasion.
El general dicta y su secretario apunta.	The general dictates and his secretary takes notes.
Apuntar un discurso.	To take down a speech.
Averiguar la verdad de un asunto.	To find out the truth of a matter.
Quiero averiguar si es verdad.	I wish to find out if it is true.
Esta cantidad basta y sobra.	This quantity is enough and more than enough.
Falta un volumen de la enciclopedia.	A volume of the encyclopedia is missing.
No faltarán compradores.	There will be no lack of purchasers.
Los niños no quieren callar.	The children will not be still.
La historia calla sobre este punto.	History is silent on this point.
¿Quién cuida la casa de V. ahora?	Who takes care of your house now?
El arsenal dista tres millas.	The arsenal is three miles distant.
No escucha mis consejos.	He does not listen to my advice.
Escuchar la música, un discurso.	To listen to the music, to a speech.
¿Qué hace V.? —Espero el ómnibus.	What are you doing? —I am waiting for the omnibus.

Ignoro el origen de la costumbre. — I do not know the origin of the custom.

Los conspiradores han incendiado el palacio. — The conspirators have set fire to the palace.

Quita la silla y mete al caballo en la cuadra. — He takes off the saddle and puts the horse in the stable.

La criada ha quitado el mantel. — The servant has taken off the tablecloth.

Sacar un diente. — To pull out a tooth.

Sacar una copia, una fotografía de algo. — To take a copy, a photograph of anything.

¿Quieren VV. presenciar la ejecución del asesino? — Do you wish to be present at the execution of the murderer?

Mira atentamente el retrato. — He looks attentively at the portrait.

Necesito repasar mis lecciones antes de salir. — I need to look over my lessons before going out.

27.4. **Abusar de** is *to abuse* in the sense of using wrongfully or excessively. **Maltratar** is *to abuse* in the sense of ill-treat. **Denostar, decir injurias a** *to abuse* with words only:

Hay individuos a quienes no pueden permitirse privilegios sin que abusen de ellos. — There are some persons who cannot be allowed privileges without abusing them.

Maltrata atrozmente a sus niños. — He abuses his children shamefully.

Con tal que se limite a decirme injurias, poco me importa. — Provided he confines himself to abusing me, I don't care.

27.5. **Acordarse de** *to remember* is used almost interchangeably with **recordar** *to recollect* which governs its object directly. **Recuerdo** is a *souvenir, memento:*

No me acuerdo de la fecha. — I do not remember the date.

¿Se acuerda V. de la promesa que me hizo? — Do you remember the promise you made me?

No puedo recordar el apellido de aquel caballero. — I cannot recall that gentleman's name.

No recordaba ni cuándo ni dónde había visto antes al recién venido. — I did not remember when or where I had seen the newcomer before.

Conservaré esta flor como recuerdo de nuestro delicioso paseo. — I shall keep this flower as a souvenir of our delightful walk.

27.6. **Admirar** may be construed in three different ways:[1]

Admiramos la incansable laboriosidad de los antiguos egipcios.	We wonder at the untiring industry of the ancient Egyptians.
La incansable laboriosidad de los antiguos egipcios nos admira.	
Nos admiramos de la incansable laboriosidad de los antiguos egipcios.	

27.7. **Alegrarse de** means *to be glad of,* followed by a verb or noun:

Me alegro de la dicha de V.	I am glad of your good fortune.
Me alegro de saber que es verdad.	I am glad to know that it is true.
Me alegro de que no hayan venido a las manos.	I am glad they did not come to blows.

27.8. **Andar** and **ir** both correspond to the English *go.* **Andar** applies to the motion of animals and inanimate objects, and to undefined going of persons. **Ir** is *to go* in a specific direction or for a definite purpose:

Andar en mangas de camisa, en carnes, con los pies descalzos, con la cabeza al aire.	To go in one's shirt sleeves; to go naked; to go barefooted; to go bareheaded.
Andar despacio, de prisa.	To go slow, fast.
Andar a gatas; andar a tientas.	To go on all fours; to grope.
Todavía no anda con pies de mar.	He has not got his sea legs yet.
El buque anda bien, es un buen andador.	The ship sails well, is a good goer.
El reloj no anda.	The clock is not going.
Ir al despacho, a palacio.	To go to office, to the palace.
Ir de un recado, ir de campo.	To go on an errand, on a picnic.
Va de cónsul a Colón.	He goes as consul to Colon.
A eso voy.	That's what I'm driving at.

Remark. In answer to a call, the English say *I am coming,* the Spaniards **voy**, literally *I am going:*

¡Pepe! —Allá voy, señor.	Joe! —I'm coming, Sir.
Ya voy.	I'm coming right now.

[1] The same is true of **extrañar: Extrañamos verle, nos extraña verle, nos extrañamos de verle.** *We are surprised to see him.* **Sorprender** has only two constructions: **Nos sorprende verle, nos sorprendemos de verle.** *We are surprised to see him.*

Allá vamos en seguida, mamá.	We are coming in a moment, mamma.

27.9. **Antojarse** takes a person as indirect object, and is to be rendered in English by *take a notion to,* the person being subject:

Se me antojó registrar este hoyo con la punta de mi bastón.	I took a notion to feel in this hollow with the point of my stick.
Si a V. se le antoja hacer eso, le castigaré.	If you take it into your head to do that I will punish you.

27.10. **Bajar** and **subir,** like their English equivalents, may take a direct object:

Bajar el río, la cuesta, la escalera.	To go down the river, the hill, the stairs.
Subir el río, la cuesta, la escalera.	To go up the river, the hill, the stairs.

27.11. **Bajar** and **subir** are also used as transitive verbs meaning to *bring* or *take down* and *up* respectively:

Los criados van a bajar los baúles.	The servants are going to take the trunks down.
La lavandera no ha subido la ropa.	The laundress has not brought up the clothes.

27.12. **Caber,** which is literally equivalent to the English *to get into,* is usually rendered by *to hold,* the Spanish subject then becoming object. It is connected with its object by **en:**

Todos estos objetos no cabrán en el baúl.	The trunk won't hold all these things.
En cada cargador caben cinco cartuchos.	Each clip holds five cartridges.
No cabe más en el saco.	The bag won't hold any more.
Meta V. todo cuanto quepa.	Put in all it will hold.
No cabíamos ni parados.	We had not room to stand.

Caber is also used figuratively, expressing the ideas of possibility or capability:

No cabe en la imaginación lo grandioso de la perspectiva.	The imagination can form no conception of the grandeur of the view.
Me rehuso a creer que quepa en él semejante vileza.	I refuse to believe that he is capable of such a contemptible action.

Todo cabe en él.	He is capable of anything.
Es más feo que el otro, si cabe.	It is uglier than the other, if that be possible.

27.13. **Caer** *to fall* has the following usages which deserve notice here:

La levita le cae bien a V.	The coat fits you well.
Cae bien a caballo.	He looks well on horseback.
No caigo en la cosa.	I don't understand the affair.
Ya caigo en ello.	I see, I understand.
No cayó en la cuenta.	He did not see the point, catch on.
La pascua cae en abril este año.	Easter comes in April this year.
El plazo cae, mi pagaré cae mañana.	The time expires, my note falls due tomorrow.
La ventana cae a la plaza.	The window overlooks the square.
La hija menor me ha caído en gracia.	The youngest daughter has taken my fancy.
Ha caído de la gracia del príncipe.	He has fallen in the prince's esteem.
Esta fonda ha caído en mala fama.	This hotel has fallen into ill repute.

27.14. **Casar.**—The meaning and usage of **casar** varies according to the person who is its subject. When it governs the object directly it means *to join in wedlock,* and *to dispose of in marriage.* The action of either of the parties to the match is expressed by **casar(se) con,** *to marry* or *wed:*

Los casó el obispo.	The bishop married them.
Casó a su hija con un barón alemán sin seso.	She married her daughter to a brainless German baron.
¿Es V. casado? —Aun no, pero me voy a casar luego.	Are you married? —Not yet, but I am going to get married soon.
Tanto Carlos V como Felipe II casaron con princesas portuguesas. (Madariaga, **España,** I, 2, 18)	Both Charles V and Philip II married Portuguese princesses.
Su familia, por razones de vanidad mundana, la habían inducido a casarse con el viejo y acaudalado corregidor. (Alarcón, **El sombrero de tres picos,** XXX)	Her family, for reasons of worldly vanity, had induced her to marry the old and wealthy Mayor.

27.15. **Dar** has the usual values of the English *give,* except in the sense of *to make a present of,* which latter meaning is preferably expressed by **regalar:**

Me dió la carta.	He gave me the letter.
Me regaló un cortaplumas.	He gave me a penknife.
Me dará mucho gusto.	It will give me much pleasure.
Me dió, me extendió la mano.	She gave me her hand.
Me doy por vencido.	I give up.
Ella le dió un beso, un abrazo, un apretón de manos.	She gave him a kiss, an embrace, a squeeze of the hand.
Eso da motivo para quejarse.	That gives opportunity for complaint.
Dar el santo al centinela.	To give the countersign to the sentry.
Dió a la isla el nombre de San Salvador.	He gave the island the name of San Salvador.

Dar frequently has the value of *to perform:*

Dar un paseo.	To take a walk.
Dar una vuelta, vueltecita.	To take a turn, short walk.
Dió una carcajada.	He burst out laughing.
Dar saltos.	To jump about.
Dar cabezadas; dar manotadas.	To nod with drowsiness; to throw up the hands (as in falling).
Dar un nudo al pañuelo.	To tie a knot in one's handkerchief.
Dar cima, dar cabo a alguna obra.	To conclude, to finish a work.
Dar la última pincelada.	To give the finishing stroke.
Dar guerra.	To wage war.
Esta mula da coces.	This mule kicks.
Dar un chillido.	To utter a scream.
Dar voces, gritos, gemidos.	To cry out, shout, groan.

Among the numerous idiomatic meanings of **dar** an important one is *to strike, to hit,* both literally and figuratively:

Dar con la badila en los nudillos.	To rap over the knuckles *(literally,* to strike on the knuckles with the fire shovel).
Disparó dos tiros a su marido. Afortunadamente no le dió. (Baroja, **El mundo es ansí,** I, 19)	She fired two shots at her husband. Fortunately she didn't hit him.
¿Pero qué le ha dado a tu hermana? ¿Hay motivo para esto? (Benavente, **Al fin, mujer,** I, 2, 2)	But what has struck your sister? Is there any reason for this?
Le habían dado varios ataques de disnea. (Palacio Valdés, **Santa Rogelia,** II, 5)	She had had several attacks of shortness of breath.
Hoy me ha dado a mí por hablar un poco más de lo que suelo. (Pereda, **La puchera,** XIV)	Today I have felt like talking more *(or* it has struck me to be more talkative) than usual.

¿Y la señá Frasquita? ¿Has dado con ella? (Alarcón, **El sombrero de tres picos,** XXVI) — And Señá Frasquita? Have you met (*or* run into) her?

Don Justiniano y Justino dieron en menudear las visitas a don Zacarías. (Pereda, **La puchera,** XVIII) — Don Justinian and Justino fell into the habit of paying (*or* were struck with the notion of paying *or simply* began to pay) Don Zacariah frequent visits.

27.16. Dejar has the two leading meanings of *to leave* and *to let* (i.e. *to permit*):

Dejar a alguien plantado. — To leave someone in the lurch.

Déjele V. que salga. — Let him go out.

El caballo no quiere dejarse ensillar. — The horse will not let himself be saddled.

Dejar de, followed by an infinitive, means *to fail* (especially in a negative sentence) and *to leave off:*

No dejaré de decírselo. — I shall not fail to tell him so.

Deje V. de molestarme. — Stop bothering me.

Dejemos de ocuparnos de semejantes frioleras. — Let us cease to concern ourselves with such trifles.

No hay que creer que esta caza deja de tener sus peligros. — You must not believe that this kind of hunting is devoid of danger.

REMARK. After **sin(que) dejar de** + infinitive may lose its force almost completely: **No pasaban junto a ella...sin que dejasen de empujarla.** (Blasco Ibáñez, **La barraca,** V) *They never passed beside her...without pushing her.* **Dejarse** + noun or pronoun means only *to leave off, to stop, to quit,* etc.: **Dejaos de tonterías. No estoy para bromas.** (Benavente, **Las cigarras hormigas,** I, 5) *Stop the nonsense. I am in no humor for jokes.*

27.17. Doler *to ache* takes as its subject a noun expressing a part of the body, and a person as indirect object:

Me duele la cabeza. — My head aches.

Le duele el pulmón derecho. — He has a pain in his right lung.

Me dolían los pies. — My feet pained me.

27.18. Echar, while regular in form, is in meaning the most irregular verb in the language. Its primary meaning is *to throw* or *cast,* but this suffers many modifications:

Echaron al intruso.	They ejected the intruder.
Se preparaban a echar el ancla.	They were preparing to cast anchor.
Echó el documento a un lado.	He threw the document aside.
Echó mano a la espada.	He grasped his sword.
Echar las cartas.	To deal the cards.
Echar el cocido, la verdura.	To serve the meat, the vegetables.
Echó el café de una taza a otra para refrescarlo.	He poured the coffee from one cup into another to cool it.

Echar with the value of *to apply,* governing a noun:

Echar la regla.	To verify by applying a measure.
Echar el cerrojo.	To bolt.
Echar llave a la puerta.	To lock the door.
Echar la tijera.	To apply the shears, to cut.
Echar el cordel.	To use the chalk-line.
Echar un candado a la puerta.	To put a padlock on the gate.

Echar in many cases has the secondary sense of *to put forth* or *develop:*

Echar carnes; echar barriga.	To grow fleshy; to grow corpulent.
Echar bigotes; echar canas.	To begin to grow a mustache; to begin to grow gray.
Echar carrillos.	To grow fat in the cheeks.
Echar coche; echar novio.	To set up a coach; to have a beau.
Echar raíces.	To take root.
Echar botones, hojas, flores.	To put forth buds, leaves, flowers.

Echar (de) menos means *to miss* (i.e. to be sensible of the absence of):

Le echamos a V. (de) menos en el baile.	We missed you at the ball.
Echaré (de) menos nuestros paseos por la tarde.	I shall miss our evening walks.
A mí nadie me echará (de) menos cuando muera.	No one will miss me when I die.

Echar de ver means *to notice:*

Echo de ver que V. ha omitido la fecha.	I notice you have omitted the date.
Se echa de ver fácilmente que es de buena alcurnia.	It is easy to see that he comes of good stock.

Echar(se) **a,** followed by an infinitive, is *to begin to, set to work at:*

Me eché a dormir.	I went to sleep.

Se echó a reír, a llorar, a barajar los naipes.	He began to laugh, to cry, to shuffle the cards.
Lo echó a rodar.	He sent it rolling.

Echar a perder is a stereotype expression meaning *to spoil:*

Con su indiscreción lo echará a perder todo.	He will spoil all with his indiscretion.
La lluvia ha echado a perder mi sombrero.	The rain has spoiled my hat.
Temo que se eche a perder.	I am afraid it will be spoiled.

27.19. Entender de is *to be a judge of:*

¿Entiende V. de brillantes? —Entiendo bastante de eso.	Are you a judge of diamonds? —I am a tolerable judge of them.
Yo no entiendo nada de pinturas.	I am no judge of paintings.
Entiende de vinos, de caballos.	He is a judge of wines, of horses.

27.20. Entrar requires to be supplemented by **en** (or, in older usage, preserved especially in Spanish America, by **a**) when followed by the name of the place entered:

Entra en el edificio.	He enters the building.
Entrar en una sociedad, en un colegio, en el ejército.	To enter a society, a college, the army.
Los demás entraron al despacho. (Güiraldes, **Don Segundo Sombra,** VII)	The rest entered the store.

27.21. Faltar and **hacer falta,** which are rendered into English by *need* or *want,* take a person as indirect object, the thing wanted being subject:

Sólo le hace falta a V. un poco de práctica.	You only need a little practice.
Nos faltan brazos.	We are short of hands (i.e. workmen).
No falta más.	That caps the climax.

27.22. Guardarse de, followed by an infinitive, signifies *to take care not to;* it is to be noticed that the Spanish expression lacks a negative:

Guárdese V. de caer.	Take care not to fall.
Me guardaré de decirles nada.	I will take care not to tell them anything.
Se guardará muy bien de mostrarse.	He will take good care not to show himself.

27.23. **Gustar,** in its simplest usage, as a transitive verb, means *to taste;* with this meaning it is more commonly replaced by **probar,** meaning literally *to try:*

Guste V. (pruebe V.) esta leche.	Taste this milk.
No he probado bocado desde ayer.	I haven't tasted a mouthful since yesterday.
Dejé el guisado sin probarlo.	I left the stew untasted.

The Spanish verb for representing the English *taste* as an intransitive verb referring to a thing, is **saber,** followed by **a** where the English verb takes *of* or *like:*

Esta mantequilla sabe rancia.	This butter tastes rancid.
La leche sabe fuertemente a ajo.	The milk tastes strongly of garlic.

Gustar *to please, give pleasure* is employed in connections where the English use *like,* for which there is no exact equivalent in Spanish. The construction is then reversed as follows :

Me gustan los pasteles.	I like pies.
Parece que a la anciana le gusta charlar.	It seems the old lady likes to talk.
A mí no me gustan las tragedias.	I do not like tragedies.

Gustar may be followed by the preposition **de,** with a person as subject as in English, and meaning *to be fond of:*

Yo gusto de bailar.	I am fond of dancing.
Gusta demasiado del teatro.	She is too fond of the theater.

REMARK. After **cómo, encontrar** *to find* or **parecer** *to seem* are preferable to **gustar** in asking an opinion:

¿Cómo encuentra V. el vino? *or* ¿Qué le parece a Vd. el vino?	How do you like the wine?
¿Cómo encontraron Vds. la vista? *or* ¿Qué les pareció a Vds. la vista?	How did you like the view?
¿Qué tal ha encontrado V. el estreno? *or* ¿Qué tal le ha parecido a Vd. el estreno?	How did you like the new play?

27.24. **Hacer** is used to reproduce other verbs in the same manner as the English *do;* the object of the verb is reproduced by the neuter **lo:**

No es extraño que todos se burlen del que de sí mismo lo hace.	It is not strange that every one makes fun of him who does so of himself.

La caballería española desbarató a los aztecas como lo hace a la niebla el viento. — The Spanish cavalry scattered the Aztecs as the wind does the mist.

Hacer por means *to try to, arrange it so as to:*

Haga V. por venir. — Try to come.

Hagan Vds. por permitirle todo el tiempo posible. — Arrange it so as to allow him all the time possible.

Haré por verle hoy mismo. — I shall try to see him this very day.

Hacer que or **como que** is *to act as if, to pretend:*

Las damas trabajaban en su costura o bordado; yo leía o hacía que leía. (Palacio Valdés, **La alegría del capitán Ribot,** VIII) — The ladies were working at their sewing or embroidery; I was reading or pretending to read.

Martín levantó la mano, y su novia, haciendo como que no le conocía, se retiró de la ventana. (Baroja, **Zalacaín el aventurero,** II, 11) — Martin raised his hand and his sweetheart, pretending not to know him, withdrew from the window.

27.25. **Llevar** is sometimes idiomatically used like **tener** in the manner of an auxiliary before a past participle, which then agrees with its object:

Llevan estudiadas sus lecciones. — They have studied their lessons.

Llevo escritas tres cartas. — I have got three letters written.

27.26. **Llegar a** is used with a future reference equivalent to the familiar English *get to:*

Cuando **llegue** V. **a** comprender el sistema, lo hallará muy fácil. — When you *get to* understand the system you will find it very easy.

El descuido y falta de método con que la corteza era extraída hizo temer que la producción de la quina disminuyera considerablemente, y aun **llegara a** agotarse. — The carelessness and lack of method with which the bark was removed caused fear to be entertained lest the production of cinchona would be considerably diminished and even *eventually be* exhausted.

27.27. **Meterse a,** followed by a noun, means *to set one's self up for:*

Se mete a sabio. — He pretends to be very learned.

Se metía a caballero. — He set himself up for a gentleman.

No vayan Vds. a creer que me meta a ingenio al manifestarles lo que acaban de oír.	Do not believe that I am posing as a genius in stating what you have just heard.

Meterse en is *to meddle with* or *in:*

Le gusta meterse en vidas ajenas.	He likes to meddle with other people's business.
Fulano se mete en todo.	So-and-so is in everything.
Meterse en honduras.	To "get into deep water."
Meterse en camisa de once varas.	To bite off more than one can chew.
No se meta V. de por medio.	Don't you interfere in this.

27.28. **Mirar** means *to look at, to examine with the eyes;* **mirar a** properly means *to look toward, to look in the direction of* but **a** is sometimes used for the other meaning:

(Mirando al reloj de pared). Es verdad que ése atrasa. (Mira su reloj). (Benavente, **La honradez de la cerradura,** III, 1)	(Looking at the wall clock). It's true that that one is running slow. (Looks at his watch).
No mires al cielo..., mira allá..., hacia las luces del hotel. (**idem,** II, 4, escena única)	Don't look at the sky, look off there, toward the lights of the hotel.
María mira al suelo, a León; mira la carta. (Pérez Galdós, **Mariucha,** III, 5)	Mary looks at the floor, at Leon; she examines the letter.
Tú misma, mirando a tu linaje, a nosotros, debes rechazarlo. (**idem,** IV, 6)	You, yourself, considering your ancestry, considering us, must reject it.

27.29. **Mudar** means *to change* in various acceptations:

Los pollos están mudando la pluma.	The chickens are moulting.
Mudar de ropa blanca.	To change one's linen.
Vamos a mudarnos de casa al fin del mes.	We are going to move at the end of the month.

27.30. **Nacer,** which in Spanish is active intransitive, is translated in English by *to be born,* which is used as a passive:

Nací en X, tres años antes de la guerra civil.	I was born in X, three years before the civil war.
Todo esto sucedió antes que V. naciera.	All this happened before you were born.

Quien nació para ahorcado no morirá ahogado.	He who was born to be hanged will never be drowned.
No le pesa haber nacido.	He does not regret having been born. *(Said of a conceited person.)*

27.31. Oír, entender and **comprender.—Oír** is simply to perceive a sound by the ear, and may apply to sounds of any nature whatever. **Entender** is to hear understandingly, to understand articulate speech. **Comprender** is to understand written language, ideas, and spoken language which is obscure or otherwise difficult of comprehension:

¿Oye V. repicar las campanas?	Do you hear the bells chime?
Oigame V. antes de condenarme.	Hear me before condemning me.
Oigo subir a alguno.	I hear some one coming upstairs.
Le oigo pero no le entiendo.	I hear him but do not understand him.
No entiendo lo que V. dice porque habla demasiado aprisa.	I don't understand what you say because you talk too fast.
No comprendo nada de esa jerigonza.	I don't understand a word of that gibberish.
Su razonamiento es difícil de comprender.	His reasoning is difficult to understand.

27.32. Pagar *to pay* may take as its direct object either the amount paid or the thing paid for, while the person paid is the indirect object. The thing paid for may be preceded by **por**:

He pagado el vestido, *or rarely* por el vestido.	I have paid for the suit of clothes.
He pagado cuarenta pesos por el vestido.	I paid forty pesos for the suit of clothes.
He pagado el vestido al sastre.	I have paid the tailor for the suit of clothes.
He pagado cuarenta pesos al sastre.	I paid the tailor forty pesos.
He pagado al sastre cuarenta pesos por el vestido.	I paid the tailor forty pesos for the suit of clothes.

27.33. Pasarse sin is *to do without, get along without:*

Hay muchas cosas sin las cuales tiene uno que pasarse.	There are many things that one has to do without.
Puesto que en tanto valúa sus servicios, trataremos de pasarnos sin ellos.	Since he values his services so highly, we will try to get along without them.

No podría pasarme sin mi máquina de escribir.	I could not do without my typewriter.

27.34. Pedir prestado and **tomar prestado** are equivalent to the English verb *borrow:*

Quiero pedirle a V. prestada su caña de pescar.	I want to borrow your fishing rod.
Lo siento infinito, pero mi hermano la ha tomado prestada.	I am very sorry, but my brother has borrowed it.
He tomado esta suma prestada a mi hermano.	I borrowed this sum from my brother.

27.35. Pesar, expressing regret or sorrow, is construed impersonally, the person being indirect object and the noun denoting the cause of the sorrow being preceded by **de.** This preposition, however, may be omitted before either a noun or an infinitive, which in that case is considered as subject:

Me parece que le pesa ahora [de] su grosería.	I think he is sorry now for his churlishness.
Me pesa mucho [de] haberle ofendido.	I am sorry I offended him.
¡Cuánto me pesa verla a V. tan triste!	How sorry I am to see you so sad!

27.36. Poner, meter, colocar.—Poner en is to *put on* the surface or outside of anything; **meter en,** *to put into* or *insert.* **Poner** may be accompanied by other prepositions—**sobre, encima de, enfrente de,** etc. Either verb may be replaced by **colocar,** except in figurative significations:

Puso la mano en mi hombro.	He laid his hand on my shoulder.
Metió las pulseras en la cajita de prendas.	She put the bracelets in the jewel box.
Colocó el vaso en la repisa.	She put the vase on the shelf.
El artista metió los lienzos detrás del escaparate.	The artist thrust the canvases behind the cupboard.
Puso, colocó la caja de cartón encima del armario.	She put the paper box on top of the wardrobe.
Pusieron en fuga al enemigo.	They put the enemy to flight.
Poner en música, en verso, en castellano.	To set to music, to put in verse, to render into Spanish.
Poner algo en limpio.	To make a final *or* engrossed copy of something.

Poner una cosa por escrito.	To put a thing in writing.
Las gallinas ya ponen huevos.	The hens are already laying eggs.
¿Han puesto la mesa?	Have they set the table?
Quiero poner a prueba su amistad.	I want to put his friendship to a test.

Ponerse a means *to set to work at:*

Se pusieron a reparar los perjuicios.	They set to work to repair the damages.
Se pusieron a discutir el significado de la orden.	They began to discuss the meaning of the order.
Me puse a pensar sus palabras.	I set to thinking over his words.
Se puso el salvaje a dar brincos como un endemoniado.	The savage began to leap about like one possessed.

27.37. **Querer decir** is equivalent to the English verb *to mean:*

¿Qué quiere V. decir con eso?	What do you mean by that?
¿Qué quieren decir estas señales?	What do these marks mean?
No comprendo lo que quiere V. decir.	I don't understand what you mean.
Mi papá no quiere decir que a él no le gusta V., sino que no le gusta que V. se quede tan tarde.	Papa does not mean that he does not like you, but that he does not like you to stay so late.

27.38. **Saber** and **conocer.**—**Conocer** applies to matters of perception. It expresses such knowledge as suffices to distinguish one person or thing from another. **Saber** is to know a fact, a reason or branch of learning as a subject of thought or understanding:

¿**Conoce** V. al doctor N.? —Sí, le **conozco** íntimamente, y **sé** que es un médico muy hábil.	Do you know Dr. N.? —Yes, I know him intimately, and I know that he is a very able physician.
¿**Conoce** V. el camino? —Sí, mas no **sé** si está en buen estado.	Do you know the road? —Yes, but I do not know whether it is in good condition.
¿**Sabe** V. el álgebra? ¿**Sabe** V. su tema? ¿**Sabe** V. que su hijo fuma?	Do you know algebra? Do you know your lesson? Do you know that your son smokes?
¿**Conoce** V. esta letra? ¿**Conoce** V. a España?	Do you know this handwriting? Are you acquainted with Spain?
Quiero aún a D. Carlos. Y, no obstante, **conozco** que no debo darle esperanzas. (Valera, **El comendador Mendoza,** XIX)	I still love Don Carlos. And nevertheless I recognize that I mustn't give him hopes.

Bien **conoce** el autor que tan primitivo espectáculo no es el más digno de un culto auditorio. (Benavente, **Los intereses creados, Prólogo**) — Well does the author recognize that such a primitive spectacle is not the most worthy of a cultivated audience.

27.39. **Saber** and **poder** are both used before infinitives to express ability, but with this distinction: **saber** denotes knowledge or mental ability; **poder,** purely physical ability. **Saber** may often be rendered *to know how to:*

No sabe leer (porque nunca lo ha aprendido). — He cannot read (because he never learned how).
No puede leer (porque es ciego, o porque ha perdido sus anteojos). — He cannot read (because he is blind *or* because he has lost his spectacles).
¿Sabe V. nadar? ¿Sabe V. bailar vals? ¿Sabe V. patinar? — Can you swim? Can you waltz? Can you skate?
¿Puede V. levantar ese peso? — Can you lift that weight?
¿Puede V. saltar por encima de aquel seto? — Can you jump over that hedge?

REMARK. It can hardly be said that the distinction between physical and mental ability is invariably observed, the preference being for **poder,** especially with the conditional tense form, where moreover the use of **saber** tends to soften the force of the statement.

27.40. **Seguir** is both *to follow* and *to continue, go on:*

Sígame V. de lejos. — Follow me at a distance.
Mi hijo mayor sigue las letras. — My eldest son follows the profession of literature.
Siga V. leyendo, no se interrumpa V. a causa mía. — Go on reading, don't disturb yourself on my account.
El anciano siguió con su narración. — The old man went on with his story.

27.41. **Sentir** means *to perceive* by the senses, *to feel* and also *to hear.* Followed by an infinitive, or by **que** with a subjunctive, it also means *to be sorry.* Therefore **sentimiento** means both *feeling* and *regret;* and **sensible,** when applied to things, means *regrettable,* and when applied to rational beings, *sensitive, tenderhearted:*

Sentir el frío; sentir hambre. — To feel the cold; to feel hunger.
Sentir un ruido; sentir pasos. — To hear a noise; to hear footsteps.
Sintió que su fin se acercaba. — He felt that his end was approaching.
Siento no poder ir. — I am sorry I can't go.

¡Cuánto siento que lo haya divulgado! — How sorry I am that he has divulged it!

Se siente enfermo; se siente mejor. — He feels ill; he feels better.

Decir su sentir. — To express one's feelings.

Una ocurrencia sensible; una pérdida sensible. — A lamentable occurrence; a sad loss.

Es muy sensible que... — It is much to be regretted that...

He sabido con profundo sentimiento que... — I have learned with deep sorrow that...

Los más sensibles empezaban a soltar lágrimas. (Palacio Valdés, **Marta y María,** I, end) — The most sensitive were beginning to shed tears.

27.42. Servir para, servir de, used intransitively, mean *to be of use as;* **servirse de,** *to make use of:*

¿Para qué le sirven esas botellas al amo de V.? — What does your master use those bottles for?

Este viejo carro le sirve para llevar sus legumbres al mercado. — He uses this old cart to take his vegetables to market in.

¿Sirve este papel para escribir? —No sirve para nada. — Is this paper good to write on? —It is not good for anything.

¿De qué le sirve a V. llorar? — What use is it for you to cry?

Mi paraguas me sirve de bastón. — My umbrella is of use as a cane.

¿Me permite V. que me sirva de su bicicleta? —Claro, sírvase V. todo cuanto quiera. — Will you allow me to use your bicycle? —Certainly, use it as much as you want to.

Los chinos se sirven de palillos para comer. — The Chinese use chopsticks to eat with.

REMARK. **Servir de** may be replaced by **hacer (las veces) de:**

Esta mesa me hace (las veces) de escritorio. — This table serves me as a desk.

27.43. Soler, which is employed only in the present, imperfect and perfect indicative, is variously expressed in English by *to be accustomed to, used to, usually.* This verb is never used alone, being always followed by an infinitive:

Suelo comer despacito. — I usually eat quite slowly.

Heródoto refiere que los babilonios solían vender sus niñas bonitas para dotar a las feas con los ingresos. — Herodotus relates that the Babylonians used to sell their pretty girls for money to portion the ugly ones.

Sin embargo, yo no he solido ver, en las novelas satíricas, esas semejanzas parlantes. (Pardo Bazán, **La quimera,** Prólogo) — Nevertheless, I have not been accustomed to see those speaking likenesses in the satirical novels.

27.44. Tardar en, followed by an infinitive, means *to be long in* doing something:

Tarda mucho en decidirse. — He is long in deciding.
El enfermo no tardó en experimentar alguna mejoría. — It was not long before the patient showed some improvement.

27.45. In the following expressions, **tener** *to have* is used with nouns where in English *to be* is employed with adjectives. The Spanish usage agrees with that of all the languages of Latin origin:

tener hambre to be hungry
tener sed to be thirsty
tener calor to be hot, warm
tener frío to be cold
tener miedo to be afraid
tener razón to be right
tener calma to be calm
tener sueño to be sleepy

27.46. Tratar de + infinitive means *to endeavor to;* **tratar de** + noun or pronoun means *to treat of, to deal with:*

Trate V. de ser más puntual en lo futuro. — Endeavor to be more punctual in the future.
Trataré de reparar la pérdida lo más pronto posible. — I shall try to repair the loss as soon as possible.
El primer capítulo trata de los aspectos históricos del asunto. — The first chapter treats of the historical aspects of the subject.

Tratarse de is used impersonally to express that something is under consideration:

¿De qué se trata aquí? — What is going on here?
No se trata del gusto de un individuo sino del bienestar de la comunidad. — It is not a question of the pleasure of one individual but of the welfare of the community.
No se trata de reír ahora. — It is not a laughing matter.

27.47. Valer is *to be worth,* expressing either the value of an article or the possessions of a person:

Este género vale $3 el metro. — This cloth is worth $3 a yard.
Se dice que fulano vale quince millones. — They say that So-and-so is worth fifteen millions.

Eso no vale la pena de mencionarse.	That is not worth mentioning.
No vale absolutamente nada.	It is worth absolutely nothing.
Esta navaja vale más que ésa.	This knife is worth more than that one.
No hacen nada que valga.	They do nothing of any account.

Vale más, used impersonally, is equivalent to the English expression *it is better:*

Creo que vale más callar sobre este suceso.	I think it is better to say nothing about this occurrence.
Más valdrá que guarde V. cama por algunos días.	It will be better for you to stay in bed for a few days.
Más vale tarde que nunca.	Better late than never.
Más valiera si aguardásemos un poco, me parece.	It would be better for us to wait a little, I think.

Hacer valer is *to turn to account;* **valerse de,** *to avail one's self of:*

Tiene pocos conocimientos, pero sabe hacerlos valer.	He has few acquirements, but he knows how to turn them to account.
V. no se hace valer, V. no hace valer sus conocimientos.	You do not assert yourself, you do not turn your talents to account.
El comandante se valió de esta perturbación de los salvajes para cambiar su punto de acecho.	The major availed himself of this diversion among the savages to change his place of observation.

27.48. Volver a, governing an infinitive, means to perform again the act expressed by the infinitive. It often corresponds to the Latin and English prefix *re-,* which is of limited use in Spanish:

Volver a forrar; volver a casarse.	To reline; to remarry.
Volver a visitar; volver a llenar.	To revisit; to refill.
En 1822 el mismo fenómeno volvió a suceder.	The same phenomenon again occurred in 1822.
A la una volvieron a ponerse en marcha.	At one o'clock they again set out.
Nunca más nos volveremos a ver.	We shall never see each other again.
El catorce de noviembre volvieron a encontrarse las barreras de hielo.	On the 14th of November the ice-fields were again encountered.
Hágame V. el favor de no volver a hablar del asunto.	Oblige me by not speaking of the matter again.

27.49. There is no single Spanish equivalent for the English verb *stand.* In speaking of inanimate objects, and unemphatically of men and the larger animals, **estar** is the word used. **Estar de** or **en**

pie is employed of persons and animals when required for distinction. **Mantenerse en pie** is *to stand* or *remain standing.* **Ponerse en pie** is *to stand up, to rise to one's feet;* speaking of animals, however, the expression is **alzarse en los pies** or **patas, levantarse de manos,** etc. **Sostenerse en pie** is *to stand* viewed as an effort:

No permita V. que esta señora se mantenga en pie.	Do not permit that lady to remain standing.
Estoy tan débil que apenas puedo sostenerme en pie.	I am so weak I can scarcely stand.
Esté V. quieto.	Stand still.
La iglesia está sobre una ligera eminencia.	The church stands on a slight elevation.
En medio de este claro estaba una encina majestuosa.	In the middle of this clearing stood a majestic oak.
El burro se alzó en los pies.	The donkey stood up.

27.50. There are in Spanish no single equivalents for the English verbs *ride, drive* and *walk.* The various locutions for expressing these ideas in Spanish are as follows:

andar	to walk *(unemphatic)*
ir a pie	to walk *(in opposition to* "to ride, drive")
pasearse	to walk, take a walk *(for exercise or diversion)*
dar un paseo, una vuelta	to take a walk
dar una vueltecita	to take a stroll
ir de paseo, ir a pasearse	to go for a walk
salir a paseo	to go out for a walk
sacar los niños a pasear	to take the children out walking
ir a caballo, ir en coche	to ride, to drive
montar a caballo	to ride horseback *(as an accomplishment or custom)*
montar bien a caballo, tenerse bien a caballo	to ride well
conducir, guiar [a los caballos, un coche, un automóvil]	to drive *(to act as driver)*
pasearse en coche	to take a drive
pasearse en trineo	to take a sleigh ride

These expressions are employed in conversation as follows:

Estoy rendido; no puedo andar más.	I am exhausted; I can walk no farther.

Ya hemos andado media legua.	We have already walked nearly two miles.
¿Iremos a pie o en simón?	Shall we walk or take a hack?
Hemos recorrido toda la distancia a pie.	We have walked the whole way.
Vamos a dar una vuelta al jardín.	Let's take a turn around the garden.
Los caballos caminaban al paso	The horses were going at a walk.
El cura iba montado en un asno pardo.	The priest rode a gray donkey.
El chiquillo iba a caballo en un bastón.	The little boy was riding on a cane.
Quiero que mi hija aprenda a montar a caballo.	I want my daughter to learn to ride horseback.
¿Sabe V. montar a caballo? —Sí, monto muy a menudo.	Do you know how to ride horseback? —Yes, I ride very often.
Voy a montar ese caballo. (Palacio Valdés, **La novela de un novelista,** VII)	I am going to ride that horse.
¡Qué ocurrencia ha sido la tuya de montar en un caballo tan alto y a pelo! **(idem)**	What a notion of yours to ride on such a tall horse and bareback!
Montar en pelo, a horcajadas, a mujeriegas.	To ride bareback, astraddle, sidewise (like a woman).
Mi hermano sabe conducir dos troncos.	My brother can drive a four-in-hand.
Si la nevada continúa, nos podremos pasear en trineo mañana.	If the snowstorm continues we shall be able to go sleigh riding tomorrow.

27.51. The following modes of expressing the reception of news in Spanish are equivalent to the respective English phrases placed opposite them:

entender decir que	to understand that
oír decir que	to hear that
oír hablar de	to hear of, to hear tell of
saber que	to learn that
recibir, tener noticias de	to hear from

EXAMPLES

Oigo hablar a menudo de un testamento ológrafo, pero no sé lo que es.	I often hear talk of a holographic will, but I don't know what it is.

He sabido que V. ha ganado el premio gordo. — I have learned that you have drawn the capital prize.

¿Ha recibido V. últimamente noticias de su primo? —Hace más de un mes que no tengo noticias suyas. — Have you heard from your cousin lately? —It is more than a month since I heard from him.

Oigo decir que Pepe Romero va a batirse en desafío. — I hear that Joe Romero is going to fight a duel.

Yo no he oído hablar palabra de ello. — I haven't heard a word of it.

No deje V. de darme noticias suyas de cuando en cuando. — Do not fail to let me hear from you from time to time.

Entiendo decir que ha jurado vengarse de la afrenta. — I understand that he has sworn to avenge the affront.

¿Dónde ha sabido V. eso? — Where did you learn that?

XXVIII
PARA and POR

28.1. The prepositions **para** and **por,** from the variety of their meanings and usage, deserve a chapter to themselves. They are employed in senses that have so great an apparent resemblance, that no small care is required to distinguish them. Stated roughly, **por** refers to source and **para** to destination. They involve the questions *whence* and *whither:*

Esta carta fué escrita **por** el general **para** el rey. — This letter was written *by* the general [intended] *for* the king.

REMARK. Of the two, **por** presents the most difficulty. It may be regarded as taking the places of the Latin *per* and *pro.*

Per was used in expressing the time or place *through* which anything passed; the person *through* or *by* whom, or that *on account of* which, anything was done.

The primary meaning of *pro* was *before, in front of.* But one might stand before another as a defender, advocate, friend or representative, and thus act or speak *for* or *on behalf of* him, or *for* his benefit; it also signified the taking, exchanging or substituting one person or thing *for* another.

These various senses are combined in the Spanish **por.**

Para is a combination of *pro* in the sense of *before, forward,* and *ad to,* so that its primary signification is *forward unto.* In all its uses its characteristics are purpose, object, end or intention.

POR

28.2. In passive expressions **por** indicates the agent *by* whom an action is performed; but if the action be a mental one, the preposition used is preferably **de:**

El muchacho será castigado por su padre.	The boy will be punished by his father.
Este niño es amado de sus padres.	This child is loved by its parents.
El fuerte fué tomado por el enemigo.	The fort was taken by the enemy.
El universo fué creado por Dios.	The universe was created by God.
España fué conquistada por los moros.	Spain was conquered by the Moors.
Ese actor ha sido bien recibido por el público.	That actor has been well received by the public.
Esta obra está escrita por un autor francés.	This work is by a French author.

28.3. Indicates manner or means:

El dentista me sacó el diente por fuerza.	The dentist pulled my tooth out by force.
Como V. los ha visto por sus propios ojos, puede afirmar que existen.	As you have seen them with your own eyes, you can declare that they exist.
Por Fulano conseguí el empleo.	I obtained the employment through So-and-so.
Conducía por la mano a un niño de cinco años.	She was leading a child of five years by the hand.

28.4. Indicates the reason or motive for an action:

Por eso no quiero verle.	For that reason I do not want to see him.
Este peleaba por la vida, aquél por la honra.	The one was fighting for life, the other for honor.
No fuí al baile por falta de ropa.	I did not go to the ball for want of clothes.

Por miedo de las consecuencias.	For fear of consequences.
Le han despedido por una falta leve.	They have discharged him for a slight fault.
Lo hace por vanidad.	He does it out of vanity.
No fué admitido por ser católico.	He was not admitted, because he was a Catholic.

28.5. After the verbs *to go, to come, to send, to return* and the like, it shows the immediate object of the errand:

El muchacho va por leña, por pan.	The boy goes for firewood, for bread.
Me mandó por el médico.	He sent me for the doctor.
Vino por su sueldo.	He came for his wages.

28.6. Indicates opinion, estimation or acceptation:

Le tengo por hombre de talento.	I take him for a man of talent.
Le dejaron por muerto.	They left him for dead.
Le fusilaron por espía.	They shot him for a spy.
Fué ahorcado por ladrón.	He was hanged for a thief.
Lo dan por cosa extraordinaria.	They represent it as a strange thing.
Pasa por docto.	He passes for a learned man.
Cuando yo estaba en España, pasaba a menudo por natural del país.	When I was in Spain I often passed as a native of the country.
Le ajusté por mozo de cuadra.	I engaged him as stableboy.
La adoptó por hija.	He adopted her as daughter.
Lo toma por concedido.	He takes it for granted.
Se le conocía por el tío Miserias. (Baroja, **El árbol de la ciencia,** II, 8)	He was known as Uncle Miseries.

28.7. Denotes the space of time during which an action takes place or continues:

Me ausento de la ciudad por un mes.	I leave the city for a month.
Me ha prestado el libro por ocho días.	He lent me the book for a week.
Hemos pleiteado por mucho tiempo.	We have litigated for a long time.
Eso apaciguó al rey por lo pronto.	That appeased the king for the time.
Eso basta por ahora.	That is sufficient for now.
Por esta noche no saldrás de aquí. (Pérez Galdós, **Fortunata y Jacinta,** II, 6, 3)	For tonight you shall not leave here.

La señá Frasquita, apartada de aquel laberinto, lloraba por la primera vez de su vida. (Alarcón, **El sombrero de tres picos,** XXVIII, end)	Señá Frasquita, standing aside from that confusion, was crying for the first time in her life.

28.8. Denotes the place through or along which motion takes place:

Entró por la puerta, pero yo le hice salir por la ventana.	He came in through the door, but I made him go out through the window.
Vagaba por los campos.	He was wandering about the fields.
Como andaba por la margen del río.	As I was walking along the bank of the river.
¿Por qué calle vino V.?	Through what street did you come?
Pasé por Filadelfia.	I passed through Philadelphia.
He viajado por Méjico.	I have traveled through Mexico.

28.9. Takes the place of **en,** in expressing time or place, but is more indefinite:

Temíamos encontrar por aquel paraje algún buque de guerra.	We were afraid of meeting some war vessel in that quarter.
Por diciembre del año pasado despachó a su secretario con instrucciones...	About December of last year he dispatched his secretary with instructions...
V. lo encontrará por aquí, sin duda.	You will find it around here somewhere, no doubt.
El cubano, al verse con dinero, no volvió por la barraca de su padre. (Blasco Ibáñez, **Cañas y barro,** VII)	The Cuban, seeing that he had money, didn't show up again around his father's cabin.

28.10. Indicates exchange of one thing for another:

Le he dado mi perro por su escopeta.	I have given him my dog for his shotgun.
He cambiado mi pluma por una nueva.	I have exchanged my pen for a new one.
Quiere vender su casa por $8.000.[1]	He wants to sell his house for $8,000.
Pide $8.000 por su casa.	He asks $8,000 for his house.
He pagado $9 por este diccionario.	I paid $9 for this dictionary.

---

[1] But **en** is also used to indicate the sum for which something sells: **Un perro llamado Napoleón fué vendido a un inglés en cincuenta mil pesetas.** (Sender, **Siete domingos rojos,** I) *A dog named Napoleon was sold to an Englishman for 50,000 pesetas.*

Le daré a V. $10 por los dos. — I will give you $10 for the two.

Por cada voz latina daba el librote cuatro, seis, diez o doce términos castellanos. (Unamuno, **Recuerdos de niñez y de mocedad,** II, 2) — For each Latin word the big book gave four, six, ten, or twelve Spanish terms.

28.11. Offsets one thing against another:

He traducido la frase palabra por palabra. — I have translated the phrase word for word.

Me pagó peso por peso. — He paid me peso for peso.

"Ojo por ojo y diente por diente." — "An eye for an eye and a tooth for a tooth."

28.12. Indicates unit of measure or number:

Por docenas. — By the dozen.

A diez por ciento. — At ten per cent.

Por mayor y por menor. — By wholesale and retail.

Este vapor marcha quince nudos por hora. — This steamer runs fifteen knots an hour.

Gano $1.500 por año. — I earn $1,500 per annum.

28.13. Has the signification of *in behalf of, in favor of, for the sake of, instead of:*[1]

Habló elocuentemente por su amigo. — He spoke eloquently in his friend's behalf.

Lo haré por V. con gusto. — I will do it for you with pleasure.

Votamos por Cleveland. — We voted for Cleveland.

Es menester observar por sí mismo. (Unamuno, **Recuerdos de niñez y de mocedad,** II, 7) — It is necessary to observe for oneself.

Fué elegido diputado por Guadalfranco. (Pérez de Ayala, **La caída de los Limones,** III) — He was elected representative of Guadalfranco.

Yo estoy por derechos protectores, mi hermano está por el libre cambio. — I am for protective tariff, my brother is for free trade.

Trabajo por el señor A. — I work in behalf of Mr. A.

---

[1] Possibly the use of **por** in stage directions to indicate that a speech refers to a given character should be classified under this heading. Also difficult to classify is the use of **por** in a few phrases to indicate the limitation of a statement to the person named: **¿Seguimos? Por mí, lector amigo,** hasta **que usted quiera.** (Unamuno, **Y va de cuento, in El espejo de la muerte**) *Shall we go on? For my part* (or *So far as concerns me*), *friend reader, as long as you want.*

Escribo esta carta por mi hermano. — I am writing this letter for my brother. *(in behalf of* or *instead of)*

¡Una limosna, por Dios![1] señor. — An alms for God's sake, Sir!

Yo haré la guardia por V. esta noche. — I will mount guard for you tonight.

Arial siguió publicando artículos y hasta libros, porque su hija escribía por él. (Alas, **Cambio de luz,** in **El Señor; y lo demás son cuentos**) — Arial continued to publish articles and even books, because his daughter did his writing for him.

28.14. Appeals to something in the manner of an oath, to strengthen an assertion:

¡Por el cielo que está encima de nosotros! — By the heaven above us!

Por mi conciencia no lo comprendo. — On my conscience, I don't understand it.

¡Por Dios! señor, es verdad lo que le digo. — By God! Sir, it is true what I am telling you.

28.15. Followed by an infinitive, **por** indicates what remains to be done—without implying, however, that it will be done:

Quedan seis páginas por copiar. — There remain six pages to copy.

El tratado está por ratificar. — The treaty is yet to be ratified.

Está por ver. — That is to be seen.

La contestación está por recibir. — The reply is yet to be received.

Cartas por escribir. — Letters to be written.

La mitad de la novela quedaba por leer, cuando... — Half of the novel remained to be read, when...

Sin dejar nada por decir. — Without leaving anything unsaid.

PARA

28.16. Para expresses the use, purpose or destination[2] for which anything is adapted or intended:

[1] This supplication is so much used by beggars that they have been nicknamed **pordioseros.** The term used when speaking courteously of them is **pobres** *poor persons.* **Mendigo** *beggar* is a more literary word. **Pordiosear** is *to go begging.*

[2] This use extends, in colloquial and antiquated language, to expressions that usually have **a** (for a difference of meaning see § **28.24** c): **Viejas labradoras de Cela y de Lestrove van para la feria con gallinas, con lino, con centeno.** (Valle-Inclán, **Malpocado,** in **Jardín novelesco)** *Old farm women from Cela and Lestrove are going to* (or *toward*) *the fair with chickens, with flax, with rye.* **Unas horas más tarde volvía para Madrid.** (Baroja, **El árbol de la ciencia,** III, 1) *A few hours later he was on his way back to Madrid.*

Esta carta es para el correo de la tarde.	This letter is for the evening mail.
Estos paquetes son para Sud América.	These packages are for South America.
Mañana parto para Boston.	I start for Boston tomorrow.
Aquel buque tiene destino para Nueva Zelandia.	That vessel is bound for New Zealand.
Estudiar para médico, para abogado.	To study to be a doctor, a lawyer.
He comprado un estante para mis libros.	I have bought a bookcase for my books.
Esta es buena tela para sábanas.	This is good cloth for sheets.
Un excelente coche para caminos rurales.	An excellent carriage for country roads.
Aquellos hombres son demasiado chicos para granaderos, pero servirán para la artillería.	Those men are too small for grenadiers, but they will do for the artillery.
¿Para dónde parte V.?	For what destination do you set out?
Este regalo no es para ti sino para tu hermana.	This present is not for you, but for your sister.
He comprado un traje para el baile del viernes próximo.	I have bought a suit for next Friday evening's ball.
Le di treinta pesos para ropa y diez para alfileres.	I gave her 30 pesos for clothes and 10 for pin money.

28.17. In this manner **para,** by indicating the special use of something, helps to form a multitude of compound expressions which in English are made by placing two words together without any intervening particle:

jaulas para pájaros	bird cages
un estante para libros	a bookcase
aceite para el pelo	hair oil
pinzas para agujas	needle forceps
una aguja para máquina de coser	a sewing-machine needle

28.18. With the same value of purpose or destination, **para** followed by an infinitive may be rendered by *to* or *in order to:*

Yo estudio para instruir a otros.	I study in order to teach others.
Será preciso tener paciencia para alcanzar nuestro objeto.	It will be necessary to have patience in order to obtain our object.
Quiero algo para leer.	I want something to read.

Necesito mi pluma ahora para escribir una carta.	I need my pen now to write a letter.
Busco mi sombrero para ir al mercado.	I am looking for my hat so as to go to market.

28.19. Followed by an infinitive governed by the verb **estar, para** indicates the proximity of an action or occurrence:

El viento está para cambiar.	The wind is about to change.
Está para llover.	It is going to rain.
Estamos para ir al teatro.	We are just going to the theater.
Estuve para ir a su casa, cuando entró.	I was on the point of going to his house, when in he came.

28.20. Para followed by an infinitive is used to indicate the following step in a series of events, somewhat as *only to* is used in English in affirmative phrases:

Cuando uno se tiraba al agua, los otros se volvían momentáneamente preocupados, como si recordaran algo, para olvidarse en seguida. (Quiroga, **Los buques suicidantes,** in **La gallina degollada y otros cuentos**)	When one threw himself into the water, the others turned around concerned momentarily, as if they recalled something, only to forget at once.
La luna llena salía del seno de un nubarrón negruzco para volverse a ocultar. (Baroja, **El mayorazgo de Labraz,** I, 1)	The full moon came out from the depths of a big black cloud only to hide itself again (*or* then it hid itself again).
Las iras de las *Miaus* recaían sobre una persona que entonces desapareció de la casa, para no volver a ella hasta la ocasión que ahora se refiere. (Pérez Galdós, **Miau,** X)	The anger of the Miaus fell upon a person who then disappeared from the house, not to return to it until the occasion which is now related.

28.21. Designates a point or a farthest limit of future time:

Lo difícil dejaremos para mañana.	We will leave the difficult part for tomorrow.
Tengo una cita para el jueves por la tarde.	I have an engagement for Thursday evening.
Se lo pagaré a V. para el quince del mes que viene.	I will pay you it by the fifteenth of next month.

Para el sábado estarán hechos. — They will be done by Saturday.

La sesión fué postergada para la semana próxima. — The session was postponed until the next week.

28.22. The termination of a period may be emphasized rather than the period itself (§ 28.7):

Se llevaron a la chica a Valencia, diciendo que sólo era **para** unos días. (Blasco Ibáñez, **El "femater,"** in **Cuentos valencianos**) — They took the child off to Valencia, saying that it was only *for* a few days.

Por la tarde la música se embarcaría para Catarroja, dejando al Palmar sumido en su tranquilidad **para** todo un año. (Blasco Ibáñez, **Cañas y barro,** VI) — In the afternoon the musicians would take a ship for Catarroja, leaving El Palmar sunk in its convent-like peace *for* a whole year.

Más vale ir al presidio **para** toda la vida que no denunciar a un hombre. (Baroja, **La dama errante,** X)[1] — It is better to go to prison *for* one's whole life than to denounce a man.

¡Esta subasta me ha arruinado **para** toda la vida! ¡He dejado aquí un dineral! (Benavente, **La comida de las fieras,** I, 3) — This auction has ruined me *for* my whole life! I have left a fortune here!

Dijo que él no se marchaba, que tenía un contrato **para** diez años con el dueño de la casa, y que no se iba. (Baroja, **La feria de los discretos,** X)[2] — He said that he wasn't going to leave, that he had a ten-year contract (contract *for* ten years) with the owner of the house, and that he wasn't going to go.

28.23. Para expresses a comparison of inequality—one member of the comparison being different from what the other would lead us to expect:

Para joven escribe muy bien. — For a young man he writes very well.

Le alaban poco para lo que merece. — They praise him little compared with what he deserves.

---

[1] Cf. **¡Sí, matarle, matarle, aunque fuese a presidio por toda la vida!** (Palacio Valdés, **Santa Rogelia,** I, 6) *Yes, kill him, kill him, even if he went to prison for all his life!* BUT: **Quizá el presidio para toda la vida (idem, I, 4, end)**.

[2] Cf. **No firma contrato menos de las setecientas pesetas diarias. Y cuando es por más de veinte días, un beneficio con el cincuenta limpio.** (Benavente, **Pepa Doncel,** I, 6) *She doesn't sign a contract for less than seven hundred pesetas a day. And when it is for more than twenty days, a benefit performance with fifty per cent net.*

Para la latitud elevada de Oregon, es muy suave su clima.	Considering the high latitude of Oregon, the climate is very mild.
Entonces tenía poco que confesar para lo que después tuve. (Santa Teresa, **Vida,** V)	I had then little to confess compared with what I afterwards had.
Para ser principiante no lo ha hecho V. mal.	You did not do it badly for a beginner.
Habla muy corrientemente para ser extranjero.	He speaks very fluently for a foreigner.
Esto no es nada para lo que viene.	This is nothing in comparison with what is coming.
¡Para lo que te ha de valer! (Baroja, **La dama errante,** XII)	For all the good it will do you!

28.24. In a broad sense **para** implies that something not generally or universally true, is true of or applicable to, the particular person or thing named:

Las mujeres, llevadas del nuevo, y **para ellas** nunca visto traje, rodearon a la mora.	The women, carried away by the new and *to* them strange (never seen) costume, surrounded the Moorish girl.
No hay hombre grande **para** su ayuda de cámara. (Coloma, **Pequeñeces,** I, 7)	No man is great *to* his valet de chambre.
Lo ocurrido en otros puntos de Madrid **para** ella no ofrecía el menor interés. (Baroja, **El árbol de la ciencia,** II, 8)	What happened in other parts of Madrid didn't have the slightest interest *for* her.
Para la señora Marquesa no es nada. **Para** mí es la salvación. (Benavente, **Campo de armiño,** II, 12)	*To* the Marchioness it is nothing. *To* me it is salvation.
Para ella había trabajado, para ella vivía y respiraba. El dinero **para** él no tenía positiva significación, puesto que no lo necesitaba. (Palacio Valdés, **Sinfonía pastoral, Andante con moto,** III)	For her he had worked, for her he lived and breathed. Money had no real meaning *for* him, since he didn't need it.

28.25. Both para and **por** may be followed by an infinitive or a clause with **que** if a new subject is introduced, but with the following distinction:

a. **Para** is used when the result of the action is certain, or we express our conviction of success. It means *in order to.*

b. **Por** often expresses an effort in the direction indicated, and means basically *for the sake of, in exchange for,* etc., though *in order to* is usually the most convenient translation. From its very meaning **por** may indicate less conviction of success than **para.**

c. **A** + infinitive, especially with a verb indicative of motion, conveys greater certainty of the outcome than **para** + infinitive, corresponding to *come, go,* etc. *and* in English: **Iré a verla** *I shall go to see her* = *I shall go and see her.* **Iré para verla** *I shall go (in order) to see her* (but may not be able to do so).

EXAMPLES

Voy a Nueva York para ver el puente de Brooklyn.	I am going to New York to see the Brooklyn Bridge.
Ando por ver si puedo dormir.	I walk to see if I can sleep.
Iré a España para aprender el idioma.	I will go to Spain to learn the language.
Iré a Washington por hablar al presidente.	I will go to Washington and try to talk to the president.
Ofrecen dinero por entrar.	They offer money to get in.
Dan dinero para entrar.	They give money to get in (They pay an entrance fee).
Estudio por aprender.	I study [hard] to learn.
Es preciso estudiar para aprender.	It is necessary to study in order to learn.
Trabajo por ganar la vida.	I endeavor to earn my living.
Necisito trabajar para ganar la vida.	I need to work to earn my living.
Le llevaba, sobre todo, porque se distrajera con la amistad y juegos de otros muchachos, no para que aprendiera, que sobrado tiempo le quedaba para aprender. (Pérez de Ayala, **Prometeo, V**)	He took him, above all, so that he might be distracted (because he wanted him to be distracted) with the friendship and games of other boys, not so that he might learn, for there was plenty of time left for him to learn.
Esta mano me cortaría porque tú vivieras. (Pérez de Ayala, **La caída de los Limones, VI**)	I would cut off this hand so that you might live (in exchange for your living).

Diré, por decir algo y porque no quede el asunto sin los debidos honores, que fué tan imponente como sencillo el cuadro final de aquel triste espectáculo. (Pereda, **Sotileza,** XXIX, end)	I shall say, for the sake of saying something and so that the subject receive honors due, that the final scene of that sad spectacle was as imposing as it was simple.

28.26. After **estar,** if a person is subject, **por** indicates inclination and **para,** immediate futurity.[1] **Por,** moreover, leaves the carrying out of the inclination uncertain. On the other hand, **para** implies that an action is going to be performed:

Estoy por salir.	I am inclined to go out.
Estoy para salir.	I am on the point of going out.
Estoy por creer que es guasa.	I am inclined to think it is a hoax.
Estaba para entrar cuando le llamé.	He was about to go in when I called him.

28.27. But if a thing is the subject, **por** denotes that the action is yet to be performed, and **para** that it is to be immediately performed:

La discusión está por concluir.	The discussion is as yet unfinished.
La discusión está para concluir.	The discussion is about to come to a close.
Está para llover.	It is going to rain.

28.28. Certain constructions in which **para** has a component part are treated in §§ **9.31** and **29.22** *c*.

[1] Instead of **para, al** is not infrequently used nowadays: **Deben estar al llegar.** (Benavente, **Al fin, mujer,** II, 1) *They must be on the point of arriving.*

XXIX

Remarks On Certain Prepositions

29.1. The simplest use of prepositions is to express the relations of things to each other in respect to time or place: *before, after, in, upon, under.* They extend, however, to many other relations, and especially to the relations between adjectives or verbs and the nouns or pronouns to which they apply.

NOTE. When the pronoun following a preposition admits of case inflection it assumes what is called the prepositional case (§ 3.22).

29.2. The simple prepositions are:

a at, to
ante before
bajo under
con with
contra against
de of, from
desde from, since
durante during
en in, into, at, on
entre among, between
excepto except
hacia towards
hasta until, to, up to
mediante by means of
para (§§ 28.16-28.24) for
por (§§ 28.2-28.15) for, by
salvo except, save
según according to
sin without
so under
sobre on, about
tras after

REMARK. Of these, **bajo** is an adjective serving as a preposition, and **durante, excepto, mediante** and **salvo** are parts of verbs.

29.3. The following simple prepositions are closely connected in meaning with the corresponding compound prepositions which are placed opposite them:

ante before	*with*	**delante de** in front of
tras after	*with*	**detrás de** after
bajo under, beneath	*with*	**debajo de** under, below
sobre on, upon, over	*with*	**encima de** on top of, on, over

29.4. The most general distinction between them is that the latter are used only in a literal sense expressive of location; the former have also a tropical or figurative acceptation. Used literally, there is but slight difference between the values of any pair.

29.5. **Ante** means *in the presence of*—i.e., of some person or tribunal—as if for criticism or judgment. **Delante de** signifies mere location *in front of,* without the idea of criticism implied by **ante;** any person or tangible thing may be its object:

El capitán comparece ante el consejo de guerra.	The captain appears before the court martial.
Ante una comisión de peritos.	Before a committee of experts.
Pasar ante el foro crítico de la prensa.	To pass before the critical forum of the press.
Ante el tribunal de su conciencia.	Before the tribunal of his conscience.
Ante las evidencias de la historia.	In the presence of the evidences of history.
Firma el testamento delante de testigos.	He signs the testament before witnesses.
El puesto de los trompetas es delante de la tropa.	The post of the trumpeters is in front of the troop.

REMARK. Figuratively, **ante** denotes preference:

La muerte ante la deshonra.	Death before dishonor.
Mi patria ante mi familia.	My country in preference to my family.

29.6. **Antes** and **después** mean *before* and *after* in point of time or order. **Delante** and **detrás** refer only to situation. They are followed by **de** when used as prepositions:

Quiero escribir la carta antes de mañana.	I want to write the letter before tomorrow.
Después de comprar pólvora, carga la escopeta.	After buying powder he loads the gun.
El caballo está delante del coche.	The horse is before the carriage.
El muchacho está detrás de la puerta.	The boy is behind the door.

REMARK. The antiquated preposition **so** is still used with the figurative meaning of **bajo** in a few phrases such as

so capa (color, pretexto) de	under pretext *(lit.* cloak, color) of
so pena de	under penalty of

29.7. **Luego** *then, afterwards* is more frequently used as an adverb than as part of a compound preposition, in which case it is followed by **de.** It differs from **entonces** and **después** in that, strictly speaking, it means *next (in order), immediately afterwards* and thus refers to a shorter period of time than **entonces** and **después.** It also means *therefore:*

Si hay que remendar, remiendo y luego me pongo a estudiar las lecciones. (Gallegos, **Doña Bárbara,** VII)	If there is mending to be done, I mend and then I begin to study my lessons.
A pocos pasos le disparó su escopeta a quemarropa, y luego, inmediatamente, la pistola. (Baroja, **La feria de los discretos,** VIII)	After a few steps he fired his shotgun at him point-blank and then, immediately, his pistol.
Y luego de limpiarse el sudor y dar unos pases con la piedra de afilar a la guadaña volvieron a la tarea. (Palacio Valdés, **Sinfonía pastoral, Adagio cantábile,** V)	And after wiping away the sweat and giving the scythe a few strokes with the whetstone they returned to the task.
Fray Ambrosio, luego de haber hablado, rióse abundantemente. (Valle-Inclán, **Sonata de otoño,** p. 24 of the **Opera Omnia** edition)	Fray Ambrosio, after having spoken, laughed a long time.
Los dos clérigos cambiaron una sonrisa tan discreta, que desde luego los tuve por jesuítas. (**idem,** p. 23 of **Opera Omnia** edition)	The two clerics exchanged such a discreet smile that I immediately took them for Jesuits.
No, yo no voy, desde luego. He quedado en ir a pasar la tarde con Flora. (Benavente, **Lo cursi,** I, 9)	No, I am not going, naturally. I have agreed to go and spend the afternoon with Flora.
Naverán – el otro catedrático de matemáticas – lo demuestra de otro modo. Me quedé pensativo, y diciéndome: ¡luego hay más de un modo de demostrar un teorema! (Unamuno, **Recuerdos de niñez y de mocedad,** II, 3)	Naverán – the other mathematics teacher – proves it in another way. I was left thoughtful and saying to myself: then there is more than one way to prove a theorem.

29.8. There is but little distinction between **tras** and **detrás de,** except that the former implies rather immediate proximity *behind,* and the latter is of more common occurrence. **Tras** is the word used in speaking of the succession of events or objects, as in a procession:

Detrás de la mula; tras la mula.	Behind the mule; just behind the mule.
El perro corre tras la zorra.	The dog runs after the fox.
Tras la primavera viene el verano.	After the spring comes the summer.

29.9. In its primary use, **bajo** is interchangeable with **debajo de,** although the latter is of more frequent occurrence. **Bajo** also expresses the secondary sense of the English *under* in a variety of figures of speech in which actual location is not intended:

Debajo de un árbol, de la mesa.	Under a tree, the table.
Debajo del agua, de la tierra.	Under water, underground.
Bajo el pretexto de enfermedad.	Under the pretext of sickness.
Bajo mis órdenes.	Under my orders *(fig.).*
Debajo de mi ventana.	Under my window *(lit.).*
Los documentos están bajo llave.	The documents are under lock and key.
La tarjeta está debajo de la llave.	The card is under the key.
Bajo un nombre supuesto.	Under a fictitious name.
Bajo pena de muerte.	Under penalty of death.

29.10. **Sobre,** when it denotes actual location, is distinguished from **encima de** in this, that **encima**[1] implies elevation above the general level contemplated, while **sobre** may mean *over* or *upon* something low:

Sobre la mesa; sobre el suelo.	On the table; on the floor.
Encima del campanario está una cruz.	On top of the steeple is a cross.
Encima de nuestras cabezas.	Over our heads.
La lluvia cae sobre la tierra.	The rain falls on the earth.
El atlas está encima del armario.	The atlas is on top of the bookcase.

29.11. **Sobre,** when employed in a secondary sense, has the meaning of *on* or *over* without reference to actual location; it is also equivalent to *on* with the value of *about* or *concerning:*

Estar sobre aviso.	To be on the alert.
Desgracia sobre desgracia.	Misfortune upon misfortune.
Tiene una gran ventaja sobre sus rivales.	He has a great advantage over his rivals.
Conferencias sobre química.	Lectures on chemistry.
Pronuncia un discurso sobre el nuevo arancel.	He delivers a speech on the new tariff.

[1] **Encima** is composed of **en** *on,* and **cima** *top* or *summit.* **Encima de** is therefore, literally equivalent to the English *on top of.*

29.12. The interrogative **dónde** *where* is usually preceded by the preposition **a** when it denotes *motion to* a place, and must be preceded by **de**[1] when *origin* or *egress* is intended. These two forms correspond exactly to the old English *whither* and *whence.* When it expresses stationary position it should in strict usage be preceded by **en,** but this is not always observed:

¿A dónde va V.?	Where are you going? (whither go you?)
¿De dónde viene V.?	Where do you come from? (whence come you?)
¿En dónde vive V.? *or* ¿dónde vive V.?	Where do you live?

29.13. Donde is also used relatively, in which case it does not bear the written accent. (§ 33.) The application of prepositions is the same as for its interrogative use:

La casa a donde voy.	The house where I am going.
La ciudad de donde vengo.	The city from which I come.
El arrabal en donde *(or* donde) resido.	The suburb where I live.
Vengo de donde V. viene.	I come from where you come from.
Vivo en donde *(or* donde) V. vive.	I live where you live.

29.14. Donde, as also **cuando** and more rarely **mientras,** are not infrequently used, through omission of their verb, as prepositions. In Spanish America especially **donde** often means **en casa de,** etc.:

Cano tomó sus bártulos, cambió de departamento, y entró, con gran serenidad, donde el matrimonio desconocido. (Alas, **Rivales,** in **El Señor; y lo demás son cuentos**)	Cano picked up his traps, changed compartments and very calmly went into that of the strange married couple.
Cuando la enfermedad de mi hermana Ramoncita, no salía un momento de esta casa. (Palacio Valdés, **La hermana San Sulpicio,** VI)	At the time of my sister Ramoncita's illness, he didn't leave this house a moment.
Pero ella nunca había cumplido esta orden, ni mientras colegiala ni cuando hermana. **(idem,** X)	But she had never obeyed this order, neither while a student nor when a sister.

[1] **De donde** *whence* is a queer reduplication, similar to the English pleonasm *from whence.* The Latin *unde* meant *whence,* but its value became lost in early Spanish, and was represented by *de onde;* which in turn became condensed into the modern **donde** *where.* A second **de** must now be preposed in order to restore the initial meaning; so **de donde** is literally *from from whence.*

29.15. The two prepositions of motion, **hacia** and **hasta**, merit a word of remark. **Hacia** *towards* denotes direction. **Hasta** means *up to, as far as;* on speaking of time, *until.* In connection with adverbs they form many adverbial phrases:

Hacia aquí; hacia allí.	This way; in that direction.
Hasta aquí; hasta allí.	Thus far; as far as there.
Hacia arriba, hacia abajo.	Upwards, downwards.
Hacia adelante, hacia atrás.	Forwards, backwards.
¿Hacia dónde quieren VV. ir?	Which way do you want to go?
¿Hasta dónde quieren VV. ir?	How far do you want to go?
¿Hasta cuándo?	How long? until when?
Hasta ahora, hasta entonces.	Until now, until then.
Hasta mañana.	Until tomorrow.
Hasta la vista. } *(Familiar leave-takings.)*	Until we see each other. *Au revoir.*
Hasta luego.	Until next time. "See you later."
¿Hasta qué hora?	Until what hour? How late?
Iré hasta la casa de V.	I will go as far as your house.
¿Hasta qué punto llegará su insolencia?	To what extreme will his insolence extend?
Marchan hacia la colina.	They march towards the hill.
Mira hacia el río.	He looks towards the river.

29.16. By extension of this meaning **hasta** means *even:*

Es preciso amar hasta a sus enemigos.	It is necessary to love even one's enemies.
Hasta las mujeres pelearán en defensa de la ciudad.	Even the women will fight in defense of the city.

Remark I. After a negative, **antes de** is preferred to **hasta** with regard to time:

No voy antes de mañana.	I am not going until tomorrow.
No pagaré la cuenta antes de recibir los géneros.	I shall not pay the bill until I receive the goods.

Remark II. A common correlative of **hasta** is **desde: desde...hasta** *from ...to.* The same English phrase is also rendered by **de...a**, but **desde** is preferred when the distance is important for the thought: **Piratería disimulada bajo patente de comercio lícito era la industria de aquella embarcación, desde Ciudad Bolívar, hasta Río Negro.** (Gallegos, **Doña Bárbara,** I, 3) *Piracy on the sly, under privilege of legal commerce, was the business of that boat, all the way from Ciudad Bolívar to Río Negro.*

29.17. Compound prepositions, or prepositional phrases, are formed in several ways:

a. A word, most frequently an adjective, used adverbially and followed by **a:**

adversamente a adversely to
conforme a according to
congruamente a consistent with
contrario a contrary to
correspondiente a corresponding to
frente a opposite to
junto a close to
relativamente a in relation to
respecto a with respect to
tocante a in (*or* with) regard to
concerniente a concerning

b. Simple adverbs followed by **de:**

acerca de about, concerning
además de besides, in addition to
alrededor de around
antes de before *(time, order)*
cerca de near, about
debajo de under
delante de before *(place)*
dentro de within
después de after *(time, order)*
detrás de behind, after *(place)*
encima de over, on top of
fuera de outside of
lejos de far from

REMARK. **Con** may be used after an adverb in the same manner as **a** and **de;** but its use is limited by its small range of signification:

juntamente con los otros estudiantes	jointly with the other students

c. Either of the above classes preceded by another preposition:

en cuanto a as for
a causa de on account of
a excepción de with the exception of
a fuerza de by dint of
al través de across
a menos de unless
a pesar de in spite of
con tal de provided that
en frente de in front of
en vez de instead of
en virtud de by virtue of
por causa de on account of
por razón de by reason of
sin embargo de notwithstanding

d. An alternate construction with some adverbs of place, favored especially when the object of the preposition would be a personal pronoun, retains the adverb and expresses the presumable object of the preposition as the indirect object of the verb:

Le pusieron delante un lucido almuerzo. (Pérez Galdós, **Miau,** VII)	They set a fine lunch before him.
Quiero que te me quites de delante. (Pereda, **Sotileza,** XXIV, end)	I want you to take yourself out of my presence.
Venía la señora a sentársele al lado. (Pérez de Ayala, **Luz de domingo,** I)	The lady would come and sit down by his side.

El mundo se me echaba encima. (Pérez de Ayala, **La caída de los Limones,** X)	The world was coming down on top of me.
Están contenidos por respeto al Marqués, su tío, y por miedo a que la sociedad de Moraleda se les ponga en contra. (Benavente, **Pepa Doncel,** II, 1, 3)	They are restrained by respect for the Marquis, their uncle, and for fear that Moraleda society may turn against them.
Las cabezas toman también la forma de las ideas que se les meten dentro. (Camba, **Aventuras de una peseta,** I, 7)	Heads also take the form of the ideas that are put in them.
Malicié que no podía ser nada bueno y me le fuí detrás. (Gallegos, **Doña Bárbara,** III, 8)	I suspected that it could not be anything good and I went off behind him.

e. In the spoken language particularly there is a tendency to convert some adverbs of place into nouns by the addition of the masculine singular form of the possessive adjective instead of into prepositions by the addition of **de** + personal pronoun:

Miró alrededor suyo. (Pérez de Ayala, **Prometeo,** I)	alrededor suyo = alrededor de **sí.**
Sacando coraje en las risas que oía detrás mío no me movía. (Güiraldes, **Don Segundo Sombra,** I)	detrás mío = detrás de mí.
Nunca había visto en derredor mío tanto arreglo y limpieza. (Pérez Galdós, **El amigo Manso,** XLVI, end)	en derredor mío = en derredor de mí.

NOTE. The prepositions, being few, may share among themselves a much larger number of meanings than any other class of words; for, if ten words have to express a hundred relations, each must have an average of ten different applications. The meaning of many prepositions is so limited as not to require space here. There are, however, some of widely diversified application which merit treatment in detail.

A

29.18. A is the most overworked of all the Spanish prepositions. This situation arises from the fact that it represents the Latin dative case, the Latin prepositions *ad to,* followed by the accusative, and *a, ab from,* followed by the ablative, and the locative case (represented in Latin by the ablative), besides many meanings of more recent origin.

a. **A** primarily indicates the point, whether of time, place or degree, which anything reaches, or to which it tends:

Era ya de noche cuando volvieron a la embarcación.	It was already night when they returned to the vessel.
Fué de Nueva York a Puerto Rico.	He went from New York to Puerto Rico.
Estaré en casa de las seis a las siete.	I shall be at home from six o'clock to seven.
Echamos el palo mayor al mar y seguimos navegando. (Baroja, **Las inquietudes de Shanti Andía,** IV, 7)	We threw the mainmast into the sea and sailed on.
Es un hombre de cuarenta y cinco a cincuenta años.	He is a man of from forty-five to fifty years.
La súbita transición del calor a un frío excesivo produjo consecuencias funestas entre la tripulación.	The sudden change from heat to extreme cold produced sad consequences among the crew.
El agua les llegó a la cintura.	The water reached to their waists.

b. It is as indicating the destination of an action that **a** is placed before the object of a transitive verb when the same represents a specific person or when the object requires to be distinguished from the subject (§§ **1.30-1.46**):

Aprovechó Cortés estos sucesos para acusar al emperador de perfidia.	Cortes took advantage of these occurrences to accuse the emperor of bad faith.
Los neocaledonios tenían la costumbre de quemar vivos a sus prisioneros de guerra.	The natives of New Caledonia had the custom of burning alive their prisoners of war.
No era grande la distancia que separaba a la quinta del monasterio.	The distance separating the cottage from the monastery was not great.
Las mil ruedas dentadas sin cesar se mordían las unas a las otras.	The thousand cogwheels ceaselessly bit into one another.

c. As indicating the objective point of movement or action, **a** is placed between some verbs and a dependent infinitive. Thus **ir, venir, enseñar,** and **aprender** require **a** when followed by an infinitive, as do all expressions meaning *to begin:*

Iremos a verlos.	We will go to see them.
Viene a ver a mi padre.	He comes to see my father.

Ella quiere aprender a tocar la guitarra.	She wants to learn to play the guitar.
La vida nos enseña a esperar.	Life teaches us to wait.
Echó a correr.	He started to run.
Las sospechas llegan a hacerse unánimes.	The suspicions eventually become unanimous.
Muerto yo, ¿qué vendrán a ser mis hijos?	When I am dead, what will become of my children?
Los naturales empezaron a entonar su canción de guerra.	The natives began to chant their war song.

d. Following the idea of movement or tendency to any point, is that of rest therein. This use is limited in scope, as place in which is normally expressed by **en:**

Llaman a la puerta.	Someone is knocking at the door.
Sentarse a la mesa.	To sit at the table.
A la derecha la montaña, a la izquierda la llanura, delante el mar.	To the right the mountain, to the left the plain, in front the sea.
Los acordes de un piano resonaban a lo lejos.	The tones of a piano sounded in the distance.
Casi al extremo meridional de esta costa se descubrió una ensenada.	Almost at the southern extremity of this coast an inlet was discovered.
El primero de agosto los dos buques estaban a los 25° 1′ de latitud sur y 134° 6′ de longitud oeste.	On the first of August the two ships were in latitude 25° 1′ south and longitude 134° 6′ west.

REMARK. **En,** not **a,** is used before the proper name of a city or country, in expressing location:

Vivía en Lérida; estaba en Gibraltar.	He lived in Lerida; he was at Gibraltar.
Vive en Chile, en el Canadá.	He lives in Chile; in Canada.

e. Closely connected with the above usage is its application to time, corresponding to a portion of the use of the Latin ablative:

A mediodía. Al anochecer.	At midday. At nightfall.
A últimos de setiembre.	In the latter part of September.
A las dos de la madrugada.	At two o'clock in the morning.
A su llegada.	On his arrival.
A poco llegó su marido.	In a short time her husband arrived.
A la mañana siguiente Cook abandonó aquel paraje poco hospitalario.	On the following morning Cook abandoned that inhospitable region.

REMARK. A very common expression to indicate the period of time at the end of which an act took place is made up of **a** + definite article + period of time + **de**:

A la semana de estar en el pueblo, María entró en la convalecencia. (Baroja, **La dama errante**, XXIX)	After being in the town a week Mary began to convalesce.

f. Denotes manner or means, corresponding to another usage of the Latin ablative:

Andar a gatas.	To go on all-fours.
Le mataron a sangre fría.	They killed him in cold blood.
Pereció a manos de un indígena.	He perished at the hands of a native.
Se dirigió a marchas forzadas sobre la capital.	He advanced upon the capital by forced marches.
Gritar a gaznate tendido.	To shout at the top of one's voice.
Guisar a lumbre mansa.	To cook by a slow fire.
A carrera abierta; a raja cincha.	At full speed; at full gallop.
A ojos vistas; a regañadientes; a porfía.	Visibly; reluctantly; obstinately.

g. Expresses price or rate:

¿A cuánto se vende?	How much does it sell at?
A peso el metro.	At a peso a yard.
La ajusté a doce reales diarios.	I hired her at twelve reals a day.
A quince nudos por hora.	At 15 knots an hour.
A todo vapor.	At full steam.
A seis por ciento, interés compuesto.	At 6% compound interest.

h. Expresses resemblance:

Cortó el nudo a lo Alejandro.	He cut the knot like an Alexander.
Obrar a lo caballero.	To act like a gentleman.
Vestirse a la francesa.	To dress in the French style.
A lo marinero.	In a seamanlike manner.

i. Placed between a noun and the same noun repeated **a** has in some cases a distributive value *(by)*. In the same construction **a** sometimes expresses juxtaposition *(to)*:

uno a uno; dos a dos	one by one; two by two
paso a paso; poco a poco	step by step; little by little
gota a gota	drop by drop
mano a mano; cara a cara	hand to hand; face to face

j. **A** corresponds to the Latin dative after verbs of giving, telling, showing, or otherwise imparting:

Entregó al abogado un paquete.	He handed the lawyer a package.
Después de la cena solía contar cuentos a sus nietecitos.	After supper he used to tell stories to his little grandchildren.
Ofrecieron a los ingleses ñames, caña de azúcar, y plátanos.	They offered the Englishmen yams, sugar cane and bananas.

k. After verbs of depriving or taking away, **a** has the value of Latin *ab:*

Quitaron al viajero su maleta.	They took the traveler's valise from him.
Robó a la anciana todo su dinero y ropa.	She stole all the old woman's money and clothes.
Este suplicio no arrancó al desgraciado una sola queja.	This torture did not draw a single complaint from the unfortunate man.
Cada uno se apresuró a sustraerse al furor de los demagogos...	Each one hastened to escape from the fury of the popular leaders...
Los indios cortaron las orejas a su prisionero.	The Indians cut off their prisoner's ears.

l. **A** is often employed, in a figurative sense, where *in* is used in English:

¡Tierra a la vista!	Land in sight!
Estaban a vista de tierra.	They were in sight of land.
A consecuencia de un resfriado ligero.	In consequence of a slight cold.
Trataban de apoderarse de todo lo que estaba a su alcance.	They tried to seize everything that was in their reach.
No llegaremos a tiempo.	We shall not arrive in time.
Al cuidado de los Sres. Baring Hermanos.	In care of Messrs. Baring Bros.
Los hombres hechos a imagen de Dios.	Men made in the image of God.

m. **A** is likewise often used where the English idiom demands *on:*

a bordo del buque	on board the ship
a la muerte de su padre	on the death of his father
al recibo de la carta	on the receipt of the letter
a la llegada de la comitiva	on the arrival of the party
al contrario	on the contrary
a causa de	on account of

a condición de que	on condition that
a precios moderados	on moderate terms
al entrar; al llegar al yate	on entering; on arriving at the yacht
al otro lado del Atlántico	on the other side of the Atlantic

REMARK. The examples accompanying the last two statements are not intended to be exhaustive, but merely to call attention to the fact that the secondary or figurative uses of any preposition do not necessarily coincide in two different languages.

29.19. CON

a. **Con** primarily expresses accompaniment:

La sultana iba al baño con sus doncellas.	The sultana was going to the bath with her maids.
El Mayor Pike, rodeado en breve de un destacamento de soldados mejicanos, fué hecho prisionero con toda su comitiva y conducido a Querétaro.	Major Pike, surrounded quickly by a detachment of Mexican soldiers, was taken prisoner with his entire party and conducted to Queretaro.
La expedición volvió con una multitud de pormenores interesantes sobre las costumbres, usos, historia y lengua de los indígenas.	The expedition returned with a multitude of interesting details about the customs, habits, history and language of the natives.
Pasó la noche con nosotros.	He spent the night with us.
Votó con el partido antiesclavista.	He voted with the antislavery party.

REMARK. In colloquial use, especially with **ir, venir, volver, enviar, mandar,** etc., **con** often means *to:*

A la edad de diez años me envió con usted. (Valera, **Pepita Jiménez, 22 de marzo**)	At the age of ten years he sent me to (*or* to live with) you.
Voy con mi madre, para leerla los periódicos. (Benavente, **Al fin, mujer,** II, 1, 5)	I am going to (*or* to be with) my mother to read the papers to her.

b. By extension of the above value it expresses relations, dealings or associations of any kind with another:

Las primeras relaciones con los naturales fueron excelentes; pero modificáronse repentinamente.	Their first relations with the natives were excellent; but they suddenly altered.
Llegó a la noticia del rey que el conde de Valois trataba secretamente con el rey de Aragón.	It reached the ears of the king that the Count of Valois was negotiating secretly with the king of Aragon.

Ya no correspondía con su hermano desde hacía diez años.	He had not corresponded with his brother for ten years.
Quien la moleste tendrá que habérselas conmigo.	Whoever molests her will have to deal with me.
Los indios ribereños sostienen un tráfico extensivo con las tribus del interior.	The coast Indians keep up an extensive trade with the inland tribes.

c. Expresses instrumentality:

Con su anteojo interrogaba todos los puntos del horizonte, pero no descubrió el menor indicio de la tierra.	He scanned with his spyglass all parts of the horizon, but he did not discover the slightest indication of land.
¡Animo, ánimo! repetía el marinero, quien sostenía a Jorge con un brazo y nadaba con el otro.	"Courage, courage," repeated the sailor, who supported George with one arm and swam with the other.
El guía señaló con el dedo una masa oscura que se destacaba sobre el horizonte.	The guide pointed out with his finger a dark mass which was outlined on the horizon.

d. Serves to form adverbial expressions of manner:

El arca se abrió con dificultad.	The chest was opened with difficulty.
Cumplió con empeño su deber.	He did his duty conscientiously.
El alud se deslizó con la rapidez de un tren expreso.	The avalanche slid down with the rapidity of an express train.
Los días se sucedían con una monotonía que desesperaba.	The days followed one another with a monotony that was maddening.
Con un disfraz semejante salió al mismo tiempo para Francia el conde de Toreno.	With a similar disguise the Count of Toreno set out at the same time for France.
Se sentían obligados a recibirlo con la risa en los labios.	They felt obliged to receive him with smiles on their lips.
Pálida, y con los ojos enrojecidos.	Pale and with reddened eyes.

e. Occasionally **con** has the value of *notwithstanding:*

Con todo eso.	For (notwithstanding) all that.
La vida del hombre, con ser tan corta, nos suministra abundantes pruebas de esta verdad.	The life of man, notwithstanding its being so short, furnishes us abundant proof of this truth.
Con todos sus preparativos no tuvo su experimento éxito alguno.	Notwithstanding all his preparation his experiment was fruitless.

29.20. DE

a. The primary meaning of **de** is that of origination, derivation or proceeding from, with which value it is applicable to place, time or condition:

El 6 de mayo salieron de la bahía con rumbo al Este.	On the 6th of May they set sail from the bay in an easterly course.
La palabra azúcar nos viene del árabe.	The word sugar comes to us from the Arabic.
El jinete se apeó de su caballo.	The rider dismounted from his horse.
El caballo de Berbería es veloz y hermoso.	The Barbary horse is swift and handsome.
Uno de los insectos más dañinos de Africa es la langosta.	One of the most destructive insects of Africa is the locust.
Don Quijote de la Mancha.	Don Quixote of La Mancha.
El ramal de Júcaro a Morón.	The branch (R. R.) from Jucaro to Moron.
Caminaron de las seis a las doce.	They traveled from six to twelve.
De sol a sol.	From sunrise to sunset.
De vez en cuando.	From time to time.

b. By extension of the value of origin or derivation, it expresses the material of which a thing is made:

Un capote de piel.	A fur cape.
Una plancha de latón pulido.	A plate of polished brass.
Una vela de cera, de sebo.	A wax candle, tallow candle.
Una silla de mimbres.	A wicker chair.
Un palanganero de caoba.	A mahogany washstand.
Fumaba una pipa de barro.	He was smoking a clay pipe.

c. It is equivalent to *of* in expressing ownership, and corresponds to the English possessive:

Los amigos del padre de Teodoro.	The friends of Theodore's father.
Doña Beatriz era hija de D. Pedro de la Cueva, almirante de Santo Domingo y hermano del duque.	Doña Beatrice was the daughter of Don Pedro de la Cueva, Admiral of San Domingo and the Duke's brother.
La naturaleza del terreno.	The nature of the soil.
El dictamen de la mayoría.	The decision of the majority.
Las obras de García.	The works of García.

d. By extension of the above, it expresses the relation of a part to the whole to which it pertains:

Las astas de un toro.	The horns of a bull.
La cabeza de un perno.	The head of a bolt.
Bayas de yedra.	Ivy berries.
Semilla de trébol.	Clover seed.
El badajo de una campana.	The clapper of a bell.
El asiento, el respaldo de una silla.	The seat, the back of a chair.
La albardilla de un muro.	The coping of a wall.

e. It expresses the use for which a thing is intended:

Una máquina de acepillar.	A planing machine.
Un caballo de caza.	A hunter (hunting horse).
Una caña de pescar.	A fishing rod.
Un carro de ganado, de equipaje.	A cattle car, baggage car.
Una sierra de podar.	A pruning saw.
Un molinillo de café.	A coffee mill.

f. Precedes a noun denoting a distinctive characteristic:

El hombre de la barba.	The man with the beard.
Don Pedro del lunar.	Don Pedro of the birthmark.
La estación de calenturas.	The fever season.
Un hombre de talento, de inteligencia.	A man of talent, of intelligence.
El año de la Héjira, del terremoto de Lisboa, de la erupción del Cosegüina.	The year of the Hegira, of the Lisbon earthquake, of the eruption of Coseguina.
Era niña de doce años, de pelo rubio y de natural vivo.	She was a girl of twelve, light-haired, and of a lively nature.

g. By extension it is used to restrict a general term to a special application, or to show which one of a class is intended:

Una colección de minerales, de órquides, de sellos de correo.	A collection of minerals, of orchids, of postage stamps.
Cloruro de sodio, de potasio, de magnesio.	Sodium chloride, potassium chloride, magnesium chloride.
Taladro de mano, de ballesta, de engranaje cónico, de extensión.	Hand drill, bow drill, bevel-wheel drill, expanding drill.
Sierra de mano, de vaivén, de través, de ingletes.	Handsaw, jigsaw, crosscut saw, tenon-saw.
Un puente de caballete, de contrapeso, de armadura de hierro, de riostras y pendolones.	A trestle bridge, counterpoise bridge, iron girder bridge, strut-and-truss bridge.

h. Is used before a noun restricting or specifying the extent and meaning of a preceding verb or adjective:

Cojea del pie derecho. — He limps with the right foot.

Trabaja de carpintero. — He works as a carpenter.

Es sordo de la oreja izquierda. — He is deaf in his left ear.

Alto de estatura, enjuto de carnes, ancho de espaldas, resuelto de ademanes, firme de andadura, basto de facciones. — Tall of stature, spare of flesh, broad-shouldered, resolute of mien, firm of step, coarse-featured.

i. Expresses cause, with the value of *by, for, on account of:*

Loco de alegría; ciego de cólera; medio muerto de hambre, de susto. — Wild with joy; blind with rage; half dead with hunger, with fright.

Falleció de tifo. — He died of typhus fever.

Estábamos ahogados del calor. — We were suffocated with the heat.

j. Denotes the agent of a verb in the passive, or a past participle, especially when expressing a mental action and when a past participle stands alone (cf. § 21.31):

Partió el general acompañado de cuatro de sus ayudantes. — The general set out accompanied by four of his aids.

El rey se veía odiado de sus súbditos y perseguido de los extraños. — The king found himself hated by his subjects and harassed by foreigners.

Remark. If the verb or participle expresses a *direct* physical action, the preposition to be used is **por:**

El Perú fué conquistado por los españoles. — Peru was conquered by the Spaniards.

Destruido por las injurias del tiempo. — Destroyed by the action of the weather.

k. Precedes a noun specifying the particular manner of an action represented by a past participle:

Forrado de pieles; cubierto de arena; adornado de joyas; amueblado de caoba; alfombrado de tapetes turcos; incrustado de nácar; embutido de marfil. — Lined with furs; covered with sand; adorned with jewels; furnished in mahogany; carpeted with Turkish rugs; overlaid with mother-of-pearl; inlaid with ivory.

Los picos encapotados de niebla; las cumbres coronadas de nieve eterna. — The peaks veiled in mist; the summits crowned with eternal snow.

l. It is used to express manner of action or being, thus forming many adverbial expressions:

Estaba de gala, de luto, de etiqueta.	He was in holiday attire, in mourning, in full dress.
Cayó de rodillas, de espaldas.	He fell on his knees, on his back.
Vistióse de marinero.	He dressed up as a sailor.
Hacía de presidente.	He was acting as president.
Fué de capitán don Rodrigo Meneses.	Don Rodrigo Meneses went as captain.
Les sirvió de guía.	He served them as guide.
Fué enviado de embajador a la Puerta.	He was sent as Ambassador to the Porte.
De falso; de golpe; de oídas; de buena fe; de mala gana.	Falsely; suddenly; by hearsay; in good faith; unwillingly.

m. As a substitute for **que** in comparisons (cf. §§ **8.5** ff.):

Encontróse el terreno menos accidentado de lo que se había supuesto.	The ground was found to be less uneven than had been supposed.
Más de cuatro horas se invirtieron en aquella operación penosa.	More than four hours were spent in that tedious operation.

n. Like the Latin *de,* it indicates the matter spoken or treated of:

Capítulo II. Del verbo auxiliar **haber** o **tener.**	Chapter II. On the auxiliary *haber* or *tener.*
Nada sé de aquel asunto.	I know nothing about that matter.
No hablemos de los peligros que hemos arrostrado.	Let us not speak of the dangers we have faced.
No pudo resistir a la tentación de informar a su mujer de todo lo sucedido.	He could not resist the temptation of informing his wife of all that had occurred.

o. **De** is placed between the common appellatives and the proper names of countries, provinces, towns, islands, and geographical divisions:

La República de Colombia.	The Republic of Colombia.
La provincia de Aragón.	The province of Aragon.
La ciudad del Cuzco.	The city of Cuzco.
La isla de Cuba.	The island of Cuba.
El pico de Tenerife.	The peak of Teneriffe.
El estrecho de Magallanes.	The straits of Magellan.

p. **De** is idiomatically used between a noun and a qualifying noun or adjective preceding, imparting a bantering note (cf. §§ **2.26, 30.52**):

El ladrón de Andresillo.	That thief Andrew.
El bribón del abogado.	The scoundrel of a lawyer.

El charlatán del médico.	The quack doctor.
El pobre de Tomás.	Poor Tom.
La desgraciada de Florinda.	The unfortunate Florinda.
¡Desventurados de ellos!	Unlucky they!

29.21. EN

a. **En** has primarily the values of *in,* expressing rest, and *into,* expressing motion:

Penetró en el interior hasta el lago Urre Lauquen, que nombró Lago de Salinas.	He penetrated into the interior as far as the lake Urre Lauquen, which he named Salt Lake.
Todos se metieron precipitadamente en sus casas.	All rushed precipitately into their houses.
Se decidió pasar la noche en aquella choza.	It was decided to pass the night in that hut.
En aquel paraje se establecieron relaciones amistosas con los naturales.	In that region friendly relations were established with the natives.

b. The above values are extended to many secondary or figurative applications, generally corresponding to the English:

En mangas de camisa; en paños menores.	In one's shirt sleeves; in dishabille.
La fonda ha caído en mala fama.	The hotel has fallen into ill repute.
Las aceras están en mal estado.	The sidewalks are in bad order.
Poner una cosa en boga.	To bring a thing into vogue.
Se lo daré a V. en cambio del suyo.	I will give it to you in exchange for yours.
En efecto; en debida forma; en vano; en desuso; en gran manera.	In fact; in due form; in vain; in disuse; in a high degree.
Déjesele en paz.	Let him be left in peace.
Roto en mil pedazos.	Broken in a thousand pieces.

c. **En** occasionally has the value of *on, upon:*

Ella tenía una sortija de matrimonio en el dedo.	She had a wedding ring on her finger.
Se sentó en la cama.	He sat down on the bed.
La comida ya está en la mesa.	The dinner is already on the table.
Apoyó su mano en mi hombro.	He rested his hand on my shoulder.
Cuando sus ojos descansaron en la pintura,...	When her eyes rested on the painting,...
Selkirk, durante su residencia en la isla de Juan Fernández, había visto pasar muchos buques.	Selkirk, during his stay on the island of Juan Fernandez, had seen many ships pass.

Después de dos días de marcha la expedición se encontró en los confines de Tarapacá. — After two days' journey the expedition found itself on the confines of Tarapaca.

d. Applies to time in practically the same manner as the English *in:*

Lo hizo en cuatro horas. — He did it in four hours.

En aquel momento una mala noticia vino a llevar a su colmo el desaliento de la tripulación. — At that moment bad news came to put the climax to the despair of the crew.

En breve volvieron a la carga. — In a short time they returned to the charge.

Prometió traérmelos en dos días. — He promised to bring them to me in two days.

En un año había llegado a ser una notabilidad. — In a year he had become a notable character.

29.22. COMBINATIONS OF PREPOSITIONS

a. **De a** are at times combined to express rate or denomination, though there is a strong tendency nowadays to omit **a** in the expressions which follow (**tabacos de diez centavos, sellos de quince céntimos, billetes de cinco pesos,** etc.):

Tabacos de a diez centavos, de a veinticinco. — Ten-centavo cigars, three-for-twenty-five cigars.

Una pieza de a doce, de a diez y ocho. — A twelve-pounder, an eighteen-pounder (gun).

Diez sellos de a quince céntimos y cuatro de a veinte y cinco. — Ten fifteen-centimo stamps and four twenty-five-centimos.

Un guardia de a caballo. — A mounted policeman.

Los de a pie. — The infantry.

El portero de al lado. — The porter of the next house.

Billetes de a cinco pesos. — Five-peso bills.

Bonos nacionales de a tres por ciento. — Three per cent, government bonds.

b. Prepositional compounds may be formed by placing **de** or **por** before other prepositions, each member retaining its own value:

El fuente salía de entre dos cerros elevados y roqueños. — The spring issued from between two high, rocky hills.

Las luciérnagas revoloteaban por entre las ramas. — The fireflies were dancing among the boughs.

Al pasar por delante del teatro... — On passing in front of the theater...

Un arroyuelo serpenteaba por entre las malezas.	A brook wound through among the underbrush.
Saltó una liebre de entre las matas.	A hare jumped out from among the bushes.
La bala pasó por encima de su cabeza.	The ball passed over his head.
Saltó por encima de la zanja, por encima del seto.	He jumped across the ditch, over the hedge.

c. **Para con** signifies moral direction toward:

Su conducta para con sus hijos.	His behavior towards his children.
Ha sido muy amable para conmigo.	He has been very kind toward me.
Noté que él era muy respetuoso para con su madre.	I noticed that he was very respectful towards his mother.
Este hombre es muy duro para con sus criados.	This man is very severe towards his servants.
Es afable y caritativo para con todos.	He is affable and charitable to all.
Me parece que su padre es injusto para con él.	It seems to me that his father is unjust towards him.
Es ingrato para con sus padres.	He is ungrateful towards his parents.
Se mostró cruel para con los prisioneros.	He showed himself cruel to the prisoners.
Es liberal para con sus empleados.	He is liberal towards his employes.

REMARK. In present-day language either **con** or **para** alone is more frequently used: **Es muy bueno con sus hijos, Es muy bueno para sus hijos.** *He is very good to his children.*

PREPOSITIONS REQUIRED BY VERBS, ADJECTIVES AND NOUNS

29.23. Some prepositions, especially **a, con, de, en, para** and **por,** are much used (as are their equivalents in English) to supplement certain nouns, adjectives and verbs. This subject, which is called in some grammars "regimen," is very extensive, and space cannot be here afforded for a list of all these combinations. A tolerably complete list, covering 57 pages, may be found in the "Gramática de la Lengua Castellana," of Vicente Salvá. Unfortunately the subject, though of the utmost importance, has been practically ignored by the writers of dictionaries.

In § **29.31** is presented a list especially of the prepositions used to supplement frequently used verbs.

29.24. The following examples will show the general character of the matter in question:

VERBS

Alegrarse de algo.	To rejoice at something.
El río abunda de peces.	The river abounds with fish.
Sus opiniones no tardaron en influir en las de Josefa.	His opinions were not long in influencing those of Josephine.
Pero no contó con la inexperiencia de sus pilotos.	But he did not count upon the inexperience of his pilots.
La viudez acabó con su juventud.	Widowhood put an end to her youth.
Su propiedad colinda con la mía.	His estate touches mine.
El Perú confina con el Ecuador.	Peru borders on Ecuador.
Este aposento huele a tabaco.	This rooms smells of tobacco.
Sustituyó los billetes con un lío de papel de desecho.	He substituted a package of waste paper for the bills.
Desimpresionarse de una idea.	To disabuse one's self of an idea.
Se enamoricó de la niña.	He was smitten with the girl.
Pensaba en ella de día y soñaba con ella de noche.	He thought of her by day and dreamt of her by night.

ADJECTIVES AND PAST PARTICIPLES

Extraño de la materia en cuestión.	Foreign to the matter in question.
Humano con los vencidos.	Humane towards the vanquished.
Odioso al público.	Distasteful to the public.
Soy muy aficionado a la ópera.	I am very fond of the opera.
Quedó muy alegre con la noticia.	He was very joyful over the news.
Parecía muy arrepentido de sus acciones.	He seemed very sorry for his actions.
Un hombre avanzado en años.	A man advanced in years.
Estábamos todos atónitos del suceso.	We were all astonished at the occurrence.
Convencido de su error.	Convinced of his error.
Ocupado de negocios.	Occupied with business.
Fué el primero, el último, en (a *is also found*) llegar.	He was the first, the last, to arrive.
Abismado en sus reflexiones.	Absorbed in his reflections.

NOUNS

Su afición a la música.	His fondness for music.
Un remedio contra la gota.	A cure for the gout.
El anhelo por sobresalir.	The desire to excel.
El amor a la patria.	Love for one's country.
Su indignación sobre la conducta de su hermano.	Her indignation over her brother's conduct.
Su generosidad para con sus asistentes.	His generosity towards his assistants.

Habilidad en el manejo de las armas.	Skill in the use of weapons.
Complicidad en un delito.	Complicity in a crime.
Denegó toda responsabilidad en el negocio.	He disclaimed all responsibility in the matter.
Mostraba una capacidad para los más altos puestos.	He showed a capacity for the highest positions.
No puede haber objeción alguna a ello.	There can be no objection to it.
No veo inconveniente en su plan.	I see no objection to your plan.
Ha expresado su simpatía con V. en su dolor.	He expressed his sympathy for you in your affliction.

29.25. A verb, adjective or noun is not always limited to a single, supplementary preposition; but may take, at different times, various prepositions according to its relations to the following word:

Bueno de comer.	Good to eat.
Bueno para la salud.	Good for the health.
Ha sido muy bueno con nosotros.	He has been very good to us.
Dar fin a una cosa.	To complete a thing.
Dar fin de una cosa.	To put an end to a thing.
Salió a su padre.	He turned out like his father.
Salío con su padre.	He went out with his father.
Salió de su padre.	He became of age.
Salió por su padre.	He gave bonds for his father.
Deshacerse de alguna cosa.	To get rid of something.
Deshacerse por alguna cosa.	To long for something.
Hacerse a una cosa.	To accustom one's self to a thing.
Hacerse con una cosa.	To obtain a thing.
Hacerse de una cosa.	To provide one's self with a thing.
Hacerse para una cosa.	To prepare one's self for a thing.

29.26. The question of the preposition required by a certain verb may be simplified by bearing in mind that verbs of motion may be followed by any preposition according to the direction of the motion; therefore the prepositions following such verbs are independent of the verbs themselves, and need not be considered under the subject of regimen:

Llegar a Berlín, llegar de Berlín.	To arrive at (*or* in) Berlin, to arrive from Berlin.
Correr al, en el, por el, hacia el, hasta el bosque.	To run to, in, through, towards, as far as the woods.

Saltar al agua, en tierra, de la muralla, sobre la mesa, por encima del foso.	To jump into the water, on to the land, from the wall, on the table, over the ditch.
Se colocó en la barquilla del globo, sobre el alcázar, cerca de la bitácora, delante de la puerta, debajo de la galería.	He placed himself in the car of the balloon, on the quarterdeck, near the binnacle, in front of the door, under the gallery.

29.27. Again we should distinguish between a preposition which really supplements the verb, and one forming part of an adverbial expression which merely modifies its meaning:[1]

Comer con un amigo, con apetito, en casa.	To dine with a friend, with appetite, at home.
Decir en alta voz, con voz humilde, en amistad, entre dientes.	To say aloud, in a humble tone, in friendship, between one's teeth.
Escribir a su tío, con esta fecha, con buenos caracteres, en buen estilo, de propio puño, en prosa, sobre el papel.	To write to one's uncle, under this date, in clear characters, in a good style, with one's own hand, in prose, on the paper.
Morir a cuchillo, a manos de otro, de viejo, en olor de santidad, por su patria.	To die by the knife, at the hands of another, of old age, in the odor of sanctity, for one's country.
Trabajar a destajo, con ahinco, de zapatero, en hierro, por otro.	To work by the job, with ardor, as a shoemaker, in iron, for another.

29.28. The preposition required to supplement a verb or adjective is usually the same whether the complement[2] be a noun or an infinitive:

La ocasión es propicia para ejecutar el proyecto – propicia para la ejecución del proyecto.	The occasion is favorable for carrying out the plan – for the execution of the plan.
Dedicarse a estudiar el derecho – al estudio del derecho.	To devote one's self to studying law – to the study of law

29.29. The infinitive follows impersonal expressions without being connected by any preposition:

---

[1] The list in Salvá's Grammar, above referred to, is full of examples which show a failure to make this distinction. The examples here given (§ 29.27) are taken from that list.

[2] A verb, adjective or noun, requiring a preposition to connect its meaning with what follows, must necessarily be followed by some word (a noun or infinitive) to which it applies. This word is here called *complement,* i.e. that which *completes* the clause.

Es agradable vivir en el campo.	It is pleasant to live in the country.
No es costumbre beber cerveza.	It is not the custom to drink beer.
No es posible abrir las ventanas.	It is not possible to open the windows.
Es útil leer buenos libros, pero es preciso leer con reflexión.	It is useful to read good books, but it is necessary to read with reflection.
Es siempre deseable tener buenos amigos.	It is always desirable to have good friends.
Es injusticia insistir.	It is an injustice to insist.

29.30. In English two or more verbs, adjectives or nouns, supplemented by different prepositions, may be made to apply to the same complement. In Spanish this is not usual, though occasionally found; two or more words having different regimens ordinarily have separate complements:

Gran número de buques entran en este puerto y salen de él todos los meses.	A large number of vessels enter and leave this port every month.
Los rebeldes atacaron la ciudad de X., y se apoderaron de ella.	The rebels attacked and took possession of the city of X.
Protesta contra esta medida y oposición a ella.	Protest against and opposition to this measure.
Tomó parte en esta expedición y aprovechó de ella.	He took part in and profited by this expedition.
Su acción no sólo fué diferente de las instrucciones que yo le había dado, sino contraria a ellas.	His action was not only different from, but contrary to, the instructions I had given him.
Es muy aficionado al juego de ajedrez y muy experto en él.	He is very fond of and expert in the game of chess.

REMARK. Such constructions as **entran en y salen de este puerto, atacaron y se apoderaron de la ciudad,** would be exceptional.

29.31.

A

abalanzarse a *rush to*

abandonar(se) a *give (oneself) up to*

abominar (de) *abominate, detest*

abstenerse de *refrain from*

abundar de *or* en *be abundant in, abound with*

abusar de *abuse, misuse*

acabar con *put an end to;* — de *finish, have (had) just;* — por *end up by*

acceder a *accede to*

acercarse a *approach, draw near to*

acertar a *chance to; manage to; succeed in;* — con *hit upon*

acomodarse a *agree to*

acompañado de *(occasionally* por) *accompanied by*
aconsejar *advise to*
acordar *agree to;* —se de *agree, remember*
acostumbrar (a) *be accustomed to;* —(se) a *accustom (oneself) to;* estar acostumbrado a *be accustomed to*
adelantarse a *get ahead of, be the first to, come forward to*
admirarse de *be astonished to* or *at*
adorar a *or* en *worship, adore*
adornar con *or* de *adorn with*
advertir (de) *warn (of)*
afanarse por *or* en *strive to*
aferrarse en *persist in*
aficionarse de *or* a *grow fond of;* ser aficionado a *be fond of*
afligirse de *lament*
agarrarse a *or* de *seize, clutch, catch*
agraviarse de *be grieved at*
aguardar a *wait to* or *until*
ajustarse a *agree to*
alcanzar a *reach to, extend to; suffice to; attain, succeed in*
alegrarse de *be glad to* or *of*
alentar a *or* para *encourage to*
alimentarse de *or* con *feed on, nourish oneself with*
allanarse a *submit to, acquiesce in*
amenazar *threaten to;* — con *threaten to* or *with*
anhelar *long to*
animar a *encourage to;* —se a *make up one's mind to, feel like*
ansiar *long to*
anticiparse a *take the first step to, be the first to*
aparentar *pretend to*
apelar de *appeal from*
apiadarse de *have pity on*
apoyarse en *or* sobre *lean on* or *upon*
aplicar(se) a *apply (oneself) to*
aprender a *learn to*
apresurarse a *hasten to, hurry to*
aprobar *approve of*
aprovechar(se de) *take advantage of*
apurarse por *strive to, worry about*
arrepentirse de *repent of*
arriesgarse a *risk*
arrojar a *throw into*
asirse de *seize, clutch, catch*
asistir a *be present at, witness*
asombrarse de *be* or *act astonished at*
aspirar a *aspire to*
asustarse de *be* or *act frightened at*
atinar a *manage to; succeed in*
atreverse a *dare to*
autorizar a *or* para *authorize to*
avaro de *greedy of*
avenirse a *agree to, come down to, consent to*
aventurarse a *venture to*
avergonzarse de *be ashamed of*
avezar(se) a *accustom (oneself) to*
avisar (de) *inform (of)*
ayudar a *help to, aid to*

B

bastar para *or* a *be sufficient to (when used personally);* — con *or without preposition (when used impersonally) be sufficient to*
breve de *(+ inf.) short (to)*
bueno de *or* para (comer) *good to (eat)*
burlarse de *make fun of*

C

caer a *fall into;* — a *or* hacia *face (toward)*
cansarse de *grow tired of;* — en *take the trouble to*
casar a *marry (off) to;* —(se) con *marry, become the husband* or *wife of*
ceder a *consent to*

celebrar *be glad to*
cesar de *cease to*
coger de *or* por (la mano) *seize by (the hand);* —se a *seize, clutch, catch*
cojear de un pie *be lame of one foot, be limping on one foot.*
comenzar a *commence to*
compadecerse de *have pity on*
comparar a *or* con *compare to* or *with*
complacerse en *take pleasure in*
comprometer(se) a *obligate (oneself) to*
concluir de *finish;* — por *or* present participle *end by*
condenar a *condemn to*
condescender en *condescend to*
confiar a *entrust to;* — en *confide in, trust in* or *to*
conformarse a *conform to, yield to;* — con *conform to, agree with*
conforme a *or* con *in accordance with*
congraciarse con *get into the good grace(s) of*
congratular(se) de *congratulate (oneself) on*
consagrar(se) a *devote (oneself) to*
conseguir *succeed in*
consentir (en) *consent to*
consistir en *consist of*
conspirar a *conspire to*
constar de *consist of*
contar con *count on* or *upon, rely on* or *upon*
contentarse con *content oneself with, be content with*
contento con *or* de *content with*
contestar a *(often without* a *when the object is a thing) answer*
continuar a *or* present participle *continue to*
contribuir a *contribute to*
convenir en *agree to*
convertir en *convert into*
convidar a *or* para *invite to*
correr a *run to;* — con *be responsible for;* —se de *be ashamed of*
cubrir con *or* de *(especially with the past participle) cover with*
cuidar (de) *take care to* or *of, care for;* —se de *concern oneself about, worry about*
culpar *blame;* — de *accuse of*
cumplir con *do one's duty toward; perform*

D

dar a *face (toward);* — con *hit upon, run across;* — contra *run* or *strike against;* — en *persist in, fall into the notion of, "take to," understand, "catch on"*
deber *ought to, should (obligation or conjecture);* — de *ought to (conjecture)*
decidir *decide to;* — + *object* + a *cause to decide to, decide to;* —se por *decide on, choose to;* estar decidido a *be resolved* or *determined to;* — sobre *decide upon* or *concerning*
dedicar(se) a *devote (oneself) to*
dejar *let, allow to, permit to;* — de *stop, cease to, fail to;* —se de (+ *noun) stop, quit*
deleitarse en *delight in*
depender de *depend on* or *upon*
desafiar a *dare to, challenge to*
desconfiar de *mistrust*
descontento con *or* de *discontent with*
descuidar(se) de *or* en *neglect to*
desdecirse de *take back, retract*
desear *desire to*
deshacerse de *get rid of;* — por *be wild to*

despedir *dismiss;* –se de *take leave of, say goodbye to*
desprenderse de *dispossess oneself of, get rid of*
destinar a *or* para *destine to, assign to*
desvivirse por *be crazy to* or *about, want very much to*
determinar *determine to;* – + *object* + a, *cause to determine to, decide to;* estar determinado a *or* en *be determined* or *resolved to*
difícil de (+ *inf.*) *difficult to*
dignarse *deign to*
disculparse con *excuse oneself to;* – de *or* por *excuse oneself for;* – de *excuse oneself from*
disfrutar (de) *enjoy, profit by*
disponer(se) a *get ready to, prepare to*
divertir(se) present participle, en *or* con *amuse (oneself) by*
dotado de *endowed with*
dudar (de) *doubt;* – en *hesitate*

E

echar(se) a *begin to*
elegir *elect to, choose to*
empeñarse en *insist on*
empezar a *begin to*
enamorarse de *fall* or *be in love with*
encarar(se con) *face*
encargar de *charge to, direct to;* –se de *undertake to, take charge of*
encariñarse con *be fond of, be attached to*
enfadarse de (+ *thing) be angry at;* – con (+ *person) be angry at* or *with*
enojarse de (+ *thing) be angry at;* – con (+ *person) be angry at* or *with*
enseñar a *teach (how) to*
entender de *know about*
entrar en *or* a *enter (into);* – a *enter to* or *on, begin to*
entretener(se) en, con *or* present participle, *entertain (oneself) by* or *with*
enviar a *send to*
equivaler a *be equivalent to, be equal (to)*
equivocarse de *be mistaken as to* or *about*
escandalizarse de *be scandalized to* or *at*
esforzarse a, para, por, *or* en *strive to*
esmerarse en *take pains in*
espantarse de *be astonished to*
esperar *hope, expect, wait;* – a *wait to* or *until*
esquivar *avoid*
estar para *be about to, be prepared for;* – por *be in favor of, be inclined to, be yet to (+ inf.)*
estribar en *be based on*
evitar *avoid*
examinarse de *be examined in*
exceder de *or* a *exceed, be more than*
excitar a *excite to*
excusar *excuse, avoid, dispense with;* –se con *excuse oneself with;* –se de *or* por *excuse oneself for;* –se de *excuse oneself from*
exponer(se) a *expose (oneself) to*
extrañar *be surprised to;* –se de *be surprised to* or *at*
extraño de *(+ inf.) strange to*

F

fácil de *(+ inf.) easy to*
faltar a *fail to keep; be disrespectful to*
falto de *lacking in*
felicitar(se) de *congratulate (oneself) on*

fiar en *confide in, trust in;* –se de *trust*
fijarse en *notice, pay attention to*
fingir *feign to, pretend to*
forzar a *force to*
frisar en *border on*

G

ganar a *surpass in*
gloriarse de *boast of*
gozar de *or* en *enjoy;* –(se) en, con *or* present participle *enjoy*
guardarse de *take care not to*
gustar de *be fond of*

H

haber de *have to, be going to;* – que *(impersonal) be necessary to*
hacer *make, have;* – de *serve as, play the part of;* – por *try to;* estar hecho a *be accustomed to*
hartarse de *have one's fill of*
henchir de *cram with*
huir (de) *flee from, avoid*
humillarse a *humiliate oneself to*

I

impacientarse por *grow impatient to*
imposible de *(+ inf.) impossible to*
impedir *prevent from, hinder from*
impeler a *impel to*
impropio de *inappropriate to, unbecoming to;* – para *unsuitable to* or *for*
impulsar a *impel to*
incitar a *incite to*
inclinar a *induce to;* –se a *be inclined to*
incomodarse de *be annoyed at;* – por *put oneself out to*
incurrir en *incur*
indignarse de *(+ thing) be indignant at;* – con *(+ person) be indignant at*
inducir a *induce to*
influir en *influence*
inquietarse con, por *or* de *worry about*
insistir en *insist on*
inspirar a *inspire to*
instar a *or* para *urge to*
intentar *attempt to, try to*
interesarse por *or* en *(+ person) be interested in;* – en *(+ thing) be interested in*
invitar a *or* para *invite to*
ir a *go to, be going to*

J

jactarse de *boast of*
jugar a (la pelota, etc.) *play (ball, etc.)*
jurar *swear (to), vow (to)*

L

lanzar a *hurl into*
lento en *(+ inf.) slow at*
libre de *free to, at liberty to (when used with* ser) *free of* or *from, rid of (when used with* estar)
limitar(se) a *limit (oneself) to*
lograr *succeed in*
luchar por *or* para *struggle to*

Ll

llegar a *come to, go so far as to; chance to; succeed in*
llenar con *or* de *fill with*
lleno de *full of, filled with*

M

mandar *command, order;* – a *send to*
maravillarse de *marvel at*
matarse por *strive to*
merecer *deserve to*
meterse a *set to, undertake to*
mirar a *look toward* or *to;* – por *look out for*

molestarse en *or* present participle *take the trouble to*
morirse por *be dying to*
mudar(se) de *change*

N

necesario a *or* para *necessary to* or *for*
necesitar (de) *need (to)*
negar *deny;* –se a *refuse to*
nombrar para *name to*

O

obligar a *oblige to*
obstinarse en *persist in*
ocuparse en *busy oneself at*
ofenderse de *be offended at*
ofrecer(se) a *offer to, promise to*
oler a *smell of*
olvidar *forget to;* –se de *forget to*
oponerse a *oppose, be opposed to*
optar por *choose (to)*
ordenar *order to*
osar *dare to;* ser osado a *be so bold as to*

P

parar a *stop to, come to end at;* – de *stop, cease;* –se en *bother to;* – en *lodge at*
parecer *seem to, appear to;* –(se) a (+ *person) resemble*
pasar a *proceed to, pass on to;* – de *pass (beyond);* –se de *exceed the just limits of;* –se sin *do without*
penetrar en *penetrate into*
pensar *plan, intend;* – en *think of, have in mind to*
perecerse por *be perishing to*
permitir *permit to*
perseverar en *persevere in*
persistir en *persist in*
persuadir(se) a *persuade (oneself) to,* – de *persuade of*
pesar (de) *grieve to*
placerse en *take pleasure in*
poder *be able to, can, may*
ponerse a *set oneself to, begin to*
precedido de *(occasionally* por) *preceded by*
preciarse de *boast of*
preferir *prefer to*
preguntar por *inquire for* or *after*
prendarse de *fall in love with*
preocuparse con *be concerned with;* – por *or* de *worry about*
preparar(se) a *or* para *prepare (oneself) to*
prescindir de *omit, neglect (to), do without, ignore, scorn (to)*
presidir *preside over*
prestarse a *lend oneself to*
presto a *or* para *ready to*
presumir (de) *presume to*
pretender *seek to, claim to*
preterir *neglect to*
primero en, *occasionally* a (+ *inf.) first to*
principiar a *begin to*
probar a *try to*
proceder a *proceed to*
procurar *seek to, try to*
prohibir *forbid to*
prometer *promise to*
propasarse a *go so far as to, forget oneself so far as to*
propio de *appropriate to, becoming to;* – para *suitable to* or *for*
proponer(se) *propose to*
pronto a *prone to;* – para *ready to*
provocar a *provoke to*
proyectar *plan to*
pugnar por *or* para *struggle to*

Q

quedar en *agree to, decide on;* – por *remain to be;* –se a *or* para *remain to*

quejarse de *complain of*
querer *want to*

R

rabiar por *be crazy to*
rebajarse a *lower oneself to, stoop to*
recatarse de *be cautious about*
recelar(se de) *fear to, be suspicious of*
reclinarse en *or* sobre *lean on* or *upon*
recordar *remember to, recall*
recostarse en *or* sobre *lean on* or *upon*
recrear(se) en *or* present participle *amuse oneself by*
reducir(se) a *bring (oneself) to*
referirse a *refer to*
rehuir *avoid*
rehusar *refuse to (occasionally,* rehusarse a)
reír(se de) *laugh at*
renegar de *renounce, deny*
renunciar (a) *renounce, give up*
reparar en *notice*
resignarse a *resign oneself to*
resistir(se a) *resist, refuse to*
resolver(se a) *resolve to;* — + *object* + a *cause to resolve to;* estar resuelto a *or* en *be resolved to*
responder a *respond to, answer;* — de *be responsible for, vouch for*
responsable de *responsible for*
restar por *remain to be*
retrasarse en *be behindhand in, be slow to*
reventar por *be bursting to*
romper a *begin suddenly to*
rozar(se) con *come into contact with, rub against*

S

saber a *taste of, savor of, smack of*
saciar(se) de *give one's fill of, sate with*
salir a *turn out like, take after*
seguido de *(occasionally* por) *followed by*
semejar a *resemble*
sentar a *seat at;* — en *seat on;* —se a *or* para *sit down to*
sentir *regret to, be sorry to*
servir de *serve as;* — para *be good for, be used for;* —se *be so kind as to, please;* ser servido (de) *be so kind as to, be pleased to*
soler *be accustomed to*
someterse a *submit oneself to*
soñar con *(occasionally* de, en, *or no preposition) dream of*
sordo de un oído *deaf in one ear*
sorprenderse de *be* or *act surprised to* or *at*
sospechar en *or* de (+ *person, usually) suspect, be suspicious of*
sostener *maintain*
subir (a) *ascend, climb*

T

tardar en *take long to*
tardo en (+ *inf.)* slow at
temer *fear to*
tender a *tend to*
tener miedo de *or* a *be afraid of, fear*
tentar a *tempt to*
terminar por *or* present participle *end by*
tirar a *throw into, tend to*
titubear en *hesitate to*
tocar *be one's turn to, fall to one's lot to*
topar (con) *run across* or *against*
tornar a *return to; . . . again*
trabajar por *or* para *work to* or *for, strive to* or *for;* — en *work at*
traducir a *or* en *translate into*
tratar de *try to*

trepar a *climb (into);* — por *climb (along)*
triunfar de *triumph over*
tropezar con *stumble over, run across* or *against*

U

último en, *occasionally* a (+ *inf.*) *last to*
usar (de) *use, be accustomed to*

V

vacilar en *hesitate to*
valerse de *avail oneself of*
vanagloriarse de *boast of*
vedar *forbid to*
velar por *look out for, watch over*
vengarse de *avenge oneself for*
venir a *come to, amount to;* — en *agree to, resolve to;* — de *come from, have just*
ver de *see to, look to, try to*
volar a *fly to*
volver a *return to; ...again*
votar a *or* por (López) *vote for (López)*

Z

zafarse de *get rid of*

COMPOUND PREPOSITIONS

además besides
antes before *(time, order)*
cerca near
debajo under, beneath
delante before, in front *(place)*
dentro within
después after *(time, order)*
detrás after, behind *(place)*
encima on, over, on top
enfrente opposite
fuera outside, out, beyond
lejos far, distant

29.32. The above words require **de** as a connecting link when followed by an object. When used absolutely or adverbially, they stand alone:

Además de la cerveza, quiere beber el vino.	*Besides* the beer he wants to drink the wine.
Ella es bonita y **además** rica.	She is pretty and rich *besides.*
Quiere beber **antes de** comer.	He wants to drink *before* eating.
El muchacho come **antes.**	The boy eats *first.*
Vive **cerca de** la catedral.	He lives *near* the cathedral.
La catedral está **cerca.**	The cathedral is *near.*
La carta está **dentro del** escritorio.	The letter is *inside of* the desk.
El dinero está **dentro.**	The money is *inside.*
Yo hablo **después de** mi padre.	I speak *after* my father.
Mi hermano viene **después.**	My brother is coming *afterwards.*
Después de un año.	*After* a year.
Un año **después.**	A year *after.*
El perro corre **detrás del** hombre.	The dog runs *behind* the man.
La niña viene **detrás.**	The girl comes *behind.*
Vive **enfrente de** nuestra casa.	He lives *opposite to* our house.

Su casa está **enfrente.**	His house is *opposite.*
Mi padre está **fuera de** la ciudad.	My father is *out of* town.
Mi padre está **fuera.**	My father is *out, outside.*
Su casa está **lejos de** la ciudad.	His house is *far from* the city.
La catedral no está **lejos.**	The cathedral is not *far off.*
Tengo un jardín **delante de** mi casa.	I have a garden *in front of* my house.
Mi cuñado tiene una hermosa casa con un jardín **delante.**	My brother-in-law has a fine house with a garden *in front.*
El perro está **debajo de** la mesa.	The dog is *under* the table.
El libro y la carta están en la gaveta de mi escritorio; la carta está **debajo.**	The book and the letter are in the drawer of my desk; the letter is *underneath.*
Mi tío viaja **encima del** coche.	My uncle travels *on top of* the coach.
El libro está **encima.**	The book is *on top.*

REMARK. It is worthy of note that many adverbs or adverbial phrases are converted into prepositions by the addition of **de** and thence into conjunctions by the use of **que:**

Callaron ambos, y **a poco** Abelarda miró a su padre. (Pérez Galdós, **Miau,** XXX)	Both became silent and *presently (or shortly afterward)* Abelarda cast a glance at her father.
A poco de salir tú, llamaron a la puerta. (**idem,** XXX)	Shortly *after* you went out, someone knocked at the door.
A poco que se descuidara, le rebosarían de la boca confidencias. (**idem,** XXX)	*Scarcely* was she off guard, secrets would come from her mouth in a flood.

XXX

Adverbs Conjunctions Interjections

30.1. Derivative adverbs are formed from adjectives in Spanish by the addition of **mente,** which is equivalent to the English termination *ly.*

This **mente** was originally the ablative singular of Latin *mens,* meaning (in post-classic Latin) *mode* or *manner.* As it was feminine in Latin it is joined to the feminine form of adjectives, with an analogy like this:

claramente = clara mente, *in a clear manner* = clearly
traidoramente = traidora mente, *in a treacherous manner* = treacherously

30.2. Adjectives having no separate form for the feminine, add **mente** to the common form:

felizmente happily
útilmente usefully
constantemente constantly
amablemente amiably

30.3. Adverbs thus formed by the addition of **mente** are pronounced as two words, each part retaining its original stress, both written and spoken:

sólidamente solidly
poéticamente poetically
cortésmente courteously
originalmente originally

30.4. When two or more of these adverbs occur in series, only the last receives the termination **mente,** the others assuming the form they would have if **mente** were to be added. This takes place only when the several adverbs modify the same word and when there is not an appreciable pause between the adverbs. Otherwise **mente** is repeated:

Escribe clara, concisa y elegantemente.	He writes clearly, concisely and elegantly.
gradual pero imperceptiblemente	gradually but imperceptibly
Se aleja paso a paso, lentamente, majestuosamente, por la calle. (Azorín, **Un hidalgo** in **Los pueblos**)	He moves off step by step, slowly, majestically, up the street.

30.5. When the adverbs do not modify the same word, the repetition of **mente** may be avoided by replacing one of the adverbs by an appropriate noun preceded by **con:**

Lee constantemente y estudia **con diligencia.**	He reads constantly and studies *diligently.*

30.6. This substitution of **con** and a noun is often made to avoid very long adverbs in **mente;** and, for the sake of euphony, to avoid adding **mente** to adjectives ending in **ente**; also where the termination **mente** would conflict with other words of similar sound; and generally where variety of style is desired. The substitution is not always practicable, and applies only to adverbs qualifying verbs. Examples:

industriosamente	*or*	**con industria**	industriously
orgullosamente	*or*	**con orgullo**	proudly
correctamente	*or*	**con corrección**	correctly
fácilmente	*or*	**con facilidad**	easily
perfectamente	*or*	**con perfección**	perfectly
cómodamente	*or*	**con comodidad**	comfortably
prudentemente	*or*	**con prudencia**	prudently

Ella escucha con paciencia (pacientemente) a su padre	She listens patiently to her father.
Toca con frecuencia y corrección *(for* toca frecuente y correctamente).	She plays frequently and correctly.

30.7. Further variety may be obtained by employing a phrase composed of **de una manera, de un modo,** followed by the appropriate adjective:

De una manera uniforme. De un modo uniforme.	Uniformly, in a uniform manner.
De una manera completa y satisfactoria.	Completely and satisfactorily.

30.8. Derivative adverbs in **mente** may qualify adjectives, verbs or other adverbs:

Ella es **extremamente bonita.**	She is *extremely pretty.*
Canta divinamente.	She *sings divinely.*
Dibuja **admirablemente bien.**	She draws *admirably well.*

30.9. The normal place of adverbs is before adjectives and after verbs but great variation is possible. When the verb has an object, the adverb is usually placed immediately after the verb; when the adverb is short, this is the only position admissible:

El sastre es horriblemente feo.	The tailor is horribly ugly.
Habla perfectamente el francés.	He speaks French perfectly.
Estudia con diligencia sus temas.	He studies his lessons diligently.
Hablan mal el idioma.	They speak the language badly.
V. habla bien el castellano.	You speak Spanish well.

30.10. Adverbs in general express time, place, manner, degree, doubt, affirmation and negation; but these subdivisions melt insensibly into each other.

NOTE. It would be impracticable to present a complete list of all the adverbs of the language in a work of this compass; only enough, therefore, will be given to illustrate the several classes.

30.11. In point of form it will be convenient to distinguish them as:

a. Those that may be regarded as simple and original:

así thus, so
aun (§ 36) yet, still
bien well
casi almost
hoy today
luego soon
muy very
nunca never

b. Other words used adverbially without change:

alto aloud
claro clearly
mañana tomorrow
quedo softly, gently
recio vehemently
temprano early

c. Adverbs derived from pronouns:

algo rather, somewhat
nada not at all

d. Adverbs formed from adjective by adding **-mente:**

ciertamente certainly
lentamente slowly
recientemente recently
últimamente lately

REMARK. It is obvious that adverbs formed by the addition of **mente** may be almost as numerous as adjectives of quality. The class has been treated in § **30.1** ff.

e. Those formed from other words by the help of prepositions. This class may be subdivided as follows:

PREPOSITION **A** JOINED TO A FOLLOWING WORD

abajo down
acaso perhaps
adelante forwards
afuera abroad
ahora now
anoche last night
apenas scarcely, hardly
apriesa, aprisa quickly
arriba up, aloft
atrás backwards

WITH THE DEFINITE ARTICLE

a la larga in the long run
a la ligera lightly, expeditiously
al momento instantly
al pronto at first, at the beginning

a la moda in style
a la verdad in truth
a la vista in sight
al contado in cash
al fiado on credit, on time
al menos at least
al raso in the open air
en el acto instantly
en lo sucesivo henceforth
por lo pronto for the time being
por lo regular ordinarily
por lo tanto consequently

WITHOUT THE ARTICLE, SINGULAR

a porfía persistently
con ligereza superficially
con todo notwithstanding
de balde gratis
de lado incidentally
de mala gana unwillingly
de nuevo anew
de raíz radically
de relance fortuitously
de sopetón suddenly
en balde in vain
en resumen in short
en revancha in return
en seguida at once
por consiguiente consequently
por supuesto of course
por último finally

WITHOUT THE ARTICLE, PLURAL

a cargas abundantly
a ciegas blindly
a dentelladas snappishly
a escondidas secretly
a gatas on all fours
a medias by halves
a solas alone, privately
de burlas in jest
de espaldas on one's back
de oídas by hearsay
de rodillas on one's knees
en ayunas agog, uninformed
en cueros naked
por adarmes very sparingly

f. Adverbial phrases:

a largo andar in the course of time
a manos llenas liberally
a más no poder with all one's might
a más tardar at the latest
a ojos vistas openly
a sus anchas at one's ease
cuanto antes as soon as possible
de par en par wide open *(doors)*
de vez en cuando from time to time
gota a gota drop by drop
luego a luego little by little *(time)*
mal de su grado unwillingly
poco a poco little by little *(degree)*

Many of these adverbial phrases are restricted to certain verbs:

Le miró **de hito en hito.**	He looked him through and through.
Le disparó el revólver **a quemarropa.**	He fired the revolver at him point blank.
Saber una cosa **de buena tinta.**	To know a thing definitely, reliably.
Gritar **a gaznate tendido.**	To shout at the top of one's lungs.

REMARK. Many of these adverbial expressions may be further extended by the addition of other adverbs:

muy de golpe	very suddenly
demasiado a la ligera	too superficially
bastante de raíz	radically enough

30.12. In point of meaning adverbs may be classed as:

a. Adverbs of time:

ahora now
a menudo often
de noche at night
después afterwards
entonces then
jamás never
luego soon
raras veces seldom
siempre always
últimamente lately

b. Adverbs of place:

acá hither
a la izquierda on the left
alrededor around
dentro within
detrás behind
enfrente opposite
en otra parte elsewhere
en todas partes everywhere
lejos far
por aquí near here, this way, through here

c. Adverbs of manner:

The adverbs of manner are much more numerous than all the others. The greater part of them are adverbial phrases, or adverbs formed from adjectives by the addition of **-mente:**

al por mayor by wholesale
a sabiendas wittingly
así thus
a tientas tentatively, gropingly
bien well
de antemano beforehand
de improviso unexpectedly
de propósito on purpose
despacio slowly
pasito a paso gently

d. Adverbs of degree:

algo somewhat, rather
apenas scarcely
bastante enough, tolerably
casi almost
demasiado too, too much
harto enough
más bien rather
menos less
muy very
sobradamente excessively

e. Adverbs of dubitation:

acaso perhaps, forsooth
apenas hardly, scarcely
difícilmente hardly, improbably
por ventura peradventure
quizás, quizá } perhaps
tal vez } perhaps

REMARK. **Acaso** and the antiquated **por ventura** are often mere interrogative or negative signs, expressing surprise or indignation and expecting a negative answer:

¿Acaso no sé lo que he visto por mis propios ojos? — Don't I know what I have seen with my own eyes?

¿Me tomáis por ventura por esclavo, que me tratáis de ese modo? — Do you take me for a slave, that you address me in that style?

¿Dónde está mi hermano? —¿Acaso me da cuenta de la vida que hace? (Pereda, **Don Gonzalo González de la Gonzalera**, XXIII) — Where is my brother? —He doesn't give me any account of his activities.

f. Adverbs of affirmation and negation:

claro, justo of course, just so
eso no not that
eso sí that indeed
jamás, nunca never
nada not at all
ni...ni neither...nor
por cierto certainly
por supuesto of course
sin duda undoubtedly
tampoco just as little

30.13. Adverbs do not in themselves admit of inflection or require it in other words; but a few have an appearance of inflection, being either old comparatives of Latin origin or formed upon superlatives of that character:

fidelísimamente most faithfully
máxime, máximamente especially
mejor better
óptimamente in the best manner
peor worse
pésimamente very badly

REMARK. Adverbs, however, admit of comparison in the same manner as adjectives, by means of **más** and **menos** (§ **8.1** ff.).

30.14. Adverbs expressing time or the direction of a movement, may be placed after nouns, thus forming adverbial phrases of time or place:

años antes years before
camino adelante onward
ciudad abajo down town
cuesta arriba up hill
escalera abajo down stairs
laguna adentro out towards the middle of the lake
mar afuera out to sea, seaward
meses después months afterwards
río abajo down stream
siglos atrás centuries ago
tierra adentro inland

30.15. **Recientemente** *recently* is replaced in Castilian by **recién** before past participles used adjectively:

Falleció recientemente.	He died recently.
El recién llegado.	The newcomer.
Canastillos para recién nacidos.	Baskets for newborn babies.
Los recién casados.	The newly married pair.

REMARK. Especially in the countries of the southern half of South America **recién** is used in any and all positions and means not only *a little while ago* but also *only (then)*, etc.:

¿Quién es ése que salió recién de aquí? (Lynch, **Los caranchos de la Florida,** XII)	Who is that fellow who left here a little while ago?
Machado se hizo como si recién reparara en misia Cenobia y se le acercó hecho un almíbar. (Payró, **Justicia salomónica,** in **Nuevos cuentos de Pago Chico**)	Machado pretended as if only then had he noticed Mrs. Cenobia and he went up to her as sweet as honey.
Recién cuando quise desensillar, me di cuenta de que...tenía desgarradas las manos. (Güiraldes, **Don Segundo Sombra,** IX)	Only when I tried to unsaddle did I realize that...my hands were torn.
Entonces recién se acordó La Negra de la famosa carta... La trajo Bartolo recientito. (Lynch, **El inglés de los güesos,** XVII)	Only then did la Negra remember the famous letter... Bartolo brought it a short time ago.

30.16. Adjectives derived from names of countries, districts and cities, may be used adverbially when preceded by **a la.** Or they may be regarded as still being adjectives, agreeing with some such noun as **moda** or **usanza** *style, fashion:*

a la inglesa, francesa	in the English, French fashion
a la malagueña, gaditana	in the Malaga, Cadiz style

REMARK. The same idea may be expressed more fully and literally:

al estilo mejicano	in the Mexican style
al estilo de Italia	in the Italian style
a la usanza de mi país	according to the usage of my country

30.17. Other adjectives may be used in the feminine form, preceded by **a la,** as above, when they express *manner;*[1] but add **-mente** when denoting *time:*

a la moderna; a la antigua	new-fashioned; old-fashioned
modernamente; antiguamente	in modern times; in ancient times

30.18. The affirmative adverb **sí** is much used as an expletive to emphasize an assertion. It is sometimes connected by **que** with what follows, and is generally equivalent to the English emphatic auxiliary *do,* or to the expletive *indeed:*

No creo que V. le haya visto. —**Sí que** le vi.	I don't believe you saw him. —I *did* see him.
¿Comprende V. ya? —**Sí que** comprendo.	Do you understand now? —*Indeed* I do.
Acaso preferiría V. ir en persona.— Eso **sí que** no.	Perhaps you would prefer to go in person. —Not that *by any means.*
Le rogaron que partiese en seguida, y él repuso que **sí** partiría.	They begged him to set out at once, and he answered that he *certainly* would.
Cuando mi obra se publique, que **sí** se publicará, le mandaré a V. un ejemplar.	When my work is published, for it *will* be published, I will send you a copy.

30.19. **Sí** and **no** are much used for emphasis in contrasted clauses; the nicety of the meaning is such that it is nearly impossible to render it into English:

No disimuló lo que le contrariaba el no encontrar en casa a Juanita, y **sí** a mí.	He did not conceal how it disappointed him to find *me* at home and not Juanita.
Arrancándome por fuerza la careta se encontraron más miradas todavía viendo que no me conocían, y yo **sí** a ellas.	Tearing off my domino by force they were more astonished than ever to see that they did not know me and that I *did* know them.
Observé entonces que el coronel estaba, no más triste, pero **sí** más pensativo que de costumbre.	I then noticed that the Colonel was not exactly sadder, but *certainly* more thoughtful than usual.
Lo expresaba en frases corteses, **sí,** pero firmes y severas.	He expressed it in terms, courteous *indeed,* but firm and severe.
Lo que a mí **no,** se le ocurrió a ella.	There occurred to her what did not occur to *me.*

[1] Nowadays **a lo** with the masculine form of the adjective is often used instead: **a lo moderno** *in modern style,* **a lo antiguo** *in ancient style.* With nouns only **lo** is used: **a lo señor** *in lordly style.*

30.20. The neuter **lo** enters into the construction of many phrases of an adverbial character. Among these may be mentioned the following:

(a) **lo más** at the utmost

(a) **lo menos, por lo menos**[1] at the least

todo lo más at the very most

todo lo menos at the very least

lo de arriba abajo upside down

lo de delante atrás wrong end foremost

EXAMPLES

Había estado dos horas **lo menos** arrimada a la reja hablando conmigo.	She had been two hours, *at least*, at the window talking to me.
La canoa siguió la costa a la distancia de dos cables **todo lo más.**	The boat skirted the shore at a distance of two cable-lengths, *at the utmost.*
Llevo **lo menos** cinco años de experiencia en asuntos de esta clase.	I have had *at least* five years' experience in matters of this kind.
Este verbo sólo está en uso en los pretéritos, y **a lo más** en el futuro de indicativo.	This verb is used only in the past tenses, or, *at the farthest,* in the future indicative.
A lo más no lograrán coger sino dos o tres.	*At most* they will only succeed in catching two or three.

30.21. The use of an adjective as an adverb is frequent in Spanish, particularly in the spoken language (and at all times in poetry):

Vivían felices, infelices.	They lived happily, unhappily.
Lo ataron firme a un poste.	They tied him firmly to a post.
La cordillera corre paralela con la costa.	The mountain chain runs parallel to the coast.
Diáfano y brillante está el cielo, por donde la luna vaga silenciosa.	The sky is clear and bright, across which the moon moves silently.
Uno que otro pájaro atraviesa el firmamento, volando perezoso.	Occasionally a bird crosses the sky, flying lazily.
¿No se ve bien claro? (Pereda, **Sotileza,** XXIV)	Isn't it clearly visible?
Estoy hablando muy formal. (Alarcón, **El sombrero de tres picos,** XXIII)	I am speaking very seriously.

[1] There exists also the form **al menos.** Perhaps **lo menos** is the most used in conversational language.

Don Panchito siente correr el sudor bajo sus ropas, y espanta furioso los jejenes que le atacan implacables. (Lynch, **Los caranchos de la Florida, V**)

Don Panchito feels the perspiration running under his clothes and furiously frightens away the gnats that attack him implacably.

El, que siempre se desayuna fuerte, a la inglesa; pues hoy... (Benavente, **La propia estimación, II, 1**)

He, who always breakfasts heartily, in the English fashion; well, today...

REMARK. The use of **bastante, tal** (cf. § **9.80**), **mejor, peor,** etc., as adverbs where adjectives might be expected is by no means infrequent:

No eran bastante las migajas de aquella mesa para saciar unos apetitos como los suyos. (Pereda, **La puchera, V**)

The crumbs from that table were not enough to satisfy any appetites like hers.

Si me dicen que las manzanas y las cerezas que Adán tenía a su disposición eran mejor que las que yo comía, me autorizo el dudarlo. (Palacio Valdés, **La novela de un novelista, II**)

If they tell me that the apples and cherries that Adam had at his disposal were better than those which I ate, I permit myself to doubt it.

30.22. The phrase compounded of **de** + **puro** + adjective or adverb corresponds to *from* (or *out of) sheer* + the quality expressed by the adjective or adverb:

Hay dos clases de hombres jocosos de puro serios. (Valera, **El comendador Mendoza, II**)

There are two classes of men who are jocose out of sheer seriousness.

No me hables de las hijas del notario. Si me miraban con descaro y con susto, fué de puro tontas. (Valera, **Juanita la larga, XVII**)

Don't talk to me about the notary's daughters. If they were looking at me with lack of respect and shocked, it was from sheer stupidity.

Preguntaba, no sólo cuanto deseaba saber, sino lo que, de puro sabido, tenía ya olvidado. (Pereda, **Sotileza, XXVIII**)

He asked, not only all that he wanted to know but what he had already forgotten from sheer knowledge of it.

30.23. The adverbs of place **aquí, ahí, allí,** are properly applicable only to a definite place; *vagueness* of place or at times *motion to* a place is expressed by the forms **acá, ahí, allá,** there being no other form of **ahí**. The distinction, however, is not strictly maintained, even by careful writers, but **venir acá** and **ir allá** are usual:

aquí	**acá**	here
ahí	**ahí**	there *(near you)*
allí	**allá**	there *(yonder, at a distance)*

El capitán está aquí.	The captain is here.
El capitán viene aquí *(or* acá).	The captain is coming here (hither).
Está ahí.	He is there } (where you are.)
Va ahí.	He is going there } (where you are.)
Reside allí.	He lives there } (distant from both.)
Va allá.	He is going there } (distant from both.)
Espero ver a mi padre **allí.**	I expect to see my father there.
¿Qué tiene V. ahí?	What have you got there?
¿Tiene V. amigos aquí?	Have you friends here?
No quiero acordarme de nadie. Ni los periódicos de allá quisiera leer. (Benavente, **La comida de las fieras,** last scene)	I don't want to remember anybody. I should like not even to read the newspapers from there.

Remark I. The distinction above shown between **ahí** and **allí** (or **allá**) is rigidly maintained. For instance, a merchant in Chicago writing to a correspondent in Lima would speak of his own city as **aquí,** of Lima as **ahí,** and of any other place not closely connected with these as **allí.** Custom does not, however, sanction the use of the form **allí** when followed by **en** and the name of a place; therefore we must say: **allá en Cuba, allá en Europa.**

Remark II. A common idiomatic meaning of **allá** is *that is his (her, your, their,* etc.) *affair* or *business* or *problem,* etc.: **Si su hermana lo prefiere, yo también me entenderé con don Jorge... —Allá ustedes.** (Linares Rivas, **El abolengo,** I, 6) *If your sister prefers, I too shall speak with George...—That is for you to decide.*

30.24. These adverbs are by extension sometimes employed as adverbs of time, as *here* is in English. They are then to be rendered as follows:

aquí	here, at this moment, at this point in the story
allí	then, at that moment relatively near
allá	then, at a remote period

30.25. Preceded by **de,** they express a deduction, with the following meanings:

de aquí	hence, from what I have said
de ahí	thence, from what you have said
de allí	thence, from what somebody else said

30.26. The adverb **ya,** when used positively, means *already, now* (being distinguished in its temporal use from **ahora** in that it implies a much shorter interval); with a negative it is equivalent to *no longer, not any more, no more.* It often comes to mean *of course; to be sure; yes, yes;* etc., indicating (sometimes ironically) assent to the obvious.

Ya es tarde.	It is already late *or* It is late now.
Ya voy.	I'm coming *or* I'll be right there.
¿Ya ha vendido V. su caballo?	Have you sold your horse already?
Ya está claro que ella ya no quiere venir.	Now it is clear that she no longer wants to come.
Ya comprendo; *or merely* Ya.	Now I understand *or* Of course.
Ya no toco el piano.	I do not play the piano any more.
¿Ya habla el castellano su hijo de V.?	Does your son already speak Spanish?
¿Ya no desea V. ir a casa de su hermano?	Don't you want to go to your brother's any more?
¿No desea V. ya ir a casa de su hermano?	Don't you want to go to your brother's now?
He querido decir que cuáles son las salidas principales. —Ya, ya; ya te había calado el pensamiento. (Pereda, **Peñas arriba,** V)	I meant to ask which are the principal means of egress. —Of course, of course; I had already guessed your thoughts.
Mi mujer tiene un geniecito que ya ya. (Ramós Carrión, **La careta verde,** I, 2)	My wife has a temper that words won't express.

Remark. The combinations **ya no** and **no...ya** usually mean *no longer,* **no ya** on the other hand usually means *not merely, not only:*

Mi padre replicaba que en los buenos tiempos antiguos, no ya los clérigos, sino hasta los obispos, andaban a caballo acuchillando infieles. (Valera, **Pepita Jiménez, 4 de Mayo)**	My father replied that in the good ancient times not merely clerics but even bishops went about on horseback slashing at infidels.
No ya el domingo que viene: jamás, jamás volverá. (Pérez de Ayala, **Luz de domingo,** IV)	Not only next Sunday: never, never will it come back.

30.27. **Aun** and **todavía** both mean *still* or *yet* when used positively; with **no** they mean *not yet.* When **aun** follows (and sometimes when it precedes) the verb it is pronounced as two syllables and is so written (cf. § 36). Secondarily, **aun** (but not normally **aún**) has the meaning of *even,* in which case it precedes the word it modifies:

¿Aun *(or* Todavía) tiene V. su yegua baya?	Do you still have your bay mare?
¿Tiene V. aún *(or* todavía) su yegua baya?	Have you still got your bay mare?
¿No ha llegado el coronel todavía?	Has not the colonel come yet?
Todavía no *or* Aun no.	Not yet.
Su libro es excelente, aun con las faltas de que está lleno.	His book is excellent, even with the faults of which it is full.
Lo creía todo, y aun llegó a creer más de lo conveniente. (Alas, **Protesto,** in **El Señor; y lo demás son cuentos)**	He believed it all, and even came to believe more than was desirable.

30.28. **Como** is an adverb or conjunction relating to manner. Used in direct or indirect interrogations **(cómo)** it is an adverb meaning *how;* used relatively **(como)** it is a conjunction with the meaning of *as, like;* used adverbially it also has the meaning of *as if:*

¿Cómo está V.?	How are you? How do you do?
Ignoro cómo explicar el fenómeno.	I do not know how to explain the phenomenon.
V. no es como su hermano.	You are not like your brother.
Habla como una persona de autoridad.	He speaks like a person of authority.
Consideramos su adopción como necesaria al triunfo de nuestro partido.	We consider its adoption as necessary to the success of our party.
La señora, dicen que estaba en la cama como dormida. (Benavente, **La honradez de la cerradura, I,** 2)	They say the lady lay in bed as if asleep.
...Los brazos atrás y el cuerpo hacia adelante como para lanzarse sobre su adversario. (Alarcón, **El sombrero de tres** picos, XXI)	...Arms back and body forward, as if to hurl herself upon her opponent.
Se oprimían unos contra otros como huyendo de la sombra que les alcanzaba. (Prieto, **El socio,** XXXI)	They crowded against one another as if fleeing from the shadow that extended to them.

REMARK I. Especially in Spanish America, **cómo no,** often pronounced without interrogative or exclamatory intonation, is used with the value of **sí** *yes:*

Si quiere, iremos juntos... —¡Cómo no, señor, cómo no! (Lynch, **Los caranchos de la Florida,** XI, near end)	If you want, we will go together... —Of course, sir, of course!

REMARK II. The conjunction **como que** has a variety of meanings of which perhaps the most frequent one is the meaning of *inasmuch as, since.* It is also found in the sense of *as if* mostly with forms of **hacer** and **parecer:**

Lo que allí pasa no puede ser más inocente... —¡Toma! ¡Como que va el mismísimo señor Obispo. (Alarcón, **El sombrero de tres picos,** XIII)	What goes on there can't be more innocent... —Why certainly! Inasmuch as the very Bishop goes!
Parecía como que el pequeñín al irse había dejado clavada una espina en la conciencia de los vecinos. (Blasco Ibáñez, **La barraca,** VIII)	It seemed as if the little one on departing had left a thorn fastened in the conscience of the neighbors.

ADVERBIAL PHRASES

en vez de; en lugar de	instead of
tal vez	perhaps
a veces	at times, sometimes
raras veces	rarely, seldom
casi siempre	almost always
casi nunca	hardly ever *(lit.* almost never)
de ningún modo	by no means, not at all
como de costumbre	as usual
¿de veras?	indeed? really?
de veras	indeed, really *(emphatic)*
en efecto	in fact, indeed
sin embargo	nevertheless
sin duda	no doubt, doubtless
hoy día	nowadays

30.29. **No más** *only* is not now used with any frequency in Spain but in Spanish America it is extremely common, not only with the meaning of *only* but with meanings comparable to those of English adverbial *just* or *right:*

Ayercito no más, el patrón me mandó con una carta. (Lynch, **Los caranchos de la Florida,** III)	Only yesterday the boss sent me with a letter.
¿Quién ha escrito esta noticia?... ¡Usted no más será, gallego! (Payró, **Cuentos de Pago Chico,** XI)	Who wrote this piece of news?... It can have been only you, you Galician!
¿Cómo te jué?... —¿Y?... ¡Lindo no más, mi madre!... ¿Cómo quiere que me juera?... —No; decía no más...con este día tan fiero... (Lynch, **El inglés de los güesos,** XXII)	How did things go?—Why do you say that? Just fine, mother! How did you expect things to go?—No, I was just saying...with this disagreeable day...
Dios no más debe ocupar nuestra alma. (Valera, **Pepita Jiménez, 20 de abril)**	Only God must occupy our soul.
Quedábanle dos recursos no más para combatir el tedio. (Pardo Bazán, **Los pazos de Ulloa,** XIII)	There were left to him only two recourses to combat boredom.

CONJUNCTIONS

30.30. A conjunction is a word that conjoins or connects. In general it connects two propositions, each complete in itself. The usual division into copulative, disjunctive, causal, etc., is without practical value. Pure and original conjunctions are few, while conjunctive phrases composed of prepositions or adverbs followed by **que** are very numerous. In a few instances the **que** has dropped out of use, as *that* often has in English.

30.31. The original conjunctions are:

o *(before* **o** *or* **ho, u**)	or	**ni**	nor, neither
y *(before* **i** *or* **hi, e**)	and	**que**	that
pero, mas, sino	but	**si**	if, whether

30.32. As a result of the concurrence of two like sounds, **y** becomes **e** when the following word begins with **i** or **hi,** and similarly **o** becomes **u** before **o** or **ho:**

español **e** inglés	Spanish *and* English	plata **u** oro	silver *or* gold
padre **e** hijo	father *and* son	vida **u** honor	life *or* honor

30.33. Y, however, does not change before words beginning with **hie** or with **y:**

madera y hierro wood *and* iron él y yo he *and* I

30.34. There are three words in Spanish to represent the conjunction *but,* namely **pero, mas** and **sino.** The two former are interchangeable both meaning *but nevertheless,* except that **mas** belongs rather to the literary style. **Sino** is of limited application, being only used to introduce a positive in direct contrast to a preceding negative, and is equivalent to the English *but on the contrary.* The same verb that preceded is understood but not repeated after it. If clauses containing different verb forms are contrasted, then **sino que** is used instead of **sino,** except at times in short clauses:

Tengo una pistola, pero no tengo un revólver.	I have a pistol, but I have not a revolver.
No tengo un revólver, sino una pistola.	I have not a revolver, but a pistol.
El burro no quiere vino, sino agua.	The donkey does not want wine, but water.
No se mezclaba en los juegos infantiles, sino que andaba solo, imaginando empresas nunca vistas. (Pérez de Ayala, **Prometeo,** II)	He didn't mix into the children's games but went about alone, imagining enterprises never before seen.
El lobo ya no siguió por el camino sino que se le plantó delante en actitud agresiva. (Palacio Valdés, **Sinfonía pastoral, Allegro ma non troppo,** II)	The wolf no longer followed along the road but took up a position in front of him with an aggressive attitude.
[Otra lid] fué con un sarraceno de Medinaceli, a quien no sólo venció sino mató. (Menéndez Pidal, **La España del Cid,** II, 4, 1)	[Another battle] was with a Saracen from Medinaceli, whom he not only defeated but killed.

REMARK. Occasionally, and perhaps in imitation of classical usage, **sino que** serves as the equivalent of **pero:**

Le ocurrió enamorarse de Maigualida Ladera. En realidad lo había estado desde niño, sino que bajo la forma de un aborrecimiento rencoroso por una broma inocente. (Gallegos, **Canaima,** IV: **Los Ardavines)**	It chanced to him to fall in love with Maigualida Ladera. In reality he had been since he was a child, but under the form of a grudge on account of an innocent joke.

30.35. Of the conjunctive phrases it is often more difficult than important to decide whether to call them conjunctions or relative adverbs. The following are the most usual:

a condición que on condition that
a fin de que in order that
a medida que according as
a menos que, **a no ser que** } unless
ahora que now that
antes (de) que before
así que so that, so, as soon as
aunque, **bien que** } although
como quiera que however
conque so, therefore, so then
con motivo que so that
con tal (de) que provided that
cuanto más que the more since
dado que in case that
de manera que, **de modo que**, **de suerte que** } so that
desde que since
después que after
en caso (de) que in case that
en cuanto as soon as
en tanto que while, in case that
en vez de que instead of
entre tanto que while
excepto que excepting
hasta que until
luego que as soon as
mientras (que) while
no obstante que notwithstanding
para que in order that
por...que however (§ 23.17)
porque because, in order that
pues que, **puesto que** } since
sea que whether, while
según according, as
siempre que whenever
sin que without
supuesto que granting that, since
tanto que so that
toda vez que since
ya que since

30.36. Some conjunctions consist of pairs of words, separated by other and intervening words. These pairs are called correlatives:

apenas–cuando	scarcely–when
así–como	both–and
así como–así también	just as–so too
aunque– { sin embargo (de eso), no obstante (eso), con todo (eso) }	although–nevertheless
ni–ni	neither–nor
no bien–cuando	scarcely–when
no sólo–sino, no solamente–sino, no tan sólo–sino que	not only–but
o–o	either–or
ora–ora	now–now
sea (fuera, fuese)–sea (fuera, fuese)	whether–or
ya–ya	whether–or, sometimes–sometimes

USE OF QUE

30.37. When a verb, participle, adjective or noun, which necessarily takes a preposition to connect it with what follows, governs a finite verb, the conjunction **que** is required between this verb and the preposition (§ 23.31):

Se opuso Da. Juana **a que** su marido se aventurase en semejante empresa.	Doña Juana opposed her husband's embarking in such an undertaking.
Consintió **en que** hiciesen la prueba.	He consented to their making the test.
Le persuadieron **a que** se conformase con el proyecto.	They persuaded him to agree to the project.
Quedó furioso **de que** se hubiesen burlado de su vigilancia.	He was enraged *that* they had eluded his vigilance.
El viento no está propicio **para que** nos hagamos a la mar.	The wind is not favorable to our putting to sea.
Estaba determinado **a que** se le restituyesen sus bienes.	He was determined *that* his property should be returned to him.
Aun tengo una ligera idea **de que** se menciona en eso el nombre de Vd.	I even have half an idea *that* your name is mentioned in it.

30.38. Indirect questions introduced by the verb **decir** are preceded by the conjunction **que**; after **preguntar, que** is sometimes encountered. These are the only cases in which **que** is so used:

Le dije **que** cuál era su opinión.	I asked him what was his opinion.
Me dijo **que** para cuándo necesitaba mi ama el traje.	She asked me by what time my mistress wanted the gown.
Me dijeron **que** por dónde había sabido la noticia.	They asked me whence I had learned the news.
Ella me preguntó **que** si aguardaba a alguien.	She asked me if I was waiting for anyone.
El pobre Villa había preguntado **que** cuáles eran esos obstáculos.	Poor Villa had asked what those obstacles were.
Preguntábase por todas partes **que** de dónde vendría aquel correo.	It was asked on every side where that courier could have come from.
Nos preguntaron **que** qué queríamos.	They asked us what we wanted.

30.39. **Que** is interposed before **sí** and **no,** after verbs of perceiving or declaring, and those expressing an emotion. The construction cannot be literally translated:

Dijo que sí.	He said he would, he had, etc.
Dijo que no.	He said he wouldn't, hadn't, etc.
Creo que sí.	I think so, I think he will, etc.
Creo que no.	I think not, I think he won't, etc
Me parece que sí,—que no.	I think so,—I think not.
Esperamos que sí,—que no.	We hope so,—we hope not.
Es de esperarse que no.	It is to be hoped not.

30.40. **Que** is apparently redundant after a number of asseverative adverbial expressions, and may be conveniently explained by assuming that some such expression as **parece, sigue, puede decirse,** is understood before **que:**

Ahora sí **que** tiene Vd. razon.	Now you are indeed right.
Entonces sí **que** nos veríamos en un buen enredo.	Then we surely would find ourselves in a nice fix.
Por cierto **que no** son muy raros.	They are certainly not very rare.
Ciertamente **que** se ha mostrado muy amable para con nosotros.	He has certainly shown himself very kind toward us.
Sin duda **que** lo sabremos mañana.	No doubt we shall know tomorrow.
¡Pardiez **que** es muy atrevido tu proyecto!	By Jove, your plan is a bold one!
¡A fe **que** eso sería arriesgar mucho!	Faith, that would be risking a good deal!

REMARK. The last two are equivalent to **juro, afirmo que.**

30.41. **Que** is often used elliptically at the beginning of a sentence or clause. In these cases **que** may have a considerable variety of meaning. It may be merely emphatic or intensive; it may assign a reason, or express surprise, indignation, etc.:

Que llaman a la puerta.	Someone is knocking at the door.
¡Que vienen! ¡Que me matan!	They are coming! Murder!
Que no tengo ánimo para más.	Well, I have no heart for anything more.
Iré de paseo; que no estaré todo el día metido en casa.	I'm going for a walk; I declare I won't stay in the house all day.
Estoy rendido, que he marchado cuatro leguas.	I'm done out; for I have walked ten miles.
Nos contentaremos con papas, que más valen papas que nada.	We will content ourselves with potatoes, for potatoes are better than nothing.

¿Que Vd. es el célebre artista Estébanez? — So you are the celebrated artist Estebanez?

¿Que te faltan las alforjas, Sancho? — So you have lost the saddlebags, Sancho?

30.42. **Que** is used idiomatically with the value of **a quien,** provided the redundant object pronoun be added, the construction being perhaps more colloquial than elegant:

Hay que tomarlo con calma, señá Isabel... —decía una vieja que no le pesaba nada del disgusto que la maestra padecía. (Palacio Valdés, **José,** XIV) — "One must bear up, Seña Isabel," said an old woman who wasn't at all grieved at the annoyance that the schoolteacher's wife was undergoing.

Esta señora era una de esas mujeres decididas y mandonas que les gusta disponerlo todo. (Baroja, **El árbol de la ciencia,** III, 3) — This lady was one of those positive and bossy women who like to arrange everything.

Esta mujer que se le pregunta quién la ha tirado, y dice el nombre de su marido; esta badila llena de sangre; las manchas que llegan hasta la ventana, todo hace sospechar lo que ya han comenzado a decir los vecinos. (**idem,** V, 9) — This woman who is asked who shot her, and says the name of her husband; this fire shovel covered with blood; the stains that reach the window, all make one suspect what the neighbors have already begun to say.

Vamos, no sé si me equivoco; pero el marqués es de los que no les gusta dar que hablar. (Benavente, **Al fin, mujer,** I, 1, 2) — Well, I don't know whether I am mistaken, but the marquis is one of those people who don't like to cause talk.

30.43. Another idiomatic use of **que** is with the meaning of *such that,* as though there were an ellipse of some phrase containing **tal:**

Con las continuadas y largas lecciones estoy que da lástima de agujetas. (Valera, **Pepita Jiménez,** 4 **de mayo**) — With the long and continued [riding] lessons I am in such shape that my twinges of pain are pitiful.

Como la niña le ha dado mil veces calabazas, está que trina. (**idem, Paralipómenos**) — As the girl has given him the mitten a thousand times, he is in such a state that he is raving.

No la vuelvo a dar propina: la guita se me va que vuela. (Pardo Bazán, **La quimera,** II) — I don't give her a tip any more: My money is running out so fast *(or* **in** such a way) that it is flying.

Les di una conferencia sobre las enseñas de cada oficio, que había que oírme. (Baroja, **La feria de los discretos,** X) — I gave them a lecture on the emblems of each trade of such a kind that you should have heard me.

USES OF SI

30.44. **Si** *if,* in addition to expressing a single doubt, may, before an infinitive, express an uncertainty between alternatives, being thus equivalent to *whether:*

No sabe si retirarse o no. — He does not know whether to withdraw or not.

No sé si aceptar su oferta o no. — I do not know whether to accept his offer or not.

Disputaban sobre si convenía volver o no. — They were disputing about whether it was proper to return or not.

30.45. **Si** is often employed at the beginning of a phrase or sentence with the value of *why,* expressive of surprise or expostulation:

Si debe ser loco. — Why, he must be crazy.

Si acaba de salir. — Why, he has just gone out.

Si lo escribí yo mismo. — Why, I wrote it myself.

Si no era no más que ayer que él mismo me lo dijo. — Why, it was only yesterday that he told me so himself.

REMARK. Not infrequently **si** is used after **apenas** without apparent effect on the meaning:

Diez millones de hombres pueden vivir artificialmente en sitios, donde, naturalmente, apenas si podría vivir una docena de focas. (Camba, **Aventuras de una peseta,** III, 22) — Ten million men can live artificially in places where scarcely a dozen seals could live naturally.

Pero las dos damas desconocidas no levantaban los ojos del plato y apenas si llevaron bocado a la boca. (Pérez de Ayala, **La caída de los Limones,** XI) — But the two strange ladies didn't lift their eyes from their plate and scarcely ate a bite.

INTERJECTIONS

30.46. True interjections are words, otherwise without meaning, used as exclamations denoting any strong emotion. They are:

¡Oh! ¡ah! — Oh! ah!

¡Ay! — Oh! alas! ah!

¡Ha! *(exultation)*	Ha! eh!
¡He! *(shock, start)*	Eh!
¡Ea! *(encouragement)*	Come!
¡Ea, ea! *(impatience)*	Come, come!
¡Eh! *(to attract attention,* etc.)	Eh!
¡Huy! *(pain, shock)*	Ouch! Phew!
¡Ola! *or* ¡hola! *(recognition or discovery)*	Ah! oh! hello!
¡Ole! *(approval)*	Bully! Bravo!
¡Puf! *(aversion)*	Ugh!
¡Uf! *(weariness)*	Oh!
¡Ca! *and* ¡quia! *(indignant denial or doubt)*	
¡Bah! *(incredulity or contempt)*	Pshaw!
¡Ce! *(to attract attention)*	Say! hey! listen!

REMARK. Of these ay is the most common. It is peculiarly Spanish, as distinguished from the rest of Europe, and indicates joy or delight, as well as surprise or pain.

30.47. Spanish abounds in exclamatory words, which are used as evasions of more profane terms:

<table>
<tr><td>¡Caramba!
¡Caray!
¡Caracoles!
¡Canastos!
¡Canario!</td><td>And others beginning with ca-, expressing surprise.</td><td rowspan="2">These correspond to such English exclamations as gracious! the dickens! great Scot! by jingo! etc.</td></tr>
<tr><td>¡Cáspita!
¡Córcholis!
¡Fuego!
¡Zapatazos!</td><td>And many other idle terms.</td></tr>
<tr><td colspan="2">¡Diantre! (to avoid diablo, demonio)</td><td>The deuce!</td></tr>
</table>

30.48. The names **Dios, Jesús, María,** etc., in exclamations, are not held to be profane or improper in Spanish. The priesthood has called them "the instinctive elevation of the soul to its maker." Be that as it may, they are employed profusely and upon the slightest provocation, and are to be rendered in English by some euphemism like *dear me!* (which is really *Dio mio):*

¡Dios! Gracious!
¡Por Dios! For goodness' sake!
¡Dios mío! Dear me!
¡Ay Dios mío! Oh dear me!
¡Cielos! Heavens!
¡Jesús! Oh heavens!
¡Válgame Dios! Bless me!
¡Virgen santa! Oh mercy!

REMARK. The exclamations **¡Jesús! ¡Ave María! or ¡Ave María purísima!** are often uttered on seeing or hearing anything heretical, startling or incredible. **¡Jesús!** alone, or **¡Jesús, María, José!** uttered when another sneezes or yawns, is a relic of an old form of exorcism for preventing evil spirits from entering at the opened mouth of the individual.

30.49. Some interjections are restricted, in their application to certain animals:

¡Arre! ¡Alza! ¡Anda! ¡Vamos!	(To draft animals)	Get up! come up!
¡So! ¡jo! ¡cho!	(To draft animals.)	Whoa!
¡Miz miz! ¡Zape!	(To cats)	Puss, puss! Kitty, kitty! Scat!
¡Tus tus! ¡Toma!	(To dogs)	Here, sir! here, here!

REMARK. Some of the above have the effect of imperatives.

30.50. Imperatives of verbs are sometimes regarded as interjections:

¡Anda! *(incredulity)*	Pshaw! go on!
¡Anda! *(importunity)*	Come! do!
¡Calla! ¡calle! *(command)*	Shut up! keep still!
¡Calla! ¡calle! *(incredulity)*	Nonsense!
¡Diga!	Say! do tell!
¡Oye! ¡oiga!	Hullo! hear, hear!
¡Miren!	Look!
¡Quita! ¡Quítese V.!	Let me alone! go away! get out!
¡Toma!	Indeed! really!
¡Vamos! *(conciliation)*	Come! well!
¡Vaya! *(mild vexation)*	Indeed! well! really! of course!

30.51. Some nouns and adjectives are used as interjections:

¡Al asesino!	Murder!
¡Al ladrón!	Stop thief!
¡Bravo! *(to a woman,* ¡brava!)	Bravo! good! bully!
¡Caballero!	Sir! *(in indignation)*
¡Cuidado!	Look out! take care!
¡Fuego!	Fire!

¡Socorro!	Help!
¡Alerta!	Watch out! be ready!
¡Firme!	Steady, there!
¡Alto!	Halt!
¡Ojo!	Watch out!

30.52. When adjectives are used as interjections before personal pronouns **de** is interposed (cf. **2.26, 29.20** p.):

¡Triste de mí!	Woe is me!
¡Pobre de mí!	Poor me!
¡Desgraciado de ti!	Unfortunate that you are!
¡Necios de nosotros!	Fools that we are *(or* were)!

30.53. The same holds good of the interjection **¡ay!** before nouns or pronouns:

¡Ay de mí!—de ti!	Alas for me!—for you!
¡Ay de mi Alhama! *(Not* "Ay de mí, Alhama!" *as Byron has it.)*	Alas for my Alhama!
¡Ay de los vencidos!	Woe to the vanquished!
¡Ay de sus proyectos!	Alas for his plans!

30.54. In conversation the words **hombre** *man* and **mujer** *woman,* are often introduced by way of emphasis or remonstrance:

Pero hombre, si eso es demasiado.	Why, man alive, that is too much.
¿Empiezo yo? —Sí, hombre, ande **V.**	Shall I begin? —Yes indeed, go ahead.
Pues mujer, he hecho lo posible.	Well, I assure you I did what I could.

30.55. Usted is often added to short sentences to show that they appeal to a particular person, or it may stand for a question by itself:

¿Verdad, usted?	It is true, don't you think so?
¿Cómo lo pasa V.? —Bien; ¿y usted?	How goes it with you? —First rate; and how are you getting on?

XXXI
Laws of Agreement

31.1. The fundamental principles of agreement (with which the student is already familiar) are that a verb agrees with its subject in person and number; that an adjective, or a past participle not connected with **haber,** agrees with its noun in gender and number; and that a pronoun, so far as its inflection will permit, agrees with the noun it represents in gender and number.

So long as the verb has but a single subject, and the adjective or pronoun relates to but a single noun about whose gender and number there is no uncertainty, the matter presents no difficulty. The complication arises where the noun is a collective noun, where the apparent gender is not the true gender, or where several nouns or subjects are involved. These cases will be taken up in detail.

COLLECTIVE NOUNS

31.2. A collective noun is one that is singular in form but represents a plurality in fact. The dependent verbs and adjectives of such nouns are sometimes singular and at other times plural. The primary ground of distinction is that if the aggregate acts as a unity it is singular; if the component parts act separately, they are regarded as a plurality:

La multitud **escuchó** al gobernador. — The throng listened to the governor.

La multitud **había** hecho alto delante del palacio, pero como no apareció el presidente, se **dispersaron** gradualmente. — The throng had stopped before the palace, but as the president did not appear, *they dispersed* gradually.

31.3. Still, Spanish ideas of congruity do not ordinarily permit a collective noun, though denoting a plurality, to be accompanied by a plural verb or adjective in the same clause:

La gente **huyó** *(not* huyeron) a la primera descarga de la tropa.
The people fled at the first volley from the troops.

Entró en la plaza el motín, pero a la primera descarga de la tropa, **huyeron** despavoridos.
The mob entered the square, but at the first volley from the troops, *they fled* in terror.

El ganado **fué** permitido vagar por los bosques en busca de pasto.
The cattle were permitted to roam in the woods in search of pasture.

El público **quiere** informarse de la verdad de estos rumores.
The public wish to be informed of the truth of these rumors.

La muchedumbre se **agolpó** a su rededor.
The throng crowded around him.

La soldadesca desenfrenada se **apoderó** de la correspondencia de la corte.
The ungoverned soldiery seized the correspondence of the court.

El motín **llenaba** las calles de Estocolmo, e **iban** todos los días a las puertas del palacio para gastar su aliento lanzando gritos inútiles.
The mob filled the streets of Stockholm, and came daily to the doors of the palace to waste their breath in vain shouting.

Llegó la noticia de que el destacamento bajo el mando del coronel Pérez **había** sido arrojado de su posición en las cercanías de Ojos Negros, y que **desprovistos** de bagaje y provisiones, se **veían** en el peligro de morir de frío y hambre.
News was received that the detachment under command of Col. Pérez had been driven from their position near Ojos Negros, and that, deprived of camp equipage and provisions, *they were* in danger of perishing from cold and hunger.

REMARK. If the collective expresses a homogeneous aggregate (such as **ejército, rebaño, armada, comisión,** *etc.)* the verb is preferably singular, even though placed at a distance from the subject.

31.4. When a singular collective noun is connected with a plural noun by **de,** an accompanying verb or adjective very frequently agrees with the noun with which it is most closely connected in meaning:

Un centenar de mujeres **fueron sepultadas** debajo de los escombros.
A hundred women were buried under the ruins.

La docena de huevos que V. compró en el mercado no **estaba completa.**
The dozen eggs you bought at the market *was* not a full one.

La docena de huevos que V. compró en el mercado **estaban hueros.**
The dozen eggs you bought at the market were addled.

Al fin del libro se **introduce** una serie de ejercicios.
A series of exercises is introduced at the end of the book.

Una multitud de palabras francesas se **introdujeron** en nuestro idioma.
A multitude of French words were introduced into our language.

Hay una clase de autores que se **contentan** con sólo repetir y combinar el trabajo de otros. — There is a class of authors who are content merely to repeat and combine the work of others.

La multiplicidad de jefes **produjo** entre los fenicios una confusión que contribuyó a su derrota. — The multiplicity of leaders produced among the Phoenicians a confusion that contributed to their defeat.

Una bandada de buitres se **cernían** encima de la catarata. — A flock of vultures *was* sailing over the falls.

REMARK I. When the meaning of the verb is not intimately associated with either noun in expressions of the above nature, the verb is regularly singular if it precedes:

Entró una tropa de asesinos en la cámara del rey.
Una tropa de asesinos **entraron** en la cámara del rey.
— A troop of assassins entered the king's chamber.

REMARK II. When it is difficult to decide which of the nouns the verb is most intimately associated with, the preference is for the plural when the verb follows:

Presenta un sin número de reglas con sus excepciones que **confunden** y **abaten** el entendimiento. — It presents an endless amount of rules and exceptions that confuse and demoralize the understanding.

31.5. Indeed, in such constructions, the singular collective and the plural complement may each have its own agreement, according to the connection and meaning:

La aleación de acero y níquel, **unidos** por la fusión, **posee** una gran fuerza de resistencia. — The alloy of steel and nickel, united by fusion, possesses great power of resistance.

La gran variedad de plantas **prodigadas** por la naturaleza en los Andes **ofrece** al naturalista un atractivo que apenas se ve igualado en otra parte del globo. — The great variety of plants lavished by Nature in the Andes offers an attraction to the naturalist which is hardly equalled in any other part of the globe.

La inmensidad de las aguas que **rodean** al globo **tiene** algo de incomprensible. — The immensity of the waters that surround the earth has in it something incomprehensible.

La cantidad de langostas **era** tan grande que **destruyeron** toda la cosecha. — The number of locusts *was* so great that *they* destroyed the whole crop.

31.6. But **parte, mayoría, mitad, resto, tercio,** and other similar singular nouns, may be accompanied by plural verbs in the same clause:

Iban en el buque sesenta personas; la mitad **perecieron.**	Seventy persons were on board; half of them perished.
Más de la mitad de la población **son** indios o mestizos.	More than one-half of the population are Indians or half-breeds.
Un tercio se **salvaron** en las lanchas; el resto **fueron** degollados sin piedad por los indígenas.	A third saved themselves in the boats; the rest *were* massacred without mercy by the natives.
Parte de los soldados **estaban** enfermos en el hospital, parte **estaban** ausentes con licencia, parte **habían** ido a forrajear, y resultó que era muy reducido el número de los que guardaban el campamento.	Part of the soldiers *were* sick in hospital, a part *were* absent on furlough, a part had gone foraging, and it happened that the number of those who were guarding the camp was very small.
Gran parte de las exportaciones **consisten** en seda cruda.	A large part of the exports *consist* of raw silk.
La mayor parte de las proposiciones **han** sido rechazadas.	The greater part of the propositions *has* been rejected.

REMARK. **Parte,** used adverbially after a noun, does not affect the agreement:

El terreno era parte sólido, parte arenoso.	The ground was in part solid, and in part sandy.

31.7. The expressions **más de un** and **uno y medio** are treated as singular:

Más de un viajero atrevido se **ha** perdido para siempre en aquellos páramos.	More than one adventurous traveler has been lost for ever on those moors.
Un día y medio se **invirtió** en aquellos preparativos.	A day and a half was spent in those preparations.

SUBJECT AND PREDICATE

31.8. When the verb **ser** connects two nouns of different number, the one being subject and the other predicate, the verb properly agrees in number with the subject:

Y esas mismas variaciones **son** un argumento incontrovertible en contra de la hipótesis de Vd.	And those very variations are an incontrovertible argument against your theory.

Sus partidarios **eran** la hez de la población.	His followers were the dregs of the town.
Reconoció que aquellos campos de hielo **serían** un obstáculo insuperable.	He recognized that those ice fields would be an insurmountable obstacle.

31.9. But the predicate following the verb **ser** exercises at times a kind of attraction upon it (as was common in Latin), especially when it is plural, or when it immediately follows the verb, and the subject is at some distance:

Periodista sin opinión propia política ni literaria, cuyo único provecho **son** cuatrocientos reales mensuales que le valen sus artículos.	A journalist without an opinion of his own, either political or literary, whose only gain *is* twenty dollars a month, which his articles bring him.
La única recompensa que recibe el reformista a menudo **son** el ridículo y la persecución.	The only reward which the reformer obtains *is* often ridicule and persecution.
El otro hombre que vi **erais** vos.	The other man that I saw was you.
La época más dichosa de la vida de Caldas **fueron** los años en que gozó de la plena y pacífica posesión del Observatorio de Bogotá.	The happiest period in the life of Caldas *was* the years in which he enjoyed the full and undisturbed possession of the Observatory of Bogotá.
Los ladrones, por lo regular, **es** gente bien informada. (Benavente, **La honradez de la cerradura,** I, 3)	Thieves ordinarily *are* well-informed people.

REMARK. This latter construction should be sedulously avoided when the verb is followed by the adjective **todo,** qualifying the subject:

Su urbanidad **es toda** seguridades y promesas sin ejecución.	Their politeness is all assurances and promises without fulfilment.
El terreno de esta región **era todo** rocas esparcidas y negruzcas, entre las cuales brotaban con dificultad algunos arbustos desmirriados y enfermizos.	The ground of this region was all blackened and scattered rocks, among which a few stunted and sickly shrubs grew with difficulty.

SEVERAL NOUNS COMBINED

31.10. When a verb has several subjects, or an adjective refers to several nouns, the fundamental principle is that two or more subjects are equivalent to a plural subject, and that two or more nouns of different genders are equivalent to a plural masculine:

El oro y la plata **arrancados** a los naturales.	The gold and silver wrung from the natives.
En ella el cuerpo y el alma **son** como los de la Santísima Virgen María.	In her, body and soul are like those of the blessed Virgin Mary.
El calor tropical y la atmósfera húmeda y malsana **fueron fatales** a gran número de los españoles.	The tropical heat and the moist, unhealthy atmosphere were fatal to a large number of the Spaniards.
Descubrióse al comandante que, cogido por la pared, y **fracturados** el pecho y la cabeza, estaba próximo a expirar.	They found the commandant, who, caught by the wall, and with his chest and head crushed, was about to breathe his last.

31.11. But these general rules are subject to a great many exceptions:

a. Two or more singular nouns, expressing ideas which coalesce into a single idea, are equivalent to one singular noun:

La legislación, lejos de temer, debe animar **este** flujo y reflujo del interés, sin **el cual** no puede crecer ni subsistir la agricultura.	Legislation, instead of fearing, should stimulate this ebb and flow of interest, without which agriculture can neither increase nor exist.
El recibo, trasmisión y distribución de los paquetes se **verifica** en este país por sociedades incorporadas.	The receiving, transmitting and delivery of parcels is carried on in this country by incorporated companies.
El abrir y cerrar de esta válvula **permite** que el flúido pase a la parte anterior e impide que vuelva.	The opening and closing of this valve permits the fluid to move forward and prevents its return.

Remark. In the following case the nouns are considered separately, each taking the article:[1]

El flujo y el reflujo del mar **son producidos** por la atracción de la luna y del sol.	The ebb and flow of the sea *is* produced by the attraction of the sun and moon.
La ascensión y la caída del mercurio **indican** las variaciones de la atmósfera.	The rise and fall of the mercury show the atmospheric changes.

[1] It does not follow, however, that omission of the article with the second noun (cf. § 2.10) means that the verb is necessarily singular: **La sencillez y franqueza del anciano me conmovieron.** (Palacio Valdés, **La hermana San Sulpicio, VII**) *The simplicity and the frankness of the old man touched me.*

Las importaciones y las exportaciones en este caso **son** casi iguales.	The imports and exports are in this instance nearly equal.

b. Two or more neuter subjects are equivalent to one only:

Esto y lo que habíamos oído en el restaurante nos **decidió** a dejar la ciudad sin demora.	This and what we had overheard in the restaurant induced us to leave the city without delay.
Lo que había aprendido por su propia experiencia y lo poco que por sí solo había podido recoger de los libros, **constituía** toda su educación.	What he had learned from his own experience and the little he had been able to glean unaided from books, formed his only education.
Lo castizo de su estilo y lo elevado de sus sentimientos **obtuvo** por las obras de Scott una popularidad de que ningún autor anteriormente había gozado.	The correctness of his style and the elevation of his sentiments obtained for Scott's works a popularity that no previous author had enjoyed.

Remark. A neuter phrase and a noun masculine or feminine singular, may be considered either as singular or plural:

Lo cual y su partida repentina me **hace** *(or* hacen) creer que ha desistido de su empeño.	Which [fact] and his sudden departure *make* me believe that he has desisted from his efforts.
Lo magnánimo de su conducta, y su modestia en la hora de la victoria, **granjeó** *(or* granjearon) al General Grant la estimación de todo el mundo.	The magnanimity of his conduct and his modesty in the hour of victory won for General Grant the esteem of the whole world.
La pureza de su lenguaje y lo elevado de sus sentimientos **obtuvo** *(or* obtuvieron) por las obras de Scott una popularidad, *etc.*	The purity of his language and the elevation of his sentiments, obtained for Scott's works a popularity, *etc.*

c. Two or more infinitives, being logically neuters, are treated as one singular:

A los vasallos **corresponde** únicamente callar y obedecer.	The duty of vassals is simply to keep silence and obey.
Ganar mucho y gastar poco **asegurará** las riquezas.	To earn much and spend little will insure riches.
Acostarse y levantarse temprano, y trabajar con moderación, si no **asegura** la salud, al menos **contribuye** poderosamente a su conservación.	To go to bed early, to rise early and to work moderately, if *they* do not insure health, at least contribute powerfully to its preservation.

Producir poco y consumir mucho **ocasionará** la ruina de la nación más poderosa.	To produce little and consume much will bring on the downfall of the most powerful nation.

REMARK I. This construction would be better if the definite article were placed before the first infinitive, thus making a single collective idea out of all of them:

Oí y comprendí cada palabra, y el oír y comprender, a tanta distancia, todo cuanto V. dijo, **parece** muy singular.	I heard and understood every word, and my hearing and understanding at such a distance, all that you said seems very wonderful.
El ganar mucho y gastar poco **asegurará** las riquezas.	To earn much and spend little will insure riches.
A los vasallos corresponde únicamente el callar y obedecer.	The duty of vassals is simply to keep silence and obey.
El producir poco y consumir mucho ocasionará la ruina de la nación más poderosa.	To produce little and consume much will bring on the downfall of the most powerful nation.

REMARK II. A definite article before each infinitive could make a plural of them:

El madrugar, el hacer ejercicio, y el comer moderadamente, **son** provechosísimos para la salud.	To rise early, to take exercise, and to eat moderately, are conducive to health.
El ganar mucho y el gastar poco **asegurarán** las riquezas.	To earn much and spend little will insure riches.
El producir poco y el consumir mucho **ocasionarán** la ruina de la nación más poderosa.	To produce little and to consume much will bring on the downfall of the most powerful nation.

d. When two or more entire statements are the joint subject of a verb, the latter is singular—they being considered as neuters:

El que hubiese habido una sublevación, y el que el partido eclesiástico hubiese llegado al poder, se **descubrió** ser una noticia falsa.	That there had been a revolution, and that the church party had come into power, was found to be a false report.
El que la administración haya taladrado a la profundidad de 1000 pies, y el que se hayan hallado allí petróleo y gas natural, **es** muy cierto.	That the company have bored to a depth of 1000 feet, and have found both oil and natural gas, is quite true.
Quién haya esparcido este rumor, y qué objeto haya tenido en hacerlo, se **ignora** por completo.	Who spread this rumor, and what object he had in doing so, is entirely unknown.

e. Neither of the two preceding exceptions can take effect when two neuters or two clauses are contrasted or opposed to each other:

Esto y lo que refiere la gaceta se **contradicen.**	This and what the gazette says *contradict* each other.
Que el hombre sea libre y que tenga que obedecer ciegamente a lo que se le manda, **repugnan.**	That man should be free and that he should have to obey blindly as he is ordered, *are inconsistent.*
Que un héroe fuese hecho invulnerable por una divinidad y que por otra fuese vestido de armadura impenetrable, nos **parecen** ser incompatibles.	That a hero should be made invulnerable by one deity, and that he should be clothed with impenetrable armor by another, *appear* to us incompatible.

REMARK. A further limitation is that when a verb which, for the reasons just given, would be singular, is followed by a predicate in the shape of a plural noun, the verb must be plural—and *vice versa:*

Crecer y propagarse **son propiedades** comunes a plantas y animales; sentir y moverse **son cualidades** características de éstos solos.	Growth and reproduction *are properties* common to plants and animals; sensation and motion *are characteristics* of the latter alone.
Quién haya esparcido este rumor, y qué objeto haya tenido en hacerlo, **son cosas** que todavía se ignoran.	Who spread this rumor, and what object he had in doing so, *are subjects* that are still unknown.
Si el planeta Marte está habitado, y, estándolo, si puede establecerse la comunicación con él, **son cuestiones** puramente especulativas.	Whether the planet Mars is inhabited, and, if so, whether communication with it can be established, *are* purely speculative *questions.*
El asentir en un sistema de doctrinas, y el vivir en conformidad con él, no **es lo mismo.**	To assent to a system of doctrines, and to live conformably to them, *are* not *the same thing.*

f. When the verb precedes several subjects in the singular number, connected by **y,** it is preferably plural if the agents act conjointly (especially if they be persons), and singular if they act separately:

Reinaban la confusión y el desorden por todas partes.	Confusion and disorder reigned everywhere.
No eran por entonces sólo el hambre y la sed los peligros que les aguardaban en el desierto aquel.	Hunger and thirst *were* not then the only perils which awaited them in that desert.
Aumentábase cada instante el furor de la tempestad y la oscuridad de la noche.	Every moment the violence of the storm and the darkness of the night increased.

Disminuía rápidamente el dinero del joven y el número de sus profesados amigos. — The young man's money was rapidly diminishing, and the number of his professed friends.

REMARK I. The illustrations above show the theoretical distinction. In practice the verb is likely to agree with the first (and nearer) member of the subject: **Allí no se puede vivir... Bien lo sabe Vd.** y **Balbina.** (Pérez de Ayala, **Luz de domingo,** VIII) *One can't live there. You and Balbina well know it.*

REMARK II. The verb agrees only with the first subject in number if it be understood, but not repeated, with the second:

No **es** el diente, no las garras del tigre, no el veneno mortal de las serpientes lo que más se teme en el fondo de estas selvas. — It *is* not the teeth or claws of the tiger nor the deadly venom of the serpents that is most feared in the depth of these forests.

Primeramente **aparece** el botón, luego la flor, y últimamente el fruto. — First *appears* the bud, then the flower, and last of all the fruit.

En aquellas montañas agrestes y en aquellas playas desiertas, **hallaba** un asilo la libertad y la gloria una tumba. — In those wild mountains and on those desert shores, freedom **found** a home and glory a grave.

g. When the verb follows several subjects in the singular, connected by the conjunction **y,** it should be plural; the same is the case when y is understood:

La antigüedad de la abadía, el silencio, la soledad y la desolación completa del lugar me **llenaron** de tristeza. — The antiquity of the abbey, the silence, the solitude and the complete desolation of the place filled me with sadness.

La tardanza y el disgusto **agotaron** su paciencia. — Delay and disappointment exhausted his patience.

El aire suave y embalsamado, la fragancia de las magnolias, el susurro del viento entre las copas de los árboles, el arrullo de las palomas silvestres me **invitaban** a dormir. — The soft and balmy air, the fragrance of the magnolias, the sighing of the wind through the treetops, the cooing of the wild pigeons, lulled me to sleep.

h. Where, of two subjects, the last is a mere variation of the first, the verb agrees with the second:

Su valor, su denuedo, **admiraba** a todos. — His bravery, his daring, astonished all.

En todos los períodos de la vida, el amor al trabajo, el gusto del estudio, **es** un gran alivio contra la desgracia.	At all periods of life, the love of work and a taste for study *are* a great solace for misfortune.

i. When of several subjects having a verb in common, the last includes or recapitulates the others, the verb agrees with *it:*

La agricultura, las bellas artes, el comercio, **todo está** atrasado en aquel país.	Agriculture, the fine arts, commerce, *all are* backward in that country.
Víveres, agua, medicinas, **todo fué** embarcado con una rapidez que sólo se explica por la impaciencia de volver a la patria.	Provisions, water, medicines, *were all* put on board with a celerity explicable only by the impatience to return home.
Vecinos, amigos, parientes, **cada cual prefiere** su propio interés al de otro cualquiera.	Neighbors, friends, relations, *each prefers* his own interest to that of any other person.
Grandes, ricos, pequeños y pobres, **nadie puede** sustraerse a la muerte.	The great, the rich, the little and the poor, *none can* escape Death.
Ni tierras, ni fincas, ni fondos ni acciones, **nada** le **quedaba;** todo había sido arrastrado a la vorágine de la especulación.	Neither lands, nor estates, nor funds nor stocks, *nothing was left;* everything had been swept into the vortex of speculation.

j. When a verb has several singular subjects connected by **o,** the verb may be singular, since the conjunction expresses an alternative. But the plural is more usual, especially when the subjects precede the verb:

Todos creen que V. o el señor Aguilar **ha** escrito este artículo.	Everyone thinks that either you or Mr. Aguilar wrote this article.
Mi tío o mi hermano **ha** de ser nombrado para la embajada de Londres.	Either my brother or my uncle *is* to be appointed to the embassy in London.
Que uno u otro **venga** conmigo.	Let one or other come with me.
Precisa que ese hombre o yo **deje** la casa.	Either that man or I must leave the house.
Se regocijaba o temblaba según que la esperanza o el temor **ocupaba** el ánimo de su amo.	He rejoiced or trembled according as hope or fear filled the mind of his master.
El trueno gordo estallaba cuando uno u otro **decían** algo que a su mamá le parecía sacrilegio. (Pérez Galdós, **La de Bringas,** XIII)	Heavy thunder was heard when one or the other said something that seemed sacrilegious to his mother.

El día que usted o don Quintín **señalen,** nos veremos con los oscurantistas. (Baroja, **La feria de los discretos,** XXVIII)	The day that you or Don Quintín *indicates* we shall settle things with the enemies of progress.

REMARK. If one of the subjects is plural, and stands nearest to the verb, the latter becomes plural by "attraction":

Se puede dudar si **son** más importantes las buenas leyes o su buena ejecución.	It may be doubted whether just laws or their proper enforcement *is* most important.
O el catedrático o los alumnos **han** sido muy negligentes.	Either the professor or the students *have* been very remiss.

k. In the case of two singular subjects separated by **ni,** the verb is singular (at least theoretically) if it could apply to only one of the subjects; if it could apply to both, the verb is plural. All in all, the use of the plural seems commoner in actual practice, except in combinations with **nadie:**

Ni el uno ni el otro **será** nombrado.	Neither the one nor the other will be appointed.
Ni el uno ni el otro **quisieron** probarlo.	Neither the one nor the other wished to try it.
Ni uno ni otro **es** mi padre.	Neither one nor the other *is* my father.
Ni la dulzura ni la fuerza **puede** nada con él.	Neither mildness nor force *is of* any *avail* with him.
Ni él ni su abogado **estaban** enterados de este hecho.	Neither he nor his lawyer *were* aware of this fact.

l. If the alternative subjects, with either **o** or **ni,** require different personal forms, there must be a separate verb for each when the meaning demands a singular; when the verb is plural, it must be of a form to include both persons:

Ni Vd. **es** el culpable ni lo **soy** yo.	Neither you nor I *am* the guilty one.
Ni Vd. ni yo **somos** culpables.	Neither you nor I *am* guilty.
Ni Vd. ni yo **tenemos** derecho alguno para criticar a esos hombres.	Neither you nor I *have* any right to criticize those men.

m. When a singular noun is connected with another by **con, como, tanto como, así como,** the agreement is usually singular; it is, however, sometimes plural, especially when **con** is the connecting word. But if the two nouns are at a distance from each other, the agreement is singular:

A esta época **llegó** la fragata Fulminante con dos galeones procedentes de la Habana.	At this juncture the frigate Thunderer arrived with two galleons hailing from Havana.
El lado c, con los lados AD y BD, **forman** un triángulo rectángulo.	The side c, with the sides AD and BD, *form* a right triangle.
La emperatriz misma, con su madre Prisca, **fué** condenada al destierro.	The Empress herself, with her mother Prisca, *was* condemned to exile.
El alma, como el cuerpo, no se **desarrolla** sino por medio del ejercicio.	The soul, as well as the body, *is* developed only by exercise.
Tanto el infierno como el cielo **da** pruebas de la existencia de un Dios justo.	Hell as well as heaven *offers* proof of the existence of a just God.
El avestruz tiene la cabeza, así como el cuello, **guarnecida** de plumón.	The ostrich has the head as well as the neck covered with down.
En Egipto, Grecia y Asia, Baco así como Hércules **eran considerados** como semidioses.	In Egypt, Greece and Asia, Bacchus as well as Hercules *were considered* as demi-gods.
Andrés Calvo **emigró** a América en 1746 con su mujer, su sobrina, y cuatro hijos.	Andrew Calvo emigrated to America in 1746 with his wife, niece, and four children.
Había sido, como muchos en tiempos de trastornos y revoluciones, víctima de circunstancias adversas.	Like many others in times of upheavals and revolutions, he had been the victim of adverse circumstances.

n. When the verb has two or more joint subjects of either number, it is regularly put in the plural; if the subjects are of different persons, the verb is put in that person which is said to take precedence. The second person takes precedence of the third,[1] while the first person outranks both. Thus:

V. y yo estudiamos.	You and I study.
Mi padre y yo vivimos en una casa de ladrillo.	My father and I live in a brick house.
Tú y el aya compráis flores.	You and the governess buy flowers.
La niña y su madre leen un libro.	The girl and her mother are reading a book.
V. y su hijo venden sus caballos.	You and your son sell your horses.

[1] In those parts of the Spanish-speaking world in which the **vosotros** form is not in ordinary use (§ 3.4) but is replaced by the third person form, a combination of second and third person subjects calls for a third person plural verb form: **Tú y el aya compran flores.** *You and the governess buy flowers.*

AGREEMENT OF ADJECTIVES

31.12. When a predicate adjective relates to several nouns of the same gender, it stands in the plural and agrees in gender with the nouns:

El capitán y el soldado están borra**chos**.	The captain and the soldier are drunk.
La madre y las niñas son bonit**as**.	The mother and the girls are pretty.
La botella y la taza están llen**as** de sidra.	The bottle and the cup are full of cider.

31.13. If the several nouns are of different genders, the adjective is put in the plural masculine:

El hombre y la mujer son ric**os**.	The man and the woman are rich.
El caballo y la mula son viej**os**.	The horse and the mule are old.
El escritorio y la silla son car**os**.	The desk and chairs are dear.

31.14. If the nouns refer to things and are in the plural, the adjective is plural and may agree in gender with the nearest noun:

Los escritorios y las sillas son car**os** *or* car**as**.	The desks and chairs are dear.

31.15. Some writers and some grammarians prefer to put the masculine noun last when the adjective has a separate termination for each gender, and so avoid the incongruity of a feminine noun followed immediately by a masculine adjective:

La mula y el caballo son viej**os**.	The mule and the horse are old.
Las sillas y los escritorios son car**os**.	The chairs and desks are dear.
La silla y el escritorio son car**os**.	The chair and desk are dear.

31.16. The principles exhibited above are of equal force when the adjective immediately follows the nouns as when it is separated from them by the verb *to be:*

Ella compra un traje y un velo nuev**os**.	She buys a new dress and veil.
Quiero vender mis botas y mi sombrero viej**os**.	I want to sell my old boots and hat.

31.17. An adjective agrees in number and gender with whatever it refers to, whether that be expressed in the sentence or not. In the case of personal pronouns, which often do not show a distinction of gender, the sex of the person represented must be borne in mind:

¿Por qué está V. callada?	Why are you silent?
Vds. son injustas.	You are unjust.
Yo estoy cansada.	I am tired.
Parecen pequeñas.	They seem small.

31.18. Adjectives of geographical division, when used to denote a language, are usually preceded by the masculine article **el**, except generally when governed by the verb **hablar**, *to speak:*

Hablo francés e inglés.	I speak French and English.
Estudio el alemán.	I am studying German.
Mi hijo aprende el latín.	My son is learning Latin.
El ruso es difícil.	Russian is difficult.

REMARK I. The use of the article is in accordance with § **2.7**, and its omission, today common after the more frequently used verbs (**aprender, enseñar, escribir, leer, saber**), corresponds theoretically to § **2.13**.

REMARK II. After the prepositions **de** and **en** the article is similarly not used if the idea is in any degree partitive (§ **2.13**) but is retained otherwise:

Hablar en español.	To speak in Spanish.
Un curso de francés.	A French course.
En el español del siglo quince.	In fifteenth century Spanish.
Esta palabra viene del latín.	This word comes from Latin.

31.19. When an adjective qualifies several nouns of the same gender which precede it, it will be plural and of their gender:

Odysseus era profesor de lengua y literatura griegas en la Universidad literaria de Pilares. (Pérez de Ayala, **Prometeo**, II)	Odysseus was professor of the Greek language and literature in the College of Letters of Pilares.
Ya habrá V. visto que me trata con el acatamiento y el cariño debidos a una especie de hermano mayor o segundo padre. (Alarcón, **El capitán Veneno**, II, 5).	You must have seen already that he treats me with the esteem and the affection due a kind of older brother or second father.

31.20. When an adjective qualifies several nouns of different gender which precede it, it may agree in gender and number with the last noun, if this is feminine, or may be in the masculine plural form:

Poseía talento y habilidad **extremada** (*or* **extremados**). — He possessed unusual talent and ability.

Esparciéronse por toda Europa cuentos extravagantes del oro y la plata **americana** (*or* **americanos**). — Europe was filled with extravagant stories of American gold and silver.

El fué quien primero llevó la cruz y el pendón de Castilla a un mundo y poblaciones **remotas** y **desconocidas.** — He it was who first carried the cross and the standard of Castile to a world and populations remote and unknown.

Entre el islote y la costa, **separados** por un canal de media milla de ancho, había una corriente muy rauda. — Between the islet and the shore, separated by a channel half a mile wide, was a very swift current.

Nunca he tratado de obtener injustamente los honores y la riqueza **ajenos.** — I have never sought to obtain unjustly another man's honors and wealth.

Milicias y ejército **desorganizados.** — The militia forces and the army [being] unorganized.

Maestra y niños **espantados** por el rayo. — Schoolmistress and children terrified by the lightning.

Con el rostro y la mirada **inclinados** al suelo, llegó hasta cerca de donde estaba D. Luis. (Valera, **Pepita Jiménez, Paralipómenos)** — With face and eyes directed toward the ground she went up close to where Don Luis was.

Los jinetes y amazonas **elegantísimos,** todo tenía un aire de elegancia y riqueza. (Baroja, **La ciudad de la niebla,** VII) — The very stylish horsemen and horsewomen, everything had an air of elegance and wealth.

31.21. Plural forms of adjectives with meanings like **los mismos, los dichos, los referidos,** may, especially in legal language, precede a series of nouns even when the first is singular. In the case of **dicho,** the definite article may be omitted:

Y **dichos** Gonzalo Rodríguez y Teodoro Osario prometen y convienen además conservar en buen estado **los referidos** casa, jardines, establos y oficinas. — And the *said* Gonzalo Rodríguez and Theodore Osario further promise and agree to keep the *aforesaid* house and garden, stables and offices, in good condition.

El preso declaró que había comprado **dichos** reloj y cadena. — The prisoner stated that he had bought the *aforesaid* watch and chain.

31.22. The same construction is applicable to any adjective preceded by the definite article or a possessive or demonstrative adjective, provided the following nouns are proper names, or denote persons:

Los doctos padre e hijo.	*The learned* father and son.
Las mutuamente **recelosas** Francia y Alemania.	*The* mutually *distrustful* France and Germany.
Sus lindas y **amables** hija y sobrina.	*His lovely* and *charming* daughter and niece.

31.23. In the above construction, if the nouns are of different genders, the adjective should be masculine, and a masculine noun is best placed nearest to it:

Palestina recibió muchas de sus artes y tradiciones de **los** más **antiguos** Asiria y Egipto.	Palestine received many of her arts and traditions from *the* more *ancient* Assyria and Egypt.
Los ilustres Isabel y Fernando trocaron las coronas de Castilla y Aragón por la diadema de las Españas unidas y el cetro de un imperio allende el océano.	*The illustrious* Isabel and Ferdinand exchanged the crowns of Castile and Aragon for the diadem of united Spain and the sceptre of an empire beyond the ocean.
El cuento de **los famosos** Píramo y Tisbe, o el de **los desgraciados** Romeo y Julieta.	The story of *the famous* Pyramus and Thisbe, or that of *the unfortunate* Romeo and Juliet.
Los anteriormente **ricos** y **florecientes** Corinto y Tebas.	*The* formerly *rich* and *flourishing* Corinth and Thebes.
Los artificiosos madre e hijo se habían precavido de este desenlace.	*The artful* mother and son had guarded against this outcome.
El rey Enrique fué víctima de **sus desleales** esposa e hijos.	King Henry was the victim of *his disloyal* wife and sons.

31.24. The repetition of the article or adjective is advisable—but not obligatory—before each noun, unless they express ideas which have no affinity with each other:

Su experiencia, **(sus)** riquezas y **(sus)** amigos hacían de él un rival formidable.	His experience, wealth, and friends made him a formidable rival.
Sus virtudes y **(sus)** faltas eran de una especie que apelaba igualmente a la simpatía popular.	His virtues and his faults were of a kind that appealed equally to popular sympathy.
La madre y **el** niño salvados del	The mother and child saved from

naufragio fueron llevados al hospital de Sta. María.	the wreck were taken to St. Mary's Hospital.

REMARK. If the nouns denote the same object, the article is not repeated:

El expresado convenio y tratado.	The agreement and treaty mentioned.
Un herrero y amolador de cuchillos se ha establecido en una gruta situada en la falda de la montaña, y le tiene el amor de un ermitaño.	A blacksmith and knife grinder has established himself in a cave situated in the side of the mountain, and has the love of a hermit for it.
El eminente religioso y guerrero, con la espada ceñida sobre la humilde túnica, se adelantó a recibir las llaves de la opulenta Orán.	The eminent priest and warrior, with his sword belted on over his humble robe, advanced to receive the keys of opulent Oran.

31.25. When the repetition of a noun is tacitly implied it is necessary to make the article plural or to repeat it:

El ejército de Inglaterra y Turquía.	The army of England and Turkey.
(A single army formed by the two countries.)	
El ejército de Inglaterra y **el** de Turquía.	The army of England and that of Turkey.
(Two armies, one formed by each.)	
Los ejércitos de Inglaterra y de Turquía.	The armies of England and Turkey.
(Several armies, each formed jointly by the two countries.)	
Los ejércitos de Inglaterra y **los** de Turquía.	The armies of England and of Turkey.
(Several armies, some belonging to each country.)	

REMARK. Where the meaning of the noun is of such a nature that it would be understood to be only one apiece, there is no difference between the second and the third arrangement:

El embajador inglés y **el** francés. **Los** embajadores inglés y francés.	} The English and the French Ambassador.

BUT

Los representantes diplomáticos de Francia e Inglaterra son mejor pagados que los de los Estados Unidos.	The diplomatic representatives of France and England are better paid than those of the United States.
Los cónsules de Inglaterra y de Francia.	The consuls of England and of France.
Los cónsules de Suecia y Noruega.	The consuls of Sweden and Norway.

31.26. When two nouns have separate attributives, the verb agrees with the subject which it accompanies, and is understood before the other:

Era penoso y peligroso el trabajo, y los obreros pocos y mal pagados.	The work *was* arduous and dangerous, and the laborers few and poorly paid.
El viento **estaba** tranquilo, el ambiente balsámico y agradable.	The wind *was* soft, the air pleasant and balmy.

31.27. When a plural noun, representing two distinct entities, is followed by two adjectives of which the first applies to one member of the pair and the second to the other, the adjectives are singular:

Los siglos décimo tercio y cuarto.	The thirteenth and fourteenth centuries.
Los tiempos presente y futuro.	The present and future tenses.
Entre las cordilleras central y costanera se halla el valle del Cauca.	Between the central and the coast range is the valley of the Cauca.

REMARK. In most cases the following construction is preferable:

El equinoccio vernal y el otoñal.	The vernal and autumnal equinoxes.
El océano Indico y el Pacífico.	The Indian and Pacific oceans.

31.28. When the plural embraces, not two individuals, but two classes, it is necessary to show whether the adjectives apply to these classes severally or to both collectively:

Un hondo barranco cubierto en ambas márgenes de álamos blancos y **de** negros.	A deep gully covered on both sides with white and black poplars.

(Cubierto de álamos blancos y negros *would denote that the poplars were mottled black and white.)*

Los carneros blancos y **los** negros eran mantenidos separados.	The black and the white sheep were kept apart.
Los alciones blancos y azules son aquí muy numerosos, y forman sus nidos minando en las orillas escarpadas.	The blue-and-white kingfishers are very numerous here, and form their nests by burrowing in the steep banks.
Los soldados valientes y aguerridos.	The brave and veteran soldiers.
Los soldados aguerridos y **los** indisciplinados.	The veteran and the undisciplined soldiers.

31.29. A peculiar irregularity in Spanish is the use of the masculine forms **un, medio** and **todo** (though not to the exclusion of the feminine forms) before feminine proper names of cities (cf. § **1.7**); an adjective in the predicate, referring to such a combination, is also masculine:

¿Quién diría que en **un** Segovia no se encuentra una buena posada?	Who would think that in a city like Segovia there is not a good inn to be found?
Medio Guatemala está construido de madera.	Half of Guatemala is built of wood.
Registraron **medio** Málaga para encontrarle.	They ransacked half Malaga to find him.
No indispongas a tu madre y a tu hermana con **todo** Moraleda. (Benavente, **Pepa Doncel,** I, 2)	Don't get your mother and your sister into the bad graces of all Moraleda.
En **todo** Nueva York hay prisa...en **todo** Nueva York hay ruido... (Camba, **La ciudad automática,** X)	In all New York there is haste... In all New York there is noise...

BUT

Media Moraleda estaría de nuestra parte. (Benavente, **Pepa Doncel,** III, 6)	Half of Moraleda would be on our side.

31.30. The masculine form **mismo** may be used after feminine names of places preceded by **en**; but if the name is one which regularly takes the definite article, **mismo** agrees with it:

Semejantes sucesos se verifican aquí en España **mismo.**	Such occurrences take place right here in Spain.
Una dama interpreta los clásicos en Salamanca **mismo,** y otra regenta la cátedra de retórica en la Universidad de Alcalá.	A lady expounds the classics in Salamanca itself, and another occupies the chair of rhetoric in the University of Alcalá.
En el **mismo** Perú; en la **misma** Habana; en la Guaira **misma.**	Even in Peru; even in Havana; in La Guayra itself.
En Francia **misma** tienen un gran éxito. (Camba, **La rana viajera, Alemania,** II)	Even in France they have great success.

CASES INVOLVING ARTICLES, ADJECTIVES AND PRONOUNS

31.31. When an article, adjective or adjective pronoun qualifies several nouns following, it agrees with the nearest one:

El valor y sufrimiento de las tropas fueron severamente experimentados.	The courage and endurance of the troops were severely tried.

La cordialidad y agasajo con que los recibió.	The cordiality and deference with which he received them.
En medio de **tantos** peligros e inquietudes.	In the midst of such dangers and alarms.
Era contra **toda** religión y derecho.	It was contrary to all religion and law.
El registro de mercaderías en las aduanas debe hacerse con **la** menor demora, gastos y daños posibles.	The customs examination of merchandise should be conducted with as little delay, expense and damage as possible.
Su distinguido mérito y servicios.	His distinguished merit and services.
Su extremada hermosura y talento.	Her extreme beauty and talent.
Su grande elocuencia y conocimientos.	His great eloquence and acquirements.

REMARK. If the intention were to restrict the adjective to the first noun, it would be necessary to repeat the pronoun or article before the second noun:

Su extremada hermosura y **su** talento.	Her extreme beauty and her talent.
Su grande elocuencia y **sus** conocimientos.	His great eloquence and his acquirements.

31.32. When a personal pronoun is followed immediately by a relative which is the subject of the verb in the relative clause, the verb agrees in person as well as number with the antecedent pronoun:

Yo, que hablo a V., era antes duque de Algaba.	I who speak to you was formerly Duke of Algava.
Tú que tienes tanta influencia podrás conseguirlo.	You who have so much influence will be able to obtain it.
Nosotros que somos tan despreciados.	We who are so despised.

31.33. In designating a particular person, in Spanish the appropriate noun or personal pronoun is placed as the subject of the verb **ser**; while in English it is oftener made the predicate after the impersonal expression *it is, it was,* etc. The Spanish construction is the more logical and consistent:

¿Quién es? —Soy yo; somos nosotros.	Who is it? —It is I; it is we.
¿Quién mete tanto ruido? —Son los muchachos.	Who is making such a noise? —It is the boys.
¿Quién ha roto la alcarraza? —No he sido yo.	Who has broken the decanter? —It was not I.

31.34. When such constructions are followed by a relative clause in which **quien** is subject, the relative and its verb may agree with the pronoun in number and person:

Soy yo quien he impedido la sublevación.	It is I who stopped the insurrection.
Seremos nosotros quienes mereceremos la gloria.	It will be we who will deserve the glory.
Nosotros éramos quienes presenciamos la pelea.	It was we who witnessed the combat.

31.35. When the antecedent is the logical demonstrative **el, la, los, las,** it is more usual but not obligatory to put the verb of the relative clause in the third person:

Yo soy el que lo afirma.	It is I who affirm it.
Nosotras somos las que le han cuidado y le han devuelto la vida.	We are the ones who cared for him and brought him back to life.

BUT

Vosotros sois los que tenéis que ayudarme. (Benavente, **Al fin, mujer,** II, 6)	You are the ones that *(or* It is you who) must help me.
Yo fuí la que impedí que Carmela se viese con ese chico en el molino. (Palacio Valdés, **Sinfonía pastoral, Scherzo,** V)	I was the one that prevented Carmela from seeing that boy at the mill.

31.36. But when the personal pronoun is followed by a predicate after the verb *to be,* the relative and its verb usually (but not necessarily) agree with that predicate:

Yo soy la persona que ha impedido la sublevación.	I am the person who stopped the insurrection.
Nosotros éramos los oficiales que presenciaron la pelea.	We were the officers who witnessed the combat.
Tú eres una visionaria que estás conspirando contra tu salud. (Espina, **La esfinge maragata,** XVII)	You are a visionary conspiring against your own health.
Tú que has hecho las compras eres la única que puedes saber si están bien los precios. (Martínez Sierra, **Mamá,** II)	You who have made the purchases are the only one that can know whether the prices are right.
Eres un desdichado que no entiendes	You are an unhappy wretch who

una palabra de negocios. (Palacio Valdés, **Los cármenes de Granada,** I, 15) — doesn't know a thing about business.

Los inquilinos del desván somos unos hidalgos que no envidiamos a nadie. (Camba, **La rana viajera, Variedades europeas,** I) — We tenants of the garret are nobles who do not envy anyone.

31.37. In the two contrasted examples following, the antecedent of the first is **nosotros,** understood. In the second the antecedent (that which is nearest to the relative) is **los dos,** construed as of the third person:

Somos dos los que **hemos** sido premiados. — We who have been rewarded are two [in number].

Somos los dos que **han** sido premiados. — We are the two who have been rewarded.

31.38. When a relative clause follows the expressions **yo soy** *it is I,* **somos nosotros** *it is we,* etc., an antecedent must be supplied for the relative, since the personal pronoun cannot act in the dual capacity of subject to the verb **ser** and antecedent to the relative. In other words, it is not the best Castilian to say **Seremos nosotros que serán matados, Soy yo que lo hice,** etc.:

Si no los matamos, seremos nosotros los que serán matados. — If we do not kill them, it will be we who will be killed (*Lit.* we shall be the ones who will be killed).

Soy yo quien lo hice. — I am he who did it.

¿Eres tú quien llamas? — Is it you who calls?

El era quien había imaginado tal escena vergonzosa, y él era a quien yo iba a exigir la reparación. — It was he who had devised such a shameful scene, and he it was of whom I was going to demand reparation.

Era la naturaleza y no la mano del hombre la (*or* lo) que había abierto la vasta caverna. — It was nature and not the hand of man which had hollowed out the vast cavern.

CASES INVOLVING RELATIVES AND ANTECEDENTS

31.39. A relative representing several nouns transmits, if possible, the number and gender of them all; if that cannot be done, preference is given to the plural number and the gender of the last noun:

La animación y el ruido que por todas partes **reinaban.**	The animation and hum that everywhere prevailed.
Los nombres y las palabras que **habían** sido **borradas** del acta.	The names and words that had been expunged from the minutes.
El estrecho y la isla que **fueron descubiertas** por Bering y que **llevan** su nombre.	The straits and the island that were discovered by Bering and bear his name.
Las mercaderías y otros efectos que **hayan** sido **recobrados** de algún buque náufrago o encallado, deben admitirse sin factura a la entrada en la aduana.	The merchandise and other effects which have been recovered from a wrecked or stranded vessel, should be allowed entry without invoice at the custom house.

31.40. Much nicety of meaning depends upon the gender of the demonstrative pronoun used as the antecedent to a relative. Thus, for example:

La Historia de Clavigero es **la** que derrama más luz sobre estos sucesos,	Clavigero's History is the one that throws most light on these events,

means that, as far as histories are concerned, Clavigero's is the one that throws most light on the subject. But if we substitue the neuter form for the one that agrees with the noun,

La historia de Clavigero es **lo** que derrama más luz sobre estos sucesos,	Clavigero's History is what throws most light on these events,

we convey the idea that Clavigero's work gives more information than anything else whatever.

31.41. But the relative pronoun may agree in gender and number with a preceding or following noun with which it is not necessarily connected in meaning. Thus, instead of saying:

Lo que a primera vista tomamos por una isla no descubierta, resultó ser, a una inspección más cerca, una bandada densa de aves marinas que se reposaban sobre las olas,	What we at first took for an undiscovered island, turned out to be, on closer inspection, a dense flock of seafowl resting on the water,

we may also say **la que a primera vista tomamos por una isla no descubierta,** etc., making the demonstrative agree with **isla** More examples:

Pero cuando somos actores en nuestra propia vida, entonces es sólo el corazón, es sólo el instinto **el** que nos mueve. (Benavente, **Campo de armiño,** III, 5)	When we are actors in our own life, then it is only the heart, only the instinct that moves us.

Un piano, jubilado por su respetable ancianidad en aquel retiro, fué **el** que marcó con voz cascada el compás de una mazurca. (Palacio Valdés, **Marta y María,** X)

It was a piano that, pensioned off on account of its respectable old age to that retreat, with its cracked voice marked the time for a mazurka.

Sin duda eran los obstáculos **los** que me daban antes bríos y fuerza. (Baroja, **Zalacaín,** III, 4)

Doubtless it was the obstacles that gave me spirit and strength before.

No tenía ya duda para Chisco que era "la señora", es decir, la osa, **lo** (lo *italicized in the original)* que rezongaba en el fondo del antro invisible. (Pereda, **Peñas arriba,** XX)

There was no longer any doubt for Chisco that it was "the madam", that is to say, the bear, that was growling in the depths of the invisible cave.

CONCLUSION. The question of agreement, like all the delicate points of language, is subject to great diversity of usage. The author has endeavored throughout this work to give the opinion of the majority of the best authorities, and where they have been about equally divided, to give both alternatives. But considerable liberties are taken by modern writers of repute, which would be censured in a tyro; while the classic authors of the XVIth and XVIIth centuries, though admirable for rhetoric and genius, abound in grammatical constructions which today would be considered highly incorrect.

There are generally a number of ways of stating the same thing, and where one way would lead to dangerous ground, it is preferable to avoid the difficulty by choosing some other expression; for it is better to be content with a simple style than to incur the charge of inaccuracy.

XXXII
Word-Making

SUBSTANTIVE COMBINATIONS

32.1. By *substantive combinations* are here intended two or more nouns, generally connected by prepositions, used together to denote a particular object.

The English language has a remarkable facility in using almost any noun as an adjective before other nouns, as: *clover honey, snipe shooting, school system.* When the words become habitually associated it is usual to link them together with hyphens: *foot-pound, book-folder.* When a combination has been long in use, the hyphen is dropped, and the parts become a single word: *penknife, horseman, hedgehog.*

This use of nouns is very limited in Spanish. In the few existing examples the secondary or qualifying noun, since it is used as an adjective, follows the principal noun, as an adjective would. The gender of the combination is that of the principal noun:

el cura párroco	the parish priest
la escuela modelo	the model school
la lengua madre	the mother tongue
la tierra virgen	the virgin soil
la finca modelo	the model farm
la aguagoma	the gum-arabic water

REMARK. Exceptions exist in a few neologisms which are imitations of English and contrary to the genius of Spanish; as: **la madre patria** *the mother country* (better **el país natal) el papel moneda** *the paper money.*

32.2. The principal method of combining nouns in Spanish is by placing the secondary noun last, and connecting the two by **de:**

el puerto de mar	the seaport
el traje de baile	the dance costume

la sortija de matrimonio	the wedding ring
el caballo de silla	the saddle horse
la granada de mano	the hand grenade
la cuchara de mesa	the tablespoon
el jugo de limón	the lemon juice

32.3. If, however, the secondary noun should express the purpose or use for which the first is intended, the preposition **para** *for* is properly used instead of **de:**

el vaso para cerveza	the beer glass
el molde para ladrillos	the brick mold
la prensa para sidra	the cider press
la percha para sombreros	the hatrack
el estante para libros	the bookcase
el canal para buques	the ship canal

32.4. It has been explained that the Spanish infinitive is used as a verbal noun corresponding to the English verbal in *-ing*. Consequently, in the secondary term of combinations of this character, Spanish employs the infinitive of the verb where English uses the present participle:

la prensa de copiar	the copying press
la máquina de coser	the sewing machine
la pluma de dibujar	the drawing pen
el papel de filtrar	the filtering paper
la mesa de escribir	the writing table

32.5. More complex ideas have to be expressed in Spanish word by word, the order being exactly the reverse of the English:

el aceite de semillas de algodón	the cottonseed oil
la aguja para máquina de coser	the sewing-machine needle
el sistema de abastecimiento de agua	the water-supply system
la máquina de torcer cuerdas	the rope-twisting machine
la prensa de embalar heno	the hay-packing press
la prensa de imprimir en colores	the color-printing press
el agua de blanquear la tela	the cloth-bleaching liquid
el molino de pulverizar el vidrio	the glass-pulverizing mill
el horno de fundir el mineral	the ore-smelting furnace
la máquina de hacer tipos de madera	the block-letter-cutting machine
la prensa de cilindro de entintamiento automático	the self-inking cylinder press

There are three other methods of expressing composite ideas such as we have been considering, but the learner with his present knowledge is not prepared to apply them correctly. They are:

a. The qualifying noun is replaced by a true adjective:

el agua llovediza	the rain water
un viento marero	a sea breeze

Still, in such cases two nouns connected by **de** can generally be used instead; thus **el agua de lluvia** and **un viento de mar** would be equally correct with the above.

b. A derivative is formed of the primitive word by adding a termination. These terminations will be treated of at length hereafter. (See §§ **32.16** ff.) Examples:

el azucarero	the sugar bowl
la librería	the bookstore
el rosal	the rosebush

c. The idea is expressed by an entirely different word:

la crin	the horsehair
la petaca	the cigar case

COMPOUND NOUNS

32.6. In Spanish, *compound nouns* are nouns formed by the combination of words which are also used separately. Nouns containing particles no longer in use alone, and those composed of parts that are distinct and separable only in some other language, cannot be considered as compounds in Spanish.

The class of compound nouns is not numerous. Very few are composed only of nouns; far the greater number are made by prefixing the stem of a verb to a noun, a few by the combination of a noun and adjective, while a rabble of scattering nouns are formed by the combination of almost any parts of speech:

el pasatiempo (pasa-tiempo, *pass-time*) the pastime
el mondadientes (monda-dientes, *clean-teeth*) the toothpick
el espantapájaros (espanta-pájaros, *scare-birds*) the scarecrow
el portafusil (porta-fusil, *carry-musket*) the sling (*of musket*)
la sinrazón (sin-razón, *without-reason*) the injustice
los quehaceres (que-haceres, *what-to-do's*) the chores
el quedirán (qué-dirán, *what-will-they-say*) the public opinion
el correveidile (corre-ve-y-di-le, *run-go-and-tell-him*) the tattler

el hazmerreír[1] (haz-me-reír, *make-me-laugh*) the guy, laughingstock
el pararrayos (para-rayos, *stop-lightnings*) the lightning rod
el métome en todo or **métomentodo** (meto-me en todo) the busy-body
el sábelotodo (sabe-lo-todo) the know-it-all
el limpiachimeneas (limpia-chimeneas, *clean-chimneys)* the chimney sweep
el guardapolvo (guarda-polvo, *guard-dust)* the dust protector
la enhorabuena (en-hora-buena, *in-good-hour)* the congratulation
el matasiete (mata-siete, *kill-seven)* the bully, blusterer, fire-eater

32.7. No rules can be laid down for determining the gender of a given compound noun. Those denoting males are masculine, females, feminine; otherwise the gender of each must be learned separately. However, where there are no determining circumstances, presumption is largely in favor of the masculine, especially if the first element is a verb form. Their irregularities of gender are apparent from the following list:

el abrelatas	the can opener
la aguamiel	the metheglin
el aguardiente	the brandy
el altavoz	the loud-speaker
la bocacalle	the mouth of the street
el cortafuego	the fire wall
el cortaplumas	the penknife
el cuentagotas	the medicine dropper
las enaguas	the skirt, petticoat
el ferrocarril	the railroad
el guardabarro(s)	the (automobile) fender
el guardabosque(s)	the gamekeeper
el guardafango(s)	the (automobile) fender
el guardapelo	the locket
el lavamanos	the washstand
el lavaplatos	the dishwasher
el limpiabotas	the bootblack
el lugarteniente	the lieutenant
la maniobra	the handiwork, maneuvre
la madreselva	the honeysuckle
el matacandelas	the candle snuffer, extinguisher
el matasanos	the quack
el matasellos	the canceling stamp
el mondaorejas	the ear spoon

[1] The initial **r** of **reír** is doubled in order to preserve the sound between vowels (cf. § **14**).

el paraguas	the umbrella
el parabrisas	the windshield
el paracaídas	the parachute
el pasamano	the handrail
el picaporte	the picklock, skeleton key
el picaflor	the hummingbird
el picamaderos	the woodpecker
la plumafuente	the fountain pen
el portamonedas	the purse, portemonnaie
el quitamanchas	the spot remover
el quitasol	the sunshade
el tiralíneas	the ruling pen
el tirabotas	the boot hook (for drawing on boots)
el *or* la sacabalas	the ball forceps
el sacabotas	the bootjack
el sacacorchos, el tirabuzón	the corkscrew
el sacamuelas	the (bungling) dentist
el salvavidas	the life preserver
el tocadiscos	the record player

COMPOSITE ADJECTIVE EXPRESSIONS

32.8. In English many adjective expressions are composed of an adjective connected by a hyphen with a noun which assumes the termination of a past participle—the combination meaning *provided with* whatever is expressed by the noun. The value is expressed in Spanish by the use of the preposition **de**:

una niña de ojos azules	a blue-eyed girl
un hombre de buen corazón	a kind-hearted man
un muchacho de pelo rubio	a light-haired boy
una casa de techo empinado	a steep-roofed house
un bote de fondo llano	a flat-bottomed boat
un vestido de mangas largas	a long-sleeved dress
un sombrero de alas anchas	a broad-brimmed hat

REMARK. In some of the above instances the adjective in Spanish may be made to agree with the first noun instead of the second:

un vestido largo de mangas	a long-sleeved dress
un sombrero ancho de alas	a broad-brimmed hat

32.9. Similar expressions are formed with a numeral instead of an adjective:

una espada de dos filos	a two-edged sword
una escopeta de dos cañones	a double-barreled shotgun

un buque de tres palos — a three-masted vessel
una lancha de cuatro remos — a four-oared boat

32.10. When the second part of the compound is a noun denoting material and preceded by **de, con** may be employed instead of **de** to connect it with the noun which it qualifies:

una espada con puño de oro — a gold-hilted sword
un abanico con varillas de marfil — an ivory-handled fan
quevedos con aros de acero — steel-bowed eyeglasses

32.11. When the English expression is composed of an actual past participle preceded by a noun, the Spanish employs a participle followed by **de** and the noun:

sembrado de estrellas — star-spangled
coronado de nieve — snow-capped
cubierto de musgo — moss-covered

REMARK. In naming colors, Spanish uses the noun **color,** which may or may not be preceded by **de,** where English employs the past participle *colored:*[1]

nubes de color de fuego — flame-colored clouds
una cinta color de ratón — a mouse-colored ribbon
un par de guantes color de casca — a pair of tan-colored gloves

32.12. There is, however, a class of compound adjectives (limited in number), composed of a noun followed by an adjective, of which the following will serve as examples:

barbiespeso heavy-bearded — (*from* barba *and* espeso)
barbirrucio grizzly-bearded — (*from* barba *and* rucio)
boquiabierto open-mouthed — (*from* boca *and* abierto)
boquirrubio simple, babbling — (*from* boca *and* rubio)
boquituerto crooked-mouthed — (*from* boca *and* tuerto)
cariacontecido crestfallen — (*from* cara *and* acontecido)
carilargo long-faced — (*from* cara *and* largo)
cejijunto beetle-browed — (*from* ceja *and* junto)
cuellierguido stiff-necked — (*from* cuello *and* erguido)

---

[1] In fact, the phrase with **(de) color (de)** may be omitted, leaving only a noun indicative of color: **terciopelo guinda** *cherry-colored velvet;* **vestiduras violeta** *violet vestments* (Pardo Bazán, **La sirena negra,** V); **ramilletes de flor de un rosa vivo** *clusters of flowers of a bright rose* (or *pink*) *color;* **un ramillo de flores rosa** *a branch of rose-colored* (or *pink*) *flowers* (idem, XIV); **una pareja de guacamayos escarlata** *a pair of scarlet macaws* (Gallegos, **Canaima,** XVI: **Remansos y torrentes**).

ojinegro black-eyed (*from* ojo *and* negro)
patihendido cloven-hoofed (*from* pata *and* hendido)
patimacizo *(the opposite of the above)* solid-hoofed (*from* pata *and* macizo)
patizambo bandy-legged (*from* pata *and* zambo)
pelilargo long-haired (*from* pelo *and* largo)
pelirrubio light-haired (*from* pelo *and* rubio)
perniabierto bowlegged (*from* pierna *and* abierto)
pernituerto crook-shanked (*from* pierna *and* tuerto)
puntiagudo sharp-pointed (*from* punta *and* agudo)

REMARK. Note the modification of the connecting vowel. Also the doubling of the initial **r.** (See § **14.**)

WORDS COMMON TO SPANISH AND ENGLISH

32.13. The English language being largely derived from the Latin and Greek through the medium of one or other of the Romance languages, a large number of words have nearly, and in some cases exactly, the same form and meaning in Spanish and English.

The differences, in the words here referred to, have a certain regularity, the understanding of which will greatly assist the learner.

32.14. The following orthographic peculiarities are to be observed:

Spanish admits of no doubled consonants except **cc** and, in quite a few cases, **nn** (§ **17**) —**ll** not being regarded as a doubled letter, but as the sign for a particular sound; hence *college* = **colegio.** And **cc** occurs only before **e** and **i;** hence *accommodation* = **acomodación.**

The **n** of the prefixes **in** and **con** does not change to *m* before a word beginning with **m,** as is the case in English and Latin; therefore *immersion* = **inmersión;** *immortal* = **inmortal;** *commotion* = **conmoción.**

Qu becomes **cu:** *frequent* = **frecuente;** *consequence* = **consecuencia;** *adequate* = **adecuado.**

The diphthongs *æ* and *œ* become **e:** *Cæsar* = **César;** *diæresis* = **diéresis;** *fœdus* = **feo;** *œstrum* = **estro.**

Initial *s,* followed by a consonant, takes an **e** before it: *sceptic* (or *skeptic*) = **escéptico;** *squadron* = **escuadrón;** *spiral* = **espiral;** *strict* = **estricto.**

The following modifications apply only to words of Greek origin:

Y becomes **i:** *typographic* = **tipográfico;** *sympathy* = **simpatía.**

Ph becomes **f:** *phonography* = **fonografía;** *philosophic* = **filosófico.**

Th and *rh* drop the *h*: *thesis* = **tesis**; *orthographic* = **ortográfico**; *rheumatism* = **reumatismo**; *rhapsody* = **rapsodia.**

Initial *pn, ps*[1] and *pt* drop the *p*: *pneumatic* = **neumático**; *psalmist* = **salmista**; *pterocarpus* = **terocarpo**; *Ptolemaic* = **tolemaico.**

Ch becomes **c** (except before **e** and **i**, when it is represented by **qu**): *anachronism* = **anacronismo**; *characteristic* = **característico**; *chloroform* = **cloroformo**; *choleric* = **colérico.** But, *chelonian* = **queloniano**; *chimera* = **quimera**; *chiromancy* = **quiromancia.**

32.15. The following is a list of the principal terminations common to both languages, embracing, with proper attention to the above orthographic changes, over 5,000 Spanish words:

NOTE. The accentuation is uniform throughout the entire class of words formed with any given termination. Those indicated by an asterisk (*) regularly bear the accent mark on the antepenultimate syllable. The remainder require none, unless one is shown on the termination or in the sample words.

NOUNS

GENDER OF THE CLASS		
m.	ACE	becomes **acio: palacio, prefacio**
f.	ADE	" **ada: brigada, parada**
m.	AGE	" **aje: equipaje, personaje**
m.	AL	no change: **canal, metal, coral**
f.	ANCE / ANCY	become **ancia: abundancia, repugnancia**
m.	ANT	adds **e: litigante, instante**
m.	ARIAN	becomes **ario: centenario, unitario**
m.	ARY	" **ario: adversario, sanctuario**
m.	ATOR	" **ador: orador, regulador**
m.	*CLE	" **culo: círculo, vehículo**
m.	CT	adds **o: contacto, conducto**
f.	CY	becomes **cia: aristocracia, potencia**
f.	ENCE / ENCY	become **encia: violencia, vehemencia**
m.	ENT	adds **e: accidente, regente**
m.	GE	becomes **gio: privilegio, vestigio**
f.	*IC	adds **a: música, lógica, retórica**

[1] The **p** is retained in writing, though not ordinarily pronounced in *psychology* = **psicología**, *psychiatry* = **psiquiatría**, and similar words.

GENDER OF THE CLASS		
m.	ICE	becomes **icio: edificio, servicio**
f.	INE	" **ina: doctrina, disciplina**
f.	ION	(not preceded by *t*) no change: **confusión, religión**
m.	ISK	becomes **isco: asterisco, basilisco**
m.	ISM	adds **o: paganismo, despotismo**
m.	IST	" **a: artista, florista**
m.	MENT	" **o: fragmento, monumento**
f.	MONY	becomes **monia: ceremonia, parsimonia**
m.	OID	adds **e: alcaloide, esferoide**
m.	OR	no change: **actor, horror, vapor**
m.	ORY	becomes **orio: directorio, promontorio**
m.	OT	adds **a: patriota, déspota**
f.	SIS	no change: **crisis, sinopsis**
m.	{ TER / TRE }	become **tro: centro, ministro, pilastro**
m.	TERY	becomes **terio: cauterio, misterio**
f.	TION	" **ción: condición, nación**
f.	TUDE	" **tud: multitud, solitud**
f.	TY	(Latin *tas*) becomes **dad: eternidad, sociedad**
m.	*ULE	becomes **ulo: glóbulo, ridículo**
f.	URE	" **ura: figura, agricultura**
m.	US	" **o: genio, censo, aparato**
m.	UM	" **o: geranio, premio, ateneo, museo**
f.	Y	(not otherwise provided for above) becomes **ía: artillería, energía, geografía, zoología**

ADJECTIVES[1]

ACIOUS	becomes **az: fugaz, sagaz, tenaz**
AL	no change: **moral, central, natural**
AN	adds **o: pagano, americano**
ANEOUS	becomes **áneo: cutáneo, extemporáneo**
ANT	adds **e: abundante, dominante**
AR	no change: **circular, solar**
ARIOUS	becomes **ario: vicario, precario**
ARY	" **ario: ordinario, contrario**
ATE	" **ado: duplicado, ornado**
BLE	no change: **notable, noble, soluble**
CT	adds **o: perfecto, intacto**

[1] Only the masculine singular is given.

ENSE	becomes **enso: denso, inmenso**
ENT	adds **e: evidente, prudente**
FEROUS	becomes **fero: aurífero, carbonífero**
IC } ICAL }	become **ico: público, satírico**
ID	adds **o: tórrido, sólido**
ILE	becomes **il: frágil, dócil**
INE	" **ino: aquilino, felino**
ITE	" **ito: definito, erudito**
IVE	" **ivo: activo, decisivo**
NAL	" **no: diurno, eterno**
ORY	" **orio: preparatorio, satisfactorio**
OSE	" **oso: jocoso, verboso**
OUS	" **oso: luminoso, monstruoso**
TIAL	" **cial: substancial, potencial**
TIONAL	" **cional: condicional, nacional**
ULENT	adds **o: turbulento, virulento**
UND	" **o: moribundo, rubicundo**
URE	becomes **uro: puro, futuro**

VERBS[1]

ATE	becomes **ar: calcular, investigar**
FY	" **ficar: fortificar, magnificar**
IZE	" **izar: civilizar, organizar**
E	A great many verbs of this termination, which come to us through the French, may be turned into Spanish by changing *e* to **ar: determinar, curar, causar, continuar, admirar, combinar, imaginar, observar**, etc., etc.

REMARK. The learner is cautioned against supposing that all English words having the terminations above specified, can be turned into Spanish by the respective changes indicated; or that all words spelled alike in both languages have the same meaning: e.g., Spanish **pan** (Latin *panis*) means *bread;* **red** (Latin *rete*) *a net.*

WORD-MAKING BY DERIVATIVES

32.16. The method of forming new terms by combining two or more known words into one is unusual in Spanish. The richness of that language lies in its power of developing new terms by adding syllables not generally recognizable as separate words. The extent

[1] Only the infinitive is given.

to which this method of word-making obtains in Spanish renders it one of the most conspicuous features of the language, and one of the most difficult to master in all its details.

A syllable attached to the beginning of a word is called a *prefix;* one at the end, a *suffix*. It will be convenient to consider suffixes first.

SUFFIXES

32.17. Derivatives formed by adding terminal syllables may be divided into two classes according to their effect:

1. Those which merely modify the meaning of the word to which they are applied, which remains the same part of speech and applies to the same object.

2. Those which change the word to which they are attached, either in meaning, or from one part of speech to another, or both.

Those of the first class have always an adjectival or adverbial effect, and are attached to nouns, adjectives and participles, and occasionally to adverbs. As they usually indicate size or importance greater or less than normal, they are called respectively *augmentatives* and *diminutives*. However, the force of those called augmentatives is often extended to express ugliness, grotesqueness, coarseness, etc., while diminutives frequently become terms of endearment, or imply insignificance or contemptibility. These secondary values sometimes supplant the expected meanings; but as the forms are the same, it will be convenient to treat all mere modifying terminations as augmentatives and diminutives.

MODIFICATIVE SUFFIXES

32.18. Augmentatives and diminutives are seldom admissible in the graver styles of writing, but are employed profusely in familiar conversation and in light literature. They abound in greater variety in Spanish than in either Portuguese or Italian, although in these languages they are frequent, while in French and English they are comparatively rare.

32.19. Augmentatives and diminutives are formed upon ascertainable principles, so that the learner may become able to form and apply the majority of them at pleasure. They all vary in number, and have a feminine form obtained either by adding **a** to the final consonant of the termination, or by changing the final vowel (**o** or **e**) to **a**:

-ón, -ona	-ito, -ita	-uelo, -uela
-acho, -acha	-illo, -illa	-ín, -ina
-ote, -ota; etc.	-ejo, -eja; etc.	-ete, -eta; etc.

32.20. Augmentative and diminutive terminations are added to the full form of words ending in a consonant or stressed vowel:

mujer, mujer-ota, mujer-ona
animal, animal-ejo, animal-ucho
papá, papa-íto

32.21. A final unstressed vowel is removed before the termination is added:

pequeño, pequeñ-uelo, pequeñ-ito
libro, libr-illo, libr-ote
isla, isl-illa, isl-ote
hombre, hombr-ón, hombr-ecillo

REMARK. If, in removing the final vowel of a diphthong, the remaining vowel is identical with the initial vowel of the termination, one of them is elided:

rubio, rub-ito
rosario, rosar-ito
historia, histor-illa

32.22. The diphthongs **ie** and **ue**, in the stressed syllable of certain words, change to **e** and **o** respectively when the accent is removed by reason of the addition of a termination. But in the case of augmentatives and diminutives modern usage generally retains the diphthong except when the primary word contains more than two syllables:

encuentro, encontrón
valiente, valentón
caliente, calentito
cuévano, covanillo

32.23. With regard to words of one or two syllables containing such diphthongs, the following revert to the primitive vowel; in others the usage varies, but the learner will be safe in retaining the diphthong:

bueno, bonazo, bonachón
buey, boyazo
luengo, longazo
cuerpo, corpanchón
pueblo, poblachón
puerta, portezuela
cueva, covacha
tierno, ternezuelo
ciego, ceguezuelo
viejo, vejezuelo, vejete

32.24. When terminations beginning with **e** or **i** are attached to a word-stem ending in **c, g, gu, z,** these change to **qu, gu, gü, c,** respectively, in order to preserve the sound:

chico, chiquillo, chiquito
frac, fraquecito
pedazo, pedacito
mozo, mocete, mocico
lengua, lengüecita
nuez, nuececita

DIMINUTIVES

32.25. Certain diminutive terminations vary in form to suit the word to which they are to be attached. The changes being uniform in each case, they will be noted by letters:

A	B	C	D
-ito	-cito	-ecito	-ececito
-ico	-cico	-ecico	-ececico
-illo	-cillo	-ecillo	-ececillo
-uelo	-zuelo	-ezuelo	-ecezuelo
-ete	-cete	-ecete	

32.26. Terminations of column *D* are taken only by monosyllables ending in a vowel (excluding y):

pie, pi-ececito, pi-ececico, pi-ecezuelo, pi-ececillo

32.27. Terminations of column *C* are taken by:

1. Monosyllables ending in a consonant or **y:**

red, red-ecilla
flor, flor-ecita
pan, pan-ezuelo
voz, voc-ecita
rey, rey-ezuelo
buey, buey-ecito

EXCEPTION: ruin-cillo

2. Words of two syllables whose first syllable contains one of the diphthongs **ei, ie, ue,** and whose last syllable ends in **a** or **o:**

ciego, ciegu-ecito
cuerda, cuerd-ecilla
cuero, cuer-ezuelo
cuerpo, cuerp-ecito
cuesta, cuest-ecilla
flueco, fluequ-ecillo
grieta, griet-ecilla
hueso, hues-ecillo
huevo, huev-ezuelo
lienzo, lienc-ecito
nieto, niet-ecico
nuevo, nuev-ecito
piedra, piedr-ecita
pueblo, puebl-ezuelo
reina, rein-ecita
rueca, ruequ-ecilla
tiempo, tiemp-ecillo
viejo, viej-ecito
yerba, yerb-ecilla

EXCEPTIONS:

cuesco, cuesqu-illo

juego, juegu-ito

REMARK. **Guerra, guerr-illa,** and **bueno, bon-ito,** can hardly be called exceptions, since the **u** of the former is merely orthographic, and the latter changes its stem.

3. Words of two syllables whose last syllable ends in any of the diphthongs **ia, io, ua:**

bestia, besti-ecita
fragua, fragü-ecilla
genio, geni-ecillo
gracia, graci-ecita
lengua, lengü-ecita
gloria, glori-ecilla

EXCEPTIONS:

agua, agü-ita
pascua, pascu-ita
rubio, rub-ita
agrio, agr-illo

4. All polysyllabic words ending in **e:**

conde, cond-ecito
pobre, pobr-ecillo
duende, duend-ecico
madre, madr-ecita
viaje, viaj-ecillo
aire, air-ecillo

32.28. Terminations of column *B* are taken by polysyllabic words ending in **n** or **r:**

autor, autor-cillo
doctor, doctor-zuelo
salón, salon-cito
joven, joven-cete
ladrón, ladron-zuelo
gabán, gaban-zuelo

EXCEPTIONS:

jardín, jardin-cito *or* -ito
altar, altar-illo *or* -cillo
pilar, pilar-illo *or* -cillo
jazmín, jazmin-illo *or* -cillo
sartén, sarten-illo *or* -cillo
señor, señor-ito
almacén, almacen-illo
alfiler, alfiler-ito
vasar, vasar-illo
serafín, serafin-ito

32.29. Terminations in column *A* are applied to all other words:

silla, sill-ita
almohada, almohad-illa
farol, farol-illo
abuelo, abuel-ito
raíz, raic-illa
pollo, poll-uelo
cuchara, cuchar-ita
pájaro, pajar-ico
cuaderno, cuadern-illo
baúl, baul-ito

EXCEPTIONS:

mano, man-ita *or* -ecita
prado, prad-ecito *and* prad-illo
piel, piel-ecita
llano, llan-ecillo *and* llan-ito

The leading diminutive terminations and their uses are as follows:

-ito, -cito, -ecito

32.30. These diminutives greatly exceed in frequency all the others put together. They form pet names and phrases, and are especially frequent in the conversation of women and children. They convey the idea of *pretty, sweet, dear, nice,* etc., as well as *little;* indeed size is often left out of account. The frequency of their use often becomes abuse in Spanish America (cf. § 32.32). They are therefore not to be applied to anything of an offensive or displeasing nature; but they are sometimes used ironically:

molino de viento; molinito de viento	windmill; toy windwheel
un viejecito; una mujercita	nice little old man; pleasant little woman
unas tajaditas de jamón frío	some nice thin slices of cold ham
Ya entiendo su guasita.	Now I understand his little game.
Me siento un poquito mejor.	I feel a little bit better.
¿Me hace V. el favor de un vasito de agua fresca?	Will you give me a glass of cool water? *(Modest request.)*
De vuelta te daré una gratificacioncita.	When you come back I will give you a gratuity.

32.31. This series of terminations applies to all baptismal names to indicate affection (whether or not connected with smallness), and corresponds to the English ending **-ie** or **-y:**

Carlitos; Juanito; Dieguito	Charley; Johnnie; Jimmie
Anita; Juanita; Pepita	Annie; Jennie; Josie
Inesita; Paquita; Mariquita	Aggie; Fannie; Mamie

32.32. These terminations are not confined to nouns, but may be added to adjectives, participles, adverbs, and indeed almost any kind of words, usually with a favorably intensive effect translatable by *quite, nice and,* etc.:

ahorita, lueguito, prontito	right now, right away, quite soon
cerquita, lejitos, juntito	quite near, some distance off, quite close
ahora mismito	this very minute
¡adiosito! *(South American)*	bye-bye!
¡caracoles calentitos!	snails, nice and hot! *(vendor's cry)*
Es una joven tan graciosita.	She is such a charming girl.
¡Qué simpatiquita es la prima de Vd.!	How pleasant your cousin is!
¡Belita! —Sí, papá, en seguidita.	Belita! —Yes, papa, in a minute.

La joven entró callandito.	The girl came very softly.
Vas a traerme un te hirviendito, hirviendito. (Benavente, **El automóvil**, I, 6)	Bring me a very hot cup of tea, a very hot one.
Lo mismito me sucede a mí.	The very same thing happens to me.
Poquito a poco; pasito a paso.	Little by little; step by step.
Hablemos bajito para que no se enteren esos señores.	Let us speak quite low so that those gentlemen may not overhear us.
Siga V. el corredor, tuerza a la derecha, suba otra escalerilla, y allí enfrentito tiene V. su despacho.	Keep on down the corridor, turn to the right, go up a short flight of steps and you will find his office right before you.

-ico, -cico, -ecico

32.33. This series of forms was originally a common equivalent for the foregoing. Except in dialect (Aragonese), they are now little used, at least in Spain, and then rather sarcastically or ironically; otherwise they have the same value as those preceding:

un angelico	an angel, oh yes
inocentico	innocent, over the left
Allí escuchará Vd. con éxtasi los gorrioncicos, que no le dejan a uno meter baza con su piada sempiterna.	You will listen with rapture to the sweet little sparrows, which won't let a person get in a word edgewise for their interminable chirping.

-illo, -cillo, -ecillo

32.34. Forms in **-illo** in general belittle everything they touch, without implying affection or malice. Things indifferent in quality are merely made smaller; evils are mitigated as of little importance, and virtues depreciated. They indicate a light, careless feeling about persons and things, good or bad, sometimes mingling a little of pity. They apply to nouns, adjectives and participles, but rarely to other parts of speech:

cigarro; cigarrillo	cigar; cigarette
bóveda; bovedilla	vault; small vault
agudo; agudillo	sharp; slightly sharp
campana; campanilla	bell; hand bell
nube; nubecilla	cloud; cloudlet
guerra; guerrilla	war; partisan strife
vara; varilla	rod; small rod
Déme V. una muestrecilla de ese raso.	Give me a small sample of that satin.

Su hermana de V. es una coquetilla.	Your sister is a little coquette.
En cierto lugarcillo de la provincia de Granada.	In a certain small village of the province of Granada.
El picarillo se escapó riendo.	The young rascal ran off laughing.
Estando apuradillo, tuve que solicitar un préstamo.	Being slightly embarrassed, I had to solicit a loan.
No vimos más que unos cuantos chiquillos de escuela.	We saw only a few schoolboys.

-uelo, -zuelo, -ezuelo

32.35. Forms in **-uelo** express contempt, either jestingly or in downright earnest, with or without the idea of smallness. They are but little used and apply almost exclusively to nouns:

una coquetuela	a vain coquette
la plazuela de San Miguel	St. Michael's square
arroyuelo; riachuelo	brooklet; rivulet
puerta; portezuela	door; carriage door
plancha; planchuela	smoothing iron; fluting iron
pintorzuelo	wretchedly bad artist
Sentía posarse sobre mí sus ojos pequeñuelos y malignos.	I felt his small, malicious eyes fixed upon me.
Gastaba una mantilla de tafetán con lentejuelas.	She wore a dotted silk veil.
Sus ojuelos, siempre vivos, parecían bailar ahora arrebatadamente.	His small eyes, always bright, seemed now to dance unrestrainedly.

Remark. When applied to words of more than one syllable which end in two vowels, the letter **h** or, in the speech of the untaught, the sound of **g** is inserted after removing the final one; when, however, the words end in **nio,** the **i** of the diphthong is absorbed by changing the **n** to **ñ:**

aldea hamlet
aldehuela, **aldegüela** } wretched hamlet
correa strap
correhuela, **corregüela** } small strap

fea, **feahuela** } ugly
Antonio, Antoñuelo
demonio, demoñuelo

-ete, -cete, -ecete

32.36. These forms are applied to a few nouns in a diminutive, and sometimes depreciative, sense:

burleta little trick
luneta lunette
clavete little nail, tack
historieta short story

lugarete small village
caballerete dude, dandy
placeta small [public] square
manteleta a small cape
pichelete a small pitcher

Gloria gozaba en hacer jugarretas a todo el mundo. — Gloria enjoyed playing practical jokes on everybody.

-ejo

32.37. This form is usually applied to nouns ending in **l** or **n,** and denotes decided contempt, sometimes indicating smallness also:

caballejo nag
papelejo scrap of paper
camellejo small camel
regalejo mean gift
el oficialejo, el alguacilejo — this officer, this constable (in contempt)

-ín, -ino and -iño

32.38. These diminutive endings are local or dialectic, **-ín** being Asturian, **-ino** common to Estremadura, and **-iño** a native of Galicia corresponding to the Portuguese *-inho,* which is pronounced the same. They are used in a limited degree in Castilian to denote smallness, and very generally modify the meaning of the primitive word:

chico; chiquitín	little one; baby
espada; espadín	sword; short sword
calabaza; calabacín	pumpkin; small pumpkin
espuela; espolín	spur; small spur
fuerte; fortín	fort; small fort
langosta; langostino	lobster; shrimp
paloma; palomino	dove; pigeon
cuerpo; corpiño	body; bodice

32.39. The termination **-ino** applies principally to young plants:

cebolla; cebollino	onion; young onion
col; colino	cabbage; young cabbage
lechuga; lechuguino	lettuce; young lettuce
puerro; porrino	leek; young leek

AUGMENTATIVES

The principal augmentatives and their applications are the following:

-ón, fem. -ona

32.40. Denotes large size, or an increased degree of a quality, and sometimes adds the idea of clumsiness or grotesqueness. Feminine nouns generally assume the masculine termination, unless *sex* is to be indicated:

silla; sillón	chair; easy chair
cuchara; cucharón	spoon; ladle
zagal; zagalón	lad; strapping young fellow
hombre; hombrón	man; big man
salchicha; salchichón	sausage; pudding
soltero; solterón	single man; old bachelor
soltera; solterona	unmarried woman; old maid
embustero; embusterón	liar; big liar, "Ananias"
zapatos; zapatones	shoes; big shoes, "gunboats"
noticia; notición	news; big news
No fué posible dormir, porque una plaga de moscas, moscones y mosquitos formaban a nuestros oídos un alegre terceto.	It was impossible to sleep, for a scourge of flies, bluebottles and mosquitoes formed a pleasant trio to our ears.

REMARK. In a few words **-ón** has a diminutive value:

ala; alón	wing; wing without feathers
carreta; carretón	cart; small cart
calle; callejón	street; narrow passage, alley
pluma; plumón	feather; down
torre; torreón, torrejón	tower; turret
cerro; cerrejón	hill; hillock
cáscara; cascarón	husk; rind, eggshell
planta; plantón	plant; scion, shoot
rata; ratón	rat; mouse
volantón	fledgling, young bird just able to fly

-azo, -aza

32.41. Has a value similar to **-ón,** but is less frequent. The gender of the termination corresponds to that of the noun to which the termination is applied:

buey; boyazo	ox; big ox
hombre; hombrazo	man; large man
libro; librazo	book; big book
luengo; longazo	long; "awfully" long
pícaro; picarazo	rogue; great rogue
perro; perrazo	dog; big dog

-ote, fem. -ota

32.42. **-Ote** is at times merely augmentative, but usually depreciative:

calabaza; calabazota	pumpkin; large pumpkin
palabra; palabrota	word; "cuss word"
franco; francote	frank; plain, ingenuous
manga; mangote	sleeve; large sleeve
feo; feote	ugly; "perfect fright"
libro; librote	book; ponderous old tome
pícaro; picarote	rascal; notorious rascal
discurso; discursote	speech; long-winded speech

REMARK. In a few words **-ote** has a diminutive value:

isla; islote	island; islet
cámara; camarote	chamber; [ship's] cabin
ancla; anclote	anchor; kedge anchor
palo; palote	stick, timber; drumstick
pipa; pipote	cask; firkin

-ajo

32.43. A termination of contempt, indicating meanness or extravagance in the quality of the primitive noun:

bebistrajo extravagant mixture of drinks
colgajo tatters
comistrajo extravagant mixture of viands
escobajo stump of a broom
espantajo scarcecrow
latinajo dog-Latin
terminajo low expression
pintarrajo "daub"
trapajo dirty rag

-acho and -ucho

32.44. These are purely depreciative, expressing poor quality of what is represented by the noun, or contempt or disdain felt for it:

cuarto; cuartucho	room; miserable, close room
vino; vinacho	wine; poor wine, slops
pico; picacho	peak; sharp point
rico; ricacho	rich; very rich
caldo; calducho	broth; weak broth
casa; casucha	house; shanty
sierra; serrucha	saw; dull, worthless saw
blanco; blancucho	white; dirty white
animal; animalucho	animal; ugly animal

flaco; flacucho	thin; flabby
papel; papelucho	paper; a contemptible paper *or* writing
término; terminacho	term; low term
vulgo; vulgacho	populace; dregs of the people
el populacho; un mamarracho	the masses; a botch
cogucho; meladucha	inferior sugar; a poor variety of apple

-uco, -uca

32.45. This termination is also purely depreciative; it is applied to a few nouns only in the standard language, though it is relatively frequent in the dialect of the region of Santander, where it is not necessarily unflattering:

carro; carruco	cart; a kind of small cart
casa; casuca	house; hovel
fraile; frailuco	friar; despicable friar
beata; beatuca	woman who wears a religious habit; vile hypocrite
hermano; hermanuco	brother; contemptuous term for a member of a religious order

NOTE. Depreciative too and not very frequent in the written language is **-ujo, -uja,** applied to adjectives and occasionally to nouns: **blandujo** *somewhat soft, softish;* **calentujo** *somewhat warm, warmish;* **granujo** *pimple.*

32.46. The following endings are irregularly applied, or of so rare occurrence that they need not be classified:

voz; vozarrón	voice; stentorian voice
viento; ventarrón	wind; violent wind
nube; nubarrón	cloud; threatening cloud (nimbus)
santo; santurrón	saint; bogus saint, hypocrite
bobo; bobarrón	dunce; booby
bobalías; bobalicón	dolt; great blockhead
viejo; vejancón	old; decrepit
cuerpo; corpanchón	body; carcass
lámpara; lampión	lamp; Japanese lantern
nariz; narigón	nose; big nose
raíz; raigón	root; snag
vivo; vivaracho	live; sprightly, frisky
ave; avechucho	bird; sparrow hawk
gente; gentuza; gentualla	people; low people, rabble
carne; carnuza	meat; bad meat
libro; libraco	book; bad book

pájaro; pajarraco	bird; ungainly bird
dinero; dineral	money; large sum of money
hoyo; hoyanco	pit; large pit
hueso; huesarrón	bone; large bone
paja; pajuzo; pajuz	straw; rotted straw; straw manure
aldea; aldeorro, aldeorrio	village; insignificant, rambling hamlet
boda; bodorrio	marriage; bad match
cepa; ceporro	grapevine; runt, vine stump
venta; ventorro	inn; poor tavern
villa; villorrio	town; "one-horse" town
cueva; covacha	cave; grotto, small cave
hilo; hilacha	thread; ravelling

32.47. Combinations of augmentative and diminutive terminations are not uncommon, the value being cumulative:

-ito with **-ito**

chico; chiquitito	little; teeny-weeny
poco; poquitito	a little; a tiny bit

-illo with **-ón**

grande; grandillón	big; quite biggish
pícaro; picarillón	rascal; large man who is somewhat of a rascal

-ón with **-illo**

pícaro; picaroncillo	rascal; small person who is a great rascal

-ete with **-ón**

guapo; guapetón	good-looking; very good-looking
mozo; mocetón	lad; corpulent, overgrown boy
pobre; pobretón	poor; poor old duffer

-ejo with **-ón**

calle; callejón	street; passage between walls
piedra; pedrejón	stone; large, loose stone

-acho with **-ón**

fresco; frescachón	fresh; florid, healthy (applied to person)
bueno; bonachón	good; good-humored, easy-going
fuerte; fortachón	strong; powerful
pueblo; poblachón	village; large village

-ón with **-azo**

borracho; borrachonazo	drunkard; inveterate drunkard
hombre; hombronazo	man; big, hulking, lubberly man
bergante; bergantonazo	scoundrel; villain of the deepest dye

REMARK. As a concluding example, the following may be made from **chico,** the various gradations of smallness being untranslatable in English:

chiquito	chicuelo	chiquirritín
chiquitillo	chiquillito	chiquirritito
chiquitito	chiquilluelo	chiquirritillo
chiquitín	chiquituelo	chiquirrituelo
chiquillo	chiquitilluelo	

32.48. The diminutive forms of baptismal names, such as are applied to children, near relations and intimate friends, are very irregular. Most noticeable are a number of shortened or abbreviated forms, some of which bear but little resemblance to the original (cf. Appendix I, 1):

Catalina (Catharine)	Catana, Catanla, Catuja
Cristóbal (Christopher)	Tobal
Francisco (Francis)	Frasco, Paco, Pacho, Pacorro, Pancho, Curro, Farruco
Isabel (Isabel, Elizabeth)	Belisa
José (Joseph)	Pepe, Chepe
María (Mary)	Maruca, Maruja
María de la Concepción	Concepción, Concha, Chona, Cota
María de los Dolores	Dolores, Lola
María de Jesús	Jesusa, Chucha
Pedro (Peter)	Perucho, Perico

32.49. Both the full forms and these shortened forms may receive the ordinary diminutive terminations **-ito, -ico, -illo** and **-uelo,** according to the sentiment to be conveyed. In the following cases they deviate, in the manner of their application, from the principles laid down in §§ 32.25-32.29:

José, Josefito	María, Mariquita
Antonio, Antoñito	Juan, Juanito
Diego, Dieguito	Emilio, Emillito

REMARK. It may be observed that if the original name ends in **s,** that letter is added to the diminutive form:

Carlos, Carlitos	Dolores, Dolorcitas

32.50. The names of the young of animals are sometimes formed by the addition of a diminutive termination, but are more usually expressed by a different word, from which a diminutive of secondary growth is often formed by the addition of **-illo** or **-ito.** The principal terms are given below:

caballo horse **yegua** mare	**potro, potrillo** colt
buey **toro**	**ternero** calf **novillo** bullock **utrero** two-year-old steer
vaca cow	**ternera** heifer **utrera** two-year-old heifer
oveja sheep	**cordero, corderillo** lamb, lambkin **borrego** two-year-old lamb
cabro *(Americanism)* goat	**cabrito, chivato, chivatillo** kid
cerdo pig, hog	**lechón, lechoncillo** young pig
jabalí wild boar	**jabato** wild pig
corzo deer	**corcino** fawn
liebre hare	**liebrastón, lebrato, lebratillo** leveret
gato cat	**gatito, gatita** kitten
león **tigre** **perro** **lobo** *and other carnivora*	**cachorro, cachorrillo** puppy, cub
ballena whale	**ballenato** young whale
ave fowl	**pollo, polluelo** chicken, pullet
pavo turkey	**pavipollo** turkey chick
ánade, pato duck	**anadino, anadón** duckling
ánsar, ganso goose	**ansarino** gosling
paloma pigeon, dove	**palomino** young pigeon
paloma casera domestic pigeon	**pichón** squab
perdiz partridge	**perdigón** young partridge
águila eagle	**aguilucho** eaglet
cigüeña stork	**cigoñino** young stork
rana frog	**ranacuajo, renacuajo** young frog
víbora viper	**viborezno** young viper

32.51. Some diminutive and augmentative terms, by being habitually applied to particular objects, have become accepted as their especial designations and are to be considered as independent words:

palo stick — **palillo** rolling pin
manzana apple — **manzanilla** camomile
mármol marble — **marmolejo** marble column
papel paper — **papelitos** curlpapers
paja straw — **pajuela** lucifer match
cera wax — **cerilla** wax match, vesta
laguna marsh — **lagunajo** pool of water after a rain

Remark I. There are many words whose endings have the appearance of augmentative or diminutive terminations, but nevertheless are not suffixes:

abrazo embrace
espejo mirror
jigote hash
pabellón pavilion
garlito snare, trap
colmillo tusk
botica apothecary's shop
pachón pointer dog

Remark II. The only true augmentatives and diminutives are those formed by the addition of a termination to a word now in use in the language. Words which were augmentatives or diminutives in Latin, and those whose augmentative or diminutive formation is a matter of antiquarian research, are to be considered as independent words. The following will serve as examples of what is meant:

abanico fan (Latin, *vannus)*
corazón heart (Latin, *cor)*
glóbulo globule (Latin, *globulus)*
mejilla cheek (Latin, *maxilla)*
castillo castle (Latin, *castellum)*

TRANSFORMATIVE SUFFIXES

32.52. We have now to treat of suffixes which serve to form new words, changing the word to which they are attached, either in meaning or from one part of speech to another, or both; somewhat as in English we make from *hand, handle, handy, handiness, handsome.* The class is so large and irregular that the author can undertake to present only a general illustration of its uses which will enable the learner to understand most derivatives when he meets with them, and to gain an insight into this principal source of richness of the Spanish language.

32.53. The expansion of the vowels **e, o,** into the diphthongs **ie, ue,** under the stress, which has already been alluded to (§§ **12, 8.53**), plays a noticeable part in the formation of these derivatives, as well as in the forms taken in Spanish by words directly inherited from the Latin:

LATIN	WITH STRESS	WITHOUT STRESS
bonum	**bueno** good	**bondad** goodness
corpus	**cuerpo** body	**corpudo** thick-set, stout
dentem	**diente** tooth	**dentedura** set of teeth
ferrum	**hierro** iron	**herrumbre** iron rust
herbam	**yerba** grass	**herbajar** to graze
mortem	**muerte** death	**mortandad** massacre
novum	**nuevo** new	**novedad** newness, novelty
os	**hueso** bone	**osamenta** skeleton
pontem	**puente** bridge	**pontaje** toll
sortem	**suerte** luck, lot	**sorteo** drawing by lot
tempus	**tiempo** time	**temprano** timely, early
ventum	**viento** wind	**ventana** window

REMARK. These mutations are not universal, and their practical application can be learned only as words are learned. So much may be stated, however, that the change is almost wholly restricted to those words derived directly from the Latin, and that with regard to the formation of derivatives from simple words, where the principle applies to one derivative, it also applies to all others from the same word.

NOTE. Those terminations derived from Latin which are also found in English with little or no change of form, have already been given in §§ 32.13-32.15 and need not be repeated except where some peculiarity of usage is to be noted.

32.54. We will now consider the principal suffixes in their alphabetical order:

-ada

a. Forms derivatives denoting the capacity or duration of what is expressed by the primitive noun:

carreta wagon	**carretada** wagonload
cesta basket	**cestada** basketful
cuchara spoon	**cucharada** spoonful
horno oven	**hornada** ovenful, batch (of bread)
mano hand	**manada** handful
mes month	**mesada** month's pay
pala shovel	**palada** shovelful
pluma pen	**plumada de tinta** penful of ink
tiempo time	**temporada** space of time, season
tonel cask, tun	**tonelada** tun *or* ton *(originally the same)*

b. Expresses a collection of a number of individuals or things of the same class:

arma arm, weapon	**armada** navy, fleet
buey ox	**boyada** drove of oxen
caballo horse	**cabalgada** raid, cavalcade
caña cane	**cañada** canebrake
estaca stake	**estacada** stockade, picket fence
perro dog	**perrada** pack of dogs
toro bull	**torada** drove of bulls
vaca cow	**vacada** drove of cows

c. Denotes a stroke or thrust, usually with a cutting or pointed instrument:

andana tier of guns	**andanada** broadside
boca mouth	**dar las últimas boqueadas** to give one's last gasp
cuchillo knife	**cuchillada** gash with a knife
lanza lance	**lanzada** lance-thrust
martillo hammer	**martillada** blow with a hammer
pierna leg	**pernada** fling of the leg in dancing
pluma pen	**plumada** stroke of a pen, dash
puñal dagger	**puñalada** stab

-ada, -ida

A feminine form of the past participial ending, forms nouns expressing the completed action of the verbs from which they are derived—usually verbs of motion:[1]

entrar to enter	**entrada** entrance, entry
ir to go	**ida** going
llegar to arrive	**llegada** arrival
morar to dwell, abide	**morada** dwelling, abode, stay
partir to depart	**partida** departure
retirar to withdraw, retreat	**retirada** retreat, retirement
venir to come	**venida** coming

[1] The formation of such nouns (with verbs of any meaning) and their use with common verbs like **dar, echar** and **pegar,** as a substitute for the original verb is a trait of popular speech in Spanish America especially: **—¡Eduardito! —grita entonces el joven, dejándose caer del caballo, que pega una espantada.** (Lynch, **Los caranchos de la Florida,** V) *"Edward," the young man then shouts, falling from his horse, which started.*

-ado

An extension of the use of the participial termination. Applied to nouns, forms adjectives expressing resemblance to what is designated by the primitive:

concha shell	**conchado** conchoidal, shell-like
corazón heart	**acorazonado** cordate, heart-shaped
lagarto lizard	**alagartado** variegated like a lizard
lechuga lettuce	**lechugado** having leaves like the lettuce
luna moon	**lunado** shaped like the half-moon
naranja orange	**naranjado** orange-colored
sierra saw	**serrado** saw-toothed

-ado, -ato

Form derivative nouns expressing offices and dignities, and the district or jurisdiction of the same:

arzobispo archbishop	**arzobispado** archbishopric
cardenal cardinal	**cardenalato** cardinalate
conde count	**condado** county
deán dean	**deanato** deanery
decano senior member	**decanato** dignity of senior
elector elector	**electorado** electorate
general general	**generalato** generalate, generalship
juez judge	**juzgado** judicature
papa pope	**papado** papacy
superior manager, superior	**superiorato** office of manager or superior

-ador, -edor, -idor

Applied to the stems of verbs, form nouns denoting a person who performs the action of the verb, or adjectives expressing custom:

abrazar to grasp	**abrazador** thieftaker
alborotar to disturb the peace	**alborotador** rioter; riotous
amenazar to threaten	**amenazador** one who threatens; threatening
beber to drink	**bebedor** toper
curtir to tan, dress hides	**curtidor** tanner
dar to give	**dador** giver
hablar to talk	**hablador** chatterer; talkative
trabajar to work	**trabajador** assiduous
tragar to swallow	**tragador** gluttonous

-aje

a. Forms derivative nouns expressing a fee or payment connected with the primitive noun:

almacén warehouse	**almacenaje** warehouse rent
cárcel prison	**carcelaje** jailer's fees
carreta wagon, cart	**carretaje** cartage
fogón hearth	**fogaje** hearth money
horno oven	**hornaje** money paid to bakers for private baking
[**hostel** *(obs.)* inn]	**hostelaje** hotel bill
muelle quay, wharf	**muellaje** quayage, wharfage
piloto pilot	**pilotaje** pilotage
puente bridge	**pontaje** bridge toll

b. Is used with a value approaching that of the English *-age* in forming derivative nouns—usually collective:

almena turret	**almenaje** series of turrets
ancla anchor	**anclaje** anchorage
blindar to armor-plate	**blindaje** armor-plating
bosque wood	**boscaje** boscage
correa strap	**correaje** lot of straps
fardo bundle	**fardaje** luggage, number of bundles
hierro iron	**herraje** ironwork
huésped guest, boarder	**hospedaje** board and lodging
lengua language	**lenguaje** manner of speech
marear to navigate a ship	**mareaje** art of navigating
marino mariner	**marinaje** seamanship
ventana window	**ventanaje** series of windows
yerba grass	**herbaje** herbage

-al

Forms derivatives denoting a collection of what is expressed by the primitive noun, or the place where it is found in abundance:

arena sand	**arenal** sandy ground
ceniza ashes	**cenizal** ash heap
chaparro scrub oak	**chaparral** brush, thicket
ciprés cypress	**cipresal** cypress grove
guijarro pebble, gravel	**guijarral** heap of gravel; place abounding in pebbles
junco rush	**juncal** place overgrown with rushes
mezquite mesquite	**mezquital** mesquite forest
naranjo orange tree	**naranjal** orange grove

pimiento pepper	**pimental** pepper plantation
plátano banana tree	**platanal** banana grove
romero rosemary	**romeral** bed of rosemary
salitre saltpetre	**salitral** nitrate bed
zarza bramble	**zarzal** bramble thicket

-anza

Added to the stems of verbs, forms abstract verbal nouns:

holgar to cease work	**holganza** repose, recreation
labrar to till	**labranza** tillage, husbandry
matar to kill	**matanza** slaughter
mezclar to mix	**mezclanza** mixture
mudar to change	**mudanza** change
tardar to delay	**tardanza** delay
templar to temper, moderate	**templanza** mildness, moderation
vengar to avenge	**venganza** vengeance

-ar

Forms derivatives denoting a collection of what is expressed by the primitive noun, or the place where it is found in abundance:

cebolla onion	**cebollar** bed of onions
colmena beehive	**colmenar** collection of beehives
lino flax	**linar** field of flax
manzano apple tree	**manzanar** apple orchard
melón melon	**melonar** melon patch
olivo olive tree	**olivar** olive orchard
paja straw	**pajar** straw loft
palma palm tree	**palmar** palm grove
paloma dove, pigeon	**palomar** dovecote, pigeon house
pino pine tree	**pinar** pine grove
sal salt	**salar** salt pan
teja tile	**tejar** tile works

-ario

a. Applied to nouns, forms derivatives denoting the place where a quantity of what is expressed by the primitive is kept:

campana bell	**campanario** belfry, steeple
hueso (Lat. *os*) bone	**osario** bone yard, charnel house
reliquia relic	**relicario** reliquary
[**sacro** sacred]	**sagrario** church receptacle for sacred utensils

yerba (Lat. *herba*) herb, plant	**herbario** herbarium
antífona anthem	**antifonario**
devoción prayer	**devocionario**
dicción word, expression	**diccionario**
ejemplo copy, pattern	**ejemplario**
epístola epistle, letter	**epistolario**

(antifonario, devocionario, diccionario, ejemplario, epistolario: Books containing collections of what is denoted by the primitive noun)

b. Applied to nouns and to the stems of verbs, forms derivatives expressing the person interested in some transaction:

arrendar to let for rent	**arrendatario** lessee
beneficiar to benefit	**beneficiario** beneficiary
censo instrument granting an annuity	**censatario** one who pays an annuity
cesión cession, transfer	**cesionario** assignee, transferee
concesión grant	**concesionario** grantee
consignar to consign, intrust	**consignatario** consignee, trustee
legar to bequeath	**legatario** legatee
mandar to order	**mandatario** agent, attorney
renunciar to give up, turn over to	**renunciatario** one to whom anything is resigned
uso use	**usuario** who has the sole use of anything

-astro

a. Which appears in a few English words as *-aster,* expresses inferiority or pretense:

cama bed	**camastro** poor truckle bed
crítico critic	**criticastro** pretended critic
filósofo philosopher	**filosofastro** philosophaster
poeta poet	**poetastro** poetaster
político politician	**politicastro** petty wirepuller

b. It also applies to certain degrees of relationship between persons who do not usually display much affection for each other:

hermanastro stepbrother	**hermanastra** stepsister
hijastro stepson	**hijastra** stepdaughter
padrastro stepfather	**madrastra** stepmother

-azgo

Forms derivatives expressing the office, function or jurisdiction of the person designated by the primitive noun:

albacea executor	**albaceazgo** executorship

alguacil constable	**alguacilazgo** constableship
almirante admiral	**almirantazgo** admiralty
compadre godfather	**compadrazgo** gossipred
hermano brother	**hermanazgo** brotherhood, fraternity
mayor senior	**mayorazgo** right of primogeniture, possessor of the right of primogeniture
padrino godfather	**padrinazgo** compaternity
patrón patron	**patronazgo** patronship
primo cousin	**primazgo** cousinship
villa town	**villazgo** charter of a town

-azo

Forms derivatives denoting a stroke or wound with the object designated by the primitive noun:

bala ball, bullet	**balazo** shot wound
bomba bomb, shell	**bombazo** explosion of a shell
codo elbow	**codazo** dig with the elbow
flecha arrow	**flechazo** arrow wound
garrote cudgel, club	**garrotazo** cudgelling, blow with club
hacha axe	**hachazo** blow, stroke with an axe
látigo whip	**latigazo** lash with a whip
puño fist	**puñetazo** blow with the fist
sable saber	**sablazo** saber cut
vara rod	**varazo** stroke with a rod
ventana window	**ventanaza** slap of a window
zapato shoe	**zapatazo** blow with a shoe

-dero

a. Applied to the stems of verbs, expresses locality for performing the action expressed by the primitive:

derrumbar to precipitate	**derrumbadero** precipice
desembarcar to land	**desembarcadero** landing place
fondear to cast anchor	**fondeadero** anchoring ground
lavar to wash	**lavadero** washing place
matar to kill	**matadero** slaughter house
picar to spur	**picadero** riding school
rebosar to overflow	**rebosadero** place of overflow

b. Added to stems of verbs, forms adjectives expressing fitness to perform or to undergo the action of the verb:

casar to marry	**casadero** marriageable
cobrar to collect [a debt]	**cobradero** collectible
cocer to boil	**cocedero** easily boiled
comer to eat	**comedero** eatable
contar to count	**contadero** numerable
crecer to grow	**crecedero** capable of growing
dividir to divide	**dividero** divisible
durar to last	**duradero** lasting, durable
hacer to do	**hacedero** practicable, feasible
pagar to pay	**pagadero** payable
perecer to perish	**perecedero** perishable

-dizo

Added to the stem of verbs, forms adjectives indicating susceptibility to the action expressed by the primitive:

beber to drink	**bebedizo** fit to drink
brincar to jump, leap	**brincadizo** which may be jumped over (e.g., a ditch)
caer to fall	**caedizo** ready to fall; deciduous
cerrar to close, lock	**cerradizo** which may be locked or fastened
comprar to buy	**compradizo** purchasable, venal
helar to freeze	**heladizo** which may be frozen
regar to water, irrigate	**regadizo** susceptible of irrigation
serrar to saw	**serradizo** fit to be sawed *(appl. to timber)*

-dumbre

Forms abstract nouns from adjectives:

cierto certain	**certidumbre** certitude
dulce sweet	**dulcedumbre** sweetness
grave grave	**gravedumbre** gravity
manso meek	**mansedumbre** meekness
mucho much	**muchedumbre** crowd
pesado wearisome, sad	**pesadumbre** weariness, sadness
podre pus, matter	**podredumbre** putridity, corruption
sal salt	**salsedumbre** saltiness
siervo slave, servant	**servidumbre** state of servitude; corps of servants

-dura

a. Added to nouns, forms derivatives denoting a set of whatever is expressed by the primitive:

botón button	**botonadura** set of buttons
broche hook	**brochadura** set of hooks and eyes
diente tooth	**dentadura** set of teeth

b. Added to verbs, forms nouns expressing the result of the action of the primitive:

acepillar to plane	**acepilladura** act of planing **cepilladuras** shavings
aserrar to saw	**aserradura** sawing, saw cut **aserraduras** sawdust
barrer to sweep	**barreduras** sweepings
cortar to cut	**cortadura** cut, gash
picar to puncture, prick	**picadura** puncture, bite (of insect)
quemar to burn	**quemadura** burn
rascar to scratch	**rascadura** scratch

-ear

Applied to nouns or to the stems of verbs, forms derivative verbs with generally a frequentative value:

baladrón braggart, bully	**baladronear** to act the bully
bodegón low saloon	**bodegonear** to frequent low saloons
borracho drunkard	**borrachear** to be often drunk
borrón blot	**borronear** to waste paper
garrapato pot hook	**garrapatear** to scrawl, scribble
haragán idler, loafer	**haraganear** to idle, loaf
hoja leaf	**hojear** to turn the leaves of a book
hurón ferret	**huronear** to ferret, pry into
husmo scent	**husmear** to scent, snuff
tecla piano key	**teclear** to finger the keys
ventana window	**ventanear** to be always at the window

-eda, -edo

Form nouns denoting the place where a thing grows:

acebo holly	**acebedo** grove of holly trees
álamo poplar	**alameda** grove of poplars, avenue
aliso alder	**aliseda** alder thicket
árbol tree	**arboleda** grove
castaño chestnut tree	**castañedo** grove of chestnut trees

fresno ash tree	**fresneda** grove of ash trees
olmo elm	**olmeda** grove of elm trees
peral pear tree	**peraleda** pear orchard
sauce (Lat. *salicem*) willow	**salceda** grove of willows
viña vineyard	**viñedo** vine-raising district

-eño

Forms adjectives expressing resemblance:

agraz verjuice	**agraceño** acrid, sour
águila eagle	**aguileño** aquiline
guijarro cobblestone	**guijarreño** cobbly
guijo gravel	**guijeño** gravelly
halagar to attract, allure	**halagüeño** attractive
pedir to beg	**pedigüeno** importunate
ribera bank, shore	**ribereño** riparian, pertaining to or dwelling upon the banks of a river or the seashore
risa laughter	**risueño** laughing, smiling
roca rock	**roqueño** rocky
trigo wheat	**trigueño** swarthy (color of wheat)

-eo

Forms nouns from the verbs in **-ear:**

cabecear to nod the head	**cabeceo** nod of the head
cañonear to cannonade	**cañoneo** cannonade
cuchichear to whisper	**cuchicheo** whisper
gimotear to cry frequently without cause	**gimoteo** frequent, causeless crying; whimpering
pestañear to wink	**pestañeo** winking
pisotear to trample	**pisoteo** trampling, stamping
rodear to go around	**rodeo** detour, evasion

-era

Forms derivatives expressing an article for containing what is expressed by the primitive noun:

carta letter	**cartera** portfolio
ensalada salad	**ensaladera** salad dish
leche milk	**lechera** milk pitcher
mostaza mustard	**mostacera** mustard pot
papel paper	**papelera** letter pad
ponche punch	**ponchera** punch bowl

sombrero hat — **sombrerera** hatbox
sopa soup — **sopera** soup tureen
tabaco tobacco — **tabaquera** tobacco pouch
vinagre vinegar — **vinagrera** vinegar cruet

-ero

a. Added to nouns, forms derivatives denoting the place for containing what is expressed by the primitive noun:

azúcar sugar	**azucarero** sugar bowl
chivato kid	**chivetero** kidfold
grano grain	**granero** granary
lápiz pencil	**lapicero** pencil case
pimienta pepper	**pimentero** pepper box
sal salt	**salero** saltcellar
tinta ink	**tintero** inkstand

b. Applied to nouns, forms derivatives indicating the proprietor or person in charge of what is expressed by the primitive:

cabra goat	**cabrero** goatherd
cárcel jail	**carcelero** jailer
coche coach	**cochero** coachman
dehesa pasture ground	**dehesero** keeper of a pasture ground
escudo shield	**escudero** shield-bearer, squire
ganado herd, cattle	**ganadero** drover, cattle owner
molino mill	**molinero** miller
rancho ranch	**ranchero** owner of a ranch
vaca cow	**vaquero** cowherd, cowboy
venta tavern	**ventero** tavern keeper
yegua mare	**yegüero** keeper of brood mares

c. Forms derivative adjectives from nouns:

cerro hill	**cerrero** running wild *(appl. to animals)*
chanza joke, jest	**chancero** jocose, sportful
guerra war	**guerrero** warlike
mar sea	**viento marero** sea breeze
pasaje passage	**pasajero** transitory, fleeting **ave pasajera** bird of passage
pendencia lawsuit	**pendenciero** litigious
rastro track, trail	**planta rastrera** creeping plant
ventura chance, casualty	**venturero** fortuitous, casual

d. Applied to articles of commerce, forms nouns denoting the dealers in those articles, or manufacturers of them:

alfar pottery	**alfarero** potter
cerveza beer	**cervecero** brewer
cuchillo knife	**cuchillero** cutler
guante glove	**guantero** glover
hojalata tin plate	**hojalatero** tinner, tinsmith
joya jewel	**joyero** jeweller
libro book	**librero** bookseller
pastel pie	**pastelero** pastry cook
plomo lead	**plomero** plumber
quincalla hardware	**quincallero** hardware dealer
reloj watch, clock	**relojero** watchmaker, clockmaker
vidrio glass	**vidriero** glazier, glassmaker
zapato shoe	**zapatero** shoemaker

REMARK. By adding **-ía** to the above derivatives, we obtain a secondary set denoting (1) the shop or place of business, and (2) the trade or business, of the person in question:

alfarero:	**alfarería** potter's shop; pottery trade
cervecero:	**cervecería** brewery
cuchillero:	**cuchillería** cutlery store
guantero:	**guantería** glove store; glove trade
librero:	**librería** bookstore; book trade
plomero:	**plomería** plumber's shop; plumbing trade
quincallero:	**quincallería** hardware store; hardware trade
relojero:	**relojería** clockmaker's shop; clock trade
vidriero:	**vidrería** glazier's shop, glass foundry
zapatero:	**zapatería** shoemaker's shop, shoe store; shoe trade

-ez

Forms abstract nouns from adjectives:

altivo haughty	**altivez** haughtiness
árido arid	**aridez** aridity
brillante bright	**brillantez** brightness
doble double	**doblez** duplicity
flúido fluid; fluent	**fluidez** fluidity; fluency
honrado honest	**honradez** honesty
impávido intrepid	**impavidez** intrepidity
lóbrego murky, dark	**lobreguez** murkiness, obscurity
maduro ripe	**madurez** ripeness, maturity
mudo dumb, mute	**mudez** dumbness

nítido lustrous — **nitidez** luster
pequeño small, little — **pequeñez** smallness, littleness
sencillo simple — **sencillez** simplicity

-eza

Forms abstract nouns from adjectives:

alto high — **alteza** highness
cierto certain — **certeza** certainty
grande great — **grandeza** greatness
ligero light — **ligereza** lightness
limpio clean, cleanly — **limpieza** cleanness, cleanliness
puro pure — **pureza** purity
triste sad — **tristeza** sorrow

-iento

Forms adjectives expressing resemblance:

avaro covetous — **avariento** miserly
calentura fever — **calenturiento** feverish, fevered
ceniza ashes — **ceniciento** ash-colored
hambre hunger — **hambriento** famished, hungry
polvo dust — **polvoriento** dusty
sed thirst — **sediento** thirsty
sudor sweat — **sudoriento** sweaty

-ino

Added to nouns, forms adjectives expressing resemblance:

alabastro alabaster — **alabastrino** *(poet.)* like alabaster
ámbar amber — **ambarino** like amber
azul blue — **azulino** sky blue
blanco white — **blanquecino** whitish
ciervo deer — **cervino** resembling a deer
ciprés cypress — **cipresino** resembling cypress
cuervo crow — **corvino** crowlike
elefante elephant — **elefantino** elephantine
fiera wild beast — **ferino** wild, savage
púrpura purple — **purpurino** purplish

-izo

Forms adjectives expressing a tendency towards the quality or action expressed by the primitive word:

bermejo red — **bermejizo** reddish
cobre copper — **cobrizo** coppery
enfermo sick — **enfermizo** sickly
llover to rain — **llovedizo** pertaining to rain
mover to move — **movedizo** movable, shifting
olvidar to forget — **olvidadizo** forgetful
plomo lead — **plomizo** leaden
rojo red — **rojizo** reddish

-mento, -miento

Serve to form verbal nouns expressing the action of a verb:

abatir to discourage — **abatimiento** discouragement, depression
casar to marry — **casamiento** marriage
cesar to cease — **cesamiento** cessation
crecer to increase — **crecimiento** increase
hundir to sink — **hundimiento** sinking, submersion
mantener to maintain — **mantenimiento** maintenance
nacer to be born — **nacimiento** birth
rendir to surrender — **rendimiento** rendition
salvar to save — **salvamento** safety, salvation, salvage

-ón

a. Added to stems of verbs, forms derivative nouns expressing the result of the action of the primitive:

aguijar to prick, goad — **aguijón** prick, goad, spur, sting
apretar to press — **apretón** pressure
arañar to scratch — **arañón** scratch
empujar to push — **empujón** push
estrujar to squeeze — **estrujón** squeezing; pressing (of grapes)
forcejar to struggle — **forcejón** struggle
resbalar to slip, slide — **resbalón** slip, slide
reventar to burst — **reventón** bursting
salpicar to bespatter — **salpicón** bespattering
trasquilar to shear — **trasquilón** clipping of wool

b. Forms adjectives from nouns and verbs, and has a frequentative value closely allied to the augmentatives in **-ón:**

burlar to jest — **burlón** waggish
juguete toy, plaything — **juguetón** playful, frolicsome
llorar to weep — **llorón** tearful

mandar to command — **mandón** domineering
preguntar to inquire — **preguntón** inquisitive
regañar to scold — **regañón** grumbling, faultfinding
responder to answer — **respondón** saucy
tragar to swallow — **tragón** voracious

-oso

Added to nouns or the stems of verbs, forms adjectives expressing the possession of the characteristic of the primitive:

borrasco squall, gust — **borrascoso** squally, gusty
cariño affection — **cariñoso** affectionate
enfadar to vex — **enfadoso** vexatious
engañar to deceive — **engañoso** deceitful
espantar to frighten — **espantoso** frightful
fatigar to tire — **fatigoso** tiresome
leche milk — **lechoso** milky
lodo mud — **lodoso** muddy
moho mould — **mohoso** mouldy
nieve snow — **nevoso** snowy
orgullo pride — **orgulloso** proud
pluma feather — **plumoso** feathery
sustancia substance — **sustancioso** substantial, nutritious
vello down *(as of a peach)* — **velloso** downy

-udo

Forms adjectives expressing, generally in an exaggerated sense, the characteristic quality of the primitive noun:

barba beard — **barbudo** having a heavy beard
barriga abdomen — **barrigudo** corpulent
cabello hair — **cabelludo** hairy
capricho whim, caprice — **caprichudo** stubborn
carne flesh — **carnudo** fleshy
casco hoof — **cascudo** hoofed
ceja eyebrow — **cejudo** heavy-browed
ceño frown — **ceñudo** frowning, grim
colmillo tusk, eyetooth — **colmilludo** with tusks; *(fig.)* who has cut his eyeteeth
diente tooth — **dentudo** with large, uneven teeth
hombro shoulder — **hombrudo** broad-shouldered
hueso bone — **huesudo** raw-boned
papo fleshy part of the chin — **papudo** double-chinned
zanca shank — **zancudo** long-shanked

-uno

Forms adjectives denoting species, usually applied to animals:

buey ox	**boyuno** bovine
caballo horse	**caballuno** equine
cabra goat	**cabruno** caprine
carnero sheep	**carneruno** ovine
[**chotar** *(obs.)* to suck]	**chotuno** sucking
ciervo deer	**cervuno** cervine
hombre man	**hombruno** manful
liebre hare	**lebruno** leprine
oveja ewe	**ovejuno** pertaining to ewes
puerco pig	**porcuno** porcine
vaca cow	**vacuno** pertaining to cows

-ura

Forms abstract nouns from adjectives:

alto high	**altura** height
amargo bitter	**amargura** bitterness
bravo brave	**bravura** bravery
dulce sweet	**dulzura** sweetness
grueso coarse	**grosura** coarseness
largo long	**largura** length
liso smooth, even	**lisura** smoothness, evenness

-zón

Applied to nouns and stems of verbs, forms derivative nouns of allied meaning:

armar to set up	**armazón** framework, skeleton
arrumar to stow, pack	**arrumazón** stowing; cloud rack
barbechar to plow in the fall	**barbechazón** time for fall plowing
cargar to load	**cargazón** cargo
clavar to nail	**clavazón** nailing; lot of nails
ligar to bind	**ligazón** bond, ligament
palo mast	**palazón** masting, masts of a ship
pollo chicken	**pollazón** hatching, brood
segar to reap	**segazón** reaping, harvest time
trabar to join	**trabazón** connection, coherence
tragar to swallow	**tragazón** gluttony, voracity

32.55. From names of arts and sciences ending in **-ía** corresponding derivatives may be formed by changing that termination into **-o:**

agronomía science of agriculture — **agrónomo** writer on agriculture
arqueología archeology — **arqueólogo** archeologist
astronomía astronomy — **astrónomo** astronomer
filosofía philosophy — **filósofo** philosopher
fotografía photography — **fotógrafo** photographer
geografía geography — **geógrafo** geographer
geología geology — **geólogo** geologist
geometría geometry — **geómetro** geometrician
litografía lithography — **litógrafo** lithographer
teología theology — **teólogo** theologian

32.56. From feminine nouns in **-ica**, denoting arts and sciences, titles for those who are experts therein may be formed by changing the final **a** into **o**:

aritmética arithmetic — **aritmético** arithmetician
botánica botany — **botánico** botanist
física physics — **físico** physicist
gramática grammar — **gramático** grammarian
lógica logic — **lógico** logician
mecánica mechanics — **mecánico** mechanician
música music — **músico** musician
óptica optics — **óptico** optician
política politics — **político** politician
química chemistry — **químico** chemist
retórica rhetoric — **retórico** rhetorician

32.57. The names of many fruit trees, ending in **-o**, become names of the fruits when the termination is changed to **-a**:

almendro almond tree — **almendra** almond
castaño chestnut tree — **castaña** chestnut
cerezo cherry tree — **cereza** cherry
ciruelo plum tree — **ciruela** plum
manzano apple tree — **manzana** apple
naranjo orange tree — **naranja** orange

NOTE. Many of the preceding derivative terminations have other values (usually an extension of some principal value), the examples of which are not sufficiently numerous and regular to deserve classification in this work.

32.58. The development of words by means of suffixes will be appreciated best by seeing the luxuriant growth arising from a single common word (which, however, is exceptionally prolific):

TIERRA, EARTH, LAND[1]

terráceo made of earth
terráqueo terraqueous (applied to the globe)
terrada cement of ochre and glue
terradillo a small terrace
terrado a terrace, platform
terraje rent of land
terrajero a tenant
terral from the land (applied to wind blowing from the land and lightning going upwards from the earth)
terraza a terrace, a glazed earthen jar
terrazgo arable land; land-tax or rent
terrazguero a tenant
terrazo ground (of a painting)
terrazuela a little earthen jar
terrear to show the ground (said of thin crops)
terregoso full of clods
terrenal terrene (pertaining to the earth in contradistinction to the heavens)
terrenidad quality of the soil
terreno earthly
terreno ground, field
térreo earthly
terrera a sloping piece of ground
terrero terrace, mound
terrero touching or approaching the ground (applied to creeping plants, low-flying birds, trailing boughs, etc.), *metaph.,* humble
terrestre terrestrial
terrestridad earthiness
terrezuelo a poor bit of ground
terrín a peasant
terrino earthy
territorial territorial
territorio territory
terrizo earthen
terrón a clod, lump of earth
terronazo a large clod; blow with a clod
terroncillo a small clod
terrontera a break in a mountain
terrosidad earthiness
terroso earthy (mixed with earth)
terruño piece of ground

By employing prefixes, the following are produced:

aterraje *(naut.)* drifting ashore
aterramiento ruin, destruction
aterrar to throw to the ground; *naut.,* to stand inshore
aterronar to clod, gather into clods
conterráneo belonging to the same district
desenterrador a body snatcher
desenterramiento disinterment
desenterrar to disinter
desterradero a retired part of the town; isolated residence
desterrado exile, outcast
desterrado exiled, banished
desterrar to exile, banish
desterronar to break clods
destierro exile, banishment
enterrador gravedigger

---

[1] **País, campo, tierra, patria.—País** is a country in its political or natural aspect; **campo** in its primitive sense is a *field,* and means also the *country* in its agricultural aspect as distinguished from the town or village. **Patria** is one's native land as distinguished from other countries **(países). Tierra** means earth, soil, land, the earth, or a large tract of country.

enterramiento interment
enterrar to inter, bury
entierro burial, funeral
soterrable that which may be put underground
soterrador one who puts under ground
soterráneo subterranean
soterrar to put under ground

PREFIXES

32.59. The prefixes used in the formation of derivatives in Spanish are the Latin prefixes which are also found in English. As they will be recognized at sight, space need not be occupied by giving a list of them here. The application of certain prefixes in the formation of verbs from nouns and adjectives, is, however, a subject deserving of some attention.

FORMATION OF VERBS FROM NOUNS

32.60. All derivative verbs of this nature are of the first conjugation, made by adding **-ar** to the primitive after removing the final vowel. In some cases a prefix is required.

32.61. The general principles under which prefixes are applied are as follows:

1. When an implement is to be used on anything, or something is to be applied so as not to adhere or remain attached, **a-** or **ad-** is prefixed to the derivative verb.

2. The prefix **en-** is added when the thing represented by the noun is to be made to adhere or remain attached; or is to be put into or stored in some receptacle.

3. When the thing named is to be removed or taken away, the prefix **des-** is added.

But, as the language is never wholly consistent, these are only prevailing usages and not absolute rules. The majority of verbs of the first class, and a large number of verbs of a miscellaneous character, do not take any prefix.

32.62. To apply or use an implement:

bozal muzzle — **abozalar** to muzzle
clavo nail — **clavar** to nail
cepillo plane, brush — (a)**cepillar** to plane, to brush
lima file — **limar** to file

martillo hammer — **martillar** to hammer
patín skate — **patinar** to skate
peine comb — **peinar** to comb
puntal prop — **apuntalar** to prop
rastrillo rake — **rastrillar** to rake
señal signal — **señalar** to signal
sierra saw — **serrar** to saw
taladro auger — **taladrar** to bore, pierce
tamiz sieve — **tamizar** to sift
taruga plug — **atarugar** to plug
tornillo screw — **atornillar** to screw

32.63. To affix or lay on something:

alfombra carpet — **alfombrar** to carpet
arena sand — **enarenar** to sand
baldosa flooring tile — **baldosar** to tile (floors)
barniza varnish — **barnizar** to varnish
brida bridle — **embridar** to bridle
cebo bait — **cebar** to bait
césped sod — **encespedar** to sod
chapa veneer — **enchapar** to veneer
goma gum — **engomar** to gum
jabón soap — **enjabonar** to soap
jaeces harness — **enjaezar** to harness
pizarra slate — **empizarrar** to slate
sal salt — **salar** to salt
silla saddle — **ensillar** to saddle
techo roof — **techar** to roof
teja roofing tile — **tejar** to tile (roofs)

32.64. To put into something—with the prefix **en:**

alforja saddlebag — **enalforjar** to put into saddlebags
bala bale — **embalar** to bale
barril barrel — **embarrilar** to barrel
bolsa purse — **embolsar** to put into a purse
botella bottle — **embotellar** to bottle
cajón box — **encajonar** to box
canasta, canasto basket, hamper — **encanastar** to put into baskets
cántaro pitcher — **encantarar** to pour into a pitcher
cubo bucket — **encubar** to put into buckets
fardo bundle — **enfardar** to make into a bundle
papel paper — **empapelar** to wrap up in paper
paquete package — **empaquetar** to make a package of

saco sack, bag — **ensacar** to put into sacks *or* bags
tierra ground — **enterrar** to put into the ground, to bury

32.65. To strip off or take away—with the prefix **des**:

cabeza head — **descabezar** to behead
canto stone — **descantar** to remove the stones from (a field)
cáscara husk — **descascarar** to husk
corteza bark — **descortezar** to bark
golleta neck (of bottle) — **desgolletar** to knock off the neck
hilo thread — **deshilarse** to ravel
hoja leaf — **deshojar** to strip off the leaves
hollín soot — **deshollinar** to clean (chimneys)
hueso bone — **desosar, deshuesar** to bone
nata cream — **desnatar** to skim (milk)
paja straw, chaff — **despajar** to winnow
pellejo skin — **despellejar** to skin
pluma feather — **desplumar** to pluck (fowls)
techo roof — **destechar** to unroof

32.66. Des, added to verbs, forms derivatives of negative or opposite meaning:

agradar to please — **desagradar** to displease
aguar to water — **desaguar** to drain
ayunar to fast — **desayunar** to breakfast
cansar to tire — **descansar** to rest
colgar to hang up — **descolgar** to take down
coser to sew — **descoser** to rip
emborrachar to intoxicate — **desemborrachar** to sober
empeñar to pawn — **desempeñar** to redeem (a pledge)
encadenar to chain — **desencadenar** to unchain
enredar to tangle — **desenredar** to untangle
esperar to hope — **desesperar** to despair
hacer to do — **deshacer** to undo
helar to freeze — **deshelar** to thaw
mandar to order — **desmandar** to revoke (an order)
pegar to glue — **despegar** to unglue, separate
pintar to paint — **despintar** to paint out
poblar to people — **despoblar** to depopulate
prender to fasten — **desprender** to unfasten
tapar to cork — **destapar** to uncork

tetar to suckle — **destetar** to wean
torcer to twist, plait — **destorcer** to untwist, unplait

32.67. Derivative verbs of miscellaneous meaning:

amenaza threat — **amenazar** to threaten
apodo nickname — **apodar** to nickname
arruga wrinkle — **arrugar** to wrinkle
atrás backwards — **atrasar** to retrograde
beneficio benefit — **beneficiar** to benefit
bloqueo blockade — **bloquear** to blockade
botón button — **abotonar** to button
boya buoy — **boyar** to buoy
carbón charcoal — **carbonar** to char
cimiento foundation — **cimentar** to found, lay the foundation
columpio swing — **columpiar** to swing
cruz cross — **cruzar** to cross
cuajo curd — **cuajar** to curdle
dictamen report — **dictaminar** to report
número number — **numerar** to number
oriente east — **orientar** to turn towards the east
página page — **paginar** to paginate
represa dam — **represar** to dam
sobre over — **sobrar** to remain over

FORMATION OF VERBS FROM ADJECTIVES

32.68. Derivative verbs meaning to impart the characteristic expressed by a primitive adjective, are formed in two principal ways—leaving out of account certain miscellaneous examples.

1. By adding the infinitive termination **-ecer** in place of the final vowel, with or without prefixing **en-**. These are called inceptive verbs and have been treated of in Chapter XXI.

2. By adding the infinitive termination **-ar,** with or without prefixing **a-** or **en-**.

EXAMPLES

agrio sour — **agriar** to sour
blando soft — **ablandar** to soften
chico small, little — **achicar** to lessen, diminish
ciego blind — **cegar** to blind
dulce sweet — **endulzar** to sweeten
duro hard — **endurar** to harden
espeso thick — **espesar** to thicken
flojo weak, loose — **aflojar** to loosen, slacken

frío cold
gordo fat
largo long
ligero light
limpio clean
raso smooth, level
seco dry
seguro secure, safe
sucio dirty
tieso stiff

enfriar to cool
engordar to fatten
alargar to lengthen, protract
aligerar to lighten
limpiar to clean
arrasar to smooth, level
secar to dry
asegurar to secure, assure
ensuciar to soil
atiesar to stiffen

XXXIII
Order Of Words

33.1. In the arrangement characteristic of everyday speech the noun precedes its adjective; the verb precedes the adverb which modifies it; the subject precedes the verb; the governing word precedes the one governed; the object follows the verb, and the adverb, if there be one; but an objective personal pronoun precedes its governing verb, unless attached to it as an enclitic.

In the more ornate construction of formal written style, the order depends largely upon the sound of words, the expression of emphasis, and the desire to avoid monotony of arrangement. In every sentence there are two places of honor—the front and the rear—where words of great dignity are placed; the common herd of vocables are crowded in between. Prominence is given to a word by placing it at the beginning or at the end. A word that is usually last is made conspicuous by placing it first, and for the same reason the first may be put last—in general any change from the natural order attracts attention.

In English the meaning depends so much on the order of words, that we have but little choice as to their arrangement, but in languages derived from Latin there is much greater freedom of movement. In Spanish words are selected and put together with more reference to harmony of sound or rhetorical effect, while the meaning is not generally affected by a change in the order of words; so long as obscurity does not result, they may be placed in almost any order. The following transpositions may serve as an example:

Halley ocupaba en Inglaterra el primer puesto entre los astrónomos y físicos. Ocupaba Halley en Inglaterra el primer puesto entre los astrónomos y físicos. En Inglaterra ocupaba Halley el primer puesto entre los astrónomos y físicos. Entre los astrónomos y físicos ocupaba Halley el primer puesto en Inglaterra.	Halley occupied the first place in England among astronomers and physicists.

33.2. The subject is frequently placed after the verb without affecting the meaning, but merely giving animation and variety to the sentence:

Llama la madre a la niña.	The mother calls the girl.
Aprendemos nosotros el castellano.	We are learning Spanish.
Necesita V. comprar una gramática elemental.	You need to buy an elementary grammar.
No quiero yo el caballo.	I do not want the horse.

33.3. The direct and indirect objects may generally assume any location:

Los indígenas tenían estos puentes antes de la llegada de los españoles. Estos puentes tenían los indígenas antes de la llegada de los españoles. Tenían los indígenas estos puentes antes de la llegada de los españoles. Antes de la llegada de los españoles tenían los indígenas estos puentes.	The natives had these bridges before the advent of the Spaniards.

A todos nos causó mal efecto aquella escena. Nos causó a todos mal efecto aquella escena. Mal efecto nos causó a todos aquella escena. Aquella escena nos causó a todos mal efecto. Aquella escena nos causó mal efecto a todos.	That scene produced a bad effect on all of us.

33.4. The natural order of words is seldom conformed to by elegant writers except in the simplest sentences. In the more complex forms of speech, where the verb has several objects and there are many dependent clauses, a more inverted style is preferred:

La iglesia acudió con el remedio.	The Church came forward with the remedy.
Contra este gentílico contagio acudió presurosa la iglesia con el remedio.	The Church came promptly forward with the remedy for this pagan corruption.
Los árabes adoptaron un sistema distinto.	The Arabs adopted a different system.
Muy distinto sistema que los godos adoptaron los árabes para hacerse dueños de la península española.	The Arabs adopted a very different system from the Goths to make themselves masters of the Spanish peninsula.

REMARK. In this excessive freedom of arrangement, care should be taken that perspicuity is not sacrificed for rhetorical effect. Words belonging together should not be too widely separated; as the noun from its adjective, the relative from its antecedent, the verb from its subject and object, etc. And words forming a phrase, or a composite idea, should not be separated or reversed; as, for instance, the compound tenses of verbs, nouns connected by a preposition, etc.

33.5. A sentence, therefore, may be separated into sections according to meaning, and the order of the sections changed according to taste; but each section should remain unchanged:

El‿cielo | se‿presentaba | por‿todos‿lados | a‿nuestra‿mirada | como‿un‿océano‿de‿llamas.	The sky on all sides appeared to our gaze like an ocean of flames.
Tres‿grandes‿faltas‿políticas | cometieron | los‿árabes | al‿llegar‿a‿nuestro‿suelo.	The Arabs, on arriving in our territory, committed three grave political errors.

33.6. An English sentence may be likened to an algebraic equation, the verb representing the sign of equality, and something must be on each side of the verb; when the entire sentence is placed after the verb, the word *there* precedes it. This principle does not apply in Spanish:

Apareció a lo lejos una pequeña nube de polvo.	*There* appeared in the distance a small cloud of dust.
Vivía en esta aldea un orífice que tenía tres hijas muy lindas.	*There* lived in this hamlet a goldsmith who had three beautiful daughters.

33.7. Attention may be focused on the subject by removing it to the beginning of the sentence or clause, the break in continuity often being restored by the use of **que:**

¿Tú qué sabes? (Sender, **Siete domingos rojos,** XXVIII)	What do you know about it?
Yo era la primera vez que viajaba por esa parte de la montaña, y, la verdad, tenía miedo. (Baroja, **El trasgo,** in **Vidas sombrías**)	It was the first time that I had traveled through that part of the mountain country of Asturias and, to tell the truth, I was afraid.
La sangre parece que se me pone como metal derretido. (Pérez Galdós, **Miau,** XLIV)	My blood seems to turn *(or* It seems that my blood turns) into molten metal.
Se confortó durmiendo profundamente la siesta, durante la cual sus desventuras y sus penas se diría que se habían sumergido en aquel arroyo como si fuese el Leteo. (Valera, **Juanita la larga,** XXIX, end)	He comforted himself by a sound nap, during which it might be said that his misfortunes and griefs had been plunged into that stream as if it were Lethe.

INTERROGATIVE SENTENCES

33.8. A question is regularly formed in Spanish by placing the verb before its subject, which in English is done only in the case of the verbs *be, have,* and the auxiliaries:[1]

¿A qué hora sale el tren?	When does the train leave?
¿Ha tomado usted los billetes?	Have you bought the tickets?

[1] But the rule for Spanish is violated for rhetorical effect or in local usages: **¿Cómo los seres que hemos amado tanto pueden desaparecer de este modo tan rápido y brutal?** (Azorín, **Sarrió,** in **Los Pueblos**) *How can the beings we have so loved disappear in this swift and brutal manner?* **¿Teófilo se ha propuesto que nos pasemos aquí la vida?** (Benavente, **La comida de las fieras,** I, 3) *Has Theophilus proposed that we spend our lives here?*

Although the usage of modern English is to retain the affirmative order with all other verbs, and prefix *do*—"do you want?" "do you eat?" and not "want you?" "eat you?"—this latter order was more common in English of a few centuries ago; e.g.:

"Ride you this afternoon?...Goes Fleance with you?"
MACBETH, Act iii, Sc. 1.

"Thinkest thou that David doth honour thy father?"—2 *Sam.*, x. 3.

The Spaniards never use any auxiliary corresponding to the English *do*, in any of its parts.

33.9. In the predicate of questions, the usual place of the adjective is immediately after the subject in Spanish, as it is before it in English. When prominence is to be given to the adjective, it is removed from its usual place. In either case the Spanish construction is the opposite of the English:

¿Es viejo el capitán?	Is the captain old?
¿Es el capitán viejo?	Is it the old captain?
¿Es alto su hermano de V.?	Is your brother tall?
¿Es su hermano alto de V.?	Is it your tall brother?

33.10. In interrogative sentences it is considered more elegant to place the predicate before the subject:

¿Es nuevo el sombrero de V.?	Is your hat new?
¿Es clara y fresca el agua?	Is the water clear and cool?
¿Es soldado su hermano de V.?	Is your brother a soldier?

33.11. In questions the object is more elegantly placed before the subject, provided the clause containing it is no longer than that containing the subject:

¿Tiene vino | el‿hombre?	Has the man any wine?
¿Tiene el‿hombre | un‿cigarro?	Has the man a cigar?
¿Tiene un‿cigarro | su‿padre‿de‿V.?	Has your father a cigar?
¿Tiene su‿padre‿de‿V. | una‿pipa‿y‿tabaco?	Has your father a pipe and tobacco?
¿Tiene cigarros‿y‿tabaco | el‿hijo de‿su‿amigo‿de‿V.?	Has your friend's son cigars and tobacco?
¿Tiene el‿hijo‿de‿su‿amigo‿de‿V. | la‿corona‿de‿oro‿y‿las‿alhajas‿de‿la‿princesa?	Has your friend's son the gold crown and jewels of the princess?

LOCATION OF ADJECTIVES

33.12. In Spanish, qualifying adjectives generally follow the noun, especially when of primary importance (from the speaker's point of view); thus when denoting a physical quality (color, size, shape, strength, etc.), or geographical division, or when qualified by a long adverb, the adjective ordinarily follows the noun:

café negro y te verde	black coffee and green tea
Bebemos vinos franceses.	We drink French wines.
las mujeres habladoras y los hombres holgazanes	the talkative women and the lazy men

33.13. On the other hand, when the adjective is used as a mere general epithet, or is employed oratorically, or in a secondary, figurative or poetic sense, it preferably precedes the noun:

el pobre indio	the poor Indian
un dulce zéfiro	a mild zephyr
los soberbios reyes	the proud kings

33.14. The tendency of an adjective placed before its noun is to express its quality as belonging to the noun as a matter of course, and not distinguishing one individual from another, which it does when placed after the noun:

las olorosas flores	the fragrant flowers *(fragrancy being considered an inherent quality)*
las flores olorosas	the fragrant flowers *(those varieties which are fragrant)*
los salvajes indios	the savage Indians *(Indians in general, considered as uncivilized)*
los indios salvajes	the savage Indians *(those Indians who are in a savage state)*
mis nuevos vestidos	my new clothes *(not my new books or anything else that I may have)*
mis vestidos nuevos	my new clothes *(not my old ones)*

33.15. An adjective placed before a noun loses much of its force; its quality is applied as if it were a matter of course. Its omission does not essentially alter the thought. On the other hand, when placed after the noun it specifies and indicates a particular kind of the thing represented by the noun. The former order, therefore, savors of a poetic style, where it is customary to use a number of adjectives merely to add coloring. When the adjective precedes the noun is the principal word; when it follows it assumes the chief importance. In English this result is attained by the stress of voice called emphasis:

los vivos colores	the bright colors
los colores vivos	the *bright* colors
las olorosas flores	the fragrant flowers
las flores olorosas	the *fragrant* flowers
desnudas peñas	barren rocks
peñas desnudas	*barren* rocks
la blanca azucena	the white water lily
la azucena blanca	the *white* water lily

33.16. The following examples will serve further to show the lack of distinguishing force of an adjective placed before a noun:

La inconstante luna; su hirviente humor; lóbrega noche; el hondo abismo; cano invierno; la tímida liebre; fresca sombra; el ronco trueno; vastas e incultas selvas.

The inconstant moon; his bubbling humor; sombre night; the deep abyss; hoary winter; the timid hare; cool shade; the hoarse thunder; vast and unbroken wilds.

Apenas había el rubicundo Apolo tendido por la faz de la ancha y espaciosa tierra las doradas hebras de sus hermosos cabellos; y apenas los pequeños y pintados pajarillos con sus arpadas lenguas habían saludado con dulce y meliflua armonía la venida de la rosada aurora, cuando el famoso caballero don Quijote de la Mancha, dejando las ociosas plumas, subió sobre su famoso caballo Rocinante, y comenzó a caminar por el antiguo y conocido campo de Montiel. (Cervantes)

Scarcely had ruddy Apollo spread over the face of the wide and spacious earth the golden strands of his hair; and scarcely had the little bright-feathered songsters with their harp-like tongues greeted with sweet and mellifluous harmony the coming of rosy Dawn, when the famous knight Don Quixote de la Mancha, leaving his downy couch, mounted his famous horse Rozinante, and commenced a journey across the ancient and well-known country of Montiel.

Remark. But adjective pronouns, demonstratives and possessives, since they do not specify quality but identity, regularly precede the noun.

33.17. Depending upon whether they stand before or after their noun, some adjectives usually have a different meaning, often calling for unlike equivalents in English:

	AFTER	BEFORE
antiguo	old, ancient *(but occasionally,* former, etc.)	former, of long standing
cierto	definite, reliable, sure	certain
diferente	dissimilar, differing	various
grande	big, large	great, grand
medio	average	half
mismo	-self *(without definite article)*	same, very, -self *(with definite article)*
nuevo	newly made, new kind of	another, different
pobre	impecunious, needy	pitiable
propio	-self, characteristic, suitable	same, own, very
puro	pure, undefiled	sheer
simple	simple-minded	mere
único	unique	only, sole, single
varios	miscellaneous	several

33.18. When two adjectives relate to one noun, they are placed according to the above principles;[1] so that both may come before, one before and one after, or both may follow the noun:

Compro libros nuevos y útiles.	I buy useful new books.
Tiene una casa pequeña y bonita.	He has a pretty little house.
un hombre pobre y desgraciado	a poor and unfortunate man
un velo largo y negro	a long, black veil
Era un viejecito de barba gris recortada. (Baroja, **El árbol de la ciencia, II,** 8)	He was a little old man with a clipped gray beard.
literatura española moderna	modern Spanish literature
un amigo mío italiano	an Italian friend of mine
una pequeña taza azul	a little blue cup
el pobre caballo ciego	the poor blind horse
¡Pobre y desvalida niña!	Poor and helpless child!
Se alzaba como elevadísima y solitaria torre. (Valera, **Morsamor,** I)	It rose like a very tall, solitary tower.
Emilio cerró al fin las carpetas sin dejar sus largas, prolijas explicaciones. (Palacio Valdés, **El capitán Ribot,** IX)	Emil finally closed the portfolios without ceasing his long, tedious explanations.

[1] The same is true when there are more than two adjectives: **los altos muros negros y carcomidos** (Palacio Valdés, **Marta y María,** X) *the tall, dark, eroded walls.*

Los falsos antiguos ideales de la Edad Media habían caído por tierra. (Valera, **Morsamor,** I)	The false former ideals of the Middle Ages had fallen to earth.

REMARK. Unless there is a break in the thought and the consequent sign of punctuation, y *and* is used to connect two adjectives when they are of equal value. When two adjectives are neither separated by a sign of punctuation nor connected by y, they are not of equal value, the adjective standing closer to the noun forming with it a single concept, which is then modified by the second adjective. For two adjectives thus to stand before a noun is not at all frequent, unless one of them is a possessive, a numeral, or an indefinite: **mi único hijo** *my only son;* **los tres primeros capítulos** *the first three chapters;* **ninguna buena ocasión** *no good occasion;* etc.

33.19. In both Spanish and English, the adjective most permanently connected with the noun stands nearest to it; but as in Spanish both adjectives very often follow, the order is apparently reversed:

un soldado viejo y borracho	a drunken old soldier
las niñas bonitas y felices	the happy, pretty girls
el Banco Nacional Central	the Central National Bank

LOCATION OF RELATIVES

33.20. A relative pronoun is never omitted as it often is in English, and when there is a governing preposition it must precede the relative:

La nación que me cabe la honra de representar.	The nation I have the honor to represent.
Los resultados a que ya hemos llegado nos hacen esperar un éxito propicio.	The results we have already attained make us hope for success.

33.21. The sentence should be arranged so that the antecedent may stand as close before the relative as possible. In the following pairs the first version is hardly the best style:

Encuentro máximas en sus discursos que son contrarias a la moral.	I find maxims in his speeches which are contrary to good morals.
Encuentro en sus discursos máximas que son contrarias a la moral.	I find in his speeches maxims which are contrary to good morals.

(In the first, **que** *would relate to* **discursos;** *in the second, to* **máximas.)**

La pescadora dice que tiene una cantidad de arenques en su carreta que venderá en dos pesos.	The fishwife says she has a lot of herrings in her cart which she will sell for two pesos.

La pescadora dice que tiene en su carreta una cantidad de arenques que venderá en dos pesos.

The fishwife says she has in her cart a lot of herrings which she will sell for two pesos.

(In the first example, **que** *would relate to* **carreta.)**

Cicerón ha imitado a Demóstenes en todo lo que tiene de más elocuente.

Cicero has imitated Demosthenes in all his most eloquent passages.

Cicerón, en todo lo que tiene de más elocuente, ha imitado a Demóstenes.

Cicero, in all his most eloquent passages, has imitated Demosthenes.

33.22. The abbreviated and impersonal forms of expression so common in English are often inadmissible in Spanish in connection with relative clauses. The first version of the following is incorrect:

Es a la hora de la adversidad que se conocen los verdaderos amigos.

It is in the hour of adversity that we know our true friends.

La hora de la adversidad es la en que se conocen los verdaderos amigos *or* Es en la hora de la adversidad en (la) que, *etc.* (cf. § 33.25).

The hour of adversity is the one in which we know our true friends.

REMARK. The difference in construction is that in the first the principal verb is impersonal; in the second the subject is "**hora.**"

33.23. When both antecedent and relative are governed by identical or equivalent prepositions, the second preposition may be omitted:

En el momento (en) que iban a alcanzarle, el roedor despareció bajo las aguas del pantano.

At the moment they were about to seize him, the rodent disappeared under the waters of the swamp.

33.24. With **ser,** especially when used impersonally, the preposition is preferably used before both noun or pronoun and relative clause:

¿Será por eso por lo que no quiere entrar? (Pérez Galdós, **Fortunata y Jacinta,** III, 6, 3)

Can it be on account of that that she doesn't want to come in?

A ésta es a quien ha de acompañar usté. (Pereda, **Sotileza,** I)

It is this lady whom you are to accompany.

Es en mi hija en la que han pensado. (Benavente, **Pepa Doncel,** I, 6)

It is of my daughter that they have thought.

A tu tío es el primero al que le parece mal. (Benavente, **Al fin, mujer,** III, 2, 1) — Your uncle is the first one to whom it seems bad.

La primera persona con quien tropezó fué con el tío Felipe de la Casuca. (Palacio Valdés, **Sinfonía pastoral, Presto finale,** VI) — The first person whom he ran into was old Felipe de la Casuca.

33.25. When the relative **que,** governed by a preposition, has as its antecedent the demonstrative pronoun **el,** the order of the three words is frequently changed:

Esta vieja casa es **la en que** pasé mi infancia.
Esta vieja casa es **en la que** pasé mi infancia.
This old house is *the one in which* I spent my childhood.

No son días de fe **los en que** vivimos.
No son días de fe **en los que** vivimos.
They are not days of faith, *those in which* we live.

El estilo en que se expone un lance dramático debe ser más conciso y enérgico que **el en que (en el que)** se presenta una disertación filosófica. — The style in which a dramatic occurrence is depicted should be more concise and energetic than *that in which* a philosophical dissertation is presented.

La hora de la adversidad es **la en que (en la que)** se conocen los verdaderos amigos. — The hour of adversity is *the one in which* we know our true friends.

Remark. Such constructions are neatly replaced by an adverb, when there is one that expresses the meaning:

Esta vieja casa es **donde** pasé mi infancia. — This old house is *where* I spent my childhood.

La hora de la adversidad es **cuando** se conocen los verdaderos amigos. — The hour of adversity is *when* we know our true friends.

33.26. The verb of a relative clause usually precedes the noun, whether this be subject or object; while in English, when the noun is subject it is placed first:

El mineral que había recogido el ingeniero era muy puro y rico. — The ore which the engineer had picked up was very pure and rich.

Los faros que revisten la costa de Holanda están todos construidos sobre cimientos artificiales. — The lighthouses which line the coast of Holland are all built on artificial foundations.

La barranca que han cavado las aguas del Colorado tiene aquí más de 500 metros de profundidad.	The ravine which the waters of the Colorado have excavated is here more than 1,500 feet deep.
Bajo la bóveda impenetrable de verdura que formaban los árboles, no se adivinaba cuánto había adelantado el sol en su carrera.	Under the impenetrable vault of foliage which the trees formed, it could not be told how far the sun had advanced in his course.

33.27. In speaking of things or ideas, nothing but a difference in number between the antecedent and the noun in the relative clause will show whether the latter or the relative is the subject of the verb; when both are of the same number there is no clue except the meaning:

Las riquezas que **brindan** los **bosques** centrales de Sud América encuentran fácilmente un mercado en todas las partes del globo civilizado.	The treasures which the inland *forests* of South America *afford* easily find a market in all parts of the civilized globe.
El camino **que recorre** la parte inferior de la montaña se bifurca en esta altura.	The road *which skirts* the lower part of the mountain forks at this altitude.
Quizás hay nuevos continentes que en este momento **están fabricando** millones y millones de estos **infusorios** del coral.	Perhaps there are new continents which millions upon millions of these coral *insects are building* at this moment.
Durante largo tiempo permanecieron en silencio, entregados a todos los temores y esperanzas que **podían** producir en ellos estos **incidentes.**	For a long time they remained in silence, given over to all the fears and hopes which these *occurrences might* produce in them.
Esa parte de la playa estaba ribeteada de árboles magníficos, unos rectos, otros inclinados, cuyas raíces **venían** a bañar las largas **ondulaciones** del mar.	This part of the beach was lined with magnificent trees, some erect, some leaning, whose roots were lapped by the long undulations of the sea (...whose roots the long *undulations* of the sea *lapped).*
El poder que le **había granjeado** esta **victoria.**	The power which this *victory had gained* for him.
El poder **que** le **había granjeado** esta victoria.	The power *which had gained* him this victory.

Remark. The verb and its subject are distinguished above by bold-faced type.

33.28. The student will often find the relative as object of a following verb in cases where in English, to avoid placing the verb at the end, the relative clause would take the passive form:

Cuando el gitano penetró en el corredor, dió un silbido bajo, al cual respondió otro idéntico.	When the gypsy entered the passage he gave a low whistle, which *was answered* by another like it.
Los colonos siguieron una larga playa que bañaba el vasto mar.	The colonists followed a long beach which *was bathed* by the open sea.
La cabeza de este distrito es la aldea de Tandil, situada al pie de las laderas setentrionales de la sierra, que protege el fuerte "Independencia."	The county seat of this district is the village of Tandil, situated at the foot of the northern slopes of the sierra, which *is protected* by Fort Independence.
Un europeo en estas comarcas es un ser útil cuyo valor conocen los salvajes.	A European in these regions is a useful being, whose worth *is* well *known* to the savages.

33.29. In such constructions in English the relative and the auxiliary verb *to be* may frequently be omitted:

La navegación de los afluentes del Amazonas está sujeta a restricciones que embarazan el franco trasporte de las riquezas **que brindan** los bosques centrales de Sud América; y no sé si los tratados **que existen** para la navegación de los ríos Orinoco, Paraná, Plata y otros, estipulan todas las garantías **que demanda** el crecimiento vertiginoso del comercio y de las explotaciones agrícolas.	The navigation of the tributaries of the Amazon is subject to restrictions which impede the free transportation of the treasures *produced* by the inland forests of South America; and I do not know whether the *existing* treaties concerning the navigation of the rivers Orinoco, Paraná, La Plata and others afford all the guarantees *demanded* by the amazing growth of commerce and agricultural enterprises.

33.30. Isolated details of word order are discussed in §§ 3.35-3.36; 3.54; 3.56-3.57; 4.17; 5.46; 5.65; 7.8; 8.61; 9.41; 12.14, note 2; 18.7, 19.50; 20.14-20.16; 20.6; 21.6-21.9; 30.9.

Appendices

Appendix

I. SPANISH FORMS OF ADDRESS

Señor *(abbrev.* **Sr.**) Lord, Sir, Mr.
Señorito Mr., "Master"
Caballero gentleman, Sir
Don *(abbrev.* **Dn.** *or* **D.**) Mr.
Señora *(abbrev.* **Sra.**) lady, Madam
Señorita *(abbrev.* **Srta.** *or* **Sta.**) Miss young lady
Doña *(abbrev.* **Dña.** *or* **Da.**) Miss *or* Mrs.

a. In their original signification, **señor** meant *senior* or *elder;* **caballero,** *horseman* or *knight;* while **don** was the title of nobility. Their modern usage is quite different, and depends in some degree on whether they are employed *directly* in speaking *to* a person or *indirectly,* in speaking *about* a person.

Señor, in the pulpit and often in exclamations, means *Lord,* is written with a capital, and may or may not have the article, as in English: **el Señor** *the Lord.* As a noun it indicates the master or owner of a thing: **servir a dos señores** *to serve two masters.* **El señor** is used familiarly by servants in speaking of the master of the house (who is also called **el amo** *"the boss").* **El** is then at times omitted.

Señor, followed by a family name, is equivalent to English *Mr.;* when so used indirectly, it must be accompanied by the definite article (except at times when accompanying a noun in apposition, cf. § 2.39):

DIRECT ADDRESS:	**Señor Varas**	Mr. Varas
INDIRECT ADDRESS:	**El señor Varas**	Mr. Varas

b. **Caballero,** as a noun, corresponds to English *gentleman:*

Este caballero es mi hijo.	This gentleman is my son.
Es usted un caballero.	You are a gentleman.

When employed by themselves in direct address, **señor** and **caballero** correspond to the English *Sir*—in the plural, *Gentlemen.* There is but little difference in their usage among equals, except that **caballero** is slightly more formal. **Señor,** moreover, has an inherent meaning of respect; it is therefore the word used by servants and inferiors, and by children to their elders. An indignant young lady would say to a presumptuous admirer: **¡Caballero!** *Sir!* and not **¡Señor!** which would imply respect.

c. **Señora** is the feminine equivalent of both **señor** and **caballero** in all their meanings:

Nuestra Señora	Our Lady (the Virgin Mary)
La señora	The mistress, lady of the house
Buenos días, señora.	Good day, ma'am.
La señora Fortuna	Dame Fortune
Ella es una verdadera señora.	She is a true lady.

A gentleman, in speaking politely of his wife, may say **mi señora,** although **mi esposa** is more usual, or even **mi mujer,** which some consider undignified; but in referring to the wife of another he will, if formal and conservative, use **señora:**

¿Cómo está la señora de V.?	How is Mrs. So-and-so?
El señor Sánchez no viene hoy; su señora está mala.	Mr. Sánchez is not coming today; his wife is ill.

REMARK. The wife may refer jocularly to her husband as **mi señor,** but the usual expression is **mi marido** or, more formally, **mi esposo.** In speaking *to* his wife, the husband generally says **mujer** *wife.*

d. **Señorito** is merely a diminutive form of **señor.** In Spain it is used to designate an idle, frivolous young gentleman. It is seldom used otherwise, except familiarly and by servants, and corresponds to English *Master* (as *Master Tommy)* or *young gentleman.*

e. **Señorita,** diminutive of **señora,** in direct address corresponds to English *Miss:* **buenos días, señorita** *good day, Miss.* **Sí señorita** *yes, Miss.* Indirectly it is equivalent to *young lady.* It is also used by family servants to refer to the lady of the house **(la señora),** even if she is not young.

Una señorita está a la puerta.	There is a young lady at the door.

f. **Don** and **Doña** are peculiarly Spanish, and are properly used only in conjunction with baptismal or given names. It is more usual in Spain to speak of persons by their Christian name preceded by **Don** or **Doña,** than by their family name preceded by **Señor, Señora.** The author remembers many acquaintances in Spain whom he daily addressed as **Don Ramón, Don Joaquín, Doña Concha,** etc., whose family names he never learned. (In Spanish America the practice of using **Señor, Señora** at the expense of **Don** has gained much ground, the latter having lost its dignified value to several humble applications.)

1. **Doña** is applied to any lady, of some age and social position, whether married or single, though its use with the names of single women is antiquated.

2. **Don,** which, like **Doña,** implies a certain age or distinction, may be preceded by **Señor,** and **Doña** by **Señora** or **Señorita,** thus conveying more respect, and in the last case showing whether the lady is married or not.

g. There are theoretically four proper ways of addressing a given gentleman or lady, as follows (supposing the lady to be single):

Señor Don Ricardo Villafranca	Señorita (doña) Laura Tascón
Señor Villafranca	Señorita Tascón
Don Ricardo	Doña Laura
Señor Don Ricardo	Señorita (doña) Laura

h. In referring to the near relatives of a person with whom one is speaking, formal (and old-fashioned) politeness demands that their names be preceded by **Señor, Señora** or **Señorita,** as the case may require:

He recibido una carta del Sr. padre de Vd. (*or* de su Sr. padre).	I have received a letter from your father.
¿Han llegado las señoritas hermanas de Vd. (*or* sus señoritas hermanas)?	Have your sisters arrived?
He visto hoy a la Sra. madre de Vd. (*or* a su Sra. madre).	I have seen your mother today.

i. It is desirable to give some explanation of the complex Spanish family names. Let the following example suffice:

A gentleman, **el Sr. D. Juan Francisco Velarde y Núñez** (**Velarde** being the family name of his father, and **Núñez** that of his mother[1]) marries **la señorita Doña Luisa Gutiérrez y Romero.** On entering the state of matrimony the lady's name is changed to **Señora Doña Luisa Gutiérrez de Velarde.** The children of this union, assuming the family names of both parents, are called as follows:

Señor Don José Velarde y Gutiérrez
Señor Don Manuel Velarde y Gutiérrez
Señorita Doña Elena Velarde y Gutiérrez

[1] The mother's name is sometimes represented by an initial; thus supposing two brothers bearing the name **López y Valdés,** the one marrying **la Srta. de Pacheco y Díaz,** and the other **la Srta. de Mutis y Ochoa,** and each having a son named **Juan,** these two cousins would be perfectly distinguishable if they signed themselves respectively **Juan López P.** and **Juan López M.**

REMARK. The y connecting the last two names is sometimes omitted, producing names like the following:

Sr. D. Carlos Martínez Silva	Sr. D. Joaquín Arrieta Rossi

Occasionally a man is commonly known by merely his father's name, as in English; still in all formal cases the mother's family name is necessary.

In Spain gentlemen of landed estate frequently, and noblemen generally, assume the name of their estate preceded by **de:**[1]

Sr. D. Diego Hurtado de Mendoza	Sr. D. Tomás García de Villanueva

The family name, unaccompanied by title or baptismal name, is used familiarly among men just as in English. But it is always the paternal name which is so used; thus **el Sr. D. Joaquín Arrieta Rossi** and **el Sr. D. Juan Francisco Durán** y **Gómez** would call each other **Arrieta** and **Durán.** It is a peculiarity worthy of notice that ladies make use of the same mode of expression in speaking of or to their intimate gentlemen friends, implying no discourtesy thereby, but merely friendly confidence.

j. In direct reference the Spanish use the definite article before all titles when followed by the names of persons. The article is omitted in direct address [as it often is nowadays in indirect reference to one's relatives: **Un día tía Valentina le dijo a su marido: "Mira, Gasparito."** (Benavente, **Lo cursi,** I, 3) *One day Aunt Valentina said to her husband, "Look, Gasparito."*]:

el rey don Alfonso doce	King Alphonso the Twelfth
el general Caamaño	General Caamaño
el presidente Núñez	President Núñez
el padre Nicolás	Father Nicholas

k. In direct address, **señor** precedes the title, which it sometimes does in indirect reference:

Buenos días, señor Doctor.	Good day, Doctor.
¿Cómo está V., señor General?	How are you, General?
Señorita, tengo el honor de presentar a V. el señor coronel Quevedo de nuestro regimiento.	I have the honor, Miss, to present to you Colonel Quevedo of our regiment.

l. There are four peculiar words in Spanish, **fulano, mengano, zutano** and **perengano,** employed to indicate persons whose names we either do not know or recollect, or do not care to mention, as in the *dramatis personae* of anecdotes. They are used only in the sin-

[1] The use of **de** in Spanish family names is now purely optional and is no longer an indication of nobility, as it is in French. It is, moreover, customarily, though not invariably, placed before the family names of women—the father's name if the lady is unmarried, the husband's name if she is married: **la Srta. Da. Anita de Quiroga y Ortiz, la Sra. Da. María de Torres y Adán.**

gular, and if relating to a female, change the final **o** to **a.** The last two enumerated designate additional personages only, and therefore never appear without **fulano.**

REMARK. When used without the others, **fulano** generally assumes the form of **fulano de tal,** or, in mock politeness, **Don Fulano de tal, fulano** representing the Christian name, and **tal** *(so-and-so)* the family name of the individual.

They are somewhat analogous characters to the litigious *John Doe* and *Richard Roe,* with whom law students are familiar, or to the factitious *Smith, Brown* and *Robinson* of the humorous column.

SOME USUAL SPANISH BAPTISMAL NAMES

Alfonso Alphonso
Andrés Andrew
Benito Benedict
Carlos Charles
Diego James
Enrique Henry
Fernando Ferdinand
Francisco Francis
  Paco Frank *(familiar)*
Gerónimo Jerome
Joaquín Joachim
José Joseph
  Pepe Joe *(familiar)*
Juan John
Manuel Emmanuel
Miguel Michael
Pedro Peter
Ramón Raymond
Vicente Vincent

Ana Anne, Anna
Catalina Catherine
Elena Helen
Enriqueta Harriet
Francisca Frances
  Paca Fanny *(familiar)*
Inés Agnes
Isabel Isabella, Elisabeth
Josefa Josephine
  Pepa Josie *(familiar)*
Juana Jane
Manuela Emma
María Mary
The following are common, but have no equivalents in English:
Concha *for* **María de la Concepción**
Dolores *for* **María de los Dolores**
Lola *for* **Dolores**
Mercedes *for* **María de las Mercedes**
Rosario *for* **María del Rosario**
Tula *for* **Gertrudis**[1]

II. SOCIAL AND EPISTOLARY USAGES

The many polite phrases employed in conversation and correspondence do not come within the province of Grammar, but still are indispensable to the practical use of any language. Especially is this the case in Spanish, a language abounding in courtly expressions and complimentary phrases many of which to be sure have become old-

[1] See also §§ **32.48-32.49.**

fashioned and not often heard in everyday social intercourse nowadays. A complete exhibition of the language of formal Spanish courtesy and etiquette is beyond the scope of the present work; still there are many peculiarities, differing from English usage, which the student cannot afford to ignore.

The following are some of the usual forms of ceremonious salutation among gentlemen:

Beso a V. la mano.	I kiss your hand.
Servidor de V., caballero.	Your servant, sir.
A la orden de V.	At your orders.
Tenga V. muy buenos días.	Good day to you.
¡Adiós!	How do you do?

REMARK. A gentleman, in greeting a lady, may say **a los pies de V., señora** or **señorita** (literally *at your feet, madam,* or *miss*). The lady's reply, if she is equally ceremonious, is, **beso a V. la mano, caballero** *I kiss your hand, sir.*

The following expressions are usual in inquiring after another's health:

¿Cómo lo pasa V.? *or* ¿Cómo está V.?	How do you do?
¿Cómo se halla V.?	How are you?
¿Cómo sigue V.?	How are you getting along?
¡Hola! ¿Qué tal?	Hullo! How are you?

The following expressions are employed in replying to the above:

Medianamente bien.	Fairly well. Tolerably well.
Así así. Tal cual.	So so.
Perfectamente bien, para servir a V.	Perfectly well, thank you.
Muy bien, gracias, ¿y V.?	Very well, thank you; how are you?
Así así, *or* tal cual; y V., ¿cómo lo pasa?	So so; and how do you do?
Sin novedad.	As usual.
Regular.	Fairly well.

REMARK. The expression **sin novedad,** literally *without novelty,* is of universal usage, and can be best rendered in English by *as usual.*

The following are some of the commoner expressions of leave-taking, the latter two now being somewhat old-fashioned:

¡Adiós! ¡(Que) V. lo pase bien! ¡Vaya V. con Dios! *(said to one who is going away.)* ¡Quede V. con Dios! *(to one who remains behind.)*	Good-bye!

Hasta luego.	Good-bye until I see you again *or* I'll see you later.
Hasta la vista.	
Hasta otra.	
Hasta más ver.	

REMARK. An infrequently used leave-taking is **agur,** occurring in the forms **ahur, abur** and **abul** (said to be from the Latin *bonum augurium, good luck).*

The following will serve as samples of introductions:

Señor don A., tengo el honor de presentarle al señor don B.	Mr. A., I have the honor of introducing you to Mr. B.
Permítaseme tener el gusto de presentar a V. mi amigo don X.	Let me have the pleasure of introducing to you my friend Mr. X.
Permita V. que le presente a mi esposa.	Let me introduce you to my wife.

The following are employed in acknowledgment:

Tanto gusto (en conocer a Vd.).	(I am) glad to know you.
Encantado, -a!	Delighted!
Caballero, celebro la ocasión de conocer a V.	I am glad to make your acquaintance.
Me considero muy feliz en conocer(le) a usted, caballero.	I am very happy to make your acquaintance.
Reconózcame V. por un servidor suyo.	Consider me at your service.

In asking or requesting:

Tenga V. la bondad de decirme...	Please *(lit.* Have the goodness to) tell me...
Hágame V. el favor de darme...	Please *(lit.* Do me the favor to) give me...
Tenga V. la complacencia de indicarme...	Please *(lit.* Have the kindness to) show me...
Se lo agradecería mucho si V. me diese...	I should be much obliged if you would give me...
Sírvase V. tomar un ejemplar.	Please take a copy.

In returning thanks:

Muchísimas gracias.	Many thanks.
Mil gracias *or* Un millón de gracias.	A thousand thanks.
Se lo agradezco a V. infinito.	I am very much obliged to you.
De nada.	You are welcome *or* Don't mention it.
No las merece.	
No hay de qué *(lit.* There is no cause why).	

It is the custom in Spanish—among those addicted to formal courtesies—when anyone admires something we possess, politely to make him a present of it, although he is not expected to accept. He will decline, not by saying that he does not care to have the gift, but by intimating that it is better under the present ownership:

Tiene V. un reloj muy precioso.	You have a very handsome watch.
Está a la disposición de V. A la disposición de V.	It is at your service.
Un millón de gracias; no podría mejorar de dueño.	A thousand thanks; but it couldn't have a better owner.
Es un alfiler bonito el que tiene Vd. puesto.	That is a very pretty pin you have on.
Permítame que se lo ofrezca a Vd. Permítame que lo ponga a la disposición de Vd.	Permit me to offer it to you.
Es V. muy buena, pero a nadie podría sentarle tanto.	You are very kind, but it would become no one else so well.

So, when asked by any one where we live, in alluding to our residence, we should call it *his,* or else tell him he is welcome there—which does not amount to an invitation to call:

¿Dónde reside V. ahora?	Where do you live now?
Su casa de V. está número 19, Calle de las Fresnas.	"Your" house is No. 19 Ash Street.
Resido número 19, Calle de las Fresnas, donde tiene V. su casa, *or* donde será V. el bienvenido.	I live at No. 19 Ash Street, where you will be welcome, *or* where you must consider yourself at home.
Aquí tiene V. su casa; ¿no quiere V. entrar y descansar un rato?	Here is my house; won't you come in and rest a while?

a. It is not polite to begin a meal, to take a drink, or even to eat an orange without inviting those who are near by to partake, whether we are acquainted with them or not. They are expected to decline unless pressed more urgently.[1] The shortest invitation is one of the following: **¿V. gusta? ¿Vds. gustan? ¿V. quiere? ¿Vds. quieren? ¿A V. le gusta? ¿A Vds. les gusta?** Suitable replies are: **Muchas gracias, que le aproveche a V.** *Thanks, may it benefit you.* **Buen provecho le haga a V.** *(Thanks), I hope you enjoy it.*

b. On entering the dining room, before taking our seat, we should greet

[1] Foreigners must bear in mind that if they do not press their offer, it will be understood to be a mere empty compliment. The author has known cases where Spanish visitors, who were invited to stay to dinner, went away disappointed because the invitation was not repeated. And, *per contra,* instances are known where foreigners unwittingly caused Spaniards much inconvenience by accepting an invitation which they were expected to decline.

those who are already at the table with **buenos días** or **buenas noches,** as the hour may require. In leaving before the others, we should say: **con permiso de Vds.** *by your leave* or **que les aproveche a Vds.,** as above.

EPISTOLARY USAGES

The only epistolary forms which can be given here are the complimentary expressions usual in beginning and terminating a formal letter, and a few miscellaneous phrases of frequent occurrence.

The opening phrase is usually one of the following:

Muy estimado señor Calvo:	Dear Mr. Calvo:
Muy señor mío: Muy señor nuestro: *(from a firm)*	Dear Sir:
Muy señores míos: Muy señores nuestros: *(from a firm)*	Gentlemen:
Muy señora mía:	Madam:

In more familiar style:

Muy señor mío y amigo:	Dear Sir and Friend:
Mi querido amigo:	My dear Friend:
Querido González:	Dear González:
Mi general:	General:

a. The letter of one's correspondent is referred to as **la favorecida, apreciable,** or **estimada de V.** *your favor* or *your esteemed communication* (**carta** being understood). These are often abbreviated to **la favor^{da}, la ap^{ble}, la est^{da} de V.**

b. Other common abbreviations are **f^{da}** for **fechada** *dated;* **pp^{do}** for **próximo pasado** *ultimo;* **cor^{te}** for **corriente** *instant;* **af^{mo}** for **afectísimo** *very devoted.*

The following are miscellaneous phrases usual at the commencement of a letter:

Tengo el honor de acusar a V. el recibo de su ap^{ble} carta f^{da} el 31 del pp^{do}.	I beg to acknowledge the receipt of your letter dated the 31st ultimo.
He tenido el gusto de recibir la apreciable de V., fecha de ayer, y en contestación me apresuro a manifestarle que...	I have received your favor dated yesterday, and hasten to say in reply that...
En contestación a la ap^{ble} de V., fecha del 8, me apresuro a manifestarle que...	In reply to your esteemed letter of the 8th, I hasten to inform you that...
Me permito llamar la atención de V. sobre el circular incluso.	I beg to call your attention to the enclosed circular.

Incluyo a V. mi tarifa.	I enclose herewith my price list.
Hemos recibido la atenta carta que nos ha hecho V. el honor de dirigirnos con fecha del 30 del pp^{do}.	We have received the obliging letter which you did us the honor of addressing to us under date of the 30th ult.
Es en nuestro poder la est^{da} de V. f^{da} el dos del actual, en la que manifiesta V. que...	We have your favor of the 2nd inst. in which you state that...
Confirmando a V. nuestra última, fecha del 15, tenemos el honor de anunciarle que...	Referring to our last letter, dated the 15th inst., we beg to announce that...
Me apresuro a acusar a V. competente recibo de la remesa que me ha hecho de $210.	I hasten to acknowledge the receipt in due time, of the remittance of $210 forwarded by you.

a. Immediately before the signature of a letter addressed to a gentleman, the initials **Q.B.S.M.** or **Q.S.M.B.** are often found, though **Q.L.E.L.M.** and **Q.E.S.M.** are nowadays more usual. These stand for **que besa sus manos, que sus manos besa** *(who kisses your hand),* **que le estrecha la mano, que estrecha su mano** *(who shakes your hand),* respectively. If the letter is addressed to a lady, the initials are **Q.B.S.P.** or **Q.S.P.B. que besa sus pies, que sus pies besa** *(who kisses your feet).*

b. The expression **su seguro servidor** *your obedient servant* is invariably abbreviated **S.S.S.**

The following will serve as examples of complimentary terminations:

Soy de Vd. af^{mo} atento y S.S. José Blanco.	I am Very sincerely yours, Joseph White.
Se repite a las órdenes de V. S.S.S. Q.S.M.B. José Blanco.	I am, Sir, Very respectfully, Joseph White.
Soy, excelentísimo señor, con el más profundo respeto, Su más humilde y atento servidor, José Blanco.	I am, Sir, Very respectfully, Your obedient servant, Joseph White.
Reciba V., señora, la profunda expresión de mi afecto respetuoso. B.S.P. José Blanco.	Accept, Madam, the expression of my deep devotion. Very respectfully, Joseph White.

Tengo el honor de reiterarle el sincero afecto con que soy de V. atento y S.S. Q.S.M.B. José Blanco.	I have the honor to be, with profound esteem, Yours very respectfully, Joseph White.
Se repite de V. Af^{mo} atento y S.S. José Blanco.	I remain Very truly yours, Joseph White.
Con este motivo tengo el honor de repetirme de V. atento y S.S. José Blanco.	I have the honor to subscribe myself Yours very respectfully, Joseph White.
Quedan de Vds. af^{mos} seguros servidores, J. Blanco y Cía.	Very truly yours, Jos. White & Co.
Permítanos Vd. le ofrezcamos los más sinceros votos por su felicidad, juntamente con la seguridad de nuestro sincero afecto y la consideración más perfecta de sus atentos servidores. Q.B.S.M. José Blanco y Cía.	Allow us to offer you our best wishes for your success, together with the assurances of our highest esteem. Very respectfully, Your ob'd't s'v'ts, Joseph White & Co.
Saludan a Vd. sus af^{mos} seguros servidores, José Blanco y Cía.	Believe us to remain Very cordially yours, Joseph White & Co.
Entretanto disponga V. de su atento y S.S. José Blanco.	In the meantime, awaiting your commands, I am Yours, etc. Joseph White.
Dándole mis anticipadas gracias por este favor, me repito de V. Af^{mo} atento y S.S. José Blanco.	Thanking you in advance for the favor, I remain Very sincerely yours, Joseph White.
Mande V. con entera libertad *(or* con toda franqueza) a su af^{mo} S.S. Q.S.M.B. José Blanco.	Do not hesitate to command me. Yours very truly, Joseph White.

Deseando a V. mucha salud y felicidades durante el año nuevo, me repito,
su af^{mo} atento y S.S.
José Blanco.

Wishing you health and happiness during the New Year, I remain
Very sincerely yours,
Joseph White.

Con motivo de la entrada de año, formamos los votos más sinceros por su prosperidad, y le reiteramos la expresión de nuestro afecto.
Sus muy atentos servidores,
José Blanco y Cía.

On the occasion of the New Year we beg to offer you our best wishes for your prosperity, and remain
Very cordially yours,
Joseph White & Co.

Letters sent by mail are addressed in the same manner as in English. Local letters sent by a messenger may be addressed thus:

TO A GENTLEMAN

B.L.M.
Al Sr. D. Juan Calvo.
S.S.S.
José F. Blanco.

TO A LADY

B.L.P.
A la Sra. Da. Juana Calvo.
S.S.S.
José F. Blanco.

III. DERIVATIVE GEOGRAPHICAL ADJECTIVES

The practice of forming adjectives from names of places is so extensive in Spanish, that a list of the principal examples seems desirable. Where the Spanish proper name is so near to the English form that the student will have no difficulty in recognizing it, the English has been omitted:

Alava	alavés, alaveño
Alcalá	alcalaíno; complutense *(applied to the University of Alcalá)*
Alcántara	alcantarino
Alcarria	alcarreño
Alcázar	alcazareño
Alcoy	alcoyano
Alemania *(Germany)*	alemán
Algeciras	algecireño
Alicante	alicantino
Alpujarra	alpujarreño
Amazonas	amazonio, amazoniano
Andalucía	andaluz
Antequera	antequerano
Antioquia	antioqueño, antioquense
Arabia	árabe, arábigo

Aragón	aragonés
Argel *(Algiers)*	argelino
Armenia	armenio
Artemisa	artemisense
Arrecibo	arrecibeño
Asiria	asirio
Asturias	asturiano
Atacama	atacamense
Atenas *(Athens)*	ateniense
Austria	austriaco
Avila	abulense
Badajoz	pacense
Barajas	barajeño
Barcelona	barcelonés
Baviera *(Bavaria)*	bávaro
Bayamo	bayamés
Bélgica *(Belgium)*	belga
Bilbao	bilbaíno
Bogotá	bogotano
Bohemia	bohemio, bohémico
Bolívar	bolivarense
Bolivia	boliviano
Boloña	boloñés
Borgoña *(Burgundy)*	borgoñón
Borja	borjeño
el Brasil	brasileño, brasilero
Bretaña *(Britain, Brittany)*	bretón
Buenos Aires	bonariense, porteño
Bulgaria	búlgaro
Burgos	burgalés
Cádiz	gaditano, cadizeño
Calabria	calabrés
Calatrava	calatraveño
Campeche	campechano
el Canadá	canadiense
Canarias *(Canary Islands)*	canario
Cantabria	cántabro
Caracas	caraqueño
Cárdenas	cardense
Carolina	carolino
Cartagena	cartagenero, cartagenense
Cartago *(Carthage)*	cartaginés
Castilla	castellano

Cataluña	catalán
Cayo Hueso *(Key West)*	cayohuesero
Cerdeña *(Sardinia)*	sardo
Checo(e)slovaquia	checo(e)slovaco
Chicla	chiclanero
Chihuahua	chihuahuense
Chile	chileno
China	chino
Cienfuegos	cienfueguero
Colima	colimense
Colombia	colombiano
Copán	copaneco
Copiapó	copiapino
Córcega *(Corsica)*	corso
Córdoba	cordobés
la Coruña	coruñés
Costa Rica	costarricense, costarriquense, costarriqueño
Cuba	cubano
Cuenca	conquense
Cuernavaca	cuernavaqués
Cundinamarca	cundinamarqués
Dinamarca *(Denmark)*	dinamarqués, danés
Durango	durangueño
Ecuador	ecuatoriano
Egipto	egipcio
Escocia *(Scotland)*	escocés
España *(Spain)*	español
Estados Unidos	estadounidense, norteamericano
Europa	europeo
Estremadura	estremeño
Ferrol	ferrolano
Finlandia	finlandés, finés
Flandes *(Flanders)*	flamenco
Florencia	florentino
Francia	francés
Gales *(Wales)*	galés, galense
Galicia	gallego
Génova *(Genoa)*	genovés
Gerona	gerundense
Gibraltar	gibraltareño, calpense
Gijón	gijonés
Granada	granadino

Grecia	griego
Groenlandia *(Greenland)*	groenlandés
Guadalajara	guadalajareño
Guadalupe	guadalupense
Guamacaro	guamacareño
Guanabacoa	guanabacoero
Guanajuato	guanajuatense
Guantánamo	guantanamero
Guatemala	guatemalteco
Guayana *(Guiana)*	guayanense
Guayaquil	guayaquileño
Guipúzcoa	guipuzcoano
la Habana	habanero
Haití	haitiano
Hamburgo	hamburgués
Hidalgo	hidalguense
Holanda	holandés
Holguín	holguinero
Honduras	hondureño
Huelva	onubense
Humacao	humacaeño
Hungría *(Hungary)*	húngaro
Ibiza	ibicenco
Ibros	ibreño
India	indio
Inglaterra *(England)*	inglés
Irlanda *(Ireland)*	irlandés
Isla de Pinos	pinero
Islandia *(Iceland)*	islandés, islándico
Jalapa	jalapeño
Jalisco	jaliscense
Jamay	jamaiquino, jamaiqueño
Japón *(Japan)*	japonés
Jarama	jarameño
Jaruco	jaruqueño
Jerez	jerezano
Jibara *(or* Gibara)	jibareño *(or* gibareño)
Júcaro	jucareño
Laponia *(Lapland)*	lapón
Leganiel	leganito
León	leonés
Lérida	leridano
Lima	limeño

Lisboa *(Lisbon)*	lisbonense
Londres *(London)*	londinense
Lorca	lorqueño
Lugo	lucense
Madrid	madrileño, matritense
Málaga	malagueño
Malta	maltés
Mallorca *(Majorca)*	mallorquín
la Mancha	manchego
Manila	manileño
Manzanillo	manzanillero
Maracaibo	maracaibero
Marruecos *(Morocco)*	marroquí
Matanzas	matancero
Mayagüez	mayagüezano
Medellín	medellinés
Méjico	mejicano
Menorca	menorquín
Milano *(Milan)*	milanés
Montevideo	montevidense
Mora	morato
Morelos	morelense
Murcia	murciano
Nápoles *(Naples)*	napolitano
Navarra	navarro
Nicaragua	nicaragüense
Normandia	normando
Noruega *(Norway)*	noruego
Nueva Granada	neogranadino
Nueva Orleáns	neorlanés, nuevaorleanés
Nueva York	neoyorkino, nuevayorkino
Nueva Zelandia	neocelandés
Oajaca	oajaqueño
Oviedo	ovetense
Palencia	palentino
Pamplona	pamplonés
Panamá	panameño, panamense
el Paraguay	paraguayo
Páramo	paramés
París	parisiense
Pas	pasiego
Patagonia	patagón
la Paz	pacense, paceño

Persia	persa
el Perú	peruano
Piamonte *(Piedmont)*	piamontés
la Plata	platense
Polonia *(Poland)*	polaco
Ponce	ponceño
Popayán	popayanés
Portugal	portugués
la Puebla	poblano
Puerto Príncipe	puertoprincipense, camagüeyano
Puerto Rico	portorriqueño
Querétaro	queretano
Quito	quiteño
Regla	reglano
República Argentina	argentino
Rioja	riojano
Rusia	ruso
Saboya *(Savoy)*	saboyano, saboyardo
Sagua la Grande	sagüero
Sajonia *(Saxony)*	sajón
Salamanca	salamanquino, salmantino; salmaticense *(applied to the University of Salamanca)*
Salvador	salvadoreño, salvatorense
Sanabria	sanabrés
Sancti Spíritus	espirituano
San Juan de los Remedios	remediano, cayero
San Luis Potosí	potosino
Santa Fe (Colombia)	santafereño
Santander	santanderino
Santiago	santiagués, santiaguero, santiaguense
Santo Domingo	dominicano
Sigüenza	seguntino
Sinaloa	sinaloense
Suecia *(Sweden)*	sueco
Suiza *(Switzerland)*	suizo
Tabasco	tabascense
Talavera	talaverano
Tamaulipas	tamaulipeño
Tampico	tampiqueño
Tarancón	taranconero
Tarapacá	tarapaqueño

Tarazona	tarazonero
Tarifa	tarifeño
Tartaria	tártaro
Tarragona	tarraconense
Terranova *(Newfoundland)*	terranovés
Tierra del Fuego	fueguense
Tlascala	tlascalteca
Toledo	toledano
Toro	toresano
Tortosa	tortosino, tortosano
Toscana *(Tuscany)*	toscano
Trinidad	trinitario
Trujillo	trujillano
las Tunas	tunero
Túnez *(Tunis)*	tunecino
Turquía *(Turkey)*	turco
Tuy	tudense
el Uruguay	uruguayo
Valdivia	valdiviense
Valencia	valenciano
Valladolid	vallisoletano
Venecia *(Venice)*	veneciano
Venezuela	venezolano
Vera Cruz	veracruzano
Vizcaya *(Biscay)*	vizcaíno
Yucatán	yucateco
Yugo(e)slavia	yugo(e)slavo
Zacatecas	zacatecano
Zaragoza *(Saragossa)*	zaragozano

INDEX

INDEX

The references are to sections. Section numbers without a period refer to Part I; those with period refer to Part II, the figure at the left of the period representing the chapter number. Thus 1 is the first section of Part I, 1.1 is the first section of Chapter I of Part I, 2.2 refers to the second section of Chapter II, etc.